INVESTMENT BANKING
– TEXT & CASES

Prof. Naliniprava Tripathy
Indian Institute of Management, Shillong
India.

Himalaya Publishing House
ISO 9001:2015 CERTIFIED

First Edition : 2012
Reprint : 2016, 2017, 2018
Reprint : 2021, 2022
Reprint : 2023

Published by : Mrs. Meena Pandey
for **HIMALAYA PUBLISHING HOUSE PVT. LTD.,**
"Ramdoot", Dr. Bhalerao Marg, Girgaon, Mumbai - 400 004.
Phone: 022-23860170, 23863863; **Fax:** 022-23877178
E-mail: himpub@bharatmail.co.in; **Website:** www.himpub.com

Branch Offices :

New Delhi : "Pooja Apartments", 4-B, Murari Lal Street, Ansari Road, Darya Ganj, New Delhi - 110 002. Phone: 011-23270392, 23278631; Fax: 011-23256286

Nagpur : Kundanlal Chandak Industrial Estate, Ghat Road, Nagpur - 440 018. Phone: 0712-2721215, 2721216

Bengaluru : Plot No. 91-33, 2nd Main Road, Seshadripuram, Behind Nataraja Theatre, Bengaluru - 560 020. Phone: 080-41138821; Mobile: 09379847017, 09379847005

Hyderabad : No. 3-4-184, Lingampally, Besides Raghavendra Swamy Matham, Kachiguda, Hyderabad - 500 027. Phone: 040-27560041, 27550139

Chennai : No. 34/44, Motilal Street, T. Nagar, Chennai - 600 017. Mobile: 09380460419

Pune : "Laksha" Apartment, First Floor, No. 527, Mehunpura, Shaniwarpeth (Near Prabhat Theatre), Pune - 411 030. Phone: 020-24496323, 24496333; Mobile: 09370579333

Cuttack : Plot No 5F-755/4, Sector-9, CDA Markat Nagar, Cuttack - 753 014, Odisha. Mobile: 09338746007

Kolkata : 3, S.M. Bose Road, Near Gate No. 5, Agarpara Railway Station, North 24 Parganas, West Bengal - 700109. Mobile: 09674536325

DTP by : HPH, Editorial Office, Bhandup. (Megha)

Printed at : M/s. Giriraj Printers, Hyderabad. On behalf of HPH.

"Dedicated to my Dearest
OM SIRIDI SAI
Who bestow on me the inspiration
and strength to take up this work"

Prof. Naliniprava Tripathy

Preface

Rapid progress of information technology and greater collaboration among financial regulators has led to closer links in the international capital markets. As global capital markets have become more integrated, global firms have moved to establish a local presence in major financial markets around the world. To enhance this presence, larger sums of money are moving across borders, and more countries have access to international finance. The business of investment banking is extremely competitive and is trending towards one-stop shopping and globalization. Investment banks no longer engage in investment banking operations only; they have ventured into other areas of financial services to meet clients' demands for one-stop shopping.

Today, Investment banking includes a wide variety of activities, including underwriting, selling, trading securities, private placement, providing financial advisory services, managing hedge funds, mergers and acquisitions, venture capital, private equities, market making, structured finance, syndication functions. Investment bank facilitate to various group of stakeholders, companies, governments, non-profit institutions and individuals to raise funds in the capital market. The key objective of this book is to provide students and business professionals an insight into the principles, operational policies and practices of the investment banks, to put the investment banking business in India in a perspective way to occupy a significant and distinctive competitive position in the minds of the investors and enhance investor's confidence in the coming years.

The book *Investment Banking – Text & Cases* is designed to use as an academic text for MBA students, M.Com. students, MFC students, CFAs, CAs, Ph.D. Students, researchers and academicians. Also it is used as a professional reference for business professionals.

The book entirely covers the healthy theme of investment banking. I feel quite confident that the Chapters that are included in this volume would go a long way of great value and useful to students, research scholars, academic community as well as corporate world. The text is presented in a rational manner and easy language to meet the specific needs of the object group. The text will no doubt acts as catalyst, motivator, and facilitator thereby leading the students to pursue a career in investment banking in today's competitive financial world.

I believe, this book will definitely generate sustained interest in the minds of the students and would greet by the academic community.

I wish to acknowledge the support of Mr. Bijoy Kumar Ojha, Himalaya Publishing House Pvt. Ltd., for his special effort in preparing the manuscript and bringing out the book in a record time. Last but not the least; I have to keep in record that I am solely responsible for errors/omissions that have crept in advertently in the publication. At the same time, I look forward the constructive suggestions and opinions from readers to improve the text.

Author

Contents

Detailed Contents

CHAPTER 1

Investment Banking

Introduction

Investment banking is part of the financial services industry and offers an increasingly important range of services to corporations throughout the world. Investment banking is neither an investing agency nor a banking organization. I-banking, as it is often called, is the term used to describe the business of raising capital for companies and advising them on financing and merger alternatives. Capital in this sense means money. When firms need money in order to grow and expand their businesses, I-banks sell securities to public investors in order to raise this money. Investment banks buy securities, such as bonds and stocks, from an issuer and then sell them to the final investors.

What is Investment Banking?

An investment bank is a financial institution that assists individuals, corporations and governments in raising capital by underwriting and/or acting as the client's agent in the issuance of securities. An investment bank assists companies in mergers and acquisitions, and provide ancillary services such as market making, trading of derivatives, fixed income instruments, foreign exchange, commodities, and equity securities.

Investment banks raise money by issuing and selling securities in the primary market. They assist public and private corporations in raising funds in the capital markets (both equity and debt), as well as in providing strategic advisory services for other types of financial transactions. Even though investment banks, brokerages and broker-dealers are often thought of as one and the same but investment banks are differing from them. A brokerage firm takes a commission for assisting in the purchase and sale of stocks, bonds, and mutual funds. A broker-dealer executes similar functions, but it trades for its own account. An investment bank actually is a broker-dealer that provides corporations with financial services, such as assistance with initial public offerings, mergers and acquisitions advice, and strategic planning.

Investment banks offer their services in different ways and forms. Hayes *et. al.*, (1983), however, define three investment banking services:

- Origination and management of new financial issues;
- Underwriting of issued securities;
- Distribution, involving selling securities to ultimate holders.

Merchant Banking vs. Investment Banking

Predominantly investment banks focus on initial public offerings (IPOs). Merchant banks tend to operate on small-scale companies and offer creative equity financing, bridge financing, mezzanine financing and a number of corporate credit products.

Investment banking covers both fund and fee-based activities but Merchant banking can either be a fund-based activity or a fee-based activity.

Merchant banks still offer trade financing products to their clients. Investment banks rarely offer trade financing.

Merchant banking in the US is primarily a fund-based activity while in India it is intermediation and advisory activity in connection with public floatation of securities.

Commercial Banking vs. Investment Banking

Commercial and investment banking share many aspects, but also have many fundamental differences. In recent years, though the two types of structures have become increasingly similar; commercial banks now offer more investment banking services and presenting themselves as one-stop shops.

Table 1.1: Commercial Banking vs. Investment Banking

Commercial Banking	Investment Banking
1. Commercial banking is refer to a bank that mostly deals with deposits and loans from corporations or large businesses. Commercial banking deals with day-to-day business banking of a client. It accepts deposits and lending; providing financial services for individuals and business.	1. An investment banker arranges for financing a business by selling its stock to the public, arranging a merger, or taking a business public. Investment banks underwrite equity and debt offerings, trade stocks and bonds provide advisory services. Investment banking is dealing in IPOs and Mutual Fund.
2. It deals with low risk business. Also risk taking ability of the bank is monitored by the regulator.	2. It deals with high risk, high return business.
3. It adheres strict Capital Adequacy norms (Basel-II).	3. No Capital Adequacy or any other stricter norms are there in investment banks.
4. Commercial banks are regulated by US Federal Reserve in US and RBI in India.	4. Investment banks are regulated by the SEC in US and all regulatory authority in India.

History of Investment Banking

The history of investment banking in England has a significant start in the 1500 or 1600s. In ancient times investment institutions extending credit to merchants and helping finance to foreign trade and simultaneously accumulated funds for long-term foreign investments. The nineteenth century saw the rise of several prominent banking partnerships financing the import of commodities for European manufacturers and helping them for export their finished products around the world. The 1800s also saw the birth of some of the most famous firms in investment banking, many of is still present today. By the middle of 1800, professional investment banks had sprung up in the US to help government raise funds for infrastructure projects and the Civil War. In the 1830, commercial banks started adding investment banking services to their regular banking activities in the US. Investment banking hit a milestone in the 1870s when syndicate banks from Europe and US teamed up to buy $50 million worth of US Treasury Bonds for resale to public. The syndicate sold billion dollars' worth of government bonds to large numbers of individual investors through the use of thousands of salesmen and an extensive advertising campaign. This venture marked the first mass securities-selling operation carried out in the United States. In the early 1900s, JP Morgan and Company put together another syndicate to reorganize US Steel from an array of affiliated companies into the first billion dollar corporation by trading shares of its smaller affiliates for the merged entity.

The firm of JP Morgan played a major role in the corporate mergers such as the merger of US Steel Corp and the Northern Pacific and Great Northern railroads. The firm grew to such size and prominence at the turn of the century that JP Morgan, the founder, is credited for "saving", Goldman Sachs was founded in 1869 by German Jewish immigrants. Marcus Goldman was among the pioneers of the initial public offering (IPO), and managed one of the largest IPOs at that time, for Sears, Roebuck and Company in 1906. During the period from 1890-1925, the investment banking industry was highly concentrated and dominated by an oligopoly that consisted of JP Morgan & Co.; Kuhn, Loeb & Co.; Brown Brothers; and Kidder, Peabody & Co. There was no legal requirement to separate the operations of commercial and investment banks. As a result deposits from the commercial banking side of the business constituted an in-house supply of capital that could be used to fund the underwriting business of the investment banking side.

In the early twentieth century, investment banking expanded dramatically. One reason was an increase in the number of individuals who owned stock, something that resulted from the prosperous years after the First World War. The Civil War was a crucial time in American history in many ways, including the role it played in the history of investment banking. During World War I and the period following, the investment banking business in the United States expanded spectacularly. This was mainly due to the unprecedented number of individual stock and security holders. This resulted from the great prosperity period in the early 1920s. New and inexperienced banks and firms entered the field, competed for business, and crashed during the Great Depression. However, the ensuing run-up in stock prices created an unsustainable bubble that finally collapsed with the Great Depression in 1929. The US plunged into one of the worst depressions in history. More than 11,000 banks failed or merged, and a quarter of the population was out of work. More importantly for investment banks, the government passed the Glass-Steagall Act in 1933, which compelled commercial banks to separate themselves from their securities distribution arms.

Glass-Steagall Act, 1933

The famous Glass-Steagall Act, enacted in 1934, erected barriers between commercial banking and the securities industry. Glass-Steagall was created in the aftermath of the stock market crash of 1929 and the subsequent collapse of many commercial banks. The modern concept of "Investment Bank" was created in the Glass-Steagall Act (Banking Act of 1933). Glass-Steagall separated commercial banks, investment banks, and insurance companies. The Act prohibited the combination of a depository institution, such as a bank holding company, with other financial companies, such as investment banks and brokerage houses. Reacting to the 1933 banking collapse in US, two Senators Carter Glass and Henry Bascom Steagall proposed the separation of investment banking and commercial banking. The Act passed in US Congress restricted commercial banks from investment activities. The restrictions put by GSA were not applied for foreign banks. The Act was making the banking industry riskier rather than safer by putting curb on diversifying them like JP Morgan less competitive in the US market. Carter Glass, Senator from Virginia, believed that commercial banks securities operations had contributed to the crash of 1929. Banks failed because of their securities operations and those commercial banks used their knowledge as lenders to do insider trading of securities. Prof. George Benston argued that unregulated banks have lower failure rate in comparison to regulated banks. Other countries (Germany, Switzerland) have always allowed universal banking system.

Reason for fall of Glass-Steagall

- The pressures of technological change, diversification, globalization of the banking industry
- Individual and corporate customers' desire for a "one-stop shop"
- Desire to make US investment banks competitive with foreign deposit-taking investment banks such as UBS, Deutsche Bank
- The proposed transaction violated portions of 1933s Glass-Steagall Act, which had clearly erected walls between commercial and investment banks.
- Citigroup successfully obtained a temporary waiver for its violation of the Act, and then after the merger intensified the effort to repeal Glass-Steagall.

Graham-Leach Act, 1999

Looking at the disadvantages and owing to the pressures from Lehman Brothers, Merrill Lynch, Goldman Sachs, Morgan Stanley, and Bear Stearns in 1999 the US Congress repealed the GSA with the establishment of the Graham-Leach-Bliley Act. It eliminated the GSA restrictions against affiliations between commercial and investment banks. President Clinton cancelled the Glass-Steagall Act of 1933. Republican Congress and President Clinton passed the Graham-Leach-Bliley Financial Services Modernization Act in 1999. Permission was given for insurance companies, investment banks, and commercial banks to compete on equal footing across products and markets. The increased leverage allowed by Graham-Leach-Bliley Act and proprietary trading ravaged the investment banking industry, leading to the collapse, merger, or restructuring of all five major pure-play banks on Wall Street. Consumer groups fought repeal of Glass-Steagall saying it would reduce privacy. Graham-Leach calls for a study of the issues of financial privacy. The combined entity offered all services like Banking, Insurance, Brokeraging under one roof. Graham Leach Bliley Act now allowed US commercial banks to do the work of I-Banks.

In JP Morgan's case, it created JP Morgan as a commercial bank, Morgan Stanley as an investment bank, and Morgan Grenfell, as a British merchant bank. The Glass-Steagall Act remained in force until it was repealed during the Clinton administration in 1999. In the mid-20th century, large investment banks were dominated by the dealmakers. Goldman Sachs, Morgan Stanley, Lehman Brothers, First Boston and others advising clients on mergers and acquisitions and public offerings their main objective focus of major Wall Street partnerships. But, however, that trend began to change in the 1980s due to Salomon Brothers, Merrill Lynch and Drexel Burnham Lambert into the limelight as a new focus on trading propelled firms. Investment banks earned an increasing amount of their profits from proprietary trading. Advances in computing technology also enabled banks to use more sophisticated model driven software to execute trades and generate a profit on small changes in market conditions. Investment banks profited handsomely during the boom years of the 1990s.

The US Securities Industry in 2000

Merrill Lynchs was offering full services by merging with other firms. In 1997, the investment bank Morgan Stanley merged with the retail brokerage Dean Witter. Trading powerhouse Salomon Brothers merged with retail brokerage Smith Barney. In 1999 and 2000, Salomon Smith Barney merged with the Travelers with Paine Webber, JP Morgan with Chase. The retail brokerage house primarily offers securities products and services to retail investors. The best example of a retail brokerage house was prudential securities. The trading firms derive most of their profits by putting their own capital at risk through the buying and selling of securities. The most prominent examples of trading firms were Bear Stearns and Lehman Brothers. The commercial banks since the demise of Glass-Steagall prohibitions have been leveraging their corporate relationships and securities underwriting. Ex. JP Morgan Chase, Citibank now part of a Salomon Smith Barney today.

Mergers among Commercial Banks, Investment Banks and Insurance Companies

Travelers' Group (insurance) and Citicorp (commercial bank) in 1998 jointly produce Citigroup, on anticipation that Glass-Steagall would be cancelled. Chase Manhattan Bank (commercial bank) acquires JP Morgan (investment bank) (2000) for $34.5 billion. UBS Switzerland buys Paine Webber (brokerage) 2000. Credit Suisse buys Donaldson Lufkin Jenrette (investment bank) 2000.

The repeal of the Glass-Steagall Act of 1933 effectively removed the separation that previously existed between Wall Street investment banks and depository banks. This repeal directly contributed to the severity of the financial crisis of 2007-2010.

Functional Areas of a Typical Investment Bank

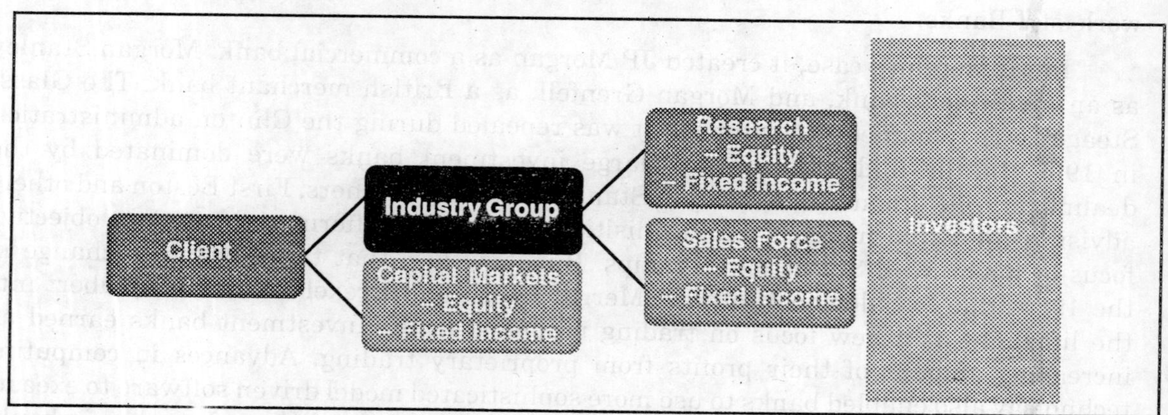

Who Needs an Investment Bank?

Any firm contemplating a significant transaction can benefit from the advice of an investment bank. A quality investment-banking firm can provide the services required to initiate and execute a major transaction, thereby empowering small to medium sized companies with financial and transaction experience without the addition of permanent overhead. Although large corporations often have sophisticated finance and corporate development departments, an investment bank provides objectivity, a valuable contact network, allows for efficient use of client personnel, and is vitally interested in watching the transaction close.

Role of Investment Banker

An investment bank performs six functions in their role as intermediary between "issuers" and "investors". An issue can be a public/private company or any other entity that sells financial assets in the form of stock or bonds. An investor can be a company or a person who buys these assets. So, issues can be viewed as a buyer of capital and an investor can be viewed as a provider of capital. Investment banking includes a wide variety of activities, including underwriting, selling, and trading securities, providing financial advisory services, restructuring, venture capital, market making, property trading, financial engineering, and asset securitization, clearing and settlement and money management. Within the bank, each groups are performing their own specialized set of activities. Investment banks cater to a diverse group of stakeholders – companies, governments, non-profit institutions, and individuals – and help them raise funds on the capital market. They perform the following major functions for their customers: serve as trading intermediaries for clients, lend and invest banks' assets, provide advice on mergers, acquisitions, and other financial transactions, research and develop opinions on securities, markets, and economies, issue, buy, sell, and trade stocks and bonds, manage investment portfolios. They are members of a team with attorneys and accountants. The investment banker's value added comes both from specific technical knowledge as well as from retrospection from the number of times they have been through the process. Investment banks help companies and governments and their agencies to raise money by issuing and selling securities in the primary market. The investment bank is act as an intermediary between issuers of securities and investors in securities. In the narrow sense, the investment banker is a specific intermediary introduced between buyers and sellers of securities in the investment and capital market. Objectively viewed, he acts as a merchant in securities, selling as rapidly as possible in varying amounts to other financial institutions or individual investors. Functionally he acts as channeling money through which saving flow into the permanent capital resources of business undertaking. Investment banker provides advice on issues such as how to raise capital through equity or debt instruments. An investment banker also deals with privatization of public entities. In addition to the above mention activities, investment bankers provide service and advice to companies on mergers and acquisitions, organizations, governments, etc.

The investment bank is an essential player in the success of the IPO offering. The investment bank heading the issuer's team of professional advisors and coordinating their roles and ensure that the company successfully completes the IPO process. Investment bank assists the company in sorting out the relevant issues and determines if an IPO indeed makes sense and is feasible.

Investment banking endeavours to build-up and strengthen client relationships by listening, understanding and providing innovative financial solutions and advice. An investment banker's main target is to help clients to accomplish their goals. Investment bankers are assisting their clients with the implementation of their chosen plan. Investment bankers identify the necessitated work of their clients and protected their own clients' accordingly. It offers a wide range of financial advisory services including underwriting the issuance of equity or debt and investment services in addition to traditional banking products. An effective investment banker is always tries to keep close relationships with each client and even devoting numerous hours to contact client and holding meetings with them. Investment bankers also look for new opportunities for existing clients. Apart from this, it is the primary role of the investment banker to balance the variable desires of the stakeholders, while appropriately representing the interests of the company. Investment bankers also design and manage a fair sale process for companies during bankruptcy situations. The investment banker's first task is to determine that their prospective client harmonizes on values and expectations need to be mutual. The investment banker and their client are developing a mutual understanding of why and where a potential buyer considering value. The investment banker must discuss openly and early in the process if there are any potential problems arises related to the company and its business. The investment banker also projecting the expenses and future performance in realistic terms about capital and other resources needed. The investment banker is also helping in recruiting or selecting other members of the teams not already in boards. The investment banker identify and evaluating potential buyer for the company at the desired price and terms. The investment banker developed marketing strategies to create an auction or alternately obtain a pre-emptive bid for mergers and acquisitions. The investment banker's next task is to identify and prioritize specific potential buyers. The investment bankers' ideal goal is to obtain personal introductions to senior management of potential buyers. Then the investment bankers' objective is to obtain a signed confidentiality or non-disclosure agreement for company. The investment banker's next step is to send prospects the "book". Confidentiality agreements notwithstanding, the book should not contain anything truly proprietary and not even identify the company by name. The investment banker's follow-up starts a week after the book is received. Investment banker also appraise the details of potential buyers regarding its company, its culture and its history, particularly with respect to prior transactions to make easier and enable the company to ask the right questions and understand why the buyer might be interested. The investment banker also obtain the buyer's schedule and checklists in advance so as to provide information to company for selection of the participants and plan formulated accordingly to handle sensitive questions. The investment banker should serve as control for incoming requests, which will help identify emerging negotiating issues. Careful consideration must be given to what is provided, especially projections, and records kept as to everything provided. The investment banker normally interface with the buyer on an letter of intent (LoI). The investment banker normally also assist in obtaining the numerous other "closing deliverables" from outside sources, e.g., consents of shareholders, lenders, landlords, leasing companies, insurance carriers, customers or government agencies; lien releases; good standing and tax clearance certificates, etc. One missing document may lead to kill a deal. A professional investment banker normally remain on the scene, on duty, until the deal finally closes. The investment banker not only is devising a broad and inclusive solicitation list of parties that are most likely to be interested in acquiring the company, but is also charged with managing the due diligence process to ensure that all potential bidders receive equal treatment and access to information. Further, the investment banker provides an unbiased view in evaluating the highest and best offers in this auction setting. Investment bankers often advise a distressed client in sensitive scenarios to explore an acceptable transaction in the given time period. So, investment banker act as a lead manager in the public and right issues of new capital, act as consultant or advisor in the public issues of new capital, underwriter offerings of new securities, provide venture capital for high technology firms, provide corporate restructure services, clearing and settling payments to facilitate trade, providing reliable price information on securities to help decentralized decision making in securities markets.

Break of an Investment Bank

Investment banks provide five main primary types of services: raising capital, advising in mergers and acquisitions, executing securities sales and trading, and performing general advisory services, syndicate and research.

Corporate Finance: Modern corporate finance teaches us that information is of critical importance when a company raises capital. It generally performs two different functions: 1. mergers and acquisitions advisory, and 2. underwriting. Investment banks often represent firms in mergers, acquisitions, and divestitures. In each case, the investment bank provides a thorough analysis of the entity bought or sold, as well as a valuation range and recommended structure. On the mergers and acquisitions (M&A), side of corporate finance, bankers assist in negotiating and structuring a merger between two companies. If, for example, a company wants to buy another firm, an investment bank will help finalize the purchase price, structure the deal, and generally ensure a smooth transaction. The underwriting involves drive the process of raising capital for a company. An investment bank is assisting a firm in raising funds to achieve a variety of objectives, such as to acquire another company, reduce its debt load, expand existing operations, or for specific project financing. Capital can include some combination of debt, common equity, preferred equity, and hybrid securities such as convertible debt or debt with warrants. The investment bank works with the client to structure the transaction to meet specific objectives which will be attractive to investors.

Sales and Trading: Sales are another core component of any investment bank. Salespeople take the form of either the classic "retail broker" or the institutional salesperson. Brokers develop relationships with individual investors, selling stocks and stock advice to customers. Institutional salespeople develop business relationships with large institutional investors, such as money managers, pension fund managers or mutual fund companies. Traders also provide a vital role for the investment bank. A trader plays two distinct roles for an investment bank: traders provide liquidity to the firm's clients, traders facilitate the buying and selling of stock is also called making a market, or acting as a market-maker. Traders are performing this function make money for the firm by selling securities at a slightly higher price than they pay for them. This price differential is known as the bid-ask spread. In addition to providing liquidity and executing trades for the firm's customers, traders also may take their own trading positions on behalf of the firm, using the firm's capital and hoping to benefit from the rise or fall in the price of securities. This is called proprietary trading. Typically, the market-making function and the proprietary trading function is performed by the same trader for each security. In recent years, executives who cut their teeth on the trading floor have risen to the top of many leading investment banking divisions. Their elevation reflects the growing importance of trading to investment bank profits.

Syndicate: Syndicate provides a vital link between salespeople and corporate finance. Syndicate exists to facilitate the placing of securities in a public offering, a knock-down drag-out affair between and among buyers of offerings and the investment banks managing the process. In a corporate or municipal debt deal, syndicate also determines the allocation of bonds.

General Advisory Services: Advisory services include assignments such as strategic planning, business valuations, assisting in financial restructurings, and providing an opinion to the fairness of a proposed transaction.

Research: Research analysts give advice regarding buy, sell or hold those securities by keeping in touch with market. They also forecast companies' future earnings. Stock analysts typically focus on one industry and will cover up to 20 companies' stocks at a time. Some research analysts work on the fixed income side such as a particular industry's high-yield bonds. The I-bank's salespeople use the research analysts' findings to convince their clients to buy or sell securities through their firm. Corporate finance bankers also rely on research teams for expert analysis and forecasts of their industry sectors.

Organizational Structure of an Investment Bank

The investment bank is organized into activities and units commonly referred to as front-office, middle-office, and back-office. The individual activities are described below:

Front-office: Investment banking is the traditional aspect of investment banks, which involves helping customers raise funds in the capital markets and advising on mergers and acquisitions. Financial markets is split into four key divisions: Sales, Trading, Research and Structuring.

Sales and trading is the most profitable area of an investment bank. Majority of revenue are generating from this area. In the process of market-making, traders will buy and sell financial products with the goal of making an incremental amount of money on each trade. In the term of investment banks sales means it is sales force. Their primary job is to call on institutional and high-net-worth investors to suggest trading ideas and take orders. Then sales desks communicate their clients' orders to the appropriate trading desks, which can price and execute trades, or structure new products that fit a specific need. Research is the division which reviews companies' reports about their prospects along with often "buy" or "sell" ratings. Research division's resources are used to assist traders in trading. In recent years the relationship between investment banking and research has become highly regulated which reducing its importance to the investment bank. Structuring is relatively a recent division due to introduction of derivatives in the market. In investment banks, highly technical and numerate employees working on creating complex structured products which typically offer much greater margins and returns than underlying cash securities.

Middle-office: Traders are considering risk management which analyzing the market and credit risk to their daily trades and taking into the balance sheet. It also setting limits on the amount of capital that they are able to trade in order to prevent 'bad' trades which will have a detrimental effect to the bank.

Back-office: Operations department generally involves data-checking trades and ensuring that they are transacting the required transfers as per requirement. It is also managing the financial information and reporting of the bank which ensures efficient function of capital markets. In other words, it provides greatest job security of the divisions of investment bank. The staff in these areas are often highly qualified understands the depth the deals of transactions that occur across all the divisions of the bank.

Technology: Technology has changed considerably in the last few years as more sales and trading desks are using electronic trading platforms nowadays. Investment banks maintain networks of frequent traders, who provide them with the information and the liquidity necessary to float new securities. Most investment banks manage large research departments working on problems similar to those faced by the network members. These departments provide the bank with a bargaining chip in its negotiations with network members, although they seem hard to justify on a standalone basis. So, every major investment bank is having considerable amounts of in-house software created by the Technology team to deal with computer and telecommunications-based support for hedging the complex model driven algorithms.

What to Look for an Investment Bank?

Customers are expecting top-notch services from the investment-banking firms. Some criteria are as follows:

Services Offered: The investment bank should provide not only "brokering" a transaction but also qualitative services for all functions except sales and trading. For example, most projects are comprise of detailed industry and financial analysis, preparation of relevant documentation such as an offering memorandum or presentation to the Board of Directors, assistance with due diligence, negotiating the terms of the transaction, coordinating legal, accounting, and other advisors, and generally assisting in all phases of the project to ensure successful completion.

Experience: It is extremely important that experienced senior members of the investment banking firm are to be active in the project on a day-to-day basis. It is always preferred to choose an investment bank that is having the background of specific industry division on the basis of the depending on the type of transaction. The investment bank is required to have a wide network of relevant contacts, such as potential investors or companies that could be approached for acquisition.

Record of Success: Although no reputable investment bank can guarantee success but the firm must have a demonstrated record of closing transactions.

Ability to Work Quickly: Often, investment banking projects have very specific deadlines. The investment bank must be willing and able to put the right people on the project and work diligently to meet critical deadlines.

Fee Structure: Generally, investment bank are charging an initial fee normally one-time or monthly and rest fees are conditional upon successful completion of the transaction. It is important to employ a fee structure that aligns the investment bank's incentive with own requirement.

Ongoing Support: An investment bank prefer to work on a transaction for the company if it intimately familiar with the business of that particular company. An investment banker also keeps on providing trusted business advisor and informal advice and support on an ongoing basis. However, an experienced, quality investment bank pays services for its fee many times more and keeps on adding significant value to a transaction.

Gaining Competitive Advantage in the Investment Banking Sector

The speed and scale of change in the investment banking industry is incredible. Increasingly sophisticated clients require increasingly sophisticated services and more stringent compliance requirements. These are combined with regulatory management makes the industry one of the most competitive today. Investment banker achieves competitive success regarding deepest understanding of the client's needs, greatest insight into the client's market dynamics, and clearest appreciation of the latest corporate and regulatory frameworks.

The modern and successful investment bank is one that is truly able to:

- Leverage its collective client contacts and relationships
- Protect ownership, sensitivities and confidentialities
- Learn and understand the client's specific business needs and objectives
- Develop, share and demonstrate deep market sector insight
- React and act quickly

Some investment banks recently have built unique overall or product-related reputations. Investment banking is more than anything else "a people's business" where relationships are critical and business success is dependent on highly personalized value-added services. People through their breadth of experience, their quality of training, as well as their integrity and dedication to the firm, generate business and add value to the firm. Such qualities of professionalism and integrity are seen as important contributors to competitive advantage. Currently the network strength of an investment bank is considered as a secondary source of competitive advantage. The investment banking industry's competitive structure is characterized by both increased concentration and increased fragmentation. Specialist corporate finance houses have focused on either local niches or specialized service niches. There are, however, two prevailing views regarding the competitive structure of the investment banking industry. The first is that a rapid polarization are taking place among the major players who are full service investment banks with a worldwide capability and specialist-niche players on a geographical or product basis.

How Investment Bankers Estimate Customer Potential?

The customer is one of the world's leading wealth management companies and a global leader in investment banking and trading across a broad range of asset classes. The investment banker estimates the companies' organic and non-organic growth prospects and the quality of management of the company. Growth prospects appear to be a very important variable and investment banks examine the degree by which the company will grow organically or develop a propensity for acquisitions. In many cases management changes are dramatically increases the business potential of a company from the investment banking point of view. However, all investment banks have a grading system for ranking customers according to their estimated future capital requirements and the organic and non-organic growth opportunities that might present themselves regarding M&A work. Investment bank positioning customer on a matrix for strategic and tactical planning purposes. A customer portfolio evaluation framework is as shown in Fig. 1.1

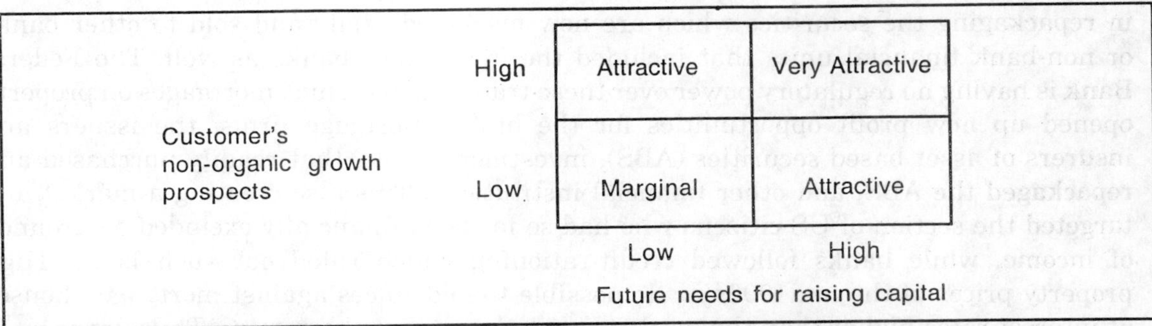

Figure 1.1: Customer Evaluation Matrix – Relationship Potential

Recent Developments in Investment Banking: The Players

JP Morgan functioned as an investment banks in earlier years but, after Glass-Steagall Act of 1933, the function of investment bank was split off from commercial banks. In 1980 commercial banks again sought and obtained permission to enter arena of Wall Street business and the Glass-Steagall Act was repealed.

In 2005, the US was the primary source of investment banking income contributing a total of 51 per cent. Europe (with Middle East and Africa) generated 31 per cent of the total, slightly more than 30% share a decade ago. Asian countries generated the remaining 18 per cent. Between 2002 and 2005, fee income from Asia increased by 98 per cent. Investment banking is one of the most global industries and is hence continuously challenged to respond to new developments and innovation in the global financial markets. Throughout the history of investment banking, many have theorized that all investment banking products and services are commoditized. New products with higher margins are constantly invented and manufactured by bankers in hopes of winning over clients and developing trading know-how in new market. Previously, investment banks had assisted lenders in raising more lending funds and having the ability to offer longer term fixed interest rates by converting the lenders' outstanding loans into bonds. For example, a mortgage lender would make a house loan, and then use the investment bank to sell bonds to fund the debt; the money from the sale of the bonds can be used to make new loans, while the lender accepts loan payments and passes the payments on to the bondholders. This process is called securitization. Another trend in investment banking is the vertical integration of debt securitization. However, lenders have begun to securitize loans themselves especially in the areas of mortgage loans. Many investment banks have focused on becoming lenders themselves making loans with the goal of securitizing them and want to be a very popular financing option for commercial property investors and developers.

The US economy is subjected to a series of credit squeeze measures which led the way to credit creation beyond the usual banking orbits. Thus, a large number of US firms started having access to short-term credit by using, as collaterals, securitized assets like commercial papers. As the movement of securitization of assets caught on, new forms of financial intermediation are provided by investment banks which lent their expertise in repackaging the securities which are now marketed easily and sold to other banks or non-bank financial units that included the investment banks as well. The Federal Bank is having no regulatory power over these transactions. Thus, mortgages on property opened up new profit opportunities for the broker-mortgage firms, the issuers and insurers of asset based securities (ABS), investment banks that readily purchased and repackaged the ABS, and other financial institutions. This also creating a market and targeted the section of US citizens who had so far been financially excluded on grounds of income, while banks followed credit-rationing which ruled out such loans. High property prices of the mid1990s made possible the advances against mortgaged houses at interest rates higher than the market rate to low income borrowers. Thus, loans were advanced by banks, via broker-dealers of mortgages, to borrowers in housing markets at subprime rates. Borrowers committed to regular instalments to parties. But house-owners failed to service debt and the prices of property fell drastically resulting in losses and foreclosure of the mortgage deal. Issuers of ABS and investment banks faced losses due to non-payment by borrowers. This was aggravated by sharp declines in ABS prices in the market. Thus, a glorious housing boom was seen in the United States and faces the collapse of American giant financial institutions which fell, one after another. The first who suffered from the increase in foreclosures were mortgage originators. Under pressure from its creditors, New Century closed its lending facility in March 2007. It was the second largest subprime lender that incurred heavy losses due to default in payment by 2.5 per cent of its borrowers on their first mortgage payment in 2006. Financial markets did not bother and remained fairly calm until early August 2007 despite having seen the downfall of two hedge funds controlled by Bear Stearns. Soon another big investment bank Lehman Brothers followed the same collapse. Before the government could realize the seriousness of the situation, another AIG (American Investment Group), the biggest insurance company with worldwide network which became bankrupt. The process did not stop here. Again three reputed investment banks followed the downfall – Merrill Lynch, Goldman Sachs and Stanley Morgan Investment. The former was taken over by the Bank of America while the latter two were converted into holding companies. Next on the chopping block was Washington Mutual, biggest bank taking deposits from and lending to ordinary clients. Everybody was shocked. The biggest investment banks include Goldman Sachs, Merrill Lynch, Morgan Stanley, Dean Witter, Salomon Smith Barney, Donaldson, Lufkin & Jenrette, JP Morgan and Lehman Brothers compete for the biggest deals both in the US and worldwide. The US housing market, which had risen steadily through 1990s, finally began to slow down. At the same time, mortgage lenders were making increasingly risky loans-approving mortgages for "subprime" customers who were at high risk of defaulting. Meanwhile, I-banks had figured out ways to securities home loans and the risks involved with them, packaging and slicing these new securities into arcane derivatives. These derivatives wound their way through the world's financial system, piling up in banks' balance sheets. This created a ticking time bomb: as people began defaulting on their mortgage payments, these assets' values evaporated, leading to massive write-downs and losses. There was a panic situation in the entire financial world. The repercussions of the fall of the financial institutions were felt in the entire economy. There was loss of confidence. Banks would not lend to each other or enter into transactions. The entire credit system crippled. The global financial crisis has passed through five stages (RBI and Bank for International Settlement, Annual Report, and 2008-09.) These are:

- The prelude, leading up to the March 2008 takeover of Bear Stearns;
- The gradual deterioration in financial conditions from mid-March to the failure of Lehman Brothers on 15th September, 2008;
- From mid-September to late October, a global loss of confidence, a massive flight to quality and the near collapse of the financial system;
- From late October, the severe decline in the global economy; and
- Beginning in mid-March 2009, the deepening downturn and the first signs of stabilization.

This is also illustrated in the Table 1.2 and Figure 1.2 below:

Table 1.2: The Global Financial Crisis: Evolution and Stages

Stages of the crisis	Markets and institutions	Macroeconomic conditions	
		Industrial economies	**Emerging market economies**
Pre-March 2008: **prelude to the crisis**	Subprime mortgage defaults create widespread financial stress. Uncertainty about size and distribution of losses. Crisis starts when interbank markets are disrupted in August 2007; waves of increasing intensity until March 2008.	Growth weakens.	Robust growth with inflation rising. Many Inflation targeters above their targets.
Mid-March to mid-September 2008: **towards the Lehman bankruptcy**	Takeover of Bear Stearns in March slows decline, but bank losses and write downs accumulate as downturn weights on asset prices. More countries affected. Liquidity crisis reveals underlying solvency crisis, increasing pressure on financial institutions.	G3 economies contract even as oil prices fall steeply after August	GDP growth slows after June but remains positive. Exports weaken in central Europe.
15th September, 2008 to late October 2008: **Global loss of confidence**	Demise of Lehman Brothers on 15th September, 2008 triggers a bigger run on key funding markets. More financial institutions fail or are rescued. Loss of confidence affects markets and countries globally. Reprieve only after unprecedented and broad-based policy intervention.	As confidence falls and financing conditions tighten, forecasts are revised down sharply.	Confidence slumps. Financing conditions tighten. Steep currency depreciations.
Late October 2008 to mid-March 2009: **Global Downturn**	Markets remain volatile, with increasingly dire economic data releases, weak earnings reports and uncertainties over ongoing government intervention. Downturn	Spending drops, leading to declines in goods trade and GDP. Inflation falls, with the price level declining in some countries.	GDP growth declines sharply in 04, 2008 as exports slump. Capital inflows reverse.

	means that credit losses keep mounting.		
Since mid-March 2009: **Downturn deepens but loses speed**	Asset prices recover somewhat after more policy action. But signs of market dysfunction remain, as official efforts have failed to fully restore confidence in the global financial system. Continued credit losses.	Consumption and production continue to decline, with possible signs of bottoming out.	Equity markets recover, and exchange rates stabilise.

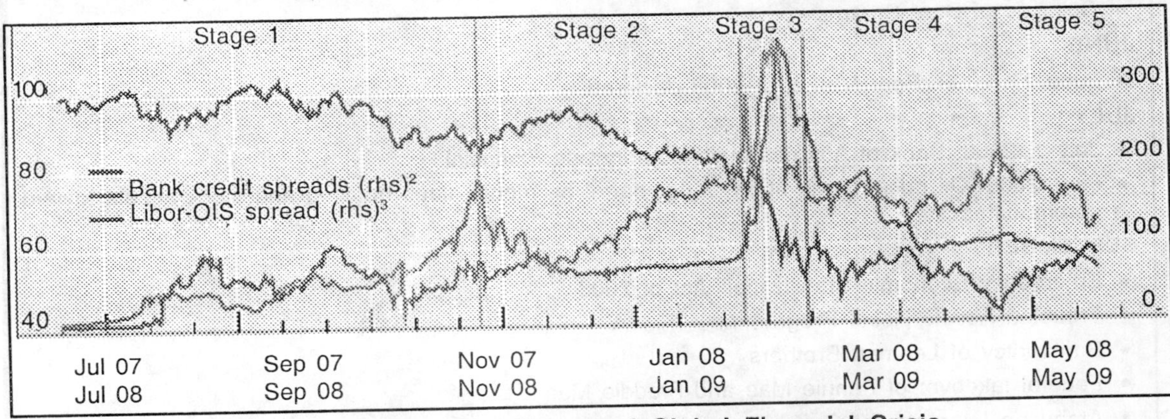

Figure 1.2: The Five Stages of Global Financial Crisis

[1] Morgan Stanley Capital International index, in US dollar terms; 1st June, 2007 = 100.

[2] Equally weighted average of CDS spreads (in basis points) for 18 major international banks; includes Lehman Brothers until 15th September, 2008 and Merrill Lynch until 31st December, 2008.

[3] Three-month US dollar Libor minus overnight index swap (OIS) rates, in basis points.

Source: Bank for International Settlement, Annual Report, 2008-09.

In the first stage, during which the main focus was on funding liquidity, bank losses and write downs continued to accumulate as the cyclical deterioration slowly translated into renewed asset price weakness. As a result, in the second stage of the crisis, from March to mid-September 2008, funding problems morphed into concerns about solvency, giving rise to the risk of outright bank failures. One such failure, Lehman Brothers on 15th September, triggered the third and most intense stage of the crisis. Stage four, from late October 2008 to mid-March 2009, saw markets adjust to an increasingly gloomy global growth outlook amid uncertainties over the effects of ongoing government intervention in markets and the economy. Stage five, beginning in mid-March 2009, has been marked by signs that markets are starting to show some optimism in the face of still largely negative macroeconomic and financial news, even as true normalization – the end of the crisis – still appears some way off (BIS, 2009).

Table 1.3: Global Financial Crisis: A Timeline of Important Events (Events of 2008, 2009)

JANUARY

- Stock Market Volatility

FEBRUARY

- Nationalization of Northern Rock

MARCH

- Collapse of Bear Stearns

JUNE

- June 27, 2008: Bear Market of 2008 declared

JULY

- July 1, 2008: Bank of America buys Countrywide Financial
- July, 2008: Oil prices peak at $147 per barrel as money flees housing and stock assets toward commodities

SEPTEMBER

- Emergency Economic Stabilization Act of 2008
- Troubled Assets Relief Programme
- Bankruptcy of Lehman Brothers
- Federal takeover of Fannie Mae and Freddie Mac
- American International Group Federal Reserve bailout
- Merrill Lynch sold to Bank of America Corporation
- Morgan Stanley and Goldman Sachs confirmed that they would become traditional bank holding companies
- Partial nationalization of Fortis Holding

OCTOBER

- Large losses in financial markets worldwide throughout September and October
- Passage of EESA of 2008
- Iceland's major banks nationalized

NOVEMBER

- China creates a stimulus plan
- Dow Jones Industrial Average (DJIA) touches recent low point of 7,507 points

DECEMBER

- The Australian Government injects 'economic stimulus package to avoid the country going into recession, December, 2008
- Madoff Ponzi scheme scandal erupts
- Belgium government resigns as a result of Fortis nationalization

JANUARY

- Blue Monday Crash 2009
- US President Barack Obama proposes federal spending bill approaching $1 trillion in value in an attempt to remedy financial crisis

- Lawmakers propose massive bailout of failing US banks
- The US House of Representatives passes the above mentioned spending bill.
- Government of Iceland collapses.

FEBRUARY

- Canada's Parliament passes an early budget with a $40 billion stimulus package.
- JP Morgan Chase and Citigroup formally announce a temporary moratorium on residential foreclosures. The moratoriums will remain in effect until March 6 for JP Morgan and March 12 for Citigroup.
- US President Barack Obama signs the $787 billion American Recovery and Reinvestment Act of 2009 into law.
- The Australian Government seeks to enact another "economic stimulus package".
- 2009 Eastern European financial crisis arises.
- The Bank of Antigua is taken over by the Eastern Caribbean Central Bank after Sir Allen Stanford is accused by US financial authorities of involvement in an $8bn (£5.6bn) investment fraud. Peru, Venezuela, and Ecuador, had earlier suspended operations at banks owned by the group.
- February 23, 2009: The Dow Jones Industrial Average and the S&P 500 indexes stumbled to lows not seen since 1997.
- February 27, 2009: The S&P index closes at a level not seen since December 1996, and also closes the two months period beginning January 1 with the worst two months opening to a year in its history with a loss in value of 18.62%

MARCH

- March 2, 2009: The S&P index finishes the first trading day of March with a drop of 4.7%, the worst opening to a March in NYSE history.
- March 6, 2009: The UK Government takes a controlling interest in Lloyds Banking Group by insuring their debt.
- March 8, 2009: United States bear market of 2007-2009 declared.
- March 18, 2009: The Federal Reserve announced that it will purchase $1.15 trillion in US assets ($750 billion in mortgage backed securities, $300 billion in Treasuries, $100 billion in Agencies) in a bid to prop up liquidity and lending to spur economic growth. The markets initially rallied on the news, however concerns began to grow regarding long-term devaluation of the US dollar and subsequent inflation.
- March 23, 2009: In the United States, the FDIC, the Federal Reserve, and the Treasury Department jointly announce the Public-Private Investment Programme to leverage $75-$100 billion of TARP funds with private capital to purchase $500 billion of Legacy Assets (A.K.A. Toxic Assets).

Source: ASSOCHAM FINANCIAL PULSE STUDY, "Indian Banking Sector: Capital Adequacy under Basel-II", June 2009, Assocham Research Bureau.

Economic environment of the world began to weaken in the middle of 2008 and continued through the second quarter of 2009. According to the *World Economic Outlook*, October 2009 Report by IMF, the global economy has been projected to contract by 1.1 per cent in 2009. The global economy is, however, projected to recover and expand by 3.1 per cent in 2010 (RBI, 2010). The severity and suddenness of the crisis can be judged from the IMF's forecast for the global economy. The report has projected real GDP of the US to shrink by 2.7 per cent in 2009 depicted in Table 1.4. It estimates that the global credit crunch would be deep and long lasting as deleveraging accelerates in advanced economies with corresponding balance sheet adjustment till end-2010. The build-up of leverage that preceded the recent crisis was substantial.

Table 1.4: Global GDP Growth

(Per cent)

Country / Region	2007	2008	2009	2010
US	2.1	0.4	(–)2.7	1.5
UK	2.6	0.7	(–)4.4	0.9
Euro Area	2.7	0.7	(–)4.2	0.3
Japan	2.3	–0.7	(–)5.4	1.7
China	13.0	9.0	8.5	9.6
India	9.4	7.3	5.4	6.4
Advanced Economies	2.7	0.6	(–)3.4	1.3
Emerging and Developing Economies	8.3	6.0	1.7	5.1
World	5.2	3.0	(–)1.1	3.1

Source: *World Economic Outlook*, October 2009, IMF.

Although the decline in bank profits was a global phenomenon, pretax profits of the US Banks in 2008 reduced to more than fifty per cent compared with the previous year (Table 1.5). There was sharp deterioration in the second half. Net interest margins also came under pressure, especially for smaller banks that found it hard to reduce their deposit rates. A total number of 25 deposit taking institutions in US failed in 2008, with combined assets of US$ 372 billion, about 10 times higher than during the previous peak in bank failures in 1993. The failure of Washington Mutual accounted for US$ 307 billion of the total. It was the largest US bank failure in history. Besides the failed banks, the number of institutions on the US deposit insurer's list of problem banks had gone up to 252 with total assets of around US$ 159 billion. Further large failures were averted as weakened institutions were acquired by others with healthier balance sheets.

In Europe, the general scene of bank performance in 2008 was broadly similar to that in North America. Profits slid down rapidly, and as a group the largest banks in the Netherlands, Switzerland and the United Kingdom registered a net loss. The size of the earlier residential property boom in Ireland, Spain and the United Kingdom posed an especially large challenge to banks in those countries once real estate markets slowed. Certain German banks were also affected by real estate exposures, albeit mainly indirectly through securities positions and exposures to commercial property. French and Italian banks were less affected by losses on structured finance investments, given their stronger focus on the domestic retail market. The profitability of Japanese banks remained poor, partly because of their structurally narrow net interest margins. Consequently, their capital base remained weak.

Table 1.5: Profitability of Major Banks
(As a percentage of total average assets)

	Pre-tax profits			Net interest margin			Loan loss provisions			Operating costs		
	2006	2007	2008	2006	2007	2008	2006	2007	2008	2006	2007	2008
Australia	1.54	1.42	0.95	1.87	1.70	1.66	0.12	0.13	0.26	1.56	1.38	1.51
Austria	1.48	1.12	0.66	1.72	1.95	2.10	0.34	0.24	0.45	2.17	2.11	2.29
Canada	1.22	1.12	0.48	1.52	1.48	1.42	0.09	0.13	0.21	2.37	2.27	2.00
France	0.73	0.41	0.05	0.59	0.49	0.70	0.05	0.09	0.21	1.20	1.19	1.23
Germany	0.43	0.25	–	0.51	0.51	0.63	0.05	0.05	0.19	0.96	0.88	1.18
Italy	1.05	0.88	0.41	1.77	1.68	1.94	0.25	0.25	0.42	2.18	1.99	2.31
Japan	0.46	0.29	0.29	0.48	0.49	0.50	0.04	0.11	0.19	0.49	0.55	0.65
Netherlands	0.48	0.30	0.12	1.03	0.85	096	0.10	0.09	0.27	1.13	1.01	1.33
Spain	1.37	1.44	–	1.64	1.72	1.83	0.31	0.37	0.53	1.75	1.77	1.89
Sweden	0.96	0.89	0.79	0.98	0.97	0.99	–	0.02	0.11	0.99	0.96	1.00
Switzerland	0.80	0.38	1.10	0.51	0.53	0.49	0.02	0.03	0.07	1.53	1.78	2.55
UK	0.90	0.74	0.67	1.16	1.02	0.81	0	0.22	0.40	1.56	1.37	1.28
US	1.71	0.98	–	2.35	2.28	2.16	0.25	0.51	1.11	2.95	3.31	3.44
			1.94				0.19					
			0.10									
			0.36									

Source: Bank for International Settlement, Annual Report, 2008-09.

As the macroeconomic situation worsened over the course of the past year, institutions faced increasing pressure on earnings and mounting losses on their credit risk exposures. Losses were intensified by illiquidity in the markets for structured finance products and securitized exposures instruments, which led to substantial reductions in their marked to market valuations shown in Table 1.6.

Table 1.6: Composition of Announced Bank Losses

In billions of US dollars

	Q3-Q4 2007	Q1-Q2 2008	Q3-Q4 2008	Q1 2009
Securities	120.5	97.0	106.1	21.0
Provisions	39.2	96.9	149.3	43.9
Real estate	3.2	11.6	55.9	3.0
Leveraged	8.3	16.4	10.4	2.0
Loans	7.4	26.5	13.7	13.3
Monolines	27.4	47.7	100.4	10.6
Others	206.0	296.0	435.8	93.7

Note: Losses have been defined as write downs in original currency converted to US dollars at end-of-period exchange rates. The classification is based on disclosures by large international banks that may not be perfectly comparable across reporting institutions.

Source: Bank for International Settlements (2009), Annual Report, 2008-09.

Compared with 2007, the rate at least doubled for Australian, French, Swiss and US banks and jumped even higher in the case of German, Dutch and Swedish lenders. European banks have also been hit nearly as strongly as their American peers by losses from subprime mortgage investments, leveraged loans, failed financial hedges and, increasingly, by a surge in conventional credit losses. As per an estimate, banks on both sides of the Atlantic so far have had to cope with combined write-downs of more than US$ 1 trillion in this crisis; they may even have to take US$ 1.3 trillion more.

Emerging countries have been increasingly integrated with the global financial markets and as such several countries have suffered from severe external imbalances, caused by fiscal imbalances and/or over-extended banking systems. These countries have become particularly vulnerable, as the crisis is transmitted through financial and trade channels. In a cross-country perspective, Indian banking sector has displayed healthy trends and so far never witnessed a banking crisis. This is due to the following reasons: (1) the growing stage of development of the credit derivatives market; (2) regulatory guidelines on securitization do not permit immediate profit recognition; (3) perseverance of prudential policies which prevent institutions from excessive risk taking and financial markets from becoming extremely volatile and turbulent; and (4) close coordination between supervision of banks and their regulation.

In fall of 2008, the world's investment banks were in a state of panic, fearing for their own–and others'– safety. Investment banks' earnings had soared through 2005, 2006 and the first half of 2007. According to Dealogic, in the first quarter of 2009, global I-bank revenue was $9.2 billion, down from $15.4 billion in the first quarter of 2008, and far from the peak of $26 billion in the second quarter of 2007. Because the United States and Europe were hardest hit by the global recession, Asia and, to an extent, the Middle East and Africa, have risen in relative importance and fee income. Some banks have begun shifting resources and attention to Asia, where private equity and a reasonably-stable financial system have kept deals flowing.

Bear Stearns was the first to collapse and the US government helped engineer a sale of Bear to JP Morgan Chase in March 2008. Lehman Brothers toppled into bankruptcy and was sold in pieces to Nomural Securities, which now owns its European and Asia-Pacific businesses, and to Barclays, which owns its North American operations. And after 94 years in business as an independent I-bank, Merrill Lynch admitted defeat and sold itself to Bank of America. That left Goldman Sachs and Morgan Stanley as the last independent bulge bracket banks on Wall Street. But even they succumbed. In late 2008, both banks received permission from US regulators to convert themselves into bank holding companies, a restructuring move that allowed them to receive government assistance-but also left them bound by strict regulations and rules regarding leverage and risk-taking. This raises an important point: in UK and in the US, banks that have taken government assistance ("bailout funds") face the imposition of new operating requirements. For the first quarter of 2009, JP Morgan; newly fattened by the addition of Bear Stearns' business– topped the Dealogic revenue rankings, earning $828 million and holding an 8.2 per cent market share. Bank of America; Merrill Lynch was No. 2, with revenue of $695 million and a 6.9 per cent market share. Citi was right behind, with revenue of $679 million and a market share of 6.8 per cent. As in the old days of the bulge brackets, big institutions continue to dominate the market. The top 10 major firms – five American, five European – accounts for over half of the industry's revenue. Representing Europe in the top 10 are UBS, Deutsche Bank, Barclays Capital, Credit Suisse and BNP Paribas. Rounding out the top 15 are the I-banking divisions of smaller European and Japanese banks, including RBS, HSBC, Nomura, Lazard and Calyon. In recent years a class of "boutique" I-banks-small, independent firms – has been on the rise, in some cases challenging their larger competitors for deals. Among the world's preeminent boutiques are Evercore Partners, Allen & Co., Moelis & Company and Perella Weinberg.

M&A Boom and Bust

Mergers and acquisitions advisory was a leading source of revenue for the global investment banking industry. In 2000 the world's volume of M&A activity totalled almost $3.5 trillion and $2.7 trillion by 2005. Both Europe and the US saw 30 to 40 per cent increases in volume. Incidentally, European M&A once accounted for just 10 per cent of the world's deal making; now, it's closer to 40 per cent. The global recession that nearly destroyed banks in 2008 took a big toll on mergers and acquisitions. The world's I-bankers did just $2.6 billion of M&A business in the first three months of 2009, way off the peak of $8 billion in the fourth quarter of 2007.

Current Scenario

Two collapses of the stock market the tech bubble and the subprime crisis have taken their toll on the investment banking industry. Landmark companies including Bear Stearns, Lehman Brothers and Merrill Lynch have been destroyed in the subprime crisis. Goldman Sachs and Morgan Stanley have moved from pure play investment banks to become commercial banks after the repealing of the Glass-Steagall Act. But still, investment banking remains a key element of our capital markets. Goldman Sachs, UBS, Credit Suisse are the major players in the global investment banking industry.

Evolution of Investment Banking in India

In 19th century, European merchant banks set-up their agency houses in the country to assist in the setting of new projects. In the early 20th century large business houses acted as issue house for securities, promoters for new projects and also provided finance to Greenfield ventures only to their companies in which they belong. In 1967, ANZ Grindlays bank set-up a separate merchant banking division. Soon in 1970 Citibank also started investment banking activities. These two banks primarily provided loan syndication, equity raising and other advisory services. In 1972, a Banking Commission report asserted the need for Merchant Banking services in India by public sector banks. SBI was the first Indian public sector bank to set up its merchant banking division in 1972. In 1972, ICICI became the first financial institution to offer merchant banking services. Initial stage the growth of the industry was very slow and by 1980, merchant banks rose to 33 numbers and were set-up by commercial banks, financial institutions and private sector. The securities scam in May 1992 was a major setback to the industry. Several leading merchant bankers, both in public and private sector were found to be involved in various irregularities. Some of the prominent public sector layers involved in the scam were Canbank financial services, SBI capital markets, Andhra Bank financial services, etc., leading private sector players involved in the scam included Fair growth financial services and Champaklal investments and finance (CIFCO). The market turned bullish again in the end of 1993 after the tainted shares problem was substantially resolved. Currently, there are 136 merchant banks registered with SEBI. Currently no person can act as a merchant banker without holding a certificate of registration granted by the Securities and Exchange Board of India. The categories for which merchant banking registration is granted by SEBI is as follows:

Category I – to carry on the activity of issue management and to act as adviser, consultant, manager, underwriter, portfolio manager

Category II – to act as adviser, consultant, co-manager, underwriter, portfolio manager.

Category III – to act as underwriter, adviser or consultant to an issue

Category IV – to act only as adviser or consultant to an issue

The capital requirement depends upon the category.

The minimum net worth requirement for acting as merchant banker are:

Category I – ₹ 5 crore,

Category II – ₹ 50 lakh,

Category III – ₹ 20 lakh, and

Category IV – Nil

Table 1.7: List of Major Investment Banks

Investment banks in the world	Investment banks in India
Barclays Capital	ICICI Securities
Blackstone Group	Ambit Corp Finance
CIBC	SBI Capital Markets
Citi group	Kotak Mahindra
Credit Suisse	Enam
Deutsche Bank	Merrill Lynch
Evercore Partners	HSBC (Blr)
Goldman Sachs	Deutsche Bank (Delhi, Bangalore, Mumbai)
HSBC	Morgan Stanley (Mumbai)
JP Morgan	ANZ
Lazard	Lehman Bros.

Moelis & Co	Goldman Sach
Morgan Stanley	UBS (Hyderabad and Mumbai)
Nikko Securities	JP Morgan (Mumbai and Bengaluru)
Bank of America	Reliance Money
Merrill lynch	

List of Top 10 Investment Banking Firms in India (11th May, 2010)

JP Morgan: JP Morgan is a pathbreaker in providing financial services and solution to its patrons in more than 100 nations across the world assisted by one of the most wide-ranging international product proposals. The firm has been assisting its patrons in commercial and business ventures, besides administering their wealth for more than two centuries. It is a division of JP Morgan Chase & Co. (NYSE: JPM) with assets worth USD 2.5 trillion.

UBS AG: UBS AG is an expanded international fiscal service provider with its main office in Zurich and Basel located in Switzerland. It is among the world's biggest individual wealth administrator besides being the second largest in Europe both in terms of market funding and productivity. The firm has its branches spread across 50 nations with around 40% staff performing business in American nations, 14% in Europe, 33% in Switzerland and 12% in Asia-Pacific. UBS's international business institutes are assets and wealth management, and investment banking.

Goldman Sach: Responsible for providing fund ideas and fiscal help to its clients, shareholders, communities, etc., Goldman Sach facilitate industrial expansion of Indian firms by investing in people, companies and our communities present across the world. The banking firm administers business risks of the firms and gives helpful suggestion in buying and selling businesses. It also assists the state and national level government in sponsoring their functions through loans and equity shares.

Deutsche Bank: With its headquarters in Frankfurt in Germany, Deutsche Bank takes pride of being the international leader in commercial banking and securities, operational banking, wealth management, asset management and retail banking. It is world's foremost global fiscal service supplier with total assets worth Euro 2.2 trillion assisted by the workforce of 80,000 employees across the globe. The bank is registered in the renowned exchange markets namely New York Stock Exchanges (NYSE) and Frankfurt (FWB)

HSBC: A subordinate of HSBC Holdings plc, HSBC Bank is ranked as the biggest banking organization by the *Forbes magazine*, besides being ranked as the seventh biggest in the world on 2009. In India HSBC controls through its various subordinates namely HSBC Operations and Processing Enterprise, HSBC Asset Management, HSBC Securities and Capital Markets, HSBC Insurance Brokers, HSBC Software Development (India) Private Limited, etc.

Morgan Stanley: MSIM offers personalized wealth management facilities and goods to administration, institutions, non-profit firms, pension funds, high income individuals, retail investors, etc. In India the firm operates many local mutual fund schemes under Morgan Stanley Mutual Fund brand for retail investors. It subsidiary Morgan Stanley Advantage Services assists Morgan Stanley's Institutional Services operations ranging from fiscal structuring to research activity, portfolio assessment to IT expansion, etc

ICICI Securities Ltd.: Is India's chief equity house. ICICI Securities Ltd. offer back-to-back banking solutions through its wide sharing network to cater to the varied needs of its retail and corporate clients. ICICI Securities meet the various requirements of its customer base. The firm operates in fiscal product supply, Equity Capital Markets Consultation Facilities, Retail Management, Organizational Equities, etc. The firm is listed under the financial power of Singapore (FPS) and Financial Services power, UK and has an reliable place in the core divisions of its functional areas such as consultant services, fiscal good sharing, Equity Capital Markets optional Services, etc.

Kotak Mahindra: Initiated in the year 1984, Kotak Mahindra is India's foremost private financial institution. The diverse financial services offered by the firm are commercial banking, life assurance, investment banking and stock broking. The bank features among the few first companies to be certified under Reserve Bank of India in 2003.

SBI Capital Markets: SBI Capital Markets is India's leading investment bank and system consultant, aiding local firms in capital recruitment activities for last so many years. SBICAP is providing stock broking facilities since the year 2001. The company is an associate of BSE and NSE capital market divisions. The brokerage facilities offered by the firm are internet broking, organizational equity, retail customer group equity, asset management solutions and equity derivatives. Asian Growth Bank (AGB) possesses 13.84% stakes in equity segment of SBICAPS.

Ambit Corp Finance: Leaders in our investment banking, Ambit Corp provide excellent financial solutions to its clients. The firm's speciality lies in offering holistic servicess to our Investment Banking customers in context of Equity Financial Markets, Mergers and Acquisitions, and Alternate Fund.

Other Investment Bank in India

Other investment bank in India offers large number of financial optional services by tracking the economic trends, besides as long as financial help to corporate and retail customers. Some of them are:

Bajaj Capital: The Bajaj Capital Group is one of the famous investment consultant and financial planning firms in India. It is expert under the Group I of Merchant Bankers by SEBI. Bajaj Capital provides specially made fiscal planning facilities and investment consultation to the investors, organizational investors, corporate, high income patrons and Non-resident Indians (NRIs).

Being one of the biggest distributors of economic goods, Bajaj Capital provides a wide range of investment schemes such as universal insurance, life insurance, mutual funds, etc., to both public and personal institutions.

IDFC: IDFC is initiated in 1997 in Chennai; IDFC undertake the liability of as long as financial support to 332 projects accruing a earnings of up to ₹ 2,20,400 million. The sectors under IDFC's financial support be infrastructure, agri-related business, transportation, health care, tourism and others.

Tata Investment Corporation Limited (TICL): A non-banking financial company (NBFC), TICL is scheduled with the Reserve Bank of India under the group of 'Investment Company'. The firm's commercial behavior constitute mostly of endour in ancient investments in equity of the firms in a variety of sectors. The chief source of go back for the firm entails income on investment trading and income accrued on dividend.

UTI Securities Ltd.: UTI Securities Ltd., authorized as a self-governing specialized body in 1994, UTI Securities Ltd., is one of the famous investment bank of India. After the annihilation of Unit Trust of India (UTI) Act, the total share fund of UTISEL is now controlled by manager of particular enterprise of UTI. The firm has been contribution all sorts of investment linked behaviour which incorporate investment banking and commercial consultation services.

YES Bank: This Investment banking friendship is busy in the categorization, understanding and execution of deals for their clients in diverse sectors and nations. Some of the typical dealings incorporate divestitures, confidential equity syndication, mergers and acquisitions and IPO discussion.

Equities and Global Investment Banking: Equities and Global Investment Banking are offered by HSBC Securities and Capital Markets (India) Private Limited. Global Investment Banking (GIB) group provides public and private sector and Government clients with strategic advice and provides critical financial advice in the areas of: Mergers and Acquisitions, Equity Capital Markets, Strategic Advice, Privatizations, Structured Financial Solutions.

HSBC is one of the market leaders in the stake enhancement business through the Open Offer and Buyback route. GIB has completed landmark deals such as:

- Book Running Lead Manager for the Public Offering by Gujarat Industrial Power Corporation of India Limited (GIPCL) - US$ 70 Mn (Ongoing)
- Book Running Lead Manager for the IPO of Jet Airways Limited - US$ 430 Mn.
- Book Running Lead Manager for the Divestment of GoI stake in GAIL India - US$ 360 Mn
- Book Running Lead Manager for the Divestment of GoI stake in CMC Ltd. - US$ 43 Mn
- Co-Book Running Lead Manager for the IPO of Biocon Ltd. - US$ 70 Mn
- Co-Book Running Lead Manager for the GoI divestment in NTPC - US$ 1 Bn
- Syndicate Member for the IPO of Tata Consultancy Services - US$ 1.1 Bn

Current transactions include advising IBP Company Ltd., on its merger with Indian Oil Corporation Ltd., and advising on the proposed restructuring of the Government of India's holdings in MTNL/BSNL.

Another top global accounting firm looking to capitalize on the growing private equity transactions in India is Deloitte Touche Tohmatsu India Pvt. Ltd., (DTTIPL) who has launched a dedicated private equity practice in India. The entity – christened as Deloitte Corporate Finance Services India Pvt. Ltd., (DCF) – is led by Sandeep Gill as Managing Director and Bimal Modi as Director. Prior to moving to India, Gill and Modi were part of the corporate finance practice of Deloitte and Touche LLP in London. Gill said: "We will provide specialist services to meet individual client needs in the private equity space which includes financial due diligence, bid support, sale and purchase agreement advisory and completion accounts work". Ernst & Young, KPMG and Price-water house coopers are already present in this area. Interestingly, a lot of private equity transactions are handled by boutique firms like Mape Group, Avendus Advisors, Spark Capital and so on. Big boys like Morgan Stanley, Kotak Mahindra, and Lehman Brothers are also expanding in this area.

ICICI Bank, India's largest private sector bank, has recast its investment banking business in order to win large, global size advisory business. The Corporate Products and Investment Banking Group of the bank has been renamed as the Global Investment Banking Group (GIBG). "The investment banking business of I-Sec as shifting to GIBG, while the retail equity brokerage part of ICICI Bank, called ICICI Direct.Com. I-Sec GIBG are having three groups. The three groups are Global Structured Finance and Advisory Group (GSFAG), Financial Institutions and Syndications Group (FISG) and International Syndications Group (ISG). The new structure is helping the I-banking division leverage ICICI Bank's balance sheet size and capital base, when structuring and syndicating M&A deals. Morgan Stanley had also raised a $515 million Asia-dedicated private equity fund in August 2005. So it plans to strengthen its private equity team in India. The fund had invested in Bengaluru's Mantri Developers and Mumbai's Oberoi Constructions. The firm employs about 900 people in India. Mergers and acquisitions (M&As) announced in India rose 38 per cent in 2006 to a record $27.8 billion, including outbound deals that trebled to $21 billion, according to data. ABN AMRO topped the Indian M&A deals table in 2006, from a distant fourteenth place in the previous year, boosted by an airport privatization deal. At the same time, Morgan Stanley slid to ninth position after topping the table in 2005, while Merrill Lynch fell to seventh from second. Merrill, Morgan Stanley and Citigroup have long dominated the Indian M&A scene, which is set to get bigger as Asia's fourth-largest economy grows at about 9 per cent a year. Goldman Sachs and Lehman Brothers are also among the global majors seeking a share of growing investment-banking revenue in India. Indian firms such as Kotak Mahindra Capital Co., and Enam Financial are also significant players in the country's M&A market.

SWOT Analysis

Strengths

Wide Range of Financial Services Offerings: Investment banking provides various types of services such as trading, private equity, venture capital, M&A, joint venture, and project finance, etc.

Efficient Employees: In investment banking all the workings are done by professionals because it requires deft and proficient personnel. The major strength of this sector is its efficient employees.

Technological Advancement: Working efficiency of employees presently has been increased tremendously due to advancement of technology. Hence, works are done quickly and easily.

Advance Infrastructure: The country is equipped with all the latest and advanced amenities such as better telecommunication, transportation, potable water, internet, land, etc. Which is a adding advantage to Investment Banks in India.

Weaknesses

Unawareness of Investors: The major weakness of this industry is not able to reach to investors. Investors are more dependent on the trading sector for their investments rather than any other field.

Opportunities

Huge Potential: The knowledge of investment banking is increasing among investors and they are diversifying their investment into many sectors besides trading. Number of mergers and acquisitions, various projects in the countries are increasing day-by-day.

Reform Policy: 1991 reform policy and recent amendments in international trade of India have widened the area and scope of investment banking activities in India.

Threats

Increasing Competition: Competition in investment banking is increasing day-by-day. New players are foraying to the market due to this market share of each existing company is getting affected and profit as well.

Decentralized Management: Each branch managers are taking decisions in their respective branches which may lead to heavy losses to the company in future if any wrong decision taken.

Top Ten Banking Groups in the World Ranked by Tier 1 Capital

There are so many investment banks in the world which offer specialized investment banking services to numerous entities. These are headquartered in different countries. Some of these investment banks because of their perfect service become a favourite in the corporate world while others struggle to improve their services. Just like other service providers, every year investment banks are rated according to their service and performance. Some hold on to their rank for a long time while some others move up and down the ladder depending on their ranking. The Banker Magazine has released the Top 1,000 world banks for 2009 based on their Tier 1 capital. The following are the Top 25 from the rankings:

Table 1.8: Top 25 Global Banks by Tier 1 Capital (2009)

Rank	Bank	Country	Ticker
1	JP Morgan Chase & Co.	US	JPM
2	Bank of America Corp.	US	BAC
3	Citigroup	US	C
4	Royal Bank of Scotland	UK	RBS
5	HSBC Holdings	UK	HBC
6	Wells Fargo & Co.	US	WFC
7	Mitsubishi UFJ Financial Group	Japan	MTU
8	ICBC	China	
9	Credit Agricole Group	France	
10	Santander Central Hispano	Spain	STD
11	Bank of China	China	
12	China Construction Bank Corp.	China	
13	Goldman Sachs	US	GS
14	BNP Paribas	France	BNPQY.PK
15	Barclays Bank	UK	BCS
16	Mizuho Financial Group	Japan	MFG
17	Morgan Stanley	US	MS
18	UniCredit	Italy	
19	Sumitomo Mitsui Financial Group	Japan	SMFJY.PK
20	ING Bank	Netherlands	ING
21	Deutsche Bank	Germany	DB
22	Rabobank Group	Netherlands	
23	Societe General	France	SCGLY.PK
24	Agricultural Bank of China	China	
25	Intesa Sanpaolo	Italy	IITSF.PK

Source: Seekingalpha.com

The Top 3 ranked banks are the US-based banks. JP Morgan Chase is the number one bank. The other two US banks are Bank of America and Citibank. Wells Fargo & Co. of the US is ranked number six. British Banks Royal Bank of Scotland and HSBC Holdings are holding the fourth and fifth spots. China's ICBC is the only in emerging market holding position in the Top 10. Other Chinese banks in the top 25 list include Bank of China, China Construction Bank Corp. and Agricultural Bank of China. This shows the strength of Chinese banks among global banks and also the growing importance of China in the world economy. Western Banks still dominate the top 25 rankings list despite huge losses due to the credit crisis. This is due to their massive recapitalization with government aid or raising capital from the markets.

Some of the key points from the *Banker Magazine* report are:

- Total profits of the top 1,000 ranked banks plunged 85.3 per cent from $780 bn to $115 bn
- Return on capital sank from 20 per cent in 2008 to a paltry 2.69 per cent
- Total Tier 1 capital has risen 9.7 per cent to $4276 bn
- Assets have grown by 6.8 per cent to $96,395 bn

The worst losses in 2008 were incurred by Royal Bank of Scotland, Citibank and Wells Fargo. Among the Western countries, "US banks made an aggregate loss of $91 bn, the EU 27 an aggregate loss of $16.1 bn, and the UK's banks lost, on aggregate, $51.2 bn." Goldman Sachs and Morgan Stanley were listed in this ranking since they converted to be bank holding companies last year.

Table 1.9: Top Nine Investment Banks, 2009

Investment Bank	Revenue (in $B)	Net Earnings (in $B)	AUM (in $Bn)
Goldman Sachs	45.2	13.4	871
JP Morgan Chase	100.4	11.8	1219
Morgan Stanley	24.74	1.7	779
Citigroup	80.3	(1.6)	556
Bank of America	121	6.3	523
Barclays	31.8	10.3	1379
Lazard	1.53	(0.18)	98
Credit Suisse	31.05	7.9	384
Deutche Bank	25.3	4.96	181
UBS	24	(1.9)	159

Source: *Balance sheet of respective banks,* 2009.

Following are the Top 10 List:

Table 1.10: Top Ten Banking Groups in the World Ranked by Tier 1 Capital

Rank	Company /bank	Tier 1 Capital (US$ million)	Country
1	Bank of America Corp.	160387.8	US
2	JP Morgan Chase & Co.	132971.0	US
3	Citigroup	127034.0	US
4	Royal Bank of Scotland	123859.0	UK
5	HSBC Holdings	122157.0	UK
6	Well Fargo & Co.	93795.0	US
7	ICBC	91110.5	China
8	BNP Paribas	90648.4	France
9	Banco Santender	81577.8	Spain
10	Barclays Bank	805867.0	UK

Source: *Banker Magazine*, July 2010.

Table 1.11: Ranking of US Largest Banks as of March 31, 2010

Rank	Company/bank	Assets (US$ million)	Country
1	Bank of America Corporation	$2,340,667,014	Charlotte, NC
2	J.P. Morgan Chase & Co	$2,135,796,000	New York,NY
3	Citigroup Inc	$2,002,213,000	New York, NY
4	Wells Fargo & Company	$1,223,630,000	San Francisco, CA
5	Goldman Sachs Group, Inc.	$880,677,000	New York, NY
6	Morgan Stanley	$819,719,000	New York, NY
7	Metlife, Inc.	$565,566,452	New York, NY
8	Barclays Group US Inc.	$427,837,000	Wilmington, DE
9	Taunus Corporation	$364,079,000	New York, NY
10	HSBC North America Holdings Inc.	$345,382,871	New York, NY

Source: Federal Reserve System, National Information Centre.

Goldman Sachs: It was founded in 1869 and is global investment banking and securities firm which engages in investment banking, securities services, investment management and other financial services primarily with institutional clients.

JP Morgan Chase: It is one of the oldest financial services firms in the world and has operations in 60 countries with assets of $2 trillion, the largest market capitalization and reports US$779 billion as assets under its management.

Morgan Stanley: It is a global financial services provider and serving a diversified group of corporations, governments, financial institutions, and individuals with US$ 779 billion as assets under its management.

Citigroup: It is a major American financial services company based in New York, NY and has the world's largest financial services network, spanning 140 countries with approximately 16,000 offices worldwide.

Bank of America (Bank of America Merrill Lynch): It is a financial services company, the largest bank holding company in the United States, by assets, and the second largest bank by market capitalization.

Barclays Capital: It is the 25th largest company in the world by Forbes Global 2000 (2008 list) and the fourth largest financial services provider in the world by Tier 1 capital ($32.5 billion). It is also the largest financial services provider globally with $3.7 trillion of assets.

Lazard: It is a pre-eminent international financial advisory and asset management firm and is one of the world's largest investment banks having a cumulative value in excess of $1 trillion and more than 250 restructurings totalling over $350 billion in debtor assets.

Credit Suisse: It was founded by Alfred Escher in 1856 and is organized into three divisions, Investment Banking, Private Banking, and Asset Management.

Deutsche Bank: It is an international universal offering financial products and services like sales, trading, and origination of debt and equity; mergers and acquisitions (M&A); risk management products, corporate finance, wealth management, retail banking, fund management, and transaction banking.

Summary

A major task for investment banks is to follow their client base, increase their technical skills continually. They must gain substantial industry expertise on an international scale, especially in the global industries and develop both multinational and local expertise through the understanding of the main economic and regulatory characteristics of the local and foreign markets. Investment banks must appear reliable, responsive to clients' needs and special requirements. They must gain customers' trust and inspire confidence in them and finally they must demonstrate empathy. Investment banks must improve and emphasize various service dimensions in order to enrich their service quality. These are customers' service demands and meeting them is the best way for an investment bank to improve its competitive position. Investment banks have to manage in a different way the outcome of the service from service process, in order to optimize the rendered service quality.

CASE ASIAN BANK LTD.

The Asian Bank is India's largest private sector banks in terms of market capitalization, assets and net profits. The bank offers a wide range of banking products and financial services to retail customers through variety of channels and also associates in the areas of investment banking and asset management. The bank is also expanded to overseas operations. It was incorporated on 31st January, 1966 as a private bank. The Bank commenced commercial operations on 12th April, 1966. Further the Bank was ranked as 'Best Bank' by the newspaper Survey among 100 nationalized, foreign and private sector banks. The Bank has a network of 20 fully computerized and automated branches covering 12 states. The principle objective of the bank was to create development financial institutions for providing medium-term and long-term project financing to Indian business. All branches are connected through the satellite to a Central Database offering the facilities of 'anywhere banking' and instant funds transfer. The bank has a deposit base of ₹ 6186.20 cr. The Bank's Certificate of Deposits Programme has been rated PRI + by CARE for the last 3 consecutive years. The total staff strength is 588 as of today. According to the *Financial Express* survey the bank has been ranked No.1 in terms of business per employee and No.3 in terms of operating profit per employee. The NPA is given in table-1

Table 1

Particulars	Amount in ₹ Crore
Standards Assets	3775.28
Substandard Assets	93.58
Doubtful Assets	3.96
Loss Assets	
Total Assets	3872.82
Provisions as per RBI norms	8.75
Net Advances	3855.32
Net Nonperforming Assets	80.04
NPAS to Net Advances	2.08%

The Capital Adequacy Position of the Bank is Given in table-2.

Table 2

(₹ in crore)

Particulars	31.03.2006	31.03.2007	31.03.2008
Risk Weighted Assets	976.56	2559.24	4331.82
Capital	323.34	465.54	558.92
Capital Adequacy Ratio	33.11%	18.19%	12.90%

Capital Adequacy Norms

All the countries establish their own guidelines for risk based capital framework known as Capital Adequacy Norms. Capital adequacy measures the strength of the bank. Capital adequacy ratio is also known as capital risk weighted assets ratio. Capital adequacy ratio (CAR) used in the bank to watch bank's health, specifically bank's capital to its risk. Capital adequacy ratio is the ratio which determines the capacity of a bank in terms of meeting the time liabilities and other risk such as credit risk, market risk, operational risk, and others. It is a measure of how much capital is used to support the banks' risk assets. Bank capital plays a very important role in the safety and soundness of individual banks and the banking system. Basel committee has prescribed a set of norms for the capital requirement for the banks in 1988 known as Basel Accord I. These norms ensure that capital should be adequate to absorb unexpected losses or risks involved. If there is higher risk, then it would be needed to back-up with capital.

The focus of Capital Adequacy Ratio under Basel I norms were on credit risk and were calculated as follows:

Capital Adequacy Ratio = Tier I Capital + Tier II Capital/Risk Weighted Assets

Tier I Capital: This is the bank's core capital comprising of share capital, disclosed reserves and minority interests. Tier II Capital: This includes supplementary Capital consisting of general loan loss reserves and revaluation reserves on investments. and properties held for investment

Minimum Requirement of Capital Adequacy Ratio (CAR):

Under Basel II norms, 8% is the prescribed Capital Adequacy Norm.

In case of Scheduled Commercial Banks CAR = 9%

For New Private Sector Banks CAR = 10%

For Banks undertaking Insurance Business CAR = 10%

and For Local Area Banks CAR = 15%

At the end of March 2008, there were 2 Scheduled Commercial Banks (1 Private Sector Bank & 1 Foreign Bank) having 0-9% of Capital Adequacy Ratio, 55 Scheduled Commercial Banks (28 Public Sector Banks,17 Private Sector Banks and 10 Foreign Banks) were having CAR between 10%-15% and 22 Scheduled Commercial Banks (19 Foreign Banks and 3 Private Sector Banks) having CAR of 15% and above according to RBI Publications.

Table 3: Credit Deposit Ratio

Particulars	Global Bank	Industry
2005-06	72.03%	54.69%
2066-07	79.39%	58.31%
2007-08	62.32%	54.91%

Table 4: Estimated Profit Forecast for 2008-09

Particulars	Amount in ₹ Crore
Interest Income	1170.5
Other Income	292.62
Total Income	1463.12
Interest Expended	898.36
Operating Expenses	159.16
Provisions and Contingencies	198.8
Total Expenses	1256.32
Net Profit	206.80

Table 5: Financial Performance for the Last Three Years

(₹ in crore)

Particulars	31.03.2006	31.03.2007	31.03.2008
Interest Income	123.06	382.44	818.60
Other Income	36.22	73.1	163.74
Total Income	159.28	455.54	982.34
Interest Expense	74.28	268.40	620.34
Operating Expense	18.46	55.02	112.30
Total Expenses	92.74	323.42	732.44
Operating Profit	66.54	132.12	249
Provisions and Contingency	22.88	40.88	103.26
Net Profit	43.66	91.24	146.64
Share Capital	2000.00	240	240
Reserves and Surplus	13.66	222.68	318.92
Net worth	213.66	462.68	558.92
Deposits	1299.6	2824.46	6186.20
Advances	1001.08	2242.38	3855.3
Investments	376.08	715	2109.08

Industry P/E Ratio for Private Sector Banks

1. Average P/E ratio 7.8
2. Highest P/E ratio 35.8
3. Lowest P/E ratio 2.6

The bank is going for Public Issue of 8,00,00,000 Shares of ₹ 10 each at a Premium of ₹ 35 per share aggregating ₹ 360,00,00,000 during April, 2008. The objective of the

Offer is to comply with the authorize condition stipulated by the RBI that the bank shall have 60% of its equity held by the public. Further dilution would take place in subsequent tranches, to augment the net worth of the bank for meeting future capital adequacy requirements, to get the bank shares listed on the stock exchanges.

You are requested to find both the qualitative and quantitative factors and also highlight risk factors for this issue. Analysts' feels that this is an underpriced issue. Narrate your views on the basic of valuation methods.

Note: The case is fictitious and any resemblance to a person/company is merely coincidental.

Review Questions

1. Explain the Investment banks' role and function and the trends in investment banking. Where does the industry come from (history of investment banking in Europe, in the US)?
2. How are investment banks organized, and how are they evolving?
3. What are the different types of services provided by investment banker?
4. **Write short notes on:**
   (a) Merchant Banking vs. Investment Banking
   (b) Commercial Banking vs. Investment Banking
   (c) Graham-Leach Act 1999
5. **Quiz**
   (a) Investment banks help companies and governments and their agencies to raise money by issuing and selling securities in _____ market.
   (b) In the year _____ commercial banks started adding investment banking services to their regular banking activities in the US.
   (c) _______ was founded in 1869 by German Jewish immigrants.
   (d) Investment banks cater to a diverse group of stakeholders i.e _____ , _____ , _____ and _____.
   (e) _____ provides a vital link between salespeople and corporate finance.
   (f) In 1972, ____ became the first financial institution to offer merchant banking services.
   (g) Glass-Steagall Act in 1933, which compelled commercial banks to separate themselves from their securities distribution arms. ***(T/F)***
   (h) Investment bank is charging an initial fee normally one-time or monthly and rest fee conditional upon successful completion of the transaction. ***(T/F)***
   (i) Currently the network strength of an investment bank is considered as a primary source of competitive advantage. ***(T/F)***
   (j) US President Barack Obama signs the $787 billion American Recovery and Reinvestment Act of 2009 into law. ***(T/F)***

2 Equity Markets, Bond Market and Private Placements

Introduction

A stock market or equity market is a system through which shares are issued and traded, either through exchanges or over-the-counter markets. It is one of the most vital areas of a market economy because it offers an opportunity to companies' access to capital and investors to participate in a company's success through an increase in its stock price.If the stock market is on the rise, it is considered as an indicator of a country's economic strength and development. Rising share prices is associated with increased business investment and *vice versa*. Share prices also affect the wealth of households and their consumption. Therefore Reserve Bank of India is always keeping an eye on the control and behaviour of the stock market for smooth operation of financial systems functions. Stock market is also act as the clearing house for each transaction and collecting and deliver the shares, and guarantee payment to the seller of a security. This eliminates the risk to an individual buyer or seller on the transaction. The smooth functioning of all these activities facilitates economic growth and promotes production of goods and services as well as employment in the economy. The size of the world stock market was estimated at about $36.6 trillion at the start of October 2008.

Why People are Investing in Equity Market?

Companies raise capital from the public and other institutions for running and mounting their businesses. They allot shares of the company to them in return. The shares have certain monetary value. In simple words, a share or stock is a document issued by a company, which give the right to its holders to be one of the owners of the company. A share represents the smallest recognized fraction of ownership in a publicly held business. Each such fraction of ownership is represented in the form of a certificate known as a share certificate. The breaking up of total ownership of a business into small fragments, each fragment represented by a share certificate, enables them to be easily bought and sold. A share is issued by a company or can be purchased from the stock market. The share price goes up or down depending on the performance of the company. The holder of the shares can buy or sell the shares through a stock exchange; this is known as share market. People invest in the stock market to gain ownership on a company and to make profits out of the upward movements in the price of a stock. By owning a share, an investor can earn a portion and getting capital gain by selling shares. So, the investors return is the dividend plus the capital gain. The equity market is one of the best asset classes for investment all over the world. The bank deposits offer a meagre return on investment which is not even enough to beat inflation, so people are looking for asset classes that return at least more than the inflation and so people look for equities as the option. People invest in the stock market to grow their wealth.

What are the Bonds?

The bond is a security issued by a borrower that obligates the issuer to make specified payments to a holder over a specific period. Bonds are debt because when an investor buys a bond they are effectively loaning the bond's issuer a sum of money and that issuer is incurring a debt. So the issuer – or seller of the bond – is a borrower and the investor – or buyer of the bond – is a lender exhibited in Fig. 2.1.

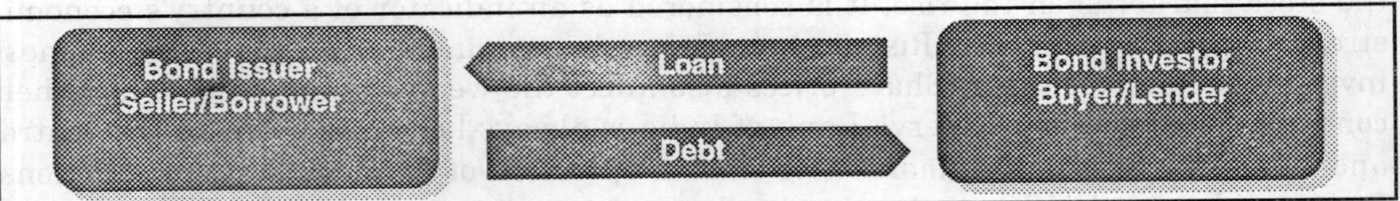

Figure 2.1

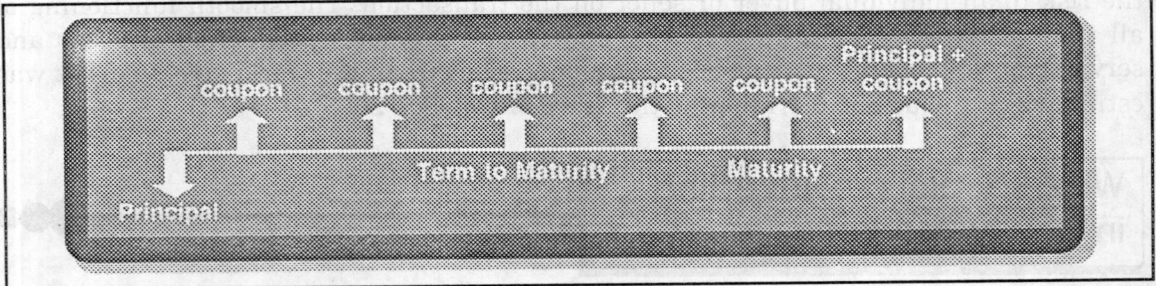

Figure 2.2

With bonds, the price you pay for the bond is known as the principal amount, or the face value of the bond. The length of the loan is referred to as its maturity. The interest paid on the loan by the borrower is called the coupon is depicted in Fig. 2.2.

Bonds are rated depending upon the financial status of the issuer of the bond. Bonds encompass the wide sweep of fixed income securities.

Bonds are also known as fixed income securities, because most bonds pay a regular income to the lender – a rate of interest on the loan. Another reason bonds are known as fixed income securities is that – unlike stocks, which makes no guarantees in terms of their returns – a company that issues a bond guarantees to payback principal plus interest.

Traditionally, the biggest issuers of bonds are government bodies. These bodies borrow money to fund their activities. Governments and municipal bodies need money to spend on public goods – roads, defence, health, social security and so on. And for governments and municipal bodies – apart from taxation and selling public assets – borrowing money is one of their few options. Business houses need cash to meet working capital shortfalls and for invest in new products and expand into new markets. Most bonds have no specific security attached to them and are called "unsecured debentures". This means that in a default situation, the bondholders' rank equally with the other unsecured creditors of the company. Since governments do not pledge specific security, most government bonds are actually debentures. An unsecured debenture usually has a "negative pledge" which prevents the issuer from having assets secured ahead of that issue.

What is Bond Market?

The bond market, also known as the debt, credit, or fixed income market, where participants buy and sell debt securities usually in the form of bonds. The majority of trading volume in the bond market takes place between broker-dealers and large institutions in a decentralized, over-the-counter (OTC) market. However, a small number of bonds, mainly corporate, are listed on exchange. "Bond market" usually refers to the government bond market because of its size, liquidity, lack of credit risk and therefore, sensitivity to interest rates. Because of the inverse relationship between bond valuation and interest rates, the bond market is often used to indicate changes in interest rates or the shape of the yield curve. Credit markets are different. They are the source of liquidity to fund operations. If they are not functioning, the economy is threatened.

As of 2009, the size of the worldwide bond market (total debt outstanding) is an estimated $82.2 trillion, of which the size of the outstanding US bond market debt was $31.2 trillion according to Bank for International Settlements (BIS).

Nearly all of the $822 billion average daily trading volume in the US bond market takes place between broker-dealers and large institutions in a decentralized, over-the-counter (OTC) market. However, a small number of bonds, primarily corporate, are listed on exchanges. Although the stock market often commands more media attention, the bond market is actually many times bigger and is vital to the ongoing operation of the public and private sector.

Important Features

The principal features of a bond are:

Maturity: Maturity of a bond refers to the date on which the bond matures, or the date on which the borrower has agreed to repay the principal amount to the lender.

Coupon: It is the rate at which interest is paid, and is usually represented as a percentage of the par value of a bond. The coupons are stated upfront either directly specifying the number (e.g., 8%) or indirectly tying with a benchmark rate (e.g., MIBOR + 0.5%)

Coupon Rate = Annual coupon/Par value

Principal: is the amount that has been borrowed, and is also called the par value or face value of the bond. All government bonds have the face value of ₹ 100, for example: GS CG2008 11.40 per cent bond refers to a Central Government bond maturing in the year 2008, and paying a coupon rate of 11.40 per cent.

Different Type of Bonds

(a) Classification on the Basis of Variability of Coupon

Zero Coupon Bonds: In such a bond, no coupons are paid. The bond is instead issued at a discount to its face value, at which it will be redeemed. There are no intermittent payments of interest. The effective interest earned by the buyer is the difference between the face value and the discounted price at which the bond is bought.

Floating Rate Bonds: Instead of a predetermined rate at which coupons are paid, it is possible to structure bonds, where the rate of interest is reset periodically, based on a benchmark rate. Such bonds whose coupon rate is not fixed, but reset with reference to a benchmark rate, are called floating rate bonds. For example, IDBI issued a 5-year floating rate bond, in July 1997, with the rates being reset semi-annually with reference to the 10-year yield on Central Government securities and a 50 basis point mark-up.

Fixed Rate Bond: Stays same until maturity; i.e., buy a ₹ 1,000 bond with 8 per cent fixed interest rate and you will receive ₹ 80 every year until maturity and at maturity you will receive the ₹ 1,000 back.

Payable at Maturity: Receive no payments until maturity and at that time you receive principal plus the total interest earned compounded semi-annually at the initial interest rate.

(b) Classification on the Basis of Variability of Maturity

Callable Bonds: Bonds that allow the issuer to alter the tenor of a bond, by redeeming it prior to the original maturity date, are called callable bonds. The inclusion of this feature in the bond's structure provides the issuer the right to fully or partially retire the bond, and is therefore in the nature of call option on the bond. It helps the issuer to reduce the costs when interest rates are falling, and when the interest rates are rising it is helpful for the holders.

Puttable Bonds: Bonds that provide the investor with the right to seek redemption from the issuer, prior to the maturity date, are called puttable bonds. The put options embedded in the bond provides the investor the rights to partially or fully sell the bonds back to the issuer, either on or before pre-specified dates. In rising interest rate scenario, the bondholder may sell a bond with low coupon rate and switch over to a bond that offers higher coupon rate.

Convertible Bonds: A convertible bond provides the investor the option to convert the value of the outstanding bond into equity of the borrowing firm, on pre-specified terms. Exercising this option leads to redemption of the bond prior to maturity, and its replacement with equity. At the time of the bond's issue, the indenture clearly specifies the conversion ratio and the conversion price. The conversion ratio refers to the number of equity shares, which will be issued in exchange for the bond that is being converted.

(c) Classification on the basis of Principal Repayment

Amortising Bonds: In amortising bond, payment includes both interest and principal is made by the borrower over the life of the bond called an amortising bond. The amortizing schedule (repayment of principal) is prepared in such a manner that whole of the principle is repaid by the maturity date of the bond and the last payment is done on the maturity date. For example: Auto loans, consumer loans and home loans are examples of amortising bonds.

Bonds with Sinking Fund Provisions: In certain bond indentures, there is a provision that calls upon the issuer to retire some amount of the outstanding bonds every year. This is done either by buying some of the outstanding bonds in the market, or as is more common, by creating a separate fund, which calls the bonds on behalf of the issuer. Such provisions that enable retiring bonds over their lives are called sinking fund provisions.

Bond Market in India

The debt market is much more popular than the equity markets in most parts of the world. In India the reverse has been true. Nevertheless, the Indian debt market has transformed itself into a much more vibrant trading field for debt instruments from the elementary market about a decade ago.

The bond market in India with the liberalization has been transformed completely. The opening up of the financial market at present has influenced several foreign investors holding up to 30 per cent of the financial in form of fixed income to invest in the bond market in India. The bond market in India has diversified to a large extent and that is a huge contributor to the stable growth of the economy. The bond market has immense potential in raising funds to support the infrastructural development undertaken by the government and expansion plans of the companies.

The major thrust of financial reforms commenced in 1992. This was when the contours of the debt market began taking shape. The idea of the financial reform movement was to have more and more different markets and not necessarily have whole financial intermediation left to the banks. The reform process attempted at doing away with regulations in favour of controls based on market forces, i.e., an era where the interest rates are governed more by the market forces of demand and supply and less by centralized supervision. Slowly, but steadily, the market grew, adding fresh players and novel instruments. Several measures have added greater transparency and have brought the issuances closer to the market levels.

The major reforms that took place in the 1990s were:

- Introduction of the auction system for sale of dated government securities in June1992. This signalled the end of the era of administered interest rates.
- The RBI moved to computerize the SGL and implement a form of a 'delivery versus payment' (DvP) system. The DvP enabled mitigating of settlement risk in securities and ensured the smoothness of settlement by synchronizing the payment and delivery of securities.
- Innovative products in form of Zero Coupon Bonds and Capital Indexed Bonds (Ex. Inflation Linked) were issued to attract a wider gamut of investors. However, the pace of innovation suffered due to non-sophistication of the markets and lack of persistence with some of the new bonds like Inflation Indexed bonds after the initial lukewarm response.
- The system of primary dealers was established in March 1995. These primary dealers have since then acquired a large chunk of share in the GoI bond market and have played the role of market-makers.
- The RBI setup "trade for trade" regime, a strong regulatory system which required that every trade must be settled with funds and bonds. All forms of netting were prohibited.
- Wholesale Debt Market (WDM) segment was set up at NSE, a limited degree of transparency came about through the WDM at NSE, where roughly half the trading volume of India's GoI bond market was reported.
- The Ways and Means agreement put an end to issuance of *ad hoc* treasury bills, the governments' favourite instrument of funding its profligacy.
- Interest income in G-Secs was exempted from the purview of TDS.
- FIIs with 100% debt schemes were allowed to invest in GoI Securities and T-Bills while other FIIs were allowed 30 per cent investment in these instruments.
- Dematerialised forms of securities in G-Secs was done through the SGL and Constituents SGL accounts.

Market Segments

The main segments in India are namely:

- **Government Securities:** This security comprises the Centre, State and State-sponsored securities. In the recent past in USA local bodies such as municipalities have also begun to tap the debt markets for funds.
- **PSU Bonds:** It is generally treated as surrogates of sovereign paper, sometimes due to explicit guarantee and often due to the comfort of public ownership. Some of the PSU bonds are tax free.
- **Corporate Securities:** This comprise of commercial paper and bonds. These bonds typically are structured to suit the requirements of investors and the issuing corporate, and include a variety of tailor-made features with respect to interest payments and redemption.
- **Short-term Paper:** This is issued by banks, mostly in the form of certificates of deposit.

Information on the size of the various segments of the debt market in India is not readily available. This is due to the fact that many debt instruments are privately placed and therefore not listed on markets. While the RBI regulates the issuance of government securities, corporate debt securities fall under the regulatory purview of SEBI. The periodic reports of issuers and investors are therefore sent to two different regulators. Therefore, aggregated data for the market as a whole is difficult to obtain. The NSE provides a trading platform for most debt instruments issued in India. The table below shows the market capitalization of different bonds in NSE Wholesale Debt Market as on March'09.

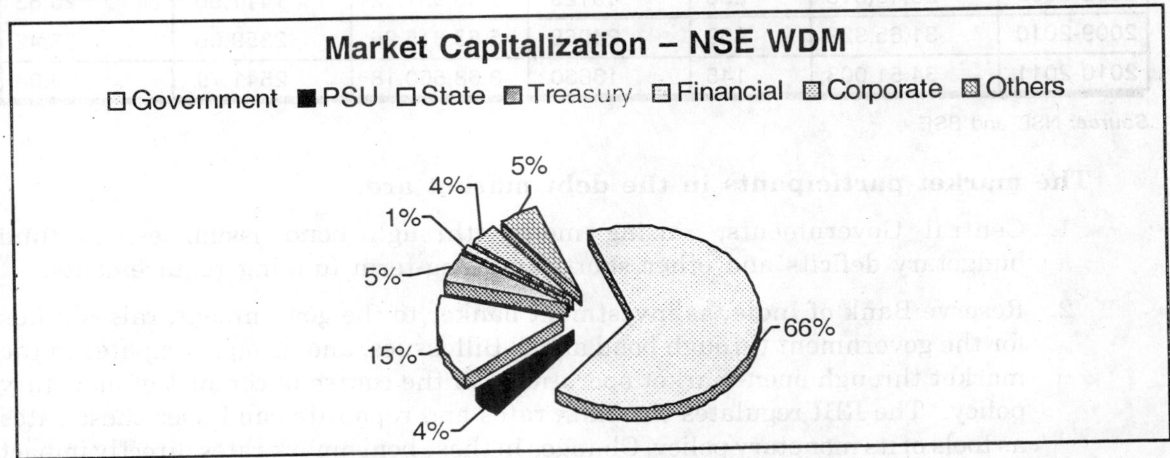

Figure 2.3: Market Capitalisation

Participants in Debt Markets

Debt markets are pre-dominantly wholesale markets, with dominant institutional investor participation. The investors in the debt markets concentrate in banks, financial institutions, mutual funds, provident funds, insurance companies and corporate.

Table 2.1: WDM Business Growth

Year	Market Capitalisation (₹ in crore)	Trading Days	Number of Trades	Net Traded Value (₹ in crore)	Average Daily Value (₹ in crore)	Average Trade Size (₹ in crore)
1994-1995	1,58,181	223	1021	6,781.15	30.41	6.64
1995-1996	2,07,783	291	2991	11,867.68	40.78	3.97
1996-1997	2,92,772	291	7804	42,277.59	145.28	5.42
1997-1998	3,43,191	289	16821	1,11,263.28	384.99	6.61
1998-1999	4,11,470	289	16092	1,05,469.13	364.95	6.55
1999-2000	4,94,033	294	46987	3,04,216.24	1034.75	6.47
2000-2001	5,80,835	289	64470	4,28,581.51	1482.98	6.65
2001-2002	7,56,794	289	144851	9,47,191.22	3277.48	6.54
2002-2003	8,64,481	297	167778	10,68,701.54	3598.32	6.37
2003-2004	12,15,864	294	189518	13,16,096.24	4476.52	6.94
2004-2005	14,61,734	293	124308	8,87,293.66	3028.31	7.14
2005-2006	15,67,574	271	61891	4,75,523.48	1754.7	7.68
2006-2007	17,84,801	244	19575	2,19,106.47	897.98	11.19
2007-2008	21,23,346	248	16179	2,82,317.02	1138.38	17.45
2008-2009	28,48,315	238	16129	3,35,951.52	1411.56	20.83
2009-2010	31,65,929	239	24069	5,63,815.95	2359.06	23.42
2010-2011	34,51,003	145	13660	3,68,560.18	2541.79	26.98

Source: NSE and BSE

The market participants in the debt market are:

1. Central Governments, raising money through bond issuances, to fund budgetary deficits and other short- and long-term funding requirements.
2. Reserve Bank of India, as investment banker to the government, raises funds for the government through bond and T-Bill issues, and also participates in the market through open-market operations, in the course of conduct of monetary policy. The RBI regulates the bank rates and repo rates and uses these rates as tools of its monetary policy. Changes in these benchmark rates directly impact debt markets and all participants in the market.
3. Primary dealers, who are market intermediaries appointed by the Reserve Bank of India who underwrite and make market in government securities, and have access to the call markets and repo markets for funds.

4. State governments, municipalities and local bodies, which issue securities in the debt markets to fund their developmental projects, as well as to finance their budgetary deficits.
5. Public sector units are large issuers of debt securities, for raising funds to meet the long term and working capital needs. These corporations are also investors in bonds issued in the debt markets.
6. Corporate treasuries issue short- and long-term paper to meet the financial requirements of the corporate sector. They are also investors in debt securities issued in the market.
7. Public sector financial institutions regularly access debt markets with bonds for funding their financing requirements and working capital needs. They also invest in bonds issued by other entities in the debt markets.
8. Banks are the largest investors in the debt markets, particularly the Treasury bond and bill markets. They have a statutory requirement to hold a certain percentage of their deposits (currently the mandatory requirement is 25% of deposits) in approved securities (all government bonds qualify) to satisfy the statutory liquidity requirements. Banks are very large participants in the call money and overnight markets. They are arrangers of commercial paper issues of corporates. They are also active in the inter-bank term markets and repo markets for their short-term funding requirements. Banks also issue CDs and bonds in the debt markets.
9. Mutual funds have emerged as another important player in the debt markets, owing primarily to the growing number of bond funds that have mobilised significant amounts from the investors. Most mutual funds also have specialised bond funds such as gilt funds and liquid funds. Mutual funds are not permitted to borrow funds, except for very short-term liquidity requirements. Therefore, they participate in the debt markets predominantly as investors, and trade on their portfolios quite regularly.
10. Foreign institutional investors are permitted to invest in Dated Government Securities and Treasury Bills within certain specified limits.
11. Provident funds are large investors in the bond markets, as the prudential regulations governing the deployment of the funds they mobilise, mandate investments predominantly in Treasury and PSU bonds. They are, however, not very active traders in their portfolio, as they are not permitted to sell their holdings, unless they have a funding requirement that cannot be met through regular accruals and contributions.
12. Charitable Institutions, Trusts and Societies are also large investors in the debt markets. They are, however, governed by their rules and bye-laws with respect to the kind of bonds they can buy and the manner in which they can trade on their debt portfolios.

Table 2.2: Participants and Products in Debt Markets

Issuer	Instrument	Maturity	Investors
Central Government	Dated Securities	2-30 years	RBI, Banks, Insurance Companies, PF, MF, Individuals
Central Government	T-Bills	91/182/364 days	RBI, Banks, Insurance Companies, PF, MF,Individuals
State Government	Dated Securities	5-13 years	RBI, Banks, Insurance Companies, PF, MF, Individuals
PSUs	Bonds, Structured Obligations	5-10 years	Banks, Insurance Companies, Corporate, PF, MF, Individuals
Corporates	Debentures	1-12 years	Banks, MF, Corporates, Individuals
Scheduled Commercial Bonds	Bank Bonds	1-10 years	Corporations, Individual Companies, Trusts, Funds, Associations, FIs, NRIs
Municipal Corporation	Municipal Bonds	0-7 years	Banks, Corporations, Individuals, Companies, Trusts, Funds, associations, FIs, NRIs

Secondary Market for Debt instrument

Wholesale Debt Market

The NSE-WDM segment provides the formal trading platform for trading of a wide range of debt securities. The WDM trading system, known as NEAT (National Exchange for Automated Trading), is a fully automated screen-based trading system that enables members across the country to trade simultaneously with enormous ease and efficiency. Most of the institutional trades are being settled through Clearing Corporation of India Limited (CCIL) with settlement guarantee.

Retail Debt Market

With a view to encouraging wider participation of all classes of investors across the country (including retail investors) in government securities, the government, RBI and SEBI have introduced trading in government securities for retail investors. Trading in this retail debt market segment (RDM) on NSE has been introduced w.e.f. January 16, 2003.

Valuation of Bonds

The value of a financial instrument is well understood as the present value of the expected future cash flows from the instrument. Valuation of a bond involves discounting these cash flows to the present point in time, by an appropriate discount rate. The cash flows expected from a bond, which is not expected to default are primarily made up of: (i) coupon payments, and (ii) redemption of principal.

Let us consider a Central Government bond with 11.75 per cent coupon, maturing after 8 years. The cash flows from this bond are the semi-annual coupon and the redemption proceeds receivable on maturity. In order to value the bond, we need the tenor for which we have to value the bond and the "required rate" for this tenor. Let us assume for simplicity, that we are valuing the bond on its issue date and the "required rate" or the 8-year rate in the market is 12 per cent. Since government bonds pay coupons semi-annually, this bond would pay (11.75/2) = ₹ 5.875, every six months as coupon. In order to value this bond, we need to list these cash flows and discount them at the required rate of 6 per cent (semi-annual rate for the comparable 12 per cent rate)

$$\textbf{Bond Price} = \frac{C}{(1+i)} + \frac{C}{(1+i)^2} + \cdots\cdots + \frac{C}{(1+i)^n} + \frac{M}{(1+i)^n}$$

Where C = coupon payment, ordinary annuity

n = number of payments

i = interest rate, or required yield

M = value at maturity, or par value

Yield

The returns to an investor in bond are made up of three components: coupon, interest from reinvestment of coupons and capital gains/loss from selling or redeeming the bond. When we are able to compare the cash inflows from these sources with the investment (cash outflows) of the investor, we can compute yield to the investor. Depending on the manner in which we treat the time value of cash flows and reinvestment of coupons, we are able to get various interpretations of the yield on an investment in bonds.

Current Yield

One of the earlier measures on yield on a bond, current yield is a very popular measure of bond returns in the Indian markets, until the early 1990s.

Current yield is measured as:

Current Yield = Annual coupon receipts/ Market price of the bond

This measure of yield does not consider the time value of money, or the complete series of expected future cash flows. It instead compares the coupon, as prespecified, with the market price at a point in time, to arrive at a measure of yield. Since it compares a prespecified coupon with the current market price, it is called as current yield.

For example, if a 12.5 per cent bond sells in the market for ₹ 104.50, current yield will be computed as

= (12.5/104.5) * 100

= 11.96%

Current yield is no longer used as a standard yield measure, because it fails to capture the future cash flows, reinvestment income and capital gains/losses on investment return. Current yield is considered a very simplistic and erroneous measure of yield.

Yield to Maturity (YTM)

YTM of a bond is that rate which equates the discounted value of the future cash flows to the present price of the bond. It is the internal rate of return of the valuation equation. Yield to maturity represents the yield on the bond, provided the bond is held to maturity and the intermittent coupons are reinvested at the same YTM rate. In other words, when we compute YTM as the rate that discounts all the cash flows from the bond, at the same YTM rate, what we are assuming in effect is that each of these cash flows can be reinvested at the YTM rate for the period until maturity.

Yield-price Relationship of Bonds

The basic bond valuation equation shows that the yield and price are inversely related. This relationship is however, not uniform for all bonds, nor is it symmetrical for increases and decreases in yield, by the same quantum.

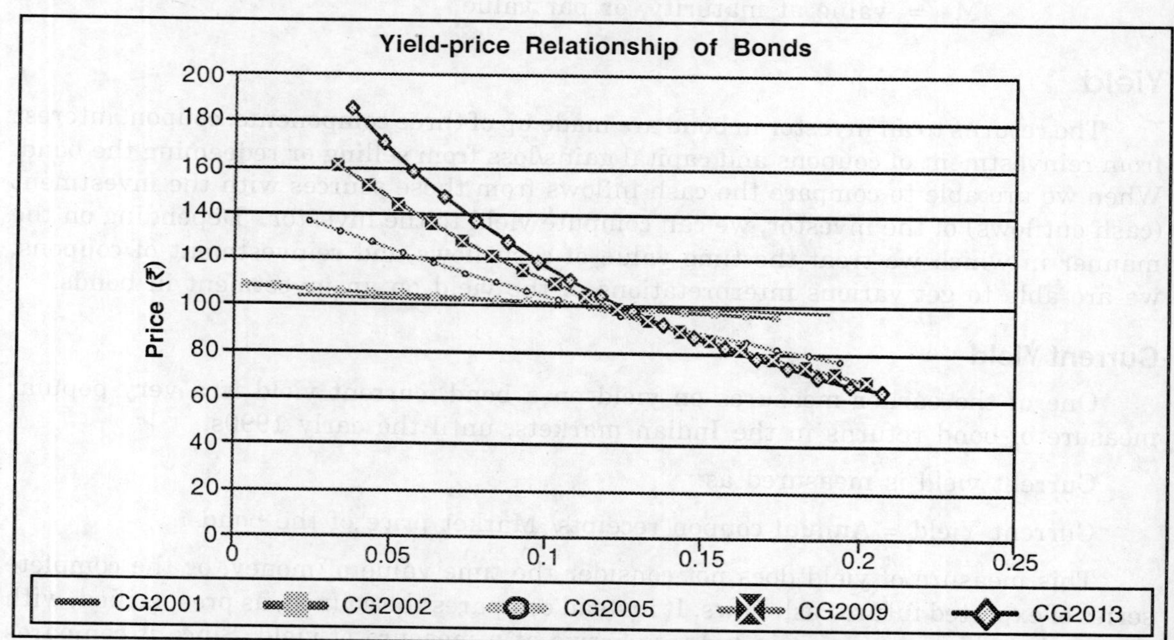

Figure 2.4: Yield-price Relationship of Bonds

Yield-price relationship between bonds is not a straight-line, but is convex. This means that price changes for yield changes are not symmetrical, for increase and decrease in yield.

The sensitivity of price changes is yield in not uniform across bonds. Therefore, for a same change in yield, depending on the kind of bond one holds, the changes in price will be different.

Higher the term to maturity of the bond is greater the price sensitivity. We notice in the above figure, that CG2013 has the steepest slope, while 2001 and 2002 are virtually flat. Price sensitivities are higher for longer tenor bonds, while in the short-term bond, one can expect relative price stability for a wide range of changes in yield.

Lower the coupon, higher the price sensitivity. Other things remaining the same, bonds with higher coupon exhibit lower price sensitivity than bonds with lower coupons.

Coupon rate is less than the required yield, i.e., Price is less than the par (Discount Bond)

Coupon rate is equal to the required yield, i.e., Price is equal to the par

Coupon rate is more than the required yield, i.e., Price is more than the par (Premium Bond)

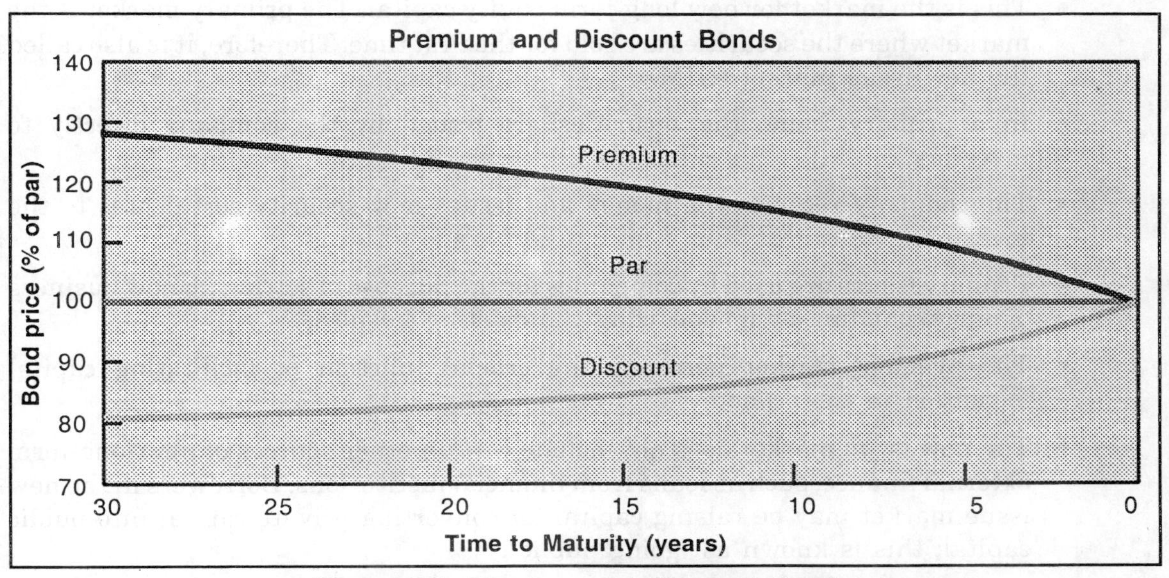

Figure 2.5: Premium and Discount Bonds

DEVT vs. Equity

At some point every company needs to raise money. To do this, companies can either borrow it from somebody or raise it by issuing stock. A company can borrow by taking a loan from a bank or by issuing bonds. Both methods fit under the umbrella of "debt financing". On the other hand, issuing stock is called "equity financing". Issuing stock is advantageous for the company because it does not require the company to payback the money or make interest payments along the way. All that the shareholders get in return for their money is the hope that the shares will someday be worth more.

Capital Market

Capital markets may be classified as primary markets and secondary markets. In primary markets, new stock or bond issues are sold to investors via a mechanism known as underwriting. In the secondary markets/stock markets, existing securities are sold and bought among investors or traders, usually on a securities exchange, over-the-counter, or elsewhere. The primary market is that part of the capital markets that deals with the issue of new securities. A market is primary if the proceeds of sales go to the issuer of the securities sold. Companies, governments or public sector institutions can obtain funding through the sale of a new stock or bond issue. This is typically done through a syndicate of securities dealers. In the case of a new stock issue, this sale is an initial public offering (IPO). Dealers earn a commission that is built into the price of the security offering, though it can be found in the prospectus. Primary markets create long-term instruments through which corporate entities borrow from capital market.

Features of Primary Markets

- This is the market for new long-term equity capital. The primary market is the market where the securities are sold for the first time. Therefore, it is also called the new issue market (NIM).
- In a primary issue, the securities are issued by the company directly to investors.
- The company receives the money and issues new security certificates to the investors.
- Primary issues are used by companies for the purpose of setting up new business or for expanding or modernizing the existing business.
- The primary market performs the crucial function of facilitating capital formation in the economy.
- The new issue market does not include certain other sources of new long-term external finance, such as loans from financial institutions. Borrowers in the new issue market may be raising capital for converting private capital into public capital; this is known as "going public".
- The financial assets sold can only be redeemed by the original holder.

Methods of issuing securities in the Primary Market are:

- Initial public offering
- Rights issue (for existing companies)
- Preferential issue

Secondary Market

The secondary market, also known as the aftermarket, is the financial market where previously issued securities and financial instruments such as stock, bonds, options, and futures are bought and sold. It is also a market where securities are traded after they are initially offered in the primary market and most of trading is done in the secondary market. The term "secondary market" is also used to refer to the market for any used goods or assets, or an alternative use for an existing product or asset where the customer base is the second market. With primary issuances of securities or financial instruments, or the primary market, investors purchase these securities directly from issuers such as corporations issuing shares in an IPO or private placement.

Types of Instrument in the Capital Market

Securities are majorly traded in the capital markets. These securities are further divided into three kinds of instruments:

Equity Capital

Equity capital is a permanent form of financing. The holders of equity capital are owners of the firm. Equity has no maturity date and never has to be repaid by the firm. Their claims cannot be paid until the claims of all creditors, including both interest and principle payments on debt have been satisfied. Because equityholders are the last to receive distributions; they expect greater returns to compensate them for the additional risk they bear. Common stockholders, who are sometimes referred to as residual owners are the true owners of the firm. As residual owners, common stockhold rs receive what is left – the residual – after all other claims on the firms' income and assets have been satisfied. Because of this uncertain position, common stockholders expect to be compensated with adequate dividends and ultimately, capital gains. Payment of dividends is at the discretion of the board of directors. Dividends may be made in cash, additional shares of stock, and even merchandise. Because stockholders are residual claimants – they receive dividend payments only after all claims have been settled with the government, creditors, and preferred stockholders. Common equityholders have voting rights that permit them to elect the firm's board of directors and to vote on special issues. Bondholders and preferred stockholders receive no such privileges. While interest paid to bondholders is tax-deductible to the issuing firm, dividends paid to preferred and common stockholders is not. The common stock of a firm can be privately owned by an individual, closely owned by a small group of investors, or publicly owned by a broad group of investors. Typically, small corporations are privately or closely owned and if their shares are traded, this occurs infrequently and in small amounts. Large corporations are typically publicly owned and have shares that are actively traded on major securities exchanges. A preemptive right allows common stockholders to maintain their proportionate ownership in a corporation when new shares are issued. This allows existing shareholders to maintain voting control and protect against the dilution of their ownership. In a rights offering, the firm grants rights to its existing shareholders, which permits them to purchase additional shares at a price below the current price. Each share of common stock entitles its holder to one vote in the election of directors and on special issues. Votes are generally assignable and may be cast at the annual stockholders meeting. Many firms have issued two or more classes of stock differing mainly in having unequal voting rights. The price of a stock fluctuates fundamentally due to the theory of supply and demand. However, there are many factors that influence the demand for a particular stock. The field of fundamental analysis and technical analysis attempt to understand market conditions that lead to price changes, or even predict future price levels.

Example:

Avon Ltd., has currently 30,00,000 shares outstanding. The market price is ₹ 65 per share. The Avon Ltd., plan to issue 10,00,000 additional shares at a issue price of ₹ 40 per share. What is the number of rights to buy a new share? How much is the market price of share after rights issue? Let us assume that Mr. X owns 300 shares of AVON Ltd. What will happen if Mr. X does not enjoy the pre-emptive right?

The number of rights to buy a new share = 30/10 = 3. The market price of a share after right issue = 30,00,000 × 65 + 10,00,000 × 40/30,00,000 + 10,00,000 = ₹ 58.75. A shareholder can buy one new share for ₹ 40 plus 3 rights. The total value of three rights = ₹ 58.75 – ₹ 40 = ₹ 18.75. The value of each right is 18.75/3 = 6.25.

Let us assume that Mr. X owns 300 shares of AVON Ltd. His total financial interest is ₹[300 × 65] = 19,500. After exercising his right, his holding will be [300/3 = 100] 300 + 100 = 400 shares. His total wealth would be 400 × 58.75 = 23,500 he has spent 100 × 40 = 4,000. So his net financial benefit is 23,500 – 4,000 = 19,500, which is equal to his rights issue.

If the person Mr. X does not exercise his right, he is going to suffer dilution of financial interest. 300 × 58.75 = 17,625. So, 19,500 – 17,625 = 1,875.

Strengths of Equity Share

- A company need not have the forced obligation to pay dividend to equity shareholders. This obligation arises only when the company earns sufficient divisible profits.
- The obligation to repay the equity capital arises only at the time of liquidation of the company.
- An equity share attracts dynamic investors who desirous to have both capital gain as well as the higher percentage of profits.
- Equity shares help the holders to participate in the management of the company through voting rights.

Demerits/Problem

- Raising only equity shares does not facilitate the company to enjoy debt equity ratio.
- Equity shareholders may create a position in the smooth running of the organization. Huge reserves will attract more problems from equity shareholders.

Equity shares will not attract passive investors who always prefer to have steady income and the safety of their investments.

- Another disadvantage of equity capital is that it cannot be recovered and repaid at the time of liquidation of the company.

Example 1:

Delhi Manufacturers (DMs) intend to raise ₹ 40,00,000 of equity capital through a rights offering. It currently has 10,00,000 shares outstanding which have been most recently selling/trading for ₹ 50 and ₹ 56 per share. In consultation with the SEBI Caps, the DM has set the subscription price for the rights at ₹ 50 per share. You are required to determine the number of new shares DM should sell to raise the desired amount of capital. Ascertain the number of shares each right would entitle a holder of one share to purchase. How many additional shares can an investor who holds 10,000 shares of DM purchase? Compute the theoretical value of a right if the current market price is ₹ 54 with rights and the subscription price is ₹ 50 for both shares selling with rights and shares selling ex-rights, (i.e., the value of the right is not included in the market price of shares).

Solution:

Number of new shares

= ₹ 40,00,000 (to be raised)/₹ 50 (subscription price) = 80,000 shares

Number of shares per right

= 80,000 (new shares)/10,00,000 (shares outstanding) = 0.08 share

Additional shares = 0.08 shares/right × 1 right/share × 10,000 shares

= 800 shares

Theoretical value of right with rights, R_w:

$R_w = (M_w - S)/(N + 1)$

R_w = theoretical value of a right when the share is selling with rights/cum-rights

M_w = market value of the stock with rights/cum-rights

S = subscription price of the shares

N = number of rights needed to purchase one share

Substituting the values,

R_w = (₹ 54 – ₹ 50)/(12.5 + 1) = ₹ 4/13.5 = ₹ 0.296

N = 1/.08 = 12.5 rights need to purchase one new share.

Theoretical value of right/ex-right,

$R_e = (M_e - S)/N$

Where,

R_e = theoretical value of a right when the share is trading ex-right

M_e = market value of shares trading ex-right

Substituting the values,

₹ 53.704 – ₹ 50/12.5 = ₹ 3.704/12.5 = ₹ 0.296

$M_w - R_w$ = ₹ 54 – ₹ 0.296 = ₹ 53.704

The investor would receive at least the theoretical value of ₹ 0.296 per right × 10,000 shares = ₹ 2,960. If he expects the price of DMs shares to increase during the period the rights are exercisable, the market value of the rights would be more than their theoretical value.

Example 2:

The Standard Company (SC) wishes to raise ₹ 30,00,000 through a rights offering. It has currently 2,40,000 shares outstanding which have been most recently trading between ₹ 106 and ₹ 116 per share. On the advice of the SBI Caps, the SC has set the subscription price for the rights at ₹ 100 per share on the assumption that they will be fully subscribed. You are required to find how many new shares should SC sell to raise the desired amount? How many shares will each right entitle a holder of one share to purchase? What is the theoretical value of a right if the current market price is ₹ 109 with rights and the subscription price is ₹ 100? Answer for both shares selling with rights and shares selling ex-rights?

Solution:

(a) Number of new shares

= ₹ 30,00,000/30,000 shares = ₹ 100

(b) Number of shares per right

= 2,40,000/30,000 = 8, that is, 8 shares rights are needed to purchase a new share at ₹ 100. Each right entitles its holder to purchase one-right of a share.

(c) Value of a right, with rights

= (₹ 109 – ₹ 100)/8 + 1 = Rupee one

Value of a right, ex-right

= (₹ 108 – ₹ 100)/8 = Rupee one

₹ 109 – Rupee one

Thus, the theoretical value of the right when the share is selling with rights or ex-rights is the same.

Preference Share

Preference capital is generally regarded as part of net worth. So, it strengthens its financial position. Issue of preference shares does not create any short of charge against assets of the company. Thus, the assets are freely available for raising additional funds from any other sources. Preferred stock is an equity instrument that usually pays a fixed dividend and has a prior claim on the firm's earnings and assets in case of liquidation. If a firm fails to pay a preferred stock dividend, the dividend is said to be in arrears. In general arrear, must be paid before common stockholders receive a dividend. Preferred stocks which possess this characteristic are called cumulative preferred stocks. Preferred stocks are also often referred to as hybrid securities because they possess the characteristics of both common stocks and bonds. Preferred stocks are like common stock because they are perpetual securities with no maturity date. Preferred stocks are like bonds because they are fixed income securities. Preference shares do not carry voting rights. So, they are not materially disturbing the existing pattern of control of the company. Financing through preference shares is cheaper as compared to financing through equity shares. In addition, some preferred stocks have mandatory sinking funds which allow the firm to retire the issue overtime. Finally, participating preferred stock allows preferred stockholders to participate with common stockholders in the receipt of dividends beyond a specified amount. One of the principal disadvantages of financing through preference shares is that preference dividend is not deductible as an expense for taxation purpose out of the profits of the company. As a result, financing through preference shares is costly to the company.

Strengths of Preference Share

Payment of dividend is not a legal obligation of the company so financing through preference shares is a flexible financing arrangement. If the earnings decline and the financial condition of the company deteriorate, the company can omit to pay dividend.

Preference shares have no final maturity date (except redeemable preference shares) so the funds provided by them is a sort of perpetual loan.

Preference capital is generally regarded as part of net worth. So it strengthens its financial position.

Issue of preference shares does not create any short of charge against assets of the company. Thus, the assets are freely available for raising additional funds from any other sources.

Preference shares do not carry voting rights. So, they are not materially disturbing the existing pattern of control of the company.

Financing through preference shares is cheaper as compared to financing through equity shares.

Preference shares are particularly useful for those investors who want fixed rate of return with comparatively lower risk.

Demerits/Problem

One of the principal disadvantages of financing through preference shares is that preference dividend is not deductible as an expense for taxation purpose out of the profits of the company. As a result, financing through preference shares is costly to the company.

Though there is no legal obligation to pay preference dividend, skipping them can adversely affect the image of the firm in the capital market.

Debt

Debt securities are also called debentures depending on their maturity and certain other characteristics. The holder of a debt security is typically entitled to the payment of principal and interest, together with other contractual rights under the terms of the issue. Debt securities are generally issued for a fixed term and redeemable by the issuer at the end of that term. For the investors, debentures offer stable return, have a fixed maturity and protected by the debenture-trust-deed and enjoy preferential claim on the assets in relation to shareholders. Debentures enable the company to take advantage of trading on equity thus pay to the equity shareholders dividend at a higher rate than overall return on investment. Debentures are more suitable for investors who particularly prefer a stable rate of return. Issue costs of debt are significantly lower than these on equity and preference capital. It is legally enforceable contract obligation in respect of interest payments and repayments, increased financial risk. Debentures are particularly not suitable for companies whose earnings fluctuate considerably. In case of such company raising funds through debentures may lead to considerable fluctuations in the rate of dividend payable to the equity shareholders. Debentures do not carry voting rights.

Strengths of Debentures

It is lower cost due to lower risk and tax deductibility of interest payments. No dilutions of control is there as debentures do not carry voting rights.

For the investors, debentures offer stable return, have a fixed maturity and protected by the debenture-trust-deed and enjoy preferential claim on the assets in relation to shareholders.

Debentures enable the company to take advantage of trading on equity and thus pay to the equity shareholders dividend at a rate higher than overall return on investment.

Debentures are more suitable for investors who particularly prefer a stable rate of return. Issue costs of debt are significantly lower than these on equity and preference capital.

Demerits/Problem

It is legally enforceable contract obligation in respect of interest payments and repayments, increased financial risk.

Debentures are particularly not suitable for companies' whose earnings fluctuate considerably. In case of such company raising funds through debentures may lead to considerable fluctuations in the rate of dividend payable to the equity shareholders.

Corporate Bonds

Corporate bonds represent the debt of commercial or industrial entities. Debentures have a long maturity, typically at least ten years, whereas notes have a shorter maturity. commercial paper is a simple form of debt security that essentially represents a post-dated cheque with a maturity of not more than 270 days.

Money Market Instruments

Money market is a market for short-term loan or financial assets. It is a market for the lending and borrowing of short-term funds. Money market is the centre for dealing mainly in short-term money assets. It meets the short-term requirements of borrowers and provides liquidity or cash to lenders. It is the place where short-term surplus funds at the disposal of financial institutions and individuals are borrowed by individuals, institutions and also the Government. Money market instruments are short-term debt instruments that is having characteristics of deposit accounts, such as certificates of deposit, and certain bills of exchange. They are highly liquid and are sometimes referred to as "near cash". Commercial paper is also often highly liquid.

Euro Debt Securities

Euro debt securities are securities issued internationally outside their domestic market in a denomination different from that of the issuer's domicile. These include Eurobonds and euronotes. Eurobonds are characteristically underwritten, and not secured, and interest is paid in gross. A euronote may take the form of euro-commercial paper (ECP) or euro-certificates of deposit.

Government Bonds

Government bonds are medium- or long-term debt securities issued by sovereign governments or their agencies. Typically it carries a lower rate of interest than corporate bonds, and serves as a source of finance for governments. US federal government bonds are called treasuries. Because of their liquidity and perceived low risk, treasuries are used to manage the money supply in the open.

Convertibles

Convertibles are bonds or preferred stock that can be converted into the common stock of the issuing company. The convertibility, however, may be forced if the convertible is a callable bond, and the issuer calls the bond. The bondholder has about one month to convert it, or the company will call the bond by giving the holder the call price, which may be less than the value of the converted stock. This is referred to as a forced conversion.

Equity Warrants

Equity warrants are options issued by the company that allow the holder of the warrant to purchase a specific number of shares at a specified price within a specified time. They are often issued together with bonds or existing equities, and are, sometimes, detachable from them and separately tradable. When the holder of the warrant exercises it, he pays the money directly to the company, and the company issues new shares to the holder.

Warrants, like other convertible securities, increases the number of shares outstanding, and are always accounted for in financial reports as fully diluted earnings per share, which assumes that all warrants and convertibles will be exercised.

What is Bull and Bear Market?

There are two classic market types, i.e., Bull market and Bear markets. When the stock market is rising and shows high economic growth and strong investor confidence in the economy, it is called bull market. A bull market is a financial market, where prices of stocks are, on average higher and investor confidence, expectations rising and aspires to obtain further capital gains. At Goldman Sachs, a bull market is said to occur when stocks exhibit expanding multiples. Bull markets are generally characterized by high trading volume. During this time, economic production is high, jobs are plentiful and inflation is low. The market shows prices will continue moving upward. A key to successful investing during a bull market is to take advantage of prices rising. During this period large numbers of stocks are performing very good leads to moving upward to the market. Investors believe in buying and selling stocks and change their portfolios accordingly. Speculators and risk-takers are relatively done well in bull markets. They believe they can make profits from rising prices and they buy stocks, options, futures and currencies to gain value. Bear markets are the opposite. Bear market are occurred when stock prices are falling continuously, bad economic news, and low investor confidence in the economy. If an investor is "bearish" they are referred to as a bear because they believe a particular company, industry, sector, or market in general is going to go down.

Stock Market Indices

A stock market index provides a statistical summary of the value of the component stocks/shares. A stock market index is a method of measuring the relative value of a group of stocks. Changing the value of the stocks leads to changes value of the index also. If an index goes up by 1% then that means the total value of the securities which make up the index have gone up by 1% in value. Indices are used to monitor the direction of share price movements in the market as a whole. The most widely publicised, most widely traded and most widely tracked stock index in the world is the Dow Jones Industrial Average, created in 1896. The Dow Jones is composed of 30 major US companies. The Standard & Poor's 500 Index (S&P 500) provides a broader based yardstick of the US stock prices. The other major US stock market index is the Nasdaq

Composite, which reflects the prices of stocks quoted on the Nasdaq electronic stock market. The Standard & Poor's CRISIL NSE Index 50 or S&P CNX Nifty (nicknamed Nifty 50 or simply Nifty), is the leading index for large companies on the National Stock Exchange of India. The Nifty is a well diversified 50 stock index accounting for 21 sectors of the economy. The Stock Exchange in Mumbai, popularly known as "BSE" was established in 1875 as "The Native Share and Stock Brokers Association", as a voluntary non-profit making association. It has evolved over the years into its present status as the premier Stock Exchange in the country. It may be noted that the Stock Exchanges is the oldest one in Asia, even older than the Tokyo Stock Exchange, which was founded in 1878.The main index of BSE is called BSE SENSEX or simply SENSEX. It is composed of 30 financially sound company stocks which are liable to be reviewed and modified from time-to-time. These companies account for around one-fifth of the market capitalization of the BSE. The base value of the sensex is 100 on April 1, 1979, and the base year of BSE-SENSEX is 1978-79. At irregular intervals, the BSE authorities review and modify its composition to make sure it reflects current market conditions. The index calculation is done on the methodology of "Free-float Market Capitalization" method. This method is also followed by the leading bourses like Dow-Jones. SENSEX reflects the splendorous performance of Indian Inc. and the consequent success story of the Indian economy.

The Exchange, while providing an efficient and transparent market for trading in securities, upholds the interests of the investors and ensures redressal of their grievances, whether against the companies or its own member-brokers. It also strives to educate and enlighten the investors by making available necessary informative inputs and conducting investor education programmes. BSE is spread all over India and is present in 417 towns and cities. The total number of companies listed in BSE is around 3,500. Bombay Stock Exchange's trading system is popularly known as BOLT (BSE's Online Trading System). It makes the trade efficient, transparent and time saving. In BSE, the following trades take place:

- Equity or Shares
- Derivatives (Futures and Options)
- Debt Instruments

At present, there are 23 stock exchanges in India, the largest among them being the Bombay Stock Exchange. BSE alone accounts for over 80% of the total volume of transactions in shares.

What Moves the Stock Market?

Share prices and the stock market, are affected by a wide range of factors (e.g., interest rates, social unrest, changes in government policy), some of which defy prediction. Financial analysts are using historical data and mathematical calculations, such as moving averages, on balance volume and the stochastic oscillator, to try to predict future changes in the stock market. Stock prices change everyday by market forces. By this we mean that share prices change because of supply and demand. If more people want to buy a stock (demand) than sell it (supply), then the price moves up. Conversely, if more people wanted to sell a stock than buy it, there would be greater supply than demand, and the price would fall. Understanding supply and demand is easy. What is difficult to comprehend is what makes people like a particular stock and dislike another stock. This comes down to figuring out what news is positive for a company and what news is negative. The principal theory is that the price movement of a stock indicates what investors feel a company's worth. So, it is not advisable to equate a company's value with the stock price. The value of a company is its market capitalization, which is the stock price multiplied by the number of shares outstanding. Market capitalisation is a good indicator of the health of capital markets of an economy. Leading economies of the world have huge market capitalisation in relation to their gross domestic product (GDP). This indicates not only the investor confidence, domestic and international, but also the strength of their economies. Market capitalisation, as the name implies, in very simple terms, is the capital of a market. To begin with, market capitalisation of a particular stock is the total number of outstanding shares of the company multiplied by the share price of that stock. Thus, stock market capitalisation would mean the summation of the market capitalisation of all the individual stocks that are listed on the exchange. For example, a company that trades at $100 per share and has 10,00,000 shares outstanding has a lesser value than a company that trades at $50 but has 50,00,000 shares outstanding ($100 × 10,00,000 = $10,00,00,000 while $50 × 50,00,000 = $25,00,00,000). To further complicate things, the price of a stock doesn't only reflect a company's current value — it also reflects the growth that investors expect in the future.

The most important factor that affects the value of a company is its earnings.

Earnings are the profit of companies, and in the long-run no company can survive without them. Public companies are required to report their earnings four times a year (once each quarter). The reason behind this is that analysts base their future value of a company on their earnings projection. If a company's results surprise (are better than expected), the price jumps up. If a company's results disappoint (are worse than expected), then the price will fall. Of course, it's not just earnings that can change the sentiment towards a stock (which, in turn, changes its price). Investors have developed literally hundreds of these variables, ratios and indicators.

Big-cap and Small-cap

At a basic level, market capitalisation or market cap represents the company's value according to the market, and is calculated by multiplying the total number of shares by share price. (This is the equity value of the company). Companies and their stocks tend to be categorised into three broad categories: big-cap, mid-cap and small-cap. While there are no hard and fast rules, in UK a company with a market cap greater than £2 billion will generally be classified as a big-cap stock. These companies tend to be established, mature companies sometimes huge companies, for example the US corporations GE and Microsoft, are called mega-cap stocks. Small-cap stocks tend to be riskier, but are also often the faster growing companies. Roughly speaking, a small-cap stock includes those companies with market caps less than £100 million. As one might expect, the stocks in between £100 million and £2 billion are referred to as mid-cap stocks.

Analysis of Financial Market

Financial Market Analysis deals with the performance of a particular financial market and the performance of a financial market depends upon the performance of the total number of securities that are traded in that market. Performances is reflected in a market indicator called Index which tracks the performance of some of the more popular and steady securities that are traded in that particular financial market. The financial market index has become particularly important in today's market economy, which is integrating very fast on a global scale. Traders do not confine trading in securities to just one or two markets in the country of their origin but invest in a large number of markets across the globe. As a result, analysis of the financial markets has become one of the main activities covering a very large number of factors both within the market and outside.

Companies raise long-term funds from the capital market. Financial manager should therefore know the ways in which securities are traded and priced in the capital markets. They should also know the procedures to be followed in issuing securities. To maximise share price, the financial manager must learn to assets two key determinants. Risk and return. Each financial decision presents certain risk and return characteristics and the unique combination of these characteristics have an impact on share price. A proper understanding of the process of valuation is necessary for any financial investment decision. The valuation technique provides the investors/companies a benchmark of comparison between assets and firms. It enables investors to appraise the relative attractiveness of assets and firms. Much effort has gone into the study of financial markets and how prices vary with time. The scale of changes in price over some unit of time is called the volatility. Large changes up or down are more likely that what one would calculate using a Gaussian distribution with an estimated standard deviation. Only negative stories about financial markets tend to make the news.

For analysis, we begin with evaluating the risk and return characteristics of individual assets, and end by looking at portfolios of assets.

Savings make available funds for emergencies and for making specific purchases in the relatively near future. The primary aim is to stock up funds and keep them protected. The objective of investing is generally to increase net worth and work toward long-term goals. Investing entails risk. Every investment involves two important aspects – returns and risk. And every investor wants to get the maximum returns with minimum risk.

What is Risk?

Risk means it is a state of uncertainty where some of the possibilities involve a loss, catastrophe, or other undesirable outcome. Risk arises when there is variability in returns from an investment. The larger is the variability the larger the risk. Hence, investors are generally reluctant to take the risk. In the context of business and finance, risk is defined as the chance of suffering a financial loss. In statistics, the notion of risk is often modelled as the expected value of some outcome seen as undesirable. So risk is then:

Risk = (Probability of an accident occurring) × (expected loss in case of accident)

Risk may be used interchangeably with the term uncertainty to refer to the variability of returns associated with a given asset. But however uncertainty means the lack of complete certainty, that is, the existence of more than one possibility.

So far risk versus uncertainty is concerned, Risk and uncertainty go together. Risk suggests that the decision maker knows that there is some possible consequence of an investment decision, but uncertainty involves a situation where the outcome is not known to the decision maker. Therefore, the word 'Risk' is used to comprise all elements of variability of return, uncertainty of the outcome. Some risk can be controlled by the investors and some by the issuers of securities by planning. Others cannot be so controlled and they are to be borne compulsorily by the investors.

However, Frank Knight (1921) in his seminal work Risk, Uncertainty, and Profit, established the distinction between risk and uncertainty. According to Frank Knight "Uncertainty must be taken in a sense radically distinct from the familiar notion of Risk, from which it has never been properly separated. The term "risk", as loosely used in everyday speech and in economic discussion, really covers two things which, functionally at least, in their causal relations to the phenomena of economic organization, are categorically different. The essential fact is that "risk" means in some cases a quantity susceptible of measurement, while at other times it is something distinctly not of this character; and there are far-reaching and crucial differences in the bearings of the phenomenon depending on which of the two is really present and operating. It will appear that a measurable uncertainty, or "risk" proper, as we shall use the term, is so far different from an unmeasurable one that it is not in effect an uncertainty at all. We accordingly restrict the term "uncertainty" to cases of the nonquantitive type. Thus, Knightian uncertainty is unmeasurable, not possible to calculate, while in the Knightian sense risk is measurable.

What is Return?

It means income received on an investment plus any change in market price usually expressed as a per cent of the beginning market price of the investment. But from investors' point of view, the most important outcome from an investment is the rate of return. The return from an investment is the realisable cash flow earned by its owner during a given period of time. Return represents the total gain or loss on an investment. The most basic way to calculate return is as follows:

$R_t = C_t + (P_t - P_{t-1})/P_{t-1}$

Where R_t is the actual return during period t, P_t is the current price, P_{t-1} is the price during the previous time period, and C_t is any cash flow accruing from the investment.

Risk-return Trade-offs

The principle is that potential return rises with an increase in risk. Low risks are related with low potential returns, whereas high risks are associated with high potential returns. All investment decisions revolve around the trade-off between risk and return. All investors generally considered that all investment involves risk. But they are not reluctant to take risk rather they are reluctant to bear losses. If two investments have the same amount of risk, a rational investor will have a preference to the investment with a higher return. Since all rational investors want a substantial return from their investment. A forecast of a security's return is a probable or expected value which is representative of the investor's prospects of the return distribution for the security, and the expected return consists of both the expected taken in and unrealized yearly income. In this world of uncertainties, an investor cannot estimate in advance exactly what rate of return an investment will yield. However, they can formulate a probable distribution of the possible rates of return. These probable distributions could be either subjective or objective. An objective probability distribution is formed by measuring objectively historical data while the subjective probability distribution is formed by simple writing down, some one's guesses and assigning probabilities to them. Objective probabilities are a more accurate way to determine probabilities than observations based on subjective measures, such as personal estimates. Objective distribution almost always influences the development of subjective distributions and in many cases are good estimated of what the future holds. Subjective probabilities contain no formal calculations and only reflect the subject's opinions and past experience. The expected rate of return in weighted average return using the probabilities for weights it measures the central or average tendency of the probability distribution of returns. The most important relationship to understand is the risk-return trade-off. Higher the risk greater the returns/loss and lower the risk lesser the returns/loss. The risk/return trade-offs is the balance between the desire for the lowest possible risk and the highest possible return. This is demonstrated graphically in the Fig. 2.6. A higher standard deviation means a higher risk and higher possible return.

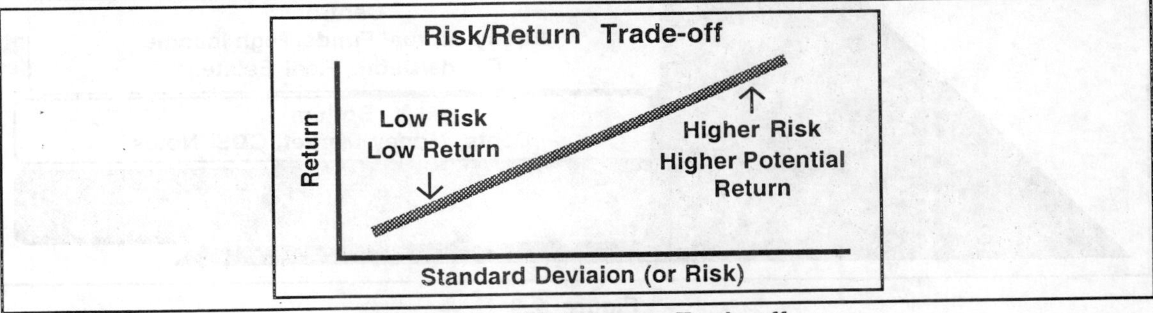

Figure 2.6: Risk/Return Trade-off

A frequent fallacy is that higher risk generates better return. The risk/return trade-offs tell us that the higher risk gives us the possibility of higher returns. Just like risk means higher potential returns, it also means higher potential losses. But, many investors do not understand how to determine the level of risk their individual portfolios should bear. For investment in securities we can frame ourselves with the different types of securities and their associated risk-reward profile shown in Fig. 2.7.

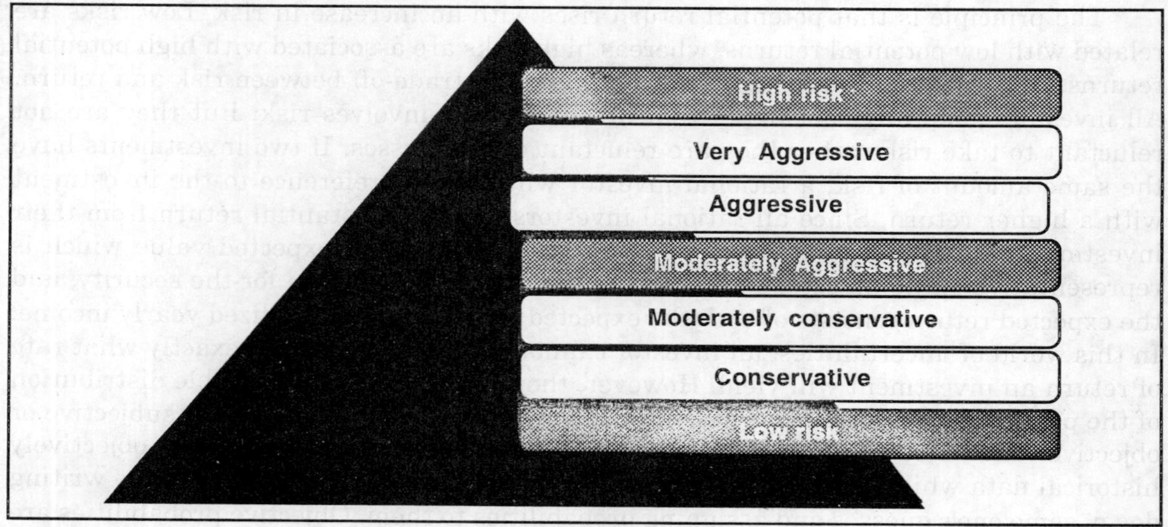

Figure 2.7

After deciding on how much risk is acceptable to an investor, one can use alternative investment options. According to risk factors investors can use to diversify their portfolio investments according to the risk profile of each security. Normally investor's portfolio has three distinct tiers:

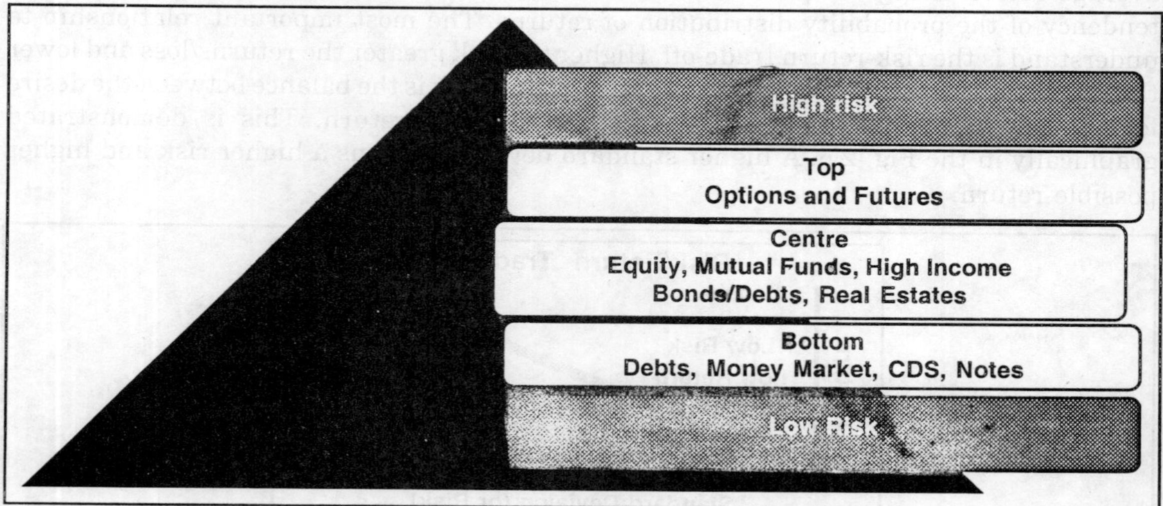

Figure 2.8

- **Bottom Line:** This area is comprised of investments that are low in risk and have probable returns. It is the prime area and composes the bulk of many investors' assets.
- **Middle Portion:** This area should be made up of medium-risk investments that offer a stable return while still allowing for capital appreciation. Although more risky than the assets creating the base, these investments should still be relatively safe.
- **Top Line:** This level is kept specifically for high-risk investments, this is the least area portfolio and should be made up of money an investor can lose without any serious repercussions.

Some investors prefer less risk, others prefer even more risk than others who have a larger net worth. Those who want more risk in their portfolios can increase the size of their investment by investing in top level investment and decreasing the other two sections, and those wanting less risk can increase the size of investment in risk-free investment. It is important for investors to understand the idea of risk and how it applies to them. To get an estimate of the securities suitable for certain levels of risk tolerance and to maximize returns, investors should have an idea of how much time and money they have to invest and the returns they are looking for.

Investment risk is categorised according to the two sources of investment return: a macro pervasive factor such as the national economy and micro, localized factors such as the company itself. Financial research has developed a useful framework, which divides the total risk of a security into two components, i.e., market risk and unique risk. The risk associated with macro factors is called systematic risk. The micro risks associated with factors particular to a company are called unsystematic risks or unique risks. The market risk or systematic risk of a security is measured by its beta, which simply reflects how the price of the security responds to change in the market. In statistical terminology, it is the covariance between the return on the security and the return on market portfolio divided by the variance of the market return.

Systematic Risk: Systematic risk is also called market risk/non-diversifiable risk. Systematic risk is associated with the movement of the overall market. Market risk arises out of changes in demand and supply pressure in the market. The market risk of a security represents that portion of its total risk, which is attributable to the fluctuations in the market as a whole. If the stock market declines, most stocks decline with it and *vice versa*. Systematic risk factors cannot be diversified away completely. This is because these factors affect the entire market in a certain direction.

Unsystematic Risk: The unsystematic risk of a security represents that portion of its total risk, which is independent of the general market movement. It arises from firm-specific factors like the manufacture of a new product, a plant break down, etc. These factors primarily affect a specific firm and not all firms in general. It is also called avoidable risk because it is possible to eliminate or diversify away this component of risk to a considerable extent by investing in a large portfolio.

How Risk is Measured?

Systematic and unsystematic risks are measured differently. Fluctuations in the security prices expose investors to risk. The most common statistical indicator of an asset's risk is the standard deviation.The standard deviation of a portfolio is calculated from the standard deviations of the individual securities that make up the portfolio. The expected returns are estimated by analyzing a reasonable set of possible returns. Variation around the expected return is measured statistically by standard deviation. Each of the possible returns is multiplied by its probability of occurrence and all of the products of the possibilities multiplied by chances are added to obtain an expected return. To calculate the expected return for standard deviation, first it is required to take the difference between possible returns and expected returns. The standard deviation of a set of numbers is simply the square root of the mean of the square of deviations around the arithmetic average. The standard deviation, sk, which measures the dispersion around the expected value.

$$\overline{K} = \sum_{j=1}^{n} k_j \times Pr_j$$

Where

K_j = return for the jth outcome

Pr_j = probability of occurrence of the jth outcome

n = number of outcomes considered

What is Standard Deviation?

The standard deviation essentially reports a fund's volatility, which indicates the tendency of the returns to rise or fall drastically in a short period of time. A security that is volatile is also considered higher risk because its performance may change quickly in either direction at any moment. The standard deviation of a fund measures this risk by measuring the degree to which the fund fluctuates in relation to its mean return, the average return of a fund over a period of time. A fund that has a consistent four-year return of 3%, for example, would have a mean, or average, of 3%. The standard deviation for this fund would then be zero because the fund's return in any given year does not differ from its four-year mean of 3%. On the other hand, a fund that in each of the last four years returned -5%, 17%, 2% and 30% will have a mean return of 11%. The fund will also exhibit a high standard deviation because each year the return of the fund differs from the mean return. This fund is therefore more risky because it fluctuates widely between negative and positive returns within a short period. A note to remember is that, because volatility is only one indicator of the risk affecting a security, a stable past performance of a fund is not necessarily a guarantee of future stability. Since unforeseen market factors can influence volatility, a fund has a standard deviation close or equal to zero in current years may behave differently in the following year. To determine how well a fund is maximizing the return received for its volatility, you can compare the fund to another with a similar investment strategy and similar returns. The fund with the lower standard deviation would be more optimal because it is maximizing the return received for the amount of risk acquired. Fig. 2.9 depicts the standard deviation.

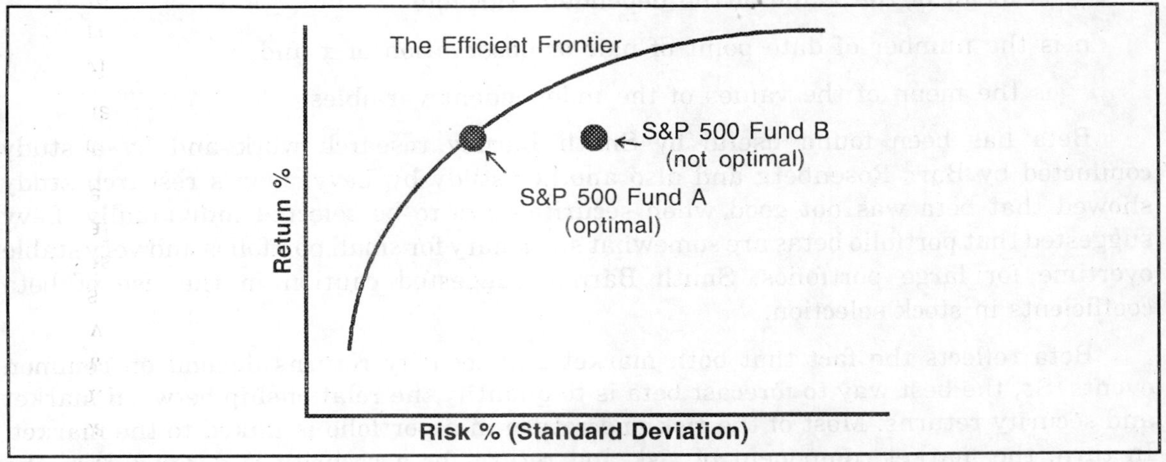

Figure 2.9

The coefficient of variation, CV, is a measure of relative dispersion that is useful in comparing risks of assets with differing expected returns.

CV = S.D/Average Return

Systematic Risk of a Security:

$B^2 \times$ variance of the market returns

Significance of Beta in Portfolio:

Alpha and beta of the stock portfolio describes the two main risks inherent in investing in stocks. Alpha relates to factors affecting the performance of an individual stock or the fund manager's skill in selecting the stocks while beta relates to market risks. Market risk is commonly measured by the "beta coefficient". Beta reflects the sensitivity of the fund's return to fluctuations in the market index. Beta is a measure of a volatility of a stock and expresses the relation of movement of stock with the movement of market as a whole. Beta of the security is nothing but the slope of the line. To calculate the beta of a portfolio, it is required to regress the rate of return of the portfolio on the rate of return of a market index. The slope of this regression line is the portfolio beta. Thus the return on market index is taken as independent variable and the return on security is taken as the dependent variable. The formula for beta is as follows:

$$\beta = \frac{\sum(X-\overline{X})(Y-\overline{Y})}{\sum(X-\overline{X})^2}$$

Where x is value of the independent variable, i.e., market portfolio return

y is value of the dependent variable, i.e., funds rate of return

$\bar{x}$ is mean of the value of the dependent variable

n is the number of date point of pair or observation of x and y

is the mean of the values of the independent variables.

Beta has been found useful by Smith Barney research work and by a study conducted by Barr Rosenberg and also another study by Levy. Levy's research study showed that beta was not good when securities are to be selected individually. Levy suggested that portfolio betas are somewhat stationary for small portfolios and very stable overtime for large portfolios. Smith Barney suggested caution in the use of beta coefficients in stock selection.

Beta reflects the fact that both market and security returns depend on common events. So, the best way to forecast beta is to quantify the relationship between market and security returns. Most of the risk and return in a portfolio is linked to the market. In turn, the market component of risk and return for a security is derived from the economic events that affect many stocks. The relationship between the returns of security and changes in the economic activity of the country are related by finding out "fundamental betas".

The fundamental betas are predicted in Barr Rosenberg study through relative response coefficient. The relative response coefficient is the ratio of market return and security return. Rosenberg found that the fundamental factors help in making an optimum portfolio. So risks are not only systematic and unsystematic but unsystematic risk can also be subdivided as "specific risk and extra market covariance". Specific risk is unrelated to events that affect other firms and is referred to as 'unique' risk of the company. Extra market covariance is the remaining component of residual risk. It shows a tendency of the stock to move together. Rosenberg prediction scheme derives estimates of both market returns and extra market covariance from a single underlying model. If Beta = 1; that means security's price will move in sync with the market. If Beta is positive; that means stock moves more than the market and is more volatile. If Beta is negative; that means stock moves less than the market and is less volatile. The beta for the average well-diversified portfolio equals 1.0. Betas greater than 1.0 indicate above average volatility – the higher the beta, the greater the risk. Beta less than 1.0 reflect below average volatility or non-aggressive portfolios. If you have a beta of 1, it is said that you have the same risk as the market. So let us say your security gets a beta of 1.20 – it has a history of fluctuating 20% more than the benchmark. If the market is up, the security is outperformed by 20%. If the market heads lower, the security is falling by 20% more. High-beta stocks are generally riskier being more volatile but provide a potential for higher returns as these are in the early stages of growth. On other side low-beta stocks pose less risk and hence lower returns. Usually utilities stocks have a beta of less than 1 while high-tech stocks have a beta of greater than 1. Beta is the index of systematic risk. It is believed that in efficient markets, only the systematic risk gets rewarded. So higher is the systematic risk index, greater the returns. The risk-averse investors should invest in scrips with beta less than 1. Aggressive risk takers would prefer scrips with greater than 1. Beta of the market is always one and beta of risk-free investment is zero. Portfolio of systematic risk can be greater than or less than one. High-beta stocks are supposed to be riskier but provide a potential for higher returns. Low-beta stocks pose less risk but also lower returns.

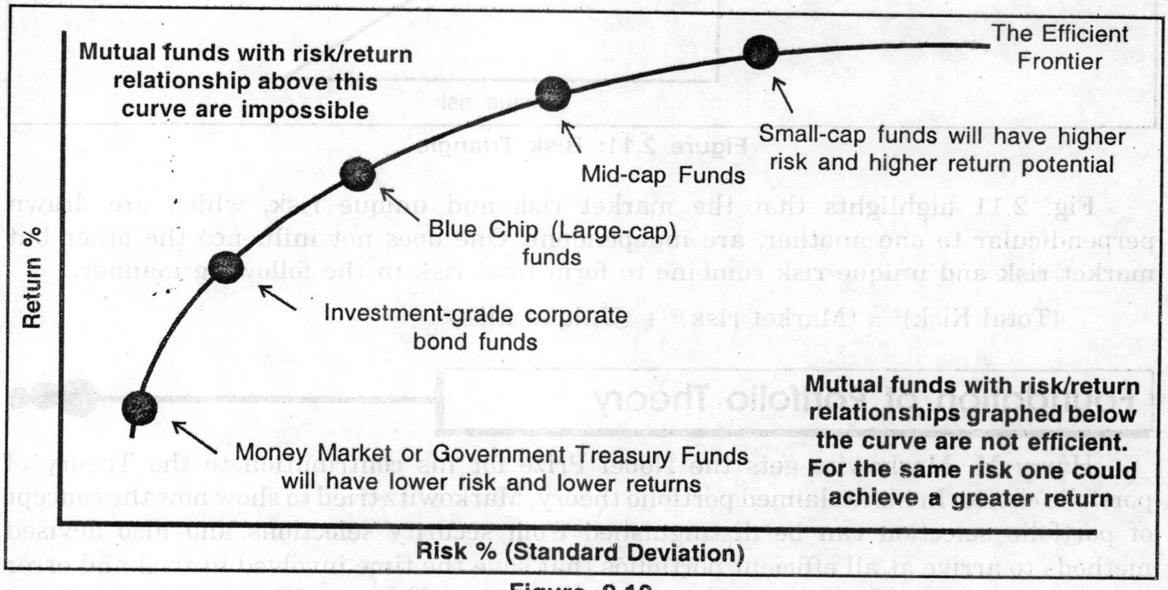

Figure 2.10

It is to be noticed that as standard deviation increases, so does the return. In the Fig. 2.10 if expected returns of a portfolio reach a certain level, an investor must take on a large amount of volatility for a small increase in return. Obviously portfolios that have a risk/return relationship plotted far below the curve are not optimal as the investor is taking on a large amount of instability for a small return. To determine if the proposed fund has an optimal return for the amount of volatility acquired, an investor needs to do an analysis of the fund's standard deviation. The modern portfolio theory and volatility are not the only means using by investors to determine and analyze risk, there are many different factors caused by market as well.

Risk Triangle:

The total risk and its components, i.e., market risk and unique risk has represented in the form of a "Risk Triangle" in Fig. 2.11.

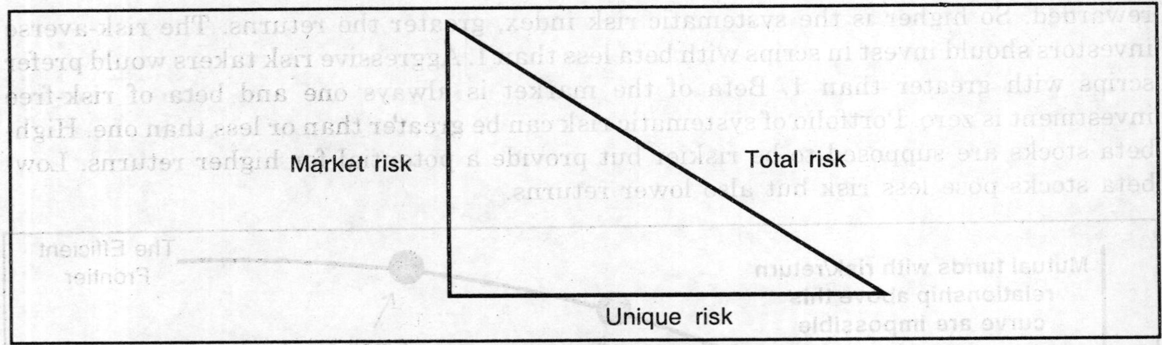

Figure 2.11: Risk Triangle

Fig. 2.11 highlights that the market risk and unique risk, which are drawn perpendicular to one another, are independent. One does not influence the other but market risk and unique risk combine to form total risk in the following manner.

$$(\text{Total Risk})^2 = (\text{Market risk})^2 + (\text{Unique Risk})^2$$

Foundation of Portfolio Theory

Harry M. Markowitz gets the Nobel Prize for his contribution to the Theory of portfolio choice. In his acclaimed portfolio theory, Markowitz tried to show how the concept of portfolio selection can be distinguished from security selections and also devised methods to arrive at all efficient portfolios that save the time involved in trial and error methods. It was on the basis of his work that William Sharp and Linter late developed the popular Capital Asset Pricing Model. So Markowitz called as the foundations of portfolio theory.

There are three major ways in which portfolio theory differs from the theory of the firm and theory of the consumer. First, it is concerned with investors rather than manufacturing firms or consumers. Second, it is concerned with economic agents who act under uncertainty. Third, it is a theory, which can be used to direct practice at least by large investors with sufficient computer and data base resources. The fact that it deals with investors rather than producers or consumers needs no further comment. Markowitz's framework led to the concept of efficient portfolios. An efficient portfolio is expected to yield the highest return for a given level of risk or lowest risk for a given level of return. Markowitz attempted to lessen the risk of an investment portfolio by mathematical methods, while maintaining the possibility of reward. This model mathematically described ways to distribute risk in an 'optimal' portfolio by diversifying investment among a number of different products, such as stocks and bonds and future contracts. This model was able to quantify risk for the first time. In the model it was called 'beta' the size of beta is supposed to convey an accurate assessment of risk. In order to generate the efficient portfolios; the Markowitz model requires the following inputs:

- The expected return on each asset being considered
- The standard deviation of returns as a measure of risk for each asset
- The coefficient of correlation as a measure of interrelationship between asset's returns.

Using these inputs the Markowitz model generates outputs in the form of weight (percentage of investible funds) to be given to each asset so as to constitute efficient portfolios. While an infinite number of portfolios are possible depending on the proportions of funds invested in the assets, these are dominated by or are inferior to the efficient portfolios. This means that these either involve greater risk for the same level of expected return or provide lower expected returns for the same level of risk. The model does not specify one optimal portfolio, but a set of efficient portfolios. The choice of a given efficient portfolio depends on the investor's own risk aversion. The inputs which are needed for portfolio optimisation are expected future values and historical values, are generally used as proxies for future values. This is based on the assumption that historical values are good approximations of future values, which may or may not be true. The quantification of risk and the need for optimisation of return with lowest risk are the contributions of Markowitz. This led to what is called the modern portfolio theory, which emphasises the trade-off between risk and return. Markowitz theory is based on the modern portfolio theory under several assumptions.

- All investors are in equal category and have the knowledge of stock market to maximise their utility with a given level of income.
- All investors are risk averse with the common objective of maximising return with minimising risk.
- The two parameters, i.e., rate of return and standard deviation is important for investors' base decisions on the expected rate of return on an investment.
- The markets are efficient and absorb the information on the returns and risk.
- Investors should aware of correct information on the returns and risk.
- Investors choose higher returns to lower returns for a given level of risk.

Portfolio Risk:

Risk on a portfolio is different from the risk on individual securities. This risk is reflected in the variability of the returns from zero to infinity. There are two measures of risk, i.e., standard deviation and variance.

If two risks are compared, then standard deviation divided by their means are compared. This is called the coefficient variation

$$\text{Coefficient Variation} = \frac{\text{SD}}{\text{x}}$$

The basic equation for calculating risk can be formulated as a regression equation

So, $y = \alpha + \beta x + e$

y = Return in the security in a given period

x = market return

α = intercept where the regression line crosses the y-axis

β = The slope of the regression line

e = error term containing all residuals

This equation is explained with the help of graph in Fig. 2.12 :

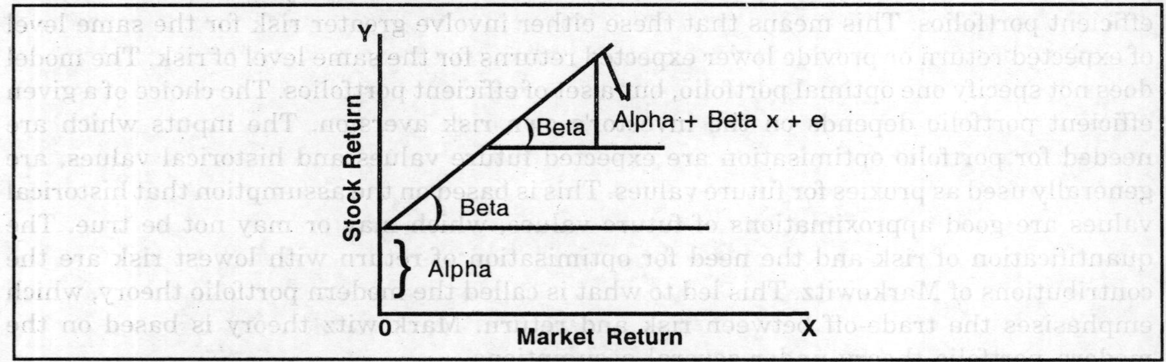

Figure 2.12

Alpha: Alpha was designed to take beta one-step further. Alpha is the risk-adjusted return on an investment. It is excess return of a stock portfolio hence is usually used to measure the performance of fund manager in managing the fund portfolio. So, usually an investor's strategy should be to buy securities with positive alpha as these may be undervalued. It looks at the relationship between a securities historical beta and its current performance. If you are trying to see if a security has beaten the performance of its relative index, you just take a look at the alpha ratio. Let us say that alpha ratio for our growth securities for last five years is 0.46. To put this in perspective, if the number is greater than 0, then it has a positive alpha. If your security has a positive alpha that means it returned more than its beta predicted. A negative alpha means it returned less. In this case, over the last five years, our growth security has been able to outperform the BSE index. The greater is the number, the greater the out-performance beta and alpha go hand-in-hand. Ideally, we want a security with a low beta and a high alpha. This means we have found a security that has outperformed the index while posing less risk than the index. The alpha coefficient is used to measure the performance of an investment firm or portfolio manager. It is a measure of excess return in investments. The difference between the fair and actually expected rates of return on a stock is called the stock's alpha. According to Alpha Stocks, the alpha coefficient is the difference between the expected value of the stock and the expected value of a risk-free asset. α is the distance between the horizontal axis and line's intersection with y-axis. If an investment outperformed the benchmark, that means more reward for a given amount of risk. In that case α > 0. If an investment underperformed the benchmark; that means the investment has earned too little for its risk. In that case α < 0. For efficient markets, the expected value of the alpha is zero, i.e., $\alpha = 0$ and the investment has earned a return adequate for the risk taken. Fund managers are rated according to how much alpha their fund generates. It is thus a measure of the fund manager's ability to generate profits in excess of market returns. Fund managers are usually paid in accordance to how much alpha their fund generates. Higher the alpha, the higher is their fees.

Alpha is calculated by the following formula:

$$\alpha = \bar{y} - \beta \bar{x}$$

Or α = [(sum of y) – ((b)(sum of x))] / n

Where:

n = number of observations

b = beta of the fund

x = rate of return for the market

y = rate of return for the fund

Residual Variance: Residual variance indicates how well the regression line is constructed fits the actual data set. It is generally used to calculate the standard error of estimate. Residual variance is another name for unexplained variation. The smaller the variance, the more accurate the predictions.

The error term or residual variance indicates that if it is high, the unsystematic risk will also be high

$$e^2 = \frac{\sum y^2 - (y) - \beta \sum xy}{n}$$

Markowitz model showed the ideal combination of securities through the efficient frontier. So, it is also called full covariance model. But when the number of observation increased, it becomes cumbersome.

Covariance: Covariance of the securities will help in the finding out the interactive risk. So, when the covariance will be positive, the interactive risk is positive, i.e., the rate of return of securities moves together either upwards or downwards. If the rates of return are independent, the covariance will be zero.

$$Cov_{xy} = \frac{\sum \left(X - \bar{X}\right)\left(Y - \bar{Y}\right)}{N - 1}$$

Cov_{xy} = Covariance between two securities.

X = return on security

Y = return on security

$\bar{X}$ = expected return to security

$\bar{Y}$ = expected return to security

N = number of observations

Coefficient of Correlation: Coefficient of correlation gives an indication of the variables being positively or negatively related to each other. A coefficient of correlation is a measure to determine how much one variable can expected to be influenced by changes in another. Correlation coefficients of one mean that the two variables are perfectly correlated.

Correlation coefficients of –1 mean that the variables are perfectly inversely correlated. If one grows the other falls. The growth in one is a negative multiple of the growth in the other. A correlation coefficient of zero means that the two variables are not related.

$$r_{xy} = \frac{Cov_{xy}}{\sigma x, \sigma y}$$

r_{xy} = Coefficient of correlation of x and y

Cov_{xy} = Co-variance between x and y

σx = standard deviation of x

σy = standard deviation of y

Correlation Effects: A correlation describes the degree of relationship between two variables.To understand the risk of the portfolio more clearly, the essence of portfolio diversification must be reviewed. When the returns of two assets are expected to move exactly like up or down, their returns are said to be perfectly positively correlated with each other. The exact opposite of perfect positive correlation is perfect negative correlation. "Zero correlation" means that no association of returns exists between the assets. If the return in one increase it cannot be predicted.

$$\text{Correlation (r)} = \frac{N\sum XY - \sum X \sum Y}{\sqrt{\left[N\sum X^2 - \left(\sum X\right)^2\right]\left[N\sum Y^2 - \left(\sum Y\right)^2\right]}}$$

Diversification

Diversification is the most important component in helping to reach long-range financial goals with minimizing risk. Diversification lowers the risk of portfolio. Coming to the modern portfolio theory, when the number of stocks in the portfolio in large, the extent of risk which the portfolio is exposed to small. This happens due to the diversification of the portfolio. As the number of stocks goes on increasing in the portfolio, the unsystematic risk of the portfolio goes on decreasing due to the diversification of risk. The major part of the risk of portfolios is exposed to be systematic in nature. Thus, to a great extent the behaviour of these portfolio are dependent on the market behaviour. About 70 per cent to 75 per cent of the behaviour of the well diversified portfolio is determined by the market index movement. So depending upon the beta value of the portfolio, the portfolio would go up when the market is bullish, whereas portfolio would go down when the market is bearish. The extent of ups and downs in the NAV of a portfolio due to market changes would be determined by the beta factor. Markowitz type diversification stresses not the number of securities but the right kind of securities, which exhibit less than perfect positive correlation. But if the investors hold a portfolio consisting of several securities, in such context, the portfolio risk is determined differently. The unique risk tends to declare if the portfolio becomes more diversified. Because in a diversified portfolio, the unique risk of different securities tends to offset portfolio risk. For a well-diversified portfolio, the risk or average deviation from the mean of each stock contributes little to portfolio risk. As a result, investors benefit from holding diversified portfolios instead of individual stocks. Now it is essential to understand the best level of diversification arises to avail diversification advantages.

The Capital Asset Pricing Model

There are many models to explain the relationship between expected risk and return for any asset when markets are equilibrium. The relationship between expected return and systematic risk and the valuation of securities is the essence of the Capital Asset Pricing Model (CAPM). Sharp defines the market portfolio as a portfolio consisting of all securities where the proportion invested in each security corresponds to its relative market value. The relative market value of a security is simply equal to the aggregate market value of the security divided by the sum of the aggregate market value of all securities. In the early 1960s, finance researchers (Sharpe, Treynor, and Lintner) developed an asset pricing model that measures only the amount of systematic risk a particular asset has. In other words, they noticed that most stocks go down when interest rates go up but some go down a whole lot more. They reasoned that if they could measure this variability – the systematic risk – then they could develop a model to price assets using only this risk. The unsystematic (company-related) risk is irrelevant because it could easily be eliminated simply by diversifying.The Capital Asset Pricing Model (CAPM) helps us to calculate investment risk and what return on investment we should expect. The following assumption underlined these models are:

- Every investor is one-period expected utilities maximize and exhibits diminishing marginal utility of terminal wealth.
- All investors have the same one-period time horizon.
- Every investor feels that he can evaluate a portfolio solely in terms of the mean and dispersion or variance of one-period returns.
- It is assumed that there are no transaction or information costs that the borrowing and lending rates are equal and the same for all individuals and those investors will only select portfolios with optimal combinations of risk and return.
- All investors hold identical or homogeneous expectations about the distributions of future returns.
- The capital market is in equilibrium.

Under these assumption, Sharpe and Lintner has shown that the expected return for asset on portfolio is related to the expected return on the market portfolio by the following equation

$R_p - R_f = \beta(R_m - R_f)$

Where,

R_p = expected return for asset on portfolio

R_f = Risk-free rate

R_m = expected return on the market portfolio

β is defined as the cov (R_p, R_m) divided by Var (R_m). The variable β is a measure of systematic risk.

The required return for all assets is composed of two parts: the risk-free rate and a risk premium. The risk premium is a function of both market conditions and the asset itself. The risk-free rate (R_f) is usually estimated from the return on T-bills. The risk premium for a stock is composed of two parts:

- The Market Risk Premium which is the return required for investing in any risky asset rather than the risk-free rate.
- Beta, a risk coefficient which measures the sensitivity of the particular stock's return to changes in market conditions.

After estimating beta, which measures a specific asset or portfolio's systematic risk, estimates of the other variables in the model may be obtained to calculate an asset or portfolio's required return.

$R_p = R_f + \beta(R_m - R_f)$

Where,

R_p = assets expected return

β = assets portfolio beta

R_m = expected return on the market portfolio

Some Comments on the CAPM

- The CAPM relies on historical data which means the betas may or may not actually reflect the future variability of returns.
- Therefore, the required returns specified by the model should be used only as rough approximations.
- The CAPM also assumes markets are efficient.
- Although the perfect world of efficient markets appears to be unrealistic, studies have provided support for the existence of the expectation relationship described by the CAPM in active markets such as the NYSE.

The Efficient Set

For every level of return, there is one portfolio that offers the lowest possible risk, and for every level of risk, there is a portfolio that offers the highest return. Modern portfolio theory suggests that if you were to borrow to acquire a risk-free stock, then the remaining stock portfolio could have a riskier profile and, therefore, a higher return you have to otherwise choose. Modern portfolio theory demonstrates that portfolio diversification can reduce investment risk. Modern portfolio theory has had a noticeable impact on how investors perceive risk, return and portfolio management. Efficient set consists of investment in the market portfolio, coupled with either risk-free borrowing or lending. The concept of risk-free rate (R_f) is central to CAPM and at equilibrium level, the amount of money borrowed or lent is the same. Efficient portfolio plot along the line starting at R_f and going through market portfolio and consist of alternative combinations of risk and return obtainable by combining the market portfolio with risk-free borrowing or lending. This linear efficient set of CAPM is known as the capital market line (CML) is depicted in the Figure 2.13.

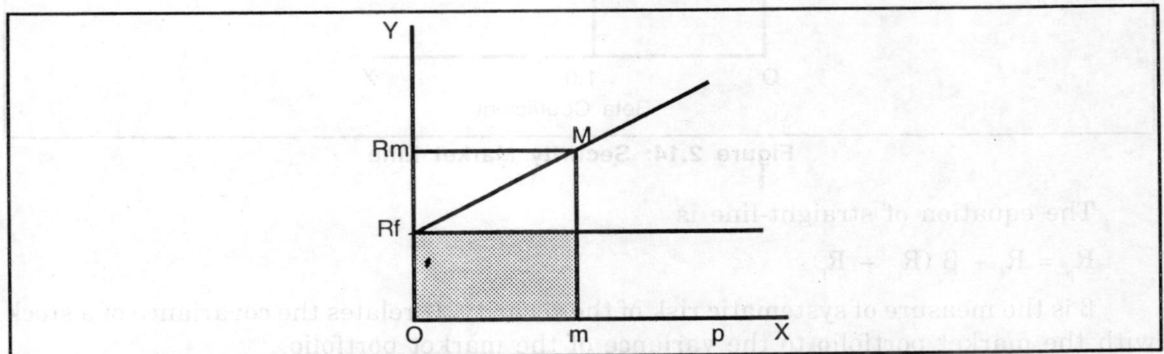

Figure 2.13: Capital Market Line

The slope of the CML is equal to the difference between the expected return on the market portfolio and the risk-free rate (R_m – R_f) divided by the difference in their risk. The straight, line characterizing the CML has the following equation:

$$R_p = R_f + \sigma_p \; [(R_m - R_f)/ \; \sigma_m]$$

Where R_p and σ_p refer to the expected return and standard deviation of a different portfolio.

The CML represents the equilibrium relationship between the expected return and standard deviation for efficient portfolios. The CAPM does not imply any particular relationship between the expected return and the standard deviation of an individual security. Under the CAPM, each investor holds the market portfolio and is concerned with its standard deviation because this will influence the slope of the CML. The contribution of each security to the standard deviation of the market portfolio depends on the size of its covariance with the market portfolio. Accordingly, each investor will note that the relevant measure of risk for a security is its covariance with the market portfolio.

Securities with larger covariance values have to provide proportionately larger expected returns to interest investors in purchasing such high-risk securities.

The relationship between covariance and expected return is known as security market line (SML). To determine the SML, it is needed to connect the intercept (beta of zero, or riskless security) and the market portfolio (beta of one and return of R_m). These two points identify the straight-line shown in the Fig. 2.14.

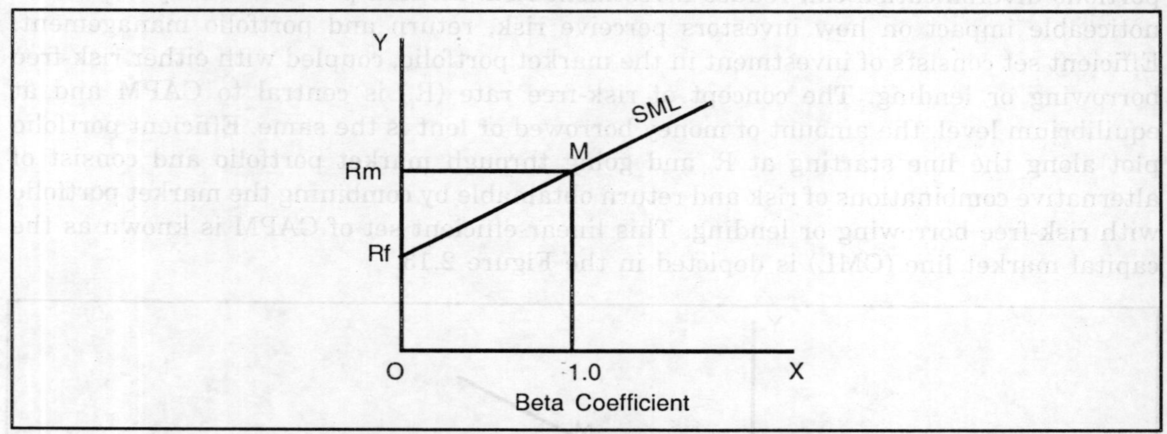

Figure 2.14: Security Market Line

The equation of straight-line is

$$R_p = R_f + \beta (R_m - R_f)$$

ß is the measure of systematic risk of the security. It relates the covariance of a stock with the market portfolio to the variance of the market portfolio.

The Characteristic Line

The systematic risk is derived from a regression model, returned to as the assets characteristic line with market portfolio:

$$R_p = \alpha + \beta_p R_m + e_p$$

Where, e_p = error term

α = constant term

β_p = systematic risk (Beta)

Though, SML and CML are for the purpose of security return, every security of the portfolio must be plotted on SML and CML. However, undiversified portfolios plot only on the SML.

Private Placements

Private placement means selling of securities in the form of stocks and sometimes bonds to a relatively small number of selected private investors rather than to public investors. Private placements provide an alternate means of using capital markets when the public market may not be appropriate or available. Private placements are the issuances of securities that do not occur on a public exchange. In reality all stock issuances by privately held companies are privately placed. Private Placement does not have to be registered with the Securities and Exchange Board of India. Investors involved in private placements are usually large banks, mutual funds, insurance companies and pension funds. Private placements are generally considered a cost-effective way for small businesses to raise capital without "going public" through an initial public offering (IPO). A private placement candidate company typically has a net worth of at least $15 million with annual sales of $30 million. This may not always be the case, however, because private placements can be used in smaller startup or seed capital rounds. A company can issue securities through Public, Rights or preferential issues also known as private placements. Private placements or preferential issues are relatively simple. The classification of issues is illustrated below:

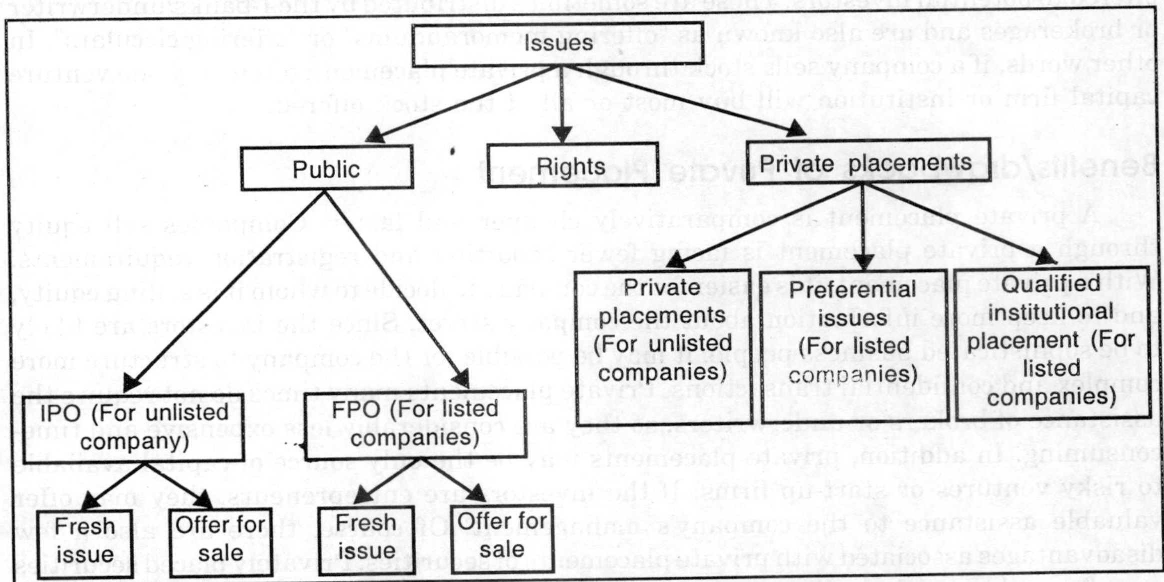

Figure 2.15: Classification of Issues

A private placement of shares or of convertible securities by a listed company is generally known by name of preferential allotment. A listed company going for preferential allotment has to comply with the requirements of SEBI guidelines. A Qualified Institutions Placement is a private placement of equity shares or securities convertible into equity shares by a listed company to Qualified Institutions Buyers only in terms of provisions of SEBI (DIP) guidelines.

Why Private Placements?

When a company in the third stage of finance is looking for growth or expansion funding looking for private placement secondly when company has completed product development, conducted a market-feasibility study and business planning also looking for private placements. Companies wishing to raise capital frequently find out that they are unable to go public for a number of reasons. The company may not be big enough; the markets may not have a desire for IPOs; the company is not ready to be a public company; or the company do not want to have its stock be publicly traded. Such companies make excellent private placement candidates. Sometimes companies advised by investment bankers to do a private placement first rather than going public as they need to gain size in order to justify an IPO. Also with the limited infusion of capital into the stock market, the private investor market is an attractive alternative for investors and small businesses. Private placement offers a viable form of business financing without the constraints of taking a company public and conceding control.The process of raising capital is only slightly different from a public deal. One difference is that private placements do not involve a road-show and do not registered with SEBI/SEC. In place of the prospectus, investment banks draft a detailed private placement memorandum (PPM) which provides material information about the company and the securities being offered to potential investors. These are sometimes distributed by the I-banks/underwriter or brokerages and are also known as "offering memorandums" or "offering circulars". In other words, if a company sells stock through a private placement, often only one venture capital firm or institution will buy most or all of the stock offered.

Benefits/drawbacks of Private Placement

A private placement is comparatively cheaper and faster. Companies sell equity through a private placement is facing fewer reporting and registration requirements. With a private placement, it is easier for the company to decide to whom it is selling equity, and to keep more information about the company secret. Since the investors are likely to be sophisticated business people, it may be possible for the company to structure more complex and confidential transactions. Private placements many times do not require the assistance of brokers or underwriters, so they are considerably less expensive and time-consuming. In addition, private placements may be the only source of capital available to risky ventures or start-up firms. If the investors are entrepreneurs, they may offer valuable assistance to the company's management. Of course, there are also a few disadvantages associated with private placements of securities. Privately placed securities are often sold at a deep discount below their market value. Companies that undertake a private placement may also have to relinquish more equity, because investors want compensation for taking a greater risk and assuming an illiquid position.

The Investment Bank's Role in Private Placements

The investment banker's profession in a private placement is to find a buyer by writing the PPM and then contacting potential strategic or financial buyers of the client. In the case of private placements, however, financial buyers are typically venture capitalists rather than buyout firms. A sale occurs when a firm sells greater than 50 per cent of its equity, but a private placement occurs usually when less than 50 per cent of its equity is sold. In private placements, the company typically offers convertible preferred stock, rather than common stock as private placements involve selling to a single buyer. Investment bankers function as negotiators for the company, helping to convince the investor of the value of the firm. Fees involved in private placements work like those in public offerings.

Private placements provide an excellent way for management and other insiders associated with the company to maintain a high degree of ownership in the listed company when they are the investors purchasing the stock. It is also a frequently used method to compensate executives and at the same time inject funds into the coffers of the company.

Summary

Financial markets have evolved significantly over several hundred years and are undergoing constant innovation to improve liquidity. India financial market promotes the savings of the economy, providing an effective channel for transmitting the financial policies. Financial markets around the world are integrating on a scale as nowadays more and more investment companies developing global dimensions. As a result, analysis of the financial markets has become one of the main activities covering a very large number of factors both within the market and outside. Each financial decision presents certain risk and return characteristics and the unique combination of these characteristics have an impact on share price. A proper understanding of the process of valuation is necessary for any financial investment decision. A portfolio is a combination of various assets and/ or instruments of investments. In general, portfolio management seeks to combine securities so that the overall return of the portfolio is enhanced and the risk to the portfolio is reduced. The determination of superior performance is made for the entire portfolio or combination of security, rather than separately for each individual security. Since portfolio management is always investor specific, the emphasis varies, some investors want income, some capital gains and some a combination of both. In spite of these variations, several objectives are considered as basic to a well executed investment programme and hence establishing the indifference curve of risk versus return for them.

CASE: PORTFOLIO RISK AND RETURN

Johnson had worked very hard in B-school to prepare himself for being a financial advisor. Johnson who is graduated with specialization in finance from a leading B-school in India operated office at Mumbai and providing investors advise services. Before joining his new business he was working with a leading broking firm in India. While working, he was finding enough challenge and crumples in this job to keep him paying attention and involved. His was given the assignment to educating the investors and small business owners about their financial alternatives and the basics of investments and portfolio theory. As the firm grew, Johnson developed a reputation with the clients and increased the business two-fold with a short span of period. He also helping other friends in the firm and giving training his associates and helping them establish themselves in the business. Johnson was used to work long hours at workplace. He was always involved in extra reading and still tries to learn about financial services, and finance in general, and he looked forward to each assignment of the firms.

At one point of time he took the decision to quit the job and started own investors services firms. Johnson already has a significant amount of knowledge in financial services sector and good number of clients. He feels that his firm will be one of the leading companies in the future reason being for this perceived future success is the research being done in the area of parallel for all financial markets.

Michael Frank is an individual investor who is currently considering the purchase of ₹ 4,000 worth of any common stock which will give good return. But he has not sufficient idea of stock market and investment. He is wondering for a good financial advisor to provide him sound advice on investment in stock market. He has been advised by one of his friend regarding Johnson who is having a small office at Mumbai and providing sound advice on investing in different financial products. Presently, Michael holds ₹ 2,000 worth of Stock A, ₹ 3,500 in Stock B, and ₹ 4,500 in Stock C.

Quarterly Closing Prices (March 2005-September 2010)

	BSE-100	TCS	CMC	Infosys	Wipro
Q1 2005	3,481.86	1,432.75	620.55	2,257.20	671.1
Q2 2005	3,800.24	1,351.90	493.05	2,358.20	765.55
Q3 2005	4,566.63	1,481.25	507.6	2,515.30	371.8
Q4 2005	4,953.28	1,702.45	507.6	2,996.80	463.45
Q1 2006	5,904.17	1,914.15	540.3	2,981.40	558.55
Q2 2006	5,382.11	1,735.65	413.5	3,078.90	513.75
Q3 2006	6,328.33	1,021.60	560.25	1,849.60	525.1
Q4 2006	6,982.56	1,218.60	674.3	2,241.80	604.55
Q1 2007	6,587.21	1,231.20	1,211.20	2,018.60	558.35
Q2 2007	7,605.37	1,149.25	1,191.55	1,929.00	518.5

Q3 2007	8,967.41	1,056.75	1,002.60	1,887.10	459.85
Q4 2007	11,154.28	1,083.35	1,379.30	1,765.00	525.6
Q1 2008	8,232.82	810.9	810.4	1,433.50	425.3
Q2 2008	7,029.74	858.8	626.95	1,726.00	437.95
Q3 2008	6,691.57	662.75	438.9	1,404.00	339.65
Q4 2008	4,988.04	478.1	308.05	1,116.10	233.55
Q1 2009	4,942.51	540	319.95	1,326.00	245.4
Q2 2009	7,571.49	389.7	775.9	1,777.60	377.65
Q3 2009	8,930.31	619.35	1,114.30	2,303.90	601.75
Q4 2009	9,229.71	749.75	1,343.00	2,604.70	679.4
Q1 2010	9,300.20	780.8	1,340.00	2,615.00	706.8
Q2 2010	9,442.58	751.15	1,433.55	2,790.00	384.75
Q3 2010	10,627.35	922.55	1,941.70	3,042.90	448.35

Michael wants advice to invest his funds in good stocks and seeking advice from Johnson to see what affect the purchase of other stocks will have on the beta of his overall portfolio.

1. Calculate the annual rate of return for each portfolio and find the average annual return for each portfolio.
2. Calculate the standard deviation of the returns from question 1 and discuss the return and risk associated with each portfolio. Which portfolio appears to be preferable?
3. Assume that the risk-free rate of interest is 3.25%, and find the return on the market. Based on CAPM, what is the required rate of return on all stocks?
4. Using your answer from question 3, if **Michael** had an expected return of 8%, would **Michael** be well advised to purchase the stock? At what minimum expected rate of return would **Michael** be encouraged to buy the stock?

Note: The case is fictitious and any resemblance to a person/company is merely coincidental.

CASE: VALUING A SHEPHERD AIRLINES CORPORATE BOND ISSUE

Shepherd Airlines is currently considering the issuance of a series of $ 1,000 par bonds. The coupon rate offered, based on current market interest rates and the ICRA's based Shepherd bond rating, will be 10%. The current interest rate is coincidentally 10% as well. Interest on the bonds will be paid semi-annually. However, Shepherd cannot decide on the maturity of the new issue. The life of the bonds will be 10, 20, or 30 years. What will the bonds sell for today if Shepherd decides to issue the bonds with a maturity of 10 years? What will the price be if the bonds have a maturity of 20 years? If the bonds are issued with 10 years to maturity and the day after they are issued, the market interest rates increase to 12%, what will be the price of Shepherd Airline's bonds? If the bonds are issued with 20 years to maturity and the day after they are issued, the market interest rates increase to 12%, what will be the price of Shepherd Airline's bonds? What if interest rates drop to 8%? What is the relationship between time to maturity and the price of the bond? What is the relationship between current interest rates, the coupon rate, and time to maturity?

CASE: PRIVATE PLACEMENT

The company has taken up an expansion project to set up a chemicals plant requiring project outlays of ₹ 930 crore. The project is intended to finance by some leading bank ₹ 160 crore through private placement of NCDs ₹ 80 crore from internal accruals and the balance through equity market in right issues. The right issues are proposed to be priced at 80% of its current market prices. The company had issued 20,00,000 17% PCDs of ₹ 240 each in Jan. 2007. Part A of ₹ 100 will be converted into 4 shares, 15 months from the date of allotment. The balance will be redeemed at the end of 5 years.

The company had raised a sum of ₹ 17.5 million by issue of 12,50,000 GDRs in March 2007. The paid-up capital of ₹ 20 crore includes 50,00,000 shares underlying the GDRs. The balance sheet of Minaco Plant Ltd. as on 31st March, 2008 is as follows:

(₹ in Crore)

Liabilities		Assets	
Share Capital (Face Value ₹ 10)	20	Land and Building	32
Reserves and surplus	136	Plant and Machinery	94
Debentures	60	Miscellaneous Fixed assets	48
Current liabilities	64	Current Assets	106
	280		280

Assuming that GDRs are quoted at 20% premium to their domestic price and the ₹/$ exchange rate is as follows: At the time of issue of GDRs ₹ 72/$, at the time of rights issue and sale by GDR holder ₹ 82/$. You are required to find the gain or loss in dollars to a GDR holder who holds 100 GDRs exercise the rights and sell his entire holdings at the prevailing GDR price. You are required to determine the ratio for issue of rights shares and the pricing and also value of rights.

Note: The case is fictitious and any resemblance to a person/company is merely coincidental.

Review Questions

1. What are the differences between stocks/equity and bonds/credit markets?
2. What are the different types of bonds are available?
3. Who are the market participants in bond market?
4. How do you analyse the financial market?
5. What is Private Placement? What are its benefits and drawbacks of Private Placement? What is investment bank's role in private placements?
6. **Quiz:**
   (a) ______ are also known as fixed income securities.
   (b) ______ is the rate at which interest is paid, and is usually represented as a percentage of the par value of a bond.
   (c) The ______ performs the crucial function of facilitating capital formation in the economy.
   (d) In ______ market where prices of stocks are, on average higher and investor expectations rising and aspires to obtain further capital gains.
   (e) ______ is defined as the chance of suffering a financial loss.
   (f) ______ represents the total gain or loss on an investment.
   (g) The risk associated with macro factors is called ______ risk.
   (h) Beta is a measure of a volatility of a stock and expresses the relation of movement of stock with the movement of market as a whole. ***(T/F)***
   (i) Portfolio of systematic risk can be greater than or less than one. ***(T/F)***
   (j) Harry M. Markowitz did not gets the Nobel Prize for his contribution to the Theory of portfolio choice. ***(T/F)***
   (k) Residual variance is another name for unexplained variation. ***(T/F)***
   (l) The relationship between covariance and expected return is known as Capital market line. ***(T/F)***
   (m) Private placement does not have to be registered with the Securities and Exchange of India. ***(T/F)***

CHAPTER 3 Initial Public Offerings

Introduction

Initial Public Offering, is the sale of shares by a company to the public for the first time. When shares are bought in an IPO it is termed primary market. After an IPO, the stocks of the company are traded publicly on stock exchanges. The primary market does not involve the stock exchanges. Buying in the primary market does not assure an investor of allotment of shares. A successful IPO is providing a company with an objective valuation of its stock create a good public image of the company which leads to lowering its cost of borrowing and provide it with a pool of publicly owned shares for future acquisitions of other companies. The IPO can be in the form of a fixed price portion or in the form of a book-building portion. The IPO paves the way for listing and trading of the issuer's securities. Book-building and Fixed Price Issue are the two types of Initial Public Offerings (IPOs) through which a public company can raise money in the capital market. In a book-building public issue the bids are offered by investors at different price levels and accordingly issue price is ascertained. In a fixed price issue the issue price is predetermined by the issuer.

Economic Condition and IPO Declaration

- Decision to go public (or getting listed) is often based on market trends
- If primary market is strong, cost of raising funds through IPO is low, hence high temptation to go public
- During boom, the company gets a high premium
- Opposite is the case during economic slow-down

Why do Companies Offer IPO?

In general, companies offer IPOs in order to raise money for their business expansion and new business opportunities. There are three main reasons behind the offering of IPOs. First motive is to mobilize savings for economic development. Second motivation is the desire to achieve liquidity. Third motivation is that going public means interactions with customers or suppliers. This is particularly important in industries where products do not represent a one-time purchase, but require ongoing service or upgrades. Apart of it the companies go public for due to the following reasons:

- Retire long pending loans and debts taken at high interest rates
- Take advantage of boom cycles in stock market and issue shares at a premium price
- Diversify the owners of the company thereby reducing the controlling rights concentrated in the hands of a few
- Rebalance their balance sheet accounts and capital structure after high growth and investment.
- Being publicly traded also opens many financial doors:
    - Because of the increased scrutiny, public companies can usually get better rates when they issue debt.
    - Trading in the open markets means liquidity. This makes it possible to implement things like employee stock ownership plans, which help to attract top talent.

While IPO sounds a good way for companies to raise money, but one of the important disadvantages is that there are heavy legal compliance and financial regulations that needs to be followed strictly.

Benefits of an IPO: The following are the benefits presented in Fig. 3.1.

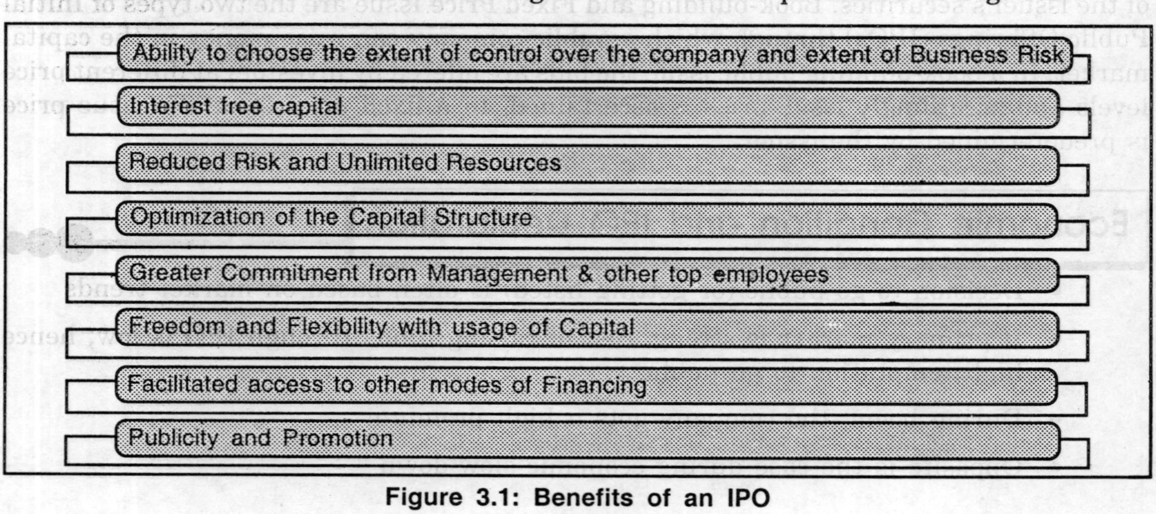

Figure 3.1: Benefits of an IPO

Significance of IPO

Pros

- New Source of Finance
- Opens Market Window and New Class of Investors called "Retail Investors"
- Liquidity Event: Exit route for existing and future investors
- Creates market capitalization for the company

Cons

- Market capitalization can act both as an enhancement or deterrent for future fund raising by the company in the equity route
- Open up gate for hostile takeover attempts
- Future acquisition cost by promoters become expensive
- The company is subjective to more regulation and restrictions on future capital transactions

The Role of the Underwriter

Every public offering must be managed by an underwriter. Usually, two brokerage houses are sharing this role, so that there is a lead underwriter and a co-manager. The underwriter acts as the company's agent. The underwriter and the company agree on a number of shares and a price per share, and the underwriter basically buys all the new stock at the agreed price and sells it into the market. Generally, an estimated price range is determined a couple of months ahead of time; the final price is set the day before trading begins. At the time of pricing, the deal can still be run by either the company or the underwriter. Once the pricing is committed, the underwriter carries the risk if the price is too high.

How to Choose an Underwriter?

The following points are to be considered while choosing underwriter depicted in Fig. 3.2.

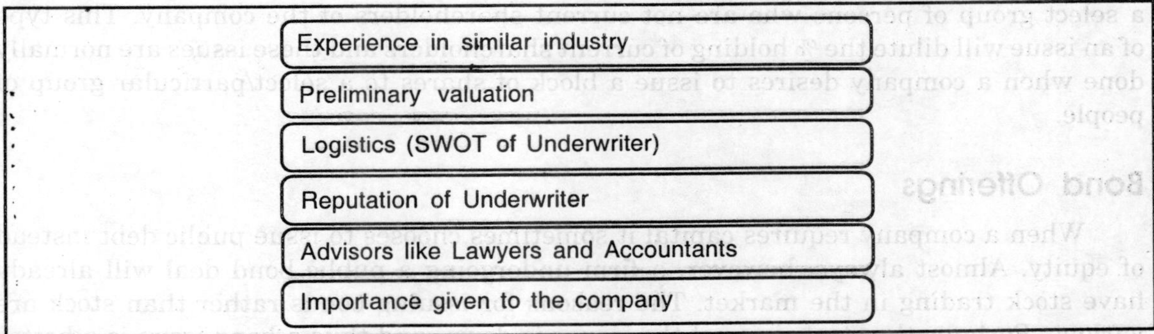

Figure 3.2

Types of IPO

- The plain vanilla IPO is undertaken by a privately held company, mostly owned by management, who want to secure additional funding and determine the company's fair market value.
- A venture capital-backed IPO refers to a company who has sold its shares to one or more groups of private investors in return for funding and advice. These enable the venture capitalists to exit after the company financially viable in the market in which they have invested.
- In a reverse-leveraged buyout, when a company was privatized after a previous listing on an exchange, the IPO are used to pay-off the debt accumulated. This process enables owners to privatize their publicly trading firms, which are undervalued in the market. Owners realizing financial gains after the public were informed of the high intrinsic value of the private firm.

IPO – Different Types of Issues

Different types of issues that a promoter use for his business to raise capital is: Initial Public Offer, Offer for Sale, Follow-on Offer, Rights Issue, Preferential Issue.

Initial Public Offer (IPO): An unlisted company invites the public to buy its fresh issue of shares, which will be listed on a stock exchange like NSE or BSE is called an IPO.

Offer for Sale: Existing shareholders of an unlisted company invite the public to buy their shares which will be listed on the stock exchange is called an Offer for Sale.

Follow-on Public Offer (FPO): When a listed company makes either a fresh issue of shares to the public or an offer for sale of existing shares to the public, it is referred to as a follow on public offer.

Rights Issue: When a listed company issue fresh shares to its existing shareholders, it is called as a rights issue. Rights shares are normally offered to existing investors in a particular ratio corresponding to the number of shares they already hold with the company.

Preferential Issue: A Preferential issue means a listed company issue shares to a select group of persons who are not current shareholders of the company. This type of an issue will dilute the % holding of current shareholders and these issues are normally done when a company desires to issue a block of shares to a select/particular group of people.

Bond Offerings

When a company requires capital it sometimes chooses to issue public debt instead of equity. Almost always, however, a firm undergoing a public bond deal will already have stock trading in the market. The reasons for issuing bonds rather than stock are various. Perhaps the stock price of the issuer is down, and thus a bond issue is a better alternative. Or perhaps the firm does not wish to dilute its existing shareholders by issuing more equity. Or perhaps a company is quite profitable and wants the tax deduction from paying bond interest, while issuing stock offers no tax deduction. These are all valid reasons for issuing bonds rather than equity.

The bond offering process resembles the IPO process. The primary difference lies in: (1) the focus of the prospectus, and (2) the importance of the bond's credit rating. Clearly, a firm issuing debt will want to have the highest possible bond rating, and hence pay a lower interest rate. As with stock offerings; investment banks earn underwriting fees on bond offerings in the form of an underwriting discount on the proceeds of the offering. The percentage fee for bond underwriting tends to be lower than for stock underwriting.

The IPO Process

A company goes through a three-part IPO transformation process: a pre-IPO transformation phase, an IPO transaction phase and a post-IPO transaction phase. In pre-IPO transformation phase, company starts the groundwork toward becoming a publicly-traded company. The IPO transaction phase usually takes place just before the shares are sold. The key issue of this phase is to maximize investor confidence and credibility to ensure that the issue will be successful. The post-IPO transaction phase involves the execution of the promises and business strategies the company committed. This phase is typically a very long phase, because companies always try to prove the market that they are a strong performer.

The first step in the going public process is the announcement of intent and then selection of the underwriter. This is done roughly three months before the IPO date.

Table 3.1: One Year Action Plan for an IPO

Month-1	File prospectus with SEC /SEBI issues press release and sell the company to investors
Month-2	Outside auditors opinion is issued. Membership with stock exchange is complete
Month-3	Convene new Board of Directors. Audit of interim financials should be complete
Month-4	Finalize performa and interim financial statements. Make revision to drafts prospectus
Month-5	Finalize historical financial statements. Start preparing interim financial statements of current period
Month-6	Establish transition contracts for newly formed public company, such as independent audits of financial statements
Month-7	Circulate draft prospectus for comments
Month-8	Draft three-year historical financial statements
Month-9	Establish a Board of Directors for the newly formed public company

Month-10	Start drafting the prospectus. Coordinate data collection to minimize duplications
Month-11	Due diligence work-worthless assets written-off, in consistencies with GAPP resolved
Month-12	Form a core team for the IPO process, compiling the financial information

Key Terms Realted to IPO Process

- **Bought Deal:** an offering in which the lead underwriter buys all the shares from a company and becomes financially responsible for selling them. Also called firm commitment.
- **Direct Public Offering (DPO):** an offering in which a company sells its shares directly to the public without the help of underwriters. Can be done over the Internet. Liquidity or the ability to sell shares, in a DPO is usually extremely limited.
- **Flipping:** Buying an IPO at the offering price and then selling the stock soon after it starts trading on the open market. Greatly discouraged by underwriters, especially if done by individual investors.
- **Green Shoe:** Part of the underwriting agreement which allows the underwriters to buy more shares — typically 15% — of an IPO. Usually done if a deal is extremely popular or was overbooked by the underwriters. Also called the overallotment option.
- **Gross Spread:** The difference between an IPO's offering price and the price the members of the syndicate pay for the shares. Usually represents a discount of 7% to 8%, about half of which goes to the broker who sells the shares. Also called the underwriting discount.
- **Lock-up Period:** The time period after an IPO when insiders at the newly public company are restricted by the lead underwriter from selling their shares. Usually lasts 180 days.
- **Offering Price:** The price that investors must pay for allocated shares in an IPO. Not the same as the opening price, which is the first trade price of a new stock.
- **Opening Price:** The price at which a new stock starts trading. Also called the first trade price. Underwriters hope that the opening price is above the offering price, giving investors in the IPO a premium.
- **Prospectus:** The document, included in a company's S-1 registration statement, which explains all aspects of a company's business, including financial results, growth strategy, and risk factors.
- **Road-show:** A tour taken by a company preparing for an IPO in order to attract interest in the deal. Attended by institutional investors, analysts, and money managers by invitation only. Members of the media are forbidden.

- **S-1 Document:** Document filed with the Securities and Exchange Commission announcing a company's intent to go public. Includes the prospectus; also called the registration statement.

The following steps are involved in the process:

- **Announcement of Intent:** Generally, the intent to make a public offering will be announced prior to making an SEBI filing
- **Selecting an Underwriter:** It is desirable to have a well-respected firm as the underwriter.
- **Prospectus:** A formal prospectus must be written and filed with the SEBI
- **Road-show:** With the prospectus in hand, a representative of the underwriter travels with company management to give presentations to people to persuade them to take an allocation of the new stock.
- **Allocations:** The new stock is sold by the company to the underwriter at an agreed-upon fixed price. The underwriter usually allocates a significant fraction of the stock to other brokerages, who can offer it to their best clients at the fixed price.
- **Pricing:** The company management and the underwriter's group have to set the price below their assessment of a realistic long-term price, in order to make sure that the underwriter won't lose money.
- **First Day:** A stock with a lot of hype and great public interest may continue to float up during the day; it may close at three times the issue price and keep rising for the next week or two.
- **Unloading by Underwriter:** Over the next week or two, the underwriter will slowly release the stock offering into the market at a controlled rate.
- **Quiet Period:** The SEBI insists that the prospectus is the only information from the brokerage houses to potential investors and this restriction is relaxed after about 3 weeks. This period is known as "the quiet period".
- **Regular Coverage:** After the quiet period ends, analysts at the brokerage houses can start recommending the stock in their newsletters, etc.

The company is to approach several investment banks as underwriters to offer an IPO. Underwriters do not necessarily make guarantees concerning selling an initial public offering (IPO). The two most common types of **underwriting are** bought deals and best effort deals. In a bought deal, the underwriter purchase company's entire IPO issue and resells it to the investing public. The underwriter bears the entire risk of selling the stock issue. Underwriter acquired the stock from the issuer usually at a discounted price and sells the shares to public at face value. In a best effort deal, the underwriter does not necessarily purchase any of the IPO issue, and only makes a guarantee to the company issuing the stock that it will use its "best efforts" to sell the issue to the investing public at the best price possible. However, that depends on the type of underwriting that is agreed upon with the stock's issuer. In many cases, company select multiple underwriters to manage the offering. These might include, for instance, a smaller investment bank that specialise in market segment or a particular industry and a larger bank with the ability to market equities very effectively to institutions. Only one of the banks, however, will be designated as the lead, or book, underwriter. The underwriters provide the issuing firm with procedural and financial advice. The company is responsible for the most critical function, the management of the records of who desires shares in the new offering and the allocation of the shares among investors. The managing or co-managing banks normally recruit other banks and brokerage houses to join the "syndicate". The function of the underwriters is to assess the business, operational and financial background of the company in order to determine the value of the company's shares to be sold to the public. The underwriter plays several important roles before the offering is marketed to the public. These include undertaking due diligence on the company to insure that there are no "skeletons in the closet", determining the offering size, and preparing the marketing material. The investment bank also assists in the preparation of regulatory filings in collaboration with the law firms. In India permission from SEBI (Securities Exchange Board of India) is required before a firm going public. In the United States, Securities and Exchange Commission (SEC) and state regulatory bodies focuses on whether the company has disclosed all material information and whether the offering is priced appropriately or not. The firm and the investment banker decide upon an offer price (also called issue price) and prepare a prospectus. This takes place roughly 5 months before the issue date. The face value of all shares in India is usually ₹10. The difference between the face value and the offer price is called 'premium'. Pricing of equity is allowed only when the company has made profits for the last three years. After this criterion is satisfied, there is no further restriction on deciding the price of the offer by the firm from the regulatory bodies. The prospectus is submitted to SEBI for approval. It is not necessary for the firm to declare the exact offer price to SEBI during the submission of the prospectus. If the company specifies an offer price of x, then the actual offer price could be anywhere in between x and 1.2x, i.e., a margin of 20% is allowed. In case of oversubscription the underwriters can sell additional shares up to 15% of the total shares offered is called *Green Shoe*. The prospectus is a legal document describing the securities to be offered to participants and buyers. Underwriters provides information such as the types of stock to be issued, biographies of officers and directors with detailed information about their compensation, any litigation in place, and any other material information required by regulatory body. Once the agreement is made between the companies and the lead underwriter to sell shares in the market, the underwriters can proceed to sell these shares to any interested investors. These underwrites are paid commissions for the shares that they sell. The investment bank begins the process of marketing the offering after regulatory scrutiny is over. It typically circulates a preliminary prospectus, or "red herring" to prospective institutional and individual investors in the firm. Initial prospectus containing all the information about the company except for the offer price and the effective date, which aren't known at that time is called Red Herring.

In many cases, the firm also undertake a "road-show," in which the management team describes the company's lines of business and prospects to potential investors. In the United States, "book-building" is the most frequently employed approach. In particular, the underwriter learns from potential investors how many shares will be demanded at each proposed price, which enables him to set the best price for the company. In India, i.e., book-building and fixed price issue are employed. Investment bank and company bring together all the information about demand in order to determine the price of share which will be sold to the public. In determining a price, the bankers are also likely to factor in information about valuation comparable firms, as well as discounted cash-flow analyses of the firm's projected cash flows. Roughly before a month of the issue, a massive campaign is organized to capture the attention of the investors. The issue closes for four to ten days after it opens. Subscription takes place in this window, i.e., investors apply for shares and pay an amount that is less than the offer price. If there is oversubscription, then the money paid at the time of application is returned after a few months. After the issue closes, allotment of shares takes place. In case of an oversubscription, the allotment of shares is delayed. Then the investors receive their shares if they are allotted some or the cheques if they have been denied shares due to a heavy over subscription. The first day of trading takes place after a considerable time of the issue date.

IPO Price Discovery Mechanism

The most important part of the initial public offering (IPO) process is setting the offer price. To estimate the market price issuers and their advisers conduct a costly analysis to estimate the value of the firm, this is known as "price discovery" mechanism.

There are three popular ways of carrying out this price discovery process:

- Fixed Price Method
- Book-building method
- Dutch auction method

Fixed Price Method

The traditional method of bringing out an IPO is the fixed price offering. Here, the issuer and the merchant banker agree on a fixed price known as "issue price" – e.g., ₹ 100. After this the investors are provided with a choice of filling in an application form at this price and subscribing to the issue.

Extensive research has revealed that the fixed price offering is a very poor way of doing IPOs. Fixed price offerings, all over the world including India, suffer from 'IPO under-pricing'. In India, on average, the fixed-price seems to be around 50% below the price at first listing; i.e., the issuer obtains 50% lower issue proceeds as compared to what might have been the case if the book-building method of price discovery had been followed. This average masks a steady stream of dubious IPOs which get an issue price which is much higher than the price at first listing. Hence, fixed price offerings are weak in two directions: Dubious issues get overpriced, and good issues get underpriced, with a prevalence of under-pricing on average.

Book-building Method

Book-building is a method employed by companies raising capital through Public Offerings-both through Initial Public Offers (IPOs) or Follow-on Public Offers. Book-building is a technique used for marketing a public offer of equity shares of a company. It refers to collection of bids from investors, which is based on a price range. The issue price is fixed after the closing date of the bid. The price at which securities is allotted is not known in case of offer of shares through book-building. In case of book-building, the demand can be known everyday as the book is built. Also, the costs of public issue are much reduced and the time taken for completion of the entire process is much less than in the normal public issue. The principal intermediaries involved in a book-building process are the company, Book Running Lead Manager (BRLM) and syndicate members. The intermediaries are normally registered with SEBI and eligible to act as underwriters. Syndicate members are appointed by the BRLM. The process begins with consultations between issuer company, the fund managers and the institutional investors. The Issuer who is planning an offer selects lead merchant banker(s) as 'book runners'. After that the issuer specifies the number of securities to be issued and the price band for the bids. The advertisement announcing the bidding contains the date of the opening of the offer and the closing date. The issuer also nominates syndicate members with whom orders are to be placed by the investors. The syndicate members input the orders into an 'electronic book', through a process known as 'bidding'. This is similar to open auction.

In an open book system, it is mandatory to have an online display of the demand and bids during the bidding period. As per SEBI, only electronic facility is allowed to be used in case of book-building. SEBI has introduced an additional method of book-building for FPOs where the issuer is required to decide on a floor price and mention the floor price in the red herring prospectus. If the floor price is not mentioned in the red herring prospectus, the issuer has to announce the floor price at least one working day before opening of the bid in all the newspapers in which the pre-issue advertisement released. Qualified institutional buyers can bid at any price above the floor price. The bidder who bids at the highest price shall be allotted the number of securities that he has bidded for and then the bidder who has bidded at the second highest price and so on, until all the specified securities on offer are exhausted. Allotment is to be done on price priority basis for qualified institutional buyers. Allotment to retail individual investors, non-institutional investors and employees of the issuer shall be made proportionately. If the number of specified securities bidded for at a price is more than available quantity, then allotment shall be done on proportionate basis.

The book normally remains open for a period of 3 to 7 days and can be extended by another three days if the issuer decides to revise the floor price and the band. Bids have to be entered within the given price band. Bids are subject to revision by the bidders before the book closes. After the close of the book-building period, the book runners evaluate the bids on the basis of the demand at various price levels. The book runners in consultation with the issuer decide the final price at which the securities shall be issued. This price is known as the cut-off price. The cut-off price is the price discovered by the market. It is the price at which the shares are issued to the investors. Investors bidding at a price below the cut-off price are ignored. So, those investors who apply at a price higher than the cut-off price have a higher chance of getting the stock. The cut-off price is arrived at by the method of Dutch auction.

Dutch Auction Method

Dutch Auction Method is a technique employed for pricing shares whereby the price of the shares offered is lowered until there are enough bids available to sell all shares. In Dutch auction underwriters used an auction IPO is an alternative to the traditional negotiated pricing process to set IPO prices. Under this method the underwriter solicit bids from potential investors. Investors specify the number of shares that they want and the price that they are willing to pay per share. Since the allocation of shares are based on the bid price and amount of shares, The company choose to offer the shares at the maximum offering price, or they apply a discount price and offer shares at less than the maximum. This pricing method does not distinguish between institutions and individuals with regard to allocations. This process endeavours to reflect a price of what investors are truly willing to pay for a stock. In a Dutch auction the price of an item is lowered, until it gets its first bid and then the item is sold at that price. Let's say a company wants to issue one million shares. The floor price for one share of face value, ₹ 10, is ₹ 48 and the band is between ₹ 48 and ₹ 55. At ₹ 55, on the basis of the bids received. So the cut-off price cannot be set at ₹ 55. So the price is lowered to ₹ 54. At ₹ 54, investors are ready to buy 4,00,000 shares. So if the cut-off price is set at ₹ 5,46,00,000 shares will be sold. This still leaves 4,00,000 shares to be sold. The price is now lowered to ₹ 53. At ₹ 53, investors are ready to buy 4,00,000 shares. Now if the cut-off price is set at ₹ 53, all one million shares will be sold. Investors who had applied for shares at ₹ 55 and ₹ 54 will also be issued shares at ₹ 53. The extra money paid by these investors while applying will be returned to them. Generally, the number of shares is fixed, and thus, the issue size gets frozen based on the final price per share. Allocation of securities is made to the successful bidders, while the rest get refund orders. There are three kinds of investors in a book-building issue. The retail individual investor (RII), the non-institutional investor (NII) and the qualified institutional buyers (QIBs). RII is an investor who applies for stocks for a value of not more than ₹ 1,00,000. Any bid exceeding this amount is considered in the NII category. NIIs are commonly referred to as high net worth individuals. On the other hand QIBs are institutional investors who possess the expertise and the financial muscle to invest in the securities market. Thus, it is observed that in case the bid is below the cut-off price, the investor will not receive any allotment. However, the investor can avoid this situation by submitting the bid without indicating any price. In such cases, the investor has to simply indicate in the bid that she is ready to accept the offer of shares at whatever cut-off price the company fixes in the book-building process. This option is open only to retail investors and most of them submit their bid at the cut-off price.

Difference between shares offered through book-building and offer of shares through fixed price method is exhibited in Table 3.2.

Table 3.2: Difference Between Fixed Price Process and Book-building Process

Features	Fixed Price process	Book-building process
Pricing	Price at which the securities are offered or allotted is known in advance to the investor	Price at which securities will be offered or allotted is not known in advance to the investor, just an indicative price range is known
Demand	Demand for the securities offered is known only after the issue has reached closure	Demand for the securities offered can be known everyday as the book is being built
Payment	Payment if made at the time of subscription has to be paid back in case of non-allocation	Payment is made only after allocation

The success driver of IPO is shown in Fig. 3.3.

Offer structure	Due diligence and documentations	Syndicate structure	Investment case and valuation	Marketing and book-building	After-market support
• Size • Shareholder structure • Listing strategy • Type of shares • Timing	• Due diligence • Legal • Business • Bring down • Prospectus • Stock exchange admission	• Beauty contest • Lead manager/ book-runner • Syndicate composition • Steering committee and project organization • Legal counsel	• Company fundamentals • Business plan • Growth potential • Management • Valuation	• Investor targeting • Pre-marketing • Marketing • Order taking • Pricing • Allocation	• Encourage after-market interest • Execution of green shoe • Ensure market liquidity • Ongoing research coverage

Preparation → Execution

Prerequisites for an IPO Issue (BSE)

The prerequisite is presented in Table 3.3.

Table 3.3

Eligibility Criteria	Large-cap Companies	Small-cap Companies
Minimum post-issue Paid-up capital	₹ 3 crore	₹ 3 crore
Minimum issue size	₹ 10 crore	₹ 3 crore
Minimum market capitalization of the Company	₹ 25 crore	₹ 5 crore

Additional conditions for Small Cap companies is that the minimum income/turnover of the Company shall be ₹ 3 crore in each of the preceding three 12 months period; and the minimum number of public shareholders after the issue shall be 1,000.

Factors keep in Mind before Applying for IPO

Track Record of the Promoters: The main factors considered while applying for IPOs is the background and experience of the promoters, the management team and their expertise as they are responsible for the profitability of the company.

Financials: The company's balance sheet is a very important document and investors should look the current balance sheet as well as last three to four years balance sheet to get an idea of the company's growth and focus.

Prospectus: The investor should read the prospectus of the company carefully which has to file with the SEBI. The prospectus has all the details about the company, the risk factors and the company's financials.

Issue Price: Investors need to decide if the issue is worth-investing in at that price. So, he /she needs to check the price-earnings (P/E) multiple of the company. P/E of the issue should be compared with the industry average and the other companies in that sector.

Apart from these important points other factors like amount to be paid on application, the lead managers for the issue, the stock exchanges that issue plans to list on and the current market sentiment are other factors to watch out for.

Underpricing

Underpricing is most likely happening in the book-building method. If the closing price on the first day of listing is higher than the IPO price then stock issue is deemed to be underpriced. Underpricing refers to the price jog up of the IPO on the first day of trading. It is also known as the initial return or first-day return of the IPO. The issuing company loses money if an IPO is significantly underpriced. The loss is determined as the number of shares in the offering multiplied by the difference between the first day opening price and the offer price. This is an expression of market inefficiency caused by the irrational behaviours of investors and IPO issuing firms.

Underpricing = [(First-day closing price – Offer price)]/Offer price × 100%

The first-day closing price signifies what the investors are willing to pay for the firm's shares. If the offer price is lower than the first-day closing price, the IPO is said to be underpriced. Since existing shareholders resolve for a lower offer price/proceeds than what they could have got, the money is left on the table for new investor represents that wealth transfer from existing shareholders to new shareholders.

Money left on the table = (First-day closing price – Offer price) × Number of shares

On average, the amount of money left on the table is about twice the amount of direct underwriting fees, and for many IPO firms it can equal several years of operating profit. Generally, underpricing is a good thing. Most IPOs worldwide are underpriced. This makes the initial face value of the IPO very fascinating in the stock market. First publicly traded leads to enormous increases for those investors who jumped on the IPO early. The negative aspect to underpriced IPOs is lost capital. Although underpriced IPOs can have a down side, overpriced IPOs seem to carry more risks. If a particular stock is made available to the public at a greater price than the market is willing to pay, underwriters can face difficulty keeping their promise to sell shares. Even when everything runs smoothly and all the issued shares of an overpriced IPO have been sold, if the stock market decreases in value on the initial day of trading, the IPO's marketability and value may be lost.

Systematic Underpricing

- **Reduce Capital Loss:** The most obvious reason that underwriters systematically underpriced new stock is to make it easier for them to market the issue. This intentional underpricing reduces the chances that the issue will be undersubscribed which results in capital loss to the underwriters. Aversion to loss also influences the pricing behaviour of IPOs by the underwriting firm.
- **Diversified Ownership:** A firm going public is willing to underprice its shares in order to generate excess demand for the offering. With excess demand, the firm could spread the shares among many different investors, with no single investor holding a significant block of stock. This widely dispersed ownership structure may benefit the firm by providing the company with a more liquid market for their shares.
- **Underwriter's Long-term Warrants:** Firms might also be encouraged to under price their shares by the underwriter if the investment bank holds long-term warrants to buy more shares from the firm if excess demand is present.
- **Higher Stock Valuations:** Firms are under-price their IPOs to achieve higher stock valuations for the future seasoned secondary offerings. A firm with excellent prospects for growth is willing to leave "money on the table" in the initial offering. If investors recognize and respond to this signal, then the long-term value of the firm's shares will be higher, and it can recoup the initial underpricing costs in future equity offerings.
- **Winners Curse:** From the behavioural finance perspective, the following explanations for this irrational behaviour are plausible. Given the problem of the winner's curse, firms may have to underprice shares, on average, to keep the market for IPOs functioning by providing liquidity to investors and owners. Generally, relatively unsophisticated investors receive larger allocations of the IPOs with negative returns and smaller allocations of those with positive returns. Unless these investors receive winners at an acceptable frequency, they would eventually cease participating in the market.
- **Investment Bank Reputation:** Another theory is that investment banks underprice the issue. Because oversubscribed offering increases the attractiveness

of the issuing firm. As a result, underwriters have an incentive to underprice the IPO to ensure that investors will fully subscribe to the offering. On the down side, if an offering is not oversubscribed, the reputation of the underwriting syndicate may be damaged.

Overpricing of IPO

The danger of overpricing is also an important consideration. If a stock is offered to the public at a higher price than the market will pay, the underwriters may have trouble meeting their commitments to sell shares. Even if they sell all of the issued shares, if the stock falls in value on the first day of trading, it may lose its marketability and hence even more of its value.

Google IPO was a very good example of overpricing of IPO, which received loads of critical reviews. Google has been in the focus of attention of most Wall Street experts. However, when Google decided to issue the IPO in its own manner, most specialists were not very satisfied since Google decided to go straight to the investor. It bypassed the traditional network for which it won much of the dissatisfaction. Instead of using the traditional way of issuing IPO through investment banking establishments and major brokers, it addressed directly the investors. Under the traditional approach investment bankers decide which brokers to get packages of stocks. Under such conditions individual investors are forced to purchase stocks well above the original offering price, after the stocks have gone through several hands. Behind Google's concern that individual investors are given the opportunity to take their fair share at the original offering price, some negative implications may be hidden. One of them is that the price may get overpriced. A good tactic for acquiring stocks that you really want to bid as high as you can afford. In this way you will ensure a greater chance for purchasing the stock. However, since this tactic is not a secret to anyone, this might lead to artificially high bids. Especially when there are many people who desperately want to own Google's shares. As a result the stock becomes overpriced. Thus, overpricing of IPO's is not that prevalent but generally does take place when the launch takes some different route from the traditional ones or some special measures being taken by the underwriter.

Selection of an Exchange

- Different exchanges have different listing requirements. In general, they require minimum levels of pre-tax income, net tangible assets, and number of stockholders. For example, a New York Stock Exchange listing requires an income of either US$2.5 million before federal income taxes for the most recent year or US$2 million pre-tax for the each of the preceding two years. The firm must have been profitable in the two years before a listing.
- The NASDAQ (National Association of Securities Dealers Automated Quotations), the largest electronic screen-based equity securities trading market in the United States, has lower listing requirements than the NYSE. Other markets, such as the NASDAQ Small Cap Market and the American Stock Exchange,

offer even lower listing requirements. Thus, an IPO firm needs to assess its own strengths and weaknesses in order to pick the right exchange on which to list its shares.

- A firm also needs to select a trading symbol for use on the exchange. For example, Microsoft trades as MSFT. A fee, which varies for each exchange, has to be paid for the services provided.

BSE Specific Requirements for a Company before Making an IPO Offer

- Companies desiring to list their securities offered through a public issue are required to obtain prior permission of BSE to use the name of BSE in their prospectus or offer for sale documents before filing the same with the concerned office of the Registrar of Companies.
- As per Section 73 of the Companies Act, 1956, a company seeking listing of its securities on BSE is required to submit a Letter of Application to all the stock exchanges where it proposes to have its securities listed before filing the prospectus with the Registrar of Companies.
- Companies making public/rights issues are required to deposit 1% of the issue amount with the Designated Stock Exchange before the issue opens. This amount is liable to be forfeited in the event of the company not resolving the complaints of investors regarding delay in sending refund orders/share certificates, non-payment of commission to underwriters, brokers, etc.

Eligibility Criteria for Primary Issuance (IPO or Offer for Sale)

The following eligibility criteria have been prescribed effective August 1, 2006 for listing of companies on BSE, through Initial Public Offerings (IPOs):

1. Companies have been classified as large cap companies and small cap companies. A large cap company is a company with a minimum issue size of ₹ 10 crore and market capitalization of not less than ₹ 25 crore. A small cap company is a company other than a large cap company.

(a) In respect of Large Cap Companies

(i) The minimum post-issue paid-up capital of the applicant company (hereinafter referred to as "the Company") shall be ₹ 3 crore; and

(ii) The minimum issue size shall be ₹ 10 crore; and

(iii) The minimum market capitalization of the company shall be ₹ 25 crore (market capitalization shall be calculated by multiplying the post-issue paid-up number of equity shares with the issue price).

(b) In respect of Small Cap Companies

(i) The minimum post-issue paid-up capital of the company shall be ₹ 3 crore; and

(ii) The minimum issue size shall be ₹ 3 crore; and

(iii) The minimum market capitalization of the company shall be ₹ 5 crore (market capitalization shall be calculated by multiplying the post-issue paid-up number of equity shares with the issue price); and

(iv) The minimum income/turnover of the company shall be ₹ 3 crore in each of the preceding three 12 months period; and

(v) The minimum number of public shareholders after the issue shall be 1,000.

(vi) A due diligence study may be conducted by an independent team of Chartered Accountants or Merchant Bankers appointed by BSE, the cost of which will be borne by the company. The requirement of a due diligence study may be waived if a financial institution or a scheduled commercial bank has appraised the project in the preceding 12 months.

2. For all companies:

(a) In respect of the requirement of paid-up capital and market capitalization, the issuers shall be required to include in the disclaimer clause forming a part of the offer document that in the event of the market capitalization (product of issue price and the post-issue number of shares) requirement of BSE not being met, the securities of the issuer would not be listed on BSE.

(b) The applicant, promoters and/or group companies, shall not be in default in compliance of the listing agreement.

(c) The above eligibility criteria would be in addition to the conditions prescribed under SEBI (Disclosure and Investor Protection) Guidelines, 2000.

SEBI Gidelines for Issuing IPOS

IPOs of Small Companies

Public issue of less than five crore has to be through OTCEI and separate guidelines apply for floating and listing of these issues.

OTCEI (Over-the-counter Exchange of India) was incorporated in 1990 as a Section 25 company under the Companies Act, 1956 and is recognized as a stock exchange under Section 4 of the Securities Contracts Regulation Act, 1956. The exchange was set up to aid enterprising promoters in raising finance for new projects in a cost-effective manner and to provide investors with a transparent and efficient mode of trading.

Modelled along the lines of the NASDAQ market of USA, OTCEI introduced many novel concepts to the Indian capital markets such as screen-based nationwide trading, sponsorship of companies, market-making and scripless trading. As a measure of success of these efforts, the exchange today has 115 listings and has assisted in providing capital for enterprises that have gone on to build successful brands for themselves like VIP Advanta, Sonora Tiles and Brilliant Mineral Water, etc.

Size of the Public Issue

Issue of shares to general public cannot be less than 25% of the total issue, in case of information technology, media and telecommunication sectors this stipulation is reduced subject to the conditions that:

- Offer to the public is not less than 10% of the securities issued.
- A minimum number of 20 lakh securities is offered to the public, and
- Size of the net offer to the public is not less than ₹ 30 crore

Promoter Contribution

- Promoters should bring in their contribution including premium fully before the issue
- Minimum promoters contribution is 20-25% of the public issue.
- Minimum lock-in period for promoters contribution is five years
- Minimum lock-in period for firm allotments is three years

Collection Centres for Receiving Applications

- There should be at least 30 mandatory collection centres, which should include invariably the places where stock exchanges have been established.
- For issues not exceeding ₹ 10 crore (including premium, if any), the collection centres shall be situated at:
  — The four metropolitan centres, viz., Mumbai, Delhi, Kolkata, Chennai; and
  — All such centres where stock exchanges are located in the region in which the registered office of the company is situated.

Regarding Allotment of Shares

- Net offer to the general public has to be at least 25% of the total issue size for listing on a Stock exchange.
- It is mandatory for a company to get its shares listed at the regional stock exchange where the registered office of the issuer is located.
- In an issue of more than ₹ 25 crore the issuer is allowed to place the whole issue by book-building
- Minimum of 50% of the net offer to the public has to be reserved for investors applying for less than 1,000 shares.
- There should be at least 5 investors for every 1 lakh of equity offered (not applicable to infrastructure companies).
- Quoting of Permanent Account Number or GIR Number in application for allotment of securities is compulsory where monetary value of investment is ₹ 50,000 or above.

- Indian development financial institutions and mutual fund can be allotted securities up to 75% of the issue amount.
- A Venture Capital Fund shall not be entitled to get its securities listed on any stock exchange till the expiry of 3 years from the date of issuance of securities.
- Allotment to categories of FIIs and NRIs/OCBs is up to a maximum of 24%, which can be further extended to 30% by an application to the RBI-supported by a resolution passed in the General Meeting.

Time Frames for the Issue and Post-issue Formalities

- The minimum period for which a public issue has to be kept open is 3 working days and the maximum for which it can be kept open is 10 working days. The minimum period for a rights issue is 15 working days and the maximum is 60 working days.
- A public issue is affected if the issue is able to procure 90% of the total issue size within 60 days from the date of earliest closure of the public issue. In case of oversubscription the company may have the right to retain the excess application money and allot shares more than the proposed issue, which is referred to as the 'green shoe' option.
- A rights issue has to procure 90% subscription in 60 days of the opening of the issue.
- Allotment has to be made within 30 days of the closure of the public issue and 42 days in case of a rights issue.
- All the listing formalities for a public issue has to be completed within 70 days from the date of closure of the subscription list.

Dispatch of Refund Orders

- Refund orders have to be dispatched within 30 days of the closure of the public issue.
- Refunds of excess application money, i.e., for unallotted shares have to be made within 30 days of the closure of the public issue.

Other Regulations Pertaining to IPO

- Underwriting is not mandatory but 90% subscription is mandatory for each issue of capital to public unless it is disinvestment in which case it is not applicable.
- If the issue is undersubscribed then the collected amount should be returned back (not valid for disinvestment issues).
- If the issue size is more than ₹ 500 crore voluntary disclosures should be made regarding the deployment of the funds and an adequate monitoring mechanism to be put in place to ensure compliance.

- There should not be any outstanding warrants or financial instruments of any other nature, at the time of initial public offer.
- In the event of the initial public offer being at a premium, and if the rights under warrants or other instruments have been exercised within the twelve months prior to such offer, the resultant shares will not be taken into account for reckoning the minimum promoter's contribution and further, the same will also be subject to lock-in period.
- Code of advertisement specified by SEBI should be adhered to.
- Draft prospectus submitted to SEBI should also be submitted simultaneously to all stock exchanges where it is proposed to be listed.

Restrictions on Other Allotments

- Firm allotments to mutual funds, FIIs and employees not subject to any lock-in period.
- Within twelve months of the public/rights issue no bonus issue should be made.
- Maximum percentage of shares, which can be distributed to employees, cannot be more than 5% and maximum shares to be allotted to each employee cannot be more than 200.

Relaxations to Public Issues by Infrastructure Companies

These relaxations would be applicable to infrastructure companies as defined under Section 10 (23G) of the Income Tax Act, 1961, provided their projects are appraised by any Developmental Financial Institution (DFI) or IDFC or IL&FS. The projects must also have a participation of at least 5% of the project cost (in debt and/or equity) by the appraising institution.

- The infrastructure companies will be exempted from the requirement of making a minimum public offer of 25 per cent of its securities.
- The requirement of 5 shareholders per ₹ 1 lakh of offer is also waived in case of offerings by infrastructure companies.
- For public issues by infrastructure companies, minimum subscription of 90% would no longer be mandatory provided disclosure is made about the alternate source of funding which the company has considered, in the event of under subscription in the public issue.
- Infrastructure companies are permitted to freely price the offerings in the domestic market provided that the promoter companies along with equipment suppliers and other strategic investors subscribe to 50% of the equity at the same or a higher price than what is being offered to the public. Adequate disclosures about the justification for the pricing will be required to be made in the offer documents.

- The infrastructure companies would be allowed to keep their issues open for 21 days. The relaxation would give infrastructure companies sufficient time to mobilize funds for their issues.
- Infrastructure companies would not be required to create and maintain a Debenture Redemption Reserve (DRR) in case of debenture issues.

Over the past few months, a number of initiatives have been taken by SEBI towards bolstering the IPO and mutual fund segments. The initiatives taken by SEBI in the past few months include opening up gates for longer trading hours for stock exchanges by allowing the bourses to extend market hours by around two-and-a-half hours between 9 a.m. and 5 p.m. Market regulator SEBI, said on Wednesday, that companies should list themselves within seven days of their IPOs — a move that would lower the risks and costs associated with a longer gestation period currently in place.

Indian IPO Market

In a developing economy like India, there is no dearth of enthusiastic entrepreneurs who have nurtured their small business ventures and dreamt of making them 'go-public' one day. This is the reason behind the energetic Indian IPO market. The scope of the primary market is enormous because of the large-scale direct participation in the primary market by millions of retail investors is unlike that in any other country in the world. Besides, there is a lot of media hype related to IPOs in India. Every company betting its fate on an IPO is made to undergo strict scrutiny in the eyes of the retail and institutional investor alike.

Procedure of Going-public in India

Behavioural Dynamics of the Indian IPO Market

IPO is a very significant moment for all the stakeholders of the company, which included the management and the underwriters. This has been analyzed in detail below:

- **Stake of the Managers:** In the case of a small start-up the manager is often the promoter of the company and has a long-term stake in the company. So the managers are going to stay invested for a long time to come and are not interested in any short-term gains as such.
- **Underwriter:** The underwriter is the investment banker who has been hired to carry-out the Initial Public Offering on behalf of the firm. It is the onus of the underwriter to see that the IPO is oversubscribed by a wide margin and that it succeeds. If the IPO fails, the reputation of the underwriter is invariably tarnished. If the IPO succeeds on the other hand, the underwriter enhances its chances of attracting more prospective clients. Hence, the underwriter would do anything for the success of the IPO and has short-term interests with the company.

Effect of Recession on IPO Market

The liquidity crunch has had an adverse impact on global IPO market with firms and financial institutions running low on cash. Prevalent pessimism has also had a negative impact on the launching of new IPOs which have sufficiently decreased in number since the economic meltdown. The recession and shuttered IPO market have placed tremendous pressure on portfolio companies to restructure and plan the future course of action.

Russia

The current global trend is such that regional companies prefer to choose local floors. In Russia, in 2007, about 38% of the total volume of placements (about 11.7 billion dollars) is accounted for by Russian floors. This figure considerably exceeds the results of 2006, when the volume of placements in the domestic market reached only 1.2 billion dollars. There were quite a few so-called dual IPOs, when companies make their placements on both Russian and Western floors. In 2007, the volume of dual IPOs reached about 16.2 billion dollars.

The mortgage crisis in the United States and the destabilization of the global financial market resulted in the decline of the value of various companies' stocks. As far as Russia is concerned it is in a somewhat privileged position, because Russia has all prerequisites for further stable economic growth. The speed at which the population is getting involved in the stock market is very high. Despite today's increased volatility of the stock market, about 2,500 individuals begin to participate in trading on the MICEX Stock Exchange each week. Thus, the size of the investment base doubled in one year. So it has been estimated that in the near future up to 5 million individual Russian investors are likely to enter the stock market. Domestic investors will be investing primarily in the Russian market, where they are protected by the law and the regulator against all kinds of legal risks and where they know the companies in which they decide to invest. This means Russian issuers have a very powerful incentive to make their placements in the domestic market.

USA

The US economy relies on a steady stream of venture-backed companies, who collectively produce more than one-fifth of the US gross domestic product. In fact, public companies that were VC funded currently account for more than 12 million US jobs and $2.9 trillion in revenues.

Research firm Global Insight estimates that 92 per cent of job growth at these companies occurs once the company enters the public market. However, economic uncertainty, and an adversity to risk has substantially reduced the IPO pipeline, and broken this cycle. In order to survive, VCs need to rethink *how* and *where* they can help their portfolio companies remain innovative and profitable in the current economy.

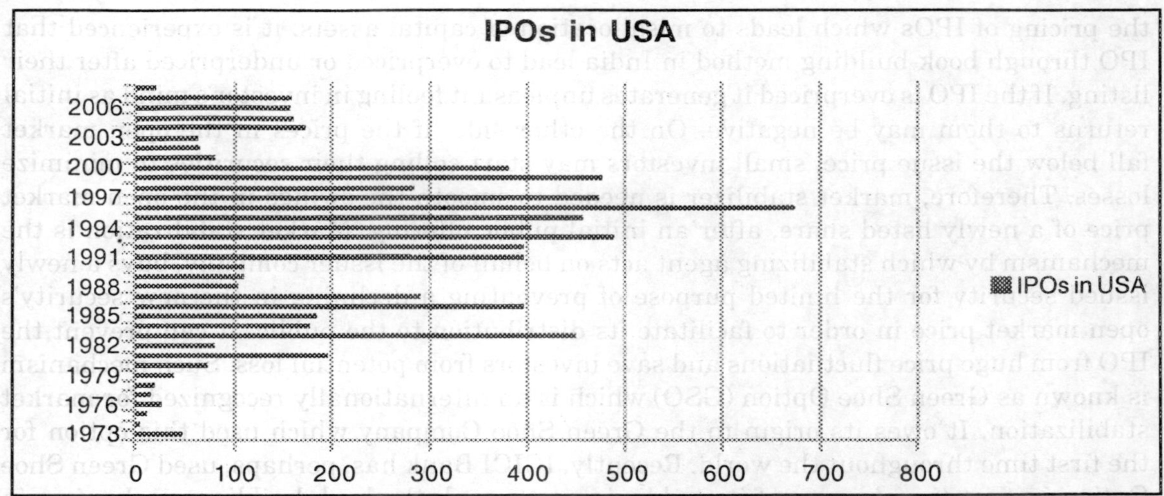

India

India has too suffered a drastic decrease in the number of IPOs due to recession with few companies going public. Even the existing companies have been cutting down on costs to generate the necessary working capital to see through the bad economic climate[1]. The meltdown has decreased the number of IPO launches significantly in India with both the companies and the investors being more cautious.

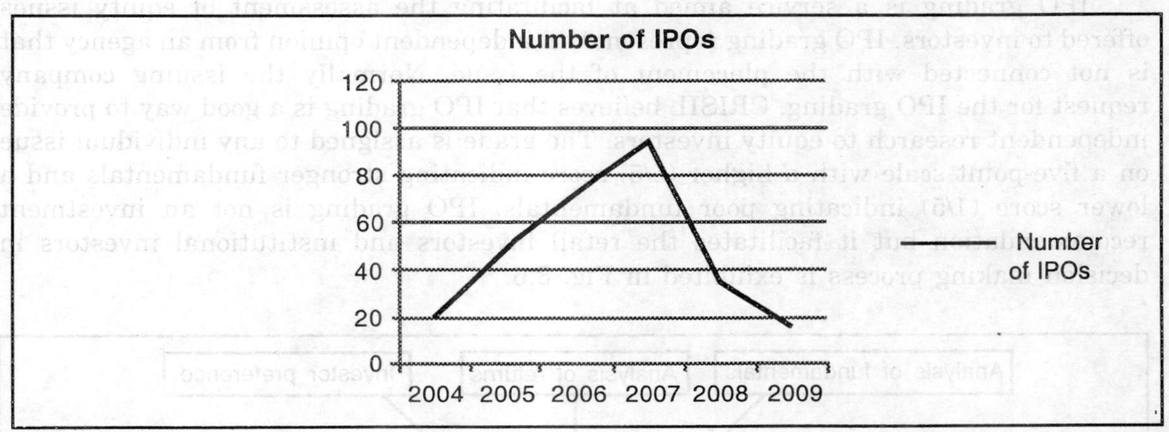

IPO: Improvements Required

IPO issuance, due diligence, structure, marketing and after-market support: all these steps have considerable room for reforms and improvement. Inefficiencies arise out of poor operational structure of the whole process of an initial public offering and also from

1 http://www.bseindia.com/bookbuilding/bookbuilding_hist.asp?ir_flag=ipo

the pricing of IPOs which leads to misallocation of capital assets. it is experienced that IPO through book-building method in India lead to overpriced or underpriced after their listing. If the IPO is overpriced it generates unpleasant feeling in investor's mind as initial returns to them may be negative. On the other side, if the prices in the open market fall below the issue price, small investors may start selling their securities to minimize losses. Therefore, market stabilizer is needed to smooth the swings in the open market price of a newly listed share, after an initial public offering. Market stabilization is the mechanism by which stabilizing agent acts on behalf of the issuer company, buys a newly issued security for the limited purpose of preventing a declining in the new security's open market price in order to facilitate its distribution to the public. It can prevent the IPO from huge price fluctuations and save investors from potential loss. Such mechanism is known as Green Shoe Option (GSO) which is an internationally recognized for market stabilization. It owes its origin to the Green Shoe Company which used this option for the first time throughout the world. Recently, ICICI Bank has, perhaps, used Green Shoe Option in first time in case of its public issue through the book-building mechanism in India. SEBI is primarily concerned with reforms in IPO process. SEBI has also commissioned two committees: Securities Markets Infrastructure Leveraging Expert Task Force (SMILE) and Primary Market Advisory Committee (PMAC) to minutely follow the primary markets of India and suggest reforms.

IPO Grading

IPO grading is a service aimed at facilitating the assessment of equity issues offered to investors. IPO grading represents an independent opinion from an agency that is not connected with the placement of the issue. Normally the issuing company request for the IPO grading. CRISIL believes that IPO grading is a good way to provide independent research to equity investors. The grade is assigned to any individual issue on a five-point scale with a higher (5/5) score indicating stronger fundamentals and a lower score (1/5) indicating poor fundamentals. IPO grading is not an investment recommendation but it facilitates the retail investors and institutional investors in decision making process is exhibited in Fig. 3.6.

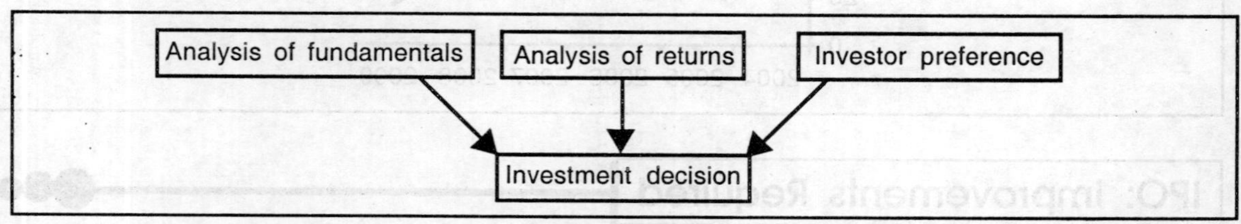

Figure 3.6

IPO grading is a one-time exercise. It does not have an ongoing validity. CRISIL believes that IPO grading is to be emerging as a useful valuation tool for equity shares just as credit ratings are used for the valuation of 'buy/sell/hold' recommendations of bonds. CRISIL IPO grading is based on the assessed future performance. The assessed future performance is based on the business plan of the company's management. **CRISIL IPO grading is also based on** Business Prospects, Financial Prospects, Management quality and corporate governance. It is mandatory for the issuers to disclose the IPO grading in the Red Herring prospectus, advertisements and Offer Document released during the IPO period. CRISIL also makes a press release after every IPO grading that it assigns. This press release is sent to all leading print and electronic media engaged in reporting about India.

Case Examples of IPO Process

MIC Electronics

MIC Electronics, the Hyderabad-based ISO 9000:2000 certified company, engaged in the design and manufacture of True Colour LED video display systems, opened for subscription with an initial public offer (IPO) of 5,100,000 equity shares of ₹ 10 for cash at a price to be decided through the 100% book-building process for listing on both Bombay Stock Exchange and National Stock Exchange.

The price band for the offer was fixed between ₹ 129 and ₹ 150 per equity share for IPO which closed on May 8, 2007. The public offer constituted 25.34% of the company's fully diluted post-issue paid-up equity capital.

Up to 50% of the issue was allocated on a proportionate basis to the qualified institutional buyers, of which 5% of the issue was available for allocation to mutual funds. Further, 15% of the issue was available for non-institutional bidders and 35% of the issue available for allocation on a proportionate basis to the retail individual bidders.

MIC Electronics has three divisions — Media, Info-Tech, Communications and Electronics. It is engaged in the design, development and production of True Colour LED video Display Systems, telecom software solutions and communication equipment such as Digital Loop Carrier on optical fibre including voice, video/data applications, and Hand Held Computers. MIC is the only company in India to have the "Design-to-manufacture" capability for the manufacture of LED Video Display Systems.

The unconsolidated total income, of the company for the 6 months ended December 31, 2006, was ₹ 654.56 million and net profit after tax was ₹ 108.91 million. During the year ended June 30, 2006, the total income posted was ₹ 1,044.12 million while the net profit after tax was ₹ 154.76 million. MIC has a confirmed order book of worth ₹ 1,678.55 million as on December 31, 2006.

The sole book running lead manager to the issue was Edelweiss Capital.

Maytas Infra

The initial public offer of Infrastructure development firm Maytas Infra got subscribed 5.73 times on the fourth day of its issue. A total of 5.06 crore bids were received for 8.85 lakh shares on offer, latest data available on the stock exchanges shows.

Maytas had fixed the price-band at ₹ 320 to ₹ 370 a share and expected to raise about ₹ 327 crore from the issue.

The portion reserved for Qualified Institutional Buyers (QIBs) got subscribed 9.35 times, while the Retail Individual Investors (RIIs) section and the Non-institutional Investors segment got marginally subscribed. The company plans to use the proceeds towards various built-operate-transfer (BOT) projects that are under development.

Out of the total proceeds from the issue, the company would use ₹ 27.7 crore in the Bangalore-Hosur elevated expressway, ₹ 127 crore in the 300 MW coal-based KVK Nilachal power project in Odisha and ₹ 34.25 crore in the 56 MW coal washery reject-based SV power plants and 2.5 million MT per annum coal washery at Korba in Chhattisgarh.

It would utilize ₹ 33.29 crore for buying construction equipments, while the remaining amount would be kept for other projects and capex purpose.

Advanta India

Advanta India, an international agronomic seed company and a subsidiary of United Phosphorus, has received good response from investors, especially foreign institutional investors; their portion has subscribed 1.48 times, till March 29, 2007.

More than 1.34 crore bids have been put against its issue size, which includes 2.45 lakh bids at cut-off price. The issue was subscribed 3.98 times, till 5.30 pm on March 30, as per NSE website.

It has been received good response from investors, especially foreign institutional investors; their portion has subscribed 1.48 times, till March 29.

The company had entered capital market with an initial public offering, IPO of 33,80,000 equity shares of ₹ 10 for cash at a premium to be decided through the 100% book-building process.

The price band was between ₹ 600 and ₹ 650 per equity share. The issue constituted 20.08% of the post-issue paid-up capital of the company. The shares are listed on the National Stock Exchange and Bombay Stock Exchange.

The issue was made through the 100% book-building process, wherein at least 60% of the issue must be allotted on a proportionate basis to qualified institutional buyers (QIBs). Further, 5% of the QIB portion must be available for allocation to mutual funds only and the remaining QIB portion must be available for allocation to the QIB bidders including mutual funds, subject to valid bids being received at or above the issue price.

Further, up to 10% of the issue must be available for allocation on a proportionate basis to non-institutional bidders and up to 30% of the issue must be available for allocation on a proportionate basis to retail individual bidders, subject to valid bids being received at or above the issue price. The company has allotted 16,77,000 equity shares to a group of investors at a price of ₹ 625 per equity share under the pre-issue placement pursuant to a resolution of the board of directors dated February 23, 2007.

Headquartered in Bengaluru, Advanta India is a wholly-owned subsidiary of United Phosphorous, one of the leading generic agrochemical companies in the world with operations in the United States, Australia, China, Latin America and Europe. The company, including its operating subsidiaries, is engaged in the research, production and sales of a range of hybrid seeds for cereals and oilseed crops; and is a global leader in technical plant breeding and in the application of biotechnology to develop new hybrids and varieties of field crops and broad acre vegetable seed products.

For the year ended March 31, 2006, the company posted unconsolidated income of ₹ 435.44 million and profit after tax of ₹ 44.52 million. During the seven month period ended October 31, 2006, the company posted unconsolidated income of ₹ 598.79 million and profit after tax of ₹ 282.38 million. The results for the seven months period ended October 31, 2006 include the business of USBPL, which was amalgamated with the company with effect from April 1, 2006.

The book running lead managers to the issue are YES Bank, UBS Securities India and SSKI Corporate Finance.

Jet Airways

Jet Airways has announced the details of its IPO. The Jet Airways IPO will be of 1.72 crore shares of ₹ 10 each to raise a maximum of up to ₹ 1942.50 crore. The fully book-built issue is opening 100 per cent book built issue will open for bids on February 18 and close on February 24.

The price band for the issue has been fixed at ₹ 950 and ₹ 1,125 per share. Of the total offer, Jet Airways is making fresh issue of 1.42 crore equity shares and balance 30.21 lakh shares are an offer for sale by Tail Wings Ltd.

The combined offer constitutes 20 per cent of fully diluted post-offer paid-up equity capital of the company. A part of the proceeds of IPO would be used to retire some debt of the company.

Deutsche Bank (India) was one of the lead managers for issue. The valuation of Jet Airways assets was done by UBS Securities Ltd., and the pricing based on fair valuation done by comparing with listed airlines abroad like Ryan Air and Singapore Airlines.

Out of total offer, 12 lakh shares were reserved for Jet Airways employees. There was 60 per cent allocation for institutional investors, up to 15 per cent to high net worth individuals and up to 25 per cent to retail investors.

Deutsche Equities India Pvt Ltd., HSBC Securities and Capital Markets (India), UBS Securities India Pvt Ltd., Citigroup Global Markets India, DSP Merrill Lynch Ltd., and Kotak Mahindra Capital Company Ltd., are book running lead managers for the IPO.

Summary

IPO is the tool or mechanism to generate funds for companies. Initial Public Offering is means to an end, not an end itself. They provide access to capital markets to finance future growth as primary objective. Book-building process aims at fair pricing of the issue which is supposed to emerge out of offers made by various investors. More such reforms are necessary in days to come to ensure better functioning of primary market.

CASE: OSWAL NETWORKING LTD.

Mr. Kamat is an industrial engineer working in a large international chemical firm. He has worked in the company for a period of 20 years. With nearly twenty years 'working for other company Kamat started his own company with hopes of eventually taking the firm public. Oswald Networking had been founded in 1994 by Mr. Kamat. During 2000 there was a tremendous demand for integrated networks of desktop computers, and the development of new software. Kamat was familiar with the design of both local – and wide – area networks at his former job. So the period was very favourable to Kamat and his businesses expanded rapidly. Kamat was doing majority of the network design at the firm himself. Then he employed one network engineer and three technicians. As the business had expanded, the staff had grown in proportion. His earlier experience was helped him a lot and attracted customers to his shop. He was also maintained business relationships by being involved in several community groups in his city. He also helped the people during their crisis period. Because of this social involvement he gained the confidence and respect from the community. Through his involvement in charity and other groups, when he had the time, he quickly made a name for himself as someone who could be trusted. Kamat constantly worked recruit and train new engineers and technicians to provide good services to his company. Oswald Networking is providing generous continuing education programme for employees. Many employees who are working since its early years with Oswald Networking have earned MBAs in addition to their technical certifications and degrees.

The technology bubble of the late 2004 having a unfavourable impact on demand for distributed computing and networking services. Over the last five years (1998-2002) revenue growth has been strong, and the average cost of goods sold as a per cent of sales has decreased somewhat. Net profit growth has been irregular due to the unpredictable behaviour of selling and general administrative expenses, which increased sharply for some firms and declined slightly or stayed the same for others. Net income after-tax as a per cent of sales has been in the range of 1.0% to 4.5%.

But however Oswald Networking by 2005 become a recognized leader in its own city and begun to expand regionally. Kamat finally started to take the firm public with an issue of stock. He started to discuss with investment banker city investment banker with the aim of designing a public offering of the company's stock. Since, Kamat's reputation is very good in the community and recognized as a good employer, city investment banker is agree and suggests to issue both bonds and shares. So he asked companies operating and financial operations to take prospective financial decision for company.

Exhibit 1: Oswald Networking Balance Sheet, December 31, 2005

Current Asset	₹ 2400
Fixed Assets	₹ 18400
Total Assets	₹ 20800

Current Liabilities	₹ 2200
Mortgage Loans	₹ 1840
Common Stock ($1 par value)	₹ 2200
Retained Earnings	₹ 14560
Total Liabilities and Equity	₹ 20800

Exhibit 2: Revenue and Income Information

Year	Revenue	Net Income (after taxes)
1995	₹ 14448000	₹ 472000
1996	₹ 15248000	₹ 532000
1997	₹ 15680000	₹ 548000
1998	₹ 159200000	₹ 572000
1999	₹ 16400000	₹ 620000
2000	₹ 17296000	₹ 656000
2001	₹ 20752000	₹ 788000
2002	₹ 24004000	₹ 912000
2003	₹ 28040000	₹ 1092000
2004	₹ 30000000	₹ 1200000
2005	₹ 31200000	₹ 1248000

Exhibit 3: Oswald Networking

Total debt as a percentage of total assets	20%-32%
Compound growth in sales	9%
Compound growth in net income	8%
Dividend payout range	15%-30%
Return on equity	15%
Average earnings per share	$3.00
Industry data for publicly-traded networking firms	Firms' earnings were 20% more volatile than a benchmark market portfolio such as the Standard & Poor's 500
10-year US government bonds yielded	5.01%
10-year Industry average coupon rate	8%
New bonds today's market rate	6%
Historical 10 years yield on a broad market index of common stocks	14%

You required to evaluate the current market conditions. What is the likely initial public offering (IPO) price for the company's stock? (For the stock price calculation, assume that the relevant industry data will also apply to Oswald.) Assume that an investor's required return on a stock of this type can be derived from the capital market data given and the information in Exhibit 3. Does the comparable bond's price give any useful information regarding the proposed stock IPO? Does the change in interest rates (for the industry) suggest that a debt issue might be preferable to a stock issue?

Note: The case is fictitious and any resemblance to a person/company is merely coincidental.

Review Questions

1. What is IPOs? What is its Significance? What is its IPO Process?
2. Why are companies offering IPO?
3. What is the role of investment banker in IPO Process?
4. Discuss about IPO Price Discovery Mechanism
5. What are the BSE specific requirements for a company before making an IPO offer?
6. **Quiz:**

   (a) ____ and ____ are the two types of Initial Public Offerings (IPOs) through which a public company can raise money in the capital market.

   (b) When a listed company makes either a fresh issue of shares to the public or an offer for sale of existing shares to the public, it is referred to as a _____.

   (c) The book normally remains open for a period of ____ to ___ days and can be extended by another three days if the issuer decides to revise the floor price and the band.

   (d) If the closing price on the first day of listing is higher than the IPO price then stock issue is deemed to be _____.

   (e) In case of oversubscription the underwriters can sell additional shares up to 15% of the total shares offered is called _____.

   (f) Initial prospectus containing all the information about the company except for the offer price and the effective date, which aren't known at that time is called ____.

   (g) Recently, ICICI Bank has, perhaps, used Green Shoe Option in first time in case of its public issue through the book-building mechanism in India. *(T/F)*

   (h) Underwriting is not mandatory but 90% subscription is mandatory for each issue of capital to public unless it is disinvestment in which case it is not applicable. *(T/F)*

   (i) IPO grading is an investment recommendation but it does not facilitates the retail investors and institutional investors in decision-making process. *(T/F)*

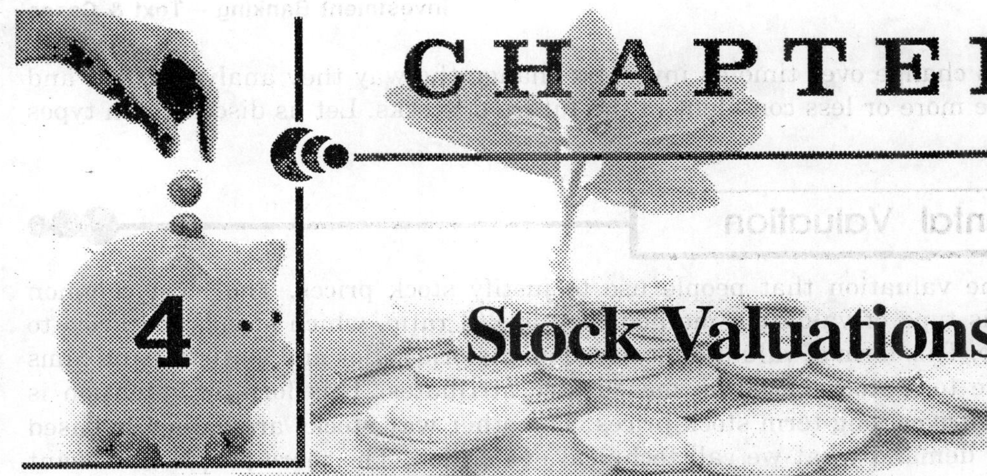

CHAPTER 4

Stock Valuations

Introduction

Valuations are more of an art than a science. A valuation technique focuses on specific part of a company's financial performances. Valuation is simply the process of determining how much to pay to invest in a company. The different range of valuation methods is grouped into three general approaches.

1. **Approaches Based on Accounting Tallies:** Book value per share, Tangible net worth per share, Replacement value of equity per share,
2. **Approaches Based on Earnings Multiples:** Price-earnings multiple – widely used by investment bankers based on an analysis of comparable companies, Stock price to EBIT-buyers of commercial real estate and some insurance companies use this for valuing securities,
3. **Approaches Based on Discounting Cash Flow:** Extensively used by corporations to evaluate projects, investors and financial intermediaries to evaluate financial securities such as equity and bonds,
4. **Dividend Growth Model:** A mathematically summary of discounted cash flow based on an assumption of a constant growth rate of dividends. It is very widely used.
5. **Dividend Capitalisation Model:** A mathematically summary of discounted cash flow assuming zero growth in dividends in the future.

Stocks have two types of valuations. One is a value created using some type of cash flow, sales or fundamental earnings analysis. The other value is dictated by how much an investor is willing to pay for a particular share of stock and by how much other investors are willing to sell a stock for (in other words, by supply and demand). Both of these values change over time as investors change the way they analyze stocks and as they become more or less confident in the future of stocks. Let us discuss both types of valuations.

Fundamental Valuation

This is the valuation that people use to justify stock prices. The most common example of this type of valuation methodology is P/E ratio, which stands for Price to Earnings Ratio. This form of valuation is based on historic ratios and statistics and aims to assign value to a stock based on measurable attributes. This form of valuation is typically what drives long-term stock prices. The other way stocks are valued is based on supply and demand what we call technical evaluation. The more people that want to buy the stock, the higher its price will be. And conversely, the more people that want to sell the stock, the lower the price will be. This form of valuation is very hard to understand or predict, and is often drives the short-term stock market trends. In short, there are many different ways to value stocks.

Valuation techniques focus on a specific part of a company's financial performance and three types of techniques are available, i.e., Balance Sheet Analysis, Income Statement Multiples and Discounted Cash Flows.

1. Balance Sheet Analysis

A balance sheet valuation is trying to calculating the worth of the underlying assets of a business as recorded in the accounting statements. Three techniques are used for this valuation.

Book Value: It is one of the simplest techniques in valuation. The book value of a company is the company's net worth, as measured by its total assets minus its total liabilities. This is how much the company would have left over in assets if it went out of business immediately. Many times the book value of an organisation's assets rarely equals the true market value of the corresponding assets. Therefore, book value is rarely used to determine the final price of an organisation. There is a problem in the value of some assets, such as buildings, equipment and furniture/fixtures, may be overstated on the books, and may not reflect the maintenance and/or replacement costs for older assets. As a result, some business valuation experts will use an adjusted book value.

Adjusted Book Value: Adjusted value is the book value of a company's balance sheet after assets and liabilities are adjusted to market value. One of the most important dimensions of using an adjusted book value is that a business could be worth more than its stated assets or liabilities because it fails to value intangible assets, account for discounts or factor in contingent t liabilities. The adjusted book value method of valuation is most often used to assign value to distressed companies facing potential liquidation.

Liquidation Value: This approach is similar to the book valuation method, except that the value of assets at liquidation is used instead of the book or market value of the assets. Liquidation value is an estimate of the worth of the assets and liabilities assuming that the company will cease its operation and the assets will be auctioned immediately. Liquidation values are typically lower than fair market value. Using this approach, the liabilities of the business are deducted from the liquidation value of the assets to determine the liquidation value of the business. If the liquidation value per share for a company is greater than the current share price then the company should go out of business.

Example:

The book value of assets ten years from now is expected to be $ 4 billion, the average age of the assets at that point is 5 years and the expected inflation rate is 3%, the expected liquidation value is

Expected Liquidation value = Book Value of Assets Term yr (1 + inflation rate) Average life of assets

= $ 4 billion (1.03)5 = $ 4.64 billion

The limitation of this approach is that it is based upon accounting book value and does not reflect the earning power of the assets.

2. Income Statement Valuations

Income statements multiples attempt to value an opportunity by capitalizing its earnings stream.

Earnings per Share (EPS): EPS is the total net income of the company divided by the number of shares outstanding. It sounds simple but unfortunately it gets quite a bit more complicated. Earnings are important to investors because they give an indication of the company's expected dividends and its potential for growth and capital appreciation. That does not necessarily mean, however, that low or negative earnings always indicate a bad stock. The most important thing to look for in the EPS figure is the overall quality of earnings. In order to make earnings comparisons more useful across companies, fundamental analysts instead look at a company's earnings per share (EPS). It is important to look at the growth in EPS over the past several quarters/years to understand how volatile their EPS is.

P/E Ratio (Price-Earning: EPS is a great way to compare earnings across companies, but it doesn't tell one, anything about how the market values the stock. That's why fundamental analysts use the price-to-earnings ratio, more commonly known as the P/E ratio, to figure out how much the market is willing to pay for a company's earnings. One can calculate a stock's P/E ratio by taking its price per share and dividing by its EPS. Historical P/Es are computed by taking the current price divided by the sum of the EPS for the last four quarters, or for the previous year. Forward P/Es are probably the single most important valuation method because they reflect the future growth of the company into the figure. And remember, all stocks are priced based on their future earnings, not on their past earnings. However, past earnings are sometimes a good indicator for future earnings. Forward P/Es are computed by taking the current stock price divided by the sum of the EPS estimates for the next four quarters, or for the EPS estimate for next calendar of fiscal year or two. Also, it is important to remember that P/Es change constantly. If there is a large price change in a stock you are watching, or if the earnings (EPS) estimates change, be sure to recompute the ratio.

PEG Ratio (Projected Earnings Growth): This valuation technique has really become popular over the past decade or so. It is better than P/E because it takes three factors into account; the price, earnings, and earnings growth rates. This ratio takes into consideration of a stock's projected earnings growth. PEG is calculated by taking a stock's P/E ratio and dividing by its expected percentage earnings growth for the next year. So, a stock with a P/E ratio of 40 that is expected to grow its earnings by 20% the next year would have a PEG of 2. The theory goes that as the percentage rises over 100% the stock becomes more and more overvalued, and as the PEG ratio falls below 100% the stock becomes more and more undervalued. The theory is based on a belief that P/E ratios should approximate the long-term growth rate of a company's earnings. Suppose we are comparing two stocks: Stock A is trading at a forward P/E of 20 and expected to grow at 25%. Stock B is trading at a forward P/E of 35 and expected to grow at 30%. The PEG ratio for Stock A is 80% (20/25) and for Stock B is 117% (35/30). According to the PEG ratio, Stock A is a better purchase because it has a lower PEG ratio than that of Stock B.

Return on Equity (RoE): Return on equity (RoE) shows one, how much profits a company generates in comparison to its book value. The ratio is calculated by taking a company's after-tax income (after preferred stock dividends but before common stock dividends) and dividing by its book value (which is equal to its assets minus its liabilities). It is used as a general indication of the company's efficiency; in other words, how much profit it is able to generate given the resources provided by its stockholders. Investors usually look for companies with RoEs that are high and growing.

Example:

Return on Equity = Net Income/Book Value of Equity

For example, Reliance Industries reported net income of ₹ 25,000 million in 2000 on book value of equity of ₹ 1,20,000 million, using its effective tax rate of 25%, resulting in an average return on equity of 21%.

Return on Invested Capital (RoIC): This valuation technique measures how much money the company makes each year out of its invested capital. Invested capital is the amount of money invested in the company by both stockholders and debtors. This ratio measures the investment return that management is able to get for its capital. The higher is the number, the better the return. This ratio is calculated by taking net income/ EPS and divides it by the invested capital. Invested capital can be estimated by adding together the stockholders equity, the total long and short-term debt and accounts payable, and then subtracting accounts receivable and cash.

Return on Assets (RoA): RoA measures the company's ability to make money from its assets. The ratio is calculated by taking net income divided by the total assets. However, because of very common irregularities in balance sheets due to intangible assets this ratio is not always a good indicator of the company's potential.

Price to Sales (P/S): By using this ratio one can find out how much the market is valuing a company by comparing the company's price to its annual sales. To compute it, take the current stock price divided by the annual sales per share. The price to sales ratio is useful, but it does not take into account any debt of the company. For example, if a company is heavily financed by debt instead of equity, then the sales per share will be high and the P/S will be lower and lower P/S ratio is better. However, P/S, like P/E ratios and P/B ratios, are numbers that are subject to much interpretation and debate. Sales obviously don't reveal the whole picture: a company is having huge sales but be terribly unprofitable. Because of the limitations, P/S ratios are usually used only for unprofitable companies, since such companies don't have a P/E ratio.

Price/Book: A company's price-to-book ratio (P/B ratio) is determined by taking the company's per share stock price and dividing by the company's book value per share. For instance, if a company currently trades at $100 and has a book value per share of $5, then that company has a P/B ratio of 20. The higher the ratio, the higher the premium the market is willing to pay for the company above its hard assets. Price-to-book ratio is of more interest to value investors than growth investors.

Market Capitalisation: Market cap is the value of all of the company's stock. The market cap is only the value of the stock so it always advised to look at the Enterprise Value. By definition: number of shares × price per share.

Enterprise Value (EV): Enterprise value is equal to the total value of the company. By definition: equity+ debt-cash. The enterprise value is the best approximation of what a company is worth at any point in time because it takes into account the actual stock price instead of balance sheet prices.

Let us take an example: Price per share is ₹ 3 and number of shares is 10,00,000. Debt of company is ₹ 3,50,000.Equity value or market capitalisation is (price per share × No. of shares) = ₹ 30,00,000 so TEV = 33,50,000. Enterprise value fluctuates rapidly based on stock price changes.

EV to Sales: This ratio measures the total value of the company as compared to its annual sales. A high ratio means that the company's value is much more than its sales. It is calculated by divide the EV with the net sales for the last four quarters. This ratio is especially useful when valuing companies that do not have earnings or bad situations.

EBITDA: EBITDA is a preferable measure to EBIT. EBITDA by definition does not account for depreciation and amortization. For some industries, accounting principles accurately depict the useful economic life of the depreciate assets. In these industries the choice between EBIT and EBITDA is arbitrary. Earnings before interest, taxes, depreciation and amortization are used for valuing both public and private companies. EBITDA is calculated by use a company's income statement then net income and then add back interest, taxes, depreciation, amortization and any other non-cash or one-time charges. It is one of the best methods to measure of a company's cash flow position.

EV to EBITDA: This method is used to measure of whether a company is cheap or expensive one. To compute, divide the EV by EBITDA. The higher the number, the more expensive the company is. However, it has been observed that more expensive companies are often valued higher because they are growing faster.

Dividend Discount Model (DD): This model suits best for income investors. The idea is to project future dividend distribution based on the average historical dividend payout ratio and discount it back to present value. Although this is the simplest among all, it works best for high dividend yield stocks.

When an investor buys stock generally expects to get two types of cash flows-dividends during the holding period of stock and an expected price at the end of the holding period. Since the expected price is determined by future dividends, so the value of a stock is the present value of dividends through infinity

Example:

$$\text{Value per share of stock} = \sum_{t=1}^{\infty} \frac{E(DPS_t)}{(1+k_e)^t}$$

where, DPSt = Expected dividends per share

k_e = Cost of equity

There are two basic inputs to the model – expected dividends and the cost on equity.

A stock is with an expected dividend per share next period of $ 5.0, a cost of equity of 18%, and an expected growth rate of 5% forever. The value of this stock is:

Value = 5.00/0.18 – 0.05 = 5. 00/.13 = $ 38.46

Example:

Aravinda Mills is a textile firm that is currently reporting after-tax operating income of $ 100 million. The firm has a return on capital currently of 10% and reinvests 50% of its earnings back into the firm, giving it an expected growth rate of 10% for the next five years:

Expected Growth rate = 10% × 50% = 5%

After year 5, the growth rate is expected to drop to 5% and the return on capital is expected to stay at 10%. The terminal value can be estimated as follows:

Expected operating income in year 6 = 100 (1.10)5(1.05) = $ 338 million

Expected reinvestment rate from year 5 = g/RoC = 5%/10% = 50%

Terminal value in year 5 = $ 338 (1 – 0.5)/0.10 – 0.05 = $ 3,380 million

The value of the firm today would then be:

Value of firm today = $ 55/1.10 + $ 60.5/(1.10)2 + $ 66.55/(1.10)3 + $ 73.21/(1.10)4 + $ 80.53/(1.10)5 + $ 3,380/(1.10)5

$ 2349.38 million

3. Discounted Cash Flow (DCF)

This is probably the most common model of stock valuation. This method is used in valuing stock by projecting future cash flow; from the sales and costs, and discount back to current value with Weighted Average Cost of Capital (WACC). Stock valuation models are methods to value stock. These valuation models are advised to use by investor while purchasing decision taken. Four steps need to be followed to use these valuation techniques: projecting the cash flow stream, choosing a discount rate, determining a terminal value for the business at the end of the projections and applying the discount rate to the projected cash flow stream and the terminal value.

Free Cash Flow (FCF): Free cash flow equals the sum of NOPAT (net operating profits after taxes) plus depreciation and non-cash charges less capital investment in working capital. Free cash flow is the residual return to shareholders after expenditures for maintains operations and financing the company. Free cash flow (FCF) represents the cash that a company is able to generate after laying out the money required to maintain or expand its asset base. Free cash flow is important because it enable the company to pursue opportunities for enhancing shareholder value.

Free Cash Flow = EBITDA – (Tax) – (Changes of working capital) – (capital expenditures)

FCF = NOPAT + depreciation – CAPEX – Δ NWC

Where, NOPAT is equal to EBIT (1 – t) where t is the appropriate marginal cash tax rate

Depreciation is non-cash operating charges including depreciation, depletion and amortization recognized for tax purposes

CAPEX is capital expenditures for fixed assets.

Δ NWC is the increase in networking capital defined as current assets less the non-interest bearing current liabilities.

If free cash flow is negative, it is a sign that a company is making large investments.

A convenient way to think about value creation is whenever the return on net assets (RONA) exceeds the weighted average cost of capital (WACC) RONA is divided into an income statement component and a balance sheet component:

RONA = NOPAT/Net assets

= NOPAT/Sales × Sales/Net Assets

Choosing a Discount Rate: The discount rate should reflect the weighted average of investors' opportunity cost on comparable investments. The WACC matches the business risk, expected inflation and currency of the cash flows to be discounted. Currently financial analysts are using the weighted average cost of capital which accounts for industry risk, the company specific risk and the financial risk for the target company.

WACC = Ke[E/(E + D)] + Kd[D/(E + D)] (1 – t)

Where,

WACC = the weighted average cost of capital

E = Target amount of equity in the company

D = Amount of debt in the company

Ke = Cost of equity

Kd = Cost of debt

t = Corporate tax rate

For determining cost of equity financial analyst are using capital asset pricing model.

$K_e = R_f + B_L \times (R_m - R_f)$

Where,

K_e = Cost of equity

R_f = Risk free asset

B_L = Beta adjusted for the company's projected use of leverage

R_m = Excepted market return

Conceptually return on equity is a function of the risk-free asset and an excess return for business and financial risk. Treasury bills can be used as risk-free rate.

Beta is a measure of how company covaries with market and is approximated using the betas of comparables of public companies in the same industry. Beta is a function of both the business risk and the degree of leverage. If the beta of a comparable company is used to determine the target beta, it has a different financial structure. So, it is essential to find the unlevered beta.

$B_{UL} = B_L/[(1 + D/E) \times (1 - t)]$

Where,

B_{UL} = Unlevered beta of the comparable company

B_L = Levered beta of the comparable company

E = Amount of equity in the comparable company

D = Amount of debt in the comparable company

t = Corporate tax

The unlevered beta can be relevered using the parameters of the target company.

BL = BUL/[(1 + D/E × (1 – t)]

Where,

BL = Levered beta of the comparable company

BUL = Unlevered beta of the comparable company

E = Amount of equity in the comparable company

D = Amount of debt in the comparable company

t = Corporate tax

Another mechanism to estimate the discount rate is to the opportunity cost of capital.

Terminal Value: Terminal value can represent a large portion of valuation. At one point rather than forecasting the varying cash flow for individual year, one use a single value representing a discounted value of all subsequent cash flows. This single value is referred as terminal value. A terminal value is the worth of the enterprise at the end of the projected cash flow stream. The terminal value is the present value at a future point in time of all future cash flows become stable growth rate forever. There are three ways to calculate terminal value. First the cash flow in the final year can be treated as perpetuity and therefore divided by the chosen discount rate. Second, EBITDA multiple can be applied to the final year's cash flow streams. Third an appropriate price earnings multiple can be applied to projected or historic earnings.

A standard estimator of the terminal value (TV) in the final year of the cash flow forecast is the constant growth valuation formula

Terminal value = $FCF^{steadystate} \div (WACC - g)$, where

$FCF^{steadystate}$ is the steady expected free cash flow for the year after the final year if the cash forecast

WACC is the weighted average cost of capital

G is the expected constant annual growth rate of $FCF^{steadystate}$ in perpetuity

Discounted the Cash Flow Stream: The adjusted present value method is a variation of the NPV method. APV is preferred over the NPV method where a firm's capital structure is changing. APV initially assumes that the capital structure of a venture will consist entirely of equity. Under APV method the valuation task is dividing into three steps. By ignoring capital structures the cash flows of the firms are discounted by using different discount rate. This discount rate is calculated by using unlevered beta since it is assumed that the company is financed by equity capital. AVP accounts for the leverage of a venture by separately projecting the net effects of the interest on the debt. Since interest payments are a pre-tax expense, they reduce the tax burden of company. The cash flows discounted using the cost of equity plus the discounted net effects of debt equal the total value of the opportunity. In scenarios where the corporate debt to equity ratio is expected to remain constant WACC is preferred. However, in situations where the debt to equity ratio will change overtime, APV is more important.

Which Method to Use?

1. B/S techniques provide a quick starting point for the valuation process. These techniques however provide the least relevant valuation estimates. B/S calculations are most appropriate for industries characterized by high asset intensity.
2. Income statement multiples is the valuation techniques most frequently used since it is the easiest to use and to communicate. Finally this method is sometimes viewed as too simple and sophisticated. It is most suitable for moderate growth services industries with little or no capital equipment
3. Discounted cash flows are also frequently used.

The discounted cash flow method however is far from perfect. First future earnings may be difficult to estimate. Second betas can vary between companies in the same industry and are derived from historical rather than forward looking data. Finally, in case where the terminal value is substantial portion of the total valuation and an EBIT multiplies is used to compute the terminal value.

All these techniques are appropriate for start-up companies with a limited operating history and only discounted cash flows is used when the company does not have an operating history. So for start-up companies' two methods are available for valuations, i.e., Comparables and Required Rates of Return.

Comparables

This method is most common used in the venture capital valuations. Comparables method means determining the valuations of company of interest by examining the values known to have been placed on like companies in like transactions. Suppose an internet company is seeking financial and other information will compare it with other internet company having similar line of business. In using the comparables method, the VC company must first find out the comparables company which is compatible with VC company. Secondly, also it is essential to know the size of revenue of the company at par with VC comparable company. Also it is to know the whether the cost structure, growth rates, distribution strategies, prospects and other matrices is similar or not.

What Metrics to Use for Comparables?

Once the comparable companies have been settling on and the data collected about them, then which metrics approach to use.

Table 4.1: Metric and Uses

Metric	Use
P/E	Always useful but seldom available
TEV/EBITDA	Always useful but in venture investment EBITDA negative
TEV/Revenue	Useful if revenue is available with company
TEV/Gross profit	Useful where there are gross profits.

Required Rate of Return

The risk of failure of start-up companies is high. William E. Wetzel, an authority on entrepreneurship proposed following rates of returns for start-up companies in his analysis on venture capital financings presented in Table 4.2.

Table 4.2

Stage (Risk)	Stage	Expected Return
Seed	Capital to prove concept	80%
Start-up	Capital requirement for product development and initial marketing	60%
First-stage	Capital to initiate full-scale manufacturing and sales	50%
Second-stage	Working capital for productions	40%
Third-stage	Capital for increasing sales and at least for break-even	30%
Bridge	Capital for going public in six months	25%

Risk investors use these rates to project their required return in the future. Venture capitalist normally using different rate instead of using required rate of return.

Many concepts look similar so it is very important to consider how valuations are made. There are two parties to a transaction: an acquire/buyer/bidder and target firm/ seller/acquired. Many times we are asking questions ourselves when purchase a company, is it a good investment?

Sources of gain and cost savings achieved through combination are called synergies. Sometimes cash flow projections for the target firm may or may not include cost savings gained from merger, if it so they are referred to as standalone cash flow. Examining the value of a target on a standalone basis can be valuable for several reasons. Standalone DCF valuation can be compared to the targets current market value. This is useful in assessing weather target is under or overvalued in the market.

If one follow the standalone analysis while targeting a company, what discount rate to take. Here the most appropriate cost of capital is the WACC of the target firm. One way to estimate the target's WACC is to compute the WACCs of firms in the target's industry and average them. An acquirer may intend to increase the debt level of the target significantly after the merger. However, WACC still reflect the business risk of the target.

Unlevered the Beta

$\beta_u = \beta_L/[1 + (1 - T)\ D/E]$

Where,

D/E is the targets debt-equity ratio before acquisitions

β_u is the targets unlevered beta

β_L is the target's pre-merger beta

Levered the Beta

$\beta_L = \beta_u[1 + (1 - T)\ D/E]$

Where,

D/E is the targets debt-equity ratio after re levering

β_L is the target's post-merger target beta

How the synergies incorporate in DCF analysis. Operating synergies are reflected in enterprise value by changing the standalone cash flows to incorporate the benefits and costs of the combinations. Since debt and equity are the sources capital, it follows that enterprise value equals to the sum of debt and equity values.

Technical Analysis Method

Technical analysis differs from fundamental analysis. Technical analysis focuses more on analyzing trends in the stock price movement. Proponents of this method rely heavily on charts that show a stock's past performance and almost every investor follows it. Technical analysts believe that stock prices move according to a predictable pattern and that has nothing to do with underlying fundamentals. Technical analysis is a method of evaluating securities by analyzing past prices and volume. Technical analysts use charts and other tools to identify patterns that can suggest future activity. There are also many different types of technical traders. Some rely on chart patterns; others use technical indicators and oscillators, and most use some combination of the two. Unlike fundamental analysts, technical analysts never care whether a stock is undervalued. They are only concerned for securities past trading data which guide them about the security movement in the future.

The field of technical analysis is based on three assumptions: 1. The market discounts everything. 2. Price moves in trends. 3. History tends to repeat itself.

1. **The Market Discounts Everything:** A major criticism of technical analysis is that it only considers price movement, ignoring the fundamental factors of the company. Technical analysts believe that along with company's fundamentals.

broader economic factors and market psychology are taking into consideration while pricing the stock.

2. **Price Moves in Trends:** Most technical trading strategies are based on the assumption that price movements are believed to follow trends. This means that after a trend has been established, the future price movement is more likely to be in the same direction.
3. **History Tends to Repeat Itself:** Another important idea in technical analysis is that history tends to repeat itself, mainly in terms of price movement and this repetitive nature of price movements is attributed to market psychology. Technical analysis applies chart patterns to analyze market movements and realize trends. Although many of these charts have been used for more than 100 years, they are still believed to be pertinent because they demonstrate patterns in price movements that often repeat themselves.

Summary

Stock market analysis is crucial when deciding to buy investments and when evaluating investment strategies. There are various tools and techniques available to do stock analysis. While some investors use fundamental analysis while others use stock market technical analysis or stock technical analysis to evaluate their stocks. It is advised to stay alert and evaluate investments regularly. Stock analysis is complex and there are several techniques used by investors and financial experts.

CASE: VALUATION OF MICA COMPANY LTD.

Mica is a leading company in cosmetics. Despite its numerous problems the company, has shown consistently good performance. The company is the market leader in its product line with a 40 per cent market share. The chairman and major shareholder of the company Mr. Rohan is thought of two plans. Either to sell-off the company and retire from business or diversify its business to technology products and give to its nephew for looks after the business. As a part of this process, Mr. Rohan is seeking to buy technology subsidiary company of Infotech Ltd., so he has asked his chief financial officer Mr. Ravikant to approach investment banker to value Iinfoteck Ltd., using NPV method. Mr. Ravikant is graduated from a top business school in India with specialization in finance. He is having special interest in the stock market and used to read stock market reports, periodicals and always keep an eye on market. He is regularly receiving research reports from the investment banker keen to take the company public. Mr. Vivek, investment banker and mica management have agreed on the followings projections:

	Year-1	Year-2	Year-3	Year-4	Year-5	Year-6	Year-7	Year-8	Year-9
Revenue	200	280	420	500	580	760	100	1300	1800
Costs	460	480	520	550	580	620	700	800	940
EBIT	–260	–200	–100	–50	–0	140	300	500	860

The company has $100 million of NOLs that can be carried forward and offset against future income. The tax rate is 40%. The average unlevered beta of five comparable high-technology companies is 1.2. Infotec Ltd., has no long-term debt. Treasury yields for ten-year bonds are 6%. Capital expenditures requirements are assumed to be equal to depreciations. The market risk premium is assumed to be 7.5%. Net working capital requirements are forecast as 10% of sales. EBIT is projected to grow at 3% per year in perpetuity after year 9. As an investment banker you are required to give advice on basis of WACC, Terminal value and FCFM calculation.

He has asked his chief financial officer Mr. Ravikant to calculate the value of the company as he is also interested to sale of the company. The two main options that he is entertaining are the sale of his interest to an employee share ownership plan and to one of the firm's publicly traded competitors. From the reports he is able to compare the following information for mica company and other two leading cosmetics company operating in same region. The following data is for the 2011 financial year is as follows:

	Avon company	Lora company	Eely company
Balance Sheet			
Assets	320	600	760
Long-term debt	10	200	0
Net worth	160	24	350

Income Statement			
Revenues	700	840	1700
EBITDA	90	110	260
Net Income	60	40	150
Market Data			
EPS	6	1.34	4.28
Price Earnings Ratio	n/a	42	29
Share Outstanding	20	60	70
Number of members	1,00,000	12,00,000	22,00,000

From the above information you as a Mr. Ravikant calculate the multiples and implied valuations for Avon Company.

Note: The case is fictitious and any resemblance to a person/company is merely coincidental.

Review Questions

1. What is Fundamental Valuation?
2. Which valuation method is used?
3. What is technical analysis method?
4. **Quiz:**

   (a) ________ is simply the process of determining how much to pay to invest in a company.

   (b) The book value of a company is the company's net worth, as measured by its total ________ minus its ________ liabilities

   (c) ________ values are typically lower than fair market value.

   (d) ________ measures the investment return that management is able to get for its capital.

   (e) Enterprise value is equal to the total value of the company. ***(T/F)***

   (f) Free cash flow represents the cash that a company is able to generate after laying out the money required to maintain or expand its asset base. ***(T/F)***

   (g) Comparables do not used in the venture capital valuations. ***(T/F)***

CHAPTER 5

Mergers, Acquisitions and Reorganizations

Introduction

Mergers, acquisitions and corporate restructuring have attained considerable significance in corporate finance world today. Merger and acquisition are getting popular because of the efficient ways of corporate growth and diversification. The underlying objective behind buying a company is to create shareholder value over and above that of the sum of the two companies. Since the introduction of Indian economic reform in 1991, Indian companies were exposed to glut of challenges both nationally and internationally. The cut-throat competition in international market compelled the Indian firms to opt for mergers and acquisitions strategies, making it a vital planned option. The real momentum was gained after 1994 when the new takeover code was formulated. Everyday investment bankers coordinate M&A transactions to bring separate companies together to form larger ones. Corporate mergers and acquisitions have a great impact on the industry and economy of any country. Mergers and acquisitions also increase the market competition and also work as 'engines of growth'. Mergers and acquisitions involve skill transfer and other sharing activities. Besides, these also result in increase in production, which again lead to rapid growth of the corporation.

What is Merger and Acquisition?

When two companies are of same size decide to move forward as a single new company instead of operating business separately is called merger.

Acquisitions are actions through which companies seek economies of scale, efficiencies and enhanced market visibility. Unlike all mergers, all acquisitions involve one firm purchasing another and there is no exchange of stock or consolidation as a new company. Acquisitions are often congenial, and all parties feel satisfied with the deal. Other times, acquisitions are more hostile. In an acquisition, as in some of the merger deals a company can buy another company with cash, stock or a combination of the two. Another type of acquisition is a reverse merger, a deal that enables a private company to get publicly-listed in a relatively short time period. A reverse merger occurs when a private company that has strong prospects and is eager to raise finance for buying a publicly-listed shell company.

Types of Mergers

Horizontal Merger: In horizontal merger, the two companies are in direct competition and share the same market and sell the same products/services.

Vertical Merger: These involve integration of companies having supplementary relationships. Ex: Either production or distribution of products or services, on the other hand customer and company or supplier and company

Conglomeration Merger: This refers to alliance of different kinds of business under one flagship company. Two/more companies merged that have no common business areas.

Product-Extension Merger: Two companies selling different but related products in the same market.

Market Extension Merger: Here participating companies sell same products in different markets.

Purchase Mergers: This kind of merger take place when one company purchases another company. The purchase is made with cash or through the issue of some kind of debt instrument. The sale is taxable.

Consolidation Mergers: In consolidation merger, both companies are bought and combined under the new entity and a new company is formed. The tax terms are the same as those of a purchase merger.

Merger Waves

The economic history has been divided into merger waves based on the merger activities in the business world as:

Table 5.1: Merger Waves

Period	Name	Facet
1889 - 1904	First Wave	Horizontal mergers
1916 - 1929	Second Wave	Vertical mergers
1965 - 1989	Third Wave	Diversified conglomerate mergers
1992 - 1998	Fourth Wave	Cogeneric mergers; Hostile takeovers; Corporate Raiding
2000 onwards - ?	Fifth Wave	Cross-border mergers

Distinction Between Mergers and Acquisitions

Though merger and acquisition were synonymous but there is slightly different between them.When one company takes over another and establishes a new owner, the purchase is called an acquisition. From a legal point of view, the target company ceases to exist, the buyer "swallows" the business and the buyer's stock continues to be traded. The difference between mergers and acquisitions is presented in Table 5.2.

Table 5.2: Difference between Mergers and Acquisitions

Merger	Acquisition
When two companies are of same size decide move forward as a single new company instead of operating business separately.	When one company takes over another and to establishe itself as the new owner of the business.
The stocks of both the companies are surrendered, while new stocks are issued afresh.	The buyer company "swallows" the business of the target company, which ceases to exist.
A purchase deal is also called a merger when both CEOs agree that joining together is in the best interest of both of their companies. For example, Glaxo Wellcome and SmithKline Beechcam ceased to exist and merged to become a new company, known as Glaxo SmithKline.	But when the deal is unfriendly – that is, when the target company does not want to be purchased – it is always regarded as an acquisition. Dr. Reddy's Labs acquired Betapharm through an agreement amounting $597 million.

Takeover and Acquisitions

Takeover and acquisitions are used as synonyms. The meaning of takeover is that one company acquires another company's total or controlling interest. Thus, the separate identity of the acquired company is lost and it is observed within the administrative frame-work of the acquired company. To increase its competitiveness and consulted its position in the market. Takeover can be either by friendly or hostile. In case of friendly takeover the management of acquired and the acquiring companies agree mutually for the takeover. As against this in case of hostile takeover an aggressive firm tries to acquire a firm against the latter's desire. Hostile takeovers are generally linked with poor management and performance. The risk of hostile takeover has increased following the liberalization of the rules and regulations governing takeovers in India in recent years. This has forced many large business houses to restructure and consolidate their holdings in their diverse fields of industrial activity.

Why Do Mergers Occur?

There are a number of reasons that mergers and acquisitions occur. These issues generally relate to business concerns such as competition, efficiency, marketing, product, resource, and tax issues. They can also occur because of some very personal reasons such as retirement and family concerns. The main goal is to increase the business and market share as well as to improve the financial performance of the corporation. The primary objective of a firm is to maximize profits, and thereby maximize shareholder wealth. M&As increases the size by joining hands with some other company and enables the firm to reap economies of scale. As a result, the firm would be able to expand its market spread, increase its profit margins and competitive strength by reducing cost of production, at times, a good target for takeover. Takeover prospects are also good if there are synergy prospects resulting in potential economies of scope. An economy of scale arises from the merger, allowing the combined firm to become more cost-efficient and profitable. If the average cost of production falls while the level of production increases then it is said to be an economy of scale. Operating economies can be gained from vertical combinations as well as from horizontal combinations. The main purpose of vertical acquisitions is to make coordination of closely related operating activities easier. Mergers occurred due to competitions. To stay competitive, companies need to stay on top of technological developments and their business applications. By buying a smaller company with unique technologies, a large company can maintain or develop a competitive edge. Deregulation in the 1990s has promoted competition in many industries. Typical examples are the liberalization of interest rates and fees, elimination of barriers to entry for subsidiaries in the financial services industry, and abolition of the provisional measures for imports of specific petroleum products in the petroleum industry. These environmental changes, combined with the prolonged post-bubble recession, caused earnings to deteriorate and threatened the survival of companies unless they improved management efficiency. One solution was the merger. By acquiring ailing companies or merging with equals, companies sought to improve earnings by achieving merits of scale and consolidating production facilities. A merge may expand two companies' marketing and distribution, giving them new sales opportunities. Mergers and acquisitions occur because the greedy corporations want to acquire everything. Acquiring a competitor is an excellent way to improve a firm's position in the marketplace. Consequently, whenever a merger is proposed, a major part of the resulting press release often deals with how this combination of firms is not anti-competitive, and is done to better serve the consumer. Through corporate mergers and acquisitions, duplicate departments can be eliminated in the combined company, which would help to reduce its fixed costs. As a result, the profit margins would go up. Due to technology and market conditions, firms may benefit on a cost basis from being a certain size. Clearly, one way to grow is to combine with other small firms until the firm is optimally sized. Generally, the assumption is that larger firms are more cost-effective than are smaller firms. It helps the organization to increase revenue and market share. Greater operating revenues can be produced from improved marketing. Improvements can be made in: (a) Previously ineffective media programming and advertising efforts, (b) A weak existing distribution network, and (c) An unbalanced product mix. Acquisitions promise a strategic advantage, i.e., an opportunity to take advantage of the competitive environment if certain situations materialize. One firm may acquire another to reduce competition. If so, prices can be increased and monopoly benefits obtained. It also helps the cross-selling of products/services. A profitable corporation also buys a loss-making company in order to use the 'losses' of the target company to lessen its tax liability. Some diversification occurs when firms merge, so the cost of financial distress is likely to be less for the combined firm than is the sum of these present values for the two separate firms. Thus, the acquiring firm might be able to increase its debt-equity ratio after a merger, creating additional tax benefits — and additional value. The costs of issuing both debt and equity are much lower for larger issues than for smaller issues. A merger can also improve a company's standing in the investment community: bigger firms often have an easier time raising capital than smaller ones. Mergers and acquisitions also let the companies to transfer resources and one company may use the specialized skills of the others. Companies also go for mergers/ acquisitions for vertical integration, where the vertically integrated company can gather one deadweight loss by setting the output of the upstream company to the competitive level. Many acquisitions and some large strategic investments are often justified with the argument that they create synergy.

"Bad" Reasons for Mergers

Earnings Growth: An acquisition can create the appearance of earnings growth, which may fool investors into thinking that the firm is worth more than it really is. The merger creates no additional value. If the market is smart it will realize that the combined firm is worth the sum of the values of the separate firms.

Diversification: Diversification often is mentioned as a benefit of one firm acquiring another. However, it cannot produce increases in value by itself. This can be seen through business's variability of return which can be separated into two parts: (a) what is specific to the business and called unsystematic, and (b) what is systematic because it is common to all businesses. Systematic variability cannot be eliminated by diversification, so mergers will not eliminate this risk at all. By contrast, unsystematic risk can be diversified away through mergers. Diversification can produce gains to the acquiring firms only if two things are true:

Diversification decreases the systematic variability at lower costs than by investors via adjustments to personal portfolios.

Diversification reduces risk and thereby increases debt capacity.

Defensive Tactics: These are the various tactics adopted by target firm managers to resist a possible takeover. Resistance usually starts with press releases and mailings to shareholders that present the view point of the company. Also target managers try to resist takeovers in order to preserve their job. The various factors that board of directors considers before it decides to defend are:

- The attitudes of present major shareholders
- The present and future impact on the value of the stock
- The ability of the company is to go for a negotiated transaction with friendly bidders.

The various defensive tactics used by target management to resist unfriendly takeover attempts are:

Divestitures: Divestment is release of assets. It can be considered as reverse of investment. Often a company sells off a business unit to concentrate more on profitable units. This narrowing down of strategic focus increases stock price, hence makes the takeover very expensive. The primary motive is to increase corporate focus. Generally ,there are three kinds of divestitures:

- **Sale of Assets:** It is usually done for cash.
- **Spin-off:** It means company distributes shares of a subsidiary to its shareholders.
- **Tracking Stock:** Tracking stock is different from spin-off because it does not involve any change in the business structure and the company pays dividend based upon the performance of a specific portion of the whole company. The company can track the performance of the divisions based on the shareholder's interest. Sometimes a company issues tracking stock when it feels that it has a very successful division but is undervalued in the market and is not fully reflected in the company's stock price.

The Corporate Charter: It refers to articles and corporate bye-laws that govern the firm which establishes the conditions for a takeover. Firms frequently modify contracts to make acquisition more difficult. Usually two-thirds of the shareholders must approve a merger and the firms can make it more difficult by changing the requirement to 80% approval of shareholders. This is called supermajority amendment.

Repurchase Standstill Agreements: Standstill agreements are contracts where the bidding firm agrees to limit its holdings. Here a firm buyback its own stock from a potential bidder usually at a higher premium. These premiums can be considered as payments to potential bidders to delay or stop unfriendly takeover attempts. Such payments are often labelled as greenmail. Standstill agreements are contracts where the bidding firm agrees to limit its holdings. The announcement of such agreements has negative impact on the stock price.

Exclusionary Self-tenders: The firm makes a tender offer of its own stock for a given amount (higher than the prevailing market price) while excluding targeted stockholders.

Going Private and Leveraged Buyouts: When a publicly owned stock in a firm is purchased by a private group (usually composed of existing management) is called as going private. The stock is taken off or is delisted. Shareholders are forced to accept cash for their shares.

These types of transactions are called as leveraged buyouts (LBOs). The cash offer price is generally financed with large amounts of debts. The stockholders are paid a premium above market price in an LBO. LBO can create value due to:

- Tax deduction due to extra debt,
- It turns previous managers to owners' thereby increasing incentive to work hard.

Also one cannot be completely sure whether LBOs have created value or not as the stock price can no more be observed once the company has been taken private.

Merger's Effect on Stock Prices Varies by Industry: Merger announcements have a significant impact on the affected industries and investors, and are often met with large fluctuations in the stock price. Under the assumption of efficient market, if a merger raises (or lowers) expectations of business results, stock prices should rise (or fall) to reflect the change in expectations. The following figures show the effect of mergers on various stocks.

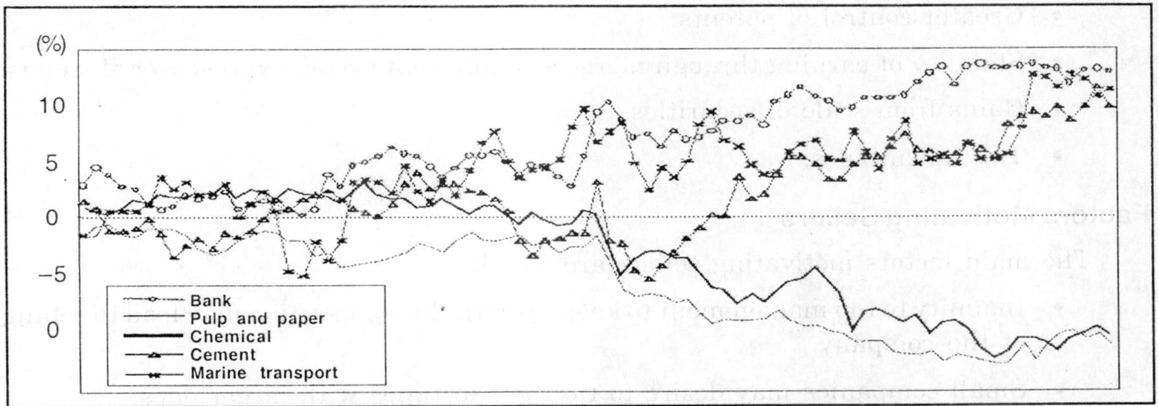

Figure 5.1: Cumulative Stock Price Divergence Rate for Acquiring Company[1]

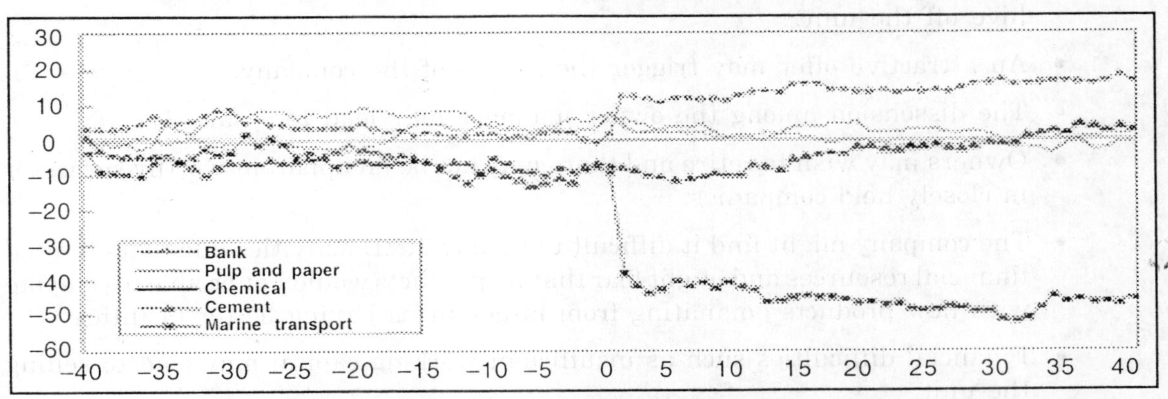

Figure 5.2: Cumulative Stock Price Divergence Rate for Acquired Company[2]

1. K. Komoto, *"The Effect of Mergers on Corporate Performance and Stock Prices"*, Economic and Industrial Research Group, No. 136, 99.
2. K. Komoto, *"The Effect of Mergers on Corporate Performance and Stock Prices"*, Economic and Industrial Research Group, No. 136, 99.

Factors Motivating Buyers

The main factors motivating the buyers for mergers and acquisitions are follows:

- Acquisition of a new product, new planned capacity, technological skills or new production organization.
- Greater degree of vertical integration, synergy, and growth.
- Shift addition facilities, products, personnel and processes
- Increased market control, economies of scale of production, distribution and advertisement and benefits from multiunit operation.
- Improved marketability of stock or increased availability of outside capital (i.e., financial advantage of larger size)
- Greater control of patents.
- Stability of earning through mergers of different cyclical and seasonal trends.
- Gains from scale of securities.
- Tax advantages.

Factors Motivating Sellers

The main factors motivating sellers are as follows:

- Inability to top management to keep up with the competition may lead to selling of the company.
- Small companies may desire to tie their fortunes with larger ones.
- The company might be incurring losses and the management might decide to hive off the unit.
- An attractive offer may trigger the selling of the company.
- The dissension among the owner manager may lead to a sale.
- Owners may wish to retire and there may not be an apparent worthy successor in closely held companies.
- The company might find it difficult to finance R&D activities due to its limited financial resources and might fear that its products would not be able to compete with new products emanating from larger firms having better facilities.
- Financial difficulties such as insufficient working capital may lead to selling the unit.
- The owners of the company may like to diversify their personal investment. They might feel that instead of continuing as a separate unit, it would be more profitable to join hands with a larger (and more diversified) company.
- High taxation rate may hamper the potential and growth of small companies.

Advantage of Merger and Acquisition

The following advantages may be derived from the merger of acquisition.

- high net profit
- high earnings per share (EPS)
- return on net assets (including human asset)
- solvency (short and long-term)
- high rating for companies debt securities
- growing sales (excluding price cutting and discount sales)
- low average collection period (proper receivable management)
- asset/liability management
- economic value addition
- market value addition

Impact of Mergers and Acquisitions

Mergers and acquisitions bring a number of changes, i.e., sizes of the organizations change, stocks, shares and assets change, ownership change within the organization., the impact of mergers and acquisitions varies from entity-to-entity and impact of mergers and acquisitions also depend on the structure of the deal. Although large corporation are gain substantially from merger and acquisition, the M&A process have often proved to be a lengthy one. In the Indian context, the most compelling challenge facing a company taking the M&A route is the integration of people in the companies concerned. While substantial time, money and energy are spend on working out the strategy and route of merger detailed plans, too little emphasis is placed on "integrating" the employees of the two companies in a common fold in the new organization. Mergers and acquisitions may have great economic impact on the employees of the organization. After mergers and acquisitions, if the merged company is pretty sufficient in terms of business capabilities, it doesn't need the same amount of employees. The greatest fear on the minds of the employees of the acquired company is the possibility of restructuring and the resultant reduction manpower leading to unemployment for some of them. So there is a possibility of lay-offs of employees. The persons who have played an important role in building up the acquired company may find that they are being marginalized in the new set up and they may feel restless and insecure. Employees may also suffer from emotional and physical problems due to the changes in the operating environment and business procedures due to the corporate culture clash. There is a chance of higher job loss in the management level than the general employees. Shareholders are also affected economically due to mergers and acquisitions. If it is a purchase, the shareholders of the acquired company get highly benefited from the acquisition as the acquiring company pays a hefty amount for the acquisition. On the other hand, the shareholders of the acquiring company suffer some losses after the acquisition due to the acquisition premium and increased debt load. Mergers and acquisitions have different impact as far as market competitions are concerned. Different industry has different level of competitions after the mergers and acquisitions.

Failure of Merger and Acquisitions

The majority of the mergers and acquisitions are not able to create a value for the company and fails miserably in spite of highest degree of strategy, planning and investments. In 1987, the professor of Harvard, Michael Porter found that around 50% to 60% of the mergers and acquisitions ended in a failure. In 2004, McKinsey also found that only 23% acquisitions ended in a positive note on investment. There are several explanations for failure of mergers and acquisitions. One of the main reasons behind the disappointment of mergers and acquisitions is the cultural difference between the organizations. The mismatch of culture leads to deterring working environment and becomes very tough to integrate the cultures of two different companies' leads to downturn of the organization. Flawed intentions often become the main reason behind the failure of mergers and acquisitions. Top executives often tend to go for mergers under the influence of bankers, lawyers and other advisers who earn hefty fees from the clients. Often the ego of the executive can become the cause of unsuccessful merger. Sometimes technological advancement or change in economic scenario encourages the organisation to go for merger. Managers becomes busy and invest time for the deal which induce them to diverted from their main work and neglecting their core business leads to hampered the work of the organisation.

Valuation Models

For mergers and acquisition valuations, methods like Replacement Cost Method, Discounted Cash Flow (DCF) Method, Economic Profit Model, Price-Earnings Ratios (P/E Ratio), Enterprise-Value-to-sales Ratio (EV/Sales) are used. In Replacement Cost Method, cost of replacing the target company is calculated and acquisitions are based on that. Replacement cost method isn't applicable to service industry. Discounted Cash Flow (DCF) method is one of the major valuation tools in mergers and acquisitions. It calculates the current value of the organization according to the estimated future cash flows. Organization's Weighted Average Costs of Capital (WACC) is used for the calculation. DCF method is one of the strongest methods of valuation. In this model, the value of the organization is calculated by summing up the amount of capital invested and a premium equal to the current value of the value created every year moving forward.

Economic Profit = Invested Capital × (Return on Invested Capital – Weighted Average Cost of Capital)

Economic Profit = Net Operating Profit Less Adjusted Taxes – (Invested Capital × Weighted Average Cost of Capital)

Value = Invested Capital + Current Value of Estimated Economic Profit.

Price earnings ratios is one of the comparative methods adopted by the acquiring companies, based on which they put forward their offers. Here, acquiring company offers multiple of the target company's earnings. In Enterprise Value to Sales Ratio acquiring company offers multiple of the revenues. It also keeps a tab on the price-to-sales ratio of other companies.

Merger and Acquisition Movements

M&A activities are usually associated with the behaviour of the US firms over the last century. In his book *The Role of Merger in Growth of Large Firms* published in 1953, J. Fred Weston identified three major periods of merger movements in USA.

The Period 1897-1904: This period is the first merger movement and merger took place between the firms which were anti-competition and enjoyed their dominance in the market according to their productivity. Most of the mergers during this period were horizontal in nature and occurred between the steel, metal and construction.

The Period 1903-1905: Most of the mergers which took place during the first phase were considered as unsuccessful. During this phase the authorized structure was not encouraging either. Later the apex judiciary body issued its directive on the anti-competitive mergers stating that they could be de-merged by implementing the Sherman Act.

The Period 1916-1940: This period concentrated on mergers between oligopolies, rather between anti-competitive firms. The mergers and acquisitions process was triggered by the financial boom which was seen after the World War I. The government strategies laid in 1920s made the corporate ambiance supportive enough for firms to work in harmony. Financial institutions like government and private banks also played a significant part in aiding the mergers and acquisitions process. The mergers which occurred during 1916-1929 were horizontal or multinational in nature. Most of these industries were the manufacturers of metals, automobile tools, food commodities, chemicals, etc. This period witnessed much vertical integration through mergers, the motive being to achieve technical gains from integration and to avoid dependence on the firms for raw material. This phase ended in 1929 with a massive decline in stock market followed by great depression. However, the tax exemptions in 1940s encouraged the conglomerates to involve themselves in M&A activities.

The Period 1940-47: This is the third merger movement in which the phenomenon of mergers and acquisitions required a new pace resulting in disappearance of above 2,500 firms.

From 1965-1970: Most of the mergers from 1965-70 were horizontal mergers and were triggered by elevating stock and interest rates, and stern implementation of anti-trust rules and regulations. During this phase the bidding companies were small in size. In 1968, the Attorney General decided to break the multinationals which resulted in the end of merging activities. The decision was triggered by the inefficient performance of the multinationals. But 1970s saw the emergence of mergers which made their mark by performing effectively. Some of them were INCO merging with ESB, OTIS Elevator with United Technologies and Colt Industries with Garlock Industries.

From 1981-1989: This phase saw the acquisition of the companies which were much bigger in size as compared to the firms in previous phases. Industries like oil and gas, pharmaceuticals, banking, aviation combined their business with their national and international counterparts. Cross-border buyouts became regular with most of them being unfriendly in nature.

In the 1990s scholars classified the M&A a movement in US into 5 ways:

1890s for monopoly

1920s for oligopoly

1960s for conglomerate takeover

1980s hostile bust up takeover

1990s driven by strategic synergetic factors

From 1992 till Present: This period was stimulated by globalization, upsurge in stock market boom and deregulation policies. Major mergers were taking place between telecom and banking giants. There was a change in the attitude of the industrialists, who opted for mergers and acquisitions for long-term profitability rather than short lived benefits. Promising economic trends, investments by corporate and revised government policies motivated the participation of many conglomerates to contribute in the acquisition trend. Until the second half of 1997, the rapid growth in consumption of oil in the Asian region was increasing prices and boosting spending on exploration and production around the world. After the Asian debacle, the region's demand had been expected to grow by almost one million barrels per day in 1998. As a result, prices fell by more than 40% between 1997 and 1998. Thus, the oil companies had no option but to cut down their costs to survive. During this time M&A emerged as a strong possibility to accomplish this objective. The rapid evolution of IT, M&A was taking place worldwide during the last few years to take the advantage of knowledge and efficiencies.

International Mergers and Acquisitions

Economic reforms opened up opportunities for international mergers and acquisitions. International mergers and acquisitions also received a major boost. The European economy also opened up to foreign mergers and acquisitions in the 1990s, which resulted in M&A (merger and acquisition) activities of large volumes taking place across Europe. USA has always been the pioneer in merger and acquisition activities, UK too have registered high levels of mergers and acquisitions. Firms are accruing various benefits due to international mergers and acquisitions. Cross-border mergers and acquisitions are effective in boosting Foreign Direct Investment (FDI). Through international mergers and acquisitions access to local markets of different countries is possible. For international investors, it is easier to invest through a merger or an acquisition. International mergers and acquisitions provide access to developing countries to improved technologies and more productive operative mechanisms. However, there are certain impediments to international mergers and acquisitions. Regulations of different countries play an important role. In some countries certain sectors are prohibited from international mergers and acquisitions, while for some other sectors certain conditions need to be fulfilled.

Table 5.3: Top 10 M&A Deals Worldwide by Value (in million US$) from 1990 to 1999

Rank	Year	Purchaser	Purchased	Transaction value (in million US$)
1	1999	Vodafone Airtouch PLC	Mannesmann	183,000
2	1999	Pfizer	Warner-Lambert	90,000
3	1998	Exxon	Mobil	77,200
4	1998	Citicorp	Travellers Group	73,000
5	1999	SBC Communications	Ameritech Corporation	63,000
6	1999	Vodafone Group	AirTouch Communications	60,000
7	1998	Bell Atlantic[20]	GTE	53,360
8	1998	BP[21]	Amoco	53,000
9	1999	Qwest Communications	US WEST	48,000
10	1997	Worldcom	MCI Communications	42,000

Source: Institute of Mergers, Acquisitions and Alliances (IMAA), Webster University, Austria

Table 5.4: Top 10 M&A Deals Worldwide by Value (in million US$) from 2000 to 2010

Rank	Year	Purchaser	Purchased	Transaction value (in million US$)
1	2000	Fusion: America Online Inc. (AOL)	Time Warner	164,747
2	2000	Glaxo Wellcome Plc.	SmithKline Beecham Plc.	75,961
3	2004	Royal Dutch Petroleum Co.	Shell Transport & Trading Co.	74,559
4	2006	AT&T Inc.	BellSouth Corporation	72,671
5	2001	Comcast Corporation	AT&T Broadband and Internet Services	72,041
6	2009	Pfizer Inc.	Wyeth	68,000
7	2000	Spin-off: Nortel Networks Corporation		59,974
8	2002	Pfizer Inc.	Pharmacia Corporation	59,515
9	2004	JP Morgan Chase & Co.	Bank One Corp.	58,761
10	2009	Technofist Inc.	Goldspark IT Solution Pvt. Ltd., Inc.	N/A
11	2008	Inbev Inc.	Anheuser-Busch Companies, Inc.	52,000

Source: Institute of Mergers, Acquisitions and Alliances (IMAA), Webster University, Austria

Some Mergers and Acquisitions in India

India has emerged as one of the top countries with respect to mergers and acquisitions deals. The followings are merger tookplace from 1993 onwards are given below:

1993:

BBLIL acquires Kothari General Foods and Cadbury's Dollops brand

Coca-Cola Co. acquires Parle Exports Brands

S.S Pasasi acquires Remington brand.

1994:

Asea Brown Boveri acquires Flakt Brand

Aravind Mills acquires Asoka Mills

Voltas acquires Hyderabad Allwyn.

1995:

Eicher Tractor acquires Royal Enfield Motors

Electrolux acquires Maharaja International

Torrent Group acquires Ahmedabad and Surat Electricity.

1996:

BBLIL acquires Kissan

Aravind Mills acquires Rohit Mills

Goodricke Group acquires Himalaya Tea Garden

1997:

Crompton Greaves acquires Goa Electricals.

GE Capital acquires SRF Finance

Gillete acquires Parle's oralcare division

1998:

Wockhardt acquires Merind

Grasim acquires Shree Digvijay Cement Company

Pond's Inia merged with HLL.

1999-2002:

Lafarge acquires Tisco's cement division

Tata Tea acquires Etley

ICICI acquires Bank of Madura, etc..

2003-2004:

Times group forms Joint ventures with BBC Worldwide

NIC (national insurance company) merged with Sun Life

VSNL acquired by Tyco.

The important factors that contributed to the growth of mergers and acquisitions in 2005 were – Growing sense of comfort among investors about acquisitions and uncertainties exist no longer existed. Secondly, increased availability of cash with the companies, thirdly, opening up of Europe to international mergers and acquisitions. Fourthly, acquisitions helped in cost-cutting exercises.

2005:

Financial and Banking Sectors:

Acquisition of Citigroup's travellers' life insurance by MetLife

Merger of Gemplus and Axalto

Bank of America's acquisition of MBNA

Acquisition of Metris by HSBC

Food and Beverages Sector:

Acquisition of Salad Express by Chiquita

Southcorp, an Australian winemaker was acquired by Foster's – another Australian group.

Spirit group acquired by Punch Taverns of UK.

Computers and IT Sector:

Acquisition of Macromedia by Adobe.

Acquisition of Siebel by Oracle.

Acquisition of StorageTek by Sun Microsystems.

Skype acquired by eBay.

Scientific Atlanta acquired by Cisco.

Acquisition of Maxtor by Seagate.

Consumer Products Sector:

Gillette acquired by Procter & Gamble.

Acquisition of Reebok by Adidas.

Acquisition of Maytag by Whirlpool.

Pharmaceutical Sector:

Hextel and Eon Labs acquired by Novartis.

Chiron acquired by Novartis.

ID Biomedical of Canada acquired by Glaxo.

Telecom Sector:

France Telecom acquired Spain's Amena.

AT&T acquired by SBC.

Western Wireless acquired by Alltel.

Midwest Wireless acquired by Alltel.

Telesim of Turkey acquired by Vodafone.

Marconi of UK acquired by Ericsson.

Travel and Transport:

Hilton Group acquired by Hilton Hotels.

Merger of Air West and US Airways

USF acquired by Yellow Roadway.

Acquisition of Britain's P&O by Dubai Ports

2006:

Banca Intesa SpA and Sanpaolo IMI SpA for $37.54 billion

Wachovia Corp. and Golden West Financial in the banking sector worth $26 billion

Mittal Steel Co. and Arcelor SA for $22.7 billion

Xstrata Plc and Falconbridge Ltd., of mining for $21.2 billion

Anadarko Petroleum and Kerr-McGee Corp. in the energy sector for $18 billion

Johnson & Johnson Inc. acquired Pfizer Inc. Consumer Products Division for $16.6 billion in the Pharmaceuticals sector.

Softbank KK acquired Vodafone Japan KK for $15.3 billion in telecommunications

Regions Financial Corp. and AmSouth Bancorp for $10 billion in banking and finance.

AXA SA and Winterthur in the insurance sector for $9.93 billion

Goldcorp Inc. and Glamis Gold Ltd., for $8.6 billion in mining and minerals sector

Merrill, Lynch & Co., acquired BlackRock Inc. for $8 billion

Takeover of Abbey National, Life Insurance Division by Resolution Plc in the insurance sector for $6.7 billion

MTN Group Ltd., and Investcom LLC in the telecom sector for $5.5 billion in telecommunications

2007:

Mahindra and Mahindra acquired 90% stake in the German company Schoneweiss.

Corus was taken over by Tata

RSM Ambit based at Mumbai was acquired by PricewaterhouseCoopers.

Vodafone took over Hutchison-Essar in India

Ten Biggest Mergers and Acquisitions Deals in India during 2007-09

Tata Steel acquired 100% stake in Corus Group on January 30, 2007. It was an all cash deal which cumulatively amounted to $12.2 billion.

Vodafone purchased administering interest of 67% owned by Hutch-Essar for a total worth of $11.1 billion on February 11, 2007.

India Aluminium and Copper giant Hindalco Industries purchased Canada-based firm Novelis Inc. in February 2007. The total worth of the deal was $6 billion.

Indian Pharma Industry registered its first biggest in 2008 M&A deal through the acquisition of Japanese pharmaceutical company Daiichi Sankyo by Indian major Ranbaxy for $4.5 billion.

The Oil and Natural Gas Corp purchased Imperial Energy Plc. in January 2009. The deal amounted to $2.8 billion and was considered as one of the biggest takeovers after 96.8% of London based companies' shareholders acknowledged the buyout proposal.

In November 2008 NTT DoCoMo, the Japan based telecom firm acquired 26% stake in Tata Teleservices for USD 2.7 billion.

India's Financial Industry saw the merging of two prominent banks – HDFC Bank and Centurion Bank of Punjab. The deal tookplace in February 2008 for $2.4 billion.

Tata Motors acquired Jaguar and Land Rover brands from Ford Motors in March 2008. The deal amounted to $2.3 billion.

In May 2007, Suzlon Energy obtained the Germany-based wind turbine producer Repower. The 10th largest in India, the M&A deal amounted to $1.7 billion.

2009 saw the acquisition Asarco LLC by Sterlite Industries Ltd.'s for $1.8 billion making it ninth biggest-ever M&A agreement involving an Indian company.

Top 10 Mergers and Acquisitions in India for 2010

Tata Chemicals bought British Salt; a UK-based white salt producing company for about US $13 billion.

Reliance Power and Reliance Natural Resources merger is the one of the biggest deals of the year. This deal was valued at US $11 billion.

Airtel acquired Zain at about US $10.7 billion to become the third biggest telecom major in the world.

Abbott's acquisition of Piramal health care solutions at US $3.72 billion which was 9 times its sales benefited greatly by moving to leadership position in the Indian market.

GTL Infrastructure acquisition of Aircel towers about US $1.8 billion and money generated gave Aircel the funds for expansion throughout the country and also for rolling out its 3G services

ICICI Bank buys Bank of Rajasthan for a price of ₹ 3,000 cr would help ICICI improve its market share in northern as well as western India

Jindal Steel Works acquired 41% stake at ₹ 2,157 cr in Ispat Industries to make it the largest steel producer in the country.

Reckitt acquired Paras Pharma at a price of US $726 million to basically strengthen its health care business to establish itself as a strong consumer health care player in the fast growing Indian markets.

Mahindra acquired a 70% controlling stake in troubled South Korea auto major Ssang Yong at US $463 million.

Fortis Health Care, after acquiring Hong Kong's Quality Health Care Asia Ltd., for around ₹ 882 cr last month, they are planning on acquiring Dental Corp, the largest dental services provider in Australia at ₹ 450 cr.

The M&As have happened across industries in banking, automotive, health care, FMCG, Telecom, etc., indicates the dream year of Indian industry.

Financial Restructuring

Financial restructuring is the process of reshuffling of the financial assets and liabilities of a company which primarily comprises of equity capital and debt capital in order to create the most beneficial financial environment for the company. The process of financial restructuring is often associated with corporate restructuring so in that restructuring the general function and composition of the company is likely to impact the financial health of the corporation. Financial restructuring is the substantial change in a company's financial structure, or ownership or control, or business portfolio. It is designed to increase the value of the Firm. Fig. 5.4 shows the corporate restructuring.

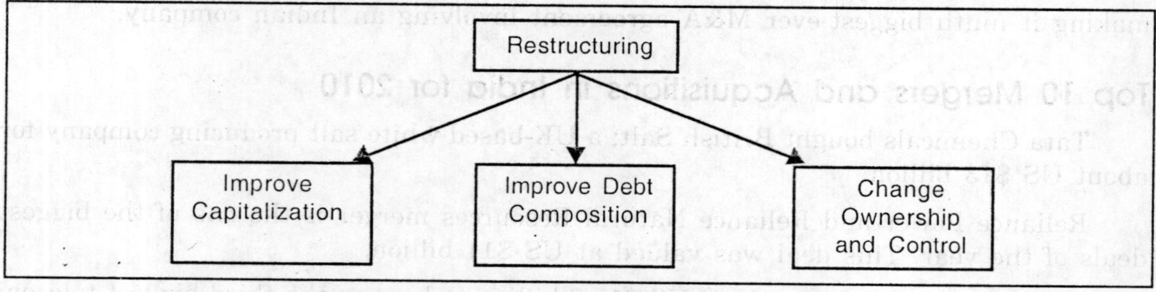

Figure 5.4: Financial Restructuring

The two components of financial restructuring are;

- Debt Restructuring
- Equity Restructuring

Debt Restructuring

Debt restructuring is the process of reshuffling the whole debt capital of the company because company's financial manager needs to minimize the cost of capital and improving the efficiency of the company. Debt restructuring can be done in three ways.

- A healthy company can go in for debt restructuring to change its debt by substituting the current high cost debt with low cost borrowings.
- A company that is facing liquidity problems can go for debt restructuring to reduce the cost of borrowing and to increase the working capital position.
- An insolvent company can go for restructuring in order to make it solvent and free it from the losses and make it viable in the future.

Reasons behind debt restructuring are as follows:

- Restructuring of secured long-term borrowings
- Restructuring of unsecured long-term borrowings
- Restructuring of secured working capital borrowings
- Restructuring of other term borrowings

Equity Restructuring

Equity restructuring is the process of reshuffling of the shareholders capital and the reserves that are appearing in the balance sheet. Equity restructuring mainly deals with the concept of capital reduction.

The following are the some of the various methods of restructuring:

- Repurchasing the shares from the shareholders for cash is to reduce the liability of the company to its shareholders resulting in a capital reduction by returning the share capital.
- Restructuring of equity share capital can be done by writing down the share capital by certain appropriate accounting entries lead to reducing the amount owed by the company to its shareholders without actually returning equity capital in cash.
- Restructuring is also be done by reducing the dues that the shareholders need to pay.
- Restructuring is also be done by consolidation of the share capital.

Reasons behind equity restructuring:

The following are the reasons for which equity restructuring is done:

- Correction of overcapitalization
- Keep-up management stakes
- To provide respectable exit mechanism for shareholders in the time of depressed markets by providing them liquidity through buyback.
- Reorganizing the capital for achieving better efficiency
- To wipe out accumulated losses
- To write-off unrecognized expenditure
- To maintain debt-equity ratio
- For revaluation of the assets
- For raising fresh finance

Fees in Restructuring Work

When an investment bank represents a bankrupt company, the burden of the work is focused on analysing and recommending financing alternatives. Thus, the fee structure resembles that of a private placement. I-bankers not only work in securing financing, but also assist in building projections for the client. They are also renegotiating credit terms with lenders, work with the company's lawyers to navigate the bankruptcy court process and help re-establish the businesses a going concern.

Corporate Advisory Services

With the growing importance of investment banking across the globe, People are looking its advisory functions with increased confidence. The core of corporate advisory services for investment banking relates to Business advisory, Restructuring advisory, Project advisory and Merger and Acquisition advisory.

With the world growing at a rapid pace, the company does not want to lose opportunities but look out for expansion opportunities, go in for strategic alliances, seek profitable mergers and acquisitions, etc., to improve upon its current standing. The transactions and formalities involved in such a case need to be professionally handled and need a specialist intermediary called Corporate Advisory Services for the proposed transaction to get the job done easily and effectively. There are several areas of the companies' business processes that need specialized advice on feasibility of the project, the environmental conditions, political aspects, and sources of financing before initiating a business plan. All this needs is done very efficiently by professionals with exposure in such areas of service by Corporate Advisory Services. Company finds the need of restructuring its financial statements, with a motto to revamp its current state of affairs.

On the other hand, it is just a financial compulsion. Corporate advisers in such cases come in as very handy in meeting these considerations.

Investment banks render the following services:

Entry Strategy Plans: Investment bankers give advice to a company when it plans a venture into a new business either in a new line of business or existing line of business. The strategy is given in terms of corporate structure of a product and pricing strategy, target market segment, strategic alliance, etc.

Project Feasibility Plans: Before any fund raising activity is carried out by the company, it is essential to examine the viability of a proposed business from a business, technology and financial perspective. An investment bank conducts such feasibility studies from a business and financial perspective since they have in-depth information on each industry space.

Corporate Plans: In order to carry-out the expansion and business strategy, companies formulate the medium to long-term corporate plans by taking the advice of investment banks. The formulations of corporate plans involve:

- In-depth examination of the industry
- In-depth examination of the business
- Identification of growth drivers
- Market positioning
- Product policies
- Diversification strategies
- Corporate and group structure, etc.

Business Alliances: This relates to joint ventures, collaborations and other such strategic relationships between two corporate entities. Investments bankers carry-out the following functions:

- Identification of partners with complementary strengths or synergies
- Due diligence and valuation aspects
- Negotiation and deal making

Cross-border Investments: Strategic business investments are made by the investing corporate in the parent country or in other foreign entities. Investment banks carry-out an in-depth examination of the financial and regulatory issues that are necessary to arrive at the optimum size of the investment, valuation methodology, investment structure and taking necessary regulatory clearances.

There has been significant restructuring of the investment banking industry as a result of the global financial crisis. Long established firms such as Bear Sterns, Lehman and Merrill Lynch are being rescued by universal banks. The capital strength of leading universal banks has been greatly reduced and the trend of major corporate and governments increasingly turning to independent advisory businesses for advice.

Summary

Corporate advisory refers to the activity of advising organizations, including corporations, institutions and government bodies, on mergers and acquisitions and other transactions that involve a change in ownership of a company or business. Booming stock market encourages merger. Corporate mergers and acquisitions have a great impact on the industry and economy of any country. Many companies find that the best way to get further on is to expand ownership boundaries through mergers and acquisitions. Mergers create synergies and economies of scale, expanding operations and cutting costs. Synergy is the main motive behind mergers and acquisitions. Mergers can fail for many reasons including a lack of management foresight, the inability to overcome practical challenges and loss of revenue momentum from a neglect of day-to-day operations. Another reason is that coping with a merger can make top managers spread their time too thinly and neglect their core business. So much of senior management's attention must be focused on developing a post-transaction strategy and integration plan that will generate the revenue enhancements and cost savings which prompted the merger or acquisition.

CASE: MERGER AND TAKEOVERS

Mega-merger was announced just hours after a three-way $19.6 billion between Delta Company and Allure Company the world leader in the aluminium industry, announced plans to buy Reynolds Metal of Allure Company for $6.6 billion. If the merger between Delta and Reynolds the second largest aluminium firm, is to happen then Delta become the market leader. Since mergers also means lay-offs, managers are always cautious about merger deals. But at the same time mergers also mean stock price will increases large for the company who are the target of merger and takeover attempts. In fact, High Fields Management Ltd., Reynolds' single largest stockholder, has taken the initiative to foster further merger consideration. They are pressuring Reynolds' management to arrange an auction to the highest bidder. Industry analysts report that these firms are scrambling in an attempt to be a part of deals while the market is in a state of frenzy. The fear of being left out could be a rational one as many feel bidding wars result in over paying for firms. Big Chandani Partners a firm who got their start in computer software has come out of the woodwork to announce interest in Reynolds.The following table reflects current data for Delta Company and Delta's expectations of the data values for Allure Company with proper management in place.

Item	Delta Company	Allure company
Earnings available for common stock	$12,80,000	$3,60,000
Number of shares of common stock outstanding	8,00,000	1,20,000
Market price per share	$64	1,20,000

Delta Company estimates that after the proposed acquisition of its Allure Company price/earnings (P/E) ratio will be 37.

1. What are the general reasons why firms merge?
2. Find the ratio of exchange in market price, and (2) the earnings per share (EPS) and price/earnings (P/E) ratio for each company on the basis of the data given in the table that accompanies discussion of the acquisition alternative.
3. Find the post-merger earnings per share (EPS) for Delta Company assuming that it acquires Allure Company under the terms given.
4. Use the estimated post-merger price/earnings (P/E) ratio and your finding in part 2 to find the post-merger share price.

Use your finding in part 3 to determine how much, if any, the total market value of Delta Company will change as a result of acquiring Allure Company.

Review Questions

1. Why does merger occurred? What are its advantages of mergers and acquisitions?
2. Explain about mergers and acquisitions movement
3. **Write short notes on:**
   (a) Distinction between mergers and acquisitions
   (b) Distinction between mergers and takeover
   (c) Equity restructuring
   (d) Corporate advisory services
4. **Quiz:**
   (a) When the two companies are in direct competition and share the same market and sell the same products are called ____ merger
   (b) Divestment is considered as reverse of ____.
   (c) ____ means company distributes shares of a subsidiary to its shareholders.
   (d) In 1987, ____ found that around 50% to 60% of the mergers and acquisitions ended in a failure.
   (e) Most of the mergers from 1965-70 were ____ mergers
   (f) Tata Steel acquired ____ stake in Corus Group on January 30, 2007
   (g) Merger of HDFC Bank and Centurion Bank of Punjab deal took place in ____ for $2.4 billion.
   (h) A company that is facing liquidity problems can go for debt restructuring to reduce the cost of borrowing and to increase the working capital position. *(T/F)*
   (i) A healthy company can go in for debt restructuring to change its debt by substituting the current low cost debt with high cost borrowings. *(T/F)*
   (j) Strategic business investments are made by the investing corporate in the parent investing corporate in the parent country or in other foreign entities. *(T/F)*

CHAPTER 6

Venture Capital

Introduction

Today's global business environment is progressively more competitive requiring conviction, broader relationship networks, ample financial resources, and a global audience in order to compete efficiently. However, starting a venture is never simple. The essential qualities like experience, integrity, prudence and a clear understanding of the market are necessitated for promoters to start a venture. However, there are other factors, which lie beyond the control of the entrepreneur is the timely infusion of funds. This is where the venture capitalist comes in, with money, business wisdom and a lot more. Venture capital in broader sense is not exclusively a booster of funds into a new firm rather than it is an input of skills needed to set up the firm, devise its marketing strategy, systematize and manage it. Thus, it is a long-term involvement with succeeding stages of company's growth under highly risky investment conditions.

What is Venture Capital?

Venture capital is largely based on the twinning concept: Financing and Business Plans. Venture capital is the capital invested in young, fast growing or changing companies that have the potential for high growth in exchange for an equity stake rather than a loan in the business hopes to get better-than-average return. Venture capital provides long-term, committed share capital, to help unquoted companies grow and succeed. Venture capital is a form of "risk capital". Venture capital is invested in exchange for an equity stake in the business. Venture capitalist prefer to invest in "entrepreneurial businesses". The VC may also invest in a firm that is unable to raise finance through the conventional means. Venture capital is a mode of providing equity finance to rapidly-growing private companies. Venture capital involves investment in new or comparatively inexperienced technology, initiated by professionally or technically qualified entrepreneurs with insufficient funds. Finance is required in many stages, i.e., start-up, development/ expansion or purchase of a company. The ultimate goal of venture capital is to build companies so that their shares become liquid (through IPO or acquisition) and provide a rate of return to the investors in the form of cash or shares keeping the level of risk taken consistent. In other words, Venture Capital Financing signifies the investment in high-risk ventures willing to share in the risk of the project, with the anticipation of proportionate levels of returns. Venture capital firms usually look to retain their investment for between three and seven years or more. The main sources of venture capital are venture capital firms and "business angels".

Most venture capital comes from a group of wealthy investors, investment banks and other financial institutions that pool such investments or partnerships. According to International Finance Corporation (IFC), venture capital is equity or equity featured capital seeking investment in new ideas, new companies, new production, new process or new services that offer the potential of high returns on investments. As defined in Regulation 2(m) of SEBI (Venture Capital Funds) Regulation, 1996 "venture capital fund means a fund established in the form of a company or trust which raises monies through loans, donations issue of securities or units as the case may be, and makes or proposes to make investments in accordance with these regulations. Jane Koloski Morris, editor of the well-known industry publication, *Venture Economics*, defines venture capital as 'providing seed, start-up and first stage financing' and also 'funding the expansion of companies that have already demonstrated their business potential but do not yet have access to the public securities market or to credit-oriented institutional funding sources.

The European Venture Capital Association describes it as risk finance for entrepreneurial growth-oriented companies. It is investment for the medium or long-term return seeking to maximize medium or long-term for both parties. It is a partnership with the entrepreneur in which the investor can add value to the company because of his knowledge, experience and contact base.

Why Venture Capital is Important?

Venture capital funding is the business of employing capital 'Patiently' to 'Maximize Returns' while managing risks in a relatively high-risk venture. Venture capital has the potential to finance start-ups as venture capitalists are generally willing to accept high levels of risks for high potential profits. Further venture capitalists do not require collateral nor charging interest payments and contribute to the management of the firm. Venture capitalists provide networking, management and marketing support as well. In the broadest sense, therefore, venture capital connotes financial as well as human capital. Venture capital provides a source of funds through investment, usually in companies or projects that are start-up or at a very early stage of product development. These projects and organizations usually are not bright to attract sources of finance such as loans and not able raise money in the major public stock markets. In various developed and developing economies venture capital has played a significant developmental role. Venture capital is needed to boost to innovative high-tech enterprise, for development of the sunrise sectors (high growth potential) and provision of technical managerial expertise by VCs. Apart of it VC is important for money, position and for non-financial contributions.

Money

- Angels provide substantial quantities of financing. Angels provide substantial early-stage financing. Recent large-scale survey of 11,000 SME (Small and Medium Enterprise) owners reveals 18% of business owners have made investments in businesses owned by third parties. Angels seek out high growth firms to compensate for risk, angels look for annualized rates of return of at least 25%. Angels apply 7-7 rule for each $1 invested angels want to exit with $7 after 7 years and only growth-oriented firms can meet these rate of return requirements, exits via IPOs (initial public offerings).

Position

- Business angels invest in most sectors and where many people say there is a 'capital market gap' – in early stage growth-oriented businesses.

Non-financial Contributions

- **Advice:** Private investors assisted by providing guidance to management, and VC also provided guidance in the development of a corporate governance process and reporting discipline. They also provided legal advice, financial negotiations and seeks business opportunities ... also brought tu company rights to exploit several new technologies which he revealed. They provided office space and office furniture as well.
- **Boards of Directors and Advisors:** VC served as directors and provided bank guarantees for the company line of credit. Also provided personal loans. They sits on the board of directors, acts as a reseller of products, provides input for development, marketing, growth opportunities.
- **Market and Business Intelligence:** VC identification of possible customers, identification of technical partners or competitors, payroll benefits, handling employees. They close working relationship with key angels – consultancy.

Who Invests in Venture Capital?

- High net worth individuals with appetite for high risk.
- Institutions diversifying investment portfolios: Financial services – Insurance companies, pension funds, banks, etc.
- Governments acting as catalysts

Feature of Venture Capital

High Risk

Venture capital financing is highly risky and chances of failure are high. It provides long-term start-up capital to high risk-high reward ventures. Venture capital believes four types of risks, i.e., Management risk, Market risk, Product risk, Operation risk.

High tech venture capital investments are made in high tech areas using new technologies or producing innovative goods by using new technology. Venture capital is available for expansion of existing business or diversification to a high risk area.

Equity Participation and Capital Gains: The funds in the form of equity help to raise term loans that are cheaper source of funds. In the early stage of business equity investment implies that investors bear the risk of venture and would earn a return commensurate with success in the form of capital gains.

Participation in Management

Venture capital provides value addition by managerial support, monitoring and follow-up assistance. Venture capitalist advises the promoters on project planning, monitoring, financial management, including working capital and public issue. Venture capital keeps a close contact with the promoters or entrepreneurs to protect their investment.

Length of Investment

Venture capitalist help companies grow, but they eventually seek to exit the investment in three to seven years. An early stage investment may take seven to ten years to mature, while most of the later stage investment takes only a few years.

Illiquid Investment

Venture capital investments are illiquid. The investment is realized only on if enterprise is liquidated for unsuccessful working. Venture capitalist understands this illiquidity and factors this in their investment decisions.

Origin of Venture Capital Funding

In the 1920s and 1930s, wealthy individuals and families provide the start-up money for companies that would later become famous. The Vanderbilts, Whitneys, Rockefellers, and Warburgs were notable investors in private companies in the first half of the century. In 1938, Laurance S. Rockefeller helped finance the creation of both Eastern Air Lines and Douglas Aircraft and the Rockefeller family had vast holdings in a variety of companies. Eric M. Warburg founded E.M. Warburg & Co., in 1938, which would ultimately become Warburg Pincus, with investments in both leveraged buyouts and venture capital. John Hay Whitney and his partner Benno Schmidt founded the J.H. Whitney & Company as the Venture capital funding and investing since the 1930s. They set up the Pioneer Pictures in 1933 and acquired 15% interest in Technicolor Corporation. Florida Foods Corporation has been one of the Whitney's most famous investments. The company developed a new method for carrying nutrition to American soldiers as Minute Maid Orange Juice, which was later sold to The Coca-Cola Company in 1960.Georges Doriot, known as the "father of venture capitalism" founded the American Research and Development fund at the Massachusetts Institute of Technology in 1946, to finance the commercial exploitation of new technologies developed in US universities. The main idea was to support private sector investments in businesses and in 1957 investment of $70,000 in Digital Equipment Corporation would be grow over $355 million after the company's initial public offering in 1968. Past employees of ARDC established several well-known venture capital firms, like Greylock Partners and Morgan, Holland Ventures, the predecessor of Flagship Ventures. ARDC continued to invest up to 1971 till the retirement of Doriot and in 1972, Doriot merged ARDC with Textron after investing in more than 150 companies. The small business Act of the US permitted license to the Small Business Administration and support financially small business investment companies for engaged in venture capital finance, to provided fuel to the growth of venture capital finance. Larger companies in the US like Xerox, 3M and General Electric entered the field with their venture capital divisions and motivated the development of venture capital throughout the world. Though the initial efforts of introducing venture capital made in the early seventies were unsuccessful but the changed environment of the eighties witnessed a phenomenal growth of hi-tech industries and provided a fertile ground for the blossoming of venture capital. J.H. Whitney & Company continued to make investments in leveraged buyout transactions, raising around $750 million for its sixth institutional private equity fund in 2005. During the late 1960s and early 1970s, more than 25% of the Fortune 500 firms attempted corporate venture programs. The typical venture programme begun in the late 1960s was dissolved after only four. The number of active venture organizations increased dramatically during the late 1970s and early 1980s. After the stock market crash of 1987, however, the market for new public offerings went into a sharp decline. By 1992, the number of corporate venture programmes had fallen by one-third and their capital under management represented only 5% of the venture pool. Corporate venture capital climbed once again in the mid-1990s, both in the United States and abroad. Once again, much of this interest was stimulated by the success of the independent venture sector, i.e., the rapid growth of funds and their attractive returns. These corporate funds have invested directly in a variety of internal and external ventures as well as in funds organized by independent venture capitalists. Venture Capital financing, a significant financial innovation of the twentieth century, is a mechanism to institutionalize innovative entrepreneurship.

How Does the VC Industry Work?

Venture capital firms typically source the majority of their funding from large investment institutions such as fund of funds, financial institutions, endowments, pension funds and banks. Their money is comprised in a fund, which is managed by the Venture Capital Company depicted in Fig. 6.1.These institutions typically invest in a venture capital fund for a period of up to ten years with the expectation of receiving very high returns on their investment and after that trying to exit through either an IPO or a merger/acquisition. So venture capitalists invest in high growth potential company and trying to promote the growth of the companies where they invest. They also managing the associated risk to protect and enhance their investors' capital. Though the venture capitalist receive some return through dividends but their primary return on investment comes from capital gains when they eventually sell their shares in the company, typically between three to five years after the investment.

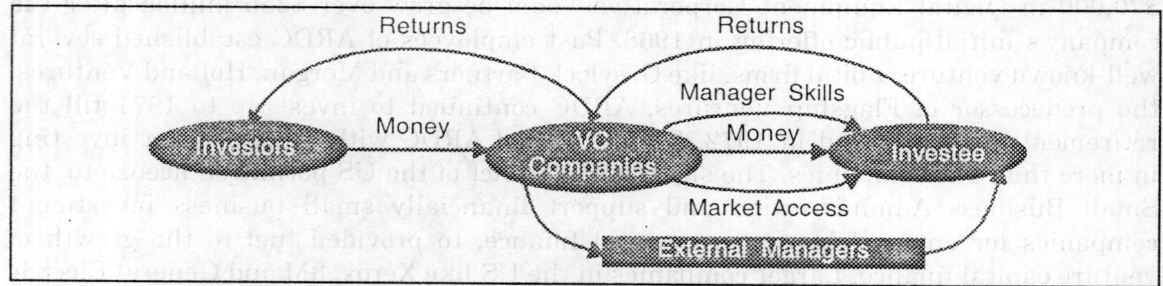

Figure 6.1

Venture Capital Investment Process

The investment process begins with the initial review of the proposal by venture capitalist to determine if it fits with the firm's investment criteria. If so, a meeting will be arranged with the entrepreneur/management team to discuss the business plan. This process is shown in Fig. 6.2

Step 1: Business Plan Submission

The first step in approaching a VC is to submit a business plan which includes: a description of the opportunity and market size, resumes of management team; a review of the competitive landscape and solutions; detailed financial projections; and a capitalization table, an executive summary of business plan. Once the VC has received the plan, it will discuss internally to proceed further or not. VCs receive an average of 200 business plans each month. Of those, less than 5 per cent is invited to meet with the VC's partners. Just 2 per cent will reach the due diligence phase, and less than one per cent will be offered a term sheet. Some 0.3 per cent of those submitting a business plan will ultimately obtain VC funding. Majority of successful proposals come from a trusted referral of the VC, such as a limited partner, another VC, a known attorney or accountant, or other professional.

Step2: Introductory Conversation/Meeting

If the firm has the potential to fit with the VC's investment preferences, firm will be contacted in order to discuss the business opportunity in more depth.

Step 3: Preliminary Screening

The initial meeting provides an opportunity for the venture capitalist to meet with the entrepreneur and key members of the management team to review the business plan and conduct initial due diligence on the project. It is an important time for the management team to reveal their understanding of their business and the strategies outlined in the plan. The venture capitalist normally looks cautiously at the team's functional skills and backgrounds.

Step 4: Due Diligence

The due diligence phase is depending upon the nature of business proposal. The venture capitalists review the quality of entrepreneur before appraising the characteristics of the product, market or technology. Most venture capitalists make an assessment of the possible risk and return of the venture.

Step 5: Term Sheets and Funding

If the due diligence phase is satisfactory, the VC will offer a term sheet to entrepreneur. This is often called memorandum of understanding (MoU) an agreement between the venture capitalist and management of the terms of the term sheet. The venture capitalist will then proceed to study the viability of the market to estimate its potentially using market forecasts which have been independently prepared by industry experts who specialize in estimating the size and growth rates of markets and market segments.

Step 6: Approvals and Investment Completed

After due diligence final investment proposal is typically submitted to the venture capital fund's board of directors. If approved, legal documents are prepared. The investment process can take up to two months, and sometimes longer for secure the required funding.

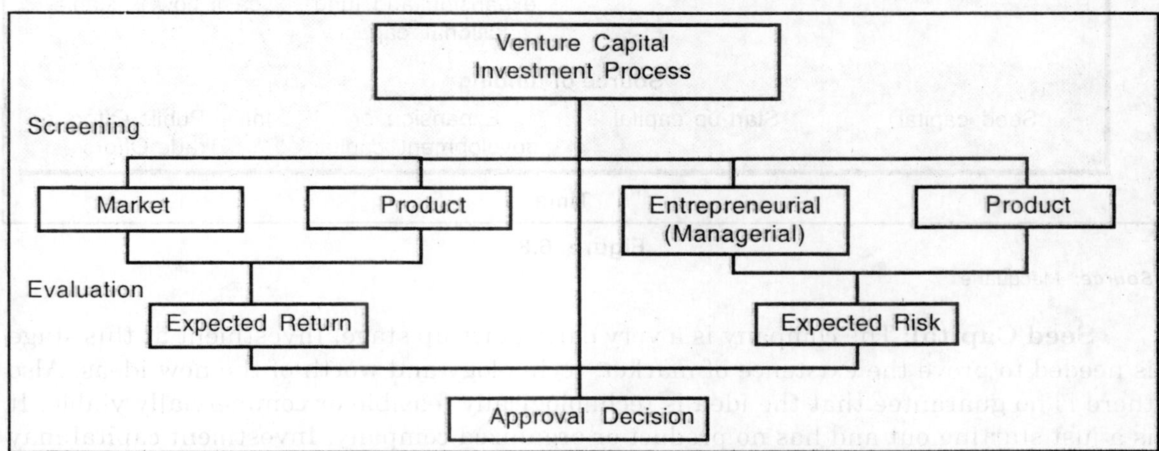

Figure 6.2: Venture Capital Investment Process

Venture Capitalists Staged Investments

Venture capital funds are available at various stages and different VCs provide funding in some or all of the stages. These characteristics change from one company to another and also depend on the condition of the given market. Also there can be several rounds of investments within one stage before the company moves on to the next stage. In this sense, the following market segments/product groups are defined:

- Seed capital
- Start-up capital
- Expansion capital
- MBO/MBI and M&A capital
- Bridge financing capital
- Rescue capital

The various stages of financing are shown in Fig. 6.3.

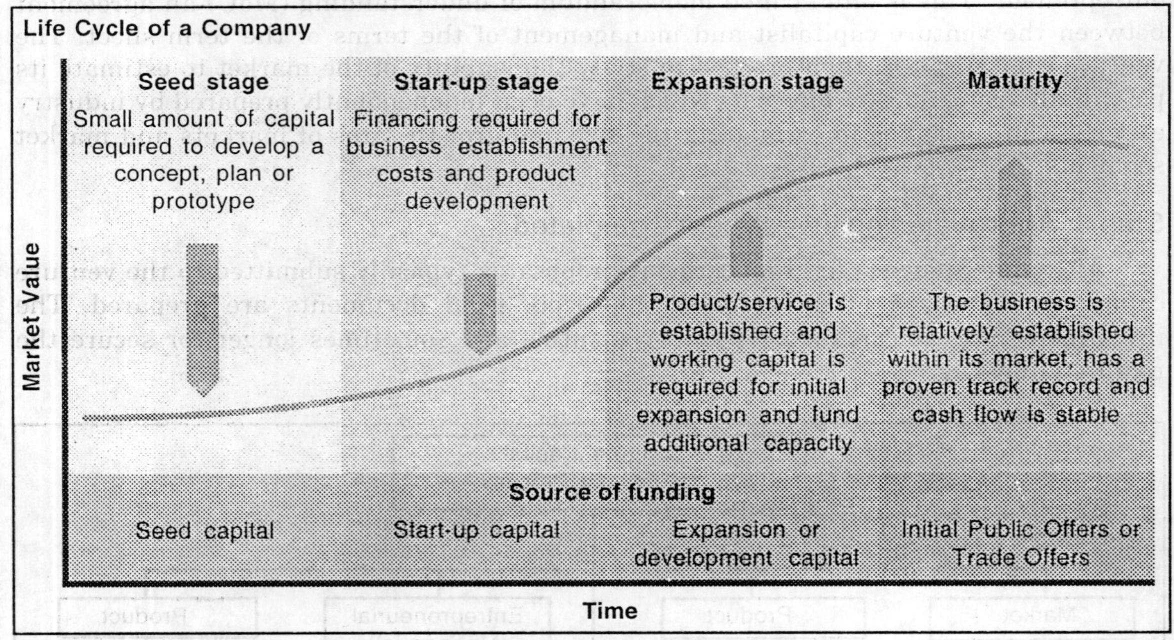

Figure 6.3

Source: Macquarie

Seed Capital: The company is a very early start-up stage. Investment at this stage is needed to prove the existence of market, technology and worth of the new ideas. Also there is no guarantee that the idea is technologically feasible or commercially viable. It is a just starting out and has no product or organized company. Investment capital may be used to create a sample product, fund market research, or cover administrative set-up costs. Seed capital is used to determine whether an idea is worth further consideration and to transform the idea into a working business concept.

Start-up Capital: At this stage, the company is already having a basic team of managers and entrepreneurs with a basic business plan. At this stage the company would have a sample product available with at least one chief working full-time. Once the feasibility of the idea is proved, capital can also be raised from private investors. Funding at this stage is also rare. It tends to cover recruitment of other key management, additional market research, and finalizing of the product or service for introduction to the marketplace.

Early Stage Capital: The company is starting to develop products and sales. Typical activities financed by start-up capital are prototype development, testing and test marketing. First stage financing is used to complete the development process and commence the commercialization process of the product. At this stage, VC funding help the firm increase sales to the break-even point, improve firms' productivity, or increase the company's efficiency.

Expansion Capital: The company has made good progress on its plan, sales have started to increase, and the business is expanding. The company is well established, and now companies are looking to a VC to help take business to the next level of growth. Funding at this stage is helping the company to enter into new markets.

Late Stage Capital: At this stage, company has already achieved impressive sales and revenue and the company have a second level of management in place. The company may be looking for funds to increase capacity, ramp up marketing, or increase working capital.

Bridge Financing: Bridge financing capital is determined to finance the expenses in the period before the IPO. The investors in this stage are often passive investors who expect to sell their stakes after the IPO, and venture capital funds, which have already invested in the company.

Acquisition/Buyout Financing: MBO/MBI and M&A capital is normally provided to more mature companies. It finances changes in the ownership of the investee. Acquisition financing is for acquiring another firm for further growth. Management buyout financing is for enabling operating group to acquire firm or part of its business. Turnaround financing is for turning around a sick unit.

Rescue Capital: Companies can also obtain venture capital to overcome economic problems. Measures to return to profitability and competitiveness are financed by rescue capital.

It is apparent that the largest volume of investments took place into companies in developing and growth phase. Possibly this is due to the industries life cycle, which is still in growth phase. Venture capital investments are spread over the market segments tentatively shown in Fig. 6.4.

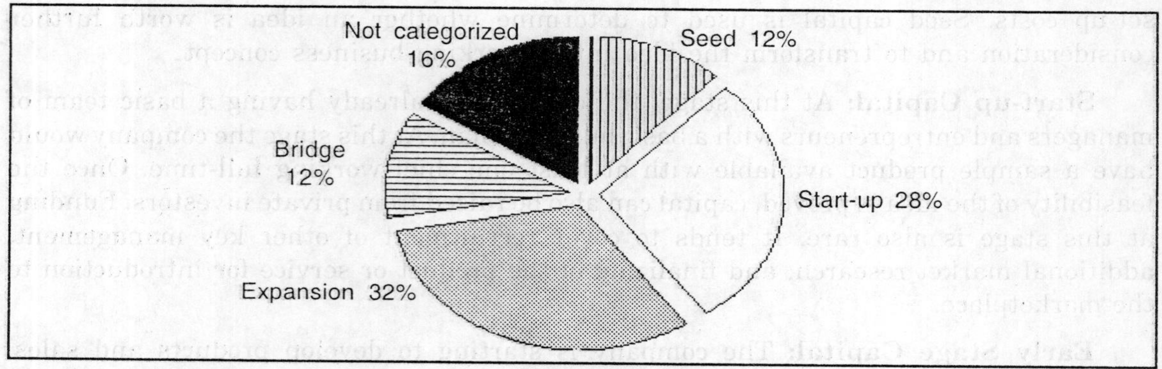

Figure 6.4

Expected returns from different financing stage is presented in Fig. 6.5.

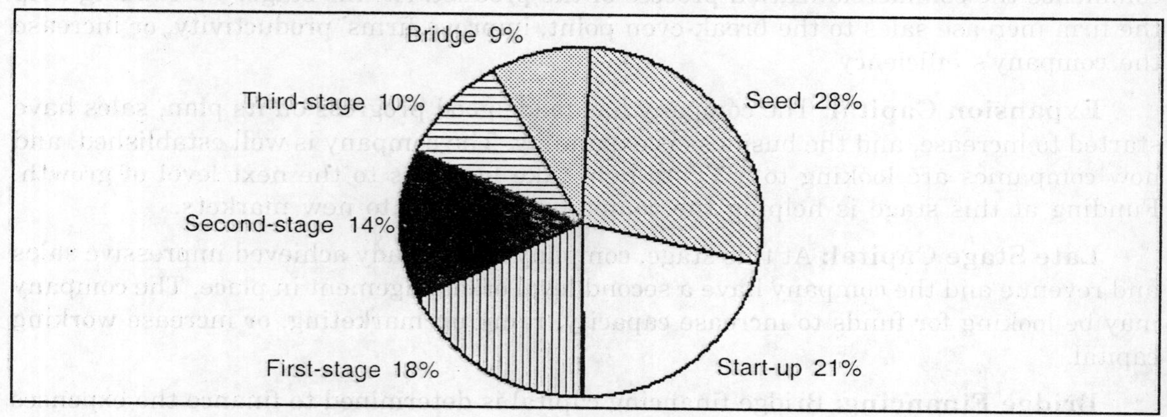

Figure 6.5

Key Success Factors

Venture capital backed companies can provide high returns. However, despite of success stories like Apple, FedEx of Microsoft, a lot of these deals fail. It is said that only one out of ten companies succeed. That's why every deal has an element of potential profit and an element of risk, depending on the deals size. To be successful, a venture capital company must manage the balance between these three factors shown in Fig. 6.5.

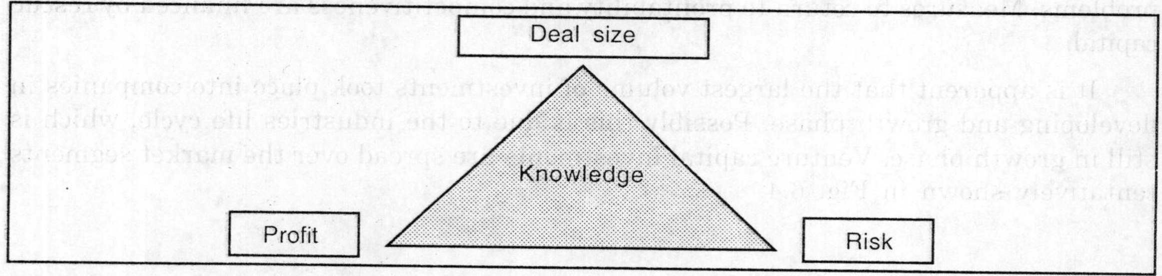

Knowledge is key, to get the balance in this "Magic Triangle". Knowledge about the financial markets and the industries to invest in is extremely important. Larger deals leads to achieve higher profits are not only important for the financial performance of the venture capital company, but they have to attract funds which are the basis for larger deals. However, larger deals imply higher risks of losses.

Advanture of Venture Capital

There are a number of advantages of venture capital over other forms of Finance which are as follows:

- It injects long-term equity finance which provides a solid capital base for future growth.
- The venture capitalist is a business partner, sharing both the risks and rewards. Venture capitalists are rewarded by business success and the capital gain.
- The venture capitalist has the capacity to provide practical advice and assistance to the company based on previous experience with other firms which were in similar situations.
- The VC also enjoys a network of connections in many areas that can add value to the company, such as in recruiting key personnel, providing contacts in international markets, introductions to strategic partners, and if needed co-investments with other venture capital firms when additional rounds of financing are required.
- The VC might be able to supply additional rounds of funding when it is required to finance growth.

What Do VCs Look for?

Venture capitalists is majorly looking for 3 key things that is people, Market potential of the product or technology, adding significant non-financial value. People must be honest, exhibit strong work ethic, understand how to make a business succeed and are invested in own business and have realistic notions of how to value the business. Secondly, they must have good business plan, the plan should concisely describe the nature of the business, the qualifications of the members of the management team, how well the business has performed, and business projections and forecasts. Venture capitalists look for businesses that have the potential to grow quickly to significant size, yielding a significant return in a relatively short period of time. The venture capitalist manages the risk/reward ratio by only investing in businesses which fit their investment criteria. For VC, a target is one that may be capable of becoming a large market leader in its industry due to some new industry opportunity and competitive advantage. Venture capitalists must be satisfied with a company's management or potential management and their plans. A strong management team and each member of the team must have adequate level of skills, commitment and motivation that creates a balance between members in areas such as marketing, finance, and operations, research and development, general management, personnel management, and legal and tax issues. It must have a management team with relevant experience, self-confidence, and expertise each member of the team, must have adequate level of skills and commitment and motivation. Venture capitalists look for companies with superior products, fast growing or untapped markets with a justifiable strategic position such as intellectual property or patents. VC will also consider factors such as results of past operations, amount of funds needed and their intended use, future earnings projections and conditions. VC is a part owner rather than a creditor, so it's looking for potential long-term capital, rather than interest income. A common rule of thumb is that a VC looks for a return of three to five times its investment in a five- to seven-year time period. So, the venture capitalist wants to see the possibility of strong management, A growing market, A unique product, IPO candidate or acquisition target, Sound business plan, significant gross profit margins, home run potential. So while approaching a venture fund one needs to be fully prepared and keep the above requirements in mind while submitting the business plan.

Types of Venture Capitals

Generally, there are three types of institutional venture capital funds: venture capital funds set up by angel investors, that is, high net worth individual investors; venture capital subsidiaries of corporations and private venture capital firms/funds. Major corporations, commercial bank holding companies and other financial institutions establish venture capital subsidiaries. Venture funds in India can be classified on the basis of the type of promoters. Financial institutions led by Industrial Credit and Investment Corporation of India (ICICI) ventures, Risk Capital and Technology Finance Corporation Ltd., (RCTC), ILFS, etc. ICICI venture is one of the largest and most successful private equity firms in India focusing mainly on private equity, buyouts, real estate and mezzanine financing with funds under management in excess of US$ 2 billion. The name of RCTC was changed to IFCI Venture Capital Funds Ltd., (IFCI Venture) in February 2000. It was set-up with a view to widen the entrepreneurial base by providing start-up capital for setting up Green Field projects. IFCI venture has provided the start-up capital and venture funding to over 400 entrepreneurs. The company was formerly known as IL&FS Invest Smart Limited and changed its name to HSBC Invest Direct (India) Limited in August 2009. HSBC Invest Direct (India) Limited was founded in 1997. HSBC Invest Direct (India) Limited engages in the securities broking, investment advisory, distribution of financial products, portfolio management services, and securities related financing businesses. It offers retail broking services, including equities, derivatives, and mutual funds, as well as online and branch trading, and NRI services; wealth management services that include IPO advisory and distribution services; advisory reports; investment tools; insurance broking; and investment banking. Private venture funds like Indus, etc.,. Regional funds: Warburg Pincus, JF Electra. Regional funds dedicated to India: Draper, Walden, etc., Offshore funds: Barings, TCW, HSBC, etc., Corporate ventures: venture capital subsidiaries of corporations, Angels: high net worth individual investors, Merchant bankers and NBFCs (Non-bank finance companies) who specialize in "bought out" deals also fund companies.

Venture Capital in India

In India, the need for VC was recognized in the 7th Five-Year Plan. In 1973 a committee on development of small and medium enterprises highlighted the need to faster VC as a source of funding new entrepreneurs and technology. VC financing really started in India in 1988 with the formation of Technology Development and Information Company of India Ltd., (TDICI) – promoted by ICICI and UTI (Unit Trust of India). The first private VC fund was sponsored by Credit Capital Finance Corporation (CFC) and promoted by Bank of India, Asian Development Bank and the Commonwealth Development Corporation, viz., Credit Capital Venture Fund. At the same time, state level financial institutions started Gujarat Venture Finance Ltd., and APIDC Venture Capital Ltd. But now, India is recognized for its globally competitive high technology and human capital. India's recent success story in software and information technology is almost a fairy tale against several odds such as inadequate infrastructure, expensive hardware, restricted access to foreign skills and capital, and limited domestic demand. India certainly needs a large pool of risk capital both from home and abroad. All this can happen provided there is the right regulatory, legal, tax and institutional environment. In 1999, US$30 billion worth of venture capital was invested in the U.S. of which technology firms got 80 per cent approximately. By contrast, in India, cumulative disbursements to date are less than US$500 million, of which technology firms have received only 36 per cent.

Some Important Venture Capital Funds in India

- APIDC Venture Capital Limited, 1102, Babukhan Estate, Hyderabad 500 001
- Canbank Venture Capital Fund Limited, IInd Floor, Kareem Towers, Bengaluru
- Gujarat Venture Capital Fund 1997, Ashram Road, Ahmedabad 380 009
- Industrial Venture Capital Limited, Thyagaraya Road, Chennai 600 017
- Auto Ancillary Fund, Opp. Signals Enclave, New Delhi 110 010
- Gujarat Venture Capital Fund 1995, Ashram Road, Ahmedabad 380 009
- Karnataka Information Technology Venture Capital Fund, Cunningham Rd., Bangalore
- India Auto Ancillary Fund, Nariman Point, Mumbai 400 021
- Information Technology Fund, Nariman Point, Mumbai 400 021
- Tamilnadu Infotech Fund, Nariman Point, Mumbai 400 021
- Orissa Venture Capital Fund, Nariman Point Mumbai 400 021
- Uttar Pradesh Venture Capital Fund, Nariman Point, Mumbai 400 021

- SICOM Venture Capital Fund, Nariman Point, Mumbai 400 021
- Punjab Infotech Venture Fund, 18 Himalaya Marg, Chandigarh 160 017
- National Venture Fund for Software and Information Technology Industry, Nariman Point, Mumbai 400 021

Top Venture Capitalists in India by Investments

The list of VCs based on number of investments, Value of their investments and total funds raised by different venture capitalists.

Table 6.1: Number of Investments

Investor	2005	2006	2007	2008	2009	Total
Sequoia Capital India	7	12	13	18	3	53
Ventureast	5	11	4	9	3	32
Intel Capital	3	7	4	8	1	23
Helion Venture Partners	0	4	8	8	2	22
DFJ India	0	3	3	9	2	17
Nexus India Capital	0	1	4	9	2	16
NEA Indo-US Ventures	0	0	5	9	0	14
IDG India Ventures	0	0	6	5	0	11
Kleiner Perkins	1	3	0	6	0	10
Norwest Venture Partners	1	3	1	2	3	10
Canaan Partners	0	1	4	4	1	10
Inventus Capital Partners	—	—	—	—	3	3

Table 6.2: Value of Investments ($ mn)

Investor	2005	2006	2007	2008	2009	Total
Sequoia Capital India	42	184	114	138	26	504
Intel Capital	19	37	15	53	7	131
Norwest Venture Partners	13.9	8.1	24.1	17.7	92.8	156.6
Helion Venture Partners	—	30	30	30	10	100
Nexus India Capital	—	7.5	16	45	7	75.5
DFJ India	—	13.75	4	33	10	61
Ventureast	7	19	2	17	9	54
NEA Indo-US Ventures	—	—	24	26	—	50
Canaan Partners	—	4	10	12	4	30
Kleiner Perkins	2	8	—	19	—	29
IDG India Ventures	—	—	14	8	—	22
Inventus Capital Partners	—	—	—	—	—	—

Table 6.3: Total Funds Raised ($ mn)

Investor	2005	2006	2007	2008	2009	Total
Sequoia Capital India	200	400	300	725		1,625
Helion Venture Partners	—	140	—	210	—	350
Nexus India Capital	—	—	100	220	—	320
Ventureast	—	—	136	86	—	222
NEA Indo-US Ventures	—	—	189	—	—	189
IDG India Ventures	—	150	—	—	—	150
Inventus Capital Partners	—	—	—	125	—	125
Norwest Venture Partners	—	—	—	—	—	—
DFJ India	—	—	—	—	—	—
Kleiner Perkins	—	—	—	—	—	—
Intel Capital	—	—	—	—	—	—
Canaan Partners	—	—	—	—	—	—

Source: *Outlook Business*, 2009

How Venture Capital Influence Economy?

Venture capital investments create jobs. On average, 75% of venture capital investment is spent on payroll, and venture capitalists generally estimate compensation per-employee at their portfolio companies to be $1,00,000 per year. Consequently, each $1 million of venture capital directly creates or sustains seven and one-half skilled, high-paying jobs.

- For every job directly created, another 2.2 jobs are indirectly created through the multiplier effect.
- Overtime, companies that are originally financed with venture capital grow to become major employers.
- Beyond jobs, venture capital drives sales, taxes, exports, and R&D.
- Per $1,000, companies backed by venture capital have approximately twice the sales, pay almost three times the federal taxes, generate almost twice the exports, and invest almost three times as much in R&D as the average company that is not backed by venture capital.

Apart from this, the other factors important for India are as follows:

- Innovation – needs risk capital in a largely regulated, conservative, legacy financial system
- Creating new industry clusters – media, retail, call centers and back-office processing, trickling down to organized effort of support services like office services, catering, and transportation
- Patient capital – not flighty, unlike FIIs

Growth Drivers of Venture Investing in India

- Knowledge-based industries growing fast and mostly global, less affected by domestic issues
- World-class engineers, professionals, entrepreneurs – success evident in the US as well
- Second largest English speaking population, science and mathematics at a premium
- India has advanced rapidly in the 90s, catching up with global markets in many sectors
- Evidence of this in the US as well —
  - — 25 per cent of small companies in the US have Indian founders
  - — Disproportional large presence of Indians in the US software sector
- Government highly supportive of growth in technology and knowledge-based sectors
- Strong and supportive legal framework — Information Technology Act, VC norms, ESOPs, Copyright, etc.
- Government controlled telecom being fully deregulated
- Capital market system amongst most advanced in Asia
- Electronic trading-through NSE and BSE the committed capital chasing India is abundant.
- The next stop for VCs, the most recent wave, has been consumer internet and mobile offerings. India's growing mass of connected consumer population is the target wallet. Travel, jobs, games, mobile payments are all segments getting substantial capital infusion. This trend is likely to continue for the next couple of years. The engineering required in building these sites is marginal, marketing being the big differentiator.
- India has a better opportunity in this field for the same reason as retail: domestic producer, domestic consumer
- Positive climate for education, R&D fuels new business opportunities and start-ups
- Tax policy can have a huge influence on investment preferences and can change the attractiveness of venture capital funds for investors in both directions
- Globalisation drives scale
- Requires huge investments in acquisitions and market development
- Need for external expertise

- Ongoing globalisation and liberalisation provide two-fold opportunities for venture capital firms
- Direct venture capital activities in new markets, e.g., eastern European entrants into the EU
- Companies go global and need funding for their international activities

Where are VCs Investing in India?

- IT and IT-enabled services
- Software Products (Mainly Enterprise-focused)
- Wireless/Telecom/Semiconductor
- Banking
- PSU Disinvestment
- Media/Entertainment
- Biotechnology/Bioinformatics
- Pharmaceuticals
- Electronic Manufacturing
- Retail

Taxation of FVCI

SEBI issued the Foreign Venture Capital Investor Regulations (FVCI) 2000 and apply to foreign venture capital investors who established outside India as well propose to invest in India. FVCIs avoided registering themselves with SEBI due to the extremely confusing regulatory and tax position. FVCIs preferred to operate from overseas, usually through a liaison office in India. Under Section 90(2) of the IT Act, a non-resident assesses based in a country with which India has a double taxation avoidance agreement (DTAA), may opt to be taxed either under the IT Act or the DTAA, whichever is more beneficial. Under Section 10(23FB) of the IT Act, any income of a registered FVCI is exempt from income tax. The FVCI can carry on business in India through a permanent establishment in India, and yet its entire income would be tax-free. On the other hand, if the FVCI opts to be taxed under the DTAA and it has a permanent establishment in India, its Indian income will not be tax-free. The tax exemption under Section 10(23FB) has to be read with Section 115U of the IT Act, which confers a pass-through status on SEBI-registered venture funds. Investors in such funds would be liable to tax in respect of the income received by them from the FVCI in the same manner as it would have been, had the investors invested directly in the venture capital undertaking. However, the Authority for Advance Ruling on March 7, 2001 held that profits made by a private equity fund or venture capital fund should be taxed as business profits and not as capital gains. Non-resident investors in an FVCI, therefore, liable to pay Indian income tax on what they receive from the FVCI as business profits. Accordingly, a non-resident investor in an FVCI, who receives dividend from the FVCI, is entitled to characterize the same as dividend under the DTAA, by opting to be taxed under the DTAA and not the IT Act. The budget 2007 has changed Indian law so that pass through status to registered VCFs is only available for nine specified sectors:

- Nano-technology
- Information technology relating to hardware and software development
- Seed research and development
- Biotechnology
- Research and development of new chemical entities in the pharmaceutical sector
- Production of biofuels
- Building and operating composite hotel-cum-convention centers with seating capacity of more than three thousand
- Dairy or poultry industry
- Infrastructure

International Scenario

In the last decade, there has been a significant increase in the globalization of the venture capital industry (Kenney *et al.* 2002). Despite the spread of venture capital globally, the US and, more particularly, Silicon Valley, remain the centre of both venture capitalism and high-technology industry. In terms of business models and economic development, Silicon Valley was the inspiration for Asian policymakers, entrepreneurs, and venture capitalists.

In 1946, the first venture capital firms were established in the US with the objective of providing financial backing and business assistance to entrepreneurs in exchange for repayments in capital gains. These pioneering VC firms soon discovered that technology-based innovations most consistently yielded the greatest returns. In 2006, entrepreneurial high-technology ventures play a significant role in the US national innovation system. Although US traditionally have developed a VC industry funding at all stages, the focus at present in VC industry is clearly on expansion and leter stage funding.

Global consumer markets, increased international competition, investment opportunities in emerging markets, the higher cost of building a company in the mature markets and advancements in technology are driving factors for the globalization of both venture funds and their portfolio companies. Collaboration among funds is also increasing. Global investors seek out local funds in the emerging innovation source for help in making the right investments and penetrating large developing consumer markets. The total funding was to the tune of US $21.7 bn in 2,939 deals in 2005 as against US $21.6 bn in 2004, which accounts for over US $17.5 bn in 2005. It is very interesting to note that though Israel does not seem to be a likely candidate of being the country, which is one of the world leaders in VC funding in the world. Israel has always been a powerhouse of R&D due to highly educated workforce, defence forces, Immigration, Ongoing Government support, venture capital performance showed positive returns across almost all investment horizons for the period ending December 31, 2006 according to Thomson Financial and the National Venture Capital Association (NVCA).

Overall venture capital performance for the five-year time horizon took more than a two point leap from Q3 2006, brining the return from 1.2% to 1% in Q4 2006. Three-year venture returns remained constant at 9.1% in Q4 2006, while one-year venture returns posted a 16.4% return in Q4 2006, up from 7.0% in Q3 2006. Ten and twenty year returns remained steady at 20.3% and 16.6%, respectively. Investment Horizon Performance through 12/31/2006 shown in Table 6.4.

Table 6.4: Investment Horizon Performance

Fund Type	1 Yr	3 Yr	5 Yr	10 Yr	20 Yr
Early/Seed VC	9.90	6.50	–3.00	36.40	20.50
Balanced VC	20.50	11.70	4.10	17.60	14.60
Later Stage VC	25.20	9.40	3.70	9.00	14.00
All Venture	16.40	9.10	1.00	20.30	16.60
NASDAQ	4.75	6.25	4.30	6.41	10.11
S & P 500	10.80	8.21	4.25	6.65	9.20
All Venture (through 09/30/2006)	7.00	9.10	–1.20	20.60	16.60

Source: Thomson Financial/National Venture Capital Association

Venture-backed company exits grew in value and number in 2005, as the United States and Israel saw increasing M&A valuations, while Europe experienced an increase in IPOs, a trend that is set to continue the year 2006 and into 2007. In the emerging markets, the increasing number of China-focused venture capital funds suggests that there is a robust population of venture-backed Chinese companies in the IPO pipeline.

According to the Ernst & Young Venture Capital Insights Report 2006, venture capital investments worldwide reached the level of US $31.3 billion. The United States, Canada, Europe, and Israel represent 93% of capital invested, while China and India account for the remainder. Venture capital firms in the United States have raised US $41 billion in new funds in the last 2004 and 2005 years. European firms closed on • 3.7 billion in 2005, more than doubled in comparison to 2004. Leading investment bankers and venture capital investors believe that the challenge of meeting Sarbanes-Oxley requirements in the United States and the increased bar to listing on NASDAQ are creating new interest among venture-backed companies in listing on global exchanges such as Hong Kong and Tokyo. Between 2000 and 2006, the overall number of firms making investments in US companies declined by 49%. During the same period, the number of firms investing in European companies dropped by 52%, while active investors in Israeli companies fell by 57%.

In the United States from 2002-2005, VC investments has ranged between 58% and 60%. Between 18% and 23% of total investments were in life sciences, while the remainder were scatted across other industries. In Europe between 51% and 57% of the total investments was in IT, while the life sciences received a further 21% to 28%. In Israel, IT has been far more dominant, receiving 70% to 76% of total VC investments. In 2006 the top three countries receiving the most venture capital investments were the United Kingdom (515 minority stakes sold for € 1.78bn), France (195 deals worth € 875m), and Germany (207 deals worth € 428m) Venture capitalists invested some $6.6 billion in 797 deals in US during the third quarter of 2006, according to the Money Tree Report by PricewaterhouseCoopers and the National Venture Capital Association. A recent National Venture Capital Association survey found that majority (69%) of venture capitalists predicts that VC investments in US will level between $20-29 billion in 2007. The investment of capitalists in Indian industries in the first half of 2006 is $3 billion and reaches $6.5 billion at the end of the year 2006.

Thirty-five US venture capital funds raised nearly $3 billion in the fourth quarter of 2010 compared to the third quarter of 2010, which saw 49 funds raise $3.2 billion during the period marks a 6% decrease, by dollar commitments. In year 2010, 157 venture capital funds raised $12.3 billion (Thomson Reuters and the National Venture Capital Association (NVCA) exhibited in Table 6.5.

Table 6.5: Fund Raising by Venture Funds, 2005-1Q 2010

Year/Quarter	Number of Funds	Venture Capital ($M)
2005	234	30,759.6
2006	235	31,860.9
2007	237	31,205.0
2008	213	26,412.2
2009	150	16,314.9
2010	157	12,304.2
4Q'08	49	2,807.9
1Q'09	57	4,942.5
2Q'09	39	4,995.5
3Q'09	32	2,310.3
4Q'09	47	4,066.9
1Q'10	46	4,007.0
2Q'10	52	2,130.3
3Q'10	49	3,177.1
4Q'10	35	2,989.9

Source: Thomson Reuters and National Venture Capital Association

There were 24 follow-on funds and 11 new funds raised in the fourth quarter of 2010 a ratio of 2.2-to-1 of follow-on to new funds. The largest first fund at a newly established firm during the fourth quarter of 2010 was Raleigh, North Carolina-based Nova Quest Health Care Investment Fund, L.P., which raised $177 million.

Table 6.6: VC Funds: New vs. Follow-on

	No. of New	No. of Follow-on	Total
2005	54	180	234
2006	63	172	235
2007	71	166	237
2008	64	149	213
2009	43	107	150
2010	52	105	157
4Q'08	17	32	49
1Q'09	10	47	57
2Q'09	14	25	39
3Q'09	13	19	32
4Q'09	14	33	47
1Q'10	16	30	46
2Q'10	19	33	52
3Q'10	18	31	49
4Q'10	11	24	35

Source: Thomson Reuters and National Venture Capital Association

The largest fund raising during the fourth quarter of 2010 was from Menlo Park, California-based Andreessen Horowitz Fund II, L.P. which raised $650 million, followed by Palo Alto, California-based Meritech Capital Partners IV, L.P., which raised $390 million.

Why Policymakers are So Fond of Venture Capital?

National Venture Capital Association (NVCA) study finds that on average every $36,000 in VC investment creates one new job. A study by the European Private Equity and Venture Capital Association (EVCA) found that VC-backed European companies generated significantly higher growth rates in sales, research spending, exports and job creation.

Venture-backed companies in the US account for more than 12 million jobs (Fig. 6.6), or 11 per cent of total private sector employment (Fig. 6.7). These numbers reflect the industry's focus on finding and funding only those companies with high growth potential. This may be one reason that job growth generated by venture-backed companies outstripped overall US job growth between 2006 and 2008 (Fig. 6.8).

According to a 2011 Global Insight study, venture-backed companies accounted for nearly 12 million jobs and $3.1 trillion in revenues in the United States in 2010. (Deloitte/ National Venture Capital Association 2011 Global Venture Capital Survey)

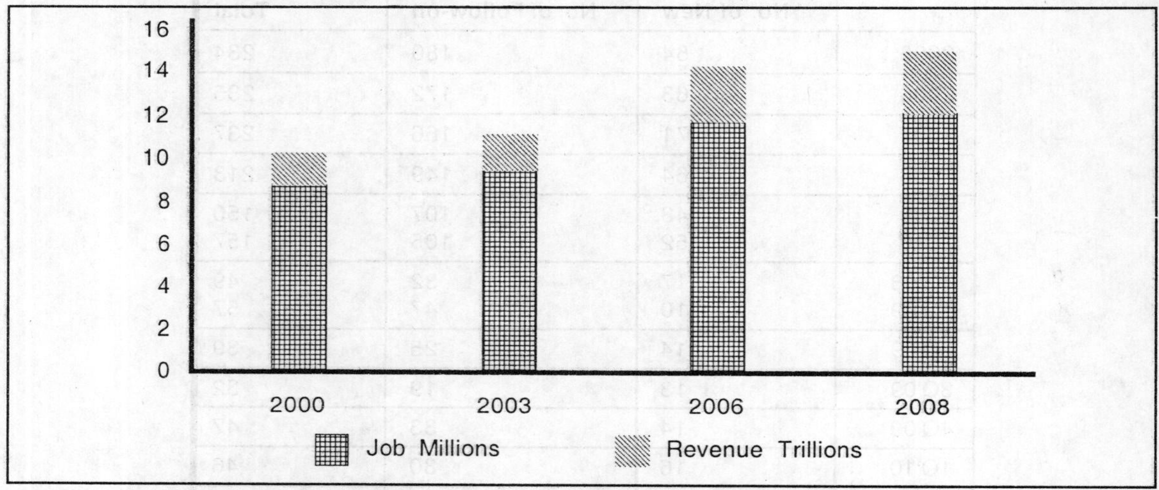

Figure 6.6: Economic Benefit of US Venture-backed Companies (2000-2008)

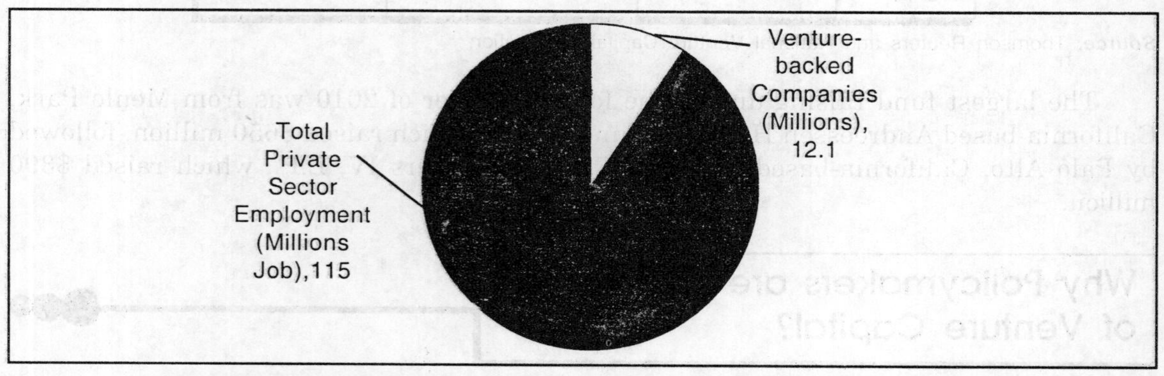

Figure 6.7: Employment at Venture-backed Companies as a Per Cent of Private Sector Employment 2008

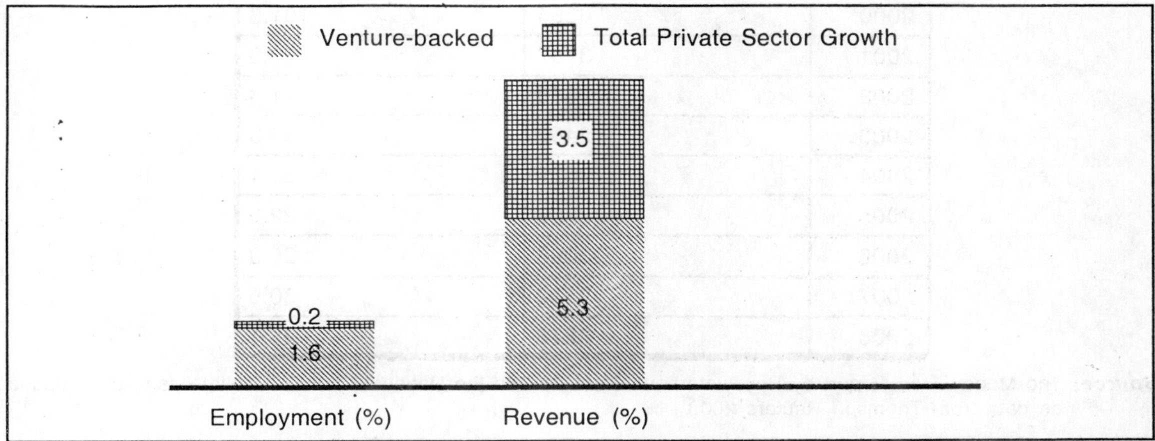

Figure 6.8: Employment and Revenue Growth at Venture-backed Companies vs. Total Economy 2006-2008

Venture-backed companies also have a significant impact on US revenue almost $3 trillion in revenue contributing one-fifth of the country's gross domestic product in 2008 (Fig. 6.9)

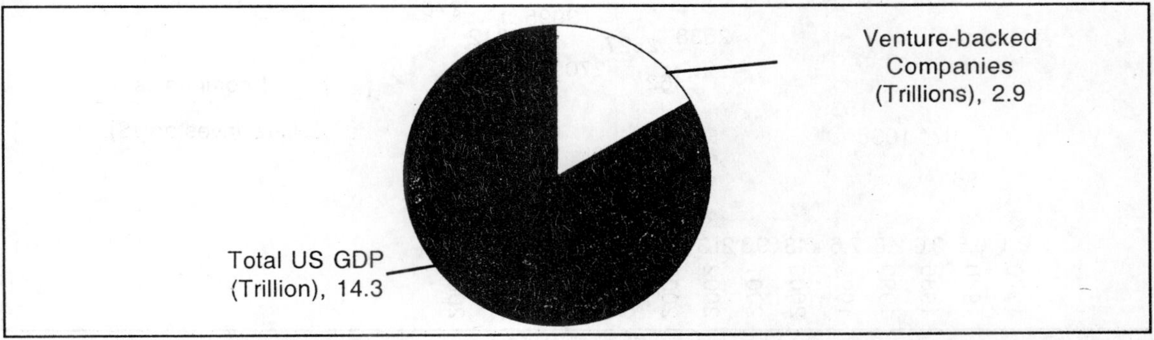

Figure 6.9: Revenue at Venture-backed Companies Relative to US GDP

Since its formative years in the early 1970s, the US venture capital industry has invested approximately $456 billion in more than 27,000 companies (Fig. 6.10). While many of these companies ultimately failed, successes like Genentech, eBay and Intel went on to create entire new industries and ways of doing business.

Table 6.7: Venture Capital Investment in the United States 1970-2008

Year	No. of companies	Dollars invested ($)
1970	116	0.1
1980	386	0.5
1985	1174	2.6
1990	1036	2.6
1995	1539	7.6

2000	6334	101.8
2001	3787	39.3
2002	2638	21.3
2003	2462	19.3
2004	2627	22.1
2005	2709	22.9
2006	3095	26.3
2007	3312	30.6
2008	3276	28.1

Source: The Money Tree Report by PricewaterhouseCoopers and the National Venture Capital Association, based on data from Thomson Reuters 2008

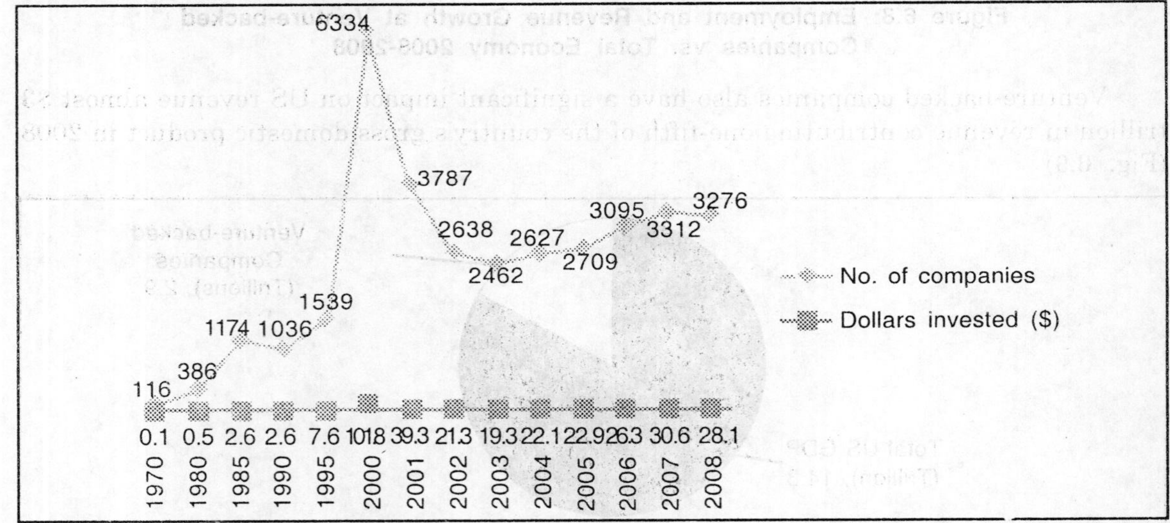

Figure 6.10

For every dollar of venture capital invested from 1970-2008, $6.36 of revenue was generated in 2008. In 2008, one US job existed for every $37,702 of venture capital invested from 1970-2008.

The Number of Deals in 2010 and 1st Q2011 is presented in Table 6.8.

Table 6.8: Number of Deals

2010		2011	
# of Deals	**Amount Invested**	**# of Deals**	**Amount Invested**
787	$ 5,16,55,40,700	736	$ 5,87,34,70,400
995	$ 7,15,24,59,300		
838	$ 5,35,34,97,500		
827	$ 5,59,14,32,000		
3,447	$ 23,26,29,29,500	736	$ 5,87,34,70,400

Invested in 2010 and 2011 is depicted in Table 6.9.

Table 6.9: Amount Invested

Stage of Development	2010 Total	2011Qtr 1 Total
Seed	$ 1,72,53,61,000	$ 12,05,40,700
Early Stage	$ 5,49,54,81,900	$ 1,73,96,31,900
Expansion	$ 9,18,74,20,200	$ 1,88,57,47,900
Later Stage	$ 6,85,46,66,400	$ 2,12,75,49,900
Grand Total	$ 23,26,29,29,500	$ 5,87,34,70,400

Investments by industry (2010) is shown in figure 6.11.

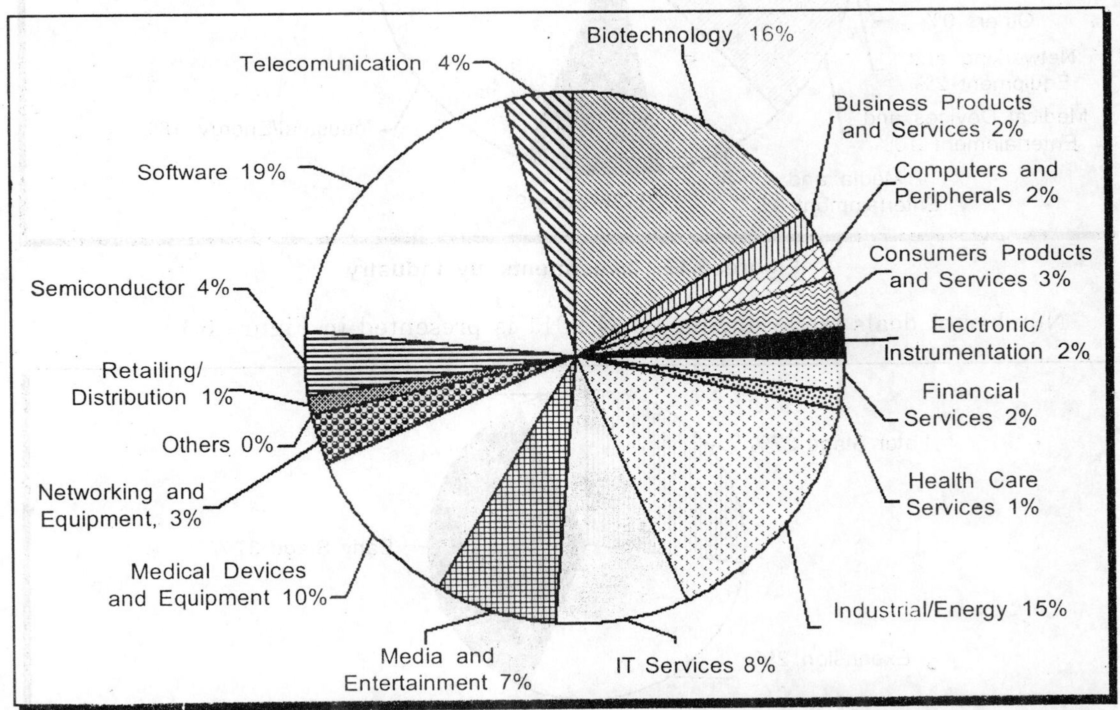

Figure 6.11: Investments by Industry

Investments by industry made during (1st Q 2011) is depicted Figure 6.12.

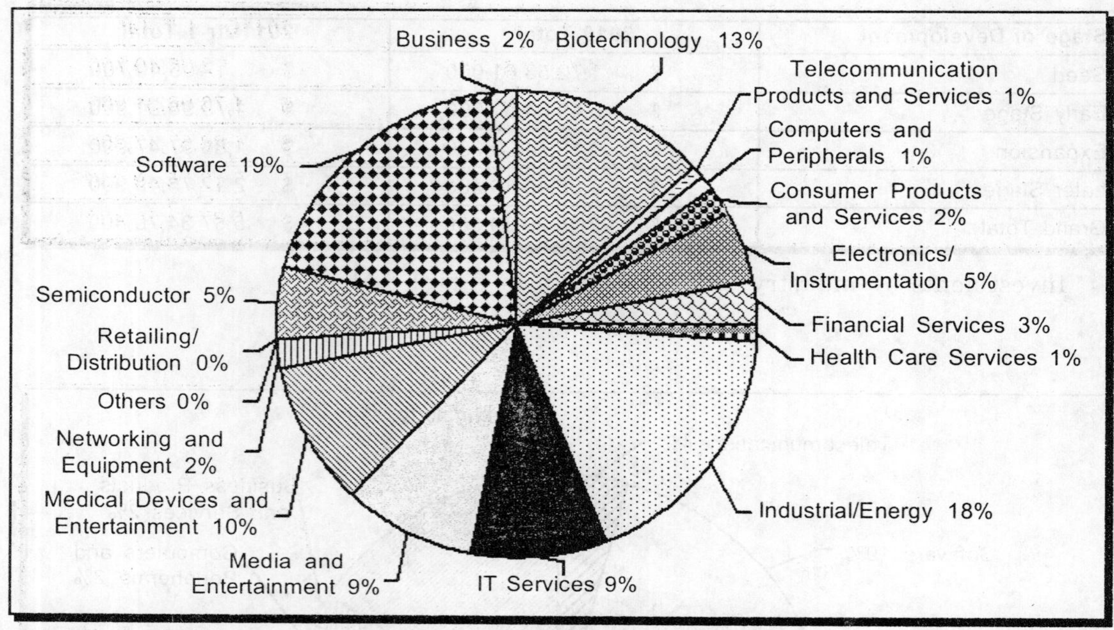

Figure 6.12: Investments by Industry

Number of deals made during 1st Q 2011 is presented in Figure 6.13.

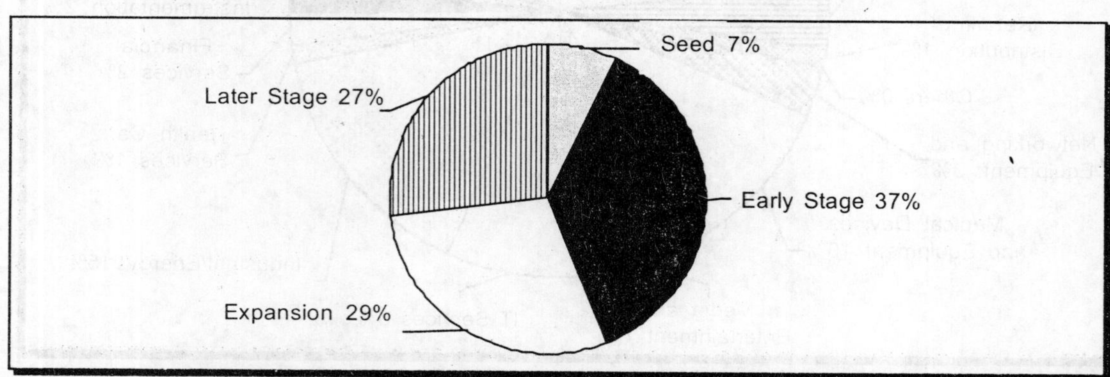

Figure 6.13: Number of Deals

Present Indian Scenario

Nasscom's vision for India states that it should become one of the top five global locations in the creation of technology ventures. The Table 6.10 demonstrates the growth of Venture Capital and Angel Investments in India's IT software and services sector.

Table 6.10: VC/Angel Investments in High-tech firms in India

Year	₹ Million	U.S. $ million
1996	700	20
1997	3,200	80
1998	6,100	150
1999	14,000	320
2000	32,000	750
2001	50,000	1200
2008	450,000	10,000

According to a Venture Intelligence in partnership with the Global-India Venture Capital Association, Venture Capital firms invested $475 million over 92 deals in India during the 12 months ending December 2009. The amount invested during 2009 was $836 million being invested across 153 deals which is lower compared to 2008. VC firms however began to increase their pace of investments in Q4'09, making 42 investments worth $265 million, significantly higher than that during the same period in 2008 (23 investments worth $102 million) as well as Q3'2009 (19 deals worth $74 million). IT and IT-enabled services (IT and ITes) industry retained its status as the favourite among VC investors during 2009, the industry's share has declined to about 43 per cent, from about 55 per cent during 2008. Within IT & ITeS, online services companies retained their status as the favourite sector accounting for about 39 per cent of the investments during 2009. Companies based in South India accounted for 50 per cent of all VC investments (47 per cent by value) during 2009. Their peers in Western India accounted for 25 per cent of the pie in 2009 (29 per cent by value). Companies based in North India accounted for 15 per cent of the investments in 2009 (12 per cent by value). Among cities, companies headquartered in Bengaluru and Mumbai were the favorite among VC investors during 2009 with the former attracting 29 investments and the latter 15. The Delhi National Capital Region (including New Delhi, Gurgaon and Noida) accounted for 11 investments followed by Hyderabad with 9.

Table 6.11: Top VC Investments

Company	Sector	Amount (US$ M)	Investors
FINO	IT Services (Banking)	20.0	HSBC PE, IFC, Intel Capital
Soham Renewable Energy	Renewable Energy	19.0	FE Clean Energy
MCX Stock Exchange	Stock Exchange	16.3	IIML

Stoke	Communications Tech	15.0	Reliance Tech Ventures, Others
Manthan Systems	Enterprise Software (Retail)	15.0	Fidelity, ePlanet Ventures, IDG Ventures India

Formerly, US-IVCA, Gobal India Venture Capital Association is a non-profit association of US-based venture capitalists interested in US-India cross-border investments. Its membership consists of venture capital firms, service providers, corporate investors and business.

Issues and Challenges

- To prepare for stable long-term developments, Venture Capital companies should seek for alliances inside and outside the industry, Grow, but avoid too rapid developments, Improve risk management systems, Continue to attract expertise for own management.
- Indian VC yet to be established as a sustainable asset class among institutional investors. Moreover, a limited amount of true "risk-capital" impacts entrepreneurial activity. Exit challenges exist mainly due to shallow capital markets and dull M&A environment for small companies. Most importantly, India is yet to create a brand-name for IP-led companies, like Israel has successfully done.
- Corporate should be encouraged to participate in the VC by providing suitable tax incentives.
- To encourage private participation in the venture capital activity, government should provide tax incentives/breaks to banks, institution, high-net worth individuals and corporate sector. In US venture funds and angel investors get such incentives.
- The government should introduce suitable legislation to allow limited partnerships and limited liability partnership for venture companies in India. Non-availability of this structure is one of the reasons for slow growth of domestic VC industry.
- At the present situations, India needs to concentrate its investment in small and medium enterprises. Government should promote a programme similar to Small Business Investment Programme of USA.

Benefits and Problems of Corporate Venture Funds

Many big companies are attracted to the Venture Capital model not only because of its impressive track record. More important is that it provides them improved access to business innovation, better retention or entrepreneurial talent and greater growth in the demand for their core products. Thus the corporations can capture more value from their strategic assets. By offering Venture Capital to companies with related businesses/ operations companies can develop clusters of supporting industries for their core operations.

However, many corporate funds do not achieve the same results as other Venture Capital funds do. Reasons are that they have:

- difficulties to establish the systems, capabilities and cultures that make good VC firms successful
- less freedom to fund innovative projects or to cancel midstream those that clearly won't live up to promise
- managerial skills for managing mature businesses but not for nurturing start-ups
- a lack of vital contacts in the start-up community
- a lack of contact to seasonal managers for the investees
- problems to find out the optimal time to sell out
- more hierarchical organisational structures that imply longer decision times than the more flexible Venture Capital funds have
- a portfolio management which is not ruthless enough in weeding out losers early; whereas Venture Capital funds are willing to cut losses on failing ventures immediately, corporate fund managers tend to perceive such actions not suitable to the companies policy or as admission of a mistake.

Problems with VCs in the Indian Context

Venture funding is so successful in USA but Indian VC faced a number of problems. The biggest problem is the mindset change from "collateral funding" to high risk high return funding. For any venture idea to succeed there should be a product with growing market along with a scalable business model. The IT industry in India is still having service centric business model. Products developed for Indian markets are of lack scale. Secondly, true venture capital is capital that is used to help launch products and ideas of tomorrow. Abroad, this problem is solved by the presence of 'Angel investors'. They are typically wealthy individuals who not only provide venture finance but also help entrepreneurs to shape their business and make their venture successful. Thirdly, Domestic venture funds are set up under the Indian Trusts Act of 1882 as per SEBI guidelines, while offshore funds routed through RBI guidelines. Abroad, such funds are made under the Limited Partnership Act, which brings advantages in terms of taxation. Fourthly, the exit routes available to the venture capitalists are restricted to the IPO route. Fifthly, exposure to fast growing intellectual property business and services sector is almost zero. All these combined factors are slow start to the industry.

The Pricing of Venture Capital Investments

Assume that the president and founder of the start-up company Internet Concepts Corporation (ICC), approaches a technology-oriented venture capital fund of ₹ 50,00,000 in new funding to support her firm's rapid growth. After intense negotiations, the parties agree that ICC is currently (prior to VC investment) worth ₹ 1,00,00,000 and that the risk of the firm is such that the venture capitalists are entitled to a 50% compound annual (expected) return. Assume further that both parties agree that ICC should plan to execute an IPO in five years, at which time the firm is expected to have net profits of ₹ 40,00,000 and to sell at a price-to-earnings ratio of 20 times, which will value the company at ₹ 8,00,00,000. The promised value of the venture capitalists stake in five years is calculated using basic future value computations, with an initial investment amount (A) of $5 million, a required return (r) of 50 per cent, and an investment horizon (n) of five years.

$FV = A\ (1 + r)^n$ = \$50,00,000 $(1.50)^5$ = \$50,00,000 (7.6) = \$3,80,00,000 ... (Eq. 1)

- To determine what fraction of the ICC's equity (% Equity) that the venture capitalist will receive, this future value (FV) is divided by ICC's expected market valuation (Exp MV) at the time of the IPO:

  % Equity = FV ÷ Exp MV = ₹ 3,80,00,000 ÷ \$8,00,00,000 = 0.475 ... (Eq. 2)

- This means that the venture capital fund will receive 47.5% of ICC's equity in exchange for its ₹ 5 million investment. If the required return on investment had instead been established as 40%, rather than fifty, the promised value of the venture capitalists share at the time of the IPO would have been $26.9 million and the fund would have claimed only one-third (33.6%) of ICC's equity, rather than almost half.

What is Venture Capital Valuation?

Valuation means the process of determining how much to pay invest in a company. There are some methods available for venture capital and entrepreneurs.

Market Capitalization: Market capitalization represents the value of equity.

Total Enterprise Value: TEV is taking into account different capital structures. It represents the total value of company not just the venture is acquiring.

TEV

Price per share	₹ 4.00
No. of Shares	20,00,000
Debt	₹ 5,00,000
Cash	₹ 1,00,000
Equity value	₹ 80,00,000

TEV = 80,00,000 + 5,00,000 – 1,00,000 = 84,00,000

Valuation methodologies differ by the stage of investment and the availability of quantitative and qualitative data. However, the venture capital valuation is universal, simple, and is well understood. Business valuation has become an intrinsic part of the corporate landscape. The valuation methods serve as roadmaps for the Angel investors, venture capitalists and corporate acquirers in order to know the true value of a company's assets. The core of a venture capital transaction is that the investor puts cash in the company in return for newly-issued shares in the company. The state of affairs immediately prior to the transaction is referred to as "pre-money", and immediately after the transaction "post-money". Pre-money value: The value of the company before the new money goes in. Post-money value: the pre-money plus the amount of the new investment.

Post-money Value:

Pre-money value	₹ 5,00,000
New money invested	₹ 3,00,000
Post money value	₹ 8,00,000

The pre-money valuation is what the investor is valuing the company today, before investment, while the post-money valuation is simply the pre-money valuation plus the contemplated aggregate investment amount. The value of the whole company before the transaction, called the "pre-money valuation" (and similar to a market capitalization) is just the share price times the number of shares outstanding before the transaction: Pre-money Valuation = Share Price × Pre-money shares. The total amount invested is just the share price times the number of shares purchased: Investment = Share Price × Shares Issued. The shares purchased in a venture capital investment are new shares, leading to a change in the number of shares outstanding: Post-money Shares = Pre-money Shares + Shares Issued.

Determining the pre-money valuation of the company, combined with the amount of capital accepted by the company, determines the amount of equity ownership sold in exchange for capital. Cash: Post-money Valuation = Pre-money Valuation + Investment.

The resulting valuation after the investment of capital is called the "post-money" valuation. For example, in a company with a pre-money value of 5 crore, a 5 crore investment would buy a 50% ownership stake in the company. Using some simple algebra there is another way to view this: Fraction Owned = Investment/Post-money Valuation = Investment/(Pre-money Valuation + Investment).

So when an investor proposes an investment of 2 crore at 3 crore "pre" this means that the investors will own 40% of the company after the transaction: 2 crore/(3crore + 2 crore) = 2/5 = 40%.

And if you have 1.5 crore shares outstanding prior to the investment, you can calculate the price per share: Share Price = Pre-money Valuation/Pre-money Shares = 3 crore/1.5 crore = 2.00

As well as the number of shares issued: Shares Issued = Investment/Share Price = 2 crore/2.00 = 1 crore.

Ther, exists a simple approach to valuations that is sometimes referred to as the venture capital method. The method is called internal rates of returns (IRR) and sometimes in terms of NPV. Take an example. A company called Kalinga Ventures is a start-up company. But it can be able to sell the company for 50 million in four years.

It needs venture capital fund from Gujarat Ventures. They need 6 million capitals. But Gujarat Ventures considers that it is a risky ventures and wants to apply a discount 50% to be adequately compensated for the risk which they bear. The entrepreneurs' also decided that whatever valuations they would get they wanted to own 2 million shares.

So, (V) terminal value is 50 million in four years, (T) Time to exit is 4 years, (I) Amount of investment is 6 million, (r) Discount return used by investors is 50% and (x) number of existing shares owned by entrepreneurs is 2 million.

Step 1:

Post-money valuation

NPV of the terminal value in 4 years is = V/(1+r)^4 = 50 million

50/(1 + .5)4 = 9,876.544 = post-money valuation.

Step 2:

Pre-money valuation = 9,876.544 – 6 million = 3,876.544

Step 3:

Ownership fraction = $6 million/$9,876.544 = 60.75 per cent

Required rate of return is 60.75 per cent.

Step 4:

No. of Shares

Let x be the number of shares owned by the entrepreneur (x = 2 million)

Number of shares required by Gujarat Ventures is = y

So, y/(20,00,000 + y) = 60.75 %

Y = 20,00,000[.6075/1 – .6075]

= 20,00,000 × .6075/.3925 = 30,95,541.40126

Step 5:

The price of the share is 6 million/30,95,541.40126 = $1.94

Sensitivity analysis with venture capital method:

If we reduce the terminal value by 10 per cent, increase IRR by 10 per cent, increase investment by 10 per cent, increase time to exit by 10 per cent.

Table 6.12

NPV method		Valuation-1	Valuation-2	
Exit value	V	5,00,00,000	4,50,00,000	5,50,00,000
Time to exit	t	4	4	
Discount rate	r	50%	50%	60%
Investment	I	60,00,000	60,00,000	60,00,000
Number of existing shares	x	20,00,000	20,00,000	20,00,000

Post-money valuation	post	9,876.544	8,888.888	7,629.394
Pre-money valuation	pre	3,876.544	2,888.888	1,629.394
Ownership fraction	F	60.75%	67.50%	78.64%
Ownership fraction of entrepreneurs	1-F	39.25%	32.50%	21.36%
Number of new shares	y	30,95,541.40126	41,53,846	73,64,698
Price per share	p	1.94	1.44	.81

The terminal value represents the value of the company at the time of an exit event be it in IPO or an acquisitions. In venture capital method of valuation the estimate of the terminal value is typically based on some kind of success scenarios.

Investment Value vs. Company Valuation

Early stage investors are always likely having their equity interest in the company diluted by later investors. For example, if Angel group members invest $5,00,000 at a pre-money valuation of $1 million, and then a venture capital firm invests $5 million the following year at $5 million pre-money valuation, the original angel group investors will now own only half as much of the company, even though the company value has increased more than three-fold. As a result, because of the early stage, Angel group members generally receive 25-50% of the company's fully diluted equity in exchange for their investment.

Venture Capital Method of Valuation Facts and Assumptions

Table 6.13: Venture Capital Method of Valuation Facts and Assumptions

Owners originally issues (t = 0)	2,000	shares				
Net Income (year 5)	$8,000	estimate				
PE ratio (year 5)	15	from similar company				
Investment required t = 0	$5,000	estimate from company				
VC target rate of return	60%					
Cash Flow and Valuation						
	0	1	2	3	4	5
Investment	5,000					
Net Income	x	x	x	x	x	$8,000
Valuation t = 5						$1,20,000
Valuation t = 0 (discounted) = Post-money valuation	$11,444					
Pre-money valuation	$ 6,444					

VC ownership requirement	43.7%	
Number of shares (owner)	2,000	56.3%
Number of shares (VC)	1,552	43.7%
Total Shares	3,552	
Price per share	$3.22	per share

Table 6.14: Simplified Model - Just One Round of Financing

Owners originally issues (t = 0)	2,000	shares			
Net Income (year 5)	$8,000	estimate			
PE ratio (year 5)	15	from similar company			
Investment required t = 0	$5,000				
Investment required t = 2	$10,000				
VC(1) target rate of return	60%	annually			
VC(2) target rate of return	40%	annually			
Cash Flow and Valuation					
	0	1	2	3	4
Investment	5,000		10,000		
Net Income	x	x	x	x	x
Valuation t = 5					
2nd Round Investor					
Valuation t = 2			$43,732		
Pre-money valuation			$33,732		
Time 5 ownership to earn targeted return			22.9%		
1st Round Investor					
Valuation t = 0 (discounted) = Post-money valuation			$11,444		
Pre-money valuation	$6,444				
VC#1 ownership requirement (t = 5)	43.7%				
Retention Ratio (1 – previous round owners %)	77.1%				

VC#1 ownership requirement (t = 0)	56.6%				
Number of shares (owner)	2,000	33.4%			
Number of shares (VC#1)	2,613	43.7%			
Number of shares (VC#2)	1,368	22.9%			
Total Shares	5,980				
Price per share (t = 0) for VC#1	$ 1.91	per share			
Price per share (t = 2) for VC#2	$ 7.31				

Some of the common valuation models for determining a start-up's terminal value and associated valuation are planned in the Table 6.14 along with their strengths and weaknesses for valuing new venture firms:

Model	Strengths	Weaknesses
Comparables (a.k.a. Market Value Approach): Price Multiples Industry heuristics Merger and Acquisition comparables	Simple in application and comparables are typically market based and understood by most investors. All valuations include a comparable valuation in calculating a terminal value.	Information on comparable private firms may be difficult or impossible to find.
Net Present Value Method (NPV)	NPV is based on the firm's Weighted Average Cost of Capital.	If using the NPV method, entrepreneurs should create several scenarios (worst case, most likely, and best case) for arriving at a range of values.
Monte Carlo Simulation	Is used in combination with the other valuation techniques to simulate multiple probable values for a single variable.	Comparable company information is required to calculate Beta and target capital structure, which may not fit the strategy and risk profile of a start-up firm.
Adjusted Present Value Method (APV)	Similar to NPV, but allows for changing capital structure and useful in situations where the effective tax rate is changing.	The relationships between variables and shapes of probability distributions make Monte Carlo Simulation difficult to apply. Complicated to calculate with many of the same weaknesses of NPV.
Venture Capital Method (VCM)	The most popular method for valuing start-up firms. Simple to understand and implement.	VCM is generally calculated with a large discount rate that can undervalue a new venture opportunity significantly.

Options Analysis	A very powerful tool that overcomes many of the weaknesses of NPV and APV. This method allows stakeholders to determine an accurate valuation in situations.	Option Analysis relies on terminal values from other methods such as NPV or APV. Weaknesses of this method include the capability of putting real world decisions into mathematically solvable problems.

Summary

Venture Capital can be used as a financial tool for development. With the global economy in the recovery phase and India spending a lot on the infrastructure development, Venture Capital has a very bright future. According to the survey conducted by Deloitte, the VC fund managers are more likely to move from IT ventures to the ventures in the space of real estate and bio-technology. Given such vast potential not only in IT and software but also in the field of service industries, biotechnology, telecommunications, media and entertainment, medical and health care services and other technology based manufacturing and product development, Venture Capital Industry can play a catalytic role to put India on the world map as a success story.

CASE 1: VENTURE CAPITAL

Mr. Arun is a partner in a very successful Mumbai-based Venture Capital firm. He is planning to invest $10 million in a start-up technology venture firm and thinking to take decision what shares of the company he should demand for his investment. He projected that the company's net income in the year seven will be of $40 million. The few profitable technology companies are trading at an average price-earnings ratio of 30. The company currently has 10,00,000 shares outstanding. Arun believes that a target rate of return of 50% is required for taking risk of this venture. What is the discounted terminal value? What is the required per cent ownership? Find the price per new share? What is implied Pre-money valuation? What is post-money valuation?

Arun feels that he needs now as much as $24 million in total outside financing to launch his new product. If he required raising the full amount in this round, how much of his company would he have to give up? What price per share would the Venture Capitalists be willing to pay if her required rate of return was 50%?

Note: The case is fictitious and any resemblance to a person/company is merely coincidental.

CASE 2: TIME SOFTWARE MULTINATIONAL COMPANY: VENTURE FUNDING

Ms. Naina Tyagi has earned her Master's degree in Management from a leading business school in 2006. She was working in Times Software Multinational company for a period of five years. In addition to her main line of business she was having the habit of doing research in her own lab. She preferred a business based on her creative ideas. She was not genuinely interested in her profession because she does not aspire to do routine work. But however she gained five years experience which helped her valuable lessions on being a better entrepreneur. After some years she was motivated to set up Reveena software jointly with a team of young technocrats. The team has developed a voice recognition software package which is completely new in the market. The estimated project cost is ` 1 cr. The team is able to invest only a sum of ` 50 lakh as equity at a face value of ` 10 each. The balance is proposed to be financed through Venture Capital. The company offers two alternative investment packages to the VC firm.

(a) Straight equity investment

(b) Fully Convertible Debentures with a coupon of 20%. At the end of 4 years, the FCD would be converted into equity. The conversion would take place at a P/E ratio of 10 on the weighted average EPS of the preceding three years with weights of 1, 2 and 3 for the EPS of 2nd, 3rd and 4th year respectively.

The company plans to tap the capital market with an IPO at the beginning of 6th year. The IPO is expected to be priced at P/E multiple of 12 on the EPS of the 5th year. The VC firm intends to divest its holding at the time of the IPO. The company proposed to maintain a Dividend Payout Ratio of 10% for all 5 years.

The expected EBIT for the 5 years is:

Probability	0.2	0.5	0.3 (₹ in crore)
Year 1	0.4	0.8	1.0
Year 2	1.2	1.6	0.8
Year 3	1.0	1.2	1.6
Year 4	2.0	1.0	1.2
Year 5	1.4	1.8	2.4

Ignore Taxes.

You are required to

Choose the alternative investment to be made by VC firm if its required rate of return is 14%.

Note: The case is fictitious and any resemblance to a person/company is merely coincidental.

Review Questions

1. How does the VC industry work? What are the features of venture capital?
2. What do venture capitals look for?
3. How does the venture capital influence the economy?
4. What are the issues and challenges Venture Capital is facing today?
5. **Quiz:**
   (a) Venture Capital financing is highly _____ and chances of failure are ______
   (b) Venture Capital is a mode of providing _____ finance to rapidly-growing private companies.
   (c) Venture capitalists look for businesses that have the potential to grow quickly to – and _____ in a relatively short period of time
   (d) _____, _____, and ______ are 3 Non-financial Benefits of Venture Capital Financing?
   (e) The first private VC fund was sponsored by _____.
   (f) Venture capitalist rejects projects when entrepreneurs' unfamiliarity with products, processes, or markets. *(T/F)*
   (g) IFCI Venture is one of the largest and most successful private equity firms in India focusing mainly on private equity, buyouts, real estate and mezzanine financing with funds under management in excess of US$ 2 billion. *(T/F)*
   (h) Venture capitalist invests in media and entertainment industry. *(T/F)*
   (i) A study by the European Private Equity and Venture Capital Association (EVCA) found that VC-backed European companies generated significantly higher growth rates in sales, research spending, exports and job creation. *(T/F)*

CHAPTER 7

Private Equity

Introduction

The robust financial markets of India are now experiencing a strong growth, encouraged by domestic and international investments. At present, sophisticated investors are looking out for more localized investment and alliance opportunities. They believed that partnering with the right team can improve company's existence and competitive edge by providing insight into the local decision-making process, overcoming cultural barriers, interpreting laws and, most importantly, maintaining important relationships that will add value to a company's expansion strategy. Another benefit of partnering with locals is that they will know how to approach and communicate to promising entrepreneurs, who might be reluctant to bring in outside capital and foreign advice to grow their young company. Access to funding, resources, operational expertise, expansion, and the lure of riches encouraged companies opted to go private. Favourable changes in the foreign trade policy in emerging markets have contributed to the growth of private equity in India. PE firms bring lot more than just capital into a company. Private equity executives face increasing professional and personal liability for the performance of their funds and portfolio companies.

Origin

The origin of PE investing can be traced back to 1960s in the US. The concept is quite old and popular in Europe and Australia. However, the investment tool is relatively new in Asia and has started gaining momentum only during the recent years. Although India had paved the path for private equity investments in 1989-90, it was during the end of 1990s that India evinced interest from major global players. As major global players started betting on emerging economies like India after witnessing dwindling returns from the developed economies, private equity space in India underwent a major transformation since 2003.

What is Private Equity?

Typically, company is looking for large amounts of capital for fund expansion and growth. But the company is reluctant to take loan route for investment which involves high risk also does not ready to go public. The company is looking for alternative option called private equity for financing its business propositions. Private equity capital infused into a company without going through public for issue of shares/stocks or bonds. Private equity refers to the manner in which the funds have been raised, namely on the private markets, as opposed to the public markets.The money comes from individual high-net worth investors or venture capital funds. Typically private equity investments are made by organisations rather than by individuals. Private equity investor is looking for higher than market returns in quick time. Private equity investors reap huge rewards when their portfolio companies are large enough and successful enough to go public in an initial public offering (IPO).Typical forms of private equity include venture capital, growth and mezzanine capital, Angel investing, and private equity funds. Private equity investors 'goal is to boost the value of the company, sell-off their investment and walk away with substantially more money than what they invest. They also take substantial interest in a company to gain control over the company's management.

Private equity falls into two broad groups: venture capital and other private equity. Private equity investing is often divided into the categories described in Fig. 7.1. Private equity is the universe of all venture and buyout investing, whether such investments are made through funds, fund of funds or secondary investments.

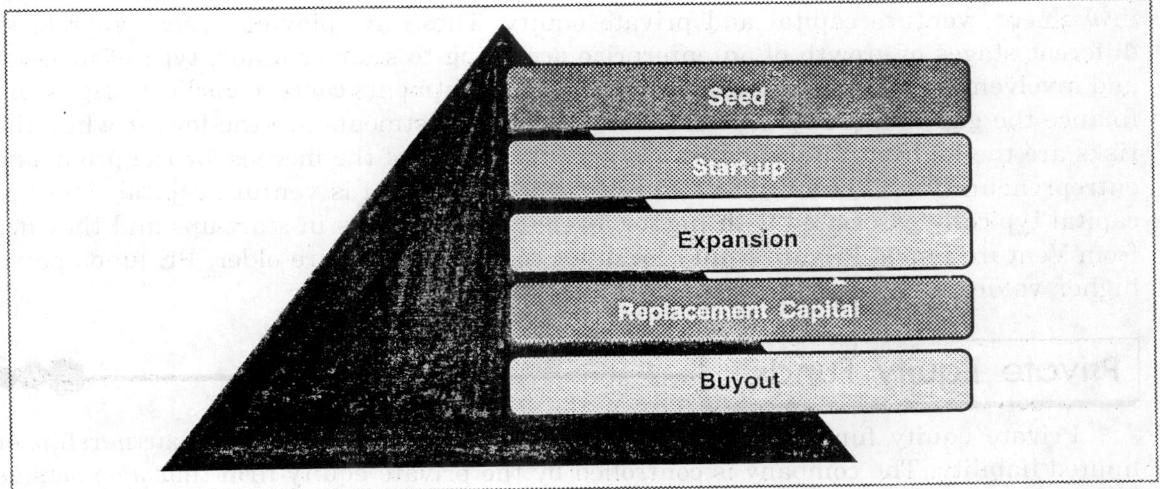

Figure 7.1: Maturity of the Company

Why Private Equity Matters?

Private equity investors are normally very wealthy individuals or institutions having significant experience on corporate strategy and governance. If private equities are funding a company, they have a significant impact on the company for better running to compete in the current business environment. They also play a significant role in company's board of directors. On a day-to-day basis, company likely to see higher expectations for sales targets and new business goals. If senior management of the company can't meet those objectives, there is every possibility for companies to see new faces in the office soon. Among larger companies, private investment is responsible for an increasing chunk of mergers and acquisitions which is a extremely disruptive to employees. Private equity firms specialize in increasing the value of their holdings by strengthening leadership, refocusing strategy, reducing cost structures, instituting growth initiatives, or even breaking up the company to sell it in parts. When it works as intended, the result is more efficient use of capital, which in turn fuels the economy and drives innovation. Private equity is gaining popularity because it provides a way for investors to have tight control over a company's strategy, management, and financial decisions without the quarterly scrutiny, public disclosure requirements, and regulatory oversight faced by publicly traded firms. It is also argued that private equity investors seek to boost the value of a company as quickly as possible, with least attention for intangible factors such as company history, culture, or workplace environment. So private equity is great for investors, it may not be so much fun for the companies they invest in or the people who work for them.

What is Angel, Venture Capital or PE?

Private equity investment of a company can come from three routes, Angel investment, venture capital and private equity. These are playing their own role in different stages of growth of an enterprise according to scale of funds, type of investor and involvement and role of the investor. Angel investments come in earliest stages and finance the gap in start-up capital. Normally the investments are the lowest while the risks are the highest. The angel investor plays the role of the mentor for the promising entrepreneur. The next stage in third party equity capital is venture capital. Venture capital typically associated with higher levels of investments in start-ups and they are from Venture funds. Private equity looks for companies that are older. PE funds pay a higher value for a minority share in the company

Private Equity Funds

Private equity funds are generally organized as either a limited partnership or limited liability. The company is controlled by the private equity firm that also acts as the general partner. The fund obtains capital commitments from certain qualified investors such as pension funds, financial institutions and wealthy individuals to invest a specified amount. As an asset class, private equity investments are very illiquid and investment commitments are having typical durations of 7 to 10 years. Private equity is generally part of an LP's overall investment strategy that may include real estate, bonds, and publicly traded company stock.

The goal of every private equity firm is to generate a higher-than-market rate of return for its investors. The private equity industry generates returns by investing in the stock of private companies. Subsequently it generates a capital gain on that stock when the company is sold or becomes publicly traded. A private equity firm typically has one or more funds that it manages. Each fund is having a stated investment strategy that describes aspects of investments it prefers. These preferences may include Industries, Geography; Stage of deals, e.g., pre-revenue or post-revenue, growing or mature, Size of total investment, each fund has a General Partner (GP). The general partner is responsible for: Selecting the best investments or portfolio companies for a fund, working with the management of these portfolio companies to increase the value of the initial investment, developing a strategy for the fund to exit the investment within a given time-frame.

Private equity firms generally receive a return on their investment through one of three ways: an IPO, a sale or merger of the company they control, or a recapitalization. Unlisted securities may be sold directly to investors by the company (called a private offering) or to a private equity fund, which pools contributions from smaller investors to create a capital pool. Private equity funds are generally less regulated than ordinary mutual funds. The majority of investment into private equity funds comes from institutional investors. According to data of London-based Private Equity Intelligent Ltd., the most prolific investors into private equity funds in 2006 were public pension funds and banks and financial institutions combined contributed 40% of all commitments made globally.

Another large investor group in private equity funds is so-called fund of funds, which are private equity funds that invest in other private equity funds in order to provide investors with a lower risk product through exposure to a large number of vehicles often of different type and regional focus. Fund of funds accounted for 14% of global commitments made to private equity funds in 2006 according to Private Equity Intelligence Ltd.

Principal means of private equity investment are: Investing in private equity funds, outsourcing selection of private equity funds, and direct investment in private companies.

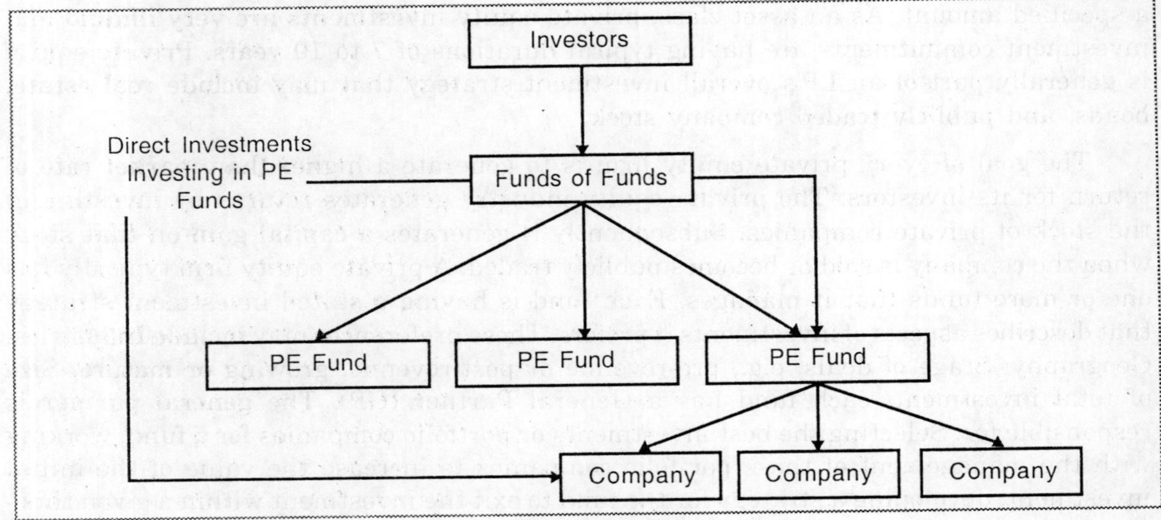

Figure 7.2

The Fig. 7.2 describes that investors can make direct investments into companies, compared with investing through funds. It requires more capital, a different skill set, more resource and different evaluation techniques. While co-investing the rewards can be high but there is higher risk involved and the chance of potential for complete loss of invested capital. This strategy is recommended only to experienced private equity investors.

Is Private Equity a Sensible Investment for the Average Investor?

Private equity is a favoured asset class for professional managers because it has historically produced superior returns. Annual returns over the past twenty years have averaged 13.7%, beating stocks, bonds, real estate, and most other forms of investment. Its risk is a spreading investment over long time periods, in multiple industry sectors, and in a large number of investments. Professional money managers know how to do so, that is why private equity has a prominent place in large investment portfolios, even in conservative ones like those of pension funds.

How Private Equity Groups Work?

In many ways, private equity groups operate just like house buyers. They are looking for bargains. They usually stump up a bit of money, a deposit; upfront, and then rely on the bank to lend them the rest. They are looking for a quick, profitable sale, usually within three to seven years. And they do things in relative privacy, often de-listing their acquisitions if they were quoted on any stock market. This means they can make tough or controversial decisions without having considered the shareholders without releasing sensitive information. Hence, they are accountable only to small groups of private investors and lenders, rather than to stock market investors and company employees. They do not even to release information to journalists making enquiries into their affairs.

What the Private Equity Investors can and cannot do for your Company?

Private equity funds can buy 100 per cent of the outstanding shares of business and founding shareholders can be retained in the business to manage or buyout by established a senior management team and board of directors to run the business. Private equity funds are having hard cash on hand to buy companies and creating less uncertainty for business owners. Typically, private equity funds are more attracted to cashing out a founder if a controlling stake is available. Sometimes, owners sell because of illness, retirement, monotony or unsolvable squabbles with investors. If business and personal asset is pledged as collateral at bank, jeopardizing the company's growth prospects and failure to compete in new environment, Private equity funds are extending their hand for acquisition and help prosperous business owners in new product-line development and geographic expansion. Private equity investors are financial investors. They are sensitive to a founder's wishes, but not sentimental in negotiating final deal terms.

In the 1960s and 1970s, partnership agreements contained few such restrictions but however during 1980 institutional investors holding a portfolio of private equity funds and demanded contractual provisions that would limit general partners' ability to deviate from their area of expertise. The first restrictions is relates to the size of investment in any one company. The general partners are not supposed to investment significant resources in a poorly performing company. This behaviour will typically do not receive a share of profits until the limited partners have received their original investment back. Consequently, the general partners' share of profits can be thought of as a call option, and its value may increase disproportionately from increasing risk of the portfolio at the expense of diversification. The second restriction is limits the use of debt particularly on venture capital funds. As option holders, the general partners may be tempted to increase the variance of their portfolio's returns by leveraging the fund. Partnership agreements may restrict debt to a set percentage of committed capital or assets, and in some instances also restrict the maturity of the debt, to insure that all borrowing is short-term. The third restriction is co-investments with the existing funds of private equity organization. Many private equity organizations manage multiple funds, which can lead to opportunistic behaviour. A fourth class of covenant relates to reinvestment of profits. Private equity investors may have several reasons to reinvest funds, rather than distribute profits to the limited partners. First, many partnerships receive fees on the basis of either the value of assets under management or adjusted committed capital. Distributing profits will reduce these fees. Second, reinvested capital gains may yield further profits for the general partners. The reinvestment of profits may require approval of the advisory board or the limited partners. Alternatively, such reinvestment may be prohibited after a certain date, or after a certain per cent of the committed capital is invested. Another restriction on the general partners is future fund raising. The raising of an additional fund will raise the management fees that the general partners receive, and may reduce the attention that they pay to existing funds. Partnership agreements may prohibit fund raising by the general partners until a set percentage of the portfolio has been invested or until a given date. Some partnership agreements restrict other actions by general partners as outside activities are likely to reduce the attention paid to investments. Private equity investors are restricted to spending "substantially all" of their time managing the partnership's investments. Alternatively, the general partners' ability to be involved in businesses other than the companies in which the private equity fund has invested is restricted. These limitations are often confined to the first years of the partnership.

Comparison of Private Equity with Alternate Source of Financing

A provider of debt is rewarded by interest and capital repayment of the loan and it is usually secured either on business assets or own personal assets. As a last resort, if the company defaults on its repayments, the lender can put his business into receivership, which may lead to the liquidation of any assets. Debt which is secured in this way and which has a higher priority for repayment than that of general unsecured creditors is referred to as "senior debt". By contrast, private equity is not secured on any assets although part of the non-equity funding package provided by the private equity firm may seek some security. The private equity firm, therefore, often faces the risk of failure just like the other shareholders. The private equity firm is an equity business partner and is rewarded by the company's success, generally achieving its principle return through realizing a capital gain through an "exit" which may include:

- Selling their shares back to the management
- Selling the shares to another investor (such as another private equity firm)
- A trade sale (the sale of company shares to another)
- The company achieving a stock market listing

Although private equity is generally provided as part of a financing package, to simplify comparison we compare private equity with senior debt.

Private Equity Compared to Senior Debt

Private equity	Senior debt
Medium to long-term.	Short to long-term.
Committed until "exit".	Not likely to be committed if the safety of the loan is threatened. Overdrafts are payable on demand; loan facilities can be payable on demand if the covenants are not met.
Provides a solid, flexible, capital base to meet your future growth and development plans.	A useful source of finance if the debt to equity ratio is conservatively balanced and the company has good cash flow.
Good for cash flow, as capital repayment, dividend and interest costs (if relevant) are tailored to the company's needs and to what it can afford.	Requires regular good cash flow to service interest and capital repayments.

The returns to the private equity investor depend on the business growth and success. The more successful the company is, the better the returns all investors will receive.	Depends on the company continuing to service its interest costs and to maintain the value of the assets on which the debt is secured.
If the business fails, private equity investors will rank alongside other shareholders, after the banks and other lenders, and stand to lose their investment.	If the business fails, the lender generally has first call on the company's assets.
If the business runs into difficulties, the private equity firm will work hard to ensure that the company is turned around.	If the business appears likely to fail, the lender could put your business into receivership in order to safeguard its loan, and could make you personally bankrupt if personal guarantees have been given.
A true business partner, sharing in your risks and rewards, with practical advice and expertise (as required) to assist your business success.	Assistance available varies considerably.

What are Investment Features of Private Equity?

Most private equity funds requiring substantial entry requirements. Legal form of private equity investment is referred to as illiquid investments since investors' capital is locked-up for long-term investments but however earns a premium over traditional securities such as stocks and bonds. Limited partners typically have no right to demand for sales to be made. All investors in private equity are passive and trust on the manager to make investments and generate liquidity from those investments. An investor can lose all of its investment since private equity investments associated with risks. If private equity managers significantly outperforming the public markets, private equity can provide high returns.

PE Industry Overview in India

The industry wise split-up of total investments for the ten industry classes over the five-year period are given in Fig. 7.3. Figures in the brackets indicate the investments in a given industry as a percentage of total investments in that particular year. In 2004, a majority of PE-VC investments were in the IT& ITes sector accounting 43% of the total investments. However, this picture has dramatically changed and during the years 2004-2008, there was robust growth in PE investments in technology-led, capital intensive sectors like Telecom, Energy, Transportation and Infrastructure in addition to the initial drivers like IT& ITes, BPO, Health care and Biotechnology. The industry-wise share of total PE investments in India over the five-year period is given in Fig. 7.5. India had seen tremendous growth in overall Private Equity funding. In 2004, the total value of PE deals was $1.8 billion which grew tremendously to $22 billion in 2007 and then falling down to $8.1 billion in 2008.

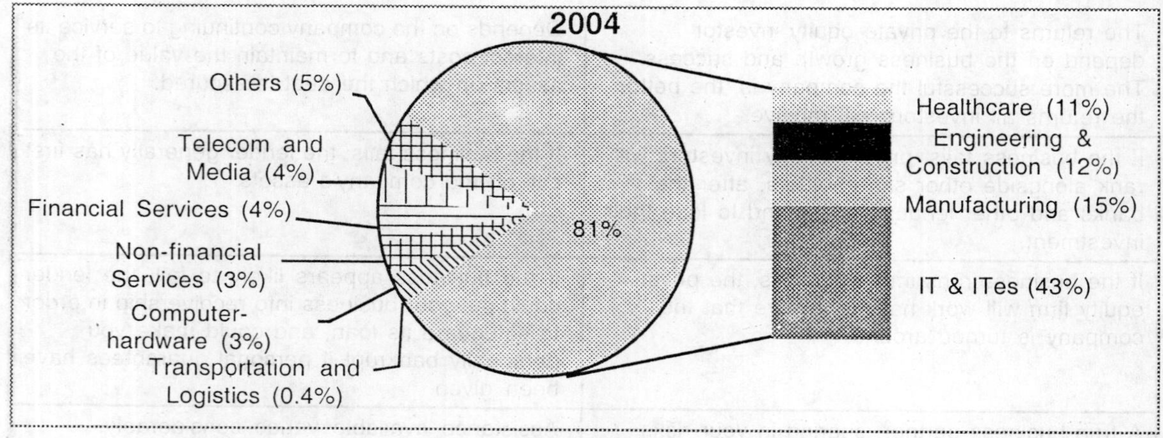

Figure 7.3

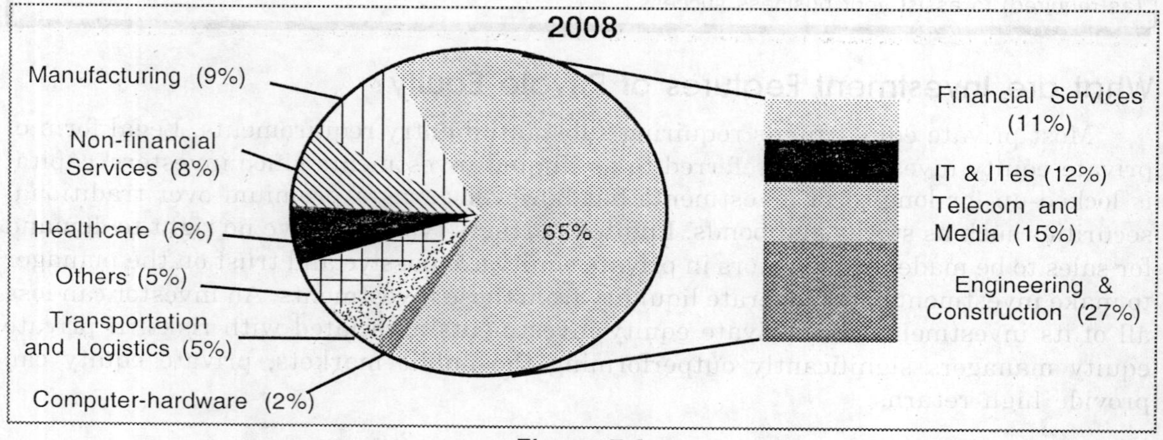

Figure 7.4

Industry-wise Private Equity Investment breakup by amounts (2004-2008)

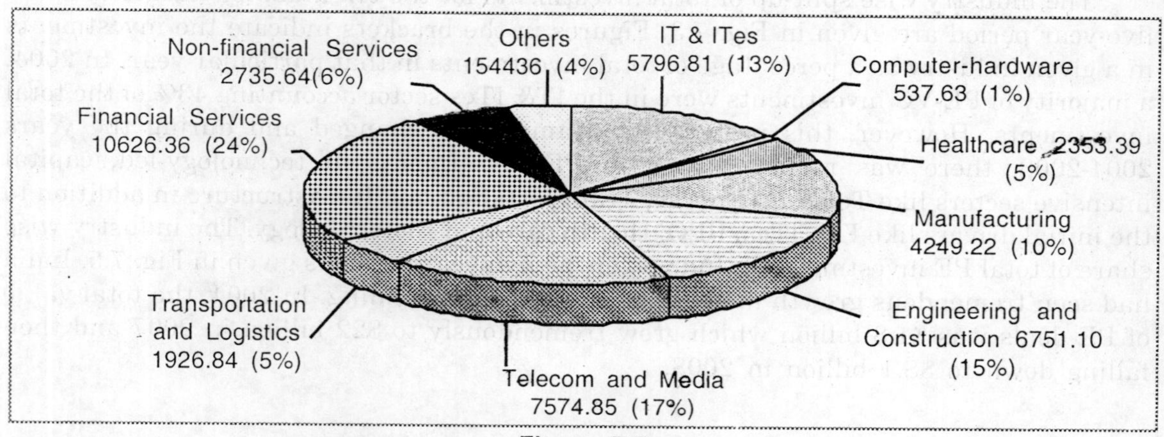

Figure 7.5

Financial Services Sector constitutes (24%) the biggest share of Investment, followed by Telecom and Media (17%), Engineering and Construction (15%) and IT& ITes (13%).

Financing Stage

The financing stage wise split-up of total investments for six different stages over the five-year period are given in Fig. 7.6. It is seen from the Fig. 7.7 that late stage investments and Private investments in Public Equity (PIPE) deals constitute a majority of the investments and consistently account for more than 50% of total amount invested in each of the five years.

Another distinguishing feature about late stage deals is that they are least affected in terms of both value and volume during the slow-down period. The amount invested in late stage deals fell only by 7% as compared to dip of 63% in total investments in 2008 over previous year 2007. In fact late stage investments are most preferred in the period of economic downturn as it is evident from the fact that more than 62% investments in 2008 are late stage investments. On the contrary, early stage investments suffered the most during the economic crisis with steep decline of 91% in the amount invested in 2008 over 2007.

Though it is quite obvious for investors to become risk-averse and hence sceptical about new ventures in period of economic slow-down, the steep decline is definitely a cause of worry. Another critical factor concerning early stage investments is that the Y-o-Y growth in number of deals is very slow as compared to Y-o-Y growth in amount invested even during good times. So it is suggesting that very few new ventures are receiving funding although average amount of funding received by a new venture has gone up. The category which is attracting substantial investment apart from late stage is PIPE. This is one of the most favoured routes by foreign investors for entering Indian PE market as it allows them to tap the growth potential of already well-established public-listed enterprises with minimum risk.

The other two stages, i.e., Pre-IPO and buyout have attracted lowest investments in Indian markets so far. Pre-IPO stage funding witnessed a spurt especially in 2006 and 2007 when Indian IPO market was at its peak generating very attractive returns. During that time there was considerable increase in PE-backed IPO exits happening. Buyouts are one of the most favoured PE investments in developed markets but they are comparatively exceptional in India (accounting for only 9% of total funds invested and 3% of total number of deals) and this trend has been consistent over the five-year period. This may be due to the fact that PE investors play an active role in the market for corporate control in developed economies like the US. But due to regulatory and other constraints such opportunities are unusual in India.

The financing stage-wise share of total PE-VC investments in India over the five-year period is given in Fig. 7.6.

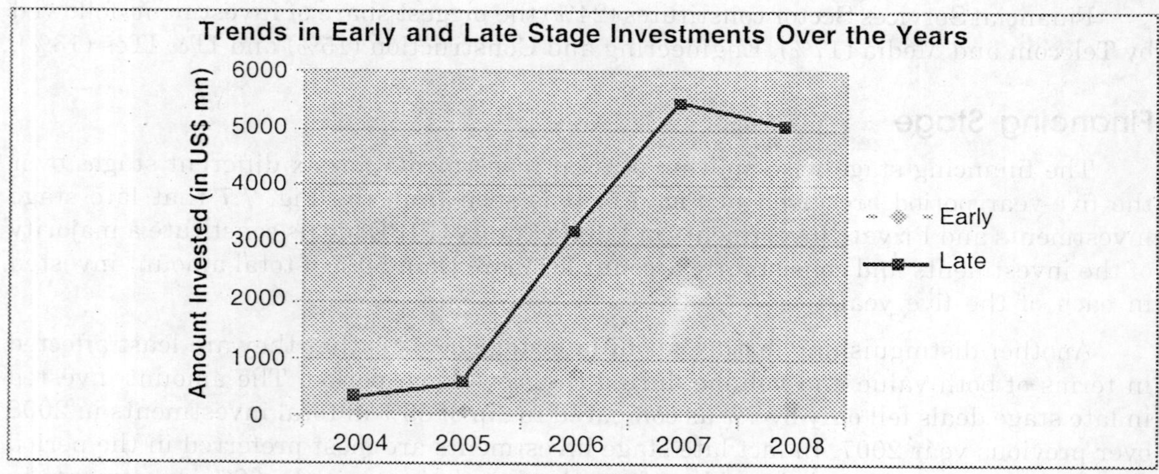

Figure 7.6

Source: India Venture Capital and Private Equity Report 2009

Stage-wise Private Equity Investment between 2004 to 2008

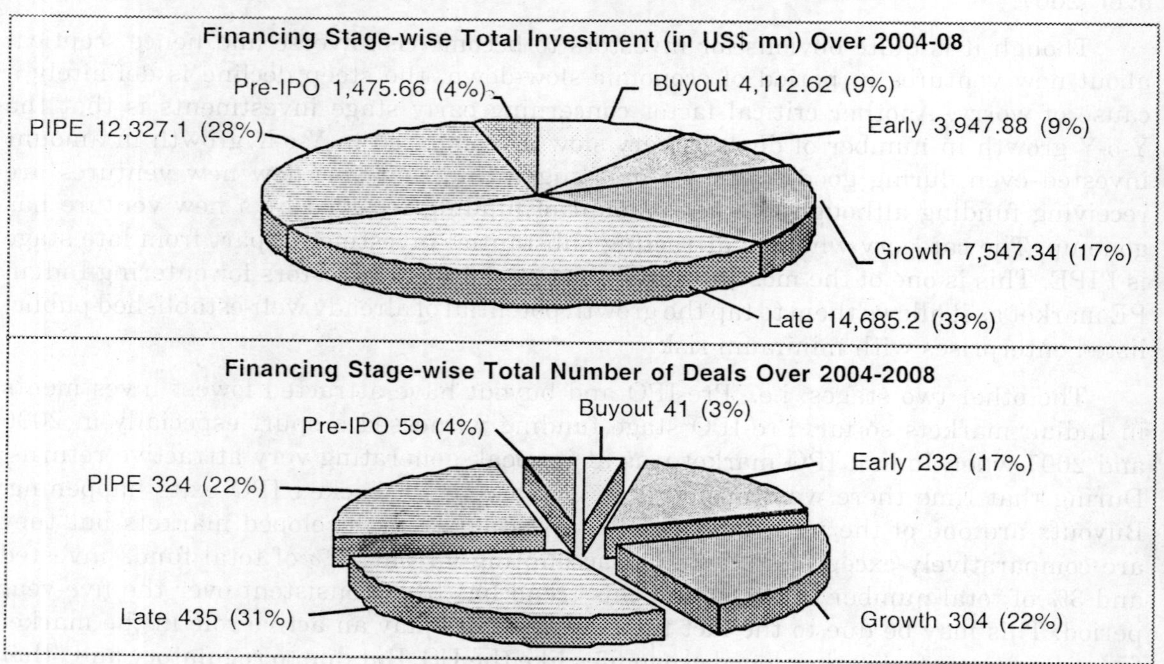

Figure 7.7

Source: India Venture Capital and Private Equity Report 2009

If total investments over the five-year period are considered, it was found from Fig. 7.7 that late stage investments constitute one-third of the total investments closely followed by PIPE deals, which account for 28% investment of the total investment. The number of deals also follow similar pattern of proportion across the different stages except for early stage investments where share by value (amount invested) is only 9%

(US$ 3.94 billion) as against share by volume (number of deals) of 17% (232 deals). This is more surprising given the fact that number of early-stage deals was growing at very slow clip as pointed out earlier. As far as average amount per deal is concerned, it is fairly constant across the stages (varying between US$ 20 million to 35 million) except for buyout deals, where the average deal size is much higher in the range of US$ 100 million and above.

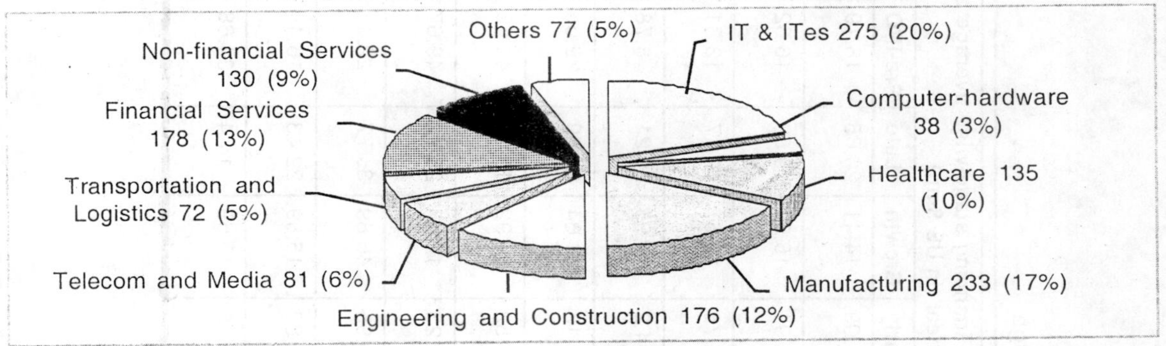

Figure 7.8

Source: Venture Intelligence India

Industry-wise Private Equity Investment break-up by Deal Numbers (2004-2008)

It is evident from Fig. 7.8 that IT & ITes sector lead in the total PE investment amount accounting (20%) generated maximum number of deals followed by manufacturing (17%) and financial services (13%).

Industry vs. Financing Stage

It is exhibited in the previous analysis that late and PIPE stages have biggest share in investment pie and this trend is clearly visible across almost all the industry classes in terms of amount invested as well as number of deals except IT & ITes and Computer-Hardware industries. Another interesting observation about IT&ITes industry is that while buyout stage deals forms a major chunk of investments by value (42.6%), early stage deals grab the highest share by volume (43.6%) of total investment in the industry over the period, thus defying the trends observed across most of the other industries, both in terms of value and volume investments.

In early stage investments, financial services has attracted considerably higher seed/early stage funding as compared to other industries most probably owing to emergence and growth of numerous new firms in BFSI sector during the strong economic growth period of 2005-2007.

Region-wise Distribution of PE Investment

There appears a characteristic trend in PE-VC investments when the deals are classified by the region of incorporation of investee firm. While the West has attracted the highest investment by value, the South has the most number of deals (largest share by volume) during the five-year period ending 2008. Tables below presents the region-wise split-up for 1033 PE-VC investment deals for which region-specific data was available.

Table 7.1: Industry vs. Financing Stage

Industry	Financing stage-wise number of deals (% of Total number of deals in the industry)						Financing stage-wise average amount per deal (in US $mn)					
	Early	Growth	Late	Pre-IPO	PIPE	Buyout	Early	Growth	Late	Pre-IPO	PIPE	Buyout
IT & ITes	120 (43.64%)	68 (24.73%)	40 (14.55%)	4 (1.45%)	36 (13.09%)	7 (2.55%)	5.09	14.41	26.65	18.19	16.53	353.29
Computer-hardware	12 (31.58%)	15 (39.47%)	6 (15.79%)	2 (5.26%)	2 (5.26%)	1 (2.63%)	4.91	15.97	19.58	16.62	31.7	25
Healthcare	21 (15.56%)	27 (20%)	51 (37.78%)	4 (2.96%)	31 (22.96%)	1 (0.74%)	5.78	15.67	21.7	13.81	19.81	33
Manufacturing	7 (3%)	31 (13.3%)	83 (35.62%)	6 (2.58%)	99 (42.49%)	7 (3%)	4.2	11.95	20.21	8.78	19.24	30.65
Engineering and Construction	16 (9.09%)	31 (17.61%)	78 (44.32%)	14 (7.95%)	32 (18.18%)	5 (2.84%)	44.13	51.64	34.69	29.06	37.93	23.45
Telecom and Media	8 (9.88%)	21 (25.93%)	37 (45.68%)	3 (3.7%)	10 (12.35%)	2 (2.47%)	10.52	29.92	119.04	44.63	220.84	57.77
Transportation and Logistics	8 (11.11%)	12 (16.67%)	31 (43.06%)	3 (4.17%)	14 (19.44%)	4 (5.56%)	23	12.67	25.72	49.67	31.21	51.84
Financial services	17 (9.55%)	51 (28.65%)	43 (24.16%)	8 (4.49%)	55 (30.9%)	4 (2.25%)	106.95	46.89	35.77	22.43	79.08	87.44
Non-financial Services	22 (16.92%)	41 (31.54%)	40 (30.77%)	7 (5.38%)	13 (10%)	7 (5.38%)	14.89	15.89	22.43	16.44	31.34	48.1
Others	1 (1.3%)	7 (9.09%)	26 (33.77%)	8 (10.39%)	32 (41.56%)	3 (3.9%)	7.8	15.69	14.4	34.68	16.7	80.17

Source: Venture Intelligence India

Table 7.2: Region-wise Distribution of PE Investments in India (Number of Deals)

Region	2004		2005		2006		2007		2008		Total	
East	2	2.90%	6	4.17%	8	3.29%	17	5.76%	8	2.84%	41	3.97%
North	18	26.09%	26	18.06%	45	18.52%	57	19.32%	61	21.63%	207	20.04%
South	32	46.38%	54	37.50%	98	40.33%	113	38.31%	114	40.43%	411	39.79%
West	17	24.64%	58	40.28%	92	37.86%	108	36.61%	99	35.11%	374	36.21%
Total	**69**	**100%**	**144**	**100%**	**243**	**100%**	**295**	**100%**	**282**	**100%**	**1033**	**100%**

Table 7.3: Amount Invested (in $mn)

Region	2004		2005		2006		2007		2008		Total	
East	20.9	1.95%	71.8	3.64%	76.09	1.29%	393.9	4.08%	83.7	1.07%	646.39	2.45%
North	494.4	46.22%	357.4	18.11%	1674.95	28.35%	2346.75	24.31%	2371.3	30.29%	7244.8	27.41%
South	348.89	32.62%	578.82	29.33%	1222.71	20.70%	3074.21	31.84%	2710.2	34.62%	7934.83	30.02%
West	205.46	19.21%	965.32	48.92%	2934	49.66%	3839.62	39.77%	2663.06	34.02%	10607.46	40.13%
Total	**1069.65**	**100%**	**1973.34**	**100%**	**5907.75**	**100%**	**9654.48**	**100%**	**7828.26**	**100%**	**26433.48**	**100%**

Table 7.3 shows that overall distribution of investments across different regions is quite skewed with very low PE-VC investments in East as compared to other three regions. But this may be more due to low levels of industrial activity in the region as a whole *vis-à-vis* the rest of India. More importantly, PE-VC funding has shown almost constant distribution pattern across the regions over the five years.

Another notable aspect of region-wise distribution of PE investments in India is that there is considerably higher preference for few industries over the other in a given region. For e.g., while Financial Services and Telecom are prime drivers in West, Engineering and Construction and IT&ITes are most sought-after industries in North. Similarly, manufacturing and non-financial services have attracted relatively more investments in East. The investments are more evenly distributed across the industries in South region where 4 to 5 industry classes including Health care and IT & ITes account for a major share of the total investments in the region. As far as stage-wise investments across the regions are concerned, there was no discernible trend towards any particular stage in any given region.

Comparison with Leading PE Markets

The industry-wise investment for all the industry classes as a percentage of total investment for India, US, UK and Europe over the five-year period are consolidated in Table 7.4. The investment appears relatively more uniformly spread across different industries for India and Europe as a whole (which includes 20 European countries along with UK). However, the investments are skewed in favour of certain industries in US and UK with only 3 industry classes accounting for more than 70% investments as reflected. While financial services has highest share (24.1%) of PE-VC investments in India as mentioned earlier, it is health care (29.4%) in US, non-financial services (43.7%) in UK and manufacturing (29%) in Europe which have attracted the highest investments.

Table 7.4: Industry-wise Investment in Different Countries

Industry	India	US	UK#	Europe#
IT & ITes	13.15%	24.62%	3.96%	NA*
Computers-hardware	1.22%	16.30%	2.01%	6.88%
Healthcare	5.34%	29.44%	9.01%	10.36%
Manufacturing	9.64%	3.48%	4.91%	29.03%
Engineering and Construction	15.31%	8.79%	24.06%	6.43%
Telecom and Media	17.18%	14.04%	0.89%	12.97%
Transportation and Logistics	4.37%	0.97%	NA*	3.82%
Financial Services	24.10%	2.28%	10.97%	4.09%
Non-financial Services	6.20%	NA*	43.79%	19.30%
Others	3.50%	0.07%	0.40%	7.11%

Table 7.5: Financing Stage in Different Countries

Financing Stage	India	Asia	North America	Europe
Early	12.50%	8.00%	6.00%	3.00%
Expansion (Growth + Late)	45.30%	20.00%	11.00%	13.00%
Others (PIPE + Pre-IPO)	37.20%	24.00%	12.00%	5.00%
Buyout	5.00%	48.00%	71.00%	79.00%

Y-o-Y Growth Rate

India has experienced consistent positive growth in PE-VC investments for all the sectors except IT & ITes, Computer-hardware and Health care for each of the years during 2004-2007 over the previous year shown in Table 7.6. On the other hand, the US has consistent positive growth only for Engineering and Construction industry. Table below compares the Y-o-Y growth rates for industry-wise investments in India and US over the five-year period.

Table 7.6: Industry-wise Y-o-Y Growth Rate in PE Investment

	2004-05		2005-06		2006-07		2007-08	
Industry	India	US	India	US	India	US	India	US
IT & ITes	–65%	–4%	827%	7%	–41%	12%	–34%	–5%
Computers-hardware	–17%	–6%	69%	1%	269%	4%	–47%	–29%
Healthcare	70%	0%	77%	20%	27%	21%	–35%	–14%
Manufacturing	46%	6%	203%	25%	41%	23%	–55%	–24%
Engineering and Const	-34%	10%	752%	128%	142%	69%	–24%	43%
Telecomand media	38%	21%	1484%	22%	214%	–1%	–74%	–15%
Transportation and Logistics	1496%	31%	606%	–13%	80%	81%	–57%	–32%
Financial Services	316%	75%	482%	–49%	365%	21%	–88%	–6%
Non-financial services	353%	NA*	136%	NA*	96%	NA*	–48%	NA*
Total	**20%**	**3%**	**379%**	**14%**	**118%**	**16%**	**–63%**	**–8%**

While Indian PE-VC investments has grown at a astonishingly high rates of 378% and 118% in 2006 and 2007 over the previous years, the deceleration in investments by 63% in 2008 after the global economic crisis has been equally severe with all the sectors showing a negative investment growth of more than 30% over the previous year.

Top PE Deals

The top PE deals accounted for more than 25% of the total PE deal value in 2009 as against 21% in 2008. This year saw top investments in varied sectors such as Media, Power and Shipping. In 2008, 3 of the top 6 deals were in the Real Estate sector. Fire Capital's investment in Fire Arcor Infrastructure for a 75% stake valued at US $250 million was the largest PE deal in 2009. This was followed by 3i's investment in Krishnapatnam Port and Oman Sovereign Fund's investment in Mohtisham.

Acquire	Target	Sector	% State	US $ mn
Blackstone	Moser Baer Projects Pvt. Ltd.	Power and Energy	N.A.	300.0
Quadrangle Cpital Partners LLC and a consortium of international investors	Tower Vision India Pvt. Ltd.	Telecom	N.A.	300.0
3i India Infrastructure Fund	GVK Energy Limited	Power and Energy	21%	255.3
Temasek Holdings	GMR Energy Ltd.	Power and Energy	N.A.	200.0
Kolberg Kravis Roberts and Co.	Dalmia Cement (Bharat) Ltd.	Cement	N.A.	159.6
Unnamed Investors	Tikona Digital Networks	Telecom	N.A.	148.9
Eton Park Cpital	JSW Infrastructure	Shipping and Ports	10%	125.0
TPG Growth and Others	Greenko Group Plc.	Power and Energy	N.A.	116.0

Figure 7.9: Top PE Deals

TPG Growth and Others Greenko Group plc. Power and Energy N.A. 116.0

PE Top Sector Insights

The real estate sector has been the private equity investor's favoured sector for the last 3 years. 2009 was no different with medium to large size deals in the infrastructure and real estate development sectors. The power and energy sector also seems to be a popular destination in recent times, garnering deal values of US $413 million in 2009. It is interesting to note that there were 6 deals in towards clean technology valued at close to US $100 million in 2009. Microfinance has found its way to the portfolios of most large PE players in the recent past. In 2009, there were 15 investments by PE players into companies involved in microfinance valued at US $90 million found its way to the portfolios of most large PE players in the recent past. In 2009, there were 15 investments by PE players into companies involved in microfinance valued at US $90 million.

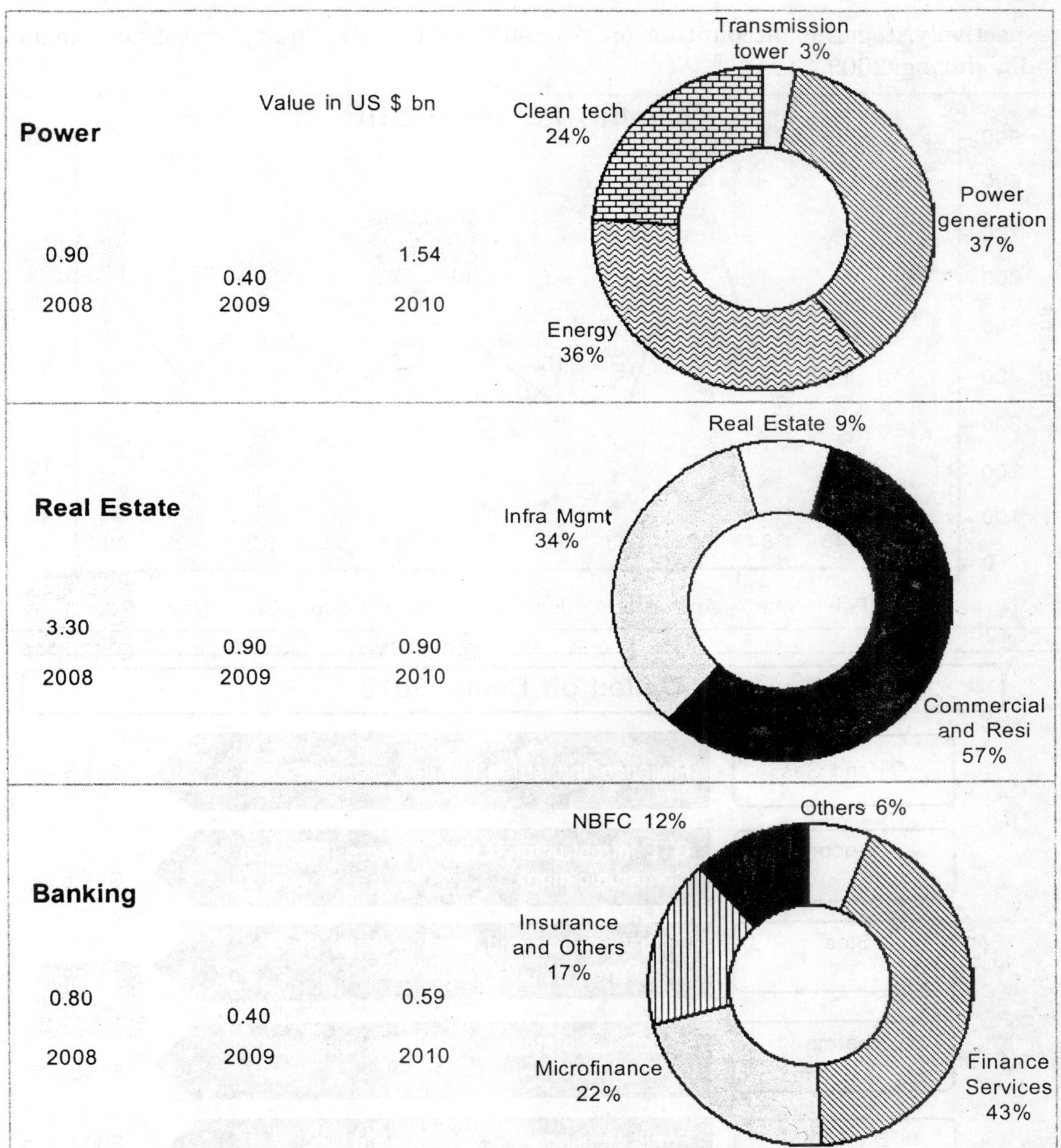

Figure 7.10: PE Sector Trends

Source: IVCA

Private Equity Investments increased from US $3.45 billion in 2009 to US $6.23 billion in 2010 registering a growth of 81%. The highest proportion of PE investment was made in the Power and Energy and Real Estate and Infrastructure Management sectors which garnered investments worth US $1.5 billion and US $945 million respectively, together accounting for over 40% of Private Equity investment made in India during 2009.

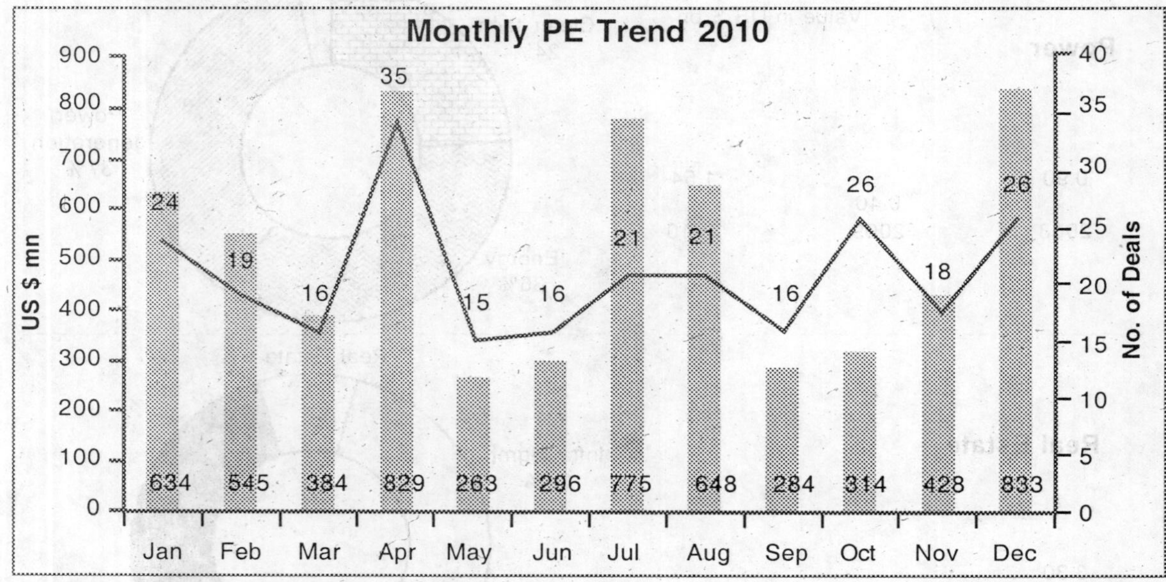

Called off Deals: 2010

Sector	Deal	Value
Oil and Gas	Reliance Industries Ltd. – LoyondellBasell	$14.5 bn
Telecom	GTL Infrastructure Ltd. – Towers (Reliance Communication)	$11 bn
Steel	Zimbabwe Iron and Steel – Jindal Steel and Power	$1 bn
Pharma	Abbott Laboratories – Nutrition Business of Wockhardt	$130 mn
Banking	Fortis Healthcare – GIC Special Investments	$80.5 mn
Media	Scripts Networks Interactive Inc – NDTV Lifestyle	$55 mn
Media	PVR – DT Cinemas	$10.6 mn

Source: IVCA

Sector wise PE Investment

According to study by Venture Intelligence, Private Equity firms invested about US $2,000 million in India across 56 deals during the quarter ended March 2010, which is highest in last 6 quarters. The figure for corresponding quarter last year was only $620 million. It is also noticed from Fig. 7.11 that IT & ITes accounted for 23% of all deals led by Actis' $50 million investment into BPO Company Integreon Managed Solutions. The IT&ITes industry registered 13 deals worth $193 million during Q1'10. BSFI sector garnered 16% of all PE investments with 9 deals worth $94 million. Energy (13%), Health care and Life sciences (9%) and Manufacturing (9%) rounded up the top 5 sectors which saw PE investments. The largest investment reported during the year was the $425m raised by power generation firm Asian Genco from investors including General Atlantic, Goldman Sachs, Morgan Stanley, Everstone and Norwest with 34 investments worth $2.14bn, energy companies came top in terms of investment value during 2010, while Information Technology with 79 investments worth $696m were first in terms of volume. Further it is noticed that Quadrangle Capital Partners' $300 million investment into telecom tower infrastructure company Tower Vision India. Also StanChart PE, KKR and New Silk Route's $217 million invested in Coffee Day Resorts. TPG Growth's $115 million invested into Clean Tech firm Greenko Group.

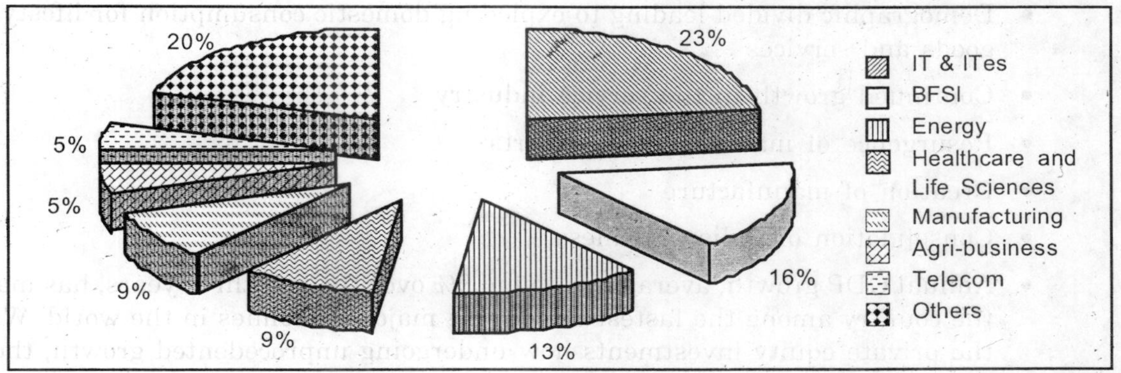

Figure 7.11

Source: Venture Intelligence

Venture Capital and Late Stage investments accounted for 16 and 18 deals respectively during first Quarter of 2010. The largest PE-backed IPO during Q1'10 was toll road operator IL & FS Transportation Networks' (ITNL) $155 million March IPO. Trinity Capital, which had invested $9.3 million in December 2006, sold its entire holding as part of the offering. The total value of transactions providing exits to PE-investors during Q1'10 was around $858 million. These included 13 sales via public markets, 7 strategic sales, 1 secondary sale and 5 buybacks by either the company or its promoters. According to the Emerging Markets Private Equity Association (EMPEA) emerging markets have seen a 30 per cent increase in capital invested in 2010.

Private equity firms invested $7.97bn in India over 325 deals during 2010, almost double the previous year's figure, according to research by Venture Intelligence. The International Finance Corporation – the World Bank's private investment arm – continued to remain the most active PE investor in India during 2010 with 25 investments. Sequoia Capital India, with 15 investments, was the second most active. Private equity firms obtained exit routes for their investments in a record 121 companies during 2010, including 24 via IPOs. PE-backed IPOs raised about $2.20bn, with the $359m raised by SKS Microfinance ranking as the largest.

Growth Drivers of PE Investment in India

- India is having solid underpinnings for economic growth, including a democratic government, a strong education system, widespread knowledge of English and a deep pool of expatriates experienced in Western businesses leading to growth driver of PE investments in India.
- Private equity deals in India can be greatly attributed to its strong corporate performance, robust and transparent capital markets, buoyant economy, and burgeoning middle-class.
- Demographic divided leading to exploding domestic consumption for lifestyles goods and services
- Continued growth in the service industry
- Resurgence of manufacturing exports
- Creation of manufacture
- Consolidation of Indian business
- Annual GDP growth, averaging around 9% over the last three years, has made the country among the fastest developing major economies in the world. With the private equity investments now undergoing unprecedented growth, there is now even more interest around the region from investment firms.
- Main economic forces driving the estimated surge in the size of the Indian private equity market are that growing consumer class is
  - — Increasing demand in key industries, such as hospitality, retail and health care delivery
  - — Increasingly differentiated Indian skills:
- Technology skills that underpinned India's initial rise in the global economy are now evolving toward higher
- Value design engineering skills
  - — Proficiency once only found in India's services markets are now being replicated in a number of growing Indian manufacturing sectors

So the combination of a growing Indian consumer class and an evolving set of differentiated Indian skills are the fuel which attract private equity growth and investment opportunities in India.

- A rapidly growing economy with a superior rate of Return on Equity (RoE) *vis-à-vis* other markets in the region, low volatility in RoE, a strong financial system, and low gearing are a few other reasons.
- The Indian corporate sector has come out with good results for the last two consecutive years, justifying the faith of investors. The good run spilled over to the first quarter of 2005-06, with firms posting encouraging results. A sample of 1,765 companies' show that net profits for the first quarter of 2005-06 jumped up by 46%, while sales clocked at 15% growth.
- One of the biggest triggers for the rise of the Indian economy is the low interest rate regime. It has changed the face of the Indian corporate that have not only weathered global competition, but also managed to influence the steep hike in fuel prices.

The performance of stock market, possibility of fast growth and maturing of the mergers and acquisitions activity has played a key role in the development of private equity market in India.

- IPO norms are stringent and SEBI is bringing in future reforms like IPO grading and easier de-listing norms to make the investment climate attractive
- India's Sensex 30 – that country's version of the US Dow-Jones Industrial Index – broke through 12,000 in 2006, up from 3,300 in December 2002. The price-to-earning ratio for India stocks is 21, which encourage foreign private equity firms to make investment destination in India.
- India has firmly established itself as the world's IT superpower with almost all major software development companies having an Indian development centre. India is also developing some retail financial service businesses, which is attracting for PE investments.
- The nature of entrepreneurship in India is different because large numbers of Indian entrepreneurs have been able to work abroad as expatriates in many roles. This is no doubt be a manifest in the kinds of businesses they develop, particularly in information technology. Again India has an advantage in health care including biotech, pharmaceuticals, telemedicine, banking, engineering and construction attracted a significant chunk of PE investments.
- In India, many listed companies act more like privately held firms because they are under tight control, usually by founders.
- India made an all-out push to promote itself as a business-friendly environment for investment. The government lifted limits on foreign direct investment. The most notable change was in the retail sector where outside firms selling a single

brand, such as Nike, will be allowed to own a majority stake in Indian stores. The government also decided to lift the limit on foreign direct investment for the development of airports, mining for diamonds and other precious stones, and power trading which leads to growth of PE investments in India.

- The first generation of private equity players has significant success in last several years, which also encourage an ideal hunting ground for PE investments.
- There are strong PE funds in India like HDFC PE, ICICI PE, Kotak Mahindra PE, UTI Venture, GVFL Ltd., and so on who provide genuine liquidity option.
- India has had very rapid changes in the underlying policies and laws that make Western-style transactions possible. India has only recently embraced TRIPS, so the judicial infrastructure is going to have to evolve quickly in India, which attracts PE investments.
- A recent spate of mergers and acquisitions has given rise to yet another way of exiting from Indian companies for private equity investors.
- Indian companies are more strongly linked to US firms that are co-based in the United States. Investors in these firms can exit through a US sale or initial public offering. All these factors are probably a more inviting place for investment at the moment in India.

This and the changed "growth focused" mindset of Indian entrepreneurs will give rise to continue and growing demand for PE.

Problems of Private Equity

Although India is being an integral part of the global economic chain, its plan is not always matched by its ability to implement change. Changes in regulation and infrastructure developments are often sidelined due to friction and conflict. Most of private equity investors are now highly considering China, because it has provided spectacular private-equity returns in recent years. Further cheap labour and foreign direct investment have made China the world's manufacturing powerhouse and 3,00,000 firm qualify to list on NASDAQ as well. Apart from this, China also has a strong entrepreneurial culture. So China is the direct competitor of India. Most of the private equity investors draw a comparison across both the countries.

Secondly, there is no listed public market is available for the vast majority of private equity investments in India. However there is a robust and maturing secondary market available for sellers of private equity assets.

Thirdly, it is easy to invest in public companies in India through transactions that are similar to a purely private deal but it is difficult to exit. The Indian public markets are lack of liquidity and many Indian companies are thinly traded in markets controlled by powerful local brokerages.

Fourthly, mid-cap funds are often constrained by several factors, i.e., in investment circles. Liquidity of the stocks they are supposed to target becomes a major issue. Some of these stocks are also said to be under-researched.

Fifthly, India's economy is largely being built by closely held family businesses, with minority private equity investors having less scope to hire and fire.

Finally, there are also several significant challenges for private equity players in India:

- Limited availability of secondary market data
- Currently high asset valuations (as a hurdle toward buyout market creation)
- Access to leverage from government restrictions

Emerging Challenges

Indian corporate is by and large family owned business. Hence, it is imperative need for Indian business to unlock the value of their business to expand for global competition. As there are multiplayer authorities like RBI, SEBI, Finance Ministry, Foreign Investment Board, Department of Industrial Policy and Promotion, it is advisable to have separate regulatory authority to smooth growth of PE space for the development of the economy. It is needed to target the beneficiaries of a growing consumer class, forge key local relationships, leverage global networks, and plot a flexible course to exits for the growth of PE investments in India. Vast majority of private equity investments in India involve minority control, so multinational private equity funds should leverage global networks to maximize their 'network effect' and influence management teams. In India, today, there are three promising investment hypotheses need to be taken:

- Target dynamic new sectors benefiting from the rise of the consumer class, including health care, real estate, banking and credit
- Capitalize on low-cost labour resources in areas such as Software applications development, business services, engineering and technical design
- Look opportunistically at emerging industry niches, including pharmaceuticals, automotive components and metal forging, as these subsectors and these industries build global scale

However, PE firms are also facing a few challenges in India in the form of bureaucracy norms, regulatory limits in certain sectors, hitherto poor infrastructure, etc. Apart from this, cross-holdings among promoters and the stake of the promoters should be valued carefully. Also, if equity players enter into India, there were a possibility that some of them would end-up with bad promoters.

Private Equity Valuation Methodologies

Since value is often realized through a liquidity event of the entire company, Managers are to fairly value the investments in their portfolio companies on a consistent, transparent and prudent basis. The methodologies discussed in this chapter involve estimating the value of the company as a whole as an initial step for valuing the company's privately issued securities and then need to determine how the total enterprise value is distributed among the various securities of the company.

Managers are not required to use other investors' valuations since the estimate of fair value is the responsibility of the managers. On each valuation date managers need to take into account available information from market participants, the relevant marketplace and the global economy along with specific facts and circumstances in determining the fair value of their investments.

Historically, the Private Equity Industry used cost or the value of the latest round of financing as an approximation of fair value. Such an approach is incompatible with the concept of fair value.

Fair value as defined in accordance with GAAP is "the price that would be received to sell an asset or paid to transfer a liability in an orderly transaction between market participants at the measurement date" (FASB Statement No. 157, paragraph 5). The objective is to estimate the exchange price at which hypothetical willing marketplace participants would agree to transact in the principal market. No matter which market is deemed most appropriate, fair value is the estimated "exit price" in that market. Securities of private companies normally won't quote available market prices. However, private companies engage in arm's-length transactions for issuances of their equity or debt securities. So, the value of these transactions are providing as an observable market price similar to a quoted market price, the fair value determination is being made and therefore used as an estimate of the theoretical exit price. When quoted market prices or arm's-length transaction prices are not available, the estimate of fair value should incorporate all reasonably available information about the business and assumed that market participants would normally use their estimates of fair value. In determining the fair value of individual investments, managers are expected to use their judgement. But however, there is a perception that bias exists or has the potential to exist in a non-independent valuation performed by a fund's manager. Therefore, the fund manager, in consultation with the Valuation Policy Committee, should establish the written valuation parameters to be consistently followed.

Therefore, at each valuation date a manager must make a determination of fair value for each investment and best indication of fair value is provided by cost or the value of the latest round of financing. Private equity managers use three valuation techniques, "Market Approach" in most situations or Comparable Company Transactions or Performance Multiple Inputs, as the primary technique to estimate the fair value of equity securities in private companies. For Private Equity, the market approach usually is the most appropriate.

While entry prices and exit prices are different conceptually, the manager considered initial investment as near term company performance in determining investment valuation. Therefore, cost (the transaction price) may be fair value (the exit price) upon purchase. The transaction price may not represent fair value upon purchase when:

(a) The transaction is between related parties;

(b) The transaction occurs under duress;

(c) The transaction price includes transaction costs (transaction costs are expensed under GAAP);

(d) The market in which the initial transaction takes place is different than the principal or most advantageous market in which the exit transaction would take place.

After some period of time, it has been observed that cost or the latest round of financing becomes less reliable as an approximation of fair value. Therefore, the manager must assess whether fair value has changed even though there has not been a new round of financing.

Comparable Company Transactions

This methodology involves deriving the value of a company through examination of third-party investments in comparable equity securities of the company, examination of transactions in equity securities of comparable companies and direct comparisons to similar companies. These comparisons should be appropriately adjusted for any control premiums, synergistic benefits or other excess benefits or detriments that accrue to the owner when determining a proper comparable valuation. Since comparable transactions are difficult to ascertain and fair value is also not reasonably assessed, performance multiple methodology can be used. The performance multiple methodology applies a relevant multiple to derive the value of the company. This approach is most applicable for companies to achieve positive and sustainable operating performance. The valuation determined using this methodology is calculated by applying the most appropriate and reasonable multiple derived from reference to market based conditions of quoted companies or recent private transactions. The multiple to be used, which may need to be adjusted for differences in terms of growth prospects and risk attributes (depending on the size of the comparison sample, among other factors), should be one of the following:

- Current average comparable public company multiple for similar companies in the industry;
- Current average multiples for recent private transactions of similar companies in the industry; and
- The original acquisition multiple when no other similar public or private multiples can be ascertained.
- The most appropriate and reasonable multiple as determined above will be applied to the relevant operating performance metrics of the company to estimate fair value.

Other Valuation Methodologies

Discounted cash flow (DCF) methodologies is only be used for estimates and forward-looking information in limited situations using a discount rate commensurate with the risks involved. Net asset valuation methodologies is used for valuing investments in businesses whose value is derived primarily from the underlying value of their tangible assets rather than their performance.

Summary

There is tremendous potential for PE firms in India. India have distinctive advantages over countries such as China as it offers investors better trained managers and more corporate transparency in the private sector. Further PE investments in India have become more inclusive and not restricted to a few sectors. India's conducive-environment is the basis for private equity to grow and this in turn led to a worthy cycle of further improvements in the economic and infrastructural environment.

CASE: CHASE CAPITAL PARTNERS LTD.

Chase Capital Partners Ltd., a leading private equity fund has recently started its operations in the Indian market. Founded in 1999 by one state government, Chase Capital was intended to spur development of the local economy and to build an innovative economy. In the next 10 years Chase Capital gradually expanded into three regions of the country and set-up 20 regional government-backed fund. It also explores other structures of investment funds such as traditional commercial funds and joint-venture funds. However, the landscape of PE industry is rapidly changing. Chase Capital has proved extremely successfully and providing much more competitive investment environment with many foreign and local VC entering to the state of Delhi. The core business of Chase Capital is to provide private equity and mezzanine finance to corporate desiring public offering of their equity.

Williams Ltd., is a fast growing garment company based in New Delhi with factories located at Ludhiana and Lucknow. Williams Ltd., started thinking about raising around of capital to help accelerate the development of his product. In the fall 2000, as the market turned down, the founders started having concerns about cash. Williams has received a prestigious order from Changi group to supply their entire year's fashion garments at about the same time, the company was starting to receive requests from big companies wanting to install machines within their enterprises. For executing this order Williams wants to imports some high-tech machines in the hope that this could create a new revenue stream.

The current EPS of Williams is ₹ 8 and the expected growth rate of EPS as estimated by the company for the coming year is as follows:

Growth rate in EPS (%)	Probability (%)
0	5
10	20
20	30
30	45

The forecast of the Financial Analyst of Chase Capital regarding the P/E ratio for Indian garment industry is as follows:

P/E ratio	Probability (%)
10	15
14	25
18	45
22	15

The investment policies of chase capital are given below:

1. The Time horizon of all investments made is one year.
2. The target return should be 35%.
3. The probability of achieving the target return should be at least 70%.
4. Divestment is priced at industry P/E Ratio.

You are required to compute the price at which Chase Capital would invest in Williams Ltd.

Note: The case is fictitious and any resemblance to a person/company is merely coincidental.

Review Questions

1. What is private equity? Why private equity is important?
2. How do you compare the private equity with alternate source of financing?
3. Explain the overview of PE Industry in India?
4. What are the Growth drivers of PE Investment in India?
5. **Quiz:**
   (a) Typical forms of private equity include ____, _____, ____ and ____.
   (b) Angel investments come in _____ stages and finance the gap in ____ capital.
   (c) Private equity funds are generally organized as either a ____ or ____.
   (d) All investors in private equity are ____ investors.
   (e) Private Equity firms invested about US$2,000 million in India across ___ deals during the quarter ended March 2010.
   (f) Private equity deals in India can be greatly attributed to its strong corporate performance, robust and transparent capital markets, buoyant economy, and burgeoning middle-class. *(T/F)*
   (g) Most of private equity investors are now highly considering China. *(T/F)*
   (h) There is listed public market is available for the vast majority of private equity investments in India. *(T/F)*

CHAPTER 8

Leveraged Buyout – LBO

Introduction

The amount of fund raising and investment activity in the buyout industry is growing significantly. Indeed, one of the main reasons that private equity has attracted so much attention recently is that public companies have increasingly been taken private via an LBO. The size of individual funds has grown considerably – with some funds reaching $20 billion and, accordingly, larger and larger companies have become potential LBO targets. LBO activity accelerated throughout the 1980s, starting from a basis of four deals with an aggregate value of $1.7 billion in 1980 and reaching its peak in 1988, when 410 buyouts were completed with an aggregate value of $188 billion. In the years since 1988, downturns in the business cycle, the near-collapse of the junk bond market, and diminished structural advantages all contributed to dramatic changes in the LBO market. In addition, LBO fund raising has accelerated dramatically. From 1980 to 1988 LBO funds raised approximately $46 billion; from 1988 to 2000, LBO funds raised over $385 billion. In 2000 the average equity contribution to leveraged buyouts was almost 38%, and for the first three quarters of 2001 average equity contributions were above 40%. The growth of public-to-private LBOs has been most marked in the US Between 2003-08 there were 259 LBOs of companies that were listed on a US stock exchange, which had a combined transaction value of $635 billion exhibited in Table 8.1. These amounts are economically sizeable and affect both the way. Industries are restructured and the working of financial markets. Policy makers, investors and academics alike need to know more about this opaque industry.

Table 8.1: Public-to-private Leveraged Buyouts in the US

	2003	2004	2005	2006	2007	2008	2003-2008
U.S. Public-to-private LBO	22	27	43	69	70	28	259
Total Deal Value ($mn)	6,292	27,446	55,066	199,442	311,178	36,018	635,442
Average Deal Value ($mn)	286	1,017	1,281	2,890	4,445	1,286	2,453

Source: Bureau van Dijk, Zephyr Global M&A Database.

What Does Leveraged Buyout Mean?

Leveraged means largely financed by borrowed capital. Buyout means when a person or organization buys a business. A leverage buyout ('LBO') is the acquisition of a business by using a significant amount of borrowed money. In an LBO, there is usually a ratio of 80%-90% debt to 10% -20% equity. A leveraged buyout ("LBO") is an acquisition of an existing publicly listed or private company by using a significant amount of borrowed money (bonds or loans) to meet the cost of acquisition. The idea of leveraged buyouts is to allow companies to make large acquisitions without committing lot of capital. A leveraged buyout occurs when a company acquires a controlling interest in another company using mostly debt to finance the purchase. In other words the "leverage" in a "leveraged buyout" refers to a company's seeking external financing through increasing its debt (borrowed capital). LBO is a transaction in which an investor group acquires a company by taking on an extraordinary amount of debt, with plans to repay the debt with funds generated from the company or with revenue earned by selling off the newly acquired company's assets. LBOs are a way to take a public company private, or put a company in the hands of the current management, MBO. LBOs use the assets or cash flows of the company to secure debt financing, bonds or bank loans, to purchase the outstanding equity of the company. After the buyout, control of the company is concentrated in the hands of the LBO firm and management, and there is no public stock outstanding. Let take an example:

X is a leveraged buyout firm. X wants to buy Helot Inc. using an LBO.

X decides that it will cost $40 billion to purchase Helot Inc. X is attracted by Helot Inc'.s positive cash flow and number of profitable subsidiaries that could be sold. X also feels as though Helot.Inc., is being mismanaged but could make out benefit from a change in management and different operational processes. X is not putting up $40 billion dollars in cash to finance the purchase. Instead, it will put up $4 billion in cash and borrow the rest. The $36 billion in debt will be secured against the assets in Helot Inc.

If the purchase goes through, and then X will use the positive cash flow from Helot Inc., to pay the debt payments, and will most likely look at cutting expenses and possibly selling off assets to pay down the debt. This is called leveraged buyout.The LBO is presented in Fig. 8.1.

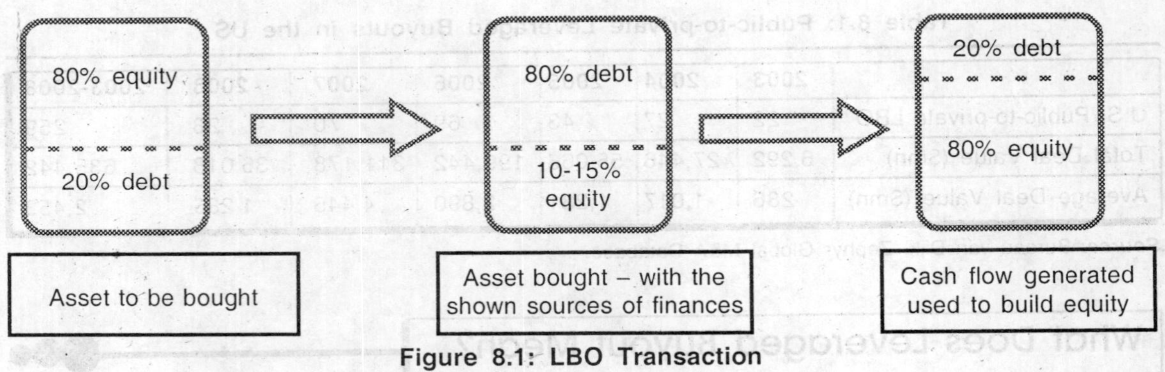

Figure 8.1: LBO Transaction

In a leveraged buyout, all of the stock, or assets, of a public corporation are bought by a small group of investors ("financial buyers"), usually including members of existing management. Financial buyers: Focus on RoE rather than RoA; Use other people's money, Succeed through improved operational performance, Focus on targets having stable cash flow to meet debt service requirements, Typical targets are in mature industries (e.g., retailing, textiles, food processing, apparel, and soft drinks).

A Brief History

It is generally agreed that the first early leveraged buyouts were carried out in the years following World War II. In the years following the end of World War II the Great Depression was still relatively fresh in the minds of America's corporate leaders, who considered it wise to keep corporate debt ratios low. As a result, for the first three decades following World War II, very few American companies relied on debt as a significant source of funding. At the same time, American business became caught up in a wave of conglomerate building that began in the early 1960s. In some cases, corporate governance guidelines were inconsistently implemented. (George P. Baker and George David Smith, 1998). The concept began in January 1955, with the purchase of Pan-Atlantic Steamship Company by McLean Industries Inc., and Waterman Steamship Corporation. For this transaction McLean borrowed $42m and raised an additional $7m through an issue of preferred stock. $20m of the cash was then used to settle debt. When the new generation of managers began to takeover American companies in the late 1970s, many companies were willing to believe debt financing as a viable substitute for financing operations. Soon LBO firms' stable pitching began to persuade some of the merits of debt-financed buyouts of their businesses. LBO saw a boom period in the 1980s. LBO activity increased from an aggregate of $1.7b in 1980 to about 410 buyouts with aggregate value of $188b in 1988. Many buyouts in this period led to bankruptcy of the accuired companies. The reason attributed to this was, nearly 100% leverage ratio which made the interest payments so large that the company's operating expenses failed to meet these obligations. By the end of 2006, new "largest buyout" records were set. In 2006, the largest LBO the acquisition of HCA Inc., by Kohlberg Kravis Roberts & Co., Bain & Co., and Merrill Lynch. The three companies reportedly paid $33b for the acquisition.

Forms of the Leverage Buyout

Hostile Leverage Buyout

Leverage buyout of a firm carried out without the wishes of the acquired firm's managers is called as Hostile Leverage Buyout. But this hardly is practised in the industry as the lenders expect that the same management has to exist with the new ownership in the acquired firm.

Reverse Leverage Buyout

An equity investment is made in the company that is already suffering with excess debt. This equity infusion by the buyout reduces the debt held by the company. A special case of leverage buyout is management buyout.

What are MBO/MBI/IBO?

MBO/MBIs are occurs because of corporate restructuring activity, leading the parent company to want to divest a subsidiary. Buyouts are the most common method of privatisation. In the private arena, if an entrepreneur has no family to succeed him/her in the business sometimes, companies' wants significant levels of business exist.

Management Buyout (MBO)

Leverage buyouts cannot only be practiced by the hostile takeovers but also by the outside corporation, private equity firm or an internal management team. Management buyouts are an important role in the corporate restructuring besides mergers and acquisitions. This is a special case of the leverage buyouts where the managers buy or acquire a large part of the company. This is to motivate the manager's interest in the company. This is supported mainly because this appreciates the fairness to its shareholders, future business plan, price and legal and tax issues. But this buyout has been criticized very badly by many of the industrialist. Take for example of some happenings: Here the companies provide the incentives to the managers who mismanage the organization (or manage less efficiently). Executive reduces the companies expected revenues and show poor reports about the organization. This automatically reduces the stock price of the organization. Then the company becomes a target for the buyout. The takeover artist who purchases this organization gains a huge profit by the buying the organization for a less amount as shown by the executive. Now the executive is provided some incentive for his work on this. Then the takeover artist concentrates on the company and by effective management increases the stock price of the company. This happens due to the information asymmetry by the executive. So the management buyout is not favoured by many industrialists.

Management buyouts is done by the managers in order to save their own job if the business is about to shut down and in the advent of the new management team to be placed if it is purchased by the new purchaser. They also receive the benefit from the success of the buyout by the company by taking up the profits. The purchase of a business by its existing management team/when sitting management team takes over firm. Recent research shows the importance of innovative behaviour, and new product development, which may not otherwise have happened. It significantly better performance over 3-5 years than comparable non-buyouts.

Management Buys In (MBI)

When outside management team acquires firm and takes it private. It typically involves extensive restructuring and performance generally less strong than MBOs.

Institutional Buyout (IBO)

Institutional buyouts are the opposite of management buyouts (MBO), in which a business's current management acquires a large part of the company. Typically, the investors in an IBO are looking to dispose of its stake in the company within a certain timeframe. In general, the private equity firm involved in the IBO will take charge in structuring and exiting the deal as well as hiring managers. New owners of delisted firm is solely institutional investors or private equity firms.

Secondary Buyouts

Secondary buyout is a leverage buyout of the company that was acquired through a leveraged buyout. Both the buyer and the seller are the private equity firms or financial sponsors. As it is a distress for both the seller and the buyer and also unattractive due to the limited partner investors, secondary buyouts are avoided by all the parties. But still secondary buyouts are practised by the firm (selling firm) when they realize that the investments have already generated enough value to the selling firm and now it is desirable to sell it than possessing it. Some of the other reasons for going with the secondary buyouts are sales to strategic buyers may not be possible for the niche or the undersized business

Secondary buyouts may generate liquidity much faster than the other routes.

Risk Factors to be Considered

The market is becoming more and more competitive with auction encouraging more of the secondary buyouts. This helps in timely exit by the fund managers. Some of the factors to be considered are: the company have to rely on the warranties and the tax covenant provided by the management. The incoming investor has to price the deal only after satisfying itself of the tax position through thorough financial due diligence. All the risk factors must be considered in context. As soon as they are inside the organization, they have to make it clear otherwise when they leave the organization, they wouldn't still be hiding it. Examples of the secondary buyout: Lee Clifford, senior associate of Pinsent Masons has advised the secondary buyout of Paragon Labels Limited and Doncaster's Group Limited. An Associate, a leading growth private equity and buyout firm, went for a secondary buyout of M and M Direct Ltd., leading online and mail order retailer in UK. ABN-AMRO capital has completed the secondary buyout of the Europe's leading specialist retailer Jessop.

Purpose of LBO

LBO facilitates larger acquisitions, as the capital requirement is less, i.e., the acquired firm's cash is used to settle the debt return to private equity sponsor increases with the use of debt. The purpose of a LBO is to allow an acquirer to make large acquisitions without having to commit a significant amount of capital. A typically transaction involves the setup of an acquisition vehicle that is jointly funded by a financial investor and management of the target company. Often the assets of the target company are used as collateral for the debt.

As the debt in LBO is relatively fixed, any return in excess of this is channelled to equity. Tax liability of the firm reduces owing to the acquisition debt and hence the value of the firm increases. The motives for LBO's is:

- Increase in debt and concentrated ownership increase incentives to maximize value.
- Non-management on board with significant equity stakes increases board effectiveness
- Advantage to being private
- Beneficial tax consequences
- Transfer wealth from other stakeholders in the firm such as employees and bondholders

Target companies that have the following operating and financial characteristics are considered ideal LBO targets are shown in Table 8.2.

Table 8.2

Operating Characteristics	Financial Characteristics
Leading market position – proven demand for product	Significant debt capacity
Strong management team	Team cash flow
Portfolio of strong brand names (if applicable)	Availability of attractive price
Strong relationships with key customers and suppliers	Low capital intensity
Favourable industry characteristics	Potential operating improvement
Fragmented industry	Ideally low operating leverage
Steady growth	Management's success in implementing substantial cost reduction programmes

India has experienced a number of buyouts and leveraged buyouts since Tata Tea's LBO of UK heavyweight brand Tetley for £271 million in 2000, the first of its kind in India presented in Table 8.3.

Table 8.3

Target Company	Country	Indian Acquirer	Value	Type
Tetley	United Kingdom	Tata Tea	271 million	LBO
Whyte & Mackay	United Kingdom	UB Group	550 million	LBO
Corus	United Kingdom	Tata Steel	$11.3 billion	LBO
Hansen Transmission	Netherlands	Suzlon Energy	465 million	LBO
American Axle[1]	United States	Tata Motors	$2 billion	LBO
Lombardini[2]	Italy	Zoom Auto Ancillaries	$225 million	LBO

[1] Potential bid [2] Buyout attempt

Characteristics of a Good LBO

Some of the characteristics of good leverage buyouts are:

- Steady and predictable cash flow ensures that interest payments will be met.
- **Low Enterprise Value/EBITDA Multiple:** Enterprise value refers to the total value of the firm (market capitalization and long-term debt). This multiple indicates the ability of the cash flow to be able to cover the purchase price.
- **Large Amount of Tangible Assets for Loan:** Tangible assets will help obtain low interest loans; this in turn will require less cash to repay loans.
- **Potential for Expense Reduction:** There is often scope for expense reduction, working on which will help free up cash and allow for faster repayment of the debt.
- **Minimal Future Capital Requirements:** Less outlay should be required to keep the company running and growing.
- **Limited Working Capital Requirements:** Increase in working capital reduces the amount of free cash for repayment of debts.
- Divestible assets
- Clean balance sheet with little debt
- Strong management team
- Strong, defensible market position
- Viable exit strategy
- Synergy opportunities
- Heavy asset base for loan collateral

Why Do Management Teams Buyouts?

Some of reasons are:

- Competitive reasons
- To acquire additional skills and competencies
- To secure a source of supply, or distribution
- To acquire new technologies
- The entrepreneurial realisation of an opportunity
- To speed market entry
- To get assets cheaply
- To acquire an opportunity in the form of an enterprise which is not realising its full potential
- Opportunity to enhance performance (commonly for privatisations)
- Retaining the management team gives additional stability
- Wealth Creation – studies prove that in the short-term after a buyout there is substantial improvements in profitability, cash flow and productivity measures
- Tax advantages associated with debt financing,
- Freedom from the scrutiny of being a public company or a captive division of a larger parent
- The ability for founders to take advantage of a liquidity event without ceding operational influence or sacrificing continued day-to-day involvement, and
- The opportunity for managers to become owners of a significant percentage of a firm's equity.

LBO Deal Structure

Advantages include the following:

- Management incentives,
- Tax savings from interest expense and depreciation from asset write-up,
- More efficient decision processes under private ownership,
- A potential improvement in operating performance, and
- Serving as a takeover defense by eliminating public investors

Disadvantages include the following:

- High fixed costs of debt,
- Vulnerability to business cycle fluctuations and competitor actions,

- Not appropriate for firms with high growth prospects or high business risk, and
- Potential difficulties in raising capital.

Pros and Cons of LBO

Leverage buyouts can have both positive and negative effects. Some are as follows: Financial analysts strongly believe there are many pros and cons in the leveraged buyout of a company.

Corporate Restructuring

One positive aspect of leveraged buyouts is the fact that poorly managed firms prior to their acquisition can undergo valuable corporate reformation when they become private. By changing their corporate structure (including modifying and replacing executive and management staff, unnecessary company sectors, and excessive expenditures), a company can refresh itself and earn substantial returns. Corporate restructuring from leveraged buyouts can greatly impact employees. This means companies may have to downsize their operations and reduce the number of paid staff, resulted into unemployment for those who will be laid-off. This will create negative influence to overall community, hindering its economic prosperity and development. Some leveraged buyouts are not friendly and it may lead to rather hostile takeovers, which goes against the wishes of the acquired firms' managers. An example of a hostile takeover occurred when the PepsiCo acquired the Quaker Oats Company, an American food company well-known for its breakfast cereals and oatmeal products. In 2001, PepsiCo, in an attempt to diversify its portfolio in non-carbonated drinks, primarily acquired Quaker Oats because QO owned the Gatorade brand. Even though this merger created the fourth-largest consumer goods company in the world, many of Quaker Oats managers were against the acquisition, claiming that such a merger was unlawful and contrary to the public interest.

Small Amount of Capital Requirements

Since this type of acquisition involves a high debt-to-equity ratio, large corporations can easily acquire smaller companies with very little capital. If the acquired company's returns are greater than the cost of the debt financing, then all stockholders can benefit from the financial returns, further increasing the value of a firm. However, if the company's returns are less than the cost of the debt financing, then corporate bankruptcy can result. In addition, the high-interest rates imposed by leveraged buyouts may be a challenge for companies whose cash flow and sale of assets are insufficient. The result can not only lead to a company's bankruptcy but can also result in a poor line of credit for the buyout investors. An example of an unsuccessful leveraged buyout is the Federated Department Stores. The Federated Department Stores had many stores nationwide and tailored primarily to high-end retailers. However, they lacked an effective marketing strategy. In 1989, Robert Campeau, a Canadian financier, bought out Federated with the hope to make considerable changes. Only one year later, and only after some reforms, Federated could not keep up with the financial burdens of high interest payments and had to file bankruptcy for 258 stores.

Management Buyout

Management buyout of a company is a common business practice. MBOs occur as a last resort to save an enterprise from permanent closure or replacement of existing management teams by an outside company. Many analysts strongly believe management buyouts greatly promote executive and shareholder interests as well as management loyalty and efficiency. Not every MBO turns out to be successful as planned. Management buyouts can generate substantial conflicts of interest among employees and managers alike. Management and executive teams can easily be lured to propose a short-term buyout for personal profit. In addition, they can also corruptly mismanage a company; leading to an enterprise's depreciated stock. An example of a successful management buyout is Springfield Remanufacturing Corporation, or SRC, an engine remanufacturing plant located in Springfield, Missouri. In 1983, SRC was at risk for permanent closure and was being bought by an outside company until their employees decided to buyout the company. The management buyout of SRC resulted in extreme success. Since 1983, it has grown exponentially from one company within $10,000 of being shut down to a proud assembly of 23 small businesses with a combined profit of over $120 million today.

Economy

Every leveraged buyout can be considered risky, especially in reference to the existing economy. If the existing economy is strong and remains solid, then the leveraged buyout can greatly improve its chances for success. On the other hand, a weak economy is highly indicative of a problematic LBO. In addition, acquisition can affect employee morale, increase hostility against the acquiring corporation, and can hinder the overall growth of a company.

The Repackaging Plan

The buying firm's goal is to repackage the company and return it to the marketplace in an initial public offering (IPO). The acquiring firm holds the company for a few years to avoid the watchful eyes of shareholders. This allows the acquiring company to repackage the company behind closed doors, making adjustments here and there and covering it up. If no major changes are made to the company, it's a zero-sum game and the new shareholders get the same financials the old company had.

The Split-up

This is fairly common with conglomerates that have acquired various businesses in relatively unrelated industries over many years. The buyer is an outsider and may use aggressive tactics. If successful, the company is dismantled after it is bought out and the parts are sold-off to the highest bidder. This method is the most feared by employees and management as they know their jobs are just numbers on a page in this situation. These deals usually involve massive lay-offs as part of the restructuring process.

The Portfolio Plan

The portfolio plan benefit to all participants, including the buyer, the management and the employees. It is also called leveraged build-up. In a competitive marketplace, a company may use leverage to acquire one of its competitors (or any company where it could achieve synergies from the acquisition). The plan is risky: the company needs to make sure the return on its invested capital exceeds its cost to acquire. If successful, all parties can benefit: the shareholders may receive a good price on their stock, current management can be retained and the company may prosper in its new, larger form.

The Saviour Plan

The saviour plan is often drawn up with good intentions, but frequently arrives too late. This scenario typically involves a plan involving management and employees to borrow money to save a failing company. If the same management stays sluggish the likelihood of success is low. On the other hand, if the company turns around after the buyout, everyone benefits.

Buyout Firm's Structure and Organisation

LBO firm invests equity in an acquisition comes from a committed capital that has been raised from institutional investors like the corporate pension plans, insurance companies and college endowments as well as individual "qualified" investors. Buyout funds are structured as limited partnerships, with the firm's principals acting as general partner and investors in the fund being limited partners. The general partner is responsible for making all investment decisions relating to the fund, with the limited partners responsible for transferring committed capital to the fund upon notice of the general partner. As a general rule, funds raised by private equity firms have a number of fairly standard provisions:

Minimum Commitment: Prospective limited partners are required to commit minimum amount of equity. Limited partners make a capital commitment, which is then drawn down by the general partner in order to make investments with the fund's equity.

Investment or Commitment Period: During the term of the commitment period, limited partners are obligated to meet capital calls upon notice by the general partner by transferring capital to the fund within an agreed-upon period of time (often 10 days). The term of the commitment period usually lasts for either five or six years after the closing of the fund or until 75 to 100% of the fund's capital has been invested, whichever comes first.

Term: The term of the partnership formed during the fund-raising process is usually ten to twelve years. The first half which represents the commitment period and the second half which is reserved for managing and exiting investments made during the commitment period.

Diversification: Most funds' partnership agreements stipulate that the partnership may not invest more than 25% of the fund's equity in any single investment. The LBO firm generates revenue in three ways:

Carried Interest: This is a share of any profits generated by acquisitions made by the fund. Once all the partners have received an amount equal to their contributed capital any remaining profits are split between the general partner and the limited partners. Normally, the general partner's carried interest is 20% of any profits remaining once all the partners' capital has been returned; although some funds guarantee the limited partners a priority return of 8% on their committed capital before the general partner's carried interest begins to accrue.

Management Fees: LBO firms charge their limited partners a management fee to cover overhead expenses associated with identifying, evaluating and executing acquisitions by the fund. The management fee is intended to cover legal, accounting, and consulting fees associated with conducting due diligence on potential targets, as well as general overhead. Other fees, such as lenders' fees and investment banking fees are generally charged to any acquired company after the closing of a transaction. Management fees range from 0.75% to 3% of committed capital, although 2% is common. Management fees are often reduced after the end of the commitment period to reflect the lower costs of monitoring and harvesting investments.

Coinvestment: Executives and employees of the leveraged buyout firm may coinvest along with the partnership on any acquisition made by the fund, provided the terms of the investment are equal to those afforded to the partnership.

Valuation of LBOs

Leverage buyouts (LBOs) are among the most risky and complex financial transactions and typically sets the floor or minimum valuation. An LBO can be evaluated from the perspective of common equity investors or of all investors and lenders. LBOs make sense from viewpoint of investors and lenders if present value of free cash flows to the firm is greater than or equal to the total investment consisting of debt and common and preferred equity. However, an LBO can make sense to common equity investors but not to other investors and lenders. The market value of debt and preferred stock held before the transaction may decline due to a perceived reduction in the firm's ability to repay such debt as the firm assumes substantial amounts of new debt and to pay interest and dividends on a timely basis. To value LBOs, several methodologies can be used: Variable Risk Method, Free Cash Flow: Calculate FCF and discount by the WACC, Adjusted Present Value Approach (APV), Capital Cash Valuation Method: Take Net Income of firm with actual debt (builds in tax shields directly) + depreciation and special charges + interest – change in NWC – incremental investment.

Variable Risk Method: Adjusts for the varying level of risk as the firm's total debt is repaid

Step 1: Project annual cash flows until target D/E achieved: Project annual cash flows until target D/E ratio achieved

- Target D/E is the level of debt relative to equity at which
  - — The firm will have to resume payment of taxes and

— The amount of leverage is likely to be acceptable to IPO investors or strategic buyers (often the prevailing industry average)

Step 2: Project debt-to-equity ratios

- Project annual debt-to-equity ratios
- The decline in D/E reflects

— the known debt repayment schedule, and

— The projected growth in the market value of the shareholders' equity (assumed to grow at the same rate as net income)

Step 3: Calculate terminal value

- Calculate terminal value of projected cash flow to equity investors (TVE) at time t, i.e., the year in which the initial investors choose to exit the business.
- TVE represents the PV of the dollar proceeds available to the firm through an IPO or sale to a strategic buyer at time t.

Step 4: Adjust discount rate to reflect changing risk

- Adjust the discount rate to reflect changing risk.
- The firm's cost of equity will decline over time as debt is repaid and equity grows, thereby reducing the leveraged β. Estimate the firm's β as follows:

$$\beta_{FL1} = \beta_{IUL1}\ (1 + (D/E)_{F1}\ (1 - t_F))$$

Where, β_{FL1} = Firm's levered beta in period 1

β_{IUL1} = Industry's unlevered beta in period 1

= $\beta_{IL1}/(1 + (D/E)_{I1}(1 - t_I))$

β_{IL1} = Industry's levered beta in period 1

$(D/E)_{I1}$ = Industry's debt-to-equity ratio in period 1

t_I = Industry's marginal tax rate in period 1

$(D/E)_{F1}$ = Firm's debt-to-equity ratio in period 1

t_F = Firm's marginal tax rate in period 1

- Recalculate each successive period's β with the D/E ratio for that period, and using that period's β, recalculate the firm's cost of equity for that period.

Step 5: Determine if deal makes sense

– Does the PV of free cash flows to equity investors (including the terminal value) equal or exceed the equity investment including transaction-related fees?

Evaluating the Variable Risk Method

- **Advantages:**
  - Adjusts the discount rate to reflect diminishing risk as the debt-to-total capital ratio declines
  - Takes into account that the deal may make sense for common equity investors but not for lenders or preferred shareholders
- **Disadvantage:** Calculations more burdensome than Adjusted Present Value Method

Discounted Cash Flow (DCF) Analysis

- Discounted Cash Flow Analysis values a company based on its future expected cash flows.
- DCF Analysis provides a theoretical valuation of the company's intrinsic value based on these future cash flows.
- The DCF Analysis is adjusted by the time value of money and the inherent risk of the cash flows.
- The DCF Analysis involves discounting these future expected cash flows to the present by a discount factor which is usually the Weighted Average Cost of Capital (WACC). These cash flows are then summed. We then find a terminal value for the company which is also discounted back to the present. The terminal value is added to the sum of the cash flows. This calculation will provide the present value of the assets or the enterprise value of the company.
- Sum of present value of unlevered free cash flow discounted at WACC + Present value of terminal value discounted at WACC = Enterprise Value.

A Discounted Cash Flow Analysis can be useful for:

- An additional reference point when valuing a company.
- Evaluating early stage companies with finite asset lives or companies that have revenues and costs that can be forecasted easily.
- Understanding the value of divisions of a conglomerate or a diversified company (for divestitures or spin-off opportunities).
- Conducting a merger valuation in the same sector or geography.
- To display potential upside to a buyer as a result of synergies and strategic opportunities.

Advantages:

- Theoretically, it is the most academically compelling valuation method.
- It is forward-looking and incorporates an expected operating strategy.
- Capital markets volatility has limited impact on the analysis.

- Recognizes the time value of money.
- Useful when there are not many comparable companies.

Disadvantages

- Highly sensitive to assumptions used (WACC, long-term growth rate, terminal value, etc.).
- Forecasted future cash flows are uncertain.
- Terminal value can have a significant impact on valuation.

Adjusted Present Value Method (APV): Separates value of the firm into: (a) its value as if it were debt free, and (b) the value of tax savings due to interest expense.

Step 1: Project annual free cash flows to equity investors and interest tax savings

- Project annual free cash flows to equity investors and interest tax savings for the period during which the firm's capital structure is changing.
  - — Interest tax savings = INT × t, where INT and t are the firm's annual interest expense on new debt and the marginal tax rate, respectively.
  - — During the terminal period, the cash flows are expected to grow at a constant rate and the capital structure is expected to remain unchanged.

Step 2: Value target without the effects of debt financing and discount projected free cash flows at the firm's estimated unlevered cost of equity.

- Value target without the effects of debt financing and discount projected cash flows at the firm's unlevered cost of equity.
  - — Apply the unlevered cost of equity for the period during which the capital structure is changing.
  - — Apply the weighted average cost of capital for the terminal period using the proportions of debt and equity that make up the firm's capital structure in the final year of the period during which the structure is changing.

Step 3: Estimate the present value of the firm's tax savings discounted at the firm's estimated unlevered cost of equity.

- Estimate the present value of the firm's annual interest tax savings.
  - — Discount the tax savings at the firm's unlevered cost of equity.
  - — Calculate PV for annual forecast period only, excluding a terminal value, since the firm is sold and any subsequent tax savings accrue to the new owners.

Step 4: Add the present value of the firm without debt and the present value of tax savings to calculate the present value of the firm including tax benefits.

- Calculate the present value of the firm including tax benefits
  - — Add the present value of the firm without debt and the PV of tax savings

Step 5: Determine if the deal makes sense.

— **Does the PV of free cash flows to equity investors plus tax benefits equal or exceed the initial equity investment including transaction-related fees?**

Evaluating the Adjusted Present Value Method

- **Advantage:**
  — Simplicity.
- **Disadvantages:**
  — Ignores the effect of changes in leverage on the discount rate as debt is repaid,
  — Implicitly ignores the potential for bankruptcy of excessively leveraged firms, and
  — Unclear whether true discount rate should be the cost of debt, unlevered cost of equity, or somewhere between the two.

Failures of Leverage Buyouts

Some of the leverage buyouts have resulted in the corporate bankruptcy. The companies affected by the leverage buyouts are Robert Campeau bought the Federated departmental stores in 1988 and Revco Drug Company in 1986, which led the company to bankruptcy due to excess of debt financing which led the company to make the interest payments more than that was generated by the company's operating cash flow. Investors holding stocks of the acquired company see a drastic reduction in the position of their company due to increased debt held by the company. Example: leveraged buyout of the R.H. Macy & Co., produced a $16 increase in the price of the stock but at the same time, the price of the debt securities fell considerably. Greater resultant debt increases the risk faced by the company which has led to many such failures. JC Flowers & Co., Friedman Fleisher & Lowe, J.P. Morgan and Bank of America purchase of Sallie Mae for $25 billion. Bain Capital Partners & Thomas H. Lee Partners purchase of Clear Channel for $17.9 billion. Value Act Capital & Silver Lake Partners purchase of Acxiom Corp for $3 billion. Tata Tea's decision to acquire Tetley through LBO seems to have many disadvantages. Main problem here to be noted is that Tata Tea wouldn't be generating any extra revenues based on this investment. It was only dilute the earnings and reduce the return on earnings. The leverage buyout failure was affecting the Tata Tea. The reasons which lead the companies that go for leverage buyouts to bankruptcy are the inability to repay the debt is due to the initial overpricing of the target firm, Overoptimistic forecast of the revenues of the target company, an attempt to increase the value of an acquired firm by selling its underperforming business units, the bought out firm faces insolvency due to the insufficiency of the fund caused by the depletion of the operating revenues. Acquired organization, though with good history of cash flows produces reduced cash flow after buyout. Optimism of the new management over the improvement of the firm to boost the cash flows in order to repay the debt turning out to be being overoptimistic. Some companies that are spotted as target of the leverage of the buyouts follow many techniques in orders to save themselves from the threat of leverage buyouts. One of the techniques is poison pill. In this case, the companies follow a self-destructing methodology in order to safeguard themselves from the takeovers.

Let us take example to understand the concept of leveraged buyouts in India using two approaches. Firstly, it has take up cases when the target company is Indian and study the impact of LBO on the stock of that company. Also another case taken when the acquirer is Indian and the impact on its stock is computed.

Indian Target Company

Dummy Case 1

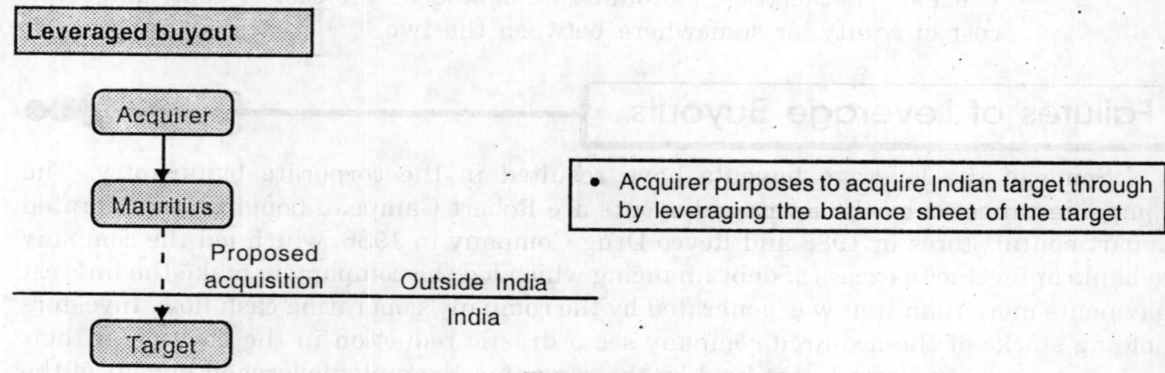

Figure 8.2

Here, the acquirer is an outside Indian company; however, the target is an Indian company. The acquirer, in Mauritius, wishes to acquire the target, based in India.

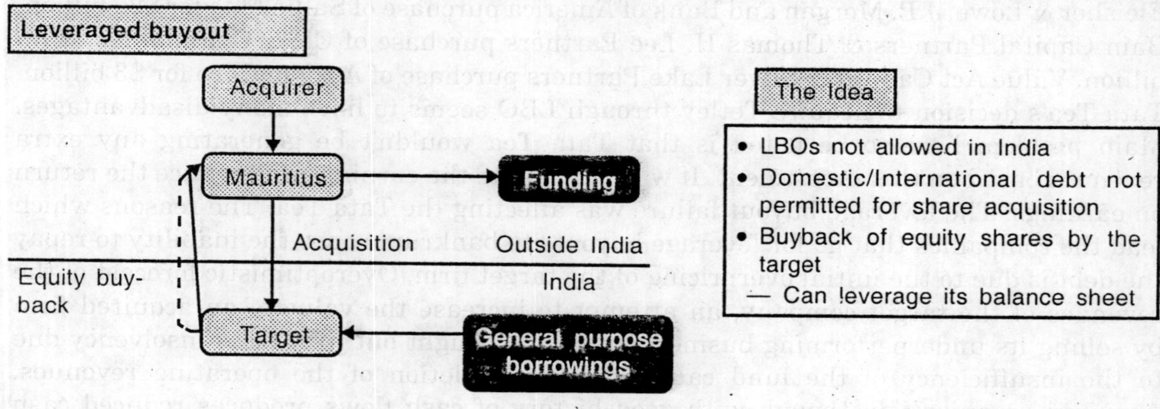

Figure 8.3

Since the rules for LBO in India are very strict and domestic/international debt is not permitted for share acquisition, the acquirer attempts to leverage the balance sheet of the target. The following steps are followed:

- The target company takes a loan from financial institutions in India, for "general purpose"?.
- The funds so received are used to buyback equity shares of itself from the shareholder.
- The acquirer takes a similar loan from a financial institution in its home country, Mauritius in this case.
- The acquirer, using the funds so collected, buys the equity bought back by the target company as an FDI investment and the LBO is indirectly effected.

Dummy Case 2

Another case in focus is when the acquirer is a foreign company and wants to acquire an Indian arm of another foreign company. This is very similar to the actual acquisition of Flextronics India by KKR through LBO. The process has been explained below:

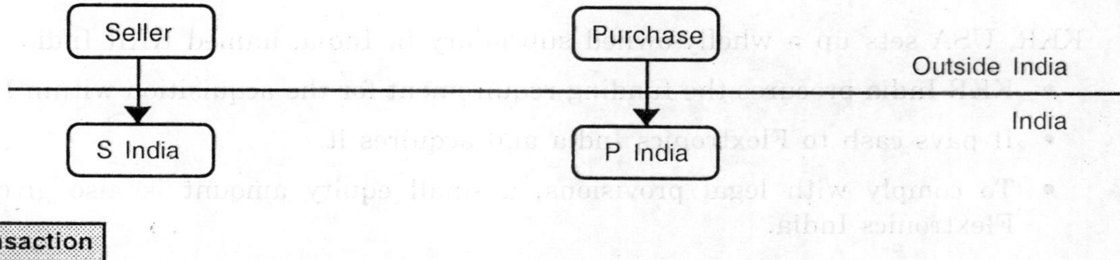

Figure 8.4

Herein, the target company, suppose "Flextronics, India? which is a subsidiary of a foreign company, Flextronics Singapore. Another foreign company, KKR (USA) wishes to acquire the Indian Arm of Flextronics USA, routed through Singapore. Since LBOs are not directly allowed in India, the following procedure would be followed:

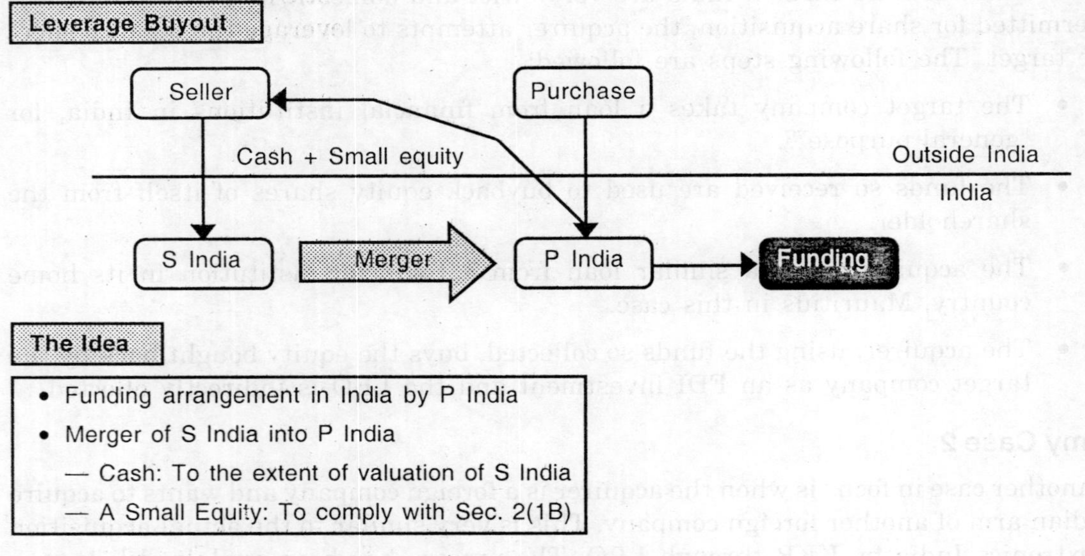

Figure 8.5

KKR, USA sets up a wholly-owned subsidiary in India, named KKR India.

- KKR India procures the funding requirement for the acquisition within India.
- It pays cash to Flextronics India and acquires it.
- To comply with legal provisions, a small equity amount is also given to Flextronics India.
- Since Flextronics India is a wholly-owned subsidiary of Flextronics USA (routed through Singapore), Flextronics India is dissolved and the amount so used for LBO is received by the foreign counterpart.
- The LBO is completed.

Recent LBOs Performance

From the Moody's study of performance of PE firms in the recent past, it is observed that LBOs are not performing well and are going through distressed phase. It is seen that

- On average, companies owned by the largest private equity firms have defaulted at roughly the same rate as similarly rated companies, but have shown higher rates of distress.
- "Mega-deals" – the top 10 private equity-sponsored leveraged buyouts (LBOs) by transaction value – have performed much worse than other private equity deals or similarly rated companies.
- Capital infusions have been rare during the past two years, and have been used mainly to help companies avoid covenant violations, not to reduce leverage.

- Companies that paidout dividends to their private equity sponsors during the first year of ownership have defaulted at rates similar to other deals that have not paid dividends during the first year, and to similarly rated companies.
- With many LBOs already in distress-rated B3 (negative outlook) or lower, it is expected that if the wave of debt maturing in the next 1 to 3 years will increase refinancing risk, and could prompt additional defaults.
- LBOs by Cerberus and Apollo are performing much worse than other private equity deals, while deals by KKR, JP Morgan and Welsh Carson have seen better performance.

The following chart from Moody's takes a sober look at the performance of the largest LBO firms. It presents the percentages of LBO deals by sponsor that are either distressed or have defaulted. Cerberus with investments such as Chrysler and IAP Worldwide (IAP provides support services, particularly for the US government/military) seems to have 2/3 of its LBO deals go bad. Apollo (with deals like Hexion, Berry Plastics, Linens'N Things, and Harrah's) is not too far behind. KKR on the other hand has done quite well. The group of sponsors as a whole is at 40% (distressed and defaulted).

Table 8.4

Performance of Large Private Equity Firms

Summary Data on Sponsored Companies

Deals Initiated Prior to 1/1/08

PE Firm	Total Deals	In Default		Distress		Default and Distress	
	Deals	%age of total	Deals	Deals	%age of total	Deals	%age of total
KKR	20	1	5%	2	10%	3	15%
Blackstone	22	3	14	3	14	6	27
JP Morgan	–		0	2	29	2	29
Welsh Carson	13	–	0	4	31	4	31
TPG	19	3	16	3	16	6	32
Providence equity	12	2	17				
Warburg Pincus	14	1	7	4	29	5	36
Goldman Sachs	21	6	29	2	10	8	38
Bain	22	5	23	5	23	10	45
Carlyle	31	5	16	11	35	16	52
Thlee	11	5	45	1	9	6	55
Apollo	20	8	40	5	25	13	65

Cerberus	6	2	33	2	33	4	67
Subtotal	229	43	19	47	21	90	39
Adj for club deals	(44)	(7)		(9)		(16)	
Total	**186**	**36**	**19**	**38**	**21**	**74**	**40**

Source: Moody's Global Corporate Finance, Nov. 2009.

Summary

LBOs are perceived as complex deals requiring teams of analysts and experts, but in reality, they just use borrowed money to buy companies. While there are forms of LBOs that lead to massive lay-offs and asset sell-offs, some LBOs can be part of a long-term plan to save a company through leveraged acquisitions. However, they are always a part of an economy as long as there are companies, potential buyers and money to lend. The Indian laws in this regard are currently very strict, and it would be interesting to see how these laws shape up in the times to come.

Case of Tata Info Media Limited

Acquirer: ICICI-payments Limited

Date of Announcement: 03rd Sep., 2003

Offer Price: ₹ 176 per share

Deal Structure: Buy 50% management stake, Open offer for 20% stake

Date of Offer Opening: 20th Oct., 2003

Date of Offer Closing: 18th Nov., 2003

Since the LBO market in India is not matured as also the corporate debt market, the effect of LBO announcements is not quite evident on the stock prices of the target company. The general perception among the shareholders is related to losing the control of the company to an outside party, as also the excessive debt involved in such transactions.

The Historical Case of RJR Nabisco LBO by KKR

Introduction

By the summer of 1988, Ross Johnson, CEO of RJR Nabisco (RJR), was becoming increasingly worried about the poor stock price performance of the conglomerate. Despite a strong earnings record, management had not been able to shake loose of its image as a tobacco company, and the stock price was languishing at $55 per share. In October 1988, Johnson and a small team of RJR's executives, backed by the Wall Street firms of Shearson Lehman Hutton and Salomon Brothers, announced a bid of $75 per share for the company. At this price, the deal would have valued at $17.6 billion, more than twice as large as the largest LBO completed up to that point. Because this deal involved the current management of the company, it falls into a special category of LBO deals called management buyouts (MBOs).The announcement focused Wall Street's attention on RJR. Even at this substantial premium, the MBO appeared to be a good deal for Johnson and his team, because soon after the offer went public, it became hotly contested. Foremost among the contenders was the firm of Kohlberg, Kravis and Roberts (KKR). KKR launched its own bid with a cash offer of $90 per share.

On November 7, the Special Committee adopted a set of rules and procedures "to determine which alternative would best serve the interests of [RJR Nabisco's] shareholders". Although not a commitment to recommend selling the company, the rules were "intended to constitute a single round of bidding. Any proposal should reflect the potential purchaser's highest offer". All bids were due by 5 p.m. on Friday, November 18. Any bid that did not conform to these rules would be considered hostile by the Special Committee. The rules for bids included the following:

- Proposals should not be conditional on the sale of any assets of RJR Nabisco.
- Proposals should provide RJR Nabisco shareholders with a "substantial common-stock related interest".
- Proposals should include details on financing arrangements, including commitment agreements and details of any noncash component of the offer.
- Proposals should be approved by the bidding firm's board of directors.

The board of directors and the Special Committee reserved the right to amend or terminate any of the rules, to terminate discussions with any bidder, and to reject any or all proposals.

The Bid War

On a per share basis, KKR's bid was $75 cash, $11 for pay-in-kind preferred stock, and $6 principal amount of pay-in-kind converting debt, which KKR valued at $8.6. The debt would convert to common stock at the end of one year unless the holder decided to retain it. If all debt was converted into common stock, it would represent 25% of the outstanding common stock of RJR Nabisco. The cash portion of the bid would be financed by $1.5 billion in equity, $3.5 billion in subordinated debt, and $12.4 billion in bank debt. KKR also planned on assuming the $5.2 billion of pre-existing debt. On a per share basis, the Management Group's bid was $90 cash, $6 of pay-in-kind preferred stock, and $4 of convertible preferred stock. The convertible preferred stock, as a class, could be converted into about 15% of the surviving company's equity, but it was callable by the company at any time for the face value and accumulated dividends. The cash portion of the bid would be financed by $2.5 billion in equity, $3 billion in subordinated debt, and $15 billion in bank debt. Like KKR, the Management Group planned on assuming the $5.2 billion of outstanding debt. The First Boston Group's offer involved the purchase of RJR Nabisco's tobacco business by the First Boston group and the sale of the food businesses. The food businesses would be sold for a $13-billion instalment note before December 31, 1988, and a right to 80% of the net proceeds of the subsequent sale of the food business in excess of the instalment note. RJR Nabisco shareholders would receive the proceeds from the sale of the food business. First Boston would purchase the tobacco business for $15.75 billion, plus warrants (valued at $2-3 per RJR Nabisco share) to acquire up to 20% of the equity of the tobacco business. On a per share basis, RJR Nabisco shareholders would receive a cash payment ranging from $98 to $110, securities valued at $5, and warrants worth $2-3. Unlike the bids by KKR and the Management Group, the First Boston proposal did not include information about its financing.

The End Result

A bidding war saw the offer price ultimately rise to $109 per share, valuing the deal at more than $25 billion. In the end, both Johnson and KKR offered very similar deals although management's final bid was slightly higher than KKR's. Eventually, RJR's board accepted KKR's bid of $109 per RJR's share. The offer price comprised $81 per share in cash, $18 per share in preferred stock, and $10 per share in debenture securities.

Conclusion

From an economic point of view, this outcome is surprising. One would think that given their inside knowledge of the company, management would be in the best position to not only value it, but also run it. Why, then, would an outsider choose to outbid an insider for a company? The answer in RJR's case appeared to point to managers themselves. As the deal proceeded, it became increasingly obvious to investors that executives (and members of the board of directors) enjoyed perks that were unprecedented. For example, Johnson had the personal use of numerous corporate apartments in different cities and literally a fleet of corporate jets that he, the top executives, and members of the corporate board personally used. In their leveraged buyout proposal, they had obtained a 4% equity stake for top executives that were worth almost $1billion, $52.5 million of golden parachutes and assurances that RJR airforce (the fleet of corporate jets) and the flamboyant Atlanta headquarters would not be subject to budget cutting.

Tata Corus Deal

Background

Let us first look at the two companies involved to understand the scale of the deal.

Tata Steel

Tata Steel was established in 1907 by an Indian Jamshetji Nusserwanji Tata. Tata Steel has quite a few firsts to its credit which include:

- Introduction of an 8-hour workday in 1912 when India was under the British rule.
- It introduced leave-with-pay in 1920, way became legally binding upon employers in India in 1945.
- Tata Steel started a Provident Fund for its employees as early in 1920 much before it became a law for all employers under the Provident Fund Act in 1952.

Tata Steel's has a unique record of the production never been disrupted because of a labour strike.

Tata played a vital role in the improvement of steel production also and hence in the development of India's economy.

Tata Steel was the world's 56th largest and India's 2nd largest steel company with an annual crude steel capacity of 3.8 million tonnes. The company was also recognized as the world's best steel producer by World Steel Dynamics in 2005.

Corus

Through the merger of two companies, British Steel and Koninklijke Hoogovens, following the privatization of many steelworks companies by UK government, Corus Group plc., was formed on 6th October, 1999. Its core business comprises of manufacturing, development and allocation of steel and aluminium products and services. The four divisions of the company were:

- Strip Products
- Long Products
- Aluminium and Distribution
- Building Systems.

The customers for Corus' products were mainly from

- Commercial and military aerospace ventures
- Automotive Industry
- Construction Industry
- Engineering
- Defence and security
- Rail and shipbuilding industry

The company was regarded the largest steel producer in UK with a workforce of 50,000 employees and £10,142 million of annual revenue in 2005.

The Deal

Timeline

October 20, 2006: Tata Steel valued Corus at US$ 8.04 billion; agreed to pick-up a 100% stake at 455 pence per share in an all cash deal

November 19, 2006: The Brazilian steel company CSN made an offer for Corus at 475 pence per share, valuing it at $8.4 billion.

December 11, 2006: Tata upped the offer to 500 pence, which was trumped by CSN's offer of 515 pence per share.

January 31, 2007: Tata Steel tookover Corus after offering 608 pence per share, valuing it at $11.3bn.

Reasons for the Deal

Tata Steel which was a low cost steel producer in fast developing region of the world and Corus which was a high value product manufacturer in the region of the world demanding value products were perfect complements for each other in many ways

- Corus was trying to keep its productions costs low and was looking for sources of iron ore which was complementary to TATA Steel which was one of the lowest cost steel producers in the world and had self-sufficiency in raw material.
- Corus could have got a way in India and SE Asia where Tata had a strong retail and distribution network in
- The companies could have benefitted from technology transfer
- There was a good culture fit between the two organizations both of which highly emphasized on continuous improvement and ethics.

Deal Funding and Structure

The initial motive behind the completion of the deal was not Corus' revenue size, but rather its market Value. Even though Corus is larger in size compared to Tata, the company was valued less than Tata (at approximately $6 billion) at the time when the deal negotiations started. Tata raised $6.17bn of debt for the deal through a new subsidiary of Corus called 'Tata Steel UK', rather than by raising the debt itself. Tata's security credit rating is investment grade, whereas the new subsidiary may not be $3.5-3.8bn infusion from Tata Steel ($2bn as its equity contribution, $1.5-1.8bn through a bridge loan)

The final deal structure was:

	US $bn
Long-term Debt on Corus	6.14
Long-term Debt on Tata Singapore	1.41
Quasi-equity on Tata Singapore	1.25
Total Funding on Corus Assets	8.8
Total Equity Contribution by Tata Steel	4.1
Total Enterprise value for Corus	12.9

$5.6bn through a LBO ($3.05bn through senior term loan, $2.6bn through high yield loan)

TATA Tetley LBO

Tata Tea acquired the United Kingdom-based Tetley Group in 2000. It was a £271 million ($432 million) leveraged buyout. Tata Tea in the process outbid the American conglomerate Sara Lee. Takeover was the largest in size by an Indian company of a foreign company that time.

Tata Tea

Tata Tea is a part of Tata group, one of India's most admired and trusted group of companies. It was incorporated in 1962 as Tata-Finlay Limited and started business in 1963. The company bought the stake belonging to the James Finlay group to form the individual entity in 1983. The company then decided to move from the commodities business to consumer branding in the same year and Tata Tea brand was introduced in the market which was followed by other brands like Kannan Devan, Agni, Gemini and Chakra Gold. In 1987, Tata Tea set up a fully-owned subsidiary, Tata Tea Inc., in the USA. In the 1990s, Tata Tea decided to take its brands into the global markets. It formed an export joint venture with Britain's Tetley Tea in 1992 and in the mid-1990s; Tata Tea attempted to buy Tetley. By 1999, Tata Tea's brands had a combined market share of 25% in India. The company had 74 tea gardens and was producing 62 million kilograms of tea a year, two-thirds of it packaged and branded.

Tetley

Established in 1837, Tetley was the first British tea company to introduce the tea bag to UK in 1953. The tea bag was followed by the first round tea bag in 1989 and the 'no drip, no mess' drawstring bag in 1997. Before the acquisition Tetley was the world's second largest tea company after Unilever's Brooke Bond-Lipton and had an annual turnover of £300 million. Tetley was the market leader in Britain and Canada and a popular brand in the United States, Australia and the Middle East.

The Deal

There are several reasons which made the deal special for corporate India, some of which are:

- It was the first ever leveraged buyout by an Indian company which made it possible for Tata Tea to minimize its cash outlay in making the purchase
- Tetley's price tag of $450 mn was nearly four times the net worth of Tata Tea ($ 114 mn)
- The deal gave Tata Tea a way into the high end tea market in Western countries

Tata Tea created a Special Purpose vehicle christened as Tata Tea (Great Britain) to acquire all the properties of Tetley. The SPV was capitalized at 70 mn pounds of which 60 mn pounds were contributed by Tata Tea and the remaining 10 mn pound by the US subsidiary of the company. The SPV leveraged the 70 mn pound equity .36 times to raise a debt of 235 mn pounds which comprised of four tranches whose tenure varied from 7 years to 9.5 years. The actual cost for the LBO came out to be $305 mn. This included the basic $271 mn for the company plus $9 mn in legal fee and $25 mn for Tetley's working capital requirement.

CASE: NAVEEN PARTNERS PVT. LTD.

Naveen partners, a private equity organizations specializing in distressed company investing, was interested in purchasing turn around. Mr. Ranold a general partner at venture used the following projections to value turnaround (all data are in ₹ crore)

	Year-1	Year-2	Year-3	Year-4	Year-5
Revenue	400	420	440	460	280
Costs	200	210	220	230	240
EBIT	200	210	220	230	240
Δ NWC	6	6	8	8	10

Turnaround had ₹ 440 crore of NOL's which were available to be offset future income. At the beginning of year-1 the company had ₹ 150 crore of 8% debt which was expected to be repaid in three ₹ 50 crore instalments beginning at the end of year one the tax rate was 40%. Mr. Ralond believed an appropriate unlevered beta for turnaround was 0.8. The ten-year treasury bond yield was 7% and the market risk premium 7.5%. Net cash flows were forecast to grow at 3% per year in perpetuity after year-5. (Growth rate is assuming 3% per annum) Calculate using Adjusted Present Value Method.

Note: The case is fictitious and any resemblance to a person/company is merely coincidental.

Review Questions

1. What are the motives of LBO? What are its Pros and Cons?
2. What are the structure and organisation of buyout firms?
3. What are the valuation method available for LBOs?
4. Write short notes on
   (a) MBO
   (b) MBI
   (c) IBO
5. **Quiz:**
   (a) Leverage buyout of a firm carried out without the wishes of the acquired firm's managers are called as ______ leverage buyout.
   (b) Management buyouts are an important role in the corporate restructuring besides ______.
   (c) Buyout funds are structured as limited partnerships, with the firm's principals acting as _____ and investors in the fund being _____.
   (d) LBO firms charge their limited partners a management fee to cover overhead expenses associated with identifying, evaluating and executing acquisitions by the fund. ***(T/F)***
   (e) Institutional buyouts are the similar of management buyouts (MBO), in which a business's current management acquires a large part of the company. ***(T/F)***

CHAPTER

9

Mezzanine Financing

Introduction

In recent times, existing lines of credit have been reduced. Traditional lenders have become stricter in providing loans. Apart of it, access to the public capital markets is virtually non-existent and the economic downturn has been financially challenging for many businesses. Favourable changes in the foreign trade policy in emerging markets have contributed to the growth of private equity in India. Mezzanine finance is an alternative source of finance to debt and equity and it can be helpful in financing the start-up and firm's expansion, innovation and business transfers. The popularity of mezzanine financing is steadily growing among many middle-market businesses. It is viewed as the best option to acquire additional capital. It often bridges the gap in corporate capital structure between senior debt and equity. Though mezzanine finance instruments are gaining importance in recent years but they still remain little used compared with loan financing. So this chapter makes an endeavour to elucidate the significance of mezzanine finance which provides medium to long-term capital without significant ownership dilution and offers flexibility to meet both the investor's and investee company's requirements. It also highlights how mezzanine capital can help the company to secure more capital by analysing the comparison of various types of securities and the effect of J-curve in mezzanine financing.

In recent years, financial markets have tightened and debts multiples have fallen to historic lows. Many companies today experience this frustration. This is where mezzanine financing comes in and successfully bridging the gap between equity and senior loan funding. Its importance has increased dramatically within the last few years because of inflexible bank criteria. However, in the face of the current credit market turmoil, mezzanine products are increasingly being considered as a viable and important source of financing in both the United States and Europe, and also in Asia and Latin

America. Mezzanine finance has traditionally been viewed in some markets as a buy and hold product that was not widely distributed or traded. Mezzanine lending has been around for more than two decades. In the 1980s, the business was dominated by insurance companies and savings and loan associations. By the 1990s, Limited Partnerships (LPs) had entered the arena. Today, investors include pension funds, hedge funds, leveraged public funds, LPs and insurance companies, as well as banks that have established standalone mezzanine efforts. Mezzanine financing is characterized by its ability to provide funding business propositions with a higher risk factor versus what regular lending institutions are willing to take. It has the ability to be subsidiary to a bank debt but Mezzanine capital has always been an important element of financing for growing companies.

What is Mezzanine Finance?

Mezzanine financing is a hybrid of debt and equity financing. It's an alternative financing instrument for corporate who are planning ambitious buyouts, turnarounds, expansions and non-asset-based borrowings. It is useful for start-ups and infrastructure projects. It is generally used to finance the expansion of existing companies. Basically, it is debt capital, with current repayment requirements, but with rights to convert to an ownership or equity interest in a company. It is usually subordinated to senior debt but ranks higher than common equity provided by senior lenders such as banks and venture capital companies. Mezzanine finance is a collective term for hybrid forms of finance. It is sometimes referred to as the "bridge" between the traditional bank debt loans and the private equity investment. It normally begins as a regular debt loan with the usual interest rates applied. But, in the event that the debt is not paid in time or in full, the loan can shift to some sort of equity loan. This means that the lender does gain a portion of principal rights to the business. Typically, mezzanine financing is structured as a note with an interest rate and a warrant to buy a number of shares in the issuing company. Thus, mezzanine providers are in a sense both lenders and investors. As lenders, they are concerned about the stability of cash flow, high interest and debt service coverage ratios, as well as the amount, amortization and collateral of the senior debt that has a higher priority. But as equity investors, they are equally interested in the "upside." or the potential ability of the company to achieve superior results and create value for shareholders. Though mezzanine finance has perceived as a bridging loan, but it is increasingly used as a standalone investment in buyouts or as a substantial investment to further expand a business. One thing that comes out clearly is that this fund is for those companies that cannot borrow from the conventional sources like banks and FIIs and don't have an asset cover to offer. Mezzanine financing is typically found with venture capital companies and/or alternative lending institutions seeking a higher rate of return. Today, mezzanine capital has evolved into a highly structured and negotiated product and assumed a much more significant role in the capital structure. Key comparisons among different classes of investment is exhibited in Table 9.1.

Table 9.1: Different Classes of Investment

	Senior Debt	High Yield Bond	Mezzanine Finance	Private Equity Venture Capital
Nature	Loan, ranks highest in times of liquidation	Loan, subordinated to senior debt but ranks higher than common equity	Loan, subordinated to senior loan and usually bonds but ranks higher than common equity	Usually common equity, however may be in the form of convertible bond with a low coupon rate
Covenants/ undertakings	Stringent	Less stringent than senior debt	Less stringent than senior debt	Least stringent
Equity component	Absent	Absent	Call option/ convertible bond to convert into common equity	Common equity. Option to convert to common equity if it is a convertible bond
Shareholding dilutive effect	Absent	Absent	Less dilutive than private equity/ venture capital	More dilutive than mezzanine finance
Return expected from investors	Market lending rate	12-14% p.a.	18-20% p.a., inclusive of 10-12% p.a. coupon rate, with the remaining return from the equity portion or higher stepped up interest rate/other formula tied to the performance of the company	30%-35% p.a.

Source: http://www.technopreneurial.com

General Characteristics of Mezzanine Finance

Layer of capital between senior debt and common equity, including subordinated debt, preference shares, convertible bonds

- Repayment of debt component through amortization or conversion
- Covenant protection and creditor rights
- Equity participations

Types of Mezzanine Finance

There are various types of mezzanine finance, each having its own unique characteristics. Mezzanine debt is taking the form of convertible debt, senior subordinated debt or private "mezzanine" securities. Mezzanine capital often is a more expensive financing source for a company than secured debt or senior debt. Private mezzanine debt securities are highly negotiated instruments, and are thus illiquid investments. No active market exists to trade these securities. As a result, any trading usually involves a negotiated process directly involving buyer and seller. Private mezzanine debt also contains a very loose covenant package. The higher cost of capital associated with mezzanine financings is the result of its location as an unsecured, subordinated obligation in a company's capital structure. The most common form of mezzanine finance is the subordinated loan, which is an unsecured loan with a lower ranking in case of bankruptcy compared to senior debt.

Participating loans are normal loans, but they do not give rise to an ownership relationship. Participation in losses is contractually excluded. In legal terms, a "silent" participation is closer to a stockholding than a subordinated or participating loan. The distinguishing feature of this form of financing is that one or more persons take an equity stake in a company, but without assuming any liability to the company's creditors. The typical "silent" participation affects only the company's internal affairs and is not apparent to outside observers. Participation in profits and losses and contractual rights of approval and control are structured flexibly. (Credit Suisse Economic Research, 2006.) There are also equity related mezzanine finance instruments. Mezzanine products with profit participation rights are more related to equity and under company law the holder is entitled to rights over the company's profits. A further equity mezzanine financing instrument is the convertible bond. In addition to the usual right to fixed interest payments and repayment of principal, holders of convertible bonds or bonds with warrants have the right to acquire shares in the company instead of accepting repayment of the bond. This right is exercisable for a defined period and at a predetermined conversion or subscription rate. This way the issuer may convert debt into equity. Another equity mezzanine financing instrument is the bond with warrants, which in principal is similar to the convertible bond. The main difference is that the warrants (subscription rights) are separate from the bond and thus can be traded independently.(Credit Suisse Economic Research, 2006.)

Mezzanine capital is typically used to fund a growth opportunity, such as an acquisition, new product-line, and new distribution channel or plant expansion. The popularity of mezzanine financing is steadily growing among many middle-market businesses. In fact, this type of financing generally assists in business fusions or mergers, business procurement, rising development opportunity, management buyouts, addition of capital or even corporate restructuring. Mezzanine debt capital generally refers to that layer of financing between a company's senior debt and equity, filling the gap between the two. Structurally, it is subordinate in priority of payment to senior debt, but senior in rank to common stock or equity which is clearly stated in Fig. 9.1.

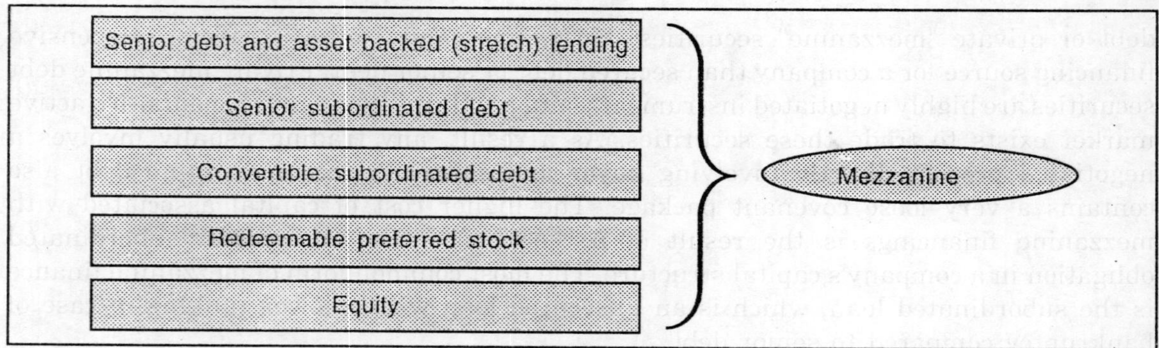

Figure 9.1

Source: Fitch Ratings

Importance of Mezzanine Capital

Mezzanine loans fill the gap between equity and senior debt and are often used to finance leveraged buyouts, to recapitalize a company's balance sheet or to fund internal growth strategies. Mezzanine loans have thus become a common alternative to conventional subordinate financing where the terms of a first position loan prohibit junior liens. Mezzanine finance instruments have been gaining in importance nowadays. Mezzanine finance products usually have the following positive features:

- Mezzanine finance is an unsecured form of financing that is principally a loan. It is subordinated to senior loans. This results in an improving leverage effect in balance sheet structure.
- A company can retain control and avoid surrendering ownership rights by choosing the appropriate form of mezzanine finance.
- In general the cost of mezzanine finance for a company is lower than for pure equity.
- Interest payments on some types of mezzanine finance are tax-deductible.
- Mezzanine finance is a very useful financial tool for business expansion, business transfer, and public to private transactions.
- Mezzanine finance providers' revenues are higher than for senior debt.
- Mezzanine finance providers' are not only offering debt finance but also advice and valuable strategic assistance when the return on the investment is partly dependent on the performance of the company.

Mezzanine Financing Structure, Terms and Pricing

- Mezzanine capital is largely unsecured risk capital which normally has to be repaid and serviced on an annual basis similar to a loan.
- Mezzanine fills the financing gap between equity and debt and can be structured with features of either debt or equity to achieve an optimal combination that matches the specific situation and requirements of the company.
- In a company's capital structure it can be a substitute for both debt and equity.
- Negotiable and interrelated are: amortization schedule; equity and/or profit participation rights; current interest rate; collateral; value of the company; and puts and calls; etc.

Equity Features

- Risk bearing through subordination
- Profit sharing and equity return participation through an "equity kicker"
- Security interest not always required
- Equity optionality through conversion rights or warrants

Debt Features

- Interest payments and principal repayment
- Financial performance ratios
- Other covenants Mezzanine Finance

Table 9.2: Mezzanine Features

Debt Component	Equity Component
• Long-term (Subordinated) Debt	Convertible Feature • Equity Options • Warrants • Profit participation tied into: — EBITDA — Net Income — Equity Value — Other Variable

The private equity market values companies on the basis of a multiple of EBITDA (Earnings before Interest, Taxes, Depreciation, and Amortization). Private equity deals use a "three layer cake" analogy consisting of senior debt, mezzanine debt and equity. This structure is the most commonly used in the private equity world. This structure is generally used in a leveraged buyout or a change in control transaction because it allows the equity provider to leverage his down payment to purchase the target company. Each layer is different and has its own unique characteristics and each layer has its own risk/ reward profile

Layer 1 – Senior Debt – Low risk, low cost, and short-term, least flexible.

Layer 2 – Mezzanine Debt – Moderate risk, moderate cost, and long-term, flexible

Layer 3 – Equity – High risk, high cost, long-term, most flexible

Just because a 3 layer cake structure is the most common structure does not mean that it is the only structure that can be used.

- Each layer of capital can be used on its own or in conjunction with other layers in varying degrees for any given transaction.
- There is no rule that requires equity to be used in every transaction nor is there a rule that requires senior debt or mezzanine debt to be used in every transaction.
- Each of these layers has advantages and disadvantages and can be mixed and matched to fit the unique needs of each business.

Mezzanine loans are typically utilized in conjunction with equity capital and senior debt and would rank second below first-lien debt, but above equity in the event of bankruptcy. Mezzanine loans are therefore a more expensive source of financing than senior debt because of the increased credit risk. Consequently, a mezzanine financier is generally looking for a 16 to 30 per cent return on investment. A mezzanine deal size typically ranges from $1 million to $25 million. Typically, mezzanine capital is priced to yield roughly an annual compounded internal rate of return of 18% to 22%, depending on the risk associated with the transaction. Mezzanine debt is typically issued with a cash pay interest rate of 12% to 14% and a maturity ranging from five to seven years with the bulk of the principal often paid toward the back-end of the loan. The remainder of the desired 18% to 22% all-in return consists of warrants to buy common stock, which the investor values based on the outlook of the company's fiscal health. In addition to an interest payment normally associated with debt, mezzanine loans will often include an option for an equity stake in the company in the form of warrants to convert the debt to equity much like that of a convertible bond. Mezzanine investors usually hold warrants for far less than 50% of any one company. The fee for raising the money runs between 2% and 3% of the transaction. Mezzanine investors are looking for an 18 to 20 per cent IRR (internal rate of return) compared to 25 to 35 per cent for equity investors, so it's more cost-effective. In Fig. 9.2, mezzanine debt is shown adding significant capital enabling a company to grow with no dilution to Company owners.

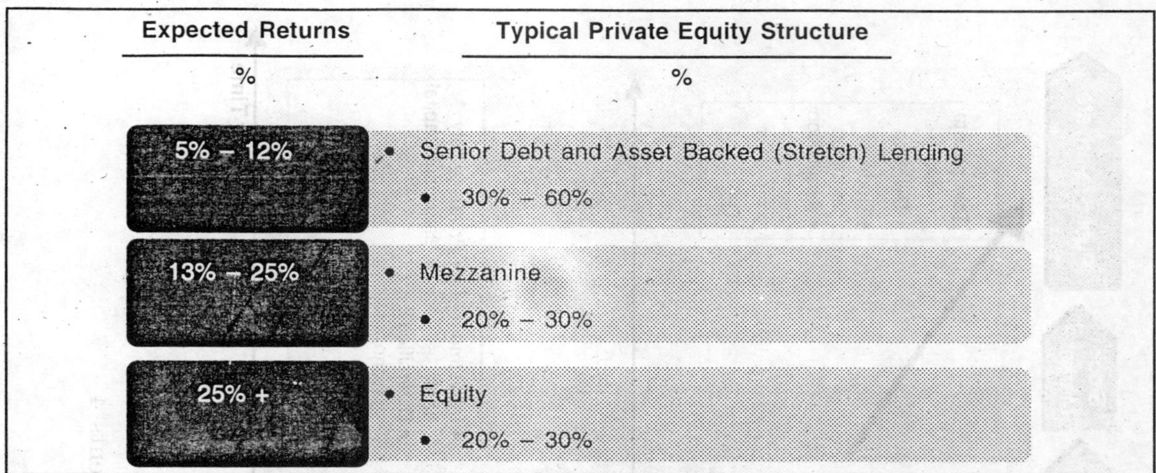

Figure 9.2

Source: *Management Magazine*, Bond Capital, January, 2006

Key Advantage of Mezzanine Capital

Normally, SMEs in the second stage of their development often require risk capital for product introduction and expansion. But many of these companies are reluctant to give up equity stakes to outside investors as it would result in the loss of control over the company. Mezzanine finance could provide a solution here.

- Many times a company is looking for business succession to be transferred to the next generation a business transfer generally requires substantial funds. Business transfers can also involve the transfer of intangible assets. Banks are often reluctant to finance such transactions for their high level of risk. There is no one fits-all solution: in each case the different interests at stake have to be taken into account and the appropriate solution will often be a specific mix of equity, quasi-equity and debt.
- Mezzanine financing is advantageous because it is treated like equity on a company's balance sheet and may make it easier to obtain standard bank financing.
- To attract mezzanine financing, a company usually must demonstrate a track record in the industry with an established reputation and product, a history of profitability and a viable expansion plan for the business (e.g., expansions, acquisitions, IPO).
- The cost of mezzanine capital (18% to 22%) is significantly lower than the returns (25% to 35%) targeted by equity investors.
- Interest on mezzanine debt is a tax-deductible expense, unlike dividends on preferred or common equity.

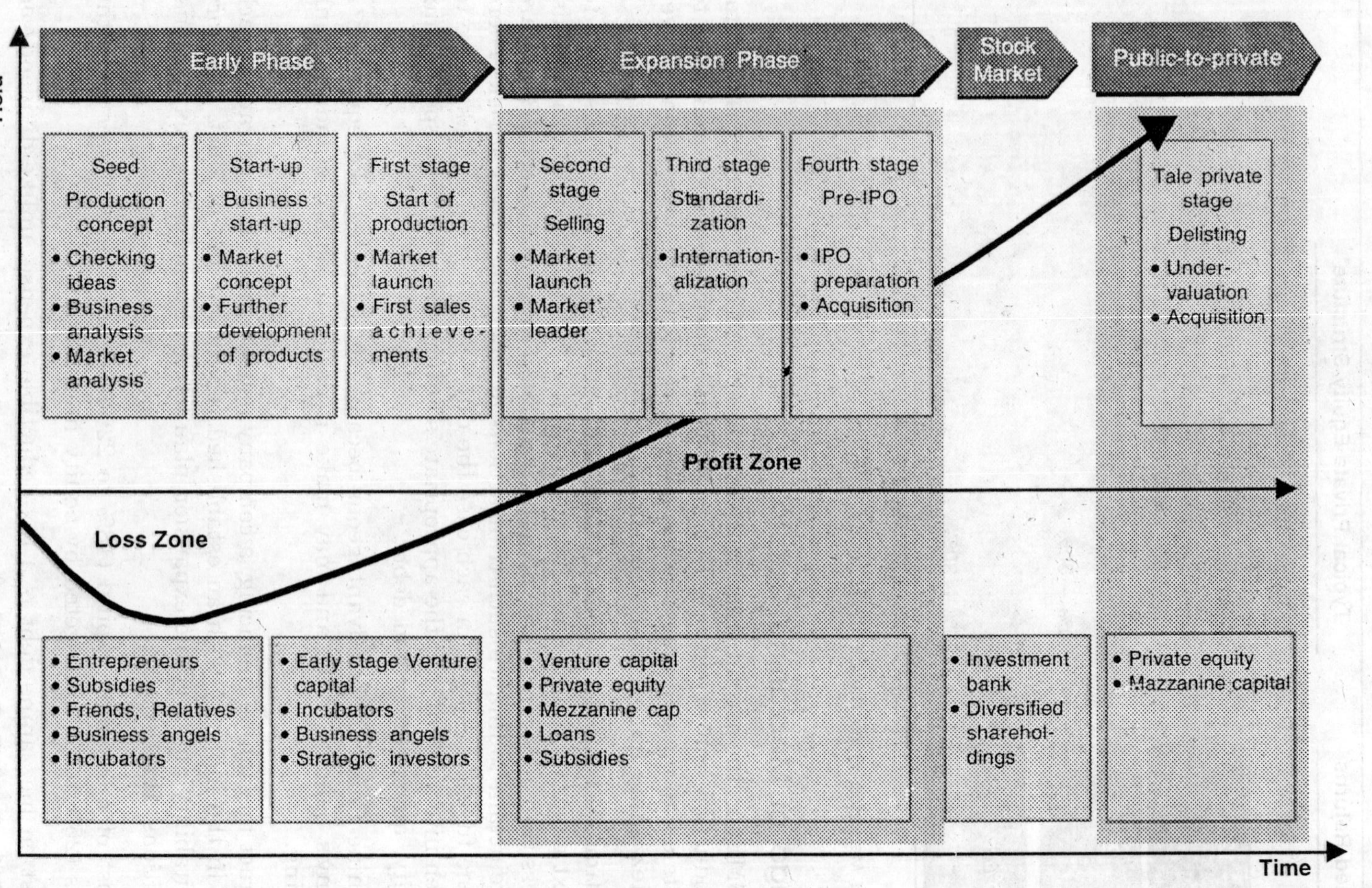

Fig. 9.3 Phases in a company's development and used financing instruments [4]

Source: Deutsche Industrie bank, presentation Dr.I. Natusch, Round Table Talks, October 23th, 2003.

- Mezzanine capital can provide an increase in senior lending potential, since most lenders regard mezzanine capital as quasi-equity.
- Mezzanine capital is usually a valuable financing alternative for management seeking to raise capital in the later phases of a company's development and is not suited for start-up financing.
- It provides access to bank funding that might not otherwise have been available.
- This kind of arrangement does not involve issuing conventional shares to the lender, so the value of any existing shareholdings in the company is not diluted.
- Debt associated with a mezzanine finance arrangement is generally redeemed in a one-off payment rather than paid monthly over a period of years.
- The repayment requirement does not put a strain on cash flow.
- It is often payable after or over a longer period of time than normal credit terms.

Disadvantages

- Mezzanine loans can be expensive, for example, if the bank is providing unsecured senior debt.
- The single redeeming payout will involve a significant sum of money.
- The exit payment could put significant strain on businesses that fail to fulfil their growth plans.

What Kind of Returns do Mezzanine Lenders Expect?

Mezzanine lenders, typically specialist mezzanine investment funds, look for a certain rate of return which can come from four sources: (each individual security can be made up of any of the following or a combination thereof):

- **Cash Interest:** A periodic payment of cash based on a percentage of the outstanding balance of the mezzanine financing. The interest rate can be either fixed throughout the term of the loan or can fluctuate (i.e., float) along with LIBOR or other base rates.
- **PIK Interest:** Payable in kind interest is a periodic form of payment in which the interest payment is not paid in cash but rather by increasing the principal amount by the amount of the interest (e.g., a $100 million bond with an 8% PIK interest rate will have a balance of $108 million at the end of the period but will not pay any cash interest). PIK income is less risky than warrants and effectively increases the defined return portion of the deal.
- **Ownership:** Along with the typical interest payment associated with debt, mezzanine capital will often include an equity stake in the form of attached

warrants or a conversion feature, similar to that of a convertible bond. The ownership component in mezzanine securities is almost always accompanied by either cash interest or PIK interest and in many cases by both.

Mezzanine lenders will also often charge an arrangement fee, payable upfront at the closing of the transaction. Arrangement fees contribute the least return and are aimed primarily to cover administrative costs and as an incentive to complete the transaction.

Mezzanine Finance from Investors Prospective

Like all lenders, mezzanine finance investors also assess the borrower's ability about service the periodic interest payments and the loan repayment. Mezzanine finance investors are less particular with collateral but more stringent in their due diligence and focus on the cash flow generation of the business. In a way, mezzanine finance investors look at parallel criteria as equity investors. The most important factor considered by them is the management team; the team must have a credible track record to run the business. Unlike equity investors, since mezzanine finance investors require consistent interest payments, the business must have a compelling growth story: not only will it meet the consistent interest payments for the investment. They are looking or the following point:

- Balances risk and return between equity and senior debt.
- Has fixed income style performance characteristics.
- Has equity type upside features and options
- Provides limited return volatility (graph)
- Has structured exits, a declining exposure profile and relatively low default risk
- Gives investment protection through covenants, security and restructuring options

Mezzanine from the Borrower's Perspective

From a borrower's perspective, mezzanine capital is more flexible than bank debt and less expensive and dilutive than common equity. If seen closely, mezzanine capital forms a very small percentage of a company's total available capital. A flexible form of risk capital that can be tailored to meet specific financing needs and cash flow profiles

- A financing layer that sits between senior debt and equity in a company's capital structure
- Long-term source of largely unsecured risk capital with debt repayment characteristics
- Flexible amortization and interest payment options
- If well structured, mezzanine will lower the average cost of capital and improve the returns of existing shareholders

- Cost of mezzanine between that of senior debt and equity
- As provider of risk capital, the lender shares in a company's financial success but without significant dilution of existing equity interests

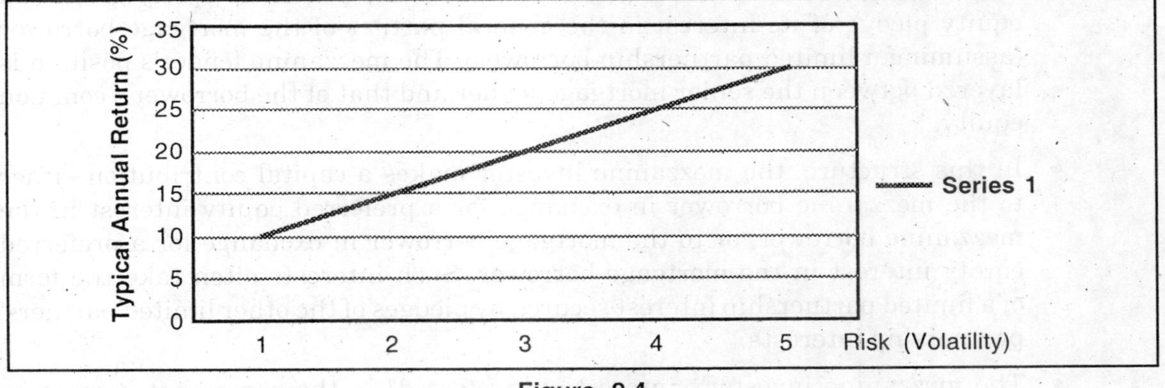

Figure 9.4

Uses of Mezzanine Capital

(a) Leveraged Buyouts: In leveraged buyouts, mezzanine capital is used in conjunction with other securities to fund the purchase price of the company being acquired. Typically, mezzanine capital will be used to fill a financing gap between less expensive forms of financing (e.g., senior loans, second lien loan, and high yield financings) and equity. Often, a financial sponsor will exhaust other sources of capital before turning to mezzanine capital. Financial sponsors will seek to use mezzanine capital in a leveraged buyout in order to reduce the amount of the capital invested by the private equity firm. Because mezzanine lenders typically have a lower target cost of capital than the private equity investor, using mezzanine capital can potentially enhance the private equity firm's investment returns. Additionally, middle market companies may be unable to access the high yield market due to high minimum size requirements, creating a need for flexible, private mezzanine capital.

(b) Real Estate Finance: In real estate finance, mezzanine loans are often used by developers to secure supplementary financing for development projects (typically in cases where the primary mortgage or construction loan equity requirements are larger than 10%). These sorts of mezzanine loans are often collateralized by the stock of the development company rather than the developed property itself (as would be the case with a traditional mortgage). This allows the lender to engage in a more rapid seizure of underlying collateral in the event of default and foreclosure. Standard mortgage foreclosure proceedings can take more than a year, whereas stock is a personal asset of the borrower and can be seized through a legal process taking as little as a few months. The essentials of a conventional mezzanine loan are as follows:

- The mezzanine lender loans the additional funding to an intermediate holding company which is either the parent of the mortgage borrower or some other upper-tier entity indirectly owning the passive equity interest (e.g., a limited partnership interest) in the mortgage borrower.

- As security, the mezzanine borrower grants an equity pledge of its interest in the mortgage borrower; the mezzanine borrower's parent company grants an equity pledge of its interest in the general partner of the mortgage borrower (assuming a limited partnership borrower). The mezzanine lender's position is layered between the senior mortgage lender and that of the borrower's common equity.
- In this structure, the mezzanine investor makes a capital contribution either to the mezzanine borrower in exchange for a preferred equity interest in the mezzanine borrower, or to the mortgage borrower in exchange for a preferred equity interest in the mortgage borrower. Such interests often take the form of a limited partnership interest secured by pledges of the other limited partners' partnership interests.
- The mezzanine investor's interest is "preferred" in the sense that it receives distributions of excess cash flow before the other partners. These distributions usually are equivalent to a coupon rate of interest, but may also include a share of profits *pro rata* with the other partners. In certain default scenarios, the preferred partner also has the right to take control of the borrower-partnership.

Mezzanine financing is an increasingly popular alternative to subordinate mortgage financing because it shifts the risk of property ownership from senior lender to mezzanine lender and proportionally compensates the mezzanine lender for such risk. Most senior mortgage lenders seek specific yield without the risks associated with property ownership. Many investment institutions, such as banks and insurance companies are penalized by regulatory authorities when a real estate investment goes from debt to equity, i.e., mortgage to foreclosure. Instead of encumbering the property with an additional mortgage, the partnership or equity interest in the mortgage borrower can be used to create a mezzanine financing opportunity. By utilizing this type of financing a real property owner, can obtain more money and greater flexibility, than through subordinate mortgage financing.

How do You Secure More Mezzanine Capital?

Some closely held companies, particularly those that are family controlled, are reluctant to consider mezzanine financing because historically it requires relinquishing a certain amount of ownership. However, a mezzanine investor's goal isn't to be a long-term shareholder, but rather to achieve a target return rate by some specified time. It's also important for a business owner to realize that a large ownership interest in a stagnant or underperforming business may not be as valuable as a smaller ownership in a growing company. What's more, having mezzanine debt in place actually can help a company secure more total capital. For e.g., if a client approached a bank and said,

'I'm buying a company for $100 million and I want all the debt to be bank debt and I'll put the rest in equity', the bank may lend $50 of that $100 million. However, with a mezzanine component, the bank may lend less, let's say $40 million and the sub-debt lender might put in $25 million, bringing the total debt raised to $65 million. As the overall level of debt increases, the actual amount of bank debt shrinks due to increased risk, but the total amount raised is higher when the mezzanine layer is added. Ultimately, this would reduce the equity requirement from $50 million to $35 million.

In addition, banks often look more favourably on companies that are backed by institutional investors and may extend credit under more attractive terms. Mezzanine lenders also may reserve a portion of their available capital in order to make additional investments in those companies that perform well. The amount of money raised for mezzanine financing has grown dramatically in recent years. Currently mezzanine providers are struggling to find good investments for billions of dollars of committed, untapped capital.

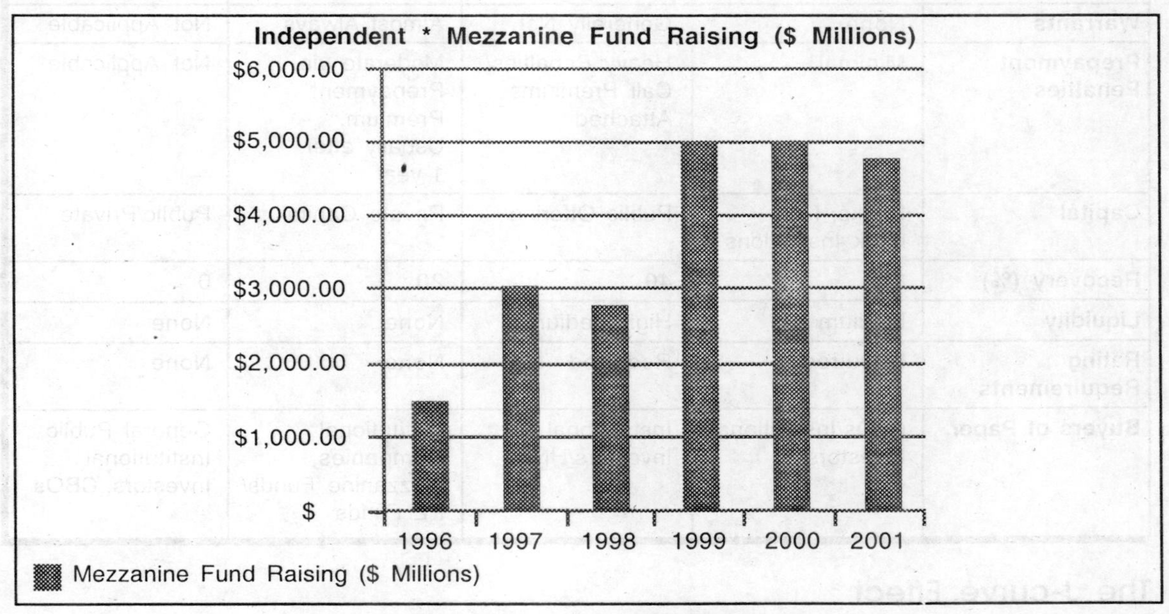

Figure 9.5: Mezzanine Fund Raising

* Excludes self-financed vehicles such as insurance companies, banks, speciality finance companies, CBOs, etc.

Source: Private Equity Analyst

Finally, a clearly defined exit strategy is pivotal to the decision since the overall return on investment hinges on the investor's ability to obtain the value of its equity position. The sale of the company, a recapitalization, a refinancing, and – less frequently these days – an initial public offering, all are potentially viable liquidity events. The private mezzanine securities market has grown from $15.2 billion raised by 1998 to more than $37.3 billion by 2002, according to Venture Economics.

Table 9.3: Comparison of Single B Security Classes

	Leveraged Loans	High Yield	Mezzanine	Public Equity
Security	First Lien	Unsecured	Unsecured	None
Ranking	Senior	Contractual Subordination	Contractual/ Structural Subordination	Junior
Covenants	Generally Comprehensive	Incurrence-based	Less Restrictive, Mostly Financial; Maintenance-Based	None
Terms	5 Years	10 Years	8 Years	Open ended
Coupon	Cash Pay – Floating	Cash Pay – Fixed	Cash Pay – Fixed/PIK	Dividends
All-in Rate	L + 437.5	T + 583	13%	Variable
Warrants	None	Generally Not	Almost Always	Not Applicable
Prepayment Penalties	Minimal	Heavy Penalties/ Call Premiums Attached	Moderate via Prepayment Premium, Usually after 1 year	Not Applicable
Capital	Banks, Non-bank Institutions	Public Offering	Private Capital	Public/Private
Recovery (%)	80	40	20	0
Liquidity	Medium	High/Medium	None	None
Rating Requirements	Required	Required	None	None
Buyers of Paper	CLOs/Institutional Investors	Institutional Investors/HNIs/	Institutional Companies, Mezzanine Funds/ PE Funds	General Public, Institutional Investors, CBOs

The J-curve Effect

The sudden attention towards mezzanine funds may be best explained by the "J-curve" phenomenon. The J-curve is a private equity investment measurement tool used to determine the rate of return for investments over a certain period of time. Typically, private equity funds experience negative returns during the first few years due to fees, overhead expenses and other costs charged to the fund. As an investment matures, expenses are recouped and valuations rise.

Correspondingly, the internal rate of return (IRR) generally rises to positive levels. In effect, you have an IRR that looks like a slanted "J", reflecting negative returns during the early life of an investment with an increasingly upward sloping return as the investment matures.

Given the spectacular crash in equity values in the technology sector, many venture capital funds are faced with the possibility of inverted J-curves. By contrast, mezzanine fund managers are attracted to the cash-on-cash returns (cash received/initial cash outlay) generated by the debt element of private mezzanine securities. Typically, an average performing mezzanine fund is able to avoid the steep negative returns compared to a pure equity fund as a result of the contractual cash coupon.

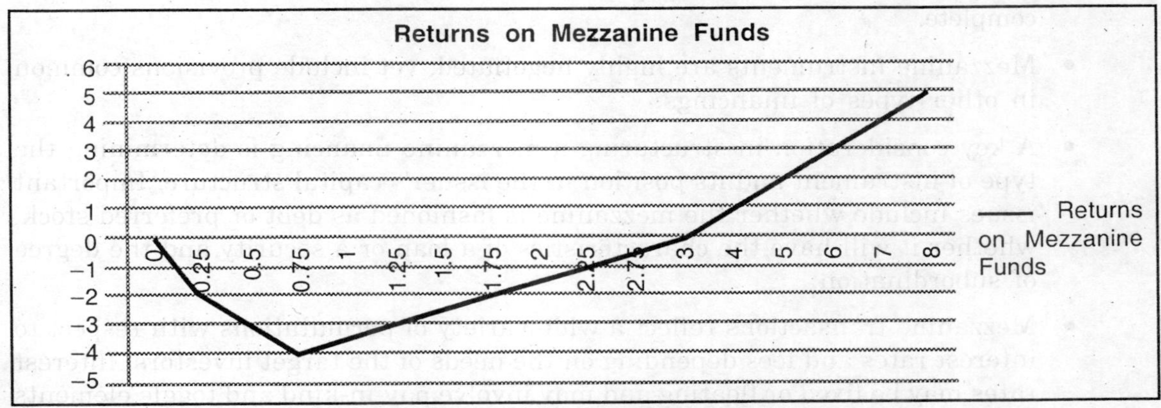

Figure 9.6: Return on Mezzanine Funds

Mezzanine CDOs and Non-traditional Funds

The growth of middle-market, private equity and other alternative asset class mezzanine collateralized debt obligations (CDOs) is on the rise. It seems that given the attractive risk-adjusted returns of mezzanine debt securities, they would be a natural fit to join this ongoing trend. Of course, the illiquid nature of assets (mezzanine debt securities) and the uncertainty of the ramp-up period are just a couple of challenges that would need to be overcome to construct a mezzanine-backed CDO. On the other hand, other non-traditional funds have started to emerge. Traditional limited partnership funds (LPs) are under increasing pressure to sustain their high level of returns in the face of lower returns experienced by equity providers. Leveraged LP structures in which LP interests are trenched may be a means of satisfying various investor return thresholds.

Issues in Mezzanine Financing

Mezzanine finance provides also some challenges for financiers and small and middle enterprises:

- Mezzanine finance is often difficult to obtain by low- and middle-tier small and middle enterprises.
- To obtain mezzanine finance the transparency requirements of companies are very high and stringent.

- Mezzanine finance is more expensive than debt financing.
- The interest component and the debt-like characteristics of mezzanine finance make it difficult for suppliers of mezzanine finance to low and middle-tier SMEs to arrange an early exit. For the upper-tier SME segment secondary markets exist.
- Individually structured mezzanine deals will often take several months to complete.
- Mezzanine instruments are highly negotiated, yet include provisions common in other types of financings.
- A key consideration in structuring a mezzanine financing is determining the type of instrument and its position in the issuer's capital structure. Important issues include whether the mezzanine is fashioned as debt or preferred stock, whether it will have the characteristics of a loan or a security and the degree of subordination.
- Mezzanine transactions reflect a wide variety of permutations with respect to interest rates and fees depending on the needs of the target investors. Interest rates may be fixed or floating and may involve pay-in-kind and toggle elements in certain circumstances. In addition, there are a wide range of possible fee alternatives that must be addressed.
- Redemption and call protection provisions vary widely in mezzanine financings. Market expectations are continually changing in this regard and it is another area where our firm's appreciation of the revealing views and practices in the United States and Europe, as well as Asia and Latin America, serves our clients particularly well.
- A key element in any mezzanine transaction is addressing the critical relationship of the mezzanine to senior and junior creditors. European transactions in particular will involve complex inter creditor arrangements, often requiring consideration of legal and other issues in multiple jurisdictions. Having counsel with an understanding of these complicated issues and the state of the market is critical to addressing the competing demands by investors at different levels of an issuer's capital structure.
- Mezzanine products often contain a co-invest option that may take a variety of forms including common equity participations and/or warrants. A range of highly-negotiated rights frequently attach to these equity components.
- The extent to which mezzanine investors have governance and/or specific information rights is another important element in which market expectations and legal requirements applicable to certain types of investors play a key role. The experience of the firm's sophisticated fund formation practice is key to our understanding the needs of mezzanine investors in the area of governance and information rights.

- As the sales and distribution methods for mezzanine have expanded from primarily privately negotiated transactions to encompass broader distributions, including jumbo syndicated deals, a number of business and legal issues relating to syndication and distribution have arisen, including disclosure, transfer restrictions and affiliate sales. It is extremely important to have knowledgeable counsel to address these issues.

Growth and Recent Trends

Mezzanine financing is characterized by its ability to provide funding business propositions with a higher risk factor versus what regular lending institutions are willing to take. It has the ability to be subsidiary to a bank debt. The absence of security does not cease chances to avail of mezzanine loans, thereby justifying the higher interest rates it requires. And, the final characteristic is the superior return in the form of percentages, shareholdings, and others. Traditionally, commercial mezzanine finance has been used as a (short-term) bridging loan. Nowadays, it is increasingly used as an instrument to improve the balance sheet structure and in cases of transfer of ownership, business succession and company expansion ('transaction mezzanine finance'). In these cases mezzanine finance is often provided in combination with senior debt and/or equity financing. A major factor influencing the development has been the growing number of management-buyins (MBIs), management-buyouts (MBOs), mergers and acquisitions. Other driving forces have been competitive pressures on traditional lending rates and the growing demand for tailor-made products. Fig. 9.7 gives a fairly good indication of the growth of the volume and value of mezzanine finance in Europe.

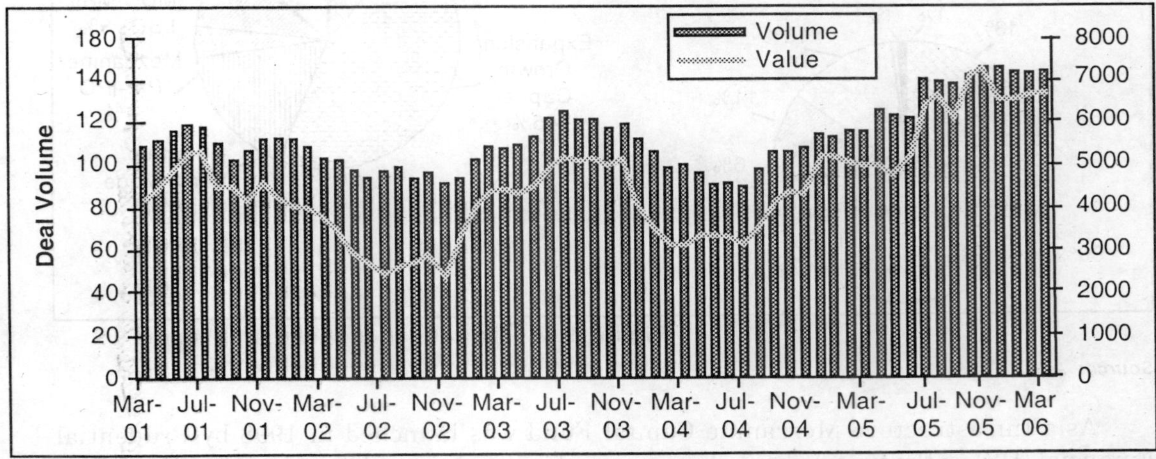

Figure 9.7: Mezzanine Volume and Value of All European Deals with Mezzanine Finance

Source: Mezzanine Monitor, Q1 2006: Mezzanine investors pause for breath?, Private equity Europe, Issue 76, May 2006

Mezzanine finance has gained considerable ground in UK following several high profile defaults of high yield bonds and some dismayed results from private equity investments. The coupon rate of mezzanine finance has remained fairly stable, but mezzanine finance has evolved to more flexible structures: mezzanine finance investors have been successful in structuring their terms to tie in with a higher interest rate compared to equity call options.

In Asia, mezzanine finance is a relatively new concept. Companies are used to either senior debt/high yield bonds or private equity, but not a sandwich tool like mezzanine finance. However, investors have turned more cautious to protect their investments compared to private equity and high yield bonds, and banks have turned more stringent in their lending policies in the present economic gloom. For entrepreneurs who are unwilling to give up much of their equity stake, need a substantial amount of funding, do not want to be tied down by stringent loan covenants, and desire a lower senior debt leverage ratio, mezzanine finance may just be an ideal tool. Fig. 9.8 depicts the stage by private equity investment volume.

Asia – Private Equity Investment Stage by Volume Break Down 2006 - YTD 2008

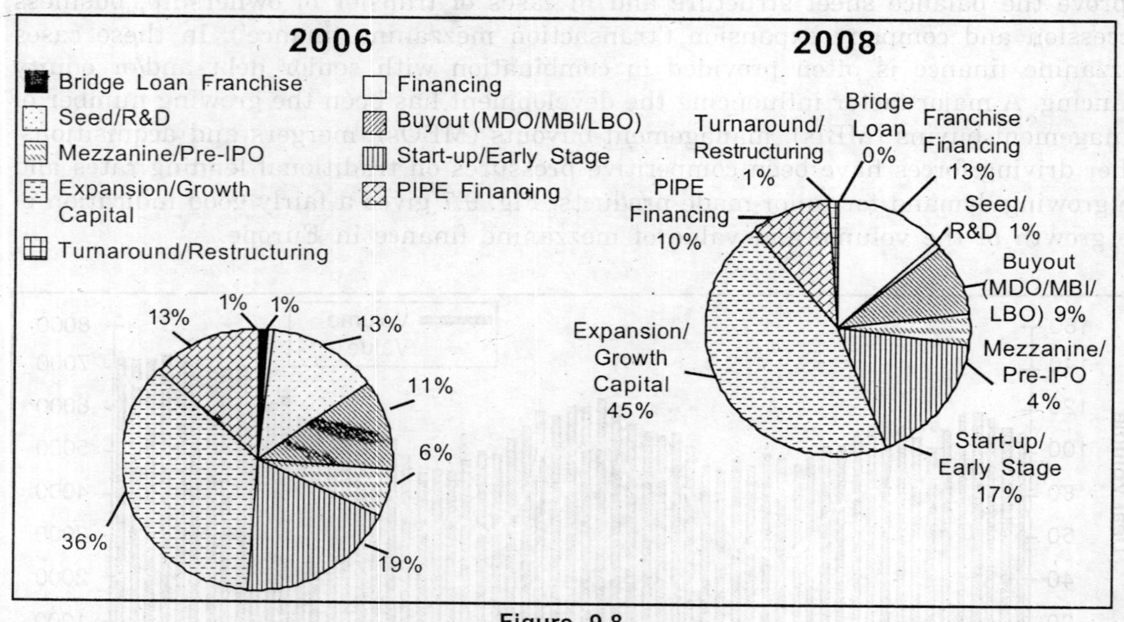

Figure 9.8

Source: AVCJ Research

Asia Infrastructure Mezzanine Capital Fund was launched in 1998 by Prudential Financial (US) as the first dedicated mezzanine fund in Asia and has played an important pioneering role in introducing this attractive form of long-term risk capital into this region.

- AIMCF's capitalization of $246 million was provided by: Prudential Financial (US and Japan), The Asian Development Bank, Nippon Life Insurance Company, Malaysia Employee Provident Fund, Asahi Mutual Life Insurance Company, The Chuo Mitsui Trust and Banking Company Ltd., Meiji-Yasuda Life Insurance Company and the Hawaiian Electric Industries, Inc.
- In March 2002, Prudential Financial sold to Darby its 100% in the Management of AIMCF while maintaining its capital commitment. The fund is managed by Darby Asia Investors (DAI). DAI has a team of five professionals based in Hong Kong. DAI assumed full responsibility for investing the fund's uninvested capital (approximately $135 million) and managing the existing portfolio. The investment ended in January 2004 and the Fund has committed $275 million for nine portfolio companies..

Exits

- Full exit via prepayment in 2001 from $ 45 million investment in Pollon Electric (China) with realized IRR of 18%.
- Full exit, via sale in public markets, from small $ 1.2 million investment in a number of managers have raised significant amounts of capital both to originate mezzanine and more senior debt for private equity and real estate investments and to buy the debt. In the second quarter, private equity fund managers alone raised $2.6 billion in aggregate capital for mezzanine funds, according to Private Equity Intelligence Ltd., a London-based data aggregator. Currently, 36 private equity mezzanine funds are on the road, raising $21.3 billion. For 2008 so far, 14 mezzanine funds have raised $20.3 billion, vs. 29 funds raising $15.7 billion for all of 2007. PEI's numbers do not include the $1 billion Barclays Structured Principal Investing Fund LP, which Barclays Capital, the New York-based investment banking division of Barclays Bank Plc. closed in early June. Goldman Sachs Private Equity Group closed a $13-billion fund, GS Mezzanine Partners V, while New York Life Capital Partners, the private equity unit of New York Life Investment Management LLC, New York, is raising another private equity mezzanine fund. Mimosa Systems, a leader in live content archiving solutions, announced that it has closed $17 million in mezzanine financing. (May 20, 2008 sabrina.sanchez@ventanapr.com)

In India

At present there are few players focused on providing mezzanine finance in India. Some of the active investors who continue to look at transactions are CLSA, ICICI Ventures and Darby. Even though the Indian mezzanine market is nascent, Indian commercial banks have been strong competitors for mezzanine investors by providing higher than desired (as per prudent financial ratios) leverage for acquisitions, bridge finance in lieu of equity and unsecured/subordinated debt. The unsecured loan portfolio of Indian banks has increased five-fold in the last five years to over $10.5bn, while the share in total advances has risen from 13.5 per cent in 2003-04 to 21.8 per cent in

2007-08. No official data is available on mezzanine finance. The availability situation has changed significantly after the collapse of Lehman Brothers and the subsequent contraction of the global credit markets. The result: mezzanine players have a good window of opportunity to strike lucrative deals.

India faces structural issues resulting from regulations relating to companies issuing foreign debt and/or convertible instruments. While foreign debt issuances have had all-in-cost caps (recently removed) and end-use restrictions, issuing convertible equity on a preferential basis is limited to a maximum conversion period of 18 months and with inflexible conversion pricing guidelines. The structural issues further compound the degree of difficulty for mezzanine investors who already face challenges of narrowing the thinking gap that Indian managements face when relating to the product while comparing it with either equity or debt. During the last five years only a handful of mezzanine deals have been concluded in India, excluding of course the unsecured/subordinated debt provided by the Indian banks. In late 2003, Arch Pharmalabs Ltd., a major player in the API and API intermediates market, concluded probably one of the first true mezzanine deals in India, primarily to finance an acquisition of a distressed asset. Indian banks at that point of time were unwilling to finance repayment of another bank's debt and this was the main reason for successful closure. The deal was structured as five-year secured debt with warrants, providing Arch Pharmalabs with very timely capital, while significantly enhancing shareholder value by limiting equity dilution. In another deal in early 2004, Alok Industries Ltd., one of India's leading textile companies, concluded a large mezzanine financing primarily for long-term working capital and short-term debt repayments. The driver of the transaction was that the financing was unsecured and allowed flexible use of capital. The deal was structured with five-year redeemable preferred stock with warrants. Other developments in the Indian mezzanine world have been investments in Escorts Construction, I-Ven Interactive and MAS Financial. ICICI Ventures has announced India's first dedicated mezzanine fund and is targeting to raise $125m. ICICI Venture is in the process of closing India Advantage Fund VII (Mezzanine Fund 1), India's first Mezzanine fund. The corpus of the fund is roughly US$ 51 million.

Summary

Although no one type of financing is the best choice for all companies or all strategies, mezzanine financing is in most cases a great fit for companies and projects that are heavy on development drilling, especially where there is a small amount of existing production at the outset. Advantages include its ability to fund rapid growth from a small base, the large majority of value retained by the managers and other equity holders, and retention of outright control by the existing owners. Promotional financial institutions are invited to develop additional products by using mezzanine instruments with profit sharing elements to finance the start-up, expansion and transfer of SMEs as well as SME innovation projects. Indian companies should consider mezzanine financing in the current environment to protect equity dilution given low valuations, reduce the overall cost of capital by replacing a part of their equity needs with mezzanine finance, build long-term investor relationships and build capital so to take advantage of attractive business opportunities and face the global recessionary situation as well as contracting credit markets. There is tremendous potential for mezzanine finance in India given the sustained economic growth drivers across sectors. India's conducive-environment is the basis for private equity to grow and this in turn led to a virtuous cycle of further improvements in the economic and infrastructures environment.

Review Questions

1. How many types of mezzanine finance are available? Explain its importance.
2. Illustrate the structure, terms and pricing of mezzanine financing
3. How do you secure more mezzanine capital?
4. **Quiz:**
   (a) Mezzanine financing is a hybrid of _____ and ____ financing
   (b) Private mezzanine debt securities are highly negotiated instruments, and are thus ______ investments.
   (c) Mezzanine debt capital generally refers to that layer of financing between a company's _____ and ______, filling the gap between the two.
   (d) Mezzanine financing is advantageous because it is treated like equity on a company's balance sheet and may make it easier to obtain standard bank financing. ***(T/F)***
   (e) Mezzanine capital is usually a valuable financing alternative for management seeking to raise capital in the later phases of a company's development and is suited for start-up financing. ***(T/F)***
   (f) Debt associated with a mezzanine finance arrangement is generally redeemed in a one-off payment rather than paid monthly over a period of years. ***(T/F)***
   (g) Mezzanine finance is cheaper than debt financing. ***(T/F)***
   (h) Redemption and call protection provisions are common in mezzanine financings. ***(T/F)***
   (i) Mezzanine products often contain a co-invest option that may take a variety of forms including common equity participations and/or warrants. ***(T/F)***

CHAPTER 10

Structured Finance

Introduction

One innovation that has gained grip as a special class of investments is known as structured products. Since the mid-1980s, structured finance has become a major segment in the financial services industry. Collateralized bond obligations (CBOs), collateralized debt obligations (CDOs), syndicated loans and synthetic financial instruments are examples of structured financial instruments. Structured finance offers the issuers' enormous flexibility in terms of maturity structure, security design and asset types, which allows issuers to provide enhanced return at a customized degree of diversification commensurate to an individual investor's appetite for risk. Hence, structured finance contributes to a more complete capital market by offering any mean-variance trade-off along the efficient frontier of optimal diversification at lower transaction cost. However, the increasing complexity of the structured finance market and the ever growing range of products being made available to investors, invariably create challenges in terms of efficient assembly, management and dissemination of information.

What are Structured Products?

Structured products originally became popular in Europe and have gained currency in the US, where they are frequently offered as SEC-registered products. They are accessible to retail investors like stocks, bonds, exchange-traded funds (ETFs) and mutual funds. Structured products are useful as a complement to other products such as option, swaps, forwards and futures. Structured products are designed to facilitate highly customized risk-return objectives by taking a conventional investment-grade bond, and replacing the of usual payment features with non-traditional pay-offs derived not from the issuer's own cash flow, but from the performance of one or more underlying assets. One of the principle attractions of structured products for retail investors is the ability to customize a variety of assumptions into one instrument. One common risk associated with structured products is lack of liquidity due to the highly customized nature of the investment. Moreover, the full extent of returns from the complex performance features is often not realized until maturity. Because of this, structured products tend to be more of a buy-and-hold investment decision. In addition to liquidity, one risk associated with structured products is the credit quality of the issuer. Although the cash flows are derived from other sources, the products themselves are legally considered to be the issuing financial institution's liabilities.

What is Structured Finance?

Many large financial institutions today offered services to the company with very unique financing needs that involves highly complex financial transactions. These financing needs usually don't match conservative financial products such as a loan. The non-standard way of raising money through complex and advanced instruments backed by some collateral asset is known as structured financing. Structured finance involves the pooling of assets and the subsequent sale to investors of tranche claims on the cash flows backed by these pools. It has become an increasingly important tool for credit risk transfer. Structured finance instruments have 3 basic characteristics:

- Firstly, pooling of assets (either cash-based or synthetically created)
- Secondly, separation of the credit risk of the collateral asset pool from the credit risk of the originator, usually through the transfer of the underlying assets to a finite-lived, standalone special purpose vehicle, and
- Thirdly, tranching of liabilities that are backed by the asset pool

While the first two characteristics are also present with classical pass-through securitisations, the tranching of liabilities sets structured finance products apart. A key aspect of the tranching process is the ability to create one or more classes of securities whose rating is higher than the average rating of the underlying collateral asset pool or to generate rated securities from a pool of unrated assets. Each of the three key characteristics of structured finance contributes to "value creation" and to the attractiveness of structured finance markets for a variety of market participants. In this context, delinking confers benefits similar to those of secured credit, with the additional feature that the income streams from the delinked assets will tend to be more predictable than those of the ongoing firm. The generation of securitized cash flows from a diversified asset portfolio represents an effective method of redistributing asset risks to investors and broader capital markets. As opposed to ordinary debt, a securitized contingent claim on a promised portfolio performance affords investors at low transaction costs to quickly adjust their investment holdings due to changes in personal risk sensitivity, market sentiment and/or consumption preferences.

Structured finance devices mean redistribution of risks/rewards or components of assets into different segments, to churn out securities with different risk/reward profiles.

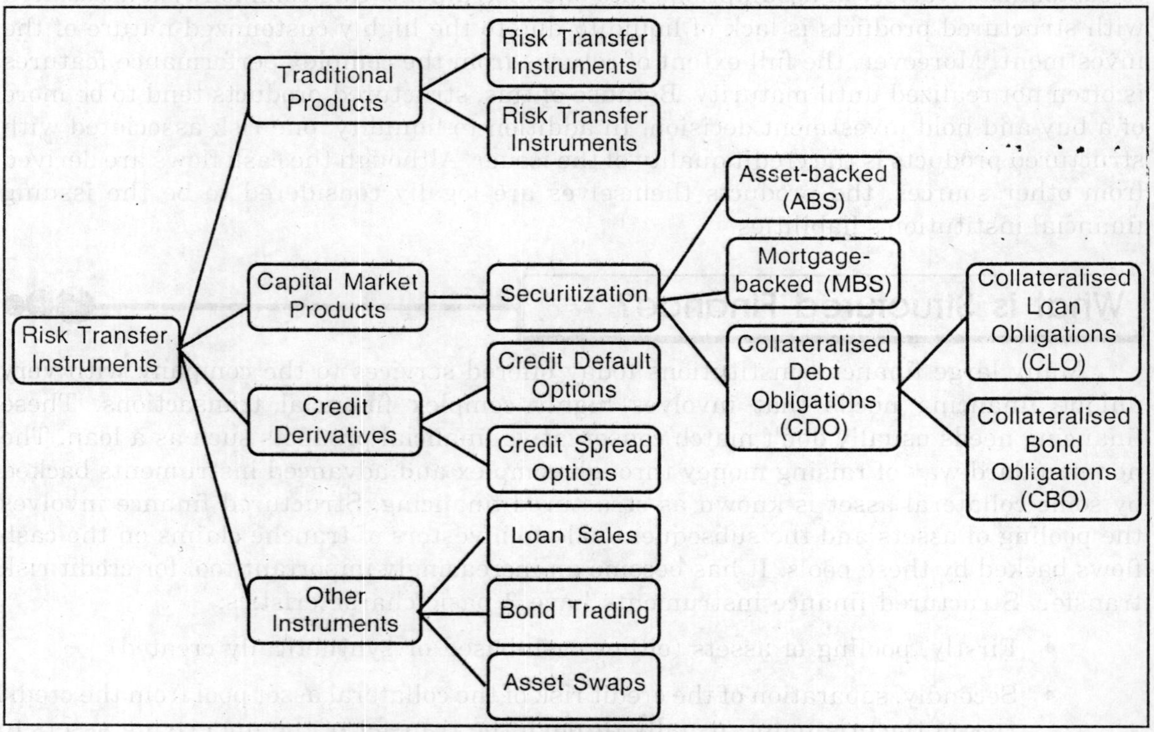

Risk Transfer Instruments
Traditional Products
Risk Transfer Instruments
Risk Transfer Instruments
Capital Market Products
Securitization
Asset-backed (ABS)
Mortgage-backed (MBS)
Collateralised Debt Obligations (CDO)
Collateralised Loan Obligations (CLO)
Collateralised Bond Obligations (CBO)
Credit Derivatives
Credit Default Options
Credit Spread Options
Other Instruments
Loan Sales
Bond Trading
Asset Swaps

Figure 10.1: Risk Transfer Instruments

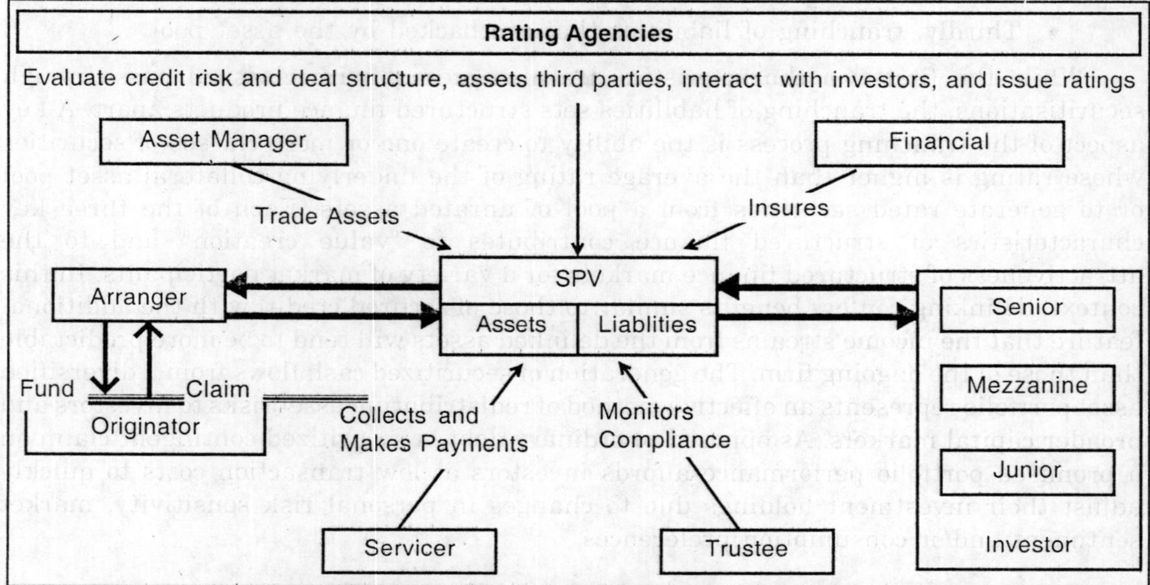

Figure 10.2: Structure Finance Market Participants

Arranger: Who sets up the structure, tranches the liabilities and markets the tranches

Originators: An entity making loans to borrowers or having receivables from customers

Servicer: Who collects payments and may track pool performance

Asset Manager: Who – in managed transactions – may assemble the initial pool and subsequently trades in and out of collateral assets

Trustee: Who oversees cash distributions to investors and monitors compliance with deal documentation; and, in certain deals

Financial Guarantors: Who provide guarantees on principal and interest payments to, or sell credit default swaps on a particular tranches as part of their business model of underwriting high-grade credit risk

Investors (Institutions or Individual): Who buy different tranches issued against the asset pool

Rating Agencies: Rating agency provide value addition to security. The provision of a structured finance rating by a rating agency can help to mitigate asymmetric information problems arising in the creation of a structured finance instrument, for example in assessing the rules governing the prioritisation of cash flows to the tranches. The rating agencies also collect and assess information on the performance of the servicer and of other third parties involved in the transaction.

Originator

- Assets removed from the balance sheet increasing scope for borrowing; servicing revenues retained
- Reduced financing costs by structuring a security of higher credit quality
- Reduction in required capital for companies facing regulatory capital requirements
- Retention of earning power of assets without sale of business
- Means of raising public debt without extensive disclosure of proprietary information
- Improved asset/liability management by transfer of funding-mismatch risk

Investor

- Superior spreads *vis-à-vis* generally available sovereign debt of similar rating
- Securitized structure is far more liquid than the loans backing the transaction
- Opportunity to diversity portfolios by participating in different asset classes
- Mitigation of event risk as high-rated ABSs, etc., are immune from event risk
- Constraints of purchasing investment grade paper can be met in the ABS market

National Economy

- Capital market development due to addition of high-quality securities to the fixed income market
- Source of funds for rapidly growing, capital-constrained, banks, finance and industrial companies whose expansion depends on the extension of credit to their customers.
- Expanded source of financing for residential home ownership
- The potential for financing of infrastructure projects, such as toll roads, that produce reliable revenue streams capable of being contractually assigned to a separate legal entity.

What are Collateralized Debt Obligations (CDOs)?

A bank lend money to borrowers for buying a house and collects monthly payments on the loan. This loan and other loans are sold to a larger bank. This larger bank then packages the loans together into a mortgage-backed security. The larger bank then issues shares of this security, called tranches to investors who buy them and ultimately collect the dividends in the form of the monthly mortgage payments. These tranches can be further repackaged and sold again as other securities, called collateralized debt obligations (CDOs).

CDO is a security backed by a diversified pool of one or more kinds of debt obligations. Party initiating a CDO is called a sponsor (e.g. financial institutions, banks). Sponsor creates a Special Purpose Vehicle (SPV) to isolate CDO investors from the credit risk of the underlying assets. SPV transfers the credit risk by issuing debt obligations (tranches). Tranche investors have the ultimate credit risk exposure to the underlying reference entities.

Collateralized debt obligations are similar to a collateralized mortgage obligation (CMO). It is type of asset backed security. It is a security backed by a diversified pool of one or more kinds of debt obligations. Party initiating a CDO is called a sponsor (e.g., financial institutions, banks). It connotes different types of debt and credit risk. These different types of debt are often referred to as 'tranches' or 'slices'. Each slice has a different maturity and risk associated with it. Sponsor creates a Special Purpose Vehicle (SPV) to isolate CDO investors from the credit risk of the underlying assets. SPV transfers the credit risk by issuing debt obligations (tranches) including bonds and loans. Each tranche offers a varying degree of risk and return so as to meet investor demand. To create a CDO, a corporate entity is constructed to hold assets as collateral and to sell packages of cash flows to investors. The higher the risk, the more the CDO pays. The tranches in a CDO are senior tranche (AAA rating), mezzanine tranche (AA–BB rating), Subordinate/equity tranche (unrated). The structure of a CDO is depicted in Fig. 10.3. CDO cash flow is depicted in Fig. 10.4

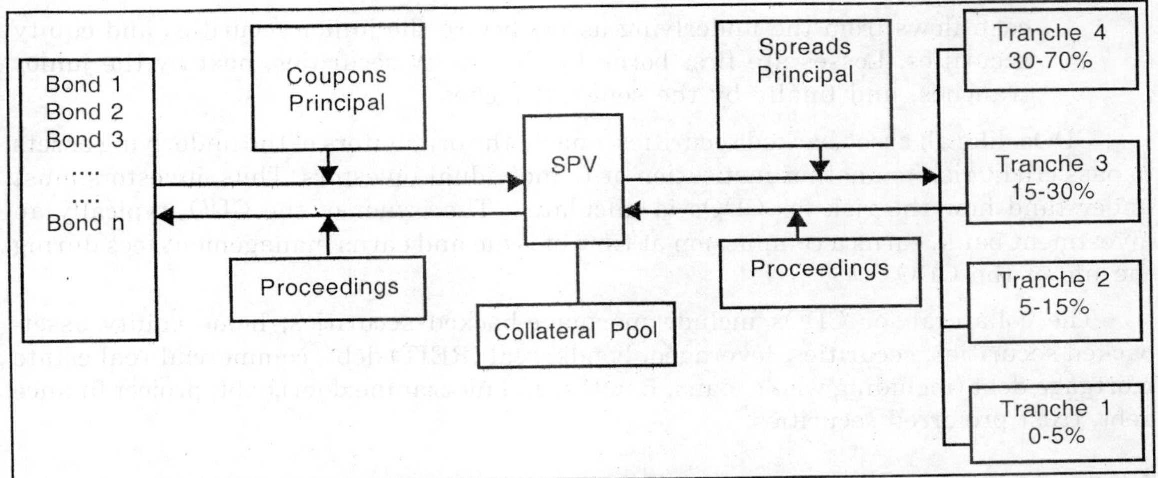

Figure 10.3: Structure of a CDO

Source: Pricing tranches of a CDO and a CDS Index by Wang, Rachev and Fabozzi, October, 2006.

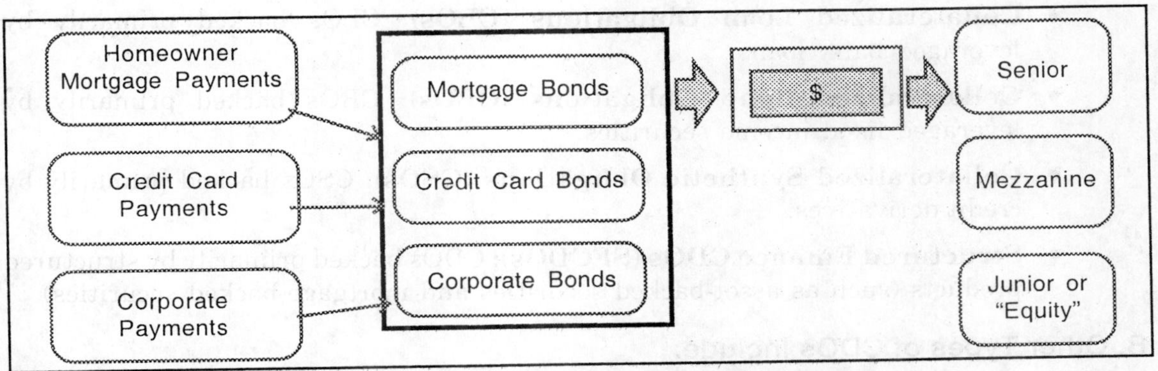

Figure 10.4: CDO Cash Flow Diagram

Senior tranches are considered the safest securities. Interest and principal payments are made in order of seniority. Junior tranches offer higher interest rates. CDO is a promise to pay cash flows to investors in a prescribed sequence, based on how much cash flow the CDO collects from the pool of bonds or other assets it owns. If cash collected by the CDO is insufficient to pay all of its investors then lower tranches suffer losses first.

A CDO is constructed as follows:

- A special purpose vehicle is designed to acquire a portfolio of underlying assets. Common underlying assets held include mortgage-backed securities commercial real estate bonds and corporate loans.
- The SPE issues bonds to investors in exchange for cash, which is used to purchase the portfolio of underlying assets. The bonds issued are in layers with different risk characteristics called tranches. Senior tranches are paid from the

cash flows from the underlying assets before the junior securities and equity securities. Losses are first borne by the equity securities, next by the junior tranches, and finally by the senior tranches.

CDOs, like all asset-backed securities, enable the originators of the underlying assets to pass credit risk to another institution or to individual investors. Thus, investors must understand how the risk for CDOs is calculated. The issuer of the CDO, typically an investment bank, earns a commission at time of issue and earns management fees during the life of the CDO.

The collateral for CDOs include mortgage-backed securities, home equity asset-backed securities, securities, leveraged, bonds, real (REIT) debt, commercial real estate mortgage debt (including whole loans, B notes, and mezzanine debt),debt, project finance debt, trust preferred securities.

Types of CDO

A. Based on the Underlying Asset:

- **Collateralized Loan Obligations (CLOs):** CLOs backed primarily by leveraged bank loans.
- **Collateralized Bond Obligations (CBOs):** CBOs backed primarily by leveraged fixed income securities.
- **Collateralized Synthetic Obligations (CSOs):** CSOs backed primarily by credit derivatives.
- **Structured Finance CDOs (SFCDOs):** CDOs backed primarily by structured products (such as asset-backed securities and mortgage-backed securities)

B. Other Types of CDOs Include:

- **Commercial Real Estate (CRE):** CDOs backed primarily by commercial real estate assets
- **Collateralized Bond Obligations (CBOs):** CDOs backed primarily by corporate bonds
- **Collateralized Insurance Obligations (CIOs):** CDOs backed by insurance or, more usually, reinsurance contracts
- **CDO-ssquared:** CDOs backed primarily by the tranches issued by other CDOs.

Classification of CDO

CDO is a broad term that can refer to several different types of products. They are categorized in several ways. CDO classification is presented in Fig. 10.5.

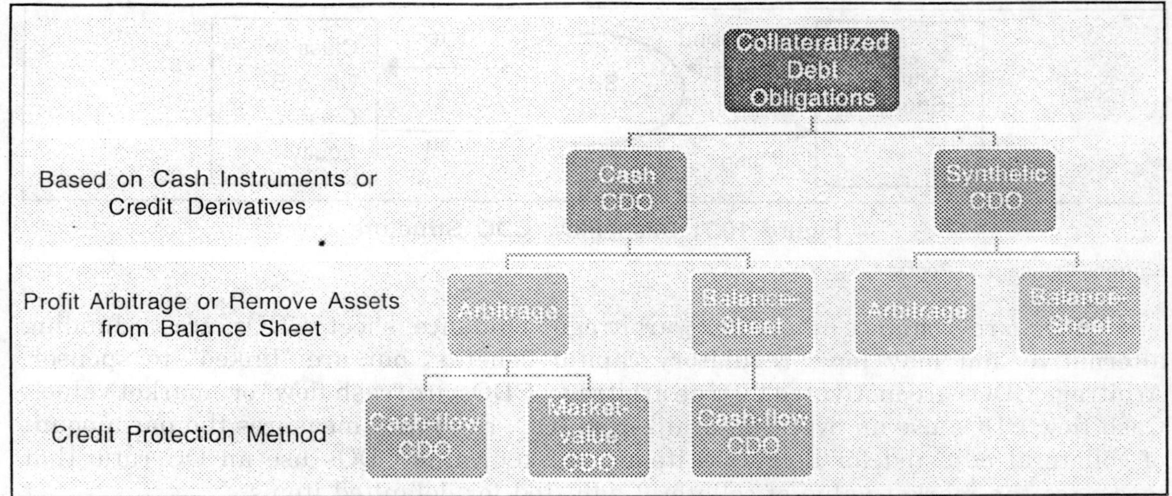

Figure 10.5: CDO Classification

Retrieved From: http://thismatter.com/money/bonds/types/cdo.htm

The CDO is cash CDO and Synthetic CDO. Cash CDO involve a portfolio of cash assets (corporate bonds). Ownership of assets is transferred to SPV, issuing the tranches and Risk of loss of assets is divided among tranches in reverse order of seniority. Synthetic CDO do not own cash assets. These CDOs gain exposure to the assets through CDS and protection seller – CDO.

The Synthetic CDO diagram is presented in Fig. 10.6.

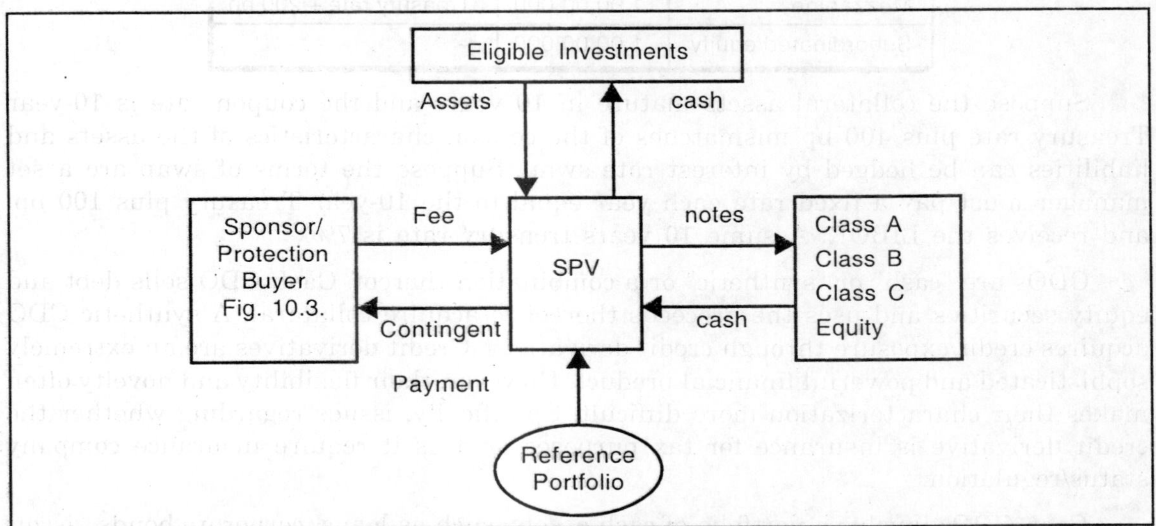

Figure 10.6: The Synthetic CDO

Source: Standard & Poor's

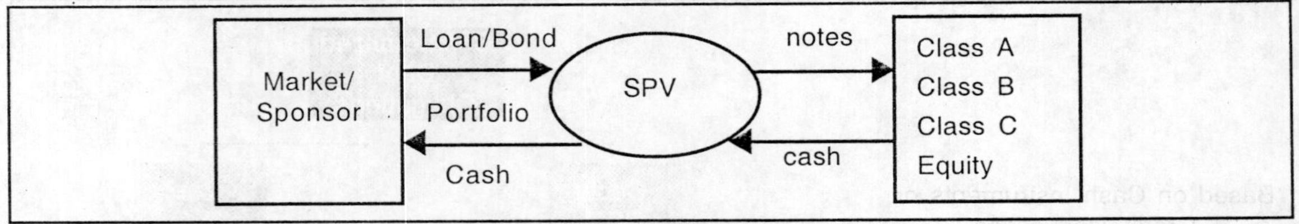

Figure 10.7: Cash Flow CDO Structure

Source: Standard & Poor's

CDOs are "balance sheet" or "arbitrage". Balance sheet CDOs are a funding alternative and may have regulatory capital benefits, but are "linked" to sponsor. Arbitrage CDOs are motivated by true arbitrage. CDOs are "cash flow" or "market value". Cash flow CDOs use an overcollateralization (OC) ratio that measures the par amount of collateral adjusted for defaulted items. Market value CDOs use an OC ratio that measures the market value of collateral adjusted for defaulted items.

In arbitrage of a CDO, excess spread is the key consideration in structuring of the CDO during underwriting process.

Excess Spread = yield – S interest payable to each tranche – management fees

Let us take an example: Consider a $100 million CDO structure with the coupon rate to be offered as follows:

Tranche	Par value	Coupon rate
Senior	$8,00,00,000	LIBOR + 70 bp
Mezzanine	1,00,00,000	Treasury rate + 200 bp
Subordinated/equity	1,00,00,000	–

Suppose the collateral assets mature in 10 years and the coupon rate is 10-year Treasury rate plus 400 bp mismatches of the coupon characteristics of the assets and liabilities can be hedged by interest rate swap. Suppose the terms of swap are asset manager must pay a fixed rate each year equal to the 10-year Treasury plus 100 bp, and receives the LIBOR. Assume 10 years treasury rate is 7%.

CDOs are "cash" or "synthetic" or a combination thereof. Cash CDO sells debt and equity securities and uses the proceeds thereof to acquire collateral. A synthetic CDO acquires credit exposure through credit derivatives. Credit derivatives are an extremely sophisticated and powerful financial product. However, their flexibility and novelty often makes their characterization more difficult. Specifically, issues regarding whether the credit derivative is insurance for tax purposes or does it require insurance company status/regulation.

Cash CDOs involve a portfolio of cash assets, such as loans, corporate bonds, asset-backed securities or mortgage-backed securities. Ownership of the assets is transferred to the legal entity (known as a special purpose vehicle) issuing the CDOs tranches. The risk of loss on the assets is divided among tranches in reverse order of seniority.

Synthetic CDOs do not own cash assets like bonds or loans. Instead, synthetic CDOs gain credit exposure to a portfolio of fixed income assets without owning those assets through the use of credit default swaps, a derivatives instrument. The Gramm-Leach-Bliley Act allowed banks to participate in 1999 in CDO transactions. Investors, the underwriter, the asset manager, the trustee and collateral administrator, accountants and attorneys are the participants in a CDO transaction.

CDOs, including Synthetic Collateralized Debt Obligations (SCDOs) are an application of securitization technology under rating agency methodology to underlying assets to result in rated securities. There are 3 Types of SCDOs: Balance Sheet SCDOs, Tranched Basket/Portfolio SCDOs, and Managed Arbitrage SCDOs.

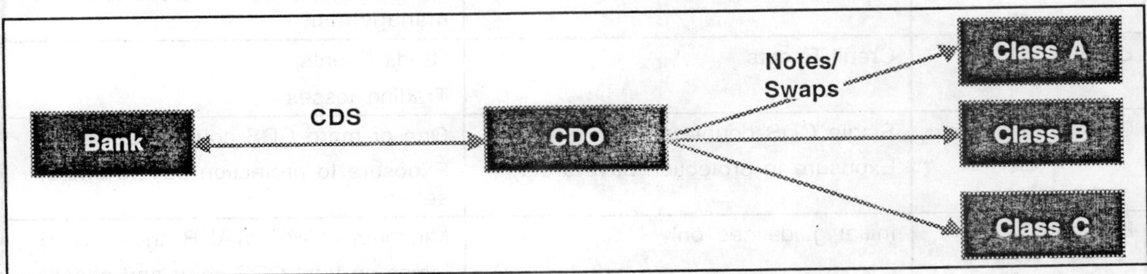

Figure 10.8: Balance Sheet SCDOs

In Balance Sheet SCDOs, Bank obtains economic and regulatory capital relief. Investors obtain credit exposure and return.

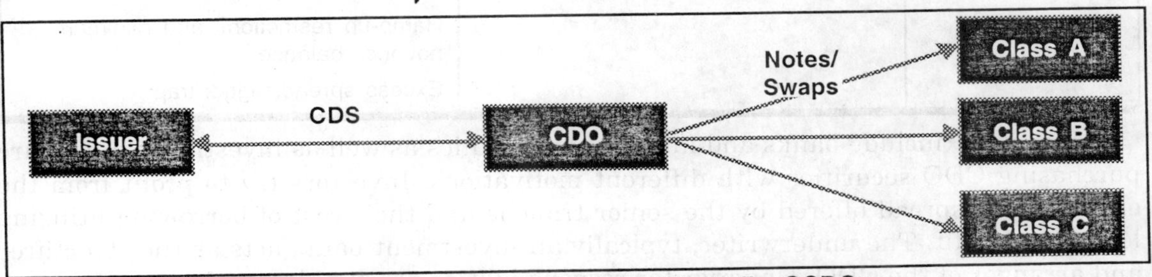

Figure 10.9: Tranched Basket/Portfolio SCDOs

In Tranched Basket/Portfolio SCDOs, Issuer reduces credit exposure. Investors obtain credit exposure and arbitrage return.

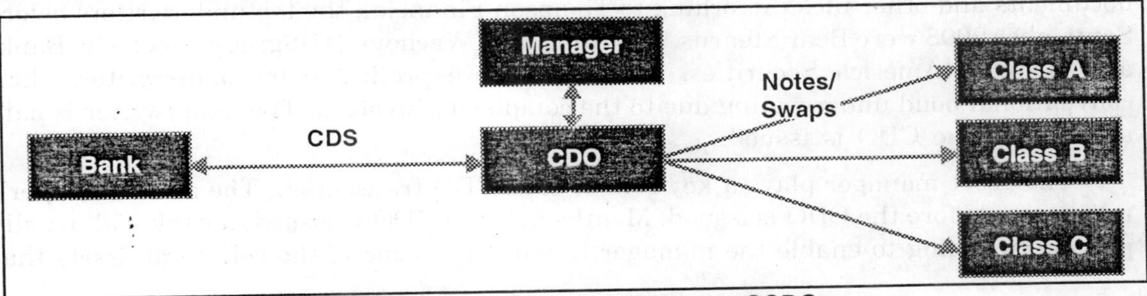

Figure 10.10: Managed Arbitrage SCDOs

In Managed Arbitrage SCDOs, Manager selects and manages portfolio to enhance arbitrage opportunity

Table 10.1: Comparison of Static and Managed SCDOs

Feature	Static	Managed
Trading	CDS Long Only No removal or substitution	CDS Long/Short Exposures added and/or removed
Excess Spread	Fixed CDS premium Credit-related premium	Excess spread released, trapped or used to offset losses CDS premium reflects credit and management
Liquidity	Credit Events	Credit Events Trading losses
Counterparty Risk	Single CDS counterparty Exposure to protection buyers only	One or more CDS counterparties Exposure to protection buyers and/or sellers
Portfolio	Initial guidelines only	Minimum WARF, WARR and/or WAS Limits on total CDS short and offset exposure, trading and concentrations
Structure	Credit enhancement only	OC and IC tests Limits on counterparties and required CDS documentation Ramp-up restrictions and minimum notional balance Excess spread trigger/trap

Investors (include banks and insurance companies as well as investment funds) are purchasing CDO securities with different motivations. Investors try to profit from the excess of the spread offered by the senior tranche and their cost of borrowing utilizing leverage benefit. The underwriter, typically an investment bank, acts as the structurer and arranger of the CDO. Underwriter responsibilities are working with a law firm and creating the special purpose legal vehicle that will purchase the assets and issue the CDOs tranches. In addition, the underwriter also works with the asset manager to determine the post-closing trading restrictions that will be included in the CDOs transaction documents and other files. According to Thomson Financial, the top underwriters before September 2008 were Bear Stearns, Merrill Lynch, Wachovia, Citigroup, Deutsche Bank, and Bank of America Securities. CDOs are more profitable for underwriters than conventional bond underwriting due to the complexity involved. The underwriter is paid a fee when the CDO is issued.

The asset manager plays a key role in each CDO transaction. The asset manager's role begins before the CDO is issued. Months before a CDO is issued, a bank will usually provide financing to enable the manager to purchase some of the collateral assets that may be used in the forthcoming CDO in a process called warehousing. During the CDOs "reinvestment period", the asset manager is authorized to reinvest principal proceeds by purchasing additional debt securities. Within the confines of the trading restrictions specified in the CDOs transaction documents, the asset manager can also make trades to maintain the credit quality of the CDOs portfolio. The manager also has a role in the redemption of a CDOs notes by auction call.

In the CDO market, the trustee also typically serves as collateral administrator. The collateral administrator produces and distributes noteholder reports, performs various compliance tests regarding the composition and liquidity of the asset portfolios in addition to constructing and executing the priority of payment models.

The underwriter typically hire an accounting firm to perform due diligence on the CDOs portfolio of debt securities. This entails verifying credit rating and coupon/spread, of each collateral security. In addition, the accountants typically calculate certain collateral tests and determine whether the portfolio is in compliance with such tests. Attorneys draft an offering document to satisfy statutory requirements to disclose certain information to investors. Attorneys ensure compliance with applicable securities law and negotiate and draft the transaction documents.

Who Buys CDOs?

Insurance companies, banks, pension funds, investment managers, investment banks and hedge funds are the typical buyers. These institutions look to outperform Treasury yields, and will take what they hope is appropriate risk to outperform Treasury returns. The simplest explanation of a CDO's structure in mortgage, credit card, auto loans, or even corporate debt, surround the fact that loans have been made and credit has been extended to borrowers that aren't as prime as the lenders thought.

Market History

The first CDO was issued in 1987 by bankers for Imperial Savings Association, a savings institution but later on it became insolvent and was taken over by the Resolution Trust Corporation on June 22, 1990. After one decade CDOs emerged as the fastest growing sector of the asset-backed synthetic securities market. CDOs offered returns that were sometimes 2-3 percentage points higher than corporate bonds with the same credit rating. A sample of 735 CDO deals originated between 1999 and 2007 showed that subprime and other less-than-prime mortgages represented an increasing percentage of CDO assets, rising from 5% in 2000 to 36% in 2007. In 2007, 47% of CDOs were backed by structured products, 45% of CDOs were backed by loans, and only less than 10% of CDOs were backed by fixed income securities. Many of the assets held by these CDOs had been subprime mortgage-backed bonds.

The CDO played a pivotal role in financing the housing bubble that peaked in the US during 2006. The CDO provided a key link between the global pool of fixed income investor capital and the US housing market. CDO volume grew significantly in between 2000-2006 and then declined dramatically in the wake of the crisis during 2007. CDO issuance grew from an estimated $20 billion in Q1 2004 to its peak of over $180 billion by Q1 2007, and then declined back under $20 billion by Q1 2008. Further, the credit quality of CDOs declined from 2000-2007, as the level of subprime and other non-prime mortgage debt increased from 5% to 36% of CDO assets. From 2000-2006, structured finance which includes CDOs accounted for 40% of the revenues of the credit rating agencies. During that time, one major rating agency had its stock increase six-fold and its earnings grew by 90%. On 24 October, 2007, Merrill Lynch reported third quarter earnings that contained $7.9 billion of losses on collateralized debt obligations. Global CDO issuance in the fourth quarter of 2007 was US$ 47.5 billion, a nearly 74 per cent decline from the US$ 180 billion issued in the fourth quarter of 2006. First quarter 2008 issuance of US$ 11.7 billion was nearly 94 per cent lower than the US$ 186 billion issued in the first quarter of 2007. Moreover, virtually all first quarter 2008 CDO issuance was in the form of collateralized loan obligations backed by middle-market or leveraged bank loans, not by home mortgage ABS. The Global CDO Issuance Volume is presented in Table 10.2.

Table 10.2: Global CDO Issuance Volume

Year	US$ bill
2004	157.4
2005	251.3
2006	520.6
2007	481.6
2008	61.9
2009	4.3
2010	8.0

Source: Securities Industry and Financial Markets Association. "Global CDO Issuance". Press release. http://sifma.org/uploadedFiles/Research/Statistics/StatisticsFiles/SF-Global-CDO-Issuance-SIFMA.xls. Retrieved 2010-011-21.

The institutions, i.e., ATC Capital Markets, Bank of New York Mellon (the Bank of New York Mellon recently also acquired the corporate trust unit of JP Morgan which is the market share leader), BNP Paribas Securities Services, Citibank, Deutsche Bank, Equity Trust, Intertrust Group, HSBC, LaSalle Bank (Recently acquired by Bank of America purchased by US Bank late 2010), Sanne Trust, State Street Corporation, US Bank (US Bank recently also acquired the corporate trust unit of Wachovia), Wells Fargo currently offer trustee services in the CDO marketplace.

What is Asset Backed Securities?

Securitization refers to a process in which the assets of a corporation or financial institution are pooled into a package of securities backed by the assets. The process starts when an originator, who owns the assets (e.g., mortgages or accounts receivable), sells them to an issuer. The issuer then creates a security backed by the assets called an asset backed security or pass through that he sells to investors. The securitization process often involves a third-party trustee who ensures that the issuer complies with the terms underlying the asset backed security. The most common types of asset backed securities are those secured by mortgages, automobile loans, credit card receivables, and home equity loans. Asset backed securities formed with mortgages are called mortgage backed securities, MBSs, or mortgage pass-through.

In Asset-backed securities (ABS), the underlying assets are collected into a pool. Pool assets are standardized. The asset pool is placed in trust. Then claims on the cash flows generated by the asset pool are structured: Pass-through structures and multi-class structures. Securities representing these claims are sold. So, asset backed securities (ABS) derive their cash flows from a pool of underlying assets. The underlying assets generate cash flows of principal and interest which can be repackaged and sold to investors.

The asset backed securities, usually backed by financial institutions typically consists of receivables other than mortgage loans such as credit cards, automobile loans, manufactured-housing contracts, home-equity loans, esoteric cash flows from aircraft leases, loans for mobile homes royalty payments, etc., and are sold in the public markets or as private placements. Payments on the loans are distributed to the holders of the lower-risk, lower-interest securities first, and then to the holders of the higher-risk securities.

These securities differ from other kinds of bonds as the source of income is other than the paying ability of the originator of the underlying assets. The originators of ABS, generally banks, auto finance companies, credit card companies and other finance companies, known as issuers but in reality are usually sponsors and not directly issuers of these securities. These financial institutions sell pools of loans to a separate institution called as a special purpose vehicle (SPV) whose only function is to carry on the securitization of asset backed securities. The concept of SPV is presented in Fig. 10.11. The special purpose vehicle, which creates and sells the securities, uses the proceeds of the sale to payback the bank that created, or originated, the underlying assets. The SPV bundles assets into specified pools that fit the risk appetite of the investors who might buy the securities, usually by transferring them to an insurance company or sells them to a trust and uses the proceeds of the sale to payback the financial institution. By selling them, the financial institution transfers the credit risk from the underlying assets from their balance sheets and receives cash in return. By doing so, they are able to reduce the amount of capital they would otherwise have to maintain under stringent capital guidelines mandated by bank regulators, improves their bank rating and also allows the bank to invest more of their capital in new loans or assets. The credit rating of the ABS depends on the assets and liabilities of the SPV and a high credit rating of the SPV to pay a lower interest rate or charge a higher price on the securities.

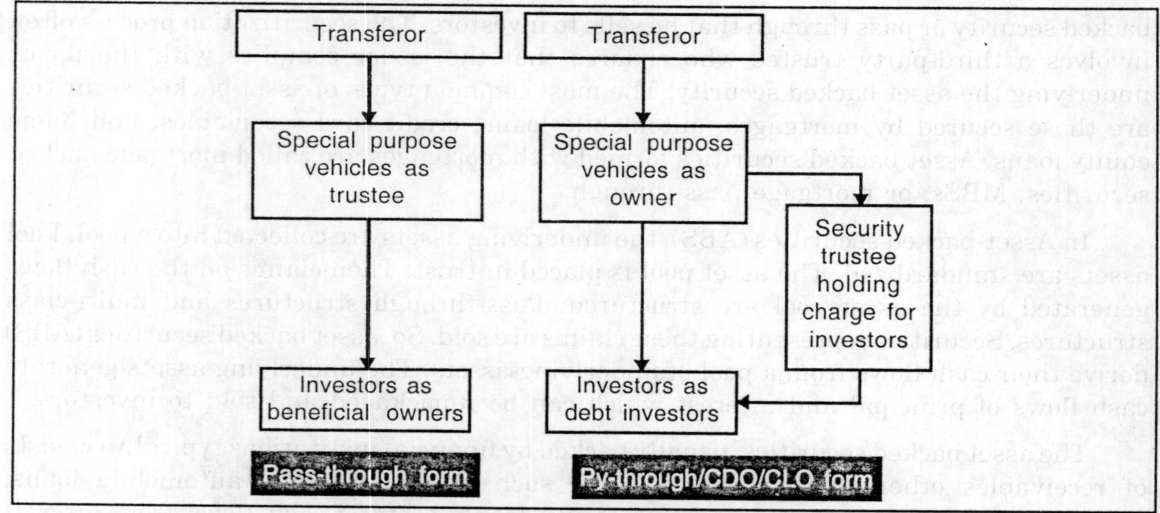

Figure 10.11: Concept of SPVs

Types

Currently, securities collateralized by home equity loans are the largest asset class within the ABS market. Subprime mortgage borrowers are required to pay interest rates higher than what would be available to a typical agency borrower. Auto loans are the second largest subsector in the ABS market. Auto finance companies issue securities backed by underlying pools of auto-related loans. Auto ABS are classified into three categories: prime, nonprime, and subprime:

- Prime auto ABS are collaterized by loans made to borrowers with strong credit histories.
- Nonprime auto ABS consist of loans made to lesser credit quality consumers, which may have higher cumulative losses.
- Subprime borrowers will typically have lower incomes, tainted credited histories, or both.

Auto loans are issuing on the basis of owner trusts allow investors to receive interest and principal on sequential basis. Deals can also be structured to pay on a *s* or combination of the two. Securities backed by credit card receivables were first introduced in 1987. Credit cardholders borrow funds pay principal and interest along with the required minimum monthly payments. Since credit card debt does not have an actual maturity date and is considered a no amortizing loan.

ABS collateralized by student loans also. It is comprise of one of the four along with home equity loans, auto loans and credit card receivables. Its core asset classes financed through asset-backed securitizations and is a benchmark subsector for most floating rate indices. The United States Congress created the Student Loan Marketing Association (Sallie Mae) as a government sponsored enterprise to purchase student loans in the secondary market and to securitize pools of student loans. Since its first issuance in 1995, Sallie Mae is now the major issuer of SLABS and its issues are viewed as the benchmark issues. There are many other cash-flow-producing assets, including manufactured housing loans, equipment leases and loans, aircraft leases, trade receivables, dealer floor plan loans, and royalties. Intangibles are another emerging asset class include in ABS.

One of the advantages of asset-backed securities for loan an originator is that they bring together a pool of financial assets that otherwise is not easily being traded in their existing form. By pooling together a large portfolio of these illiquid assets they can be converted into instruments that may be offered and sold freely in the capital markets. The tranching of these securities into instruments facilitates marketing of the bonds to investors with different risk appetites and investing time horizons.

Asset backed securities selling these financial assets to the pools reduces their risk-weighted assets and thereby frees up their capital, enabling them to originate still more loans. Sometimes the pool of assets performs very badly and owner of ABS pay the price of bankruptcy.

Market History

There is also secondary market available for trading asset backed securities. Most of the trading is done in over-the-counter markets, with telephone quotes on a security basis. At the end of 2004 in the United States and Europe, there were 74 electronic trading platforms for trading fixed-income securities and derivatives. Also 5 platforms for trading were for asset backed securities in the United States, and 8 in Europe. Since asset backed securities are not as standardized as Treasury securities so many asset backed securities are not liquid in compared to Treasury securities and mortgage backed securities. The "price" of an asset backed security is usually quoted as a spread to a corresponding swap rate.

The market for asset backed securities was born in 1985 when a SPV sold to institutional investors $192.4 million in fixed-rate notes collateralized by computer leases. The market which has seen a tremendous increase over the years saw that some $25.17 billion worth of asset backed securities were sold through March 2011. However, this amount was down from $31.54 billion over the same period last year. ABS issuance in 2011 reflects a combination of financings issuers that had postponed due to the credit crisis that began in 2008 and refinancing as outstanding issues mature. The investor acceptance of asset backed securities has grown as this market matures. While structuring these securities a careful analysis of complete tax, accounting and legal issues needs to be undertaken as issuers seek to package the securities so that the receivables will be deemed to have been sold, rather than pledged, for purposes of bankruptcy, regulatory, and generally accepted accounting principles (GAAP). That way, issuers receive "off-balance-sheet" accounting and regulatory treatment, which is significantly more favourable than "on-balance-sheet" treatment.

The average "stressed" loan-to-value ratio on bonds valued at about $8 billion offered in 2011 is 89%, up from 82% on the nearly $10 billion of bonds sold in all of 2010. Even though the market for MBS have begun recovery post the financial crisis, the major source of worry is about the declining quality of the securities offered and that most of the securities offered contain retail property.

Introduction to Mortgage

A mortgage loan is a loan secured by the collateral of some specific real estate property which obliges the borrower to make a predetermined series of payments. A mortgage is a loan and contractual agreement between the lender (mortgagee) and the borrower (mortgagor) who pledges the property to the lender as a security for the repayment of the loan through a series of payments. A mortgage design is a specification of the interest rate, term of the mortgage, and manner in which the borrowed funds are repaid. Mortgage originator (original lender) can hold the mortgage in their portfolio, sell the mortgage to an investor or use the mortgage as collateral for the issuance of a security (mortgage backed security). The borrower pays interest and repays principal in equal instalments over an agreed upon period of time (term of the mortgage). The frequency of payment is typically monthly. The servicing fee is a portion of the mortgage rate. The interest rate that the investor receives is called the net coupon. The mortgage also entitles the lender the right of foreclosure on the loan if the borrower fails to make the contracted payments.

Growing equity mortgages is a fixed-rate mortgage whose monthly mortgage payments increase overtime. Amortization schedule for a level-payment fixed-rate mortgage is as follows:

Mortgage loan : \$1,00,000

Mortgage rate : 8.125%

Monthly payment : \$747.50

Term of loan : 30 years (360 months)

Monthly payment : mortgage balance $\left[\frac{i(1+i)^n}{(1+i)^n-1}\right]$

where, i is the simple monthly interest rate

Example:

n = 360, mortgage balance = \$1,00,000, i = 0.08125/12

Mortgage payment = \$742.50

Proof of the mortgage formula

$$P[(1+i)^{n-1} + (1+i)^{n-2} + \ldots + 1] = M(1+i)^n$$

Extend one extra period:

$$P[(1+i)^{n-1} + \ldots + (1+i)] = M\,[(1+i)^{n+1}$$

Subtract the two terms:

$$P[(1 + i)^n - 1] = M\ [(1 + i)^n$$

So that

$$P = \frac{Mi(1+i)^{n+1}}{(1+i)^n - 1}$$

Months	Beginning Mortgage Balance	Monthly Payment	Monthly Interest	Principal Repayment
1	100,000.00	742.50	677.08	65.41
2	99,934.59	742.50	676.64	65.86
3	99,868.73	742.50	676.19	66.30
.	.	.	.	.
.	.	.	.	.
.	.	.	.	.
358	2,197.66	742.50	14.88	727.62
359	1,470.05	742.50	9.95	732.54
360	737.50	742.50	4.99	737.50

Interest Portion Declines and Repayment Portion Increases

The mortgages can also be divided into two types based on the loan: conventional loans and non-conventional loans. A non-conventional loan is backed by the full faith and guarantee of the Federal Government. Such loans are provided by Federal agencies such as Federal housing administration (FHA), the Veterans Administration (VA) and the Rural Development Administration (RDA) in United States. Conventional loans are those that do not carry any form of government assurance.

The market where these funds are borrowed is called the mortgage market and is divided into the primary and secondary mortgage market.

The primary market provides actual loans to borrowers, whereas the secondary market channels liquidity into the primary market by way of purchasing packages or pools of loans from lenders. Innovations have occurred in terms of design of new mortgage instruments in the primary market and the development of products that use pools of mortgages as collateral for the issuance of securities in the secondary market. Such securities are called mortgage-backed securities (MBS) and may be sold to investors either as pass-through or in structured form, known as Collateralized Mortgage Obligations (CMOs), to meet specific prepayment, maturity, and volatility trenching requirement of the investor.

The mortgage industry can be categorized into four groups: mortgage originators, mortgage servicers, mortgage insurers and mortgage investors, with the key players being commercial banks, thrift institutions, money managers, pension funds, insurance companies, security dealers, trust departments, corporate treasury departments, corporations and private investors.

Mortgage Originator: The original lender of the mortgage loan is called the mortgage originator. The three largest originators for all types of residential loan in the US are commercial banks, thrifts, and mortgage bankers, consisting of more than 95% of annual mortgage originations. Originators make their money by basically charging what they call origination fee, which is based on some percentage basis points of the par value of the loan.

Mortgage Services: Every mortgage loan, both securitized and non-securitized has to be serviced. Servicing a loan entails the collection of monthly payments and forwarding the proceeds to owners of the loan, sending payment notices to mortgagors, reminding mortgagors when payments are overdue, maintaining records of principal balances, administering an escrow balance for real estate taxes and insurance purposes, initiating foreclosure proceedings if necessary, and furnishing tax information for mortgagors if applicable. Mortgage servicers include banks and commercially related entities and mortgage bankers. Servicers receive their revenue from several sources. The primary source is called servicing fee which is some percentage of the outstanding mortgage balance, and declines overtime as the mortgage amortizes.

Mortgage Insurers: Mortgage insurance protects the lender against loss in the event of default by the borrower. Hence, insurance at the loan level minimizes the credit risk of the loan. The amount of mortgage insurance varies as it is dependent on the type of loan and term of loan but it is usually required on loans with loan-to-value ratio greater than 80%. The amount insured may be some percentage of the loan and may reduce as the LTV (Loan to Value) declines.

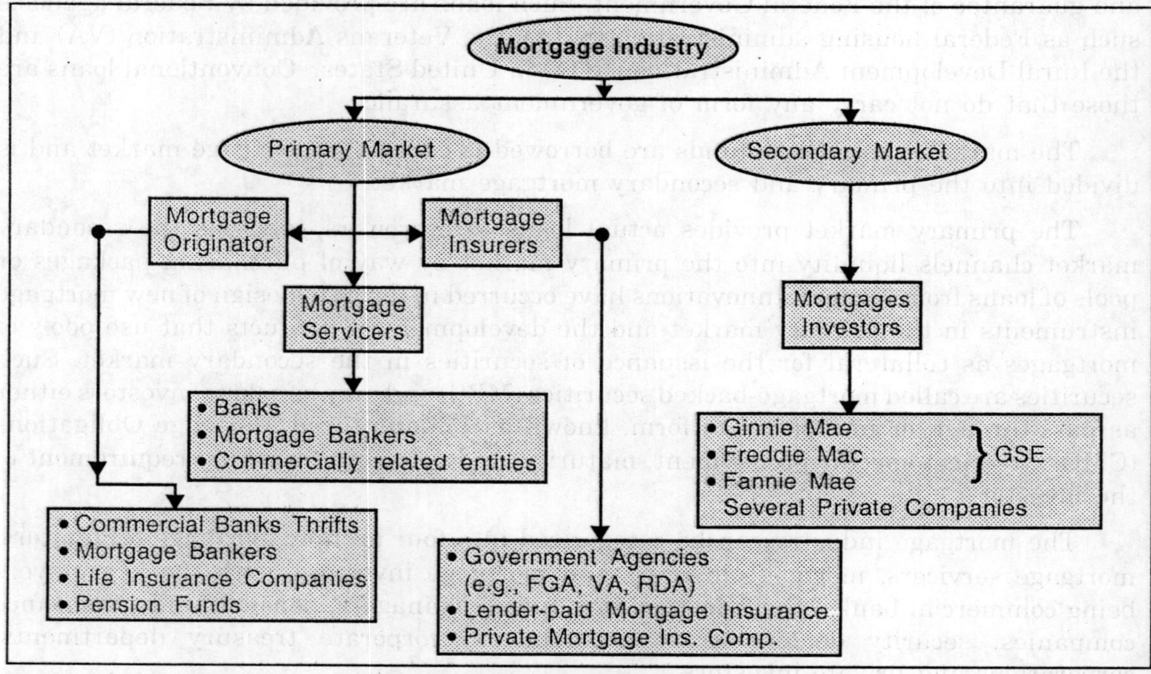

Figure 10.12: Mortgage Industry

What is Mortgage Backed Securities?

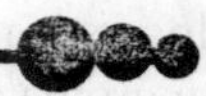

Mortgage backed securities are securities backed by a pool of mortgage loans. There are three types such as: 1. Mortgage pass through securities, 2. Collateralized mortgage obligations; 3. Stripped mortgage backed securities. The last two types are called derivative mortgage backed securities since they are created from the first type.

A mortgage pass-through security is a security created when one or more holders of mortgages form a pool of mortgages and sell shares or participation certificates in the pool. The cash flows consist of monthly mortgage payments representing interest, the scheduled repayment of principal, and any prepayments. Payments are made to security holders each month. The monthly cash flows for a pass-through are less than the monthly cash flows of the underlying mortgages by an amount equal to servicing and other fees. Not all of the mortgages that are included in the pool that are securitized have the same mortgage rate and the same maturity. A weighted average coupon rate and a weighted average maturity are determined.

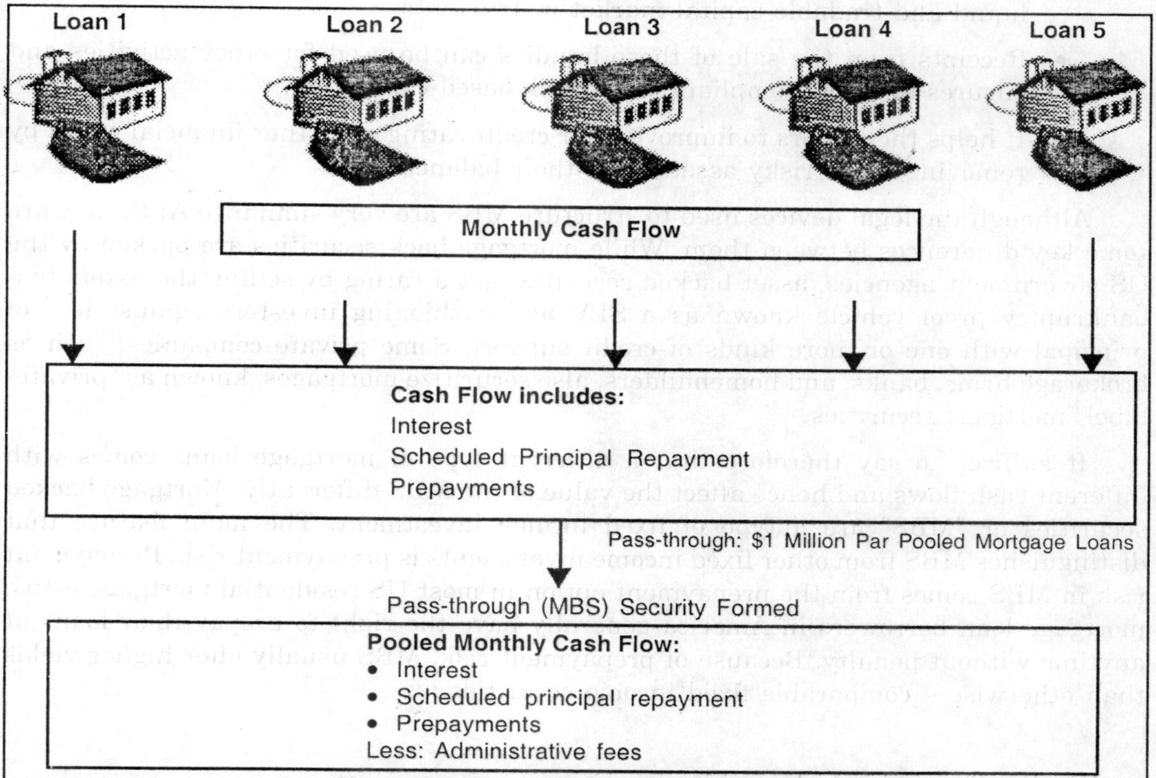

How a Pass-through Security is Created

Figure 10.13

MBSs are simply shares of a home loan sold to investors. Mortgage back security is an asset backed security that represents claims to the cash flows from pools of mortgage loans, most commonly on residential property. MBS also follow the process of securitization, wherein different mortgage loans are purchased from banks, mortgage companies and then are pooled/bundled together by a government, quasi-government or private companies. The bundling is carried on by the analysing the credit rating of the individual securities. Mortgage-backed securities usually pay periodic payments which are similar to coupon payments.

Most bonds backed by mortgages are classified as MBS. The most general type of MBS is the pass-through participation certificates, which entitle the holder to all principal and interest payments (less a servicing fee) from the pool of each month. The more unusual MBS consist of collateralized mortgage obligations or mortgage derivatives which may be designed to protect investors from or expose investors to various types of risk. An important risk with regard to residential mortgages involves prepayments, typically because homeowners refinance when interest rates fall. The originators engage in mortgage back securities as:

- It enables them to transfer relatively illiquid individual financial assets into liquid and tradable capital market instruments
- Receipts from the sale of these bundles can be used for other activities and ensures effective compliance with risk-based capital
- It helps the issuers to improve their credit rating and other financial ratios by removing these risky assets from their balance sheet

Although the legal devices used to structure MBS are very similar to ABS, they are some key differences between them. While mortgage back securities are backed by the US government agencies, asset backed securities get a rating by selling the assets to a bankruptcy proof vehicle known as a SPV and cushioning investors against loss of principal with one or more kinds of credit support. Some private companies, such as brokerage firms, banks, and homebuilders, also securitize mortgages, known as "private-label" mortgage securities.

It suffices to say therefore that a different type of mortgage loans comes with different cash flows and hence affect the value of the MBS differently. Mortgage backed securities or "MBS" are a type of fixed income investment. The main feature that distinguishes MBS from other fixed income investments is prepayment risk. Prepayment risk in MBS comes from the prepayment option in most US residential mortgage loans: mortgage loan borrowers in America generally have the right to prepay their loans at anytime without penalty. Because of prepayment risk, MBS usually offer higher yields than otherwise – comparable fixed income securities.

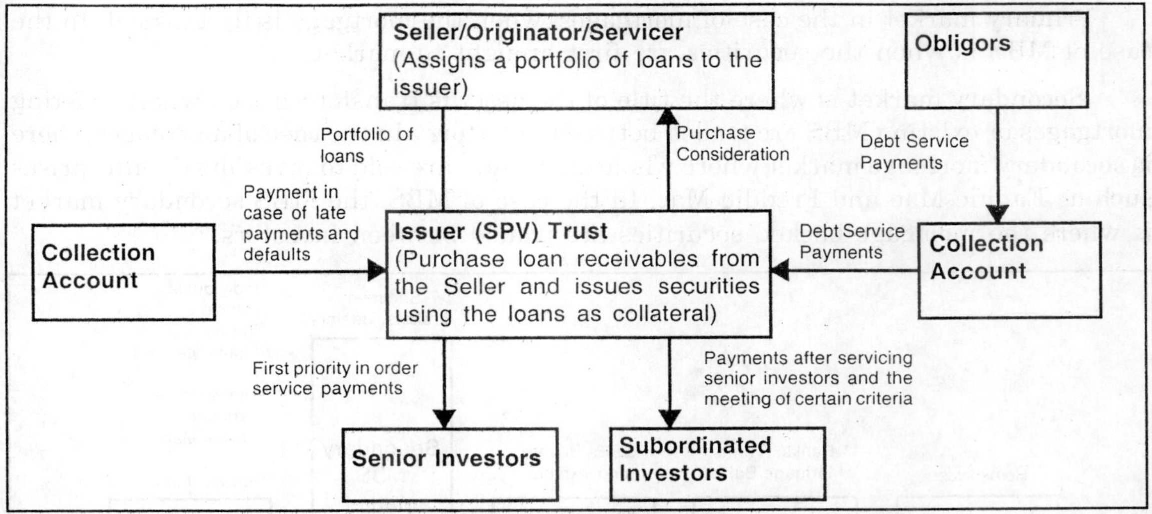

Figure 10.14: MBO Structure

A borrower's right to prepay his loan is extremely important. When interest rates fall, the borrower can take advantage of the situation by refinancing his loan at a lower rate. When interest rates rise, the borrower receives the benefit of having locked-in a lower rate in the past.

Although fixed-rate mortgage loans remain the most common, a borrower can choose a loan that has an adjustable interest rate. Such a loan is called an adjustable-rate mortgage loan or "ARM". The simplest form of ARM provides for adjustments to its interest rate annually or semi-annually. The adjustment is determined by changes in a published market index, such as LIBOR or the yield on US Treasury securities with a remaining maturity of one year. Some ARMs start with low initial interest rates that last until the first adjustment. The low initial rate is called a "teaser rate". Lenders offer teaser rates to attract new borrowers.

Features of MBS

Mortgage issuer or initial lender is a mortgage lender, usually a bank or a mortgage banker. The issuer lends money to the homeowner who is the borrower.

Guarantor guarantees the timely payment of interest and principal on the mortgage. In the case of Ginnie Mae, this guarantee is backed by the full faith and credit of the US government. Fannie Mae and Freddie Mac guarantee mortgages based on their own creditworthiness.

Mortgage Servicer: The main function of the servicer is to collect monthly payments from the mortgage borrowers and pass the cash flow to the mortgage pool or other mortgage purchaser.

MBS issuer is the institution that issues the mortgage backed security. It forwards the cash flow to the ultimate investor.

Primary market in the case of mortgages, when the mortgage is first issued. In the case of MBS is when the securities are first brought to market.

Secondary market is where the title of the asset is transferred, i.e., where existing mortgages or existing MBS are traded between investors. In the case of mortgages, there is secondary mortgage market where whole mortgages are sold to investors or enterprises such as Fannie Mae and Freddie Mac. In the case of MBS, the MBS secondary market is where the mortgage backed securities are traded between investors.

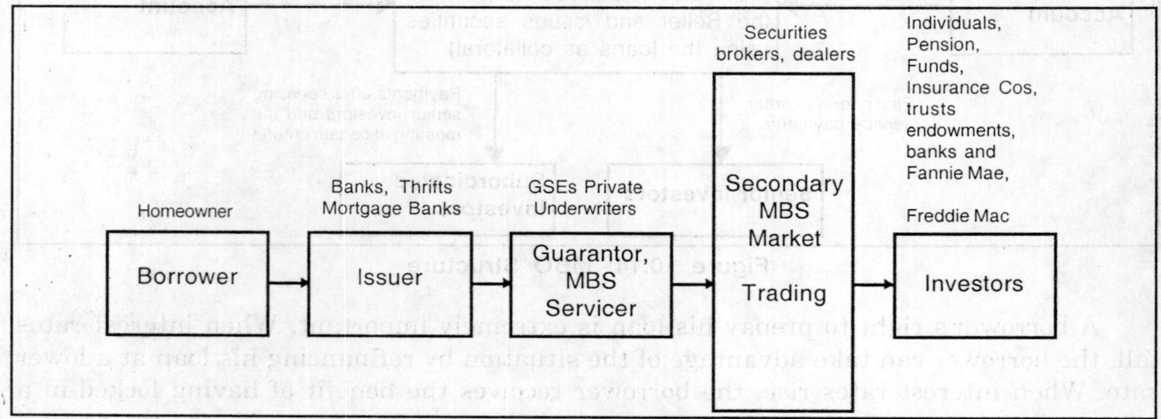

Figure 10.15

The most common type of MBS is a simple "pass-through" security that represents ownership of an underlying "pool" of mortgage loans. An investor who owns the MBS is entitled to receive collections of interest and principal, including prepayments. In MBS jargon, the payments on the loans are "passed-through" to the investors. However, a small portion of the interest collections is not passed-through. Instead, it is used to cover expenses of the deal. Thus, an MBS has a "pass-through rate", which is the net rate at which investors receive interest on the balance of the mortgage loans backing the security. For example, if the mortgage loans backing an MBS have interest rates of 6.5%, the MBS might have a pass-through rate of 6%. The difference, 0.5%, covers expenses.

Every MBS has a "servicer". The servicer is a company that collects payments from borrowers and handles the administrative task of aggregating the collected funds and distributing them to investors. Naturally, the servicer receives a fee for its services. In most MBS, the fees to the servicer consume all or nearly all of the difference between the interest rate on the mortgage loans and the pass-through rate on the security. In many cases, the lender that originated the mortgage loans becomes the servicer for the MBS comprising those loans.

Mortgage backed securities (MBS) is claims on a portfolio of mortgages. The securities entitle the holder to the cash flows from a pool of mortgages. There are three federal agencies that buy certain types of mortgage loan portfolios (e.g., FHA (Federal Housing Administration) – or VA (Veterans Administration) (-insured mortgages) and then pool them to create MBSs to sell to investors:

- Federal National Mortgage Association (FNMA)
- Government National Mortgage Association (GNMA)
- Federal Home Loan Mortgage Corporation (FHLMC)

GNMA finances FHA and VA loans. It provides typically, single family, low-income loans. GNMA pass-throughs guaranteed by GNMA and are issued by GNMA approved originators and servicers. GNMA guarantee of full and timely payment of interest and principal is backed by the full faith and credit of the US Government. Historically, prepayments are less volatile relative to other agency pass-throughs. FNMA pass-throughs buys conventional mortgages. FNMA provides guarantee of full and timely payment of interest and principal, but this guarantee is not backed by the full faith and guarantee of the US government. Mortgage pools are much more heterogeneous when compared to the pools in the GNMA. Pool may have mortgages with rates that vary by more than 200 basis points and the loans may be new or seasoned. FNMA covers both FHA and VA loans as well as conventional loans which have a much higher value. Prepayments are much more volatile. FHLMC pass-throughs buys FHA, VA, and conventional mortgages. Guarantees full and timely payment of interest and principal, not backed by a similar guarantee of the US govt. diverse mortgage pool. Prepayments are much more volatile.

Collectively, the MBSs created by these agencies are referred to as agency pass-throughs. Agency pass-throughs are guaranteed by the agencies, and the loans they purchase must be conforming loans, meaning they meet certain standards.

Types of MBS

Pass-through: In a pass-through MBS, an issuer collects monthly payments from homeowners and then passes on a proportionate share of the collected principal and interest to the investor. Pass-through MBS have three components of cash-flow:

- Scheduled principal (usually fixed)
- Scheduled interest (usually fixed)
- Prepaid principal (usually variable depending on the actions of homeowners, as governed by prevailing interest rates).

Pass-throughs represent a share of an investment pool consisting of multiple mortgages. Prepayment risk is reduced when the investment is subject to increasingly larger numbers of mortgages because each mortgage prepayment would then have a reduced effect on the total pool. Pass-through securities allow investors to reduce their prepayment risk through diversification rather than a single mortgage investment. Pass-throughs further has two subtypes:

- A residential mortgage-backed security (RMBS) is a pass-through MBS backed by mortgages on residential property
- A commercial mortgage-backed security (CMBS) is a pass-through MBS backed by mortgages on commercial property.

Collateralized Mortgage Obligations (CMOs)

A collateralized mortgage obligation or "Pay-through bond" are debt obligations of a legal entity that is collateralized by the assets it owns. Pay-through bonds are typically divided into classes that have different maturities and different priorities for the receipt of principal and in some case of interest. They often contain a sequential pay security structure with at least two classes of mortgage backed securities issued, with one class receiving scheduled principal payments and prepayments before any other class. CMOs can be less liquid than other mortgage backed securities due to the individuality of each tranche. Investors need a high level of expertise to understand the implications of tranche-specification. In addition, investors may receive more or less than the original investment upon selling a CMO. In CMO the investors are divided into three classes. They are called either class A, B or C investors. Each class differs in the order they receive principal payments, but receives interest payments as long as it is not completely paid-off. Class A investors are paid out first with prepayments and repayments until they are paid-off. Then class B investors are paid-off, followed by class C investors. In a situation like this, class A investors bear most of the prepayment risk, while class C investors bear the least.

A CMO's objective is to provide some protection against the prepayment risk associated with mortgage investments, above and beyond the protection offered by pass-through, while still offering credit quality and high yields. CMOs take the cash flows from pass-through and segregate them into different bond classes known as tranches, to provide the investor some level of payment predictability. Tranches are created in an attempt to provide a timeframe, or window, during which repayment is expected. The tranches prioritize the distribution of principal payments among various classes and serve as a series of maturities over the life of the mortgage pool.

The creation of a CMO cannot eliminate prepayment risk. It can only redistribute prepayment risk among different classes of bondholders. CMO class has a different coupon rate from that for the underlying collateral, resulting in instruments that have varying risk-return characteristics that fit the needs of fixed-income investors. Suppose investors have different preferred maturities, so they should be willing to pay different prices for securities of different expected maturities.

Sequential-pay Tranches

Total par value of $400 million

Tranches	Par amount	Coupon rate (%)
A	$19,45,00,000.00	7.5
B	$3,60,00,000.00	7.5
C	$9,65,00,000.00	7.5
D	$7,30,00,000.00	7.5
	$40,00,00,000.00	

Tranche A receives all the principal payments until the entire principal amount owed to that bond class, $19,45,00,000 is paid-off; then tranche B begins to receive principal and continues to do so until it is paid the entire $3,60,00,000. Each tranche receive interest on the respective class's outstanding balance.

Five Tranche Sequential Pay Structure with Floater, Inverse Floater, and Accrual Bond Classes*

Tranche	Par Amount	Coupon Rate (%)
A	$19,45,00,000.00	7.50
B	$3,60,00,000.00	7.50
FL	$7,23,75,000.00	1 month LIBOR + 0.50
IFL	$2,41,25,000.00	28.50 – 3 × (1 month LIBOR)
Z (accrual)	$7,30,00,000.00	7.50
	$40,00,00,000.00	

* The interest for the accrual tranche would accrue and be added to the principal balance (like zero-coupon bond). The interest that would have been paid to the accrual bond class is used to speed up pay down of the principal balance of earlier bond classes.

For Disbursement of Principal Payments

Disburse principal payments to tranche A until it is paid-off completely. After tranche A is paid-off completely, disburse principal payments to tranche B until it is paid-off completely. After tranche B is paid-off completely, disburse principal payments to tranches FL and IFL until they are paid-off completely. The principal payments between tranches FL and IFL should be made in the following way: 75% to tranche FL and 25% to tranche IFL. After tranches FL and IFL are paid-off completely, disburse principal payments to tranche Z until the original principal balance plus accrued interest is paid-off completely. Disburse periodic coupon interest to tranches A, B, FL, and IFL on the basis of the amount of principal outstanding at the beginning of the period. For tranche Z, accrue the interest based on the principal plus accrued interest in the preceding period. The interest for tranche Z is to be paid to the earlier tranches as a principal pay down. There is a cap on FL and a floor on IFL. The maximum coupon rate for FL is 10%; the minimum coupon rate for IFL is 0%. The factor 3 in IFL is called the coupon leverage.

Why CMO are Popular?

The CMO converts a long-term monthly payment instrument into a series of semi-annual payments, which are bond-like securities with short, intermediate and long maturities. The multiple maturity structure reduces the degree of uncertainty of cash flows for any particular maturity class, and provides the longer maturity classes with limited call protection. This is because shorter tranches absorb the initial burden of excess principal repayments. Investors are attracted by the broader range of investment maturities made possible by the CMO structure. The high quality of the collateral (GNMA, etc.), along with the protective structure of the trust enables these securities to generally carry the highest investment grade credit rating. Yield offer investors attractive yield premiums over Treasury and even some corporate bonds. Event risk CMO is essentially free from default risk. They are also free from events that cause price fluctuations in the corporate world.

Benefit of MBS

There are many reasons for mortgage originators to finance their activities by issuing mortgage backed securities. Mortgage backed securities:

1. Transform relatively illiquid, individual financial assets into liquid and tradable capital market instruments.
2. Allow mortgage originators to replenish their funds, which can then be used for additional origination activities.
3. Can be used by Wall Street banks to monetize the credit spread between the origination of an underlying mortgage (private market transaction) and the yield demanded by bond investors through bond issuance (typically, a public market transaction).
4. MBS are frequently a more efficient and lower cost source of financing in comparison with other bank and capital markets financing alternatives.
5. Allow issuers to diversify their financing sources, by offering alternatives to more traditional forms of debt and equity financing.
6. Allow issuers to remove assets from their balance sheet, which can help to improve various financial ratios, utilise capital more efficiently and achieve compliance with risk-based capital standards.

Risk Attached with MBS

Credit Risk: The credit risk of mortgage backed securities depends on the likelihood of the borrower paying the promised cash flows (principal and interest) on time. Credit risk arises from uncertainty of fulfil interest and principal payments. Investors in MBSs do not want to hold credit risk on the underlying mortgages, so MBS issuers provide guarantees. When Fannie Mae and Freddie Mac issue MBSs, they charge a guarantee fee that is currently between 20-30 basis points. This is taken from the gross yield on the loan so it is netted to the investor. These corporations are able reduce their risk of mortgage default by diversifying their large portfolios across the nation. Investors in these MBS thus have not the individual borrower, but Fannie Mae and Freddie Mac as a counterparty to their credit risk. Therefore, the credit risk of mortgage backed securities issued by Fannie Mae and Freddie Mac reflects the credit rating of those corporations.

Interest Rate Risk: In general, bond prices in the secondary market rise when interest rates fall and *vice versa*. Because of the prepayment risk and extension risk, the secondary market price of MBS will sometimes rise less than a typical bond when interest rates decline, but may drop more when interest rates rise. Thus, there may be greater interest rate risk with MBS than with other bonds.

Prepayment Risk: Prepayment risk is the risk that homeowners will pay-off more than their required monthly mortgage payments. Prepayment is usually precipitated by a decline in interest rates. As prepayments occur, the amount of principal retained in the bond declines faster than what otherwise may be expected – thereby shortening the average life of the bond by returning principal prematurely to the bondholder, potentially at a time when interest rates are low.

Extension Risk: Extension risk is the risk that homeowners will decide not to make prepayments on their mortgages to the extent initially expected – instead they make only the required monthly payment. Extension can be the result of an increase in interest rates. As rates rise, there is little incentive to refinance fixed rate mortgages. As the prepayments that were expected do not materialize, the average length of term (average life) originally estimated begins to creep out further along the curve, resulting in a security that is lengthier in term.

Suppose an investor buys a 10% coupon Ginnie Mae when mortgages are 10%. What would be the impact on prepayments if mortgage rates decline to 6%. The price of an option free bond will rise, but in the case of pass-rough security the rise in price is less because there is a higher prepayment. The upside price potential is truncated due to prepayments. The cash flows from prepayments are reinvested at a lower rate. What happen if the mortgage rates rise to 15%? The price of the pass-through, like the price of any bond, will decline. It declines more because the higher rates will tend to slow-down the rate of prepayment, in effect increasing the amount invested at the coupon rate, which is lower than the market rate.

Techniques for Valuing MBS

There are various models and methodologies for valuing and comparing mortgage backed securities (MBS). Valuation is also critical in applying other analytical tools such as total return analysis because the value of an MBS at the end of some investment horizon must be estimated. Some of the techniques are as follows:

Static Cash Flow Yield Analysis

The yield on any financial instrument is the interest rate that makes the present value of the expected cash flow equal to its market price plus accrued interest. For MBS, the yield calculated is called a cash flow yield. The problem in calculating the cash flow yield of an MBS is that the security's cash fows are unknown, due to the effects of prepayments.

Assumptions to Determine a Cash Flow Yield of MBS

- Compare the yield on a mortgage backed security to that of a Treasury coupon security by first calculating the MBS's bond equivalent yield.

- bond equivalent yield for a Treasury coupon security is found by doubling the semi-annual yield

Bond-equivalent yield = $2[(1 + i_M)^6 - 1]$

Where,

i_M = Mortgage Yield which is the monthly interest rate

All yield measures suffer from problems that limit their use in assessing a security's potential return. The yield to maturity has two major shortcomings as a measure of a bond's potential return. To realize the stated yield to maturity, the investor is assumed to

- Reinvest the coupon payments at a rate equal to the yield to maturity
- Hold the bond to maturity.

The reinvestment of the coupon payments is critical, and for long-term bonds can comprise as much as 80% of the bond's return. The risk of having to reinvest the interest payments at less than the computed yield is called reinvestment risk.

These shortcomings are equally applicable to the cash flow yield measure since

- The projected cash flows are assumed to be reinvested at the cash flow yield
- The MBS is assumed to be held until the final pay out based on some prepayment assumption.

The impact of reinvestment risk, that is, the risk that the cash flow will have to be reinvested at a rate less than the cash flow yield, is particularly important for many MBS, because payments are monthly and both interest and principal must be reinvested. In particular, returns for high-yielding bonds are overstated; the yield to maturity method assumes that the proceeds will be invested in similar bonds that offer the same yield. Moreover, an additional assumption is that the projected cash flow is actually realized. If the prepayment experience is different from the prepayment rate assumed, the cash flow yield will not be realized. The difference between the cash flow yield and the yield on a comparable Treasury security is called the nominal spread. The nominal spread is the most commonly quoted measure of incremental returns. However, this spread masks the fact that a portion of the nominal spread is compensation for accepting prepayment risk.

Zero-volatility Spread

A more accurate measure of spread is to compare an MBS to a portfolio of Treasury securities having the same cash flows. This spread is called the zero-volatility spread. While it does not take prepayment risk into account, it does account for the various patterns that principal payments on an MBS or CMO can take at a given prepayment speed. The zero-volatility spread or Z-spread is a measure of the spread that the investor would realize over the entire Treasury spot rate curve if the mortgage security is held to maturity. It is not a spread-off one point on the Treasury yield curve, as is the nominal spread. Rather, it is the spread that will make the present value of the cash flows from the MBS equal to the price of the MBS when discounted at the Treasury spot rate plus the spread. An iterative process is used to determine the zero-volatility spread.

Monte Carlo Simulation

The valuation of MBS depends on many variables like future interest rates, the shape of the yield curve, future interest rate volatility, prepayment rates, default rates and their timing, and recovery rates. The value of all these variables cannot be easily estimated and hence there is a high uncertainty in the valuation. Also, because of the dependence of the valuation on a large number of variables, the total range of values a MBS can take is quite large. Simulation generates a probability distribution function of the value of the MBS using various possible values for the input variable. However, just one parameter of the probability distribution model is used as the value of the mortgage backed security. This is mostly the average or the mean of the probability distribution function. While the rest of the information that is available from the probability distribution for the value of the mortgage security is generally ignored, it possesses information that can be useful in gauging the value of a security.

Prepayments are projected by feeding the refinancing rate and loan characteristics into a prepayment model. Given the projected prepayments, the cash flow along an interest rate path can be determined. The simulation works by generating many scenarios of future interest rate paths. An estimate of the value of the MBS is the average of the sample values over many simulation trials.

The following the steps in the Monte Carlo Methodology for Valuing a Mortgage Security are below:

The steps in the methodology

Step 1: Simulate short-term interest rate and refinancing rate paths.

Step 2: Project the cash flow on each interest rate path.

Step 3: Determine the present value of the cash flows on each interest rate path.

Step 4: Compute the theoretical value of the mortgage security.

Each of the steps are described in detail below:

The number of months remaining till maturity is denoted by T. Multiple such input rate paths are generated and are fed as an input to the simulator. These paths generated are called as 'trials'. The number of such trials generated is denoted as N.

The cash flow for a MBS would consist of two components the scheduled and unscheduled payments. The scheduled payments include the total amounts to be received each month based on the projected predecided mortgage payments. The unscheduled portion includes the prepayments of the principal made. This part is complicated to gauge and a prepayment model determines the amount to be assumed for each month. There is a prepayment rate for each month on a given interest rate path and the rate for a given month. Thus, the prepayment rates could vary depending on various occurrences and hence this part of the valuation process is very critical and has to be done extremely carefully.

Given the cash flows on an interest rate path, the path's present value can be calculated. The discount rate for determining the present value is the simulated spot rate for each month on the interest rate path plus an appropriate spread. The spot rate on a path can be determined from the simulated future monthly rates. The relationship that holds between the simulated spot rates for month T on path n and the simulated future 1 month rates is:

$$Z_T(n) = \{[1 + f_1(n)]\ [1 + f_2(n)]\ \dots\ [1 + f_T(n)]\}^{1/T} - 1$$

where,

$Z_T(n)$ = simulated spot rate for month T on path n

$F_j(n)$ = simulated future 1 month rate for month j on path n

Consequently, the interest rate path for the simulated future 1 month rates can be converted to the interest rate path for the simulated monthly spot rates. Therefore, the present value of the cash flows for Month T on interest rate path n discounted at the simulated spot rate for month T plus some spread is:

$$PV[C_T(n)] = \frac{C_T(n)}{[1+z_T(n)+K]^T}$$

where,

$PV[C_T(n)$ = present value of cash flows for month T on path n

$C_T(n)$ = cash flow for month T on path n

$z_T(n)$ = spot rate for month T on path n

K = spread

The present value for path n is the sum of the present value of the cash flows for each month on path n. That is,

$$PV[Path(n)] = PV\ [c_1(n)] + PV[C_2(n)] + .. + PV[C_{360}(n)]$$

The present value of a given interest rate path can be thought of as the theoretical value of a pass-through if that path was actually realized. The theoretical value of the pass-through can be determined by calculating the average of the theoretical values of all the interest rate paths.

Where N is the number of interest rate paths.

Total Return Analysis

In fact many investors do not hold these securities till maturity and hence we need a better technique so that this flaw could be corrected. A commonly used technique, called total return analysis, allows the investor to evaluate returns over different time periods and interest rate scenarios. It basically allows investors to specify additional variable which is the reinvestment rate available at different times in the future. Thus, even the reinvestment risk is considered in the valuation of these securities.The total return from a mortgage backed security is defined by the following parameters:

- Cost of the security at the time of purchase
- The security's projected cash flows, including principal payments, interest, and reinvestment income
- Projected value at the horizon date.

The total percentage return (i.e., the returns over the time horizon) can be calculated as follows:

$$\text{Periodic Total Return} = \frac{\text{Total horizon proceeds}}{\text{Total cost}} - 1$$

The return can be annualized, as shown below:

$$\text{Annualized Total Return} = [\text{Periodic total return}]^{\frac{12}{\text{Number of months in period}}}$$

The models used in the valuation techniques above use various interest rate scenarios by assuming parallel and non-parallel shifts in the yield curve. Also different assumptions for volatilities are also used.

Cash Flow from a Mortgage Portfolio

The cash flow from a portfolio of mortgages consists

- Interest payments
- Scheduled principal
- Prepaid principal

Cash Flows: Terms

- **Weighted Average Coupon Rate, (WAC):** Mortgage portfolios (collaterals) weighted average rate.
- **Weighted Average Maturity, (WAM):** Mortgage portfolios weighted average maturity.
- **Pass-through Rate, (PT Rate):** Interest rate paid on the MBS; PT rate is lower than WAC – the difference going to MBS issuer.
- **Prepayment Rate or Speed:** Assumed prepayment rate.

Example 1: Consider a bank that has a pool of current fixed rate mortgages that are:

- worth $100 million (Par, F)
- yield a WAC of 8%, and
- have a WAM of 360 months.

For the first month, the portfolio would generate an aggregate mortgage payment of $733,765

$$F_0 = \sum_{t=1}^{M} \frac{p}{(1+(R^A/12))^t}$$

$$P = \frac{\$100{,}000{,}000}{\left[\frac{1-1/(1+(.08/12))^{360}}{.08/12}\right]} = \$733{,}765 \qquad F_0 = p\left[\frac{1-1/(1+(R^A/12))^M}{R^A/12}\right]$$

$$P = \frac{F_0}{\left[\frac{1-1/(1+(R^A/12))^M}{R^A/12}\right]}$$

From the $733,765 payment, $666,667 would go towards interest and $67,098 would go towards the scheduled principal payment:

$$\text{Interest} = \left(\frac{R^A}{12}\right)F_0 = \left(\frac{.08}{12}\right)\$100{,}000{,}000 = \$666{,}667$$

Scheduled Principal Payment = p – Interest = $733,765 – $666,667 = $67098

In the standard PSA model, known as 100 PSA, the conditional prepayment rate (CPR) starts at .2% for the first month and then increases at a constant rate of .2% per month to equal 6% at the 30th month; then after the 30th month the CPR stays at a constant 6%. Thus for any month t, the CPR is

$$CPR = .06\left(\frac{t}{30}\right), \text{ if } t \le 30,$$

$$CPR = .06, \text{ if } t > 30$$

CPR is quoted on an annual basis. The monthly prepayment rate, referred to as the single monthly mortality rate, SMM, can be obtained given the annual CPR by using the following formula:

SMM = 1 – [1 – CPR]1/12

The projected first month prepaid principal can be estimated with a prepayment model. Using the 100% PSA model, the monthly prepayment rate for the first month (t = 1) is equal to SMM = .0001668:

$$CPR = \left(\frac{1}{30}\right).06 = .002$$

SMM = 1 – [1 – .002]1/12 = .0001668

Given the prepayment rate, the projected prepaid principal in the first month is found by multiplying the balance at the beginning of the month minus the scheduled principal by the SMM. By doing this yields a projected prepaid principal of $16,671 in the first month:

Prepaid principal = SMM [F_0 – Scheduled principal]

Prepaid principal = .0001668 [\$100,000,000 – \$67,098] = \$16,671

Thus, for the first month, the mortgage portfolio would generate an estimated cash flow of \$750,435, and a balance at the beginning of the next month of \$99,916,231:

CF = Interest + Scheduled principal + Prepaid principal

CF = \$666,666 + \$67,098 + \$16,671 = \$750,435

Beginning Balance for Month 2 = F_0 – Scheduled principal – Prepaid principal

Beginning Balance for Month 2 = \$100,000,000 – \$67,098 – \$16,671 = \$99,916,231

In the second month (t = 2), the projected payment would be \$733,642 with \$666,108 going to interest and \$67,534 to scheduled principal:

$$p = \frac{\$99,916,231}{\left[\dfrac{1-1/(1+(.08/12))^{359}}{.08/12}\right]} = \$733,642$$

$$\text{Interest} = \left(\frac{.08}{12}\right)(\$99,916,231) = \$666,108$$

Scheduled principal = \$733,642 – \$66,108 = \$67,534

Using the 100% PSA model, the estimated monthly prepayment rate is .000333946, yielding a projected prepaid principal in month 2 of \$33,344:

$$\text{CPR} = \left(\frac{2}{30}\right).06 = .004$$

SMM = 1 – [1 – .004]1/12 = .000333946

Prepaid principal = .000333946 [\$99,916,231 – \$67,534] = 33,344

Thus, for the second month, the mortgage portfolio would generate an estimated cash flow of \$766,986 and have a balance at the beginning of month three of \$99,815,353:

CF = \$ 666,108 + \$67,534 + \$33,344 = \$766,986

Beginning Balance for Month 3 = \$99,916,231 – \$67,534 – \$33,344

= \$99,815,353

So two points is important:

Starting in month 30 the SMM remains constant at .005143; this reflects the 100% PSA model's assumption of a constant CPR of 6% starting in month 30. The projected cash flows are based on a static analysis in which rates are assumed fixed over the time period.

Cash Flow from a Mortgage Portfolio: Example 1

Period	Balance 100000000	Interest	p	Sch. Prin.	SMM	Prepaid Prin.	CF
1	100000000	666667	733765	67098	0.0001668	16671	750435
2	99916231	666108	733642	67534	0.0003339	33344	766986
3	99815353	665436	733397	67961	0.0005014	50011	783409
4	99697380	664649	733029	68380	0.0006691	66664	799694
5	99562336	663749	732539	68790	0.0008372	83294	815833
6	99410252	662735	731926	69191	0.0010055	99892	831817
7	99241170	661608	731190	69582	0.0011742	116449	847639
23	94291147	628608	703012	74405	0.0039166	369010	1072023
24	93847732	625652	700259	74607	0.0040908	383607.	1083866
25	93389518	622597	697394	74798	0.0042653	398017	1095411
26	92916704	619445	694420	74975	0.0044402	412234	1106653
27	92429495	616197	691336	75140	0.0046154	426250	1117586
28	91928105	612854	688146	75292	0.0047909	440059	1128204
29	91412755	609418	684849	75430	0.0049668	453653	1138502
30	90883671	605891	681447	75556	0.005143	467027	1148475
31.	90341088	602274	677943	75669	0.005143	464236	1142179
32	89801183	598675	674456	75781	0.005143	461459	1135915
110	54900442	366003	451112	85109	0.005143	281916	733028
111	54533417	363556	448792	85236	0.005143	280028	728820
112	54168153	361121	446484	85363	0.005143	278148	724632
113	53804641	358698	444188	85490	0.005143	276278	720466
114	53442873	356286	441903	85617	0.005143	274417	716320
115	53082839	353886	439631	85745	0.005143	272565	712195
357	496620	3311	126231	122920	0.005143	1922	128153
358	371778	2479	125582	123103	0.005143	1279	126861
359	247395	1649	124936	123287	0.005143	638	125574
360	123470	823	124293	123470	0.005143	0	124293

Example 2

- The next exhibit shows the monthly cash flows for a MBS issue constructed from a $100M mortgage pool with the following features
  - — Current balance = $100M
  - — WAC = 8%
  - — WAM = 355 months

— PT rate = 7.5%

— Prepayment speed equal to 150% of the standard PSA model: PSA = 150

Cash flow from a MBS: Example 2

Period	Balance 100000000	Interest	p	Scheduled Principal	SMM	Prepaid Principal	Principal	CF
1	100000000	625000	736268	69601	0.0015125	151147	220748	845748
2	99779252	623620	735154	69959	0.0017671	176194	246153	869773
3	99533099	622082	733855	70301	0.0020223	201148	271449	893531
4	99261650	620385	732371	70627	0.0022783	225990	296617	917002
5	98965033	618531	730702	70936	0.002535	250701	321637	940168
6	98643396	616521	728850	71227	0.0027925	275262	346489	963011
20	91641550	572760	684341	73398	0.0064757	592971	666369	1239128
21	90975181	568595	679910	73408	0.0067447	613101	686510	1255105
22	90288672	564304	675324	73399	0.0070144	632804	706204	1270508
23	89582468	559890	670587	73370	0.0072849	652066	725436	1285327
24	88857032	555356	665702	73321	0.0075563	670873	744194	1299550
25	88112838	550705	660671	73253	0.0078284	689211	762463	1313169
26	87350375	545940	655499	73164	0.0078284	683243	756406	1302346
27	86593968	541212	650368	73075	0.0078284	677322	750397	1291609
28	85843572	536522	645277	72986	0.0078284	671448	744434	1280957
29	85099137	531870	640225	72897	0.0078284	665621	738519	1270388
30	84360619	527254	635213	72809	0.0078284	659840	732649	1259903
31	83627969	522675	630240	72721	0.0078284	654106	726826	1249501
32	82901143	518132	625307	72632	0.0078284	648416	721049	1239181
33	82180094	513626	620411	72544	0.0078284	642772	715317	1228942
100	44933791	280836	366433	66874	0.0078284	351237	418111	698947
101	44515680	278223	363564	66793	0.0078284	347965	414758	692981
102	44100923	275631	360718	66712	0.0078284	344718	411430	687061
103	43689493	273059	357894	66631	0.0078284	341498	408129	681188
200	16163713	101023	166983	59225	0.0078284	126073	185298	286321
201	15978416	99865	165676	59153	0.0078284	124623	183776	283641
353	148527	928	50171	49181	0.0078284	778	49958	50887
354	98569	616	49778	49121	0.0078284	387	49508	50124
355	49061	307	49388	49061	0.0078284	0	49061	49368

The first month's CPR for the MBS issue reflects a five-month seasoning in which t = 6, and a speed that is 150% greater than the 100 PSA. For the MBS issue, this yields a first month SMM of .0015125 and a constant SMM of .0078284 starting in month 25.

The WAC of 8% is used to determine the mortgage payment and scheduled principal, while the PT rate of 7.5% is used to determine the interest.

The monthly fees implied on the MBS issue are equal to .04167% = (8% – 7.5%)/ 12 of the monthly balance.

First Month's Payment:

$$p = \frac{\$100M}{\left[\dfrac{1-1/(1+(.08/12))^{355}}{.08/12}\right]} = \$736,268$$

From the \$736,268 payment, \$625,000 would go towards interest and \$69,601 would go towards the scheduled principal payment:

$$\text{Interest} = \left(\frac{R^A}{12}\right) F0 = \left(\frac{.075}{12}\right) \$100,000,000 = \$625,000$$

$$\text{Scheduled Principal Payment} = p - \text{Interest} = \$736,268 - [(.08/12)(\$100,000,000)] = \$69,601$$

Using 150% PSA model and seasoning of 5 months the first month SMM = .0015125:

$$CPR = 1.50\left(\frac{6}{30}\right).06 = .018$$

$$SMM = 1 - [1 - .018]1/12 = .0015125$$

Given the prepayment rate, the projected prepaid principal in the first month is \$151,147

$$\text{Prepaid principal} = SMM\,[F_0 - \text{Scheduled principal}]$$

$$\text{Prepaid principal} = .0015125[\$100,000,000 - \$69,601] = \$151,147$$

Thus, for the first month, the MBS would generate an estimated cash flow of \$845,748 and a balance at the beginning of the next month of \$99,779,252:

$$CF = \text{Interest} + \text{Scheduled principal} + \text{Prepaid principal}$$

$$CF = \$625,000 + \$69,601 + \$151,147 = \$845,748$$

$$\text{Beginning Balance for Month 2} = F_0 - \text{Scheduled principal} - \text{Prepaid principal}$$

$$\text{Beginning Balance for Month 2} = \$100,000,000 - \$69,601 - \$151,147 = \$99,779,252$$

Second Month: Payment, Interest, Scheduled Principal, Prepaid Principal, and Cash flow:

$$p = \left[\frac{\$99,779,252}{\frac{1-1/(1+(.08/12))^{354}}{.08/12}}\right] \$735,154$$

$$\text{Interest} = \left(\frac{R^A}{12}\right) F0 = \left(\frac{.075}{12}\right) \$99,779,252 = \$623,620$$

$$\text{Scheduled Principal Payment} = p - \text{Interest} = \$735,154 - [(.08/12)(\$99,779,252)] = \$69,959$$

$$CPR = 1.50\left(\frac{7}{30}\right).06 = .021$$

$$SMM = 1 - [1 - .021]^{1/12} = .001761$$

$$\text{Prepaid principal} = SMM\ [F_0 - \text{Scheduled principal}]$$

$$\text{Prepaid principal} = .0017671[\$99,779,252 - \$69,959] = \$176,194$$

$$CF = \text{Interest} + \text{Scheduled principal} + \text{Prepaid principal}$$

$$Cf = \$523,620 + \$69,959 + \$176,194 = \$869,773$$

MBS Players in India

Below are few major MBS players in Indian market:

- Deutsche Postbank Home Finance Limited
- Canfin Homes Limited
- Cholamandalam Investment and Finance Company Limited
- HDFC Limited
- ICICI Bank Limited
- Reliance Home Finance Private Limited
- Standard Chartered Bank
- Sundaram BNP Paribas Home Finance Limited

MBS Market in India

The beginning of Mortgage Backed Securities (MBS) in India was made in August 2000, when National Housing Board (NHB) issued the first MBS with issue size of INR 59.7 crore, originated by HDFC Ltd. While the number of housing loans has increased, the number of MBS issued so far has remained more or less constant for all the years since 2000, on the basis of total issue size. Also, while the volumes of securitisation in general have continued to zoom, the RMBS activity remains limited.

Issuance volume in the Indian securitisation market fell by 29% in FY2011 over the previous fiscal to ₹ 30,825 crore. While securitisation of retail loans (both Asset Backed Securitisation or ABS, and Residential Mortgage Backed Securitisation or RMBS, cumulatively) was slightly lower by about 6%, the drop in overall volume was mainly owing to single corporate loan securitisations [also known as Single Loan Collateralised Loan Obligations (CLOs) or Loan Sell-offs (LSOs)] falling out of favour. LSOs – the largest product class in FY2009, dwindled down to a trickle in FY2011, the reduction being mainly a fallout of draft regulatory guidelines.

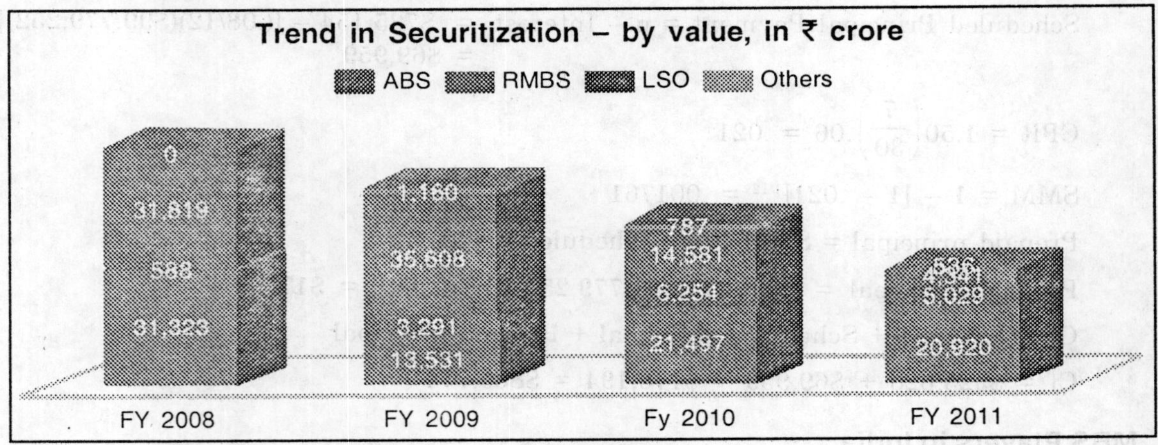

Figure 10.16

Source: ICRA's estimates (ICRA RATING FEATURE, April 2011)

As can be seen from Table 10.3, notwithstanding the decline in both the ABS and RMBS product, the overall share of retail loan securitisation increased during FY2011. The average deal size was lower in FY2011, mainly due to the greater share of the microfinance loan pools.

Table 10.3: Trend in SF Issuances – by Value, in ₹ crore

	FY2008		FY2009		FY2010		FY2011	
	Amount	**Share**	**Amount**	**Share**	**Amount**	**Share**	**Amount**	**Share**
ABS	31,323	49%	13,581	25%	21,497	50%	20,920	68%
MBS	588	1%	3,291	6%	6,254	14%	5,029	16%
Total Retail Securitization	31,911	50%	16,872	31%	27,751	64%	25,948	84%
LSO	31,819	50%	35,608	66%	14,581	34%	4,341	14%
Others	—	—	1,160	2%	787	2%	536	2%
Overall total	63,730	100%	53,640	100%	43,118	100%	30,825	100%
Growth	73%		-16%		-20%		-29%	

Source: ICRA's estimates (ICRA RATING FEATURE, April 2011)

The number of RMBS issuances remained flat at 14 in FY2011. However, the issuance volume declined by 20% in FY2011 when compared to the previous fiscal with the average deal size reducing from ₹ 447 crore in FY2010 to ₹ 359 crore in FY2011. RMBS segment continued to be highly concentrated among few Originators; HDFC Limited alone contributed to 70% of all issuances (10 of the 14 RMBS transactions).

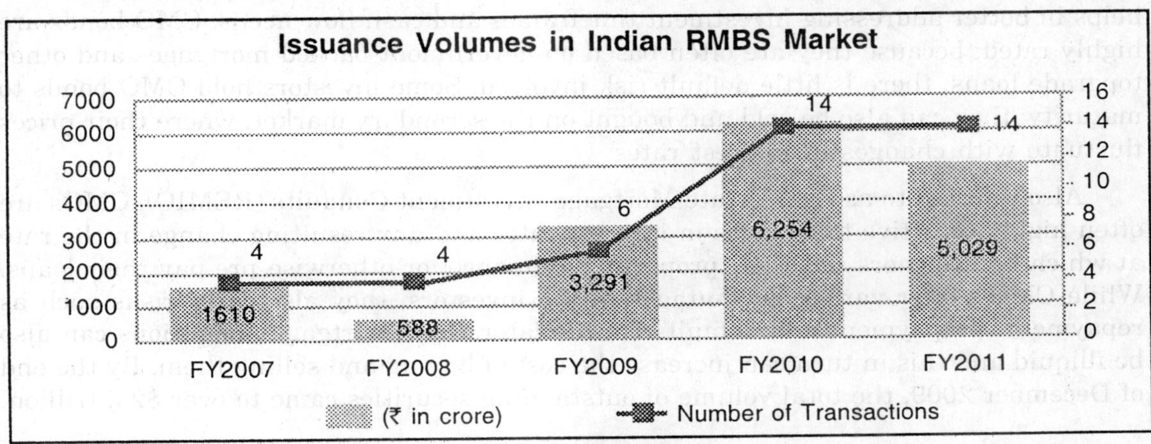

Figure 10.17

Source: ICRA's estimates (ICRA RATING FEATURE, April 2011)

The traditional obstacles to RMBS in India, viz., long tenure of RMBS paper, the lack of secondary market liquidity, high stamp duty on transfer of security, tenure uncertainty, interest rate risk and prepayment risk, continued to hinder the growth of this segment. Except for one, all the transactions in FY2011 involved direct bilateral assignment of residential mortgage loans.

Collateralized Mortgage Obligations (CMOs)

Collateralized mortgage obligations (CMOs) is a type of financial debt instrument that represents claims on specific cash flows from large pools of home mortgages. The streams of principal and interest payments on the mortgages are distributed to the different classes of CMO interests, known as tranches. Each tranche receives regular interest payments, but the principal payments received are made to the first tranche alone, until it is completely retired. Once the first tranche is retired, principal payments are applied to the second tranche until it is fully retired, and the process continues until the last tranche is retired. Each tranche may have different principal balances, coupon rates, prepayment risks, and maturity dates (ranging from a few months to twenty years). Investors in CMOs include banks, insurance companies, mutual funds, hedge funds, pension funds, government agencies, etc.

Like other mortgage backed securities — Ginnie Maes, Freddie Macs, and the like — CMOs are based on the performance of home mortgage loans that are sold by their lenders to an intermediary company. This company packages the loans as certificates that investors can buy. The interest and principal payments on the mortgages go from the home buyer through the intermediary and then to the investor – which is why they are called pass-through securities.

First developed in 1983 by the investment banks of First Boston and Salmon Brothers, this type of security helps in compartmentalization of prepayment risk and helps in better addressing investment timeframes and cash flow needs. CMO bonds are highly rated; because they are often based on government-backed mortgages and other topgrade loans, there is little default risk involved. Some investors hold CMO bonds to maturity; they can also be sold and bought on the secondary market, where their prices fluctuate with changes in interest rates.

Also referred to as Real Estate Mortgage Investment Conduits (REMIC), CMOs are often highly sensitive to changes in interest rates and any resulting change in the rate at which homeowners sell their properties, refinance, or otherwise pre-pay their loans. While CMO's offer various advantages to the investors, they also carry risks such as repayment, prepayment and default risk. Collateralized mortgage obligations can also be illiquid and this in turn can increase the cost of buying and selling them. By the end of December 2009, the total volume of outstanding securities came to over $2.5 trillion.

Collateralized Fund Obligations (CFOs)

A collateralized fund obligation is a form of securitization involving private equity fund or hedge fund assets, similar to collateralized debt obligations. CFOs are a structured form of financing for diversified private equity portfolios, layering several tranches of debt ahead of the equityholders.

The data made available to the rating agencies for analysing the underlying private equity assets of CFOs are typically less comprehensive than the data for analysing the underlying assets of other types of structured finance securitizations, including corporate bonds and mortgage backed securities.

Since the advent of CFOs, there have been only a handful of publicly announced private equity securitization transactions:

- In 2006 Temasek Holdings completed $810 million securitization of a portfolio of 46 private equity funds
- SVG capital has executed three CFO securitizations as part of its "Diamond" programme, SVG Diamond (2004), SVG Diamond II (2006) and SVG Diamond III (2007)
- Mizuho IM has launched its first CFO called Vintage I in 2007, a EUR 500 million fund investing in global buyout funds
- Tenzing (2004): Securitization of private equity fund assets by Invesco
- Pine Street (2003): Securitization of private equity fund assets by AIG
- Silver Leaf (2003): Securitization of private equity fund assets by Deutsche Bank

Indian Structured Finance Evolution

The first securitisation transaction in India was completed in 1991. The market has subsequently matured tremendously, with particular growth in the past three years, and there is now an established investor community and regular issuers. Structured finance has become a solid source of funding via the capital markets in India. Although the market remains predominantly domestic, with ratings assigned within the national scale, efforts to access the international capital markets are being explored by larger originators. Issuance volume by number of transactions is significant in India, with dozens of deals coming to market each year across all asset classes. Yet significant growth potential within this market remains, with public sector banks still not having entered the securitization arena. Indian issuers have also still to explore foreign debt capital markets and a wide range of structures and asset classes.

Securitization is a relatively new concept in India but is gaining ground quite rapidly. One of the earliest structured financing deals in India was the India Infrastructure Developer issue on BOLT structure to institutional investors. ICICI and DOT did one of the first deals for securitizing receivables. TELCO did a hire-purchase deal, where the future receivables from truck sales, along with the ownership of assets, were assigned to investors directly without an SPV. CRISIL rated the first securitization programme in India in 1991 when Citibank securitized a pool from its auto loan portfolio and placed the paper with GIC Mutual Fund. While some of the securitization transactions which took place earlier involved sale of hire purchase or loan receivables of NBFCs arising out of auto-finance activity, many manufacturing and service companies are now increasingly looking towards securitizing their deferred receivables and future flows also.

Main Characteristics of the Indian Securitisation Market

India is a significant securitisation market in Asia by number of transactions arranged each year, yet securitisation it is still largely confined to domestic issuances. The market displays a set of unique features that distinguish it from other jurisdictions. Some of the most prominent characteristics are outlined below:

- Senior notes are generally enhanced through a cash reserve or guarantee provided by a highly rated institution, usually rated 'AAA (ind)'/'AA (ind)'
- National ratings in India denote timely payment of interest as well as principal. This is probably the main difference to most other jurisdictions, where generally only timely payment of interest applies.
- The investor base is limited, comprising mutual funds, insurance companies and a few private sector banks
- Most investments in securitised paper are made on a "hold to maturity" basis

- Pass-through certificates ("PTCs") are still not classified as securities and hence are not tradable on the stock exchange
- No transaction has defaulted to date

The secondary market for securitised paper is virtually non-existent with little trading and all issuance being privately placed. Most common asset classes include:

- Asset-backed securities (ABS) such as auto loans, two-wheeler loans, commercial vehicle loans, construction equipment loans and personal loans
- Residential mortgage backed securities (RMBS)
- Credit products (single loan sell-downs and collateralised debt obligations (CDOs)/collateralised loan obligations (CLOs))

The Special-Purpose Vehicle

The most common form of special purpose vehicle (SPV) used in securitisations is the trust. A trust is formed (or declared on a specific set of assets) with a third party appointed as trustee. The formation and working of the trust is governed by a trust deed and generally has a clause allowing resignation/replacement of the trustee. The trust then buys the assets from the originator and holds the assets on behalf of the investors. Each investor has a beneficial interest in the trust assets, including all the receivables that are generated from the assets.

Current State of Structured Finance in India

In FY2009, the market for SF transactions grew by 121% y-o-y in value terms. The number of transactions increased only by 41%, pointing to a significant rise in average deal size. Within the SF domain, the ABS market showed maximum growth. This was largely due to strong increase in retail lending by banks and NBFCs. The SF scenario is largely based on ABS, accounting for 72% of the SF market in 2009, covering a variety of asset classes like cars, commercial vehicles, construction equipment, two-wheelers and personal loans.

Table 10.4: Trends in Structured Finance Volumes (₹ in Billion)

Type	2001-02	2002-03	2003-04	2004-05	2005-06	2006-07	2007-08	2008-09	2009-10
ABS	12.9	36.4	80.9	222.9	178.5	234.2	313.2	135.8	209.7
MBS	0.8	14.8	29.6	33.4	50.1	16.1	5.9	32.9	62.5
CDO/LSO/SLSD	19.1	24.3	28.3	25.8	21	119	318.2	364.4	145.8
Ohers	4	2.3	0.5	26	0		13	11.6	7.9
Total	36.8	77.8	139.3	308.1	249.6	369.3	650.3	544.7	425.9

Source: Various rating agencies like ICRA, CRISIL, etc.

ABS

ABS is the dominant type of instrument in the Indian SF market. The growth of ABS issuances in recent years has been due to a continued increase in disbursements by key retail asset financiers, investors' familiarity with the underlying asset class, relatively shorter average tenure of issuances and stability in the performance of a growing number of past pools.

FY2011 saw relatively newer asset classes such as loans for financing used cars, three-wheelers and two-wheelers which were securitized in a significant way. The average ABS deal size almost doubled y-o-y to ₹ 2.9 billion in FY2011, mainly due to large pools securitized by leading vehicle financiers like ICICI Bank and HDFC Bank. There is a growing preference for floating-rate yields, given the volatile interest rate conditions. Time-tranching is increasingly becoming the norm: during FY2011, 64% of ABS issuances involved multiple tranches with different tenures.

MBS

The largest ever MBS transaction in India, a ₹ 12 billion mortgage backed pool of ICICI Bank happened in FY2011. MBS has the potential for maximum growth, given the significant expansion in the underlying housing finance business underway. However, the long tenure of MBS papers and the lack of secondary market liquidity still deter investors.

CDO

Investment decisions influenced by the rating of the underlying corporate exposures in a CDO pool (and not purely the rating of the instrument) have impeded the growth of CDO in India. Corporate loan securitization has been far lower than that in retail securitization.

The Rational of Structured Finance to Subprime Crisis

Prior to the first decade of the 21st century, banks made an investigation into the applicant's history, i.e., income, debt, credit rating when considering lending money for a mortgage. But this was changed after the mortgage backed security (MBS) introduced. The no-document loan was created, a type of loan for which the lender didn't ask for any information and the borrower didn't offer it. The bank simply issued the loan and promptly sold it to others who ultimately took the risk if payments stopped. And since MBSs created early on were based on mortgages granted to the more dependable prime borrowers, the securities performed well. They performed so well that investors clamoured for more. In response, lenders loosened their restrictions for mortgage applicants and borrowed heavily to create cash flow for loans in order to create more mortgages. Without mortgages, after all, there are no mortgage backed securities. After MBSs hit the financial markets, they were reshaped into a wide variety of financial instruments with different amounts of risk. If interest rates rise, the return is good. If rates fall then the security loses value.

To ensure a continuous supply of credit to homebuyers, government sponsored agencies such as Fannie Mae, Freddie Mac, and Ginnie Mae were chartered to purchase mortgages originated by local banks, provided they satisfy certain size and credit quality requirements. Mortgages conforming to these requirements are repackaged by these agencies into mortgage-backed securities, and resold in capital markets with the implicit guarantee of the US government. In contrast, mortgages that do not conform to size restrictions or borrower credit quality standards are not eligible for purchase by the government-sponsored enterprises and are either held by their issuers or sold directly in secondary markets. In recent years, issuance of so-called "non-conforming" mortgages has increased significantly. For example, origination of subprime mortgages – mortgages given to those below the credit standards for the government-sponsored enterprises – grew from $96.8 billion in 1996 to approximately $600 billion in 2006, accounting for 22% of all mortgages issued that year (US Securities and Exchange Commission, 2008). During the same period, the average credit quality of subprime borrowers decreased along a number of measures, as evidenced by rising ratios of mortgage values relative to house prices, an increased incidence of second lien loans, and issuance of mortgages with low or no documentation (Ashcraft and Schuermann, 2008).

Subprime mortgage backed securities, comprised entirely from pools of loans made to subprime borrowers, were riskier, but they also offered higher dividends. Subprime borrowers are saddled with higher interest rates to offset the increased risk they pose. When borrowers stopped making payments on their mortgages, MBSs began to perform poorly.

When house prices declined, the stage was set for a significant increase in default rates as many of these borrowers found themselves holding mortgages in excess of the market value of their homes. Because subprime mortgages were ineligible for securitization by government sponsored agencies, they found their way into capital markets by way of "private label" mortgage backed securities, originated by Wall Street Banks among others (Federal Deposit Insurance Corporation, 2006). These securities carried the dual risk of high rates of default due to the low credit quality of the borrowers; and high levels of default correlation as a result of pooling mortgages from similar geographic areas and vintages. In turn, many subprime mortgage backed bonds were themselves re-securitized into what are called collateralized mortgage obligations, effectively creating a CDO. According to Moody's, the share of collateralized debt obligations that had other "structured" assets as their collateral expanded from 2.6% in 1998 to 55% in 2006 as a fraction of the total notional value of all securitizations. In 2006 alone, issuance of structured finance collateralized debt obligations reached $350 billion in notional value (Hu, 2007).

The average collateralized debt obligation (CDO) lost about half of its value between 2006 and 2008. CDOs were comprised of subprime mortgages; they became worthless after the nationwide increase in loan defaults began. Mortgage backed security brought down the Economy in the US.

Rise and Fall of Structured Finance Market

The dramatic rise and fall of structured finance products has been remarkable. In under a decade, issuance of these products within the US economy grew more than ten-fold. In the first three quarters of 2005, $25-$40 billion of structured finance products were issued in each quarter, according to data from the Securities Industry and Financial Markets Association. In the last quarter of 2006 and the first two quarters of 2007, issuance of structured finance products peaked at about $100 billion in each quarter. But by the first two quarters of 2008, these quantities had dropped to less than $5 billion per quarter. It is easy to see how the events of 2007 and 2008 compelled investors to reassess the risks they were bearing in structured products. Less obvious is how structured finance achieved such amazing growth in such a short period of time.

The rapid growth of the market for structured products coincided with fairly strong economic growth and few defaults, which gave market participants little reason to question the robustness of these products. In fact, all parties believed they were getting a good deal. Many of the structured finance securities with AAA ratings offered yields that were attractive relative to other, rating-matched alternatives, such as corporate bonds. The "rated" nature of these securities, along with their yield advantage, engendered significant interest from investors. However, these seemingly attractive yields were in fact too low given the true underlying risks:

- First, the securities' credit ratings provided a downward-biased view of their actual default risks, since they were based on the credit rating agencies' naive extrapolation of the favourable economic conditions.
- Second, the yields failed to account for the extreme exposure of structured products to declines in aggregate economic conditions.

The spuriously low yields on senior claims, in turn, allowed the holders of remaining claims to be overcompensated, incentivizing market participants to hold the "toxic" junior tranches. As a result of this mispricing, demand for structured claims of all seniorities grew explosively. The banks were eager to play along, collecting handsome fees for origination and structuring. Ultimately, the growing demand for the underlying collateral assets lead to an unprecedented reduction in the borrowing costs for homeowners and corporations alike, fuelling the real estate bubble. It seems that few investors were worried that the underlying assets were overvalued, and those who were had incentives to disregard this possibility. This changed rapidly when subprime mortgage defaults started increasing. The bulk of the blame for the rise and fall of structured finance lies on the credit rating agencies, since it was the agencies that evaluated and deemed assets created by collateralized debt obligations as "safe".

Summary

Structured products can bring many of the benefits of derivatives to investors who otherwise are not having access to them. As a complement to more traditional investment vehicles, structured products have a useful role to play in modern portfolio management. Securitization will grow in future for two significant reasons: Securitised paper is rated more creditworthy than the FI itself and strict capital requirements are imposed on the FIs. Moreover, the opening of the insurance sector for privatization can create demand for securitized paper. Most of the problems in the Structure Finance arena come from lack of compliance with legal/regulatory frameworks. There is a lack of historical data and an underdeveloped securitized assets market and different laws apply to different classes of assets in securitization. Hence necessary regulatory measures are required to be taken by the Indian financial community in a phased manner in order to make the securitization successful in the Indian financial system.

Review Questions

1. What is structure finance? Why it is important today?
2. What are the collateralized debts obligations? What are its classifications?
3. What are the Mortgaged-backed securities? Explain the different of types of MBS?
4. Write short notes on Cash CDOs and Synthetic CDOs
5. **Quiz:**
   (a) ____, ____, and ____ are examples of structured financial instruments.
   (b) Structured products are useful as a complement to other products such as ____, ____, ____ and ____.
   (c) One common risk associated with structured products is lack of ____ due to the highly customized nature of the investment.
   (d) ____ is a security backed by a diversified pool of one or more kinds of debt obligations
   (e) Collateralized debt obligations are similar to a collateralized mortgage obligation (CMO). ***(T/F)***
   (f) CBOs backed primarily by leveraged fixed income securities. ***(T/F)***
   (g) ABS is not collateralized by student loans. ***(T/F)***
   (h) Synthetic CDO sells debt and equity securities and uses the proceeds thereof to acquire collateral. ***(T/F)***
   (i) Extension risk is the risk that homeowners will pay-off more than their required monthly mortgage payments. ***(T/F)***

❖ ❖ ❖

CHAPTER 11 Loan Syndication

Introduction

Structured finance has become a key sector in the financial industry since the mid-1980s.

Often large amount of loans are required by corporate that cannot be raised from a single lender. In these cases syndicated loans are used. A syndicated facility is a lending facility defined by a single loan agreement in which several or many banks participate. Syndicated loans are essential when a borrower wants to raise a relatively large amount of money quickly and conveniently and does not want to deal with a large number of lenders and also the amount exceeds the exposure limits or appetite of any one lender. A syndicated loan is a corporate loan made by a group (or syndicate) of banks and other institutional investors. A syndicated loan is publically traded. It may be a line of credit and be "undrawn" or it may be drawn and be used by a firm. The aim of syndication is risk reduction. Syndication exposes firms to a far wider audience and allows them to have a more diversified base of lenders. Loan syndication market is major source of finance of mid-sized and large firms.The loan syndication market is huge.

Syndicated loans are always rated investment grade. However, leveraged syndicated loans are rated speculative grade. By the late 1990s syndicated loans had become a rapidly growing emerging market, and an increasingly important financing tool. Today, the syndicated loan market represents more than $2 trillion of loan commitments in the United States alone, and nearly all large, unsecuritized loans are syndicated.

What is Loan Syndication?

Loan syndication means process of involving several different lenders in providing various portion of loan. A syndicated loan is structured, arranged, administered by one or several commercial banks or investment banks and provided by a group of lenders. So syndication is an arrangement where a group of banks participate for a single loan. In simple terms, syndication is the process whereby a lending institution sells partial interests in a borrower's loan to other lending institutions. The lender chosen by the borrower to originate and arrange the syndicated loan is known as the "arranger", and is typically also act as "administrative agent", coordinating the administrative aspects of the loan. Once syndicated, the lenders are referred to as the "bank group". A loan interest is purchased either directly from the agent or from another member of the bank group. Purchasing interests in syndicated loans has become an appealing option since many lending institutions in the current market aggressively seeking to book loan assets. Further accumulating loan assets in this manner allow a firm to diversify its loan portfolio. Moreover, acquiring an interest in a syndicated loan is an attractive way for lending institutions to generate ancillary business from the borrower, such as cash management, foreign exchange, and other non-credit business. To become directly involved with the borrower, loan purchaser must become a party to the credit agreement. This can be achieved in one of two ways: by executing either the credit agreement at closing, or an assignment agreement. It is called transfer of a share in the loan from the seller to the loan purchaser. The purchaser then becomes a "lender", "co-lender", or "assignee" to the loan. Purchasing syndicated loan assets involves many legal and technical issues. The following points are the more common issues which arise in connection with the purchase of an interest in a syndicated loan.

Costs: In a syndicated transaction, however, the borrower covers only the costs of the agent.

Fees and Pricing: The arranger's compensation for syndicating the loan is generally a syndication fee, which is set forth in a separate agreement between borrower and arranger. These fees generally are not disclosed to loan purchasers to avoid disagreement among bank group lenders, and as a matter of market competition.

Generally, when a group of banks get together, they select a lead bank which handles all the dealings and negotiating the interest rates with the company. Then deal is signed between the company and the banks. The banks in the syndicate share the risk of large, inseparable investment projects. Syndicate arises because additional syndicate members provide informative opinions of investment projects or additional expertise after the funding has been extended. Loan syndication is basically done to share the total loss or liability.

Deal Partners

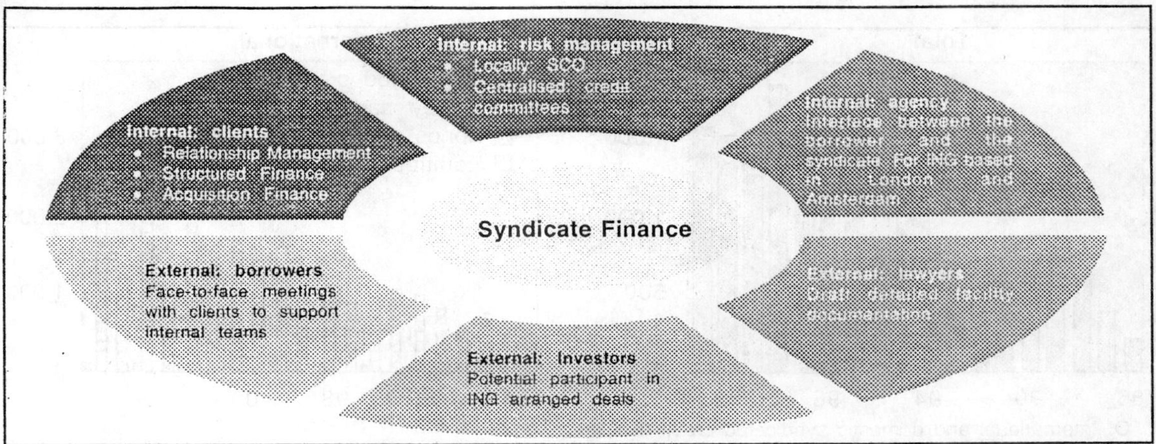

Figure 11.1: Deal Partners

History

The evolution of syndicated lending can be divided into three phases:

Credit syndications first developed in the 1970s as a sovereign business

↓

Sovereign default by Mexico in 1982 caused most of the developing countries' debt in the form of syndicated loans

↓

Payment difficulties experienced by emerging market borrowers in the 1980s resulted in the restructuring Mexican debt into Brady bonds in 1989

First phase of expansion began in the 1970s. Between 1971 and 1982; medium-term syndicated loans were widely used to channel foreign capital to the developing countries. Syndicated lending to emerging market borrowers grew from small amounts in the early 1970s to $46 billion in 1982. Lending came to an abrupt halt in August 1982, after Mexico suspended interest payments on its sovereign debt, soon followed by other countries including Brazil, Argentina. The Brady plan provided a new impetus by providing more sophisticated risk pricing to syndicate lending. Partly, lenders saw syndicated loans as a loss-leader for selling more lucrative investment banking and other services. Syndicated lending has grown strongly from the beginning of the 1990s to date. Signings of new loans – including domestic facilities – totalled $1.6 trillion in 2003, more than three times the 1993 amount. Syndicated credits have thus become a very significant source of financing. The international market accounts for about a third of all international financing, including bond, commercial paper and equity issues.

Syndicated lending since the 1980s (Gross Findings, in billions of US$)

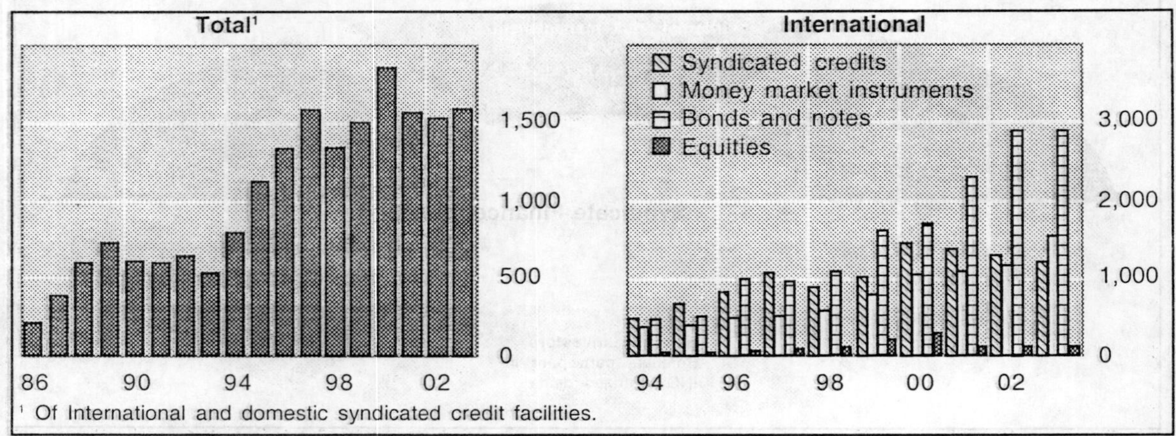

[1] Of International and domestic syndicated credit facilities.

Syndicated lending since the 1980s (Gross Signings, in billions of US$)

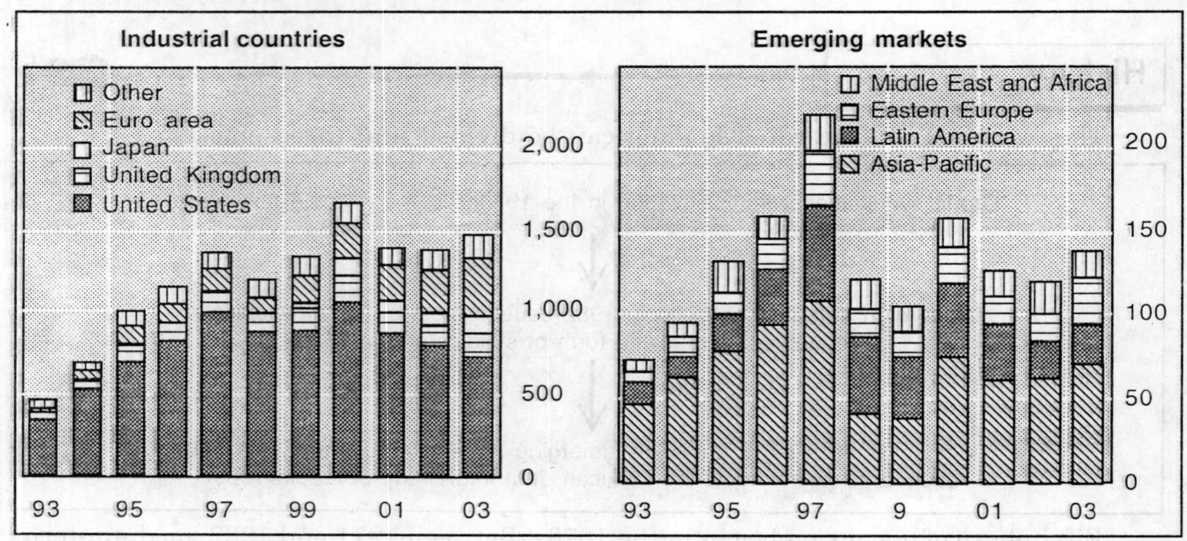

Figure 11.2

**Sources:* DealogicLoanware; Euromoney; BIS.

Types of Syndication Loan

Underwritten Deal

Sometimes the investment bank helps the other investment banks to sell the securities, forming an underwriting syndicate. The investment bank is called the originating house also known as – syndicate manager, managing underwriter, etc., which selects the members of the syndicate and determines how many shares each will get, and manages the overall process. The underwriting manager determines, along with the issuer, the offering price and the time of the offering, and controls all advertising for the new issue. Thus in an underwritten deal, the arranger guarantees the entire amount and then syndicates the loan. In this type of loan if the arranger is not able to fully subscribe to the loan they are forced to absorb the differences. This difference may then be sold to the investors. This is easy if the market rate improves otherwise the arranger has to sell at a discount and maybe take on a loss in a written deal also.

There are two variations of the best-efforts underwriting: all-or-none or mini-max. An all-or-none underwriting requires that the entire issue be sold within a specified time, or else the programme is terminated. A mini-max (a.k.a. part-or-none) underwriting is similar, except that only a specified minimum must be sold.

Thus, in best-efforts syndication the arranger group commits to underwrite less than the entire amount of the loan, leaving the credit to the vicissitudes of the market. If the loan is undersubscribed, the credit may not close-or may need major surgery to clear the market. Traditionally, best-efforts syndications were used for risky borrowers or for complex transactions. Since the late 1990s, however, the rapid acceptance of market-flex language has made best-efforts loans the rule even for investment-grade transactions.

Best Efforts Syndication

Most agreements for the sale of new securities are an underwriting, but sometimes investment bank or the arrangers agrees to a best efforts approach because the company is perceived as a risky investment for a new issue. The investment bank is doing its best to sell all of the new securities, but it does not guarantee it. The company bears the risk that the investment bank may fail to sell all of the new issue, thereby lessening the amount of money that the company receives. There are two variations of the best-efforts underwriting: all-or-none or mini-max. An all-or-none underwriting requires that the entire issue be sold within a specified time, or else the programme is terminated. A mini-max (a.k.a. part-or-none) underwriting is similar, except that only a specified minimum must be sold. Thus, in best-efforts syndication, arranger group commits to a sum less than the entire amount required and the rest are to be arranged at the market. If the loan is undersubscribed then the credit may not close. This was used for risky investments and complex transactions.

Club Deal

A club deal is a smaller loan usually $25-100 million, but as high as $150 million that is premarketed to a group of relationship lender. Each lender gets a full cut of the fees.

Types of Facility Commonly Syndicate

Following is a description about the types of facilities commonly syndicated:

Term Loan Facility

Under a term loan facility, the lenders provide a specified capital sum over a set period of time, known as the "term". Typically, the borrower is allowed a short period after executing the loan. Repayment may be in instalments or there may be one payment at the end of the facility. Once a term loan has been repaid by the borrower, it cannot be redrawn.

Revolving Loan Facility

A revolving loan facility is a particularly flexible financing tool as it may be drawn by a borrower by way of straightforward loans, but it is also possible to incorporate different types of financial accommodation within it. A revolving loan facility provides a borrower with a maximum aggregate amount of capital, available over a specified period of time. However, unlike a term loan, the revolving loan facility allows the borrower to draw down, repay and redraw loans advanced to it of the available capital during the term of the facility. Each loan is borrowed for a set period of time, usually one, and three or six months, after which it is to be technically repayable. Repayment of a revolving loan is achieved either by scheduled reductions in the total amount of the facility over time, or by all outstanding loans being repaid on the date of termination. A revolving loan made to refinance another revolving loan which matures on the same date as the drawing of the second revolving loan is known as a "rollover loan", if made in the same currency and drawn by the same borrower as the first revolving loan. The conditions to be satisfied for drawing a rollover loan are typically less onerous than for other loans.

General

Syndicated loan agreements may contain only a term or revolving facility or they can contain a combination of both or several of each type. There can be one borrower or a group of borrowers with provision allowing for the accession of new borrowers under certain circumstances from time-to-time. The facility may include a guarantor or guarantors and again provisions may be incorporated allowing for additional guarantors to accede to the agreement.

Who are Parties of the Syndication?

Borrower: A borrower is the party who wants to avail funds through the process of syndication. The syndication process is initiated by the borrower, who appoints a lender to act as an arranger.

Arranger: An arranger is a lender who has been appointed as the arranger by the borrower through a letter of grant. The arranger is also referred to as Mandated Lead Arranger. A borrower may appoint one or several arrangers. The arranger is responsible for advising the borrower as to the type of facilities it requires and then negotiating the broad terms of those facilities. It is generally found that the borrower has an established relationship with the arranger.

Lead Bank: Once the prospective borrower awarded the mandate, the lead bank is responsible for placing the syndicated loan with the other banks and ensures that the syndication is fully subscribed. They are entitled to the arrangement fee and undergo a reputation risk during this process.

Co-arranger syndication is often done in stages, with an initial group of lenders agreeing to provide a share of the facility or the total funds. This group of lenders is referred to as co-arranger. The co-arrangers then find more lenders to participate in the facility, who agree to take a share of the co-arrangers' commitment.

Underwriting Bank: This bank commits to supply the funds to the borrower – if necessary from its own resources even though the loan is not fully subscribed. In some instances, if syndications are not underwritten then the lead bank or another bank may play this role. The risk is that the loan may not be fully subscribed.

Participating Bank: This bank normally participates in the syndication by lending a portion of the total amount required so it is entitled to receive the interest and the participation fee only. But however it faces risks such as: Borrower credit risk, Passive approval and complacency.

Agent: To facilitate the process of administering the loan on a daily basis, one bank from the syndicate is appointed as agent. This agent bank acts on behalf of all the banks participating and takes care of all the administrative arrangements over the term of loan, e.g., disbursements, repayments, compliance. This bank is maintaining contact with the borrower and representing the views of the syndicate. It is also monitoring the compliance of the borrower with certain terms of the facility. It is the agent to whom the borrower is usually required to give notices. The borrower makes all payments of interest and repayments of principal and any other payments required under the loan agreement to the agent. The agent passes this money back to the banks to which they are due. Similarly, the banks advance funds to the borrower through the agent.

Why Use Syndicated Loans?

Table 11.1: Syndicated Loans vs. Bonds

	Syndicated loan	Bond
Relationship	It facilitates the borrowers to develop banking relationships and enhance their power in the marketplace	It established limited relationship with the borrower
Rating	It does not require any rating	Rating is essential by investors
Process	It believes in shorter process and targeting a specific pool of investors for exploiting existing relationship with banks	It involves regulatory approval and preparation of a prospectus hence a lengthy process.
Pricing	Pricing was determined during process time on the basis of market flex agreed by the client. But however greater flexibility in pricing offered if margin is based on a rating grid	Pricing is determined just prior to launch following 'price talk' in a book-building process
Tenor	Corporate loans is up to five years and longer for structured transactions	Loan is longer, maturity up to 30 years

Covenants	Maintenance-based	Lenient covenants. Financial covenants are incurrence-based (i.e., only tested upon the occurrence of certain events such as further debt-raising), rather than maintenance-based.
Amortisation	Either amortising through scheduled quarterly payments or maturity	It only shot
Prepayable	Yes, without penalty	Non-callable for a certain period following issuance. Thereafter various call premiums apply
Investors	Primarily commercial banks are investors though there is a mounting pool of fund investors interested in leveraged transactions	Investors are usually fund managers and institutional investors

Issues Involved

Changing Terms: The syndication process begins with the arranger sending prospective loan purchasers a proposed term sheet for the loan. Often the borrower negotiates changes in loan terms after the proposed term sheet has been delivered to prospective purchasers, creating differences between the proposed term sheet and the loan documentation. Loan purchasers should review loan documents carefully for such discrepancies, making certain that terms discussed in its internal credit-approval documents correspond with those in the final loan documents.

Standard of Care: The agent generally owes no fiduciary duty to its syndicate members, except where express language creating such a duty exists. This language is rare in practice, however. Typically the agent will expressly disclaim any fiduciary duty through an exculpation clause, which states that the agent shall be responsible to its syndicate members only for its own "gross negligence or wilful misconduct". This language may seem onerous, but actually appears in nearly all syndicated credit agreements in the United States.

Liquidity: A typical credit agreement will allow a lender to sell all or part of its share in the loan as an assignment or participation. Such sales are often conditioned upon the written consent of the agent and borrower, as well as eligibility requirements to be met by the purchaser. These limitations on transferability are typically stricter for loans with ongoing funding requirements such as lines of credit or delayed-draw term loans.

The ability to quickly sell a loan asset to a wide array of buyers without taking a substantial loss can provide the purchaser with a convenient exit to a credit; therefore, language regarding saleability is an important issue to consider before committing to a syndicated loan.

Consent: The credit agreement will require the consent of a specified percentage of lenders in order to modify the syndicated loan. This percentage is usually referred to as the "required lenders" and is typically 51% or 66%, but may be some other specified percentage.

In certain instances, material modifications may require the unanimous consent of all lenders. This unanimous consent requirement is typically in effect for modifications to items such as the loan's term, interest rate, fees, amortization schedule, collateral, or guaranty provisions.

A purchaser should understand the implications of a given required lenders percentage *vis-à-vis* the make-up of the bank group, and be comfortable with the lenders that will have collective control over the loan. If the purchase will be made by participation, special attention should be paid to the specific voting items for which participants' consent is required.

Conflicts: While the interests of agent and bank group may be aligned at the inception of a transaction, their respective interests may diverge overtime, particularly in the context of a troubled loan. For example, if the agent or its affiliates have additional business relationships with the borrower, they may have other issues to consider when evaluating decisions which affect the syndicated loan.

The possible conflicts are almost endless, and may include items relating to declaring defaults, exercising remedies, hedging agreements, and set-offs. Importantly, these conflicts can often be prevented by understanding all of the relationships the agent maintains with the borrower prior to committing to the transaction.

By maintaining awareness of these issues and understanding market standards for structures, practices, and documentation, parties can better negotiate agreements and mitigate potential problems at the outset of a transaction.

Loan Syndication Process

The loan syndication process can be divided into three steps:

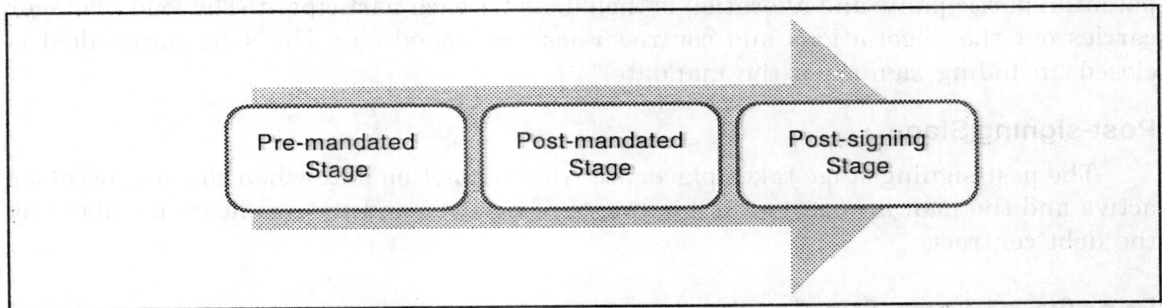

Figure 11.3: Loan Syndication Process

Pre-mandate Phase

During the pre-mandated stage, the prospective borrower liaise invite one bank or competitive bids from a number of banks. The lead bank identifies the needs of the borrower, designs an appropriate loan structure, develops a persuasive credit proposal, and obtains internal approval. The mandate is created. The documentation is created with the help of specialist lawyers. In pre-mandated stage the details of the proposed transactions are discussed and finalized. During the pre-mandated stage, after soliciting competitive offers to arrange and manage the syndication with one or more banks, the borrower chooses one or more arrangers that are mandated to form a syndicate and negotiates a preliminary loan agreement. The syndication can be sole or jointly mandated. Arranger's fees is composed of various fees.

Post-mandate Phase

The post-mandated stage the lead bank can start to sell the loan in the marketplace. It is perhaps the most crucial stage in the transaction cycle of syndication. During this stage the lead bank needs to prepare an information memorandum, term sheet, and legal documentation and approach selected banks and invite participation. The arranger prepares a documentation package for the potential syndicate members called an information memorandum (IM). IM contains the details about the creditworthiness and loan terms about the borrower.

Typically prepared by both the arranger and the borrower and sent out by the arranger to potential syndicate members. The arranger assists the borrower in writing the information memorandum on the basis of information provided by the borrower during the due diligence process. It contains a commercial description of the borrower's business, management and accounts, as well as the details of the proposed loan facilities being given. It is not a public document and all potential lenders that wish to see it usually sign a confidentiality undertaking. The previous experience with the borrower, the industry sector or the geographic area is strong drivers for being chosen by arranger to join the syndicate. The participants can then discuss and suggest and comment on the content of IM, as well as to announce closing fees and establish a timetable for commitments and closing. After this arranger makes formal announcement for the potential participants and allocation is then done for each participant. The lead manager carries out the negotiations and controversies are ironed out. The syndication deal is closed, including signing of the mandate.

Post-signing Stage

The post-signing stage takes place after the completion date when the deal becomes active and the loan is operational, binding the borrower and the syndicate members by the debt contract.

Benefits of Loan Syndication

Benefits to the Borrower: It deals with a single bank. It is quicker and simpler than other ways of raising capital. Raising loans through loan syndication is quicker and simpler than other ways of raising capital. Borrower can alternatively raise capital through other sources like issue of shares, debentures, etc. But these methods involve substantial cost and time. Syndication is a better option in this regard. In case of syndicated loan facility, the borrower has to deal only with the arranger and not each and every bank as opposed to the case when the bank tries to raise the same amount by approaching different banks individually. This saves time and administrative expense of borrower and also makes borrowing more convenient for the borrower. Syndicated loans provide borrowers with a more complete menu of financing options. In effect, the syndication market completes a continuum between traditional private bilateral bank loans and publicly traded bond markets. This has resulted in a more competitive corporate finance market, which has permitted issuers to achieve more market-oriented and cost-effective financing.

Benefits to the Arranger: Good arrangement and other fees can be earned without committing capital: Arranger earns fees because of his services to borrower. This can be done without committing any capital. Enhancement of bank's relationship with the client: Because lead banker deals with client his relationship with client enhances that can bring more business for bank in long-term.

Benefits to the Lead Banks: For lead banks good arrangement and other fees can be earned without committing capital. Syndication enhances the bank's reputation. Also it enhances the bank's relationships with the client.

Benefits to the Participating Banks: Syndication helps to access the lending opportunities with low marketing costs. It provides opportunity to participate in future syndications. In case the borrower runs into difficulties, participating banks have equal treatment. Participating banks do not find themselves at a disadvantage *vis-a-vis* a dominant bank or one with high leverage over the client. Participating banks are usually entitled to transfer their proportion of the loan to a third party without the borrower's consent. It may thus happen that a bank that originally participated in the syndicate sells its share, and a new bank – the transferee – enters the syndicate, without the borrower being aware of these transactions. Quite often, banks that participate in syndicated deals later sell their interest in those loans to other investors. One advantage of syndication loans is that this market allows the borrower to access from a diverse group of financial institutions. In general, borrowers can raise funds more cheaply in the syndicated loan market than by borrowing the same amount of money through a series of bilateral loans. This cost saving increases as the amount required rises.

Disadvantages

Managing multiple bank relationships is not an easy task. Each bank needs to understand the dynamics of conducting business and financial activities. In this transaction both parties must be at comfort level for smooth function. But it requires time and effort. Negotiating a document with four to five banks separately is a time-consuming, inefficient task. Moreover, multiple lines require an inter-creditor agreement among the banks, which takes further time to negotiate. The key figures are the number of arrangers and the concentration of the shares of the loan retained by the loan retained by the arrangers. The size of the syndicate refers to the number of arrangers in the syndicate. Both these factors have a negative impact on the syndication process duration. Greater proximity between top lenders and the borrowers may aggravate adverse selection problems, if the informational gain of the top lender is not shared with other lenders. Some of the other factors are loan size, fee, spread, maturity, guarantors, covenants, working capital, project finance, etc.

Apart of it, loan syndication has also several drawbacks as it generates potential agency problems due to informational frictions between the senior and the junior members of the syndicate. Borrower monitoring by multiple creditors may lead to cost inefficiency and free-riding. Hence, creditors usually delegate monitoring to one financial intermediary, the arranger, who acts as the syndication agent. As his monitoring effort is unobservable, the syndicate faces a moral hazard problem. Additionally, the arranger collects private information through due diligence or through a previous lending relationship. If this information cannot be credibly communicated to the participants, an adverse selection problem arises as the arranger may syndicate loans with the less favourable information. Finally, handling borrower's financial distress is more complicated in a syndicate setting because lenders must reach a collective decision. Let take an example: The sample size is determined by the information availability on the endogenous and exogenous variables. The endogenous variables are the syndication process duration, measured in days since the launching. The dependent variable is the duration of a syndication process.

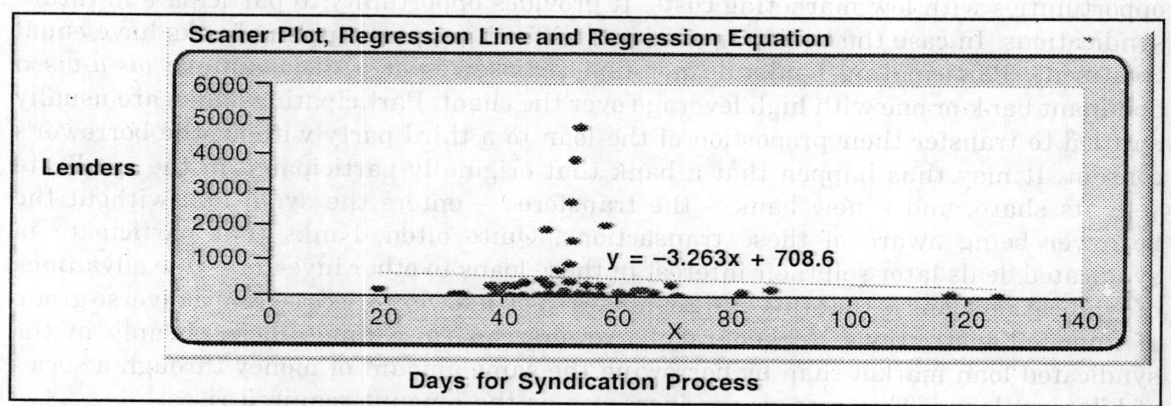

Figure 11.4: Regression Analysis

It is seen from the regression graph in Fig. 11.4 that as the number of lenders increase the time taken for syndication decreases. Except for the few exceptions, whereas the number of lenders increase time increases, the trend is constantly decreasing. Here standard deviation is 37.0186 and mean is around 55.1367 days. Further plot of loan amount and number of days show that as the size of loan increases the time taken also increases.

Structure of Fees in Syndicated Loan

Structure of Fees in a Syndicated Loan		
Fee	**Type**	**Remarks**
Arrangement fee	Front-end	Also called praecipium. Received and retained by the lead arrangers in return for putting the deal together
Legal fee	Front-end	Remuneration of the legal adviser
Underwriting fee	Front-end	Price of the commitment to obtain financing during the first level of syndication
Participation fee	Front-end	Received by the senior participants
Facility fee	Per annum	Payable to banks in return for providing the facility. Whether it is used or not
Commitment fee	Per annum, charged on undrawn part	Paid as long as the facility is not used to compensate the lender for tying up the capital corresponding to the commitment
Utilisation fee	Per annum, charged on drawn part	Boosts the lender's yield; enables. the borrower to announce actually being a lower spread to the market than what is paid. As the utilisation fee does not always need to be publicised
Agency fee	Per annum	Remuneration of the agent bank's services
Conduit Fee	Front-end	Remuneration of the conduit bank
Prepayment fee	One-off if prepayment	Penalty for prepayment

Figure 11.5: Structure of Fees

Market Trends

Syndicated loans are an integral part of capital raising. The syndicated loan market, which has developed itself with general corporate financing, is also covering specialist areas such as project finance, structured trade and commodity finance, export finance, property finance and LBOs. The banking sector is highly concentrated and the average amount of finance being raised has grown constantly. The primary market is very liquid and supplies the secondary market, which grows in importance and is an integral part of the syndicated loan market

Syndication Process and Agency Problems

Loan syndication involves several players, i.e., the arranger, the participants, the borrower and is a complex process involving specific agency costs. The latter are the consequences of informational frictions within the syndicate which can harm efficient and fast decision making. These costs can however be reduced through an adapted organization of syndicate.

Syndicate-specific agency problems are of two types. First, the arranger possesses more information about the borrower either because of the private collected through a previous lending relationship or through due diligence. This private information creates an adverse selection problem as the arranger may be inclined to syndicate loans to bad borrowers. Second, the participant banks may delegate some monitoring tasks to the arranger. This may result in moral hazard problem as the efforts of the lead bank are unobservable for participant banks.

So we can say that the presence of numerous arrangers can indeed reduce the selection problems related to private information. Greater concentration of the portion of the loan retained by the arrangers is more suited to cope with free-riding and moral hazard problems, as well as with hold-up problems in case of the borrower's distress and subsequent reorganization and renegotiation. Further it has been shown that physical distance between borrower and lenders influence the agency costs.

Syndication Loan Transfers

A lender under a syndicated loan may decide to sell its commitment in a facility for one or more of the following reasons:

Realising Capital: If the loan is a long-term facility, a lender may need to sell its share of the commitment to realise capital or take advantage of new lending opportunities;

Risk/Portfolio Management: A lender may consider that its loan portfolio is weighted with too much emphasis on a particular type of borrower or loan or may wish to alter the yield dynamics of its loan portfolio. By selling its commitment in this loan, it may lend elsewhere, thus diversifying its portfolio;

Regulatory Capital Requirements: A bank's ability to lend is subject to both internal and external requirements to retain a certain percentage of its capital as cover for its existing loan obligations. These are known as "Regulatory Capital Requirements"; and

Crystallise a Loss: The lender might decide to sell its commitment if the borrower runs into difficulties – specialists dealing in distressed debts provide a market for such loans. However, before the lender can go ahead and transfer its participation in a syndicated loan, it must consider the implications of the methods of transfer available to it under the Syndicated Loan Agreement.

Forms of Transfer

The most common forms of transfer to enable a lender to sell its loan commitment are:

Novation: Novation is the only way in which a lender can effectively 'transfer' all its rights and obligations under the loan agreement. The process of transfer effectively cancels the existing first lender's obligations and rights under the loan, while the new lender assumes identical new rights and obligations in their place. Therefore the contractual relationship between the transferring lender and the parties to the loan agreement end and the new lender enters into a direct relationship with the borrower, the agent and the other lenders. During this time, the new lender becomes a party to the loan agreement and the loan may be fully drawn, particularly if term loan facility is available. However, particularly in the case of a revolving credit facility, the new lender is assuming obligations to advance monies to the borrower. The borrower has to be a party to the novation process. The documentation required to affect a novation of a participation in a syndicated loan depends on the provisions in the loan agreement. However, most loan agreements have a transfer certificate attached as a schedule that operates by way of novation. The agent, the new lender and the existing lender are the only parties usually required to execute the transfer certificate.

Legal Assignment: Assignment involves the transfer of rights, but not obligations. For a legal assignment, S.136 of the Law of Property Act, 1925 provides that the assignment must be: absolute (i.e., the whole of the debt outstanding to the existing lender); in writing and signed by the existing lender; and notified in writing to the borrower. If any element of this requirement is missing, the assignment is likely to be impartial. In syndicated loan, a legal assignment will transfer all of the existing lender's rights under the loan agreement to the new lender. The obligation of the existing lender cannot be transferred by legal assignment and thus remains with the existing lender. The new lender pays the existing lender any funds due under the loan and the existing lender sends those funds on to the agent, who then passes such funds on to the borrower.

Equitable Assignment: In contrast to a legal assignment, the new lender, as the equitable assignee, must join the existing lender, as assignor, in any action on the debt. The most significant difference between a legal and equitable assignment arises if the borrower is not notified of the assignment. If the borrower is not notified of the assignment, the new lender will be subject to all equities which arise between the existing lender and the borrower, even after the loan has been assigned.

Funded Participation: A funded participation agreement is made between the existing lender and the participant. This creates new contractual rights between the existing lender and the participant. In a funded participation, the participant agrees that its deposit will be serviced (in terms of payment of interest) and repaid only when the borrower services and repays the loan from the existing lender. The participant has effectively taken on the risk of the first loan. The funded participation agreement must ensure that the existing bank is put in funds by the participant in time to meet the borrower's demands for drawdown in order to remove the risk. The existing lender remains liable under the Syndicated Loan Agreement.

Risk Participation: Risk participation is a form of participation which acts like a guarantee. Risk participation is provided by a new lender as an interim measure before it takes full transfer of a loan. No borrower consent is required for either a Funded Participation or a Risk Participation, so this process is confidential. There is no direct contract between the new lender and the borrower but the participant usually obtains rights of subrogation to pursue all remedies of the existing lender against the borrower.

US Syndicated Loan Market

US Syndicated and Leveraged Loan

The overall US syndicated and leveraged loan market issuance and volume for the First Quarter of 2011 is at its highest level since the same period of 2007. The First Quarter of 2007 remains the strongest on record although 2011 volume for the quarter was 87.9% of the volume of 2007. Total volume increased 134.8% to $355.3 billion and issuance increased 57.8% to 584 deals, compared to the First Quarter of 2010.

- The US leveraged loan volume for 2011 is also the strongest first quarter since the First Quarter of 2007. Total volume is up 109.1% to $149.2 billion. Issuance also increased 62.1% to 334 deals, compared to the First Quarter of 2010.
- JP Morgan ranked number one in the rankings for US Syndicated Loan Lead Arranger with 23.0% market share. Bank of America and Credit Suisse followed with 18.1% and 6.4% of the market share, respectively. In the First Quarter of 2011 the top two Lead Arrangers for the syndicated market held 41.2% of the market share.
- Bank of America ranked the highest in the Leveraged Loans Lead Arranger rankings with a market share of 16.4%. JP Morgan followed with 12.8% and Credit Suisse had 12.3% of the market share. The top three arrangers continue to command a large share of the market with 41.5% market share compared to 43.0% in 2010.
- The $20 billion bridge term loan to support AT&T's acquisition of T-Mobile from Deutsche Telekom is the largest syndicated loan for the First Quarter 2011. The loan will back the largest M&A transaction for the Quarter. JP Morgan was the Sole Book Runner on the $6.7 billion refinancing of the term loan originally issued to support Air Product's acquisition of Airgas. The deal was subsequently terminated.
- The largest leveraged deal of the First Quarter 2011 was First Data Corporation's $6.2 billion revolver and term loans. This loan refinanced the original deal signed in September 2007.

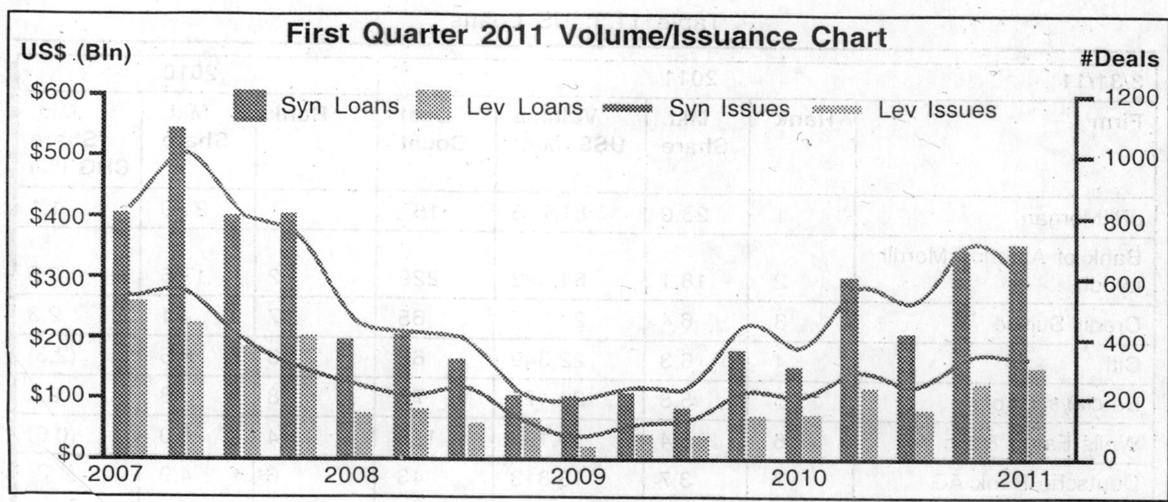

Figure 11.6: First Quarter 2011 Volumes

Table 11.2: US Syndicated and Leveraged Loan

Rankings and Market Share Underwriter	2011	2010	2009	2008	2007
Syndicated Loans					
JP Morgan	1 (23.0%)	1	2	1	1
Bank of America Merrill Lynch	2 (18.1%)	2	1	3	2
Credit Suisse	3 (6.4%)	7	13	7	7
Citi	4 (6.3%)	3	3	2	3
Barclays Capital	5 (5.8%)	8	5	8	17
Leveraged Loans					
Bank of America Merrill Lynch	1 (16.4%)	1	3	1	2
JP Morgan	2 (12.8%)	2	5	2	1
Credit Suisse	3 (12.3%)	4	9	4	7
Barclays Capital	4 (9.6%)	7	6	8	17
Deutsche Bank AG	5 (6.9%)	5	10	3	3

Source: Bloomberg 2011 Q1

Table 11.3: US Loans

3/31/11 Firm	2011 Rank	Mkt. Share	Volume US$ (Mln)	Deal Count	2010 Rank	Mkt. Share	Mkt. Share CHG (%)
JP Morgan	1	23.0	81,735	167	1	21.9	1.1
Bank of America Merrill Lynch	2	18.1	64,392	229	2	17.6	0.5
Credit Suisse	3	6.4	22,647	65	7	4.1	2.3
Citi	4	6.3	22,349	62	3	8.6	(2.3)
Barclays Capital	5	5.8	20,477	75	8	3.8	2.0
Wells Fargo & Co.	6	5.4	19,197	128	4	6.0	(0.6)
Deutsche Bank AG	7	3.7	13,313	43	6	4.9	(1.2)
Mitsubishi UFJ Financial	8	3.6	12,813	26	16	1.1	2.5
Goldman Sachs & Co.	9	3.0	10,540	26	5	5.4	(2.4)
BNP Paribas Group	10	2.8	9,870	27	9	3.0	(0.2)
RBS	11	2.7	9,456	32	11	2.4	0.3
Morgan Stanley	12	2.2	7,856	30	10	2.8	(0.6)
HSBC Bank Plc.	13	1.9	6,581	23			
General Electric Capital Corp.	14	1.6	5,736	44	12	1.8	(0.2)
UBS	15	1.3	4,581	24	13	1.5	(0.2)
SunTrust Robinson Humphrey	16	1.2	4,272	28	14	1.4	(0.2)
US Bancorp	17	1.2	4,188	36	20	0.7	0.5
BMO Capital Markets	18	1.0	3,472	25	18	0.9	0.1
RBC Capital Markets	19	0.7	2,559	18	21	0.6	0.1
PNC Bank	20	0.7	2,439	27	17	0.9	(0.2)
Total		**100%**	**3,55,300**	**584**	**1,51,306**	**100%**	

Source: Bloomberg 2011

Asia Ex-Japan Syndicated Loans: First Quarter 2011

208 Syndicated Loans are completed in the First Quarter of 2011, totalling US$ 70.9 billion. In comparison to the same period in 2010, the total volume increased by 1% from US$ 69.9 billion. Hong Kong Zhuhai Macao BR's CNY 29.4 billion (US$ 4.4 billion equivalent), was the largest Asia ex-Japan deal signed during the quarter. The Hong Kong deal is mandated by Bank of China. Five out of the top 10 issues are concluded in India. Aircel Ltd. raised INR 153 billion (US$ 3.4 billion equivalent) arranged by State

Bank of India. It was the second largest Asia ex-Japan deal during the quarter. Mumbai Metro Transport Pvt. Ltd., signed an INR 126.3 billion (US$ 2.8 billion equivalent) loan sole-led by AXIS Bank and it ranked the fifth. Total issuance for Asia ex-Japan in the first quarter is led by India with a total of 62 deals and proceeds totalling US$ 22.7 billion. Hong Kong came in second with a total of 13 issues which amounted to US$ 12.5 billion. State bank of India ranked first for the First Quarter on the Asia ex-Japan Syndicated Loans Table by arranging 21 deals, totalling US$ 9.4 billion. AXIS Bank Ltd., and Bank of China ranked second and third respectively.

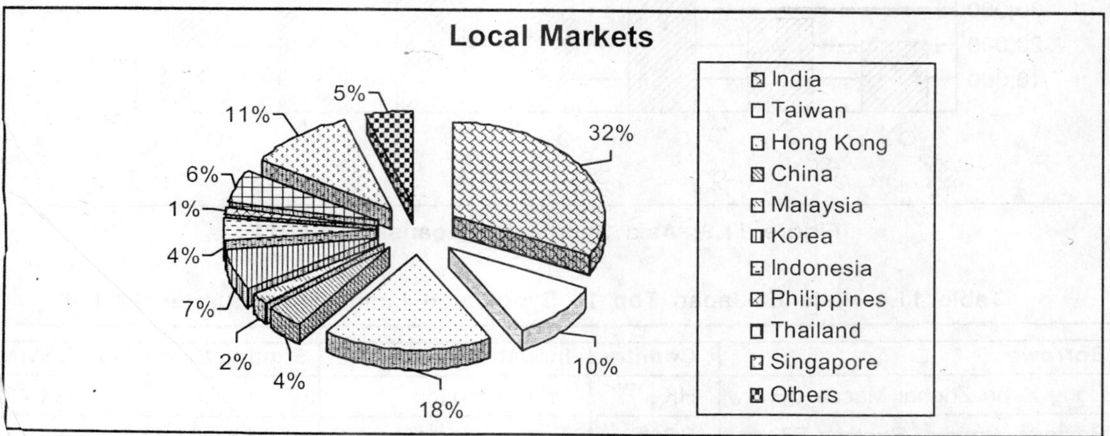

Figure 11.7: Asia Ex-Japan Syndicated Loans First Quarter 2011

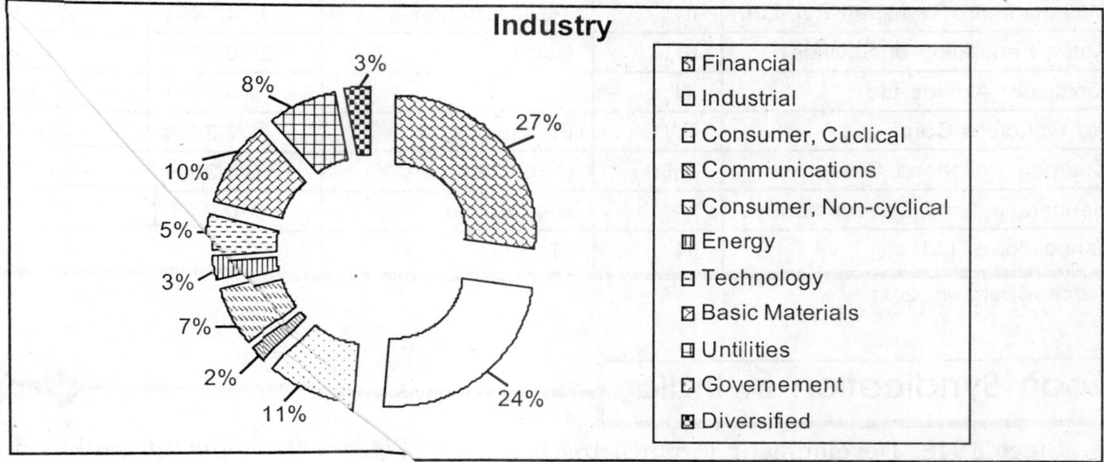

Figure 11.8

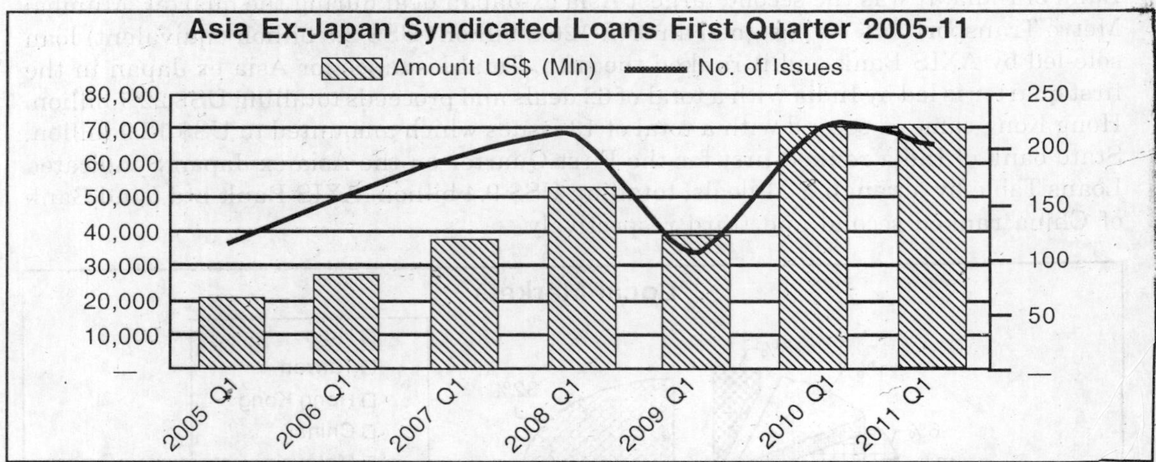

Figure 11.9: Asia Syndicated Loans 2005-2011

Table 11.4: Asia Ex-Japan Top 10 Syndicated Loans First Quarter 2011

Borrower	Country	Industry	Signing Date	Amt. US$(M)
Hong Kong Zhuhai Macao BR	HK	Transportation	1/7/2011	$4,431
Restorts World at Sentosa PT	SG	Entertainment	2/1/2011	$3,147
Hong Kong Intl Terminals	HK	Commercial Services	2/18/2011	$3,000
Mumbai Metro Transport Pvt. Ltd.	IN	Transportation	3/14/2011	$2,803
Korea Federation of Savings	KR	Banks	2/18/2011	$1,798
Kingfisher Airlines Ltd.	IN	Airlines	1/8/2011	$1,649
AU Optronics Corp.	TW	Electronics	1/7/2011	$1,532
Charoen Pokphand Group	TH	Diversified	3/4/2011	$1,485
Henderson Land Deveopment	HK	Real Estate	1/10/2011	$1,286
Lanco Power Ltd.	IN	Electric	3/25/2011	$1,243

Source: Bloomberg 2011

Loan Syndication in India

Since 1948, Development Finance Institutions (DFIs) or development banks with Industrial Finance Corporation of India and State Finance Corporations assist the promotion and financing of term loans of industrial units. DFIs have been the integral part of the capital market and have played significant role in financing the investment activity. These institutions: 1. Provide credit and other facilities for development of industries. 2. Provide term loans in Indian and foreign currencies.

An impressive 32 banks in total have signed a $1-billion syndicated loan on behalf of Mumbai-based textile producer, Reliance Industries. Seventeen book runners signed the five years deal which carries a margin of 130 basis points over LIBOR. BBVA, BNP Paribas, Bayerische Landesbank, Calyon, Citi, DBS, Fortis, HSBC, ING, Mashreqbank, Mitsubishi UFJ Financial Group, Natixis, NordLB, RBS, Rabobank, SMBC and West LB are book runners on the deal. KfW and Scotia Capital are mandated lead arrangers with China Development Bank and the Commonwealth Bank of Australia joining as arrangers. Bank of East Asia, Bank of Taiwan, Chinatrust Commercial Bank, DnB NOR Bank, E.Sun Commercial Bank, First Commercial Bank, Hua Nan Commercial Bank, Mega International Commercial Bank, Mizuho, Norinchukin Bank and Qatar National Bank joining syndication as participants. Participation fees for banks contributing $40 million are 105bp, 95bp for banks taking a $30 million plus ticket, 85bp for $20 million plus ticket and 75bp for a $10 million plus ticket.

Proceeds are for capital expenditure purposes. The borrower's last major foray into the market was in September 2007 when a considerably smaller book runner group consisting of ABN Amro, BTMU, Calyon, HSBC and Standard Chartered, led a five-year $500 million loan priced at just 39bp, or 52bp all-in. A further nine banks joined that syndication. Here the whole process involves 17 arrangers; they are BBVA, BNP Paribas, Bayerische Landesbank, Calyon, Citi, DBS, Fortis, HSBC, ING, Mashreqbank, Mitsubishi UFJ Financial Group, Natixis, NordLB, RBS, Rabobank, SMBC and WestLB. They all are charged certain fees for participation. Including 17 book runners there are 32 participants. India's Bharti Airtel is close to mandating eight lenders on a $5bn syndicated loan, raising hopes for its merger with South African mobile phone company MTN and highlighting the improvement in Asia's debt markets. State Bank of India and Kotak Mahindra are set to lead a rupee tranche worth $1.5bn, while ANZ, Barclays Capital, Bank of Tokyo-Mitsubishi UFJ, BNP Paribas, Citi, DBS, State Bank of India and Standard Chartered are to lead the $3.5bn dollar portion.

Current Scenario

Four Indian Banks, including State Bank of India and IDBI Bank, figure amongst the top five banks in the Asia-Pacific region for arranging syndicated loans in 2010. Amongst Asia-Pacific countries, Indian entities have been most active in raising funds which includes projects mostly from infrastructure in power and airports segments. SBI, the country's largest lender, with a mandate for five deals raised $ 1.58 billion followed by IDBI Bank ($ 1.41 billion in three deals), AXIS Bank ($ 980 million) and ICICI Bank ($ 686 million).

Table 11.5: Syndicated Loan: A Fact Sheet

Book runner	Year-to-date		
	Proceeds ₹	Market Share (%)	Number of Deals
Bank of Taiwan	12785.6	40.9	9
State Bank of India	1588	5.1	5
IDBI Bank	1410.2	4.5	3

AXIS Bank	980.8	3.1	4
ICICI Bank	686.5	2.2	2
Standard Chartered Plc.	633	2	7
Taiwan Coop. Bank	475.7	1.5	8
DBS Group Holdings	362	1.2	6
Fubon Financial Holding Co.	345	1.1	9
Land Bank of Taiwan	275.9	0.9	7
Top ten total	19542.7	62.5	60

Source: Thomson Reuters

State-owned banks such as Union Bank of India, Bank of India, Allahabad Bank, Corporation Bank, UCO, and United Bank of India are gradually making inroads into this domain. The prospect of earning an attractive fee income by leveraging their corporate relationships is luring banks to set up loan syndication desks.

A recent example has been the ₹ 1,300 crore loan syndication of Hutch done by ABN Amro, HSBC and Standard Chartered for three years. The issue is underwritten by the three banks equally and is thrown open for book-building. It is pitched at a rate of 7.10%. However, on the back of demand from banks, the interest rate is brought down to 7%. It is distributed among 10 banks. Hindalco raised around ₹ 6,000 crore, which is lead-managed by IDBI Bank. The loan has a tenure of 10 years with a reset after five years. It is priced at 5-year G. Sec plus 65 bps. Thirty banks participated in the issue. The largest syndication deal in the market currently is Reliance Ports at around ₹ 4,200 crore. There are also two deals in the pharmaceutical sector for ₹ 1,000 crore each, and two in the telecom sector for above ₹ 1,000 crore. Also, Delhi-based DLF is looking at raising ₹ 1,000 crore for 10 years. In India, most corporate in the market are looking at raising money for Greenfield projects. The Housing Development Finance Corporation (HDFC) has signed a loan agreement for $200 million with International Finance Corporation (IFC), the private sector development arm of the World Bank group. The loan would be available to HDFC in two tranche – the first part of $100 million to be lent directly by IFC as a multilateral tranche, and the second part as a syndicated tranche, (news release from the housing finance company). The first tranche has bullet maturity at the end of 8 years, the rate of interest being six-month LIBOR plus 100 basis points. The second tranche would be syndicated by IFC and would be placed with leading international banks. The main objective of the loan is broad-basing the medium-to-long-term funding sources for HDFC and also to reduce the overall cost of funding. The proceeds of the loan will be utilized for lending to individuals across the country for residential housing. HDFC is in the process of finalising suitable risk management arrangements to hedge against foreign exchange fluctuations.

Summary

Loan syndication are a phenomenon in extremely large loan situations, syndication allows any one lender to provide a large loan while maintaining a more prudent and manageable credit exposure because the lender isn't the only creditor. Presently the corporate are increasingly tapping the loan syndication route. But Indian companies are still underleveraged and corporate still prefer the loan route to fund their expansion plans. Hence, the loan syndication market now can expect big ticket deals in the days ahead.

CASE: ABC APPARELS LTD.

ABC Apparels Ltd., is a leading Mumbai-based software company engaged in banking software and systems integrations. Company is planning a diversified integration project and the estimated cost of which works out to be US $600 million. The company intends to finance the projects *inter alia* with a syndicated loan of US $400 million. The company proposes to finance the acquisitions by the ECB route. The company has approached to Merrily Lunch Bank for the same. The bank has agreed for the loan on the following conditions: amount $40,00,00,000, maturity 6 years from the date of loan agreement, grace period 2 years, amortisations equal half-yearly instalments after the grace period, Drawdown 505 immediate, 50% at the beginning of 2nd year.

Interest – 150 basis points over LIMEAN, management fee: 75 basis point payable upfront, commitment Fee: 25 basis points per annum payable half-yearly on undrawn balances, underwriting fees: 25 basis points payable upfront, agency fees $5,000 per annum payable at the end of each year. Security: Guarantee of Commercial Bank.

Citibank has offered to provide bank guarantee. The guarantee fee is 50 basis points per annum payable half-yearly on the outstanding balances. The fee is payable at the beginning of the period. The loan agreement is proposed to be signed on 1st January, 2005, the expected interest rate are as follows:

Particulars	LIBOR	LIBID
January-June 2005	5.1	4.6
June-December 2005	5.3	5.2
January-June 2006	5.25	4.75
June-December 2006	5.2	4.8
January-June 2007	6.1	5.9
June-December 2007	6.2	5.8
January-June 2008	4.6	4.4
June-December 2008	5.3	5.1
January-June 2009	5.6	5.4
June-December 2009	5.1	4.9
January-June 2010	5.35	5.15
June-December 2010	5.65	3.35

Give your views on its effective costs if it accepts the offer.

Review Questions

1. What is the loan syndication? Who are the parties of the syndication? What are the loan syndication processes?
2. What are the benefits and drawbacks of loan syndication?
3. What are the issues involved in loan syndication process?
4. **Quiz:**

   (a) The lender chosen by the borrower to originate and arrange the syndicated loan is known as the "arranger", and is typically also act as _____.

   (b) In a syndicated transaction the borrower covers only the _____ of the agent.

   (c) During the premandated stage, the prospective borrower liaise invite one bank or competitive bids from a number of banks. ***(T/F)***

   (d) The post-signing stage takes place after the completion date when the deal becomes active and the loan is operational. ***(T/F)***

   (e) Loan syndication generates potential agency problems due to informational frictions between the senior and the junior members of the syndicate. ***(T/F)***

   (f) PNB and Citibank figure amongst the top five banks in the Asia-Pacific region for arranging syndicated loans in 2010. ***(T/F)***

CHAPTER

12

Stock Broking

Introduction

The stock market houses are redefining themselves in every sphere and led India towards global recognition in terms of development, infrastructure and technology. A stock exchange plays an important role as indicators, reflecting the performance of the country's economic state of health. Stock market is a place where securities are bought and sold and prices are determined on the basis of demand and supply of stocks at a given time. Stock brokers are the ones who buy and sell securities on behalf of individuals and institutions for some commission. Stock broking services are widely networked and offered customer-oriented convenience through various delivery channels like e-mail, chat, SMS, phone calls, etc. Currently, progressive brokers deal in billions rather than in millions. Indian industry has now really taken off and this fact has been acknowledged globally. Nowadays brokers today have all their operations computerized and employ qualified industry specialists to advice on buying and selling of stocks. In recent years especially online banking and brokerage service has reshaped the financial landscape around the world. The business of stock broking is highly visible today.

Who is a Stock Broker?

A stock broker or an investment broker is an individual who purchases and trades stocks on behalf of another person. Individuals who perform the service as intermediary between those who want to buy stocks and those who want to sell them are called stock brokers. The stock broker charges a brokerage fee to purchase or sell shares on behalf of a client. Stock brokers also sometimes trade on their own behalf, as a principal individual speculating the increase or decline in price. In such cases the term broker trading in a principal capacity sometimes called themselves dealers, stock traders or simply traders. Stock brokers also act as financial advisors. Most broking firms have research departments and teams of client advisors who are making advice and recommendations about the share market, other investments and obtain the best price from the market and execute and settles the trades for clients. With the advent of automated stock broking systems on the internet, the stockbroker's system performs all the stock broking functions.

Need of Stock Broker

The first and most important step of an investor is to define the goals of investing activity which make easier to map the road ahead for them in terms of time, amount, type of asset and risk. The reality is that the majority of people need to purchase a home, invest in the stock market or foreign exchange, or simply to get the insurance coverage. But however many people do not have the first idea of investing activity where to begin. This is where the finance broker comes in to enable them to reach their goals and realize their dreams by helping people, connecting to the financiers and financial advisor an investor needs. At this point of time investor must also decide how much he is willing to save by include all requirements. Here are a few things that might help an investor is to set out:

- Retirement – In how many years?
- How much money will an investor need?
- How long will an investor need it for?
- Daughter's/Son's wedding – When and how much?
- Daughter's/Son's education – When and how much?
- Purchase of big ticket items, e.g., house, car, etc.
- Again, when and how much?

Some of the brokers like to perform for individual clients while others work for institutions. Many prefer to work as dealers, advisors and securities analysts. Brokers who work for institutional investors are often called securities traders. Security analysts are those who advise companies on floatation of shares. Brokers also prefer to work with banks, mutual funds, consultancies, insurance companies, pension funds and financial institutions, etc.

Functions of Stock Broker

All stock brokers do not offer full range of services. Some are concentrating in the work of institutional investors, such as superannuation funds and life insurance companies, whist others are engaged with buying and selling of securities. Normally they are:

- Providing general investment advice
- Managing investment portfolios for clients
- Giving professional/corporate advice on mergers, takeovers, etc.
- Stocks and shares trading

How Shares are Traded?

The share market is divided into two categories, i.e., primary and secondary market.

Primary ⟵ Share Market ⟶ Secondary

The main function of the primary market is to channelizing savings into issues of new securities to finance the operations of both new and existing companies. The secondary market is the place where existing shares are traded to create liquidity and convert shares into money. A person who buys company shares in the first instance is issued a share certificate by the company, which is also sold in the secondary market.

How to Place an Order?

In a share market, transactions are effected only through licensed brokers in order to have an orderly and transparent market. It is the client's savings that are invested in shares and a quasi-fiduciary relationship exists between broker and client. The brokers who work in the share market are professionally knowledgeable in accounting reports and other information of a company. The brokers are responsible for handling the paperwork involved in the transfer of shares. Brokers charge a commission for the transactions that take place in the share market through them.

Online Stock Brokerages Function

Online stock broker offers trading through the internet. It's an internet based trading facility that allows buying and selling shares through an online broker. An online stock broker is maintaining a website where customers use to enter orders in a real-time system. Once an investor joins an online trading site, he can buy and sell through the stockbroker's website. The net brings data to the investor online and netbroking enables him to trade on a click. Now information has become easily accessible to both retail as well as big investors. Today, most brokerage firms offer online services to investors. Use of online trading lowers the handling costs and therefore the commissions charged tend to be significantly lower than for traditional stock brokers. Internet and related technologies are completely different way of providing financial services. The internet also allows new financial service providers to compete more effectively for customers. They can also better stratify their customer base and allow consumers to build preference profiles online-enabling far more personalized pricing of financial services and much more effective identification of credit risks. Trading systems for equities, fixed income, and foreign exchange are consolidating and going global. Electronic trading and communication networks have lowered the costs of trading and allow for better price determination. Online trading is a boon for those who want to avoid the hassle of personally dealing with a broker.

The development of broking in India can be categorized in three phases:

- Stock brokers offering features such as live portfolio manager, live quotes, market research and news to attract more investors.
- Brokers offering customized services such as online broking and relationship management by providing and offering analysis and information to investors during broking and non-broking hours based on their profile and needs.
- Brokers (now e-brokers) offering value management services such as initial public offerings online, asset allocation, portfolio management, financial planning, tax planning, insurance services and enable the investors to take better and well-considered decisions.

Internet trading also brings total transparency between a broker and an investor in case of secondary market operations. With online trading, investors can see for themselves the price at which the deal takes place. Online trading is a major step that takes India closer to the most advanced capital markets of the world. In US markets, online brokerage has significantly changed the dynamics of the marketplace and generates biggest shifts in the individual investor's relationship with their brokers. Online brokerage provides tools to investors such as research reports to analyze the information as well. Net trading provides investors with flawless, real time online access to stock markets.

Procedure for Internet Trading

- **Step-1:** The investors who are interested for trading over internet system must approach the brokers and register with the stock broker.
- **Step-2:** After registration, the broker provides a login name, password and a personal identification number (PIN).
- **Step-3:** Actual placement of an order.
- **Step-4:** Then the investor has to review the order placed by clicking the review option. He may also reset to clear the values.
- **Step-5:** After the review has been satisfactory; the order has to be sent by clicking on the send option.
- **Step-6:** The investor receives an "Order Confirmation" message along with the order number and the value of the order.
- **Step-7:** In case the order is rejected by the broker or the stock exchange for certain reasons such as invalid price limit, an appropriate message will appear at the bottom of the screen.

- **Step-8:** Some brokers taking some advance payment from the investors to fix their trading limits. When the trade is executed, the broker asks the investors to transfer funds to his account.

SEBI Guidelines

According to SEBI guidelines on internet trading, brokers who are providing e-trading must have a minimum net worth of ₹ 50 lakh. Apart of it, they have to obtain specific permission of the stock exchange concerned. Stock exchanges should ensure that the systems used by the broker provide for security, reliability and confidentiality of data through use of the encryption technology and brokers maintain adequate back-up systems and data storage capacity. Brokers should have adequate system capacity for handling data transfer and arrange for alternate means of communication in case of internet failure.

Below are few advantages and disadvantages of Online Stock Market Trading:

Advantages of Online Stock Trading

- Real time stock trading without calling or visiting broker's office.
- Display real time market watch, historical datas, graphs, etc.
- Investment in IPOs, Mutual Funds and Bonds.
- Check the trading history; Demat account balance and bank account balance at any time.
- Provide online tools like market watch, graphs and recommendations to do analysis of stocks.
- Place offline orders for buying or selling stocks.
- Set alert to inform you certain activity on the stock through e-mail or SMS.
- Customer service through e-mail or chat.
- Secure transactions.

Disadvantages of Online Stock Trading

- Website performance – sometime the website is too slow or not enough user-friendly.
- Little long learning curve especially for people who don't know much about computer and internet.
- Brokerages are little high.

Types of Brokers

There are five categories of market professionals active on the trading floor. They are:

Commission Brokers, usually floor brokers, work for member firms. They use their experience, judgement and execution skills to buy and sell for the firm's customer for commission.

Independent Floor Brokers are individual entrepreneurs who act for a variety of clients. They execute orders for other floor brokers or for firms whose exchange members are not on the floor.

Registered Competitive Market Makers have specific obligations to trade for their own or their firm's accounts.

Competitive Traders trade for their own accounts under strict rules designed to assure that their activities contribute to market liquidity.

In addition to this, the other brokers are as follows:

- **Mortgage Brokers:** Mortgage brokers are providing valuable source of information and comfort for people who are making one of the biggest and most important investments in their lives. He always tries to find the best financing options for clients by accessing both bank and non-bank sources of financing. He always tries to provide a finance package that meets the needs of clients in every respect.
- **Insurance Brokers:** Insurance brokers has the distinct advantage of being able to help clients understand insurance; determine the insurance options that are the best for them. They also help the clients regarding the amount of coverage they need, and help them to set-up long-term insurance.
- **Forex Brokers:** Forex brokers deal in currencies and currency exchange. So he has the unique role of helping the clients by providing information about currency forecasts, foreign exchange rates, and economic indicators analysis. He links the clients' requirement to all the information need on currency trends and the factors that affect the value of currencies around the world.
- **Stock Brokers:** Stock brokers help to assess clients' needs using up to date information on the latest trends in stocks and ability to weigh the risk factors to find the options that best suit to his client. Finance broker are in the business of helping people and building relationships with them. Stock brokers' obligation towards clients is as follows:
  - — To obey the instructions of their clients
  - — To make the best deal possible for their client
  - — To issue a contract note to their client
  - — To refrain from competition with their client
  - — To exercise due care and diligence
  - — To maintain separate client accounts

What is the Advantage of Working with Finance Broker?

A broker has access to multiple lending institutions easily and quickly allowing the client to shop around with only one appointment

- A broker is able to get for the client the best interest rates.
- A broker provides all the appropriate paperwork and ensures that all the correct information is provided by both the lender and the client.
- A broker knows all the options and can sit down with the client and workout the best financing plan for any given situation.
- A broker helps clients who have credit problems.
- Usually, there are no extra fees for the client to utilize the services of a broker as the broker is paid by the lending institutions.

Besides this, mortgage, insurance, forex, and stock brokers all have specific ways to help their clients to achieve their financial goals.

The SEBI have no mechanism to protect investors from losses associated with investment risks, such as changes in value of an investment resulting from market volatility. The SEBI rsules requires that licensed intermediaries must establish a system of adequate internal controls and supervision procedures to prevent any financial loss resulting from theft, fraud, dishonest acts, misconduct or omissions. The broker must establish proper safeguards over money or securities, which are held in custody for the investor. A broker must provide accurate information. All charges and fees must be disclosed. Instructions must be stated clearly to avoid ambiguity. If the phone is used to place an order, it is better to repeat the order back to avoid any misunderstanding.

Stock Trading System

The National Stock Exchange or NSE provides nationwide trading facilities with access to investors all over the country. The automated, screen-based trading system using state-of-the-art technology makes market operations transparent. The Securities and Exchange Board of India (SEBI) has been empowered by an Act of Parliament to protect the rights of investors and ensure the promotion and regulation of the capital markets. The best stock broking houses (such as Brisk Capital Market Services, New Delhi and SSKI, Mumbai) have already redefined themselves and have introduced the compilation of a database to identify avenues for investments in industries. Some of the Indian finance service companies have already made some progress in setting up equity research for identifying growth scripts for portfolio investment and have taken up stock broking earnestly. The best firms today provide a blend of three functions: pre-sales, sales and after-sales service as well. Now brokers or stock market professionals are playing host to foreign investment bankers, who are looking for opportunities on the Indian stock market.

Problem of Stock Broking

Traditionally, the stock broking business runs on advice and this has not changed much even now. Investors who are self-motivated and do not want advice prefer internet trading. But still, the most important factor for the success of stock broking is the human face. Another reason for internet trading not being too successful is that the speed of the internet is not fast enough yet in India.

Do Stock Brokers have to Be Licenced?

Most countries have some requirement for the licensing of stock brokers. In the United States, in order to buy or sell stocks, one must register as a representative of his firm with the National Association of Securities Dealers, Inc. (NASD) and must pass the General Securities Registered Representative Examination administered by the NASD. Most states also require a second examination, the Uniform Securities Agents State Law Examination.

What is the Driving Factors Led to Changes in Stock Broking Business Today?

Traditionally, a broker's main role was just to buy and sell shares. However, with the changes in the corporate and regulatory systems, his role has changed from just execution of trades to advice along with execution. In this case, a broker has to understand the need of the client, his risk assessment, period of holding and returns expectation. He has also to provide research-based advice. There are three main factors behind the changes in the stock broking business. First, the shift from floor-based to screen-based trading in 1994, this brought transparency into trade execution and raised the confidence of investors. This has also lower transaction charges and increased convenience helped both to the investors and the brokers. The second change was dematerialization. Before this, buying or selling shares was a difficult matter. Even when an investor bought shares, he was not sure whether they would be transferred in his name. But now these concerns are no longer there. The introduction of futures and options was the third major factor that has changed the face of the stock broking business, as it is a new avenue for revenues.

Some stock brokers who are financially empowered are now tempted to trade with their own money, enjoying capital gains, instead of trading for outsiders. The level of awareness of the gains deriving from investing in securities has grown tremendously. Stock brokers have also started offering commodities trading. This business opportunity is lucrative one. But it is different from the usual equity trading in the sense that retail participation is not there. Presently, the trend started with the recapitalization of the banks, followed by the insurance subsector is also moving to the capital market. This also encourage the stock broking firms to move to this sector. This has been made possible by stock brokers' continual campaigns.

Subbrokers

An individual, a partnership firm or a body corporate can become a sub-broker provided he satisfies the criteria relating to educational qualifications, experience, etc., and is affiliated to some member(s) of the exchange. After scrutinizing the applications submitted by the subbrokers, the same are forwarded to SEBI for registration. Once a subbroker obtains certificate of registration from SEBI, he can commence business as a subbroker. It may be noted that the subbroker is an agent of the member and is allowed to issue confirmation memos to his clients for their transactions done by him through the main member-broker to whom he is affiliated.

Stock Brokers in US and UK

In US stock broker typically charges a flat fee and/or a percentage-based commission to the client while undertaking the trade as an agent. But when acting as a principal, he makes the trade with another market participant or one of the stock broker's clients. In UK stock brokers acts in the same manner as in US, except that when trading in a principal capacity with a client, the broker is obliged to inform the client and no commission is charged.

Self-regulation

Securities and Exchange Board of India (SEBI) and stock exchanges, stock brokers themselves are now part of the regulatory burden. They framed a self-regulatory organization (SRO) for the country's entire broking community. All the regulatory functions are under SEBI's control, but some of the responsibilities such as member registration and routine inspection of brokers are delegated to the SRO. The surveillance function, however, would entirely be SEBI's responsibility. The government and SEBI have been in favour of SRO culture as they can be relieve some extent of the tremendous pressure of regulatory functions. SRO is the only way out for better regulation of stock market intermediaries.

Summary

Though internet trading offers many opportunities but it is no solution. Most of the benefits, such as widening access to financial services, can be realized only if complementary reforms are made in communications infrastructure, security, contract enforcement, corporate governance, and other areas. Also, net trading relates to a variety of issues, each of which requires deeper analysis and possible changes. The volume of trading has increased tremendously in recent times. Volume has increased and the total number of stock brokers remains relatively the same. So to meet the challenges of increased volume of business, one has to train and face the challenges of the dynamics of the marketplace. Given the present complex situation of our capital markets, stock brokers have to face challenging tasks. The specialized knowledge and professional acumen is required for broking firm to remain highly skilful to meet new challenges.

CASE: MLG CAPITAL LTD.

MLG Capitals Ltd., is a leading stock broking company operating on both the Bombay Stock Exchange and National Stock Exchange. The company is offering buying and selling stocks and shares. They are also providing services which are multidimensional and multifocused and leader in providing investor relation services to clients through internet. Their services are widely networked across India and abroad with the number of trading terminals providing retail stock broking facilities as well. They offered customer-oriented convenience services to a spectrum of investors.

Mr. Rogor graduated in management from Trinity University. He started his career as a branch manager in a web designing company. While working, he was able to produced revenue of over more than ₹ 1 crore and in second year operations generating revenues of ₹ 1.5 crore for his company. Mr. Jame is also graduated from same university and was working as a consultant specializing in database application Software Company. He was also a successful employee of that organization.

Both started MLG Capitals Ltd., in 2000. Their objective is to create web design for small companies. When their company is getting little value in the market; they decided to open a special website which will only provide financial information for small investors. They put considerable effort and get big break rated top internet financial site in India for rending services to clients.

Mr. Rogor and Mr. Jame continued to upgrade and develop the stock broking site and consequently managed to hold the top financial site ranking and continued to gain recognition through different accolades and awards. In 2004 MLG Capitals Ltd., built a team of analyst headed by Mr. Roger. In less than four years MLG Capitals Ltd., had grown from two-man company to 20 staffs. Now they become a full-fledged provider of investor relations services. The team of analysts began producing economic and company specific reports for their clients. Now the company is having highly skilled research team, comprising of technical analysts as well as fundamental specialists, secure result-oriented information on market trends, market analysis and market predictions. The up dated information is given as a constant feedback to their clients regularly through daily reports. They deliver advisory services to a cross-section of customers. The service is backed by a team of dedicated and expert professionals with varied experience and background in handling investment portfolios. They are continually engaged in designing the right investment portfolio for each customer according to individual needs and budget. They usually provide valuable inputs, monitoring and managing the portfolio through varied technological initiatives. They also offer special portfolio analysis packages that provide daily technical advice on scrips for successful portfolio management and provide customized advisory services to help their clients make the right financial moves that are specifically suited to their portfolio. SRG analyst made their predictions as to the future movements of Indian stocks with varying degree of success. So in 2006 SRG management open an asset management division to invest in stocks for clients. Asset management company takes money from clients, pool the funds and then invest the funds on behalf of clients. For rendering these services asset management csompany takes a fee usually 1.5 per cent to 2 per cent of assets per year. In 2008 more than 80 per cent company's revenues are generated by fees charged to corporate clients.

But however due to high volatility of stock market many stocks are neglected and substantially discounted from anticipated actual results. Despite SRG analysts writing regular research that was being sent to clients on a daily basis but it seems they are not able to avail profit from knowledge. Mr. Gem spent most of his time managing the range of computers which ran the site, data feeds and networks upon which the site is depended. Mr. Roger consumed more time with management of the daily operations. But however Mr. Roger find it difficult to sustain companies' growth due to its operating problems. They also find difficulty in retaining qualified staffs particularly sales staffs. The commission structure put lot of pressure to sales staffs. But however MLG Capitals Ltd., the company is a closely held profit making company. The company wishes to expand its sites. The additional site means they need hardware and software needs to be upgraded constantly. They need financing to provide resources to the company to progress to the next stage of development.

The company estimated ₹ 50 crore. Mr. Roger decided to secure term loans of ₹ 20 crore and the balance ₹ 30 crore through a public issue. The company is appointed Emrald Investment Bank to advise them against tapping the market. Emrald Investment Bank suggests a boughtout deal on the following terms.

Emerald will buyout the entire issue at ₹ 125 per share. It will offload the shares through an offer for sale at the end of three years. It will be assured an IRR of 22% on their investments. In case divestment takes place at lesser price the promoters would compensate for the differential amount. In case Emerald offloads at a price which gives them an IRR of over 22%. The surplus would be shared equally by the promoters and Emerald.

The current EPS is ₹ 20 and is expected to grow by 20% annually over the next three years. The company proposes to declare dividends at 15%, 20% 25% for the next three years respectively.

The divestment takes place at a P/E multiple of 16. You are required to find the divestment price of shares. The post-issue returns to Emerald on their investment and the amount of cash outflow/inflow to the promoters on divestment.

Review Questions

1. Why we need stock broker? What are its functions?
2. What is the advantage of working with a finance broker?
3. What are the driving factors led to changes in stock broking business today?
4. **Quiz:**
   (a) Stock brokers also act as _____.
   (b) An ____ stock broker is maintaining a website where customers use to enter orders in a real-time system.
   (c) Stock brokers offering features such as ____, _____, _____ and news to attract more investors.
   (d) Stock brokers makes the best deal possible for their clients. ***(T/F)***
   (e) The SEBI rules requires that licensed intermediaries must establish a system of adequate internal controls and supervision procedures to prevent any financial loss resulting from theft, fraud, dishonest acts, misconduct or omissions. **(T/F)**

CHAPTER 13

Hedge Funds

Introduction

In an increasingly globalized world, economies are swiftly becoming highly dependent on each others, and hedge present to the investors one of the few alternatives to economic-dependent, highly correlated investments worldwide. The traditional school of financial management is based on Modern Portfolio Theory which assumes that markets are efficient. But however hedge fund managers believe that there are inefficiencies in the capital markets, performance can be increased without higher risk, and that investors should aim for superior returns regardless of the direction of major markets. The traditional efficient market hypothesis, which assumes no short selling, implies that by diversifying away non-systematic risk, investors can only increase their returns by increasing their level of systematic risk. Hedge funds, however, do the exact opposite. By hedging away systematic risk, they can generate returns that are based entirely on non-systematic risk. In other words, returns will be generated on the basis of how they are trading not on basis of what they are trading. Hedge funds do not directly finance nor do they play any essential role in the capital structure of the economy as they have no place in the capital market. Hedge funds are exempt from many of the rules and regulations governing other mutual funds, which allows them to accomplish aggressive investing goals. Hedge fund identifies as an entity that does not register its securities offerings under the Securities Act and which is not registered as an investment company under the Investment Company Act. But they are essentially just getting started as a mainstream investment option. Hedge fund is private investment limited partnership that invests in variety of securities. There are two types of partners in hedge fund: a general partner who starts the hedge fund and limited partners who supply the most of capital investment. Hedge funds are moderately liquid alternative investments. Today, hedge funds are attracting a mass of institutional money and are driving the agendas of investment banks and government regulators.

What is a Hedge Fund?

To hedge means to minimize risk. There is no exact definition to the term "Hedge Fund"; it is perhaps undefined in any securities laws. There is neither an industry wide definition nor a universal meaning for "Hedge Fund". Although there is no universally accepted definition of the term "hedge fund", the term hedge fund is widely used, the more accurate phrase is "private investment company" or "pooled investment vehicle". In simple terms a hedge fund is a pool of capital that is provided by institutional investors or wealthy individuals/families and that is deployed by a fund manager to produce substantial returns in the short-term.The primary aim of most hedge funds is to reduce volatility and risk to preserve capital and deliver positive returns under all market conditions. A hedge fund is a business that turns investment risk into investment return. Hedge funds are not regulated entities. It can take both long and short positions. It can invest in any market where it foresees inefficiencies or substantial gains at reduced risk by using arbitrage, leverage, buy and sell undervalued (overvalued) securities, trade options, bonds, OTC products. Hedge funds may invest in all markets globally and can have exposure to equities, fixed income, commodities, credit, currencies and derivatives. In fact they usually have a minimum lock-in period ranging from one to three years. A hedge fund is the popular name for an investment structure, usually in the form of a private investment vehicle such as a limited partnership, which has a flexible investment mandate. Hedge funds have experienced tremendous growth over the last decade as an asset base for institutional and individual investors. Since the hedge fund industry has indeed seen a much higher profile in recent years; it has attracted increasing interest and scrutiny from investors of all types.

History of Hedge Fund

Alfred W. Jones, noted sociologist, author, and financial journalist is credited with the creation of the first hedge fund in 1949. His unique investment strategy was to buy stocks with half his investors' money, and sell short with the other half. Jones developed his own approach, a "market neutral" fund. Jones merged two investment tools – short sales and leverage. Short selling is employed to take advantage of opportunities of stocks trading too expensively relative to fair value. Jones used leverage to obtain profits, but employed short selling through baskets of stocks to control risk. He buys undervalued securities and short sells other stocks, which provided a hedge against market risk. Jones was the first to use short selling, leverage, and incentive fees in combination. Jones believed that price movements of an individual asset and performance of the asset depends more on stock selection than market direction. He believes that during a rising market, good stock selection will identify stocks that rise more than the market, while good short stock selection will identify stocks that rise less than the market. However, in a declining market, good long selections will fall less than the market, and good short stock selection will fall more than the market, yielding a net profit in all markets. To neutralize the effect of overall market movement, he balanced his portfolio by buying securities that are expected to rise in value and selling short securities whose prices are expected to fall. He saw that price movements due to the overall market would be cancelled out, because, if the overall market rose, the loss on shorted assets would be cancelled by the additional gain on assets bought and *vice versa*. With hedge funds, the skill and luck of the manager became the only determining factor in how much money could be made, irrespective of the state of the market. In 1952, he created the first multimanager hedge fund. Other incentive-based partnerships were set up in the mid-1950s, including Warren Buffett's Omaha-based Buffett Partners and Walter Schloss's WJS Partners, but their funds were styled with a long bias after Benjamin Graham's partnership (Graham-Newman). Under today's broadened definition, these funds are also considered hedge funds. The second hedge fund after A. W. Jones was City Associates founded by Carl Jones not related to A. W. Jones in 1964 after working for A. W. Jones. A further notable entrant to the industry was Barton Biggs when he formed the third hedge fund, Fairfield Partners, with Dick Radcliffe in 1965. Many funds decomposed during the market downturns of 1969-1970 and 1973-1974 and unable to resist the temptation to be net long and leveraged during the prior Bull Run. Hedge funds lost their prior popularity, and did not recover it again until the mid-1980s. Fairfield Partners was among the victims as it suffered from an early market call of the top, selling short the Nifty Fifty leading stocks because their valuation multiples had climbed to what should have been an untenable level. A *Fortune magazine* article ("The Jones Nobody Keeps Up With") in 1966 about Jones's "hedge fund" astonished the investment community with its outperformance. That set-off a rush, and, within a few years, the number of hedge funds increased from a handful to more than 100. Jones took both long and short positions in securities to increase returns while reducing net market exposure and used leverage to further enhance the performance. Jones became employed stock pickers to supplement his own stock-picking ability. Soon he had as many as eight stock pickers autonomously managing portions of the fund. In 1954, he had converted his partnership into the first multimanager hedge fund by bringing in Dick Radcliffe to run a portion of the portfolio. By 1984, at the age of 82, he had created a fund of funds by amending his partnership agreement to reflect a formal fund of funds structure. Today the term "hedge fund" takes on a much broader context, as different funds are exposed to different kinds of risks. Over-time, hedge funds began to diversify their investment portfolios to include other financial instruments and engage in a wider variety of investment strategies. Today, in addition to trading equities, hedge funds may trade fixed income securities, convertible securities, currencies, exchange-traded futures, over-the-counter derivatives, futures contracts, commodity options and other non-securities investments. Furthermore, hedge funds today may or may not utilize the hedging and arbitrage strategies that hedge funds historically employed, and many engage in relatively traditional, long only equity strategies. It is important to note that hedging is actually the practice of attempting to reduce risk, but the goal of most hedge funds is to maximize return on investment. The name is mostly historical, as the first hedge funds tried to hedge against the downside risk of a bear market by shorting the market (mutual funds generally can't enter into short positions as one of their primary goals). Nowadays, hedge funds use dozens of different strategies, so it isn't accurate to say that hedge funds just "hedge risk". In fact, because hedge fund managers make speculative investments, these funds can carry more risk than the overall market. Over the past decade, the hedge fund industry has seen tremendous growth. This growth has led to a constantly evolving marketplace with new strategies, asset classes, and fund structures. During the 1980s, most of the hedge fund managers in the United States were not registered with the SEC and instead relied on word-of-mouth references to grow their assets depicted in Table 13.1. The hedge fund industry has grown tremendously throughout the 1990s. From 1990 to 1998, assets under management increased from $20 billion to $400 billion with the number of hedge funds increasing from 200 to over 6,000. Based on data from Hedge Fund Research, Inc. (HFRI) the hedge fund industry grew in terms of unleveraged assets under management of $38.9 billion in 1990 to $456.4 billion in 1999 and $536.9 billion at the end of 2001. From 1999 to 2004 hedge fund assets grew 46% (mutual fund assets grew 5%). The reason for their growth is due to bank regulations; the creation of new capital markets (such as energy, insurance bonds, leasing, factoring, etc.), created opportunities that smaller firms can take advantage of faster and better than the larger banks. In addition to it, there is perhaps a share of unskilled managers who are attracted to a profitable, high-fee business: 1% of the assets as management fee and 10% of the absolute gains over a benchmark standard.

Table 13.1: Hedge Fund Assets under Management in the 1980s ($ millions)

Category	1980	1985	1990
Global	$193	$517	$1,288
Macro	0	0	4,700
Market-neutral	0	78	638
Event-driven	0	29	379
Sector	0	0	2
Short selling	0	0	187
Long only	0	0	0
Fund of funds	0	190	1,339
Total (excluding fund of funds)	$193	$624	$7,194
Total (including fund of funds)	193	814	8,533

Source: Eichengreen and Mathieson (1998), Table 2.2, p. 8, based on MAR/Hedge data.

The hedge fund sector has improved by extending the investor group to institutions – as exhibited in Fig.13.1.

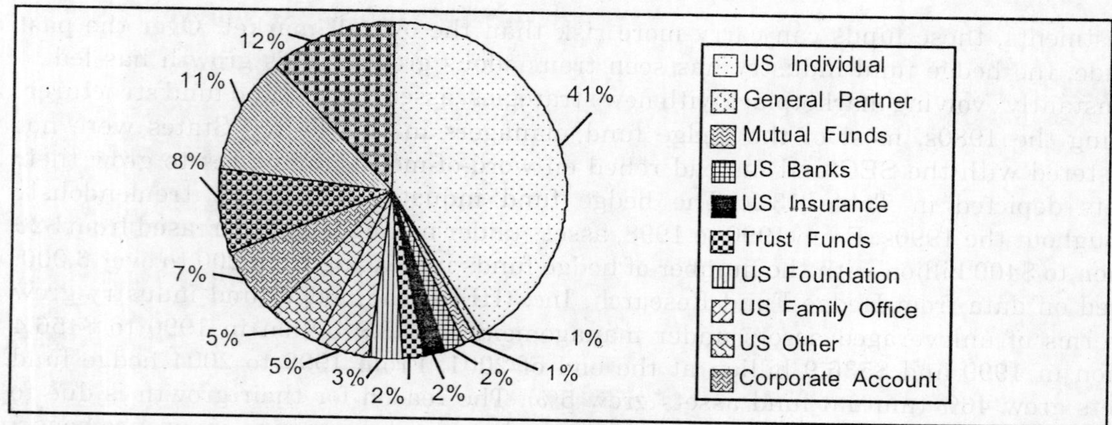

Figure 13.1

Hedge funds can provide value to high net worth individuals with a high absolute return. However, hedge funds can provide even more value (diversification) to institutional investors as an alternative asset class with lower correlations to other asset classes. Today's fund managers must also contend with fluctuating exchange rates and differing accounting standards, regulations, and tax laws.

Hedge funds play a critical role in the financial markets, broadening the use of investment strategies, increasing the number of participating investors, and enlarging the pools of capital available. For investors, hedge funds can serve a risk-management purpose since their returns are often uncorrelated to those in the equity and fixed-income markets. Their importance has been acknowledged by the President's Working Group on Financial Markets, the Commodities Futures Trading Commission, the Securities and Exchange Commission, two chairs of the Federal Reserve Board, and Members of Congress.

How are Hedge Funds Different from Traditional Asset Classes/Other Pooled Funds?

Absolute Returns

While there is no universally accepted definition, a hedge fund's main objective is to produce positive returns irrespective of market direction; that is targeting 'absolute returns'. Mutual funds are often classified as relative return products as they are benchmarked against an index or a peer group.

Skill-based Investing

Traditional mutual funds rely to a large degree on the direction of market performance; hedge funds are much more dependent on the skills of the fund managers.

Minimum Investment Levels

Hedge funds have historically targeted high net worth investors and institutions with high minimum investment levels. However, as some regulators recognise the benefits of hedge funds, there has been a relaxation of minimum investment criteria in certain markets.

Liquidity and Capacity

Hedge funds generally require a stable asset base and liquidity is often limited to monthly, quarterly or yearly 'lock-in' periods. Hedge funds therefore are taking as medium to long-term holding. Many hedge funds limit investment capacity and close to new investors once capacity is reached.

Performance Fees

The hedge fund manager fees are based on percentage of realised positive returns on predetermined minimum return target. Performance fees have helped to attract some of the best fund management talent into the asset class and act as strong incentives for producing superior returns.

Hedge Funds – Comparison to Other Pooled Funds

Hedge funds are similar to private equity funds, such as venture capital funds, commodity pools in many respects. Although all of these investment vehicles are similar and they own up investors' money and generally invest it on a collective basis, they also have characteristics that distinguish them from hedge funds.

Comparison between Hedge Funds and Private Equity

Hedge funds are similar to private equity funds are lightly regulated, private pools of capital that invest in securities and compensate their managers with a share of the fund's profits. Both private equity funds and hedge funds are typically organized as limited partnerships. The investors in private equity funds and hedge funds typically include high net worth individuals and families, pension funds, endowments, banks and insurance companies. Private equity funds, however, differ from hedge funds in terms of the manner in which contribution to the investment pool is made by the investors. Most hedge funds invest in very liquid assets, and permit investors to enter or exit the fund easily. Private equity funds invest mainly in very illiquid asset such as early-stage companies and so investors are "locked in" for the entire term of the fund. Hedge funds often invest in private equity companies' acquisition funds.

Comparison between Hedge Funds and Mutual Funds

Both hedge funds and mutual funds issue units or securities to investors, hold pools of securities to diversify investment, have professional asset manager and have similar investment strategies. However, mutual funds are highly regulated by the SEBI. Hedge funds are not required to be registered and therefore, are not subject to similar regulatory provisions.

Comparison between Hedge Funds and Venture Capital Funds

Venture capital pools are similar to hedge funds and they draw the same class of investors. But Venture capital funds invest in the start-up or early stages of a company. Unlike hedge fund advisors, general partners of venture capital funds often play an active role in the companies in which the funds invest. Hedge funds hold an investment in a portfolio security for an indefinite period based on market events and conditions but venture capital fund typically seeks to liquidate its investment once the value of the company increases above the value of the investments.

Comparison between Hedge Funds and Commodity Pools

Commodity pools are investment trusts, syndicates or similar enterprises that are operated for the purpose of trading commodity futures. The investment concentration in commodity futures distinguishes commodity pools from hedge funds.

The comparison features is exhibited in Table 13.2.

Table 13.2: Hedge Funds – Comparison to Traditional Asset Classes

Investment Class	Hedge Funds	Traditional Investment
Strategies	Long and Short	Long Only
Performance Measurement	Absolute	Benchmark
Positive Returns	Independent of Behaviour of Traditional Markets	Conditional on Rising Markets
Technique	Leverage/Deleverage	Limited Use of Leverage/ Deleverage
Manager's Own Investment	Invested	Not Invested
Risk	Absolute Risk	Tracking Error
Fees	Management and incentive fee	Management Fee Only
Transparency	Often still very low	Public information distribution
Correlation between manager	Low	High

Domestic and Offshore Hedge Funds

Domestic hedge funds are usually organized as limited partnerships to accommodate investors that are subject to domestic taxation. The fund's sponsor typically is the general partner and investment adviser. Domestic hedge funds typically maintain contractual relationships with one or more broker-dealers, which provide clearance and settlement and financing services and provides a variety of incidental services but do not have a board of directors.

Offshore funds generally attract investment of domestic tax-exempt entities, such as pension funds, charitable trusts, foundations and endowments, as well as non-US residents. An offshore hedge fund is having an independent fund administratorand located in offshore, which assist the hedge fund's adviser to value securities and calculate the fund's net asset value, maintain fund records, process investor transactions, handle fund accounting and perform other services.

Characteristics of Hedge Funds

- Hedge funds are organized as private investment partnerships use a wide variety of trading strategies involving position-taking in a range of markets.
- Hedge funds fluctuate extremely in terms of investment returns, volatility and risk. Most of hedge fund strategies tend to hedge against trading recession in the markets.
- Hedge funds are also characterized by their fee structure and pay performance fees to their managers.
- Hedge funds utilize a number of different investment styles and strategies and invest in a wide variety of financial instruments such as equity and fixed income securities, currencies, over-the-counter derivatives, futures contracts and other assets to reduce risk and enhance returns.
- Hedge funds offer investors an important risk management tool by providing valuable portfolio diversification because hedge fund returns in many cases are not correlated to the broader debt and equity markets.
- Hedge funds often provide markets and investors with substantial benefits
- Many hedge funds have the ability to deliver non-market correlated returns.
- Many hedge funds have as an objective consistency of returns and capital preservation rather than magnitude of returns.
- Hedge fund advisory personnel often invest significant amounts of their own money into the hedge funds that they manage.
- Most hedge funds are managed by experienced investment professionals who are generally disciplined and diligent.
- Pension funds, endowments, insurance companies, private banks and high net worth individuals and families invest in hedge funds to minimize overall portfolio volatility and enhance returns.
- Most hedge fund managers are highly specialized and trade only within their area of expertise and competitive advantage.
- Hedge funds typically engage one or more broker-dealers to provide a variety of services, including trade clearance and settlement, financing and custody services.

- Venture capital funds, private equity funds and commodity pools that generally are not categorized as hedge funds although similar to hedge funds.

Hedging Strategies

Wide ranges of hedging strategies are available to hedge funds. Each one is offering different degrees of risk and return. It is essential to know and understand the characteristics of the many different hedge fund strategies to capitalizing variety of investment opportunities. All hedge funds are not the same — investment returns, volatility, and risk differ extremely. Some strategies which are not correlated to equity markets are able to deliver consistent returns with extremely low risk of loss, while others may be as or more volatile than mutual funds. A successful fund of funds recognizes these differences and blends various strategies and asset classes together to create more stable long-term investment returns than any of the individual funds. There are approximately 14 distinct investment strategies used by hedge funds, each offering different degrees of risk and return.

A. Very High Risk Strategies

Emerging Markets

Emerging market strategies are attractive because of high returns. However, the risk involved in emerging markets is much higher due to political instability, less liquidity, currency volatility, higher inflation, volatile growth but potential for significant future growth. Apart of it, emerging markets are not developed the same level of standards in accounting, securities regulation, and information availability. So the risk is high due to the market's valuation inconsistencies. Also effective hedging is not available since short selling is not permitted in many emerging markets. Hedge fund manager may invest in any asset class, e.g., equities, bonds, currencies and construct his portfolio on any basis, e.g., value, growth, arbitrage. Examples of such countries are Brazil, China, India, and Russia.

Short Selling

This strategy is selling shares without owning them, hoping to buy them back at a future date at a lower price in the expectation that their price will drop and generating a profit out of it. Short selling managers typically target overvalued stocks, characterized by prices. They believe the fundamentals of the underlying companies. When it feels market is approaching a bearish cycle, It is often used as a hedge to offset long only portfolios.

Global Macro

Its strategy is to take long and short positions in major financial markets based on views influenced by economic trends and events. The macro-investing strategy aims to profit from changes in global economies typically brought about by shifts in government policy. These opportunities are realized through equity markets, fixed-income markets, commodities markets, and currency markets. Managers have substantial flexibility and invest in any country or asset class where they see an opportunity. The strategy relies on the ability to make superior forecasts compared to other market participants, and then act promptly and decisively. Macro-investing has the advantage of being able to hold a position in almost any market in any type of security. The ability to take large positions in a variety of investments in different markets gives the strategy a great deal of flexibility in its analysis. However, timing is absolutely crucial in implementing the strategy and maximizing the value of specific opportunities.

B. High Risk Strategies

Aggressive Growth

Managers employing this strategy generally utilize short selling to some degree, although a substantial long bias is common. This includes sector specialist funds such as technology, banking, or biotechnology. The manager normally considers a company's business fundamentals when investing in stocks on the basis of technical factors, such as stock price momentum.

Market Timing

The manager attempts to predict the short-term movements of various markets (or market segments) and based on those predictions, moves capital from one asset class to another in order to capture market gains and avoid market losses. The allocation of assets among investments is primarily switching between stocks, bonds, and cash depending on market and/or economic outlook. It is seeking to sell at or near the markets top and buy at or near a market trough in particular categories of investments.

C. Moderate Risk Strategies

Special Situation

The manager invests both long and short, in stocks or bonds which are expected to change in price over a short period of time due to an unusual event. Corporate transactional events such as industry consolidations, mergers and acquisitions, spin-offs, recapitalizations, share buybacks, bankruptcies, and liquidations are creating opportunities for funds to leverage profit from predicting the outcome of such events. It involves simultaneous purchase of stock in companies being acquired, and the sale of stock in its acquirer, hoping to profit from the spread between the current market price and the ultimate purchase price of the company. This will provide the opportunity to perform analysis on any price disparities of the financial instrument like equity or debt.

Value

Funds focused on value stocks look to identify equities that are trading at a discount or undervalued by the market relative their intrinsic value. These investments require a long investment horizon to realize potential gains. Value stocks trade at lower price-to-earnings ratio and may have higher than average dividends.

Funds of Hedge Funds

The manager invests in other hedge funds rather than directly investing in securities such as stocks, bonds, etc. It is a diversified portfolio of generally uncorrelated hedge funds. It provides an investment portfolio with lower levels of risk and can deliver returns uncorrelated with the performance of the stock market. It delivers more stable returns under most market conditions due to the fund-of-funds manager's ability and understanding of the various hedge strategies. Fund-of-funds are also referred to as multimanager funds. Returns, risk, and volatility can be controlled by the mix of underlying strategies and funds. Capital preservation is generally an important consideration. Volatility depends on the mix and ratio of strategies employed. It delivers more consistent returns than stock portfolios, mutual funds, unit trusts or individual hedge funds.

Distressed Securities

Companies in distress face financial or other business related complications. The announcement of restructurings or reorganizations to deal with these financial or business issues often cause a price disparity of the underlying securities, debt or equity, within the market. Negative news regarding the company led to market devaluation. Distressed security managers use their expertise to determine whether the underlying security is undervalued by analyzing the fundamental analysis of the company. The manager must determine the strength of the company's core business, operations, and management, and its ability to bounce back after the reorganization has taken place.

D. Variable Risk Strategies

Investment theme changes from strategy to strategy as opportunities arise to profit from events such as IPOs, sudden price changes often caused by an interim earnings disappointment, hostile bids, and other event-driven strategies.

Opportunistic

The manager's investment idea changes from strategy-to-strategy as opportunities arises to profit from events such as IPOs, sudden price changes often caused by an interim earnings disappointment, hostile bids, and other event-driven opportunities. The manager may also employ a combination of different approaches at a given time since asset classes' portfolio and market capitalization are likely to vary significantly from time-to-time.

Multistrategy

The manager typically utilizes many specific, predetermined investment strategies such as Value, Aggressive Growth, and Special Situations in order to better diversify their portfolio to realize short- or long-term gains. This style of investing allows the manager to overweight or underweight different strategies to best capitalize on current investment opportunities.

E. Low Risk Strategies

Arbitrage

Simultaneous buying and selling of securities is called using arbitrage to exploit pricing inefficiencies between related securities. Strategies tend to be more focused on diversification, operating independently from the direction of the market. Strategies include: Convertible Arbitrage, Equity Market Neutral and Fixed Income Arbitrage.

Convertible Arbitrage

A convertible security is a fixed income instrument issued either as debt or preferred shares. The holder receives a fixed coupon or preferred dividend payments as well as cash at maturity. In addition, the holder of the bond has the right to convert the security into a certain number of shares instead of receiving the full payment.

Convertible arbitrage strategies typically take a long position in the convertible bond and short the company's equity. In doing so, the investor takes advantage of the undervaluation of the convertible bond while reducing the exposure to the underlying stock price movement. An important parameter in this trade is delta, the proportional change in the value of the convertible bond relative to the change in the underlying stock price. If the stock price increases substantially, convertible bond prices generally increase even more rapidly. The interest on the proceeds from selling short the underlying stock is used to finance the position. Convertible arbitrage means purchase and sale strategy, i.e., purchase convertible securities and at the same time sale the underlying equity.

Fixed Income Arbitrage

The main objective of fixed income arbitrage is to identify fixed-income securities whose values are interrelated based on in-depth analysis. This strategy invests with primary focus on yield or current income rather than only on capital gains. This strategy utilizes leverage to buy bonds and sometimes fixed income derivatives in order to profit from principal appreciation and interest income. By taking a long position in the undervalued security and a short position in the overvalued security, the effect of change in interest rate is neutralized. The profit is gained when the pricing of the two securities returns to its historical equilibrium.

Merger Arbitrage or Risk Arbitrage

The focus of merger/risk arbitrage is on the securities of companies involved in mergers and takeovers. Usually, when a stock offer is announced, the target firm's share price rises, while the share price of the bidding company falls. The arbitrage strategy usually will involve buying the former and short-selling the latter. Merger or risk arbitrage strategy focuses on taking advantage of price discrepancies developed by mergers and acquisitions opportunities. If it is perceived that an acquisition has a high probability of occurring, the fund will usually take a long position in the company being acquired, and a short position in the acquirer company. On the contrary, if the probability of the deal occurring is low, the short and long positions will be reversed. When a merger or acquisition is about to happen, a price disparity between the two companies develops due to the market's uncertainty of the outcome. The target company's price is usually less than what it will be once the transaction is completed. This price difference is known as the spread. The spread will narrow as the transaction is finalized, allowing the investor to lock-in a profit.

Equity Market Neutral

The underlying principle of the equity market neutral strategy is to reduce the risk of overall market trends by holding a net portfolio exposure of zero. This strategy seeks to realize steady returns in both bull and bear markets by neutralizing the unpredictable events that affect direction of the general market. By minimizing the affects of overall market risk, the investor can focus on stock selection for both long and short positions. Long positions are taken in equities that are expected to outperform the market and short positions are taken in equities that are expected to under perform. The amount of profit realized depends on the degree to which the long positions outperform the short positions (i.e., long/short spread). Typically a strategy in which equal amounts of capital are invested long and short to "neutralize" market risk by purchasing undervalued securities and shorting the overvalued ones also it is called a "long/short" strategy.

Hedge Equities

An equity hedge fund may be global or country specific, hedging against downturns in equity markets by shorting overvalued stocks or stock indexes. A relative value hedge fund takes advantage of price or spread inefficiencies. A hedge strategy includes the use of short selling and derivatives to minimize exposure to overall market risk. In strong market conditions funds/assets are holding higher percentage in long positions is greater than that of assets held in short positions. The underlying objective is for long positions to outperform the market, while short positions under perform the market. In a weaker market, funds are choosing to decrease net long exposure by greater percentage of assets are allocated to short sales of equities of companies that are expected to decline at a greater rate than the overall market. Similarly, long holdings are expected to either appreciate or decline at a slower rate than the market. The use of various derivatives is also used to hedge market risk. Put options are purchased for individual stocks or indices that are held in long positions, allowing the underlying equities to be sold at a predetermined price (strike price) at a later date. This is used as a tool to minimize the downside of long exposure in any kind of market condition.

Table 13.3: Investment Styles of Hedge Funds

Investment Styles	Definition
Market Neutral	50% Short, 50% Long
Convertible Arbitrage	Long convertible security. Short underlying equity
Global Macro	Focus on global macroeconomic changes
Growth	Look for growth potential in earnings and revenues
Value	Invest based on assets, cash flow, book value
Sector	Focus on particular economic or industry sectors
Distressed Securities	Invest in companies undergoing reorganization or in bankruptcy
Emerging Markets	Invest in emerging foreign market equity and debt
Opportunistic	Trading oriented, takes advantage of market trends and events
Leverage Bonds	Employ leverage to invest in fixed income instruments
Short Only	Take short positions only

Source: Mar/Hedge

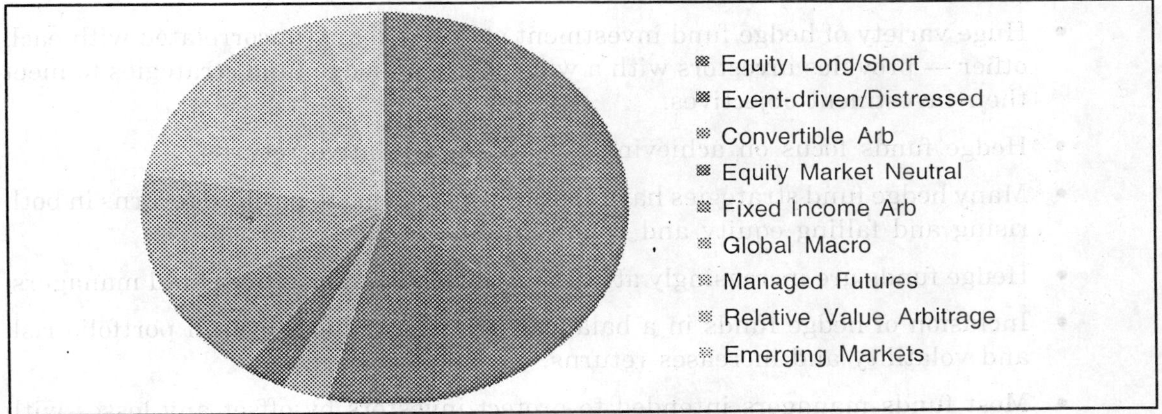

Figure 13.2

Source: HFR Industry Reports, © HFR, Inc [April 4, 2007],

The Fig.13.2 shows the general strategies as defined by Hedge Fund Research (HFR) and the percentage of the hedge fund assets attributed to each strategy. As the industry has grown, the directional strategies include Equity Hedge, Event-driven, Macro, Distressed Securities, Emerging Markets and Short Selling has increased their percentage of the total hedge fund assets. Many arbitrage strategies have limited capacity and are unable to expand at the rate of directional strategies.

Why Invest in Hedge Funds?

Hedge funds offer the following benefits:

- Hedge funds play a critical role in the financial markets, broadening the use of investment strategies, increasing the number of participating investors, and enlarging the pools of capital available.

- Hedge funds have tremendous freedom to invest in any area where their managers believe they can outperform the market. They are able to comb global markets looking for opportunities which are primarily restricted to equities, bonds, and cash.
- The most compelling reason for adding hedge funds to a traditional portfolio is that they generally have a low correlation with the stock and bond markets that comprise the core of most portfolios.
- Hedge funds managers work to change a company's leadership, encourage a merger or acquisition, overhaul the capital structure, reduce expenses, cut executive compensation, or disburse cash reserves to shareholders through dividends and buybacks to unlock shareholder value.
- The key unique feature of hedge funds is that performance is derived from managers' skill (alpha) not from the returns of the underlying markets (beta).
- Hedge funds create value by their ability to exploit structural inefficiencies in the markets.
- Huge variety of hedge fund investment styles — many uncorrelated with each other — provides investors with a wide choice of hedge fund strategies to meet their investment objectives.
- Hedge funds focus on achieving absolute not relative returns
- Many hedge fund strategies have the ability to generate positive returns in both rising and falling equity and bond markets.
- Hedge funds are increasingly attracting the best and brightest fund managers.
- Inclusion of hedge funds in a balanced portfolio reduces overall portfolio risk and volatility and increases returns.
- Most funds managers intended to protect investors by offset any losses with subsequent gains before incentive fees by safeguarding the investors from double paying for the same increase in value.
- Hedge funds enjoy çertain trading advantages and benefit from superior investment information, lower transaction costs, and better market access. Hedge funds are normally borrowed at lower interest rates than individual investors borrowed from banks.
- Hedge fund fees are high — they typically involve a management fee of 1% of assets and an incentive fee of 20% of profits (usually above a certain hurdle rate). This structure is similar to that of venture capital and other private equity partnerships.
- Hedge funds provide an ideal long-term investment solution, eliminating the need to correctly time entry and exit from markets.
- Academic research proves hedge funds have higher returns and lower overall risk than traditional investment funds.

- Hedge funds is having ability to tailor portfolios through either single strategy funds or funds of hedge funds.
- Adding hedge funds to an investment portfolio may provide diversification not otherwise available in traditional investing.
- Hedge funds are extremely flexible in their investment options. This flexibility, which includes use of hedging strategies to protect downside risk, gives hedge funds the ability to best manage investment risks.

The reasons for investing in hedge funds are exhibited in Fig.13.3 and Fig.13.4.

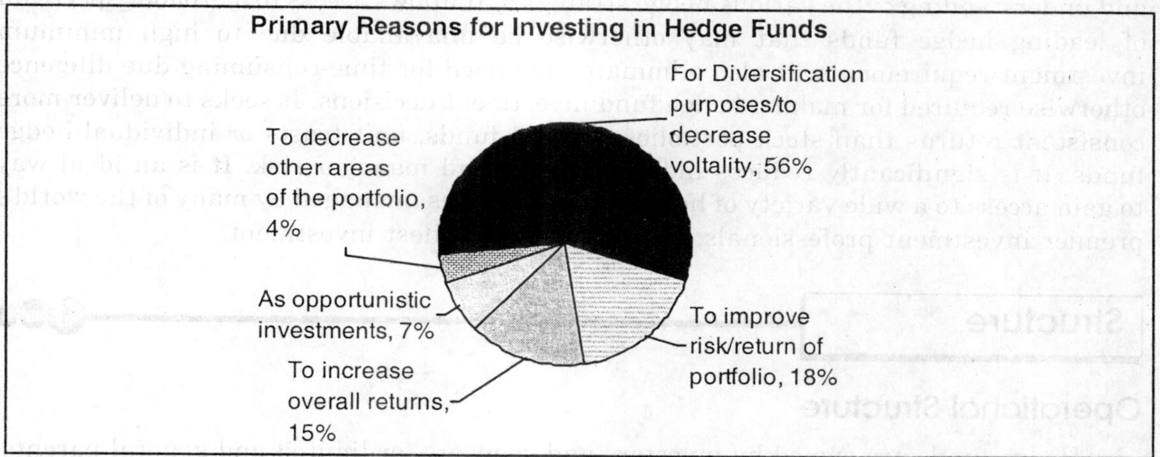

Figure13.3

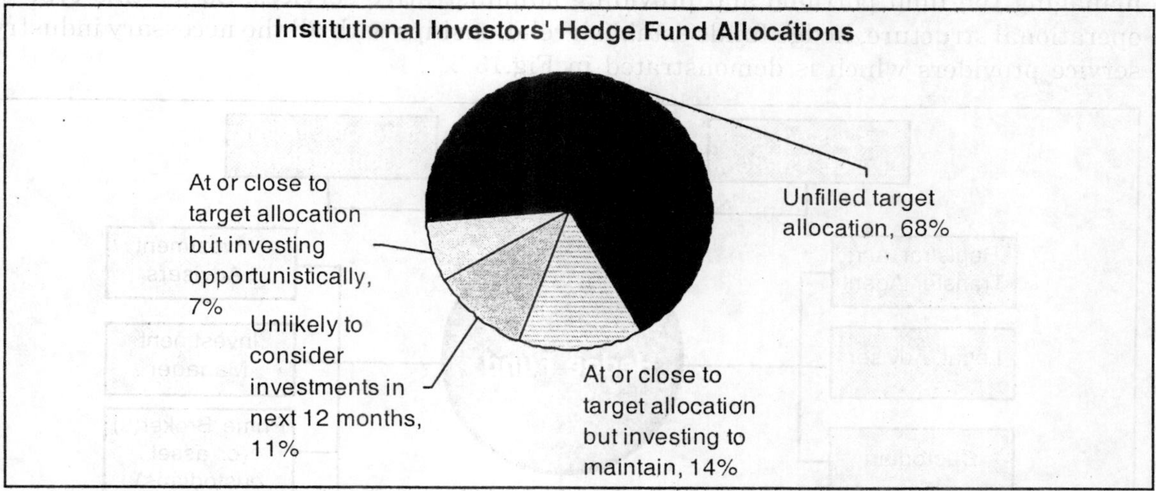

Figure 13.4

Source: *Overview of the Global Hedge Fund Institutional Investor Universe*. Special Report, November 2008.

Why Invest in Funds of Hedge Funds?

The investor is getting benefits of professional manager selection, asset allocation and portfolio construction through multimanager route. Multimanager combines several managers within one fund, known as a fund of hedge funds. Successful multi-managers typically derive their 'edge' through the quality of their ongoing due diligence and analysis of the underlying fund managers and their strategies. Typically the minimum investment criterion is lower for a fund of hedge funds than it is for a single strategy product. It provides effective diversification for investment portfolios. It delivers more stable returns under most market conditions due to the fund-of funds manager's ability and understanding of the various hedge strategies. It allows access to a broader spectrum of leading hedge funds that may otherwise be unavailable due to high minimum investment requirements. It also eliminates the need for time-consuming due diligence otherwise required for making hedge fund investment decisions. It seeks to deliver more consistent returns than stock portfolios, mutual funds, unit trusts or individual hedge funds. It is significantly reduces individual fund and manager risk. It is an ideal way to gain access to a wide variety of hedge fund strategies, managed by many of the world's premier investment professionals, for a relatively modest investment.

Structure

Operational Structure

Hedge funds are owned by investors and sponsors (or limited and general parents) and rely on external service providers to conduct the funds day-to-day business, including managing the fund portfolio and providing administrative services. So for this type of operational structure, hedge funds establish relationships with all the necessary industry service providers which is demonstrated in Fig.13.5.

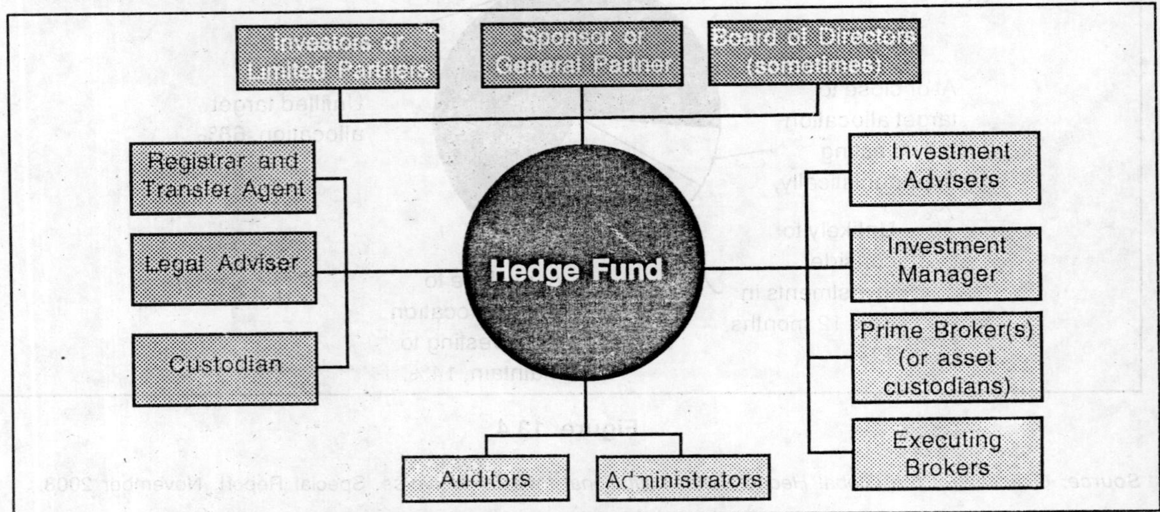

Figure 13.5: Operational Structure

Sponsor

The sponsor holds founder voting shares vested with controlling power and creator of the fund. But however they are usually not entitled to any distribution or share in the equity.

The Manager or Management Company

Manager is responsible for determining investment strategy, making choices in portfolio holdings, and making operational decisions.

The Board of Directors

The board of directors is responsible for monitoring the overall operations of the fund.

Fund Administrator

His key duty is to ensure accurate calculation of the net asset value and performs administrative services such as accounting and book-keeping and investor services or risk analysis. It is noticed recently that after wake of the financial crisis hedge funds employ recognised third-party administrators in order to attract capital from investors. The latest data reveals that assets under management by third-party hedge fund administrators increased by 6.3% in the first half of 2010, with only a few administrators reporting a decline in hedge fund assets under management exhibited in Table 13.4. Citco Fund Services retained its position as the largest hedge fund administrator with a 19.2% share of assets. It is followed by State Street with 9.5% and Citibank 9.0%.

Table 13.4: Largest Hedge Fund Administrators

Jun-10	% share
Citco Fund Services	19.2
State Street Altern. Invest. Solutions	9.5
Citibank	9
HSBC	8.7
Custome House	8.2
GlobeOp	3.9
Goldman Sachs	3.3
SEI Investment Services	3.1
Bank of New York	3.1
PNC Global Investment Servicing	2.5
Others	29.5

Source: Eurekahedge

The Investment Adviser

The role of investment adviser is simply to give professional advice on the fund's investment in a way that is consistent with the fund's investment objectives and policies, the investment adviser may be a part of the same overall organization as the hedge fund he serves, or he may be unrelated to it.

Custodian

Hedge fund assets are generally held with a custodian, including cash in the fund as well as the actual securities. The custodian's primary responsibilities include safe keeping of fund's assets, clearing and settling all trades, and monitoring corporate actions such as dividend payments. A trend since the turmoil of 2008 has been the use of multiple custody and clearing options in order to reduce risk and further protect assets.

Legal Adviser

The legal adviser or lawyer assists the fund with legal matters.

The Auditors

Most hedge funds are set up in a way that does not require them to have their financial statements audited. Some hedge funds however, may undergo annual audits if this is a part of the contract between the hedge fund and its investors. The auditors' role is to ensure that the hedge fund is in compliance with accounting practices and any applicable laws, and to verify the annual financial statement, if any.

Registrar, Transfer Agent

Its task is to keep and updates register of shareholders. He also processes and takes necessary actions for subscriptions and withdrawals of shares in the fund, as well as for the payment of any dividends and distributions.

Distributors/Placement Agents

He handles marketing and distribution of fund shares to accredited investors.

Brokers: The role of prime brokers goes beyond just replacing the hedge funds back-office. It needs to place its orders with a broker, typically using the services of several executing brokers.

Prime Brokers: It provides execution and operational services, including clearing trades, acting as global custodian, and providing both margin financing and securities lending. Prime brokers offer a diverse range of services is shown in Fig-13.6 including: financing, clearing and settlement of trades, custodial services, risk management and operational support facilities. The Table 13.5 shows the largest hedge fund prime brokers in the year 2010. Major restructuring occurred amongst prime brokers in 2008 and 2009 such as the acquisition of Bear Stearns by JP Morgan, the takeover of Lehman Brothers by Barclays Capital and the acquisition of Merrill Lynch by Bank of America. This resulted in a shift in market share from some former investment banks to commercial banks. JP Morgan and Goldman Sachs were the largest prime brokers in 2010, each with around a fifth of the market.

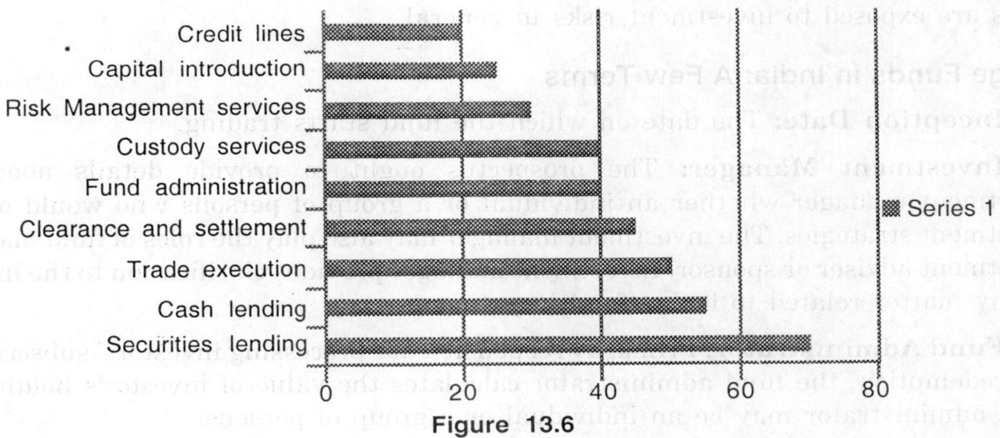

Figure 13.6

Table 13.5: Largest Hedge Fund Prime Brokers 2010

	% share
JP Morgan	21.6
Goldman Sachs	18.3
Morgan Stanley	15.9
Deutsche Bank	7.9
Credit Suisse	6.8
UBS	5.7
Citibank	4.9
Bank of America Merrill Lynch	3.6
Others	15.3

Source: Eurekahedge

Risk in Hedge Fund

Hedge funds make uncorrelated returns because they take different risks. The following is a list (not an exhaustive one) of risks categories specific to hedge funds:

Hedge funds are businesses so they do not want to disclose their strategy. Hedge funds are especially sensitive to risk type because of the unregulated and specialized nature of their transactions. Hedge funds often restrict fund redemptions hence liquidation orders take time to process. A hedge fund forced to sell securities to meet redemption orders is an easy prey to its counterparties or competitors in the financial markets. Hedge funds make money on fees; while management fees are considered generous by investment standards it is with the performance fees that most funds make their money. Hence, they are encouraged to close the fund to new investments if they see no new opportunities for return and sense that they have reached capacity. Hedge funds are exposed to investment risks in general.

Hedge Funds in India: A Few Terms

Inception Date: The date on which the fund starts trading.

Investment Manager: The prospectus ought to provide details about the investment manager whether an individual or a group of persons who would oversee investment strategies. The investment manager may also play the roles of fund manager, investment adviser or sponsor. Investment manager provides clarification to the investor on any matter related to hedge fund investment.

Fund Administrator: Primarily responsible for processing investors' subscriptions and redemption, the fund administrator calculates the value of investor's holding too. Fund administrator may be an individual or a group of persons.

Custodian: The financial entity that holds hedge fund assets. This includes cash in the fund as well as securities.

Prime Broker: There can be overlapping of roles and responsibilities with fund administrators. But prime brokers bring in investment and operational perspective to hedge funds. Prime brokers help fund manager or investment manager to decide on allocation of investment funds to different brokers.

Transaction Broker: All investment activities are executed through the transaction broker.

Typical Hedge Fund Investment

- Investor chooses and decides hedge fund investment
- Subscription amount is paid to the custodian.
- Custodian confirms receipt of payment to fund administrator.
- Fund administrator instructs issue of share to investor.
- Fund administrator issues reports on hedge fund performance.
- Investment manager instructs custodian to move funds to prime broker for investment in market.
- During the process the prime broker and custodian are in direct contact with fund administrator.

Principles of Hedging

The principle underlying hedging is different. Ideally, when you want to hedge you look at two investments that are perfectly correlated. Suppose you find that the returns of A and B are perfectly correlated. To hedge, you either buy A and sell B or do the other way. When you do so your net position is riskless. In real life, however, the correlation is often imperfect and, hence despite the hedge some residual risk exists.

Irrespective of whether the correlation is perfect or not, the manner in which a hedge is set up is the same. Imagine that you have a liability P. You want to hedge this liability by purchasing Q. Your investment in Q depends on how P and Q are related. Suppose the following relationship exists;

Expected change in the value of P = a + δ (Change in the value of Q) where a is a constant and (delta), reflecting the sensitivity of P to changes in the value of Q, is the hedge ratio. If you buy delta units of Q, you minimize your risk on account of your liability P.

An illustration may be given. Suppose that a portfolio manager has short sold ₹10 million of Reliance stock. If the market moves up, the Reliance stock is likely to rise and the portfolio manager would incur a loss on his short sale. He can mitigate the risk by purchasing the market portfolio. (In practice, since one can't buy the market portfolio, one buys the stock index futures). To decide how much he should invest in market portfolio, he must access the sensitivity of Reliance's stock prices to changes in the market index. Based on past evidence, he estimates the following regression relationship:

Change in Reliance's stock price = a + δ (Change in the market index)

= 1.20 + 1.50 (Change in the market index).

R2 = 0.55; where R2 refers to the coefficient of determination.

Note that the sensitivity factor (1.50) in the above equation is nothing but the beta of Reliance stock's stock. In order to minimize the risk of short sale, the portfolio manager must make an investment of 1.50 × 10 million = ₹ 15 million in the market portfolio.

To what extent is the risk from the short sale eliminated by the investment in the market portfolio? Since R2 is 0.55 it means only 55 per cent to the total variance in Reliance's stock price change is explained by the market movement. Put differently, 55 per cent of its risk is market risk and 45 per cent of its risk is unique risk. Thus, hedging with the market portfolio can offset only the market risk (55 per cent) and not the unique risk (45 per cent).

Suppose portfolio manager hedges 10 million rupees short position in Reliance by investing ₹ 15 million in the market portfolio. Even though he is protected against variations in the value of Reliance stock, the value of his short position in Reliance is not the same as that of his investment in the market portfolio. If he wishes to create a zero value hedge, he should borrow ₹ 5 million from the bank.

Regulation of Hedge Funds

Though the original purpose of hedge funds was to invest in equity securities and use leverage and short selling to "hedge" the portfolio's exposure to movements of the equity market, this submit has changed. Today, hedge fund advisers' use complicated investment strategies and techniques to increase investor returns and many are very active in the trading of securities, representing between nearly 20% of equity trading volume in the US securities market. Indeed, the hedge fund industry may have played more of a role in creating liquidity and making markets efficient than the mutual fund industry. The hedge fund industry is able to do so because it is generally not regulated, so that funds are free to take whatever positions they wanted and to make full use of financial innovations.

One of the most important reasons cited by the votaries of regulating the Hedge Fund industry is the incredible growth of hedge funds and the increased influence and power that hedge funds are having on the financial markets. The industry is criticized for being secretive, engaged in risky behaviour and capable of unduly influencing global economies and corporate activities. An increase in fraud cases involving hedge fund advisers, juxtapose with an increase in exposure of unsophisticated small investors to the risks of hedge fund investing has allured the policymakers and regulators to bring the hedge fund industry under greater scrutiny.

Hedge funds must also abide by the rules and regulations of markets in which they seek to buy or sell financial products. In December 2004, the SEC issued a rule change that required most hedge fund advisers to register with the SEC by February 1, 2006 as investment advisers under the Investment Advisers Act of 1940. The requirement, with minor exceptions, applied to firms managing in excess of $25 million with more than 15 investors. The SEC said it was adopting a "risk-based approach" to monitoring hedge funds as part of an evolving regulatory regime for the industry. In 2007, the SEC announced the creation of a new hedge fund task force within the Enforcement Division as part of the commission's latest initiative to "enhance its efforts to combat hedge fund insider trading. Over the last five years (2004 to 2009), the SEC brought more than 100 cases involving hedge funds. The SEC is focusing on several issues involving hedge funds and other institutional traders, including (i) possible manipulation, abusive short selling and collusion; (ii) valuation concerns with respect to illiquid assets; and (iii) potential insider trading in a host of circumstances, including prior to mergers and acquisitions and in the credit derivatives market, In January 2009, two blue-ribbon, private-sector committees established by the President's Working Group on Financial Markets issued separate yet complementary sets of policies for hedge fund investors and asset managers. The best practices for the asset managers called on hedge funds to adopt comprehensive best practices in all aspects of their business, including the critical areas of disclosure, valuation of assets, risk management, business operations, compliance, and conflicts of interest. As part of the due diligence process, investors successfully demand from hedge fund managers effective internal controls to discourage fraud, according to research published in June 2009 by professors from the University of Pennsylvania's Wharton School of Business and the University of Chicago.

The hedge fund industry presently calls for stricter regulation in recent years. Though hedge funds was not a part of emergence of the credit crisis, it is alleged that they contributed to volatility through short selling transactions and selling shares as a result of deleveraging and redemptions. The Financial Stability Board, successor to the Financial Stability Forum, was established in April 2009 following the G-20 London summit. The oversight of the new body was extended to all financial institutions important to global financial stability including for the first time large hedge funds. In the US, the Dodd-Frank Wall Street Reform and Consumer Protection Act were signed into law in July 2010. The Act was introduced in response to the financial and economic crisis. It requires investment advisers to hedge funds and other private funds to register with the SEC (Securities and Exchange Commission), unless they have no separate accounts and less than $150 million in assets under management or advice only venture capital funds. In addition, the Act will require many "mid-sized" registered advisers (those having between $25 million and $100 million of assets under management) to withdraw their SEC registration and to register instead with the applicable state or states. These statutory changes are slated to take effect in July 2011.

Self Regulations

Even though there is no statutory obligation to make a public disclosure, hedge funds provide their potential investor with a private placement memorandum that discloses information about the overview and investment strategies of the hedge fund. The memorandum also provides the adviser with the maximum flexibility in selecting, shifting and modifying its strategies and arms him with broad discretion in valuing hedge fund's assets.

Hedge Fund investors generally receive some ongoing performance information, risk analysis and portfolio profiles from their hedge fund advisers. Most hedge funds retain an auditor to conduct an independent audit which if certified is prepared using generally accepted accounting principles (GAAP). Market competition has also led to a growing demand by the investors for business-unit level SAS 70 assessment (Statement on Auditing Standards No.70 Service Organizations,) by reputed firms.

Also the manager does not receive performance fees unless the value of the fund exceeds the highest net asset value it has previously achieved. This measure is intended to link the manager's interests more closely to those of investors and to reduce the incentive for managers to seek volatile trades. The market competitive regulations are more than statutory regulations.

Regulations in India

Hedge Funds were largely held responsible for the South East Asian Economic crises in the late 1990s, the failure of the long-term Capital Management Fund in the US in 1990s and its subsequent $ 3.5 billion bailout by the Federal Reserve Bank to prevent the cascading collapse of global financial markets; and the current surge of the Bombay Stock Exchange SENSEX, which even surprised the Indian Finance Minister as to comprehend the reasons for such a surge, creates an argument that some form of regulation should be encouraged for hedge funds.

SEBI

India's stock market regulator Securities and Exchange Board of India (SEBI) is looking to provide a broad-based, registered and regulated platform to hedge funds, depending on their individual track records. Among the measures being considered is one that will allow single hedge funds (those that have a single strategy or a single investor, and, therefore, a higher degree of risk) to invest only 49% of their investment corpus in India. Hedge funds are aggressively managed portfolio investments that use strategies such as leveraging, and taking long (a bet that the underlying asset will appreciate), short (that the underlying asset will depreciate) and derivative positions in the markets in order to make high returns.

Several well-known hedge funds have already been granted entry into India. SEBI's previous chairman M. Damodaran had always maintained that the regulator was more comfortable with hedge funds coming into the domestic market through the front door, as entities registered with it. In October 2007, SEBI had clamped down on anonymous inflows of foreign money into equities through so-called participatory notes (PNs). Since clamping down on PNs, SEBI has made it easier (and quicker) for foreign investors, including hedge funds, to register themselves with it. Some prominent hedge funds such as the Old Lane LP had made investments of $45 million in a joint venture with Chennai-based infrastructure Company R.R. Industries (a Citigroup fund) have since registered their names with the regulator.

With the notification of SEBI (Mutual Fund) Regulation 1993, the asset management business under private sector took its root in India. In the same year SEBI also notified Regulations and rules governing portfolio managers who pursuant to a contract or arrangement with clients, advice clients or undertake the management of portfolio of securities or funds of the client. There are no hedge funds domiciled in India and they are not allowed to raise funds from the domestic market. Further, on account of limited convertibility, offshore hedge funds have yet to offer their products to Indian investors within India. The RBI through liberalized remittance scheme has allowed resident individuals to remit up to US $ 25,000 per year for any account or for capital account transaction. This liberalized scheme will allow individual investors to explore the possibility of investing in offshore financial products.

Hedge funds typically invested in the offshore derivatives instruments (Participatory Notes (PNs)) issued by FII against the underlying Indian securities. Through this route the hedge funds could derive economic benefits of investing in Indian securities without directly entering the Indian market as FIIs or their sub-accounts. As of October '07 there were more than 1,100 registered foreign investors and 3,447 registered sub-accounts. Through recent amendments to the FII Regulations (Regulation 15A and 20A), the

Regulatory regime has been further strengthened and periodic disclosures regime has been introduced. The Provision 15 (3)(a) of the FII Regulations relates to the prohibition on short selling of securities by FIIs. It allows that FIIs may transact business only on the basis of taking and giving deliveries of securities bought and sold, and cannot engage in short-selling securities.

Further Regulation 6(1)(b) of FII Regulations, provides that the hedge fund have to be registered with the statutory regulatory authority in their place of incorporation. Most hedge funds would fail to meet this criterion because they are not registered with any regulatory authority, nor are the managers registered with regulatory authorities. In October '07 SEBI has mandated that in the spot market, FII would not be allowed to issue P-notes that were more than 40 per cent of their assets under custody and those FII over the threshold have to freeze their holdings. FIIs that have issued P-notes below the limit may increase issuances at an incremental rate of 5 per cent of their assets under custody.

The FII regulations allow sub-accounts sponsored by registered FIIs to invest in India. Regulations 2 (k) defines "sub-account" which "includes foreign corporate or foreign individuals and those institutions, established or incorporated outside India and those funds or portfolios, established outside India, whether incorporated or not on whose behalf investments are proposed to be made in India by a foreign institutional investor".

Further provisions of Regulation 13 lay down the conditions and the procedure for granting registration to a sub-account of an FII. But the October '07 SEBI mandated new guidelines, under which FII currently registered in India would not be allowed to issue new derivatives from sub-accounts based in tax havens such as Mauritius.

However, in practice if an applicant indicates in the application that it is a hedge fund, the consideration of the application is generally withheld. Since granting of registration to FII/sub-accounts is based on the disclosure of the details and on the undertaking given by the applicant in the application form; it could be possible that the few entities who described their activities in the application form in terms other than hedge funds could have already got registration as sub-accounts. However, it is mandatory that the sub-accounts have to be sponsored by registered FIIs who are required to be regulated entities by relevant regulators in their home countries.

The FII regulations also lay down scrip-wise and fund-wise maximum limits a fund can invest. Further, through circular dated February 12, 2002 and March 9, 2004 issued in the Secondary Market Department, position limits for investment by FII in derivatives have been advised. These limits will help diversify the foreign hedge fund investments and further help in jettisoning concentration in any specific scrip. The government wants to keep the hedge funds out of short selling at least in the cash segment and thus provisions of chapter III (Regulation 15 (3) (a)) disallows short selling by FII and stipulates that all trades by FII be delivery based.

Chapter II of the SEBI (Foreign Institutional Investors) Regulations, 1995 *inter alia* lists out the instruments in which an FII/sub-account can invest. The regulation does not include currency or commodities as eligible instruments for investment for the FII. Therefore, currency trading or investment in commodity related financial products will not be an option for any hedge fund under the present FII Regulations.

The Money Laundering Act, 2003, is an endorsement of various international conventions to which India is a signatory. It adequately empowers the state authorities to declare laundering of monies a criminal offence. Working out modalities of disclosure by financial institutions regarding reportable transactions, confiscation of the proceeds of crime, declaring money laundering as an extraditable offence and promoting international cooperation in investigation of money laundering is the main aim of the Act. It also provides for reciprocal arrangement for assistance in certain matters and procedure for attachment and confiscation of property to facilitate transfer of funds involved in money laundering kept outside the country and extradition of the accused person from abroad.

Hedge Fund in International Scenario

Since 1990, the hedge fund industry has grown from 640 funds worldwide with total assets of $39 billion to an estimated 9,700 hedge funds with more than $1.7 trillion in assets under management by mid-2007. The increase translates to a compound annual growth rate of 26%, putting the industry on pace to surpass the $2 trillion mark during 2008. More than 8,900 hedge funds, or private investment companies, managed more than $1.43 trillion in assets as of June 2009. These funds serve an important role in US and global markets, providing qualified investors with opportunities to manage risks and achieve above-average gains.

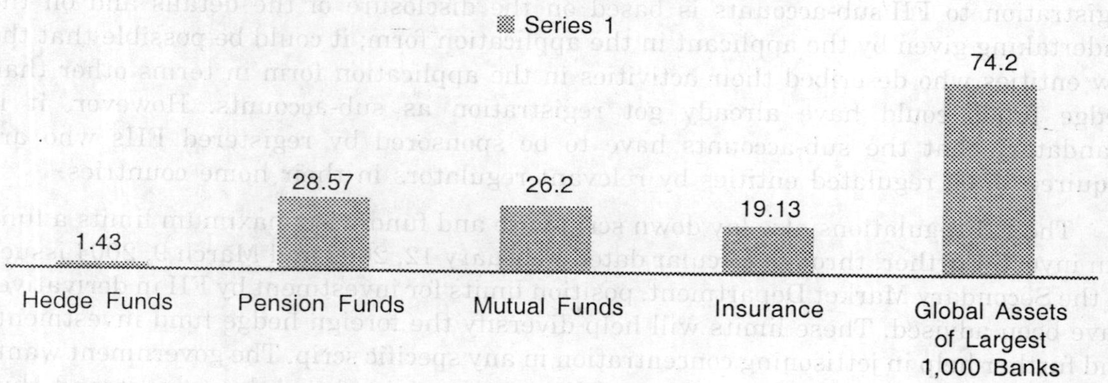

Figure 13.7

Source: McKinsey Global Institute, Mapping Global Capital Markets: Fifth Annual Report, October 2009.

Even though the assets managed by hedge funds have increased six-fold over the past decade to $1.43 trillion by June 2009, this amount is relatively small in comparison to other major global investment pools. The Fig.13.6 shows that hedge funds represent 1.1 per cent of the total funds and assets of financial institutions.

For the eleven-year period from January 1, 1998 through December 31, 2008, the average hedge fund returned 7.45 per cent a year (annualized return), compared to a 1.38 per cent loss for the Standard & Poor's 500 Index (with dividends) and a 2.79 per cent loss for the FTSE 100 Index, according to Hedge Fund Research, Inc. From January1990 through June 2009, the S&P 500 experienced 36.75 per cent negative months, dropping 3.71 per cent during these downturns, while hedge funds lost only 0.67 per cent during those general market downturns. Over the same time period, hedge funds experienced positive gains in 72.22 per cent of the months, compared to 63.25 per cent positive months for the S&P 500.

Between 2005 and 2008, 55 per cent of hedge fund managers had experienced a rise in the proportion of their capital coming from the institutional sector, with 14 per cent experiencing a decrease, according to a November 2008 survey by research firm Preqin Ltd. The global credit crisis had its origins in a bubble of rising real estate prices, followed by a sharp fall in housing prices that began in 2007 and dropped roughly 20 per cent on average nationwide by fall 2008. That led to an escalation of mortgage delinquency and default rates, which may ultimately result in losses exceeding $4 trillion.

The Growth of Hedge Funds from 1990-2009 is shown in Fig.13.8

Assets under Management and Net Asset Flow, 1990-2009* (billions of dollars)

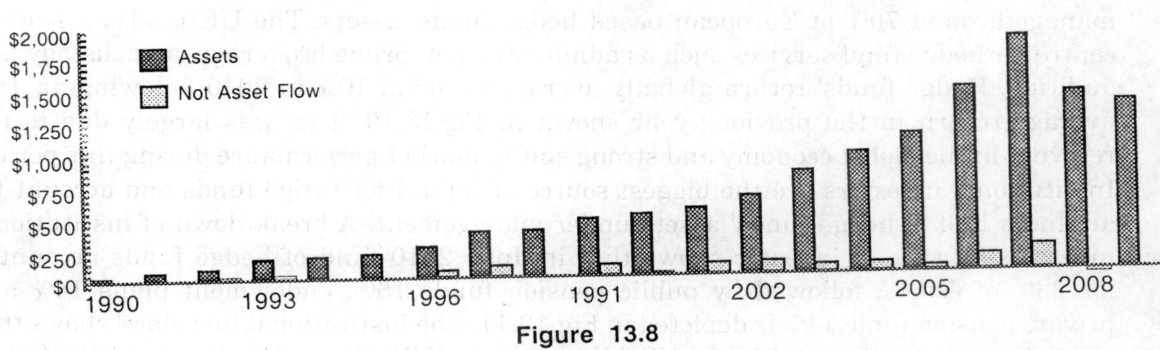

Figure 13.8

Source: Hedge Fund Research, Inc. www.hedgefundresearch.com.

Assets under management of the global hedge fund industry increased by 13% in 2010 to $1,920bn. This follows an 18% increase in the previous year. Assets under management were nevertheless still below the record $2,150bn managed at the end of 2007. Growth in assets in 2010 was due both to high returns for the second year running, as well as a net inflow of funds. The number of hedge funds totalled over 9,500 at the end of the year with new hedge funds launches outpacing fund liquidations for the first time since 2007 shown in Fig.13.9. Barring further economic turbulence, growth of hedge fund industry assets under management is likely to continue in 2011 with assets likely to recover to precrisis levels by the end of the year.

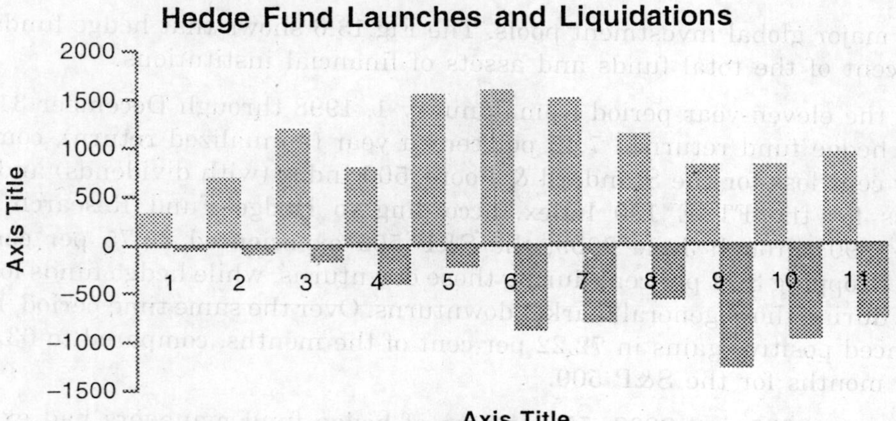

Figure 13.9: Hedge Fund Launches and Liquidations (2000-2010)

The US was the largest management centre for hedge funds with 68% of the global total at the end of 2010, down from 86% a decade earlier. Europe followed with 22% and Asia 6%. New York is the world's leading centre for hedge fund managers, followed by London. The City UK estimates that around 41% of global hedge fund assets were managed from New York in 2010, down from over a half a decade earlier. London's 19% share of the total was slightly down on the previous year mainly due to quicker growth in assets under management in the North America than in Europe during 2010. London is by far the largest centre in Europe. The 700 hedge funds located in London in 2010 manage around 70% of European based hedge funds' assets. The UK is also a leading centre for hedge fund services such as administration, prime brokerage, and custody and auditing. Hedge funds' return globally averaged around 10% in 2010 following an 18% average return in the previous year shown in Fig.13.10. This was largely due to the recovery in the global economy and strong equity market performance during this period. Institutional investors are the biggest source of capital for hedge funds and account for around a half of hedge funds' assets under management. A break down of institutional investors by type of investor shows that in June 2010 fund of hedge funds accounted for 22% of assets, followed by public pension funds 16%, endowment plans 14% and private pension funds14% is depicted in Fig.13.11. The institutional investors' shows that more than a half originates in the US followed by the UK 14% and Switzerland 5%. Public pension funds globally have increased their exposure to hedge funds by 50% in the four years up to 2011 according to a Preqin survey. The strategy focus during 2009 is shown in Fig.13.12.

It is reported that hedge funds utilize conservative leverage. Many hedge funds do not have any leverage. Most of the rest have very controlled conservative levels. Recent studies indicate that while around 72 per cent of hedge funds embody leverage, only 20 per cent have balance sheet leverage ratios of more than 2:1 is shown in Fig.13.13.

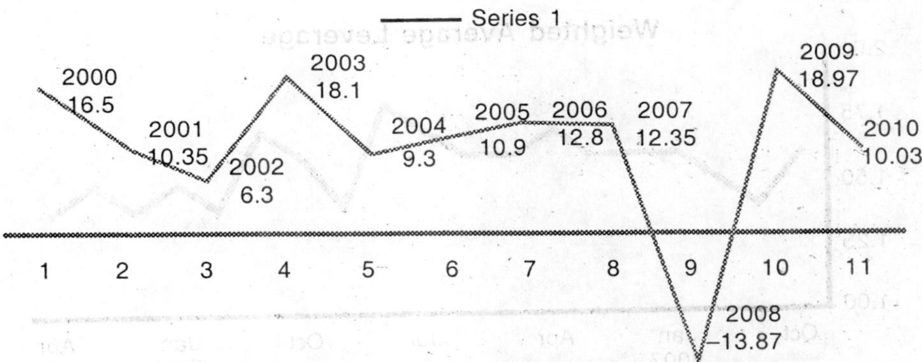

Figure 13.10: Global Hedge Fund Returns (2000-2010)

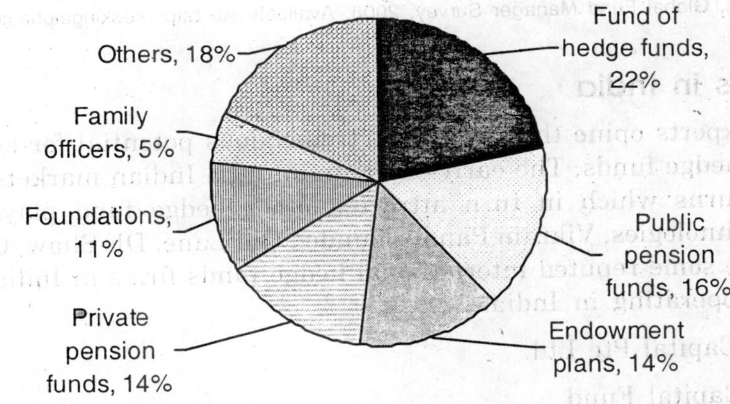

Figure 13.11: Institutional Investors in Hedge Funds % Share, 2010

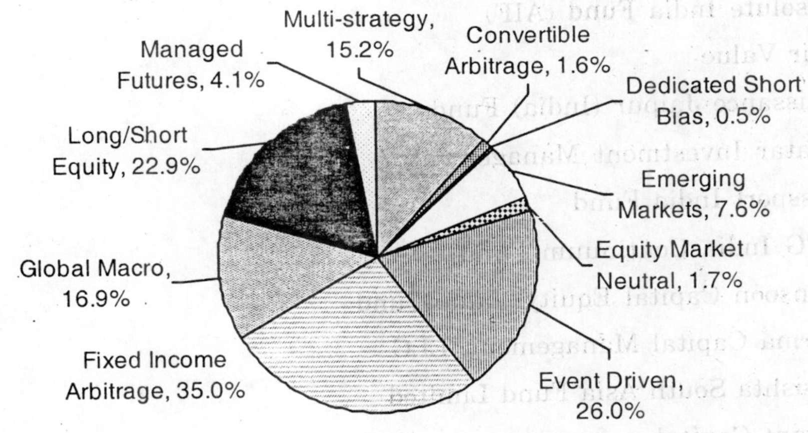

Figure 13.12: Strategy Focus Second Quarter 2009

Source: Investment Strategy Components of Credit Suisse/Tremont Hedge Fund Index. June 2009. *Available at:* http://www.hedgeindex.com

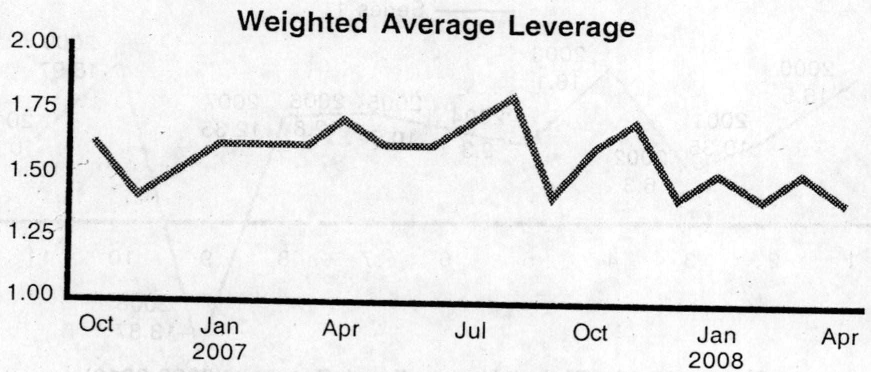

Figure 13.13: Weighted Average Leverage

Source: Merrill Lynch, Global Fund Manager Survey, 2008. Available At: http://seekingalpha.com

Recent Trends in India

Financial experts opine that India has tremendous potential for attracting global investments in hedge funds. The early entrants into the Indian markets have recorded encouraging returns which in turn attracted other hedge fund players to step in. Renaissance Technologies, Vikram Pandit-founded Old Lane, DE Shaw, Och-Ziff Capital Management are some reputed international hedge funds firms in India. Here is a list of hedge funds operating in India.

- Indea Capital Pte Ltd.
- India Capital Fund.
- India Deep Value Fund
- Absolute India Fund (AIF)
- Fair Value
- Naissance Jaipur (India) Fund
- Avatar Investment Management
- Passport India Fund
- HFG India Continuum Fund
- Monsoon Capital Equity Value Fund
- Karma Capital Management, LLC
- Vasishta South Asia Fund Limited
- Atyant Capital
- Atlantis India Opportunities Fund

1st Hedge Fund – HFG India Continuum Fund

Hudson Fairfax Group (HFG) is an investment partnership focused on India's aerospace, defence, homeland security and other strategic sectors. It is based in New York with an advisory office in New Delhi. Its team has five decades of focused experience in the sector combining investment and industry expertise. Hudson Fairfax Group, through its predecessor company, started as an investment advisory firm in 2005. It ran an investment fund, the HFG India Continuum Fund, which invested in publicly traded Indian securities. During the operation of its fund, HFG was a Registered Investment Advisor (RIA) with the US Securities and Exchange Commission and a Foreign Institutional Investor (FII) with the Securities and Exchange Board of India

2nd Hedge Fund – Avatar Investment Management

Avatar Investment Management is the investment adviser to three funds. Headquartered in Mauritius, the funds are focused on the Indian public and private equity markets. In order to meet the approval of various regulatory bodies around the world, only accredited investors may apply to invest.

3rd Hedge Fund – India Deep Value Fund

India Investment Advisers, LLC was founded by Robin Rodriguez and Raj Agarwal in 2006 to pursue the number of significant investment opportunities presented by the burgeoning Indian capital and real estate markets. As a result, the India Deep Value Fund was launched in April 2006. The fund's managers seek to achieve long-term capital gains by acting as pro-active deep value investors in publicly-traded Indian stocks.

4th Hedge Fund – Fair Value

Fair Value Capital is a highly specialized and exclusive Investment Advisory Firm focused on Deep Value Investment opportunities primarily in Indian equity markets. It seeks absolute, long-term returns for its investments while minimizing investment risks using a value-oriented approach towards our investments. Fair Value specializes in Deep Value Investments in the Indian equity markets.

5th Hedge Fund – Indea Capital Pte Ltd.

Indea Capital Pte. Ltd (Indea) is a Singapore based investment adviser. Indea was formed in 2002 to provide boutique fund management services to institutions, foundations, family offices and high net worth individuals. In July 2003, Indea launched the Indea Absolute Return Fund (IARF), a directional fund investing in India and Indian companies globally. The principals have a combined over 30 years of experience in researching and investing in India. In addition to the Singapore office, Indea has a research presence in Mumbai, India.

6th Hedge Fund – India Capital Fund

India Capital Fund SM is an open-ended Investment Company incorporated in Mauritius which has invested in India since 1994. Shares of the Indian Capital Fund SM have not been registered under the US securities Act 1933, as amended. Further it is also not registered under the US Investment Company Act of 1940, as amended: The share of the fund are not offered to Public in United States.

7th Hedge Fund – Monsoon Capital Equity Value Fund

Monsoon Capital is the adviser to onshore and offshore private investment partnerships and specializes in equity investments in India.

8th Hedge Fund – Karma Capital Management, LLC

Karma Capital Management LLC is an organization with dedicated professionals engaged in providing specialist, fundamentally based, alpha-seeking India ocused products including long-only equity and long-short products. Our wealth of experience has guided us in offering attractive risk-adjusted, performance-driven products that take advantage of market opportunities and meet specific client objectives. From diversified proprietary fund portfolios to customized programmes for a full range of global institutional investors, our capabilities and product offerings address the various investment needs of investors around the world.

9th Hedge Fund – Atlantis India Opportunities Fund

Rahul leads Atyant Capital Advisers, adviser to the Atyant Capital India Fund. In the last 10 years he's managed money exclusively in the Indian markets. His mission is to consistently identify the best 10-15 investment ideas from among the thousands of publicly-traded Indian corporations. Rahul's value-based investment philosophy stands apart due to his belief in the paramount importance of corporate governance, specifically how management operates with its minority shareholders in mind. Prior to Atyant, Rahul spent four years leading Meridian Investments, generating a 430% absolute return for the firm's high net worth clients.

Indian stocks have emerged as the most attractive bet for hedge funds, the fall guys during the recent subprime crisis, with returns better than that of the Sensex. According to a study of over 7,000 hedge funds across the world, those focused on India have emerged on top in the past five-and-a-half years.

The entire Indian hedge fund universe is modest at around 50-60 funds. The $15bn FoHF portfolio of London-based hedge fund giant Man Group, for example. is 10-15% exposed to emerging markets and 1% exposed to India. Typically, India-based hedge funds are relatively risk-averse and illiquid equity funds, which fall somewhat short of the highly liquid, short-selling, alpha-generating strategies synonymous with the 'hedge fund' tag. "The India hedge fund universe is fairly limited. There aren't many liquid India strategies. Hedging has been more difficult in India than most Asian markets. Many of the existing 50-60 India-based hedge funds focus on small/mid-cap, Private Investment in Public Equity (Pipe) and pre-IPO investments.

Hedge funds investing in India are not making as much headlines as they did during the previous Bull Run in 2007-08, but they seem to be making money for investors. Eurekahedge to be ranked among the best-performing hedge funds globally according to analysts at Singapore's fund research house. The Eurekahedge Indian Hedge Fund

Index returned over 5% in the first eight months of 2010 *vis-à-vis* 2% gains by benchmark Sensex in the same period. Asset managers attribute the decent performance of India-focused hedge funds to the buoyant stock market, 'long-only' strategies by their managers and gains in mid-cap shares. Within Indian hedge funds, 68% of the funds employ 'long-short' equity strategy — a mix of buying assets as well as short-selling them — and more than 70% of the funds invest in equities. Longer investment timeframe has helped hedge fund's log better returns in 2010. Funds belonging to asset managers like Q-India, Halbis, FMG, Baer Capital and Insynergy have all outperformed benchmarks and key hedge fund indices during the considered period 2010. Eurekahedge Indian Hedge Fund Index's returned just 52% against 76% logged by the Sensex in 2009. Most hedge funds have turned cautious and the proportion of 'long-short' strategy has come down from 80% in 2008-09 to 68% in 2010. Funds are employing broader mandates (such as multi-strategies) in their attempt not to remain dependent of price momentum of stocks. "Hedge fund managers tried complex strategies in 2008 and failed, as a result of which they been reasonably defensive in 2009 and 2010. They have now managed to get some good sectoral and stock calls. Steady investment returns have resulted in the swelling-up of asset bases of most India-focused hedge funds over the past few months. Average asset under management of an Indian hedge fund is estimated at $65 million by fund researchers. Most of the money (for India-focused funds) is coming from hedge funds, family offices and high net worth investors.

(***Source:*** *Economic Times*, 2010)

Problems

Hedge funds supposedly offer returns uncorrelated with the market but claim, however, is misleading. More important, many hedge funds simply try to exploit market imperfections and arbitrage opportunities. They are generating returns that are correlated with other actively managed portfolios. Another claim is that hedge funds are offering superior performance. This is partly true because hedge fund managers can employ trades and tactics that their mutual fund counterparts' are prevented from using. But however annual attrition rates from mutual fund are 2.53-8.22%, while hedge funds had attrition rates of13.64-26.92%. In addition, several types of hedge fund strategies had higher than expected return volatility. Hedge funds customarily lack both transparency, based on their proprietary investment strategies, and liquidity, based on their lock-in periods; however, hedge funds provide precisely what institutional investment managers' portfolio objectives demand, capital preservation, higher alphas, and lower correlations. Furthermore, with the current financial markets in turmoil, all the value enhancing synergies that hedge funds provide to a diversified portfolio become increasingly important. Liquidity is a problem for investors due in part to the investment styles of hedge funds.

Summary

In today's uncertain equity and fixed income markets, institutions and high net worth individuals are paying more attention to hedge fund strategies. Hedge funds as a whole are becoming a prominent segment of the asset management industry and gaining popularity from investors particularly from high net worth investors, universities, charitable funds, endowments, pension funds, insurance and other institutional investors. Most hedge fund managers are embracing the new sources of capital from institutional investors, who are, by their very nature, highly regulated and their investments scrutinized. The institutional market presents hedge fund managers with the opportunity for another major upswing in growth. To capitalize on this opportunity, however, hedge funds will have to compete in a highly fluid marketplace and adapt to the impacts of growing institutional dominance, including a longer and more complex sales cycle.

CASE: JOHN ASSET MANAGEMENT

John Asset Management was founded in 1980 at Mumbai by Jerry and John. John Asset Management emerged as an independent employed owned, Wealth Management Company that service both institutional and investors. It is one the largest private investment counselling firms in India. They are rendering modern portfolio management services. One of the firm's investment policies is based on the belief that superior investment results will be achieved over long years by following risk-averse, quality-oriented approach to investment management. The firm is also well-known for its commitment investor client relationship. All employees of the organisation are available over telephone or in persons to discuss issues with their clients. More than 70 per cent professional investment analysts are MBA with finance specialisation holding degree from top management schools of India. Investment decisions are taken by discussing jointly with analysts and portfolio managers. Mr. Ashoke is a dynamic fund Manager. He is managing a portfolio of ₹ 1,400 crore. He has estimated that his fund's outflows for the ensuing three years and the seed capital as follows:

Month and year	Outflows (₹ in crore)	Seed capital required (₹ in crore)
December, 2005	20.00	
December, 2006	24.00	
December, 2007	36.00	1520

To keep his fund hedge at the time, he wants to use the concept of duration and accordingly he has identified two bonds with maturity of two years and four years to invest his fund. The details of which are as follows:

Bond I: Maturing in December 2006, it is a 14% coupon bond. The par value of the bond is ₹ 100 but the current market price is ₹ 98.40

Bond II: Maturing in December 2008 it is a 13% coupon bond. The par value of the bond is ₹ 1,000. The bond is currently priced at ₹ 1,000.

The cost of the funds for Mr. Ashoke is 13% p.a.

You are required to calculate the percentage of funds to be invested in Bond I and Bond II.

Review Questions

1. How are hedge funds different from traditional asset class or other pooled funds?
2. What are the characteristics of hedge funds?
3. What are the hedging strategies?
4. Short notes on comparison between Hedge funds and Private Equity and Hedge Funds and Venture Capital Fund
5. Discuss about structure of hedge funds?
6. **Quiz:**
   (a) Hedge funds are similar to private equity funds, such as venture capital funds, commodity pools in many respects. ***(T/F)***
   (b) Hedge funds typically engage one or more broker-dealers to provide a variety of services, including trade clearance and settlement, financing and custody services. ***(T/F)***
   (c) Domestic hedge funds are usually organized as ______ to accommodate investors that are subject to domestic taxation.
   (d) The key unique feature of hedge funds is that performance is derived from ______ not from ______.
   (e) Assets under management of the global hedge fund industry increased by ______ in 2010
   (f) Hedge funds make ______ returns because they take different risks.

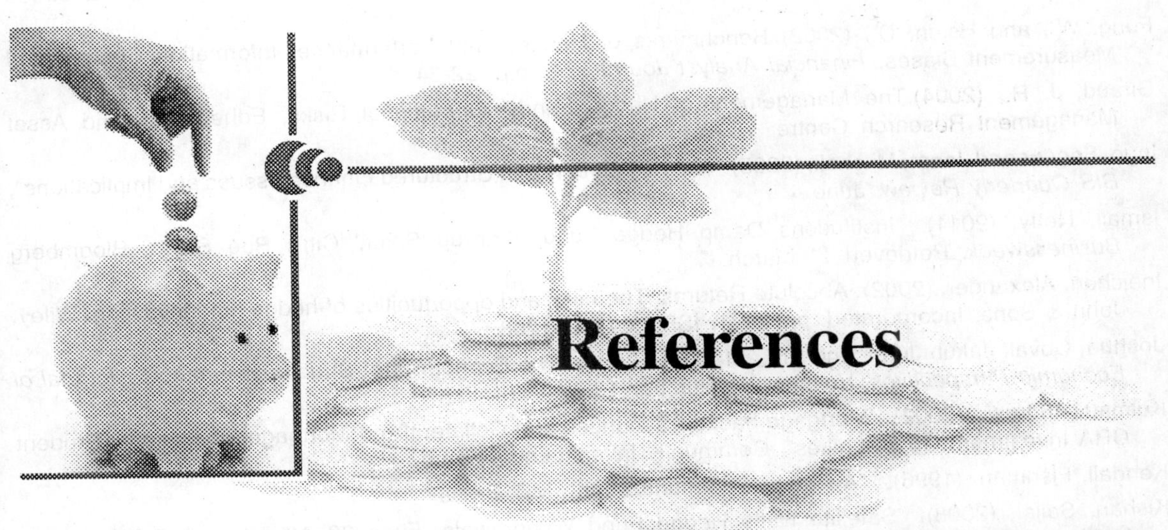

References

Journals

Ashcraft A, (2004) "How do structured finance products add value?", Federal Reserve Bank of New York,

Altman and Suggitt, E.I. Altman and Suggitt, H.J. (2000). Default rates in the syndicated bank loan market: A mortality analysis, *Journal of Banking and Finance* 24

Allen, Katrina Dean (2011), "Billion dollar club", Absolute Return. Retrieved 22 April 2011.

Brunner and Krahnen, Brunner, A., Krahnen, J.P., (2001) Multiple lenders and corporate distress: Evidence on debt restructuring. CFS Working Paper No. 2001/04. University of Frankfurt.

Buckley, I., Saunders, D., Seco, L., Portfolio optimization when assets returns have the Gaussian mixture distribution, European Journal of Optimization.

Carletti *et. al.*, Carletti, E., Cerasi, V., Daltung, S.,(2004) Multiple-bank lending: Diversification and free-riding in monitoring. CFS Working Paper No. 2004/18. Centre for Financial Studies, University of Frankfurt.

Detragiache *et. al.*, Detragiache, E., Garella P., and Guiso, L., (2000) Multiple versus single banking relationships, *Journal of Finance* 55, pp. 1133-1161.

Fung, W., and Hsieh, D., (1997) Empirical Characteristics of Dynamic Trading Strategies: The Case of Hedge Funds, Review of Financial Studies, 10, 275-302.

Fung, W., and Hsieh, D., (1997) Survivorship Bias and Investment Style in the Returns of CTAs, *Journal of Portfolio Management*, 24, 30-41.

Fung, W., and Hsieh, D., (1999) Is Mean-Variance Analysis Applicable to Hedge Funds? Economic Letters, 62, p.p. 53-58.

Fung, W., and Hsieh, D., (1999) A Primer on Hedge Funds, *Journal of Empirical Finance*, 6, p.p. 309-331.

Fung, W., and Hsieh, D., (2000) Performance Characteristics of Hedge Funds and CTA Funds: Natural versus Spurious Biases, *Journal of Quantitative and Financial Analysis*, 35, p.p. 291-307.

Fung, W., and Hsieh, D., (2000) Measuring the Market Impact of Hedge Funds, *Journal of Empirical Finance*, 7, p.p. 1-36.

Fung, W., and Hsieh, D., (2001) The Risk in Hedge Fund Strategies: Theory and Evidence from Trend Followers Review of Financial Studies, 14, p.p. 313-341.

Fung, W., and Hsieh, D., (2002) Benchmarks of Hedge Fund Performance: Information Content and Measurement Biases, *Financial Analyst Journal*, 58, p.p. 22-34.

Giraud, J. R., (2004).The Management of Hedge Funds' Operational Risks, Edhec Risk and Asset Management Research Centre.

Ingo, Fender and Janet, Mitchell, (2005) "The role of ratings in Structured Finance: Issues and Implications", *BIS Quarterly Review*, June.

Ismail, Netty, (2011). "Institutions Damp Hedge Fund 'Start-up Spirit,' Citi's Roe Says". Bloomberg *Businessweek*. Retrieved 11 March.

Ineichen, Alexander, (2002). Absolute Returns: The risks and opportunities of hedge fund investing. Wiley, John & Sons, Incorporated. pp. 8-21. ISBN 0471251208.

Joshua, Coval, Jakub Jurek and Erik, Stafford, (2009) "The Economics of Structured Finance", *Journal of Economic Perspectives*, Volume 23, Number 1.

Kelman, Andrew, (2002). "Mortgage-backed Securities and Collateralized Mortgage Obligations: Prudent CRA Investment Opportunities", Community Investments, March.

Kendall, Fishman, (1996). "A Priner of Securitization", MIT Press,

Kishan, Saijel, (2008). "Satellite Halts Hedge Fund Withdrawals, Fires 30 After Losses." Bloomberg. Retrieved 2010-08-14.

Mark, Hulbert, (2006) "That Hedge Fund May Be More Than a Flash in the Pan," *The New York Times*. June 4,. Available at: http://www.nytimes.com

Michael R., King and Philipp, Maier, (2008). "Hedge Funds and Financial Stability: Regulating Prime Brokers Will Mitigate Systemic Risks." October 30, Available at SSRN: http://ssrn.com/abstract=1297188.

Ongena and Smith, Ongena S., and Smith, D.C., (2000). What determines the number of bank relationships? Cross-country evidence, *Journal of Financial Intermediation* 9, pp. 26-56.

Ravi, Jagannathan, Alexey, Malakhov, Dmitry, Novikov, (2006). "Do Hot Hands Persist Among Hedge Fund Managers? An Empirical Evaluation," National Bureau of Economic Research working paper no. 12015, February. Available for purchase at: http://www.nber.org/papers/w12015.

Shadwick, W., and Keating, C., (2002). Omega, a universal performance measure, *Journal of portfolio Measurement*, Spring.

Sharpe, W., (1975). Adjusting for Risk in Portfolio Performance Measurement, *Journal of Portfolio Management*, Winter.

Sortino, F., and van, der, Meer, R., (1991). Downside risk-capturing what's at stake in investment situations, *Journal of Portfolio Risk*, 17.

Shyamala, Gopinath,(2010). "Securitisation markets in India – a post-crisis perspective," BIS Review.

Simons, K. Simons, (1993). Why do banks syndicate loans?, *New England Economic Review* Jan/Feb issue, pp. 45-52.

Strasberg, Jenny, Eder, Steve, (2011). "Hedge Funds Bounce Back." *Wall Street Journal Online*. Retrieved 22 April, 2011.

Tausche, Kayla, (2011). "225 Hedge Funds in Billion Dollar Club". CNBC.com. Retrieved 22 April, 2011.

Ubide, Angel, (2006), "Demystifying Hedge Funds." Finance and Development (International Monetary Fund). Retrieved 3 March, 2011.

Williams, Orice, M., (2009). "Hedge Funds: Overview of Regulatory Oversight, Counterparty Risks, and Investment Challenges". US Government Accountability Office. Retrieved 14 March, 2011.

Books

Campbell, Katherine. Smarter Ventures: A Survivor's Guide to Venture Capital through the New Cycle. *Financial Times*, Management Press. ISBN 0-273-65403-9.

Davidson, Sanders, Wolff, Ching "Securitization: Structuring and Investment Analysis", Wiley John & Sons, Incorporated 2003.

Gompers, Paul, and Josh, Lerner"The Venture Capital Cycle", 2nd ed., MIT Press, ,2004.

George P. Baker, and George, David, Smith, The New Financial Capitalists: Kohlberg.

Horwitz, R., Hedge Fund risk fundamentals, Bloomberg Press, 2004.

Hayre, Lakhbir. "Salomon Smith Barney Guide to Mortgage-backed and Asset-backed Securities", Wiley John & Sons, Incorporated 2001.

Hedge fund definition, Collins Dictionary of Business, 2006.

Hedge fund definition, Merriam-Webster's Collegiate Dictionary, 2004.

Hurn, S. Hurn, Syndicated Loans: A Handbook for Banker and Borrower, Woodhead-Faulkner Ltd. (Prentice-Hall, Europe), Cambridge, UK, 1990.

Hu, Joseph. "Basics of Mortgage-backed Securities," 2nd ed. Frank J. Fabozzi Associates, 2001.

Jaeger, L. Managing Risk in Alternative Investment Strategies, Prentice-Hall, 2002.

Investopedia: Hedge Fund Definition Retrieved July 2011.

Kravis, Roberts, and the Creation of Corporate Value, (Cambridge: Cambridge University Press), 1998.

Mitchell J, "Financial intermediation theory and structured finance markets," National Bank of Belgium, 2004.

Markowitz, H., Portfolio Selection, *Journal of Finance* 7(1):11-91,1952.

Merton, Continuous Time Finance, Blackwell Publishers, 1992.

NVCA and Venture Economics, National Venture Capital Yearbook,1999.

Nicholas, Joseph G., Hedge fund of funds investing: an investor's guide. Wiley John & Sons, Incorporated. p. 11. ISBN 1576601242,2004.

Rhodes, In: T. Rhodes, Syndicated Lending: Practice and Documentation, Euromoney Publications Plc, London, UK,1996.

Zipf, Robert. "How the Bond Market Works," 2nd ed., New York Institute of Finance, 1997.

Newsletters and Reports

Anna Katherine Barnett-Hart: The Story of the CDO Market Meltdown: An Empirical Analysis-March 2009.

A Primer on Hedge Funds, William Fung and David A. Hsieh, August 1999.

Bloomberg-Flawed Credit Ratings Reap Profits as Regulators Fail Investors-April 2009.

Bob Jesenik, Mezzanine financing could take business higher, *The Daily Journal of Commerce*, July 24, 2007.

Bookrunners of all global syndicated loans (2009) *Euroweek*, 09527036, Issue 1124.

Bookrunners of all global syndicated loans (2008). *Euroweek*, Issue 1041.

Bookrunners of all global syndicated loans (2008). *Euroweek*, Issue 1039.

Credit Suisse Economic Research, 2006.

Celent (2005) "Collateralized Debt Obligations Market." Press release. http://www.celent.com/PressReleases/20051031/CDOMarket.htm. Retrieved 2009-02-23.

Deutsche Industriebank, presentation Dr. I. Natusch, Round Table Talks October 23rd 2003 (www.finanzstandort.com.)

Economics (Summary Document), September, 1998.

Fannie Mae, Annual Report, 2003.

Grant Thornton – DealTracker for Private Equity for 2008, 2009, 2010.

Investopedia – Private Equity, Types of Private Equity.

Huffington Post-Yves Smith-Magnetar Capital-April 2010.

Hedge-Fund Firms Woo the Little Guy, Jaime Levy Pessin, *Wall Street Journal,* Dec. 6, 2010.

ICFAI Reader, April 2005.

ICFAI Reader, April 2007.

Indian Venture Capital Association – IVCA Venture Activity 1997.

KfW Research, Mezzanine-Finanzierungen für den Mittelstand: Der Markt ist in Bewegung. Issue 1, July 2005.

Merrill sells assets seized from hedge funds, CNN June 20, 2007.

Mezzanine Monitor, Q1 2006: Mezzanine investors pause for breath?, Private Equity Europe, Issue 76, May 2006.

Mezzanine Monitor, Q1 2006: Mezzanine investors pause for breath?, Private equity Europe, Issue 76, May 2006.

Nirav Mody, Mrudula, Deshingkar and Asina Ajwani, "Indian Securitisation Market Q&A," Fitch Ratings, February 2006.

NPR-The Giant Pool of Money-March 2008.

Private Placement Newsletter, January 6, 2003.

PBS-Credit and Credibility-December 2008.

Portfolio organizer, July 2006.

The Securities and Exchange Board of India – SEBI (Venture Capital Funds) Regulations, 1996.

Timeline: Subprime losses, BBC May 19, 2008.

The Financial Express, January 04, 2004

The Coming Evolution of the Hedge Fund Industry: "A Case for Growth and Restructuring", RR Capital Management Corporation, KPMG Peat Marwick LLP, March 1998.

The Economic Times daily

Lewis, Michael, The Big Short. W.W. Norton & Company. ISBN 978-0-393-07223-5,2010.

The Magnetar Trade: How One Hedge Fund Helped Keep the Bubble Going (Single Page)-April 2010.

Wall Street Journal, Bridgewater Goes Large Michael Corkery, June 22, 2011.

"Citigroup chief executive resigns". BBC News. 2007-11-05. http://news.bbc.co.uk/1/hi/business/7078251.stm. Retrieved 2010-04-30.

"CDO deals resurface but down 90 pct in Q1-report." Reuters. 2008-04-09. http://uk.reuters.com/article/marketsNewsUS/idUKN0947372020080409.

Eavis, Peter, (2007). "Merrill's $3.4 billion balance sheet bomb." CNN. http://money.cnn.com/2007/10/24/news/companies/merrill_eavis.fortune/index.htm?section=money_latest. Retrieved 2010-04-30.

Fannie, Mae, News Archive, http://www.freddiemac.com/news/archives/investors/2003/mvsrelease_102403.html

"Institutional Share Growing For Hedge Funds." FINalternatives. 10 February, 2011. Retrieved 10 March, 2011.

Hedge Fund Research, Inc., "Hedge Fund Industry Assets Surge as Performance Leads Industry Recovery." Press Release. July 21, 2009. Available at: https://www.hedgefundresearch.com/pdf/pr_20090721.pdf.

"Hedge Funds: How They Serve Investors in US and Global Markets" (PDF). Hedge Fund Facts.org. Coalition of Private Investment Companies. (2009) Retrieved 1 March, 2011.

Mezzanine Finance: Closing the Gap between Debt and Equity, Fleet Capital Corporation, www.fleetcapital.com 1-866-287-4098.

McLean, Bethany (2007). "The dangers of investing in subprime debt". *Fortune.* http://money.cnn.com/magazines/fortune/fortune_archive/2007/04/02/8403416/index.htm

Peaslee, James, M., and David Z., Nirenberg. Federal Income Taxation of Securitization and Related Topics. Frank J. Fabozzi Associates (2011, with periodic supplements, www.securitizationtax.com): 1018.

Securities Industry and Financial Markets Association. "Global CDO Issuance." Press release. http://sifma.org/uploadedFiles/Research/Statistics/StatisticsFiles/SF-Global-CDO-Issuance-SIFMA.xls. Retrieved 2010-011-21.

http://www.sifma.org/research/pdf/SIFMA_CDOIssuanceData2008.pdf

http://www.indianmba.com

http://www.sidbiventure.co.in/svc-0302.htm

http://sramanamitra.com/articles/venture-capital-in-india

http://www.investopedia.com/articles/basics/03/050203.asp#12961223977802&close

http://money.cnn.com/2007/06/20/news/companies/bear_stearns/index.htm. Retrieved May 24, 2010.

http://news.bbc.co.uk/2/hi/business/7096845.stm. Retrieved May 24, 2010.

http://www.iadb.org/exr/bs/0603/KY

http://www.bondmarkets.com , 2004.

http://www.oscn.net/applications/oscn/deliverdocument.asp?citeid=433720 Located in footnote of court documents

http://findarticles.com/p/articles/mi_hb5247/is_199012/ai_n19908728&tag=rel.res1?tag=col1;fa_related_widget.[dead link]

http://www.law.cornell.edu/supct/html/92-1370.ZO.html See Notes of Supreme Court ruling Zandi, Mark (2009). Financial Shock. FT Press. ISBN 978-0-13-701663-1.

http://infoproc.blogspot.com/2005/09/gaussian-copula-and-credit-derivatives.html

http://online.wsj.com/article/SB112649094075137685.html How a Formula Ignited Market That Burned Some Big Investors, Mark Whitehouse, *Wall Street Journal*

h http://www.indiavca.org/res_indus_stats.aspx

http://archives1.sifma.org/assets/files/SIFMA_CDOIssuanceData2007q1.pdf

http://finance.mapsofworld.com/merger-acquisition/2005.html

http://finance.mapsofworld.com/merger-acquisition/international.html

http://www.icmrindia.org/casestudies/catalogue/Finance/FINC049.htm

http://en.wikipedia.org/wiki/Mergers_and_acquisitions

http://en.wikipedia.org/wiki/Tata_Corus_acquisition

Corporate Finance: Ross, Westerfield, Jaffe; Tata McGraw Hill; 7th Ed.; pp 796-823

http://en.wikipedia.org/wiki/Keiretsu

http://en.wikipedia.org/wiki/Tata_Tea_Limited

http://corp.bankofamerica.com/public/public.portal?_pd_page_label=products/abf/capeyes/archive_index&dcCapEyes=indCE&cFile=C00110.html

http://corp.bankofamerica.com/public/public.portal?_pd_page_label=products/abf/capeyes/archive_index&dcCapEyes=indCE&cFile=C00159.html

http://economictimes.indiatimes.com/News/News-By-Industry/Indl-Goods-/-Svs/Steel/Corus-buy-Tatas-may-go-for-leveraged-buyout/articleshow/2143113.cms

www.bis.org/publ/qtrpdf/r_qt0412g.pdf

http://en.wikipedia.org/wiki/Syndicated_loan

http://ssrn.com/abstract=1267397. See also: Alon Brav, Wei Jiang, Frank Partnoy, and Randall S. Thomas, "Hedge Fund Activism, Corporate Governance and Firm Performance." Available at: http://www.fdic.gov/bank/analytical/CFR/2006/oct/hedge_fund.pdf.

http://www.svtuition.org/2010/05/list-of-hedge-funds-in-india.html

http://www.hedgefundsreview.com/hedge-funds-review/news/1566381/currying-investment-marketing-distribution-funds-india

www.sebi.gov.in

www.wikipedia.org/wiki

www.vcindia.com

www.vccircle.com

www.indiavca.org

www.themanager.org

www7.nationalacademies.org

www.indianpe.com

www.fraternityfunds.com

www.E-Hedge.com

www.hedgefundresources.com

www.hedgefundresearch.com

www.mckinsey.com.

www.absolutereturn.net

www.aima.org

www.eurekahedge.com

www.eurohedge.co.uk

www.hedgefundsreview.com

www.hedgeweek.com

www.hedgeco.net

www.hedgefund.net

www.hedgefund.com

www.hedgefundcenter.com

www.hedgefundintelligence.com

www.hedgefundnews.com

www.hedgefunds.net

www.thehedgefundjournal.com

www.institutionalinvestor.com

www.investhedge.com

www.mfainfo.org

www.thehfa.org

www.vanhedge.com
www.wisegeek.com/what-is-mezzanine-financing.htm
www.altassets.net/private-equity-features/article/nz1318.html
www.wikipedia.in
www.tatasteel.com/newsroom/press518.asp
www.tatasteel.com/Company/profile.asp
www.cfo.com/article.cfm/5541263/2/c_2984411?f=archives
www.icmrindia.org/casestudies/catalogue/Finance/Finance%20-%20The%20Leveraged%20Buy%20Out%20Deal%20of%20Tata%20&%20Tetley.htm

Acronym

TICL: Tata Investment Corporation Limited

A

ABS:Asset-backed securities

AIF: Absolute India Fund

APV: Adjusted present value

ANZ Grindlays bank: The Australia and New Zealand Banking Group Limited Grindlays bank

APIDC Venture Capital Limited: Andhra Pradesh Industrial Development Corporation Limited

AGBAsian growth Bank

AT&T – American Telephone and Telegraph Company

B

BIS: Bank for International Settlements

BBLIL:Brooke Bond Lipton India Ltd

BBVA: Banco Bilbao Vizcaya Argentaria (First Bank of Spain)

BNP Paribas: Banque Nationale de Paris

BNP: Banque Nationale de Paris Hong Kong & Shanghai Banking Corporation Bank

BRLM: Book Running Lead Manager

BOT: Built-operate-transfer

C

CAR: Capital Adequacy Ratio

CAPM: Capital Asset Pricing Model

CML: Capital market line

CIFCO: Champaklal investments and finance

Acronym

CCIL: Clearing Corporation of India Limited
CBOs: Collateralized Bond Obligations
CDOs: Collateralized Debt Obligations
CIOs: Collateralized Insurance Obligations
CMOs: Collateralized Mortgage Obligations
CSOs: Collateralized Synthetic Obligations
CMBS: Commercial Mortgage-Backed Security
CRE CDOs: Commercial Real Estate CDOs
CFC: Credit Capital Finance Corporation
CRISIL: Credit Rating Information Services of India ltd

D

DAI: Darby Asia Investors
DBS: The Development Bank of Singapore Limited
DRR: Debenture Redemption Reserve
DvP: Delivery versus Payment'
DCF: Deloitte Corporate Finance Services India Pvt. Ltd
DTTIPL: Deloitte Touche Tohmatsu India Pvt Ltd
DFIs: Development Finance Institutions
DFI: Developmental Financial Institution
DFJ India: Draper Fisher Jurvetson India
DPO: Direct Public Offering
DCF: Discounted Cash Flow
DDM: Dividend Discount Model
DJIA: Dow Jones Industrial Average
DnB NOR Bank: Den norske Bank
DTAA: Double taxation avoidance agreement

E

EBIT: Earnings Before Interest and Tax
EPS: Earnings Per Share
EBITDA: Earnings Before Interest, Taxes, Depreciation and Amortization
EMPEA: Emerging Markets Private Equity Association
EV: Enterprise Value
EVCA: European Private Equity and Venture Capital Association
ETFs: Exchange-Traded Funds

F

FDIC: Federal Deposit Insurance Corporation
FHLMC: Federal Home Loan Mortgage Corporation
FHA: Federal Housing Administration
FNMA: Federal National Mortgage Association

FISG: Financial Institutions and Syndications Group
FMCG: Fast Moving Consumer Goods
FPO: Follow on Public Offer
Foreign company, KKR Kravis and Roberts
FDI: Foreign Direct Investment
FII: Foreign Institutional Investors
FVCI: Foreign Venture Capital Investor Regulations
FCF: Free Cash Flow
FV: Future value

G

GE Capital: General Electric Ltd
GP: General Partner
GAAP: Generally Accepted Accounting Principles
GIC Mutual Fund: General Insurance Company
GIB: Global Investment Banking
GSFAG: Global Structured Finance & Advisory Group
GNMA: Government National Mortgage Association
GDP: Gross domestic product
GSA: Glass-Steagall Act
GVFL Ltd: Gujarat Venture Finance Limited

H

HCA Inc. by Kohlberg: Hospital Corporation of America Inc
HFRI: Hedge Fund Research, Inc.
HLL: Hindustan Lever Ltd.
HDFC: Housing Development Finance Corporation
HFG: Hudson Fairfax Group

I

ICICI: Industrial Credit and Investment Corporation of India
IDFC: Infrastructure Development Finance Co. Ltd
IDG India Ventures
IFCI Venture Capital Funds Ltd: Industrial Financial Corporation of India
ILFS: Infrastructure Leasing & Financial Services Limited (IL&FS)
ING: International Netherlands Group
IBO: Institutional Buyout
IRR: Internal Rate of Return
IFC: International Finance Corporation
ISG: International Syndications Group
ICC: Internet Concepts Corporation

Investors who continue to look at transactions are CLSA
IPOs: Initial Public Offerings

J

JC Flowers & Co – J. Christopher Flowers
JP Morgan Chase – John Pierpont Morgan

K

KKR: Kohlberg Kravis Roberts & Co

L

LBO: Leveraged Buyout
LPs: Limited partnerships
LLC by Sterlite: Limited Liability Company
LSOs: Loan Sell-Offs
LOI: Letter of Intent

M

MBO: Management Buyout
MBI: Management Buys In
MBNA: Maryland Bank, N.A
M&A: Mergers and Acquisitions
MICEX: Moscow Interbank Currency Exchange
MBS: Mortgage-Backed Securities
MTN Group Ltd: Mobile Telecommunications Company

N

NASDAQ: National Association of Securities Dealers Automated Quotations
NASD: National Association of Securities Dealers, Inc.
NHB: National Housing Board
NSE: National Stock Exchange of India
NVCA: National Venture Capital Association
NEA IndoUS Ventures: New Enterprise Associates
NEAT: National Exchange for Automated Trading
NPV: Net Present Value
NIM: New Issue Market
NYSE: New York Stock Exchange
NIC: National Insurance Company
NII: Non-Institutional Investor
NOPAT: Net Operating Profits After Taxes
NTT DoCoMo: Nippon Telegraph and Telephone do communications over the mobile network

O

OIS: Overnight Index Swap
OTC: Over The Counter
OC: Overcollateralization

P

PNs: Participatory Notes
PTCs: Pass-Through Certificates
PIN: Personal Identification Number
P/S: Price to Sales
P/E: Price-Earnings
P/B ratio: Price-to-Book ratio
PE: Private Equity
PIPE: Private Investments in Public Equity
PPM: Private Placement Memorandum
PEG: Projected Earnings Growth

Q

QIBs: Qualified Institutional Buyers

R

RBS: Royal Bank of Scotland
REIT: Real Debt
REMIC: Real Estate Mortgage Investment Conduits
RIA: Registered Investment Advisor
RMBS: Residential Mortgage-Backed Security
RDM: Retail Debt Market Segment
ROA: Return on Assets
ROE: Return on Equity
ROIC: Return on Invested Capital
RONA: Return on Net Assets
RCTC: Risk Capital & Technology Finance Corporation Ltd
RJR: RJR Nabisco
RDA: Rural Development Administration

S

SBC: Southwestern Bell Corporation
SBI Capital Markets: State Bank of India Capital Markets:
SEBI: Securities and Exchange Board of India
SEC: Securities Exchange Commission
SML: Security Market Line
SMBC: Sumitomo Mitsui Banking Corporation
SPV: Special Purpose Vehicle

SRF Finance: Shri Ram Fibres Ltd
SFCDOs: Structured Finance CDOs
SCDOs: Synthetic Collateralized Debt Obligations

T

TDS: Tax Deducted Source
TDICI: Technology Development and Information Company of India Ltd.
TELCO: Tata Engineering and Locomotive Company
TV: Terminal Value
RII: The Retail Individual Investor
VA: The Veterans Administration

U

UBS: Union Bank of Switzerland
UTI Securities Ltd: Unit Trust of India Securities Ltd.

V

VC: Venture Capital
VCM: Venture Capital Method
VSNL: Videsh Sanchar Nigam Limited

W

WACC: Weighted Average Cost of Capital
WDM: Wholesale Debt Market

Y

YTM: Yield to Maturity